Curriculum: Principles and Foundations

CURRICULUM
PRINCIPLES AND FOUNDATIONS

Robert S. Zais
KENT STATE UNIVERSITY

Thomas Y. Crowell
HARPER & ROW, PUBLISHERS
New York   Hagerstown   San Francisco   London

CURRICULUM: Principles and Foundations

Published simultaneously in Canada by Fitzhenry & Whiteside, Ltd., Toronto.

LIBRARY OF CONGRESS CATALOGING IN PUBLICATION DATA

Zais, Robert S
 Curriculum: principles and foundations.

 Includes bibliographies and index.
 1. Education—Curricula—History. 2. Culture.
3. Curriculum planning. I. Title.
LB1570.Z34 1976   375'.001   76-1886
ISBN 0-690-00857-0

CONTENTS

v

PART III
Anatomy of the Curriculum   295

PART IV
Curriculum Design and Engineering   393

*For
Edith, Louis,
and
Roberta*

PREFACE

Curriculum construction in the United States is generally conducted in a shockingly piecemeal and superficial fashion. "Reforms" are implemented in response to popular clamor or perceived social crises; "innovations" are often little more than jargon; and the whole process is influenced mainly by mere educational vogue. The results, of course, are school programs characterized by fragmentation, imbalance, transience, caprice, and at times, incoherence.

There are a number of reasons for this unfortunate state of affairs. One is the overwhelming complexity of the curricular enterprise; the number of interdependent variables that influence curriculum development is disconcertingly immense. A second and related reason for superficiality is the relative infancy of the curriculum field; it made its appearance as a specialized area of inquiry and systematic study less than sixty years ago. Finally, the pragmatic nature of the American temperament—as suspicious of reflection and theorizing as it is infatuated with the desire to "do anything" to "get the job done"—has been a continuing source of difficulty. Curriculum workers tend to charge ahead, making decisions and changes without really understanding the basis and nature of curricular phenomena or the effect of their actions on the total curriculum.

For these reasons and others, it is not surprising that most current writers emphasize the processes of curriculum development and/or the techniques of curriculum improvement. But important as these areas may be, one must have some understanding of the nature of the phenomenon before one can deal effectively with the problems of implementation.

This book attempts to give balanced attention to all important areas of curriculum study: (1) the dimensions of the curriculum enterprise, (2) the bases on which decisions regarding the substance of curricula are made, (3) the components of the curriculum, (4) the ways in which curricula can be organized, and (5) the processes of curriculum development and implementation. Although the approach is analytical and theoretical, it stresses the importance of the theory–practice nexus. It has been my desire to discuss curricular matters in understandable terms to teachers, school administrators, and others who may have had no prior acquaintance with the field of curriculum or one or more of its subsumed disciplines: philosophy, anthropology, sociology, and psychology.

I should like to acknowledge a profound debt of gratitude to my mentor, Dr. Philo T. Pritzkau, Emeritus Professor of Education, University of Connecticut. This undertaking would never have been initiated, much less consummated, had it not been for his concern, friendship, and wisdom. I should also like to thank my colleagues in the Department of Secondary Education, Kent State University, who in countless discussions have helped me to clarify my ideas about curriculum. Special appreciation is due Dr. John F. Ohles, Professor of Secondary Education at Kent State University, for his encouragement and help in formulating the proposal for this book. Finally, I must thank my wife, Edith, who not only typed the manuscript, but has been an influential partner in the entire effort.

I

CURRICULUM AS A FIELD OF STUDY

The four chapters of Part I present an introductory overview of curriculum as a segment of the total educational enterprise. Chapter 1 includes a brief treatment of the origin and development of curriculum as a specialized field of study, followed by a more extensive discussion that attempts to establish the scope of curriculum study and to define some of its more prominent concerns. Chapters 2 and 3 trace the evolution of curriculum in America from its earliest Puritan beginnings to the present. Chapter 4 explores the nature and function of curriculum theory and its relevance for conceptual frameworks that enhance understanding of curricular phenomena. This chapter closes with the presentation of an eclectic theoretical model that serves as a basis for the curriculum analysis that appears in Parts II, III, and IV.

CHAPTER 1

CONCEPTIONS OF CURRICULUM AND THE CURRICULUM FIELD

It is most important that those who are constructing our school curriculum shall maintain an overview of the total situation. . . .

—HAROLD RUGG

The term "curriculum," like most words in our language, is used in many different ways. Indeed, even among professional educators, it is used in so many different ways that communication often is hampered. Although curriculum specialists have, in the interest of clarity, attempted to limit the meaning of curriculum, disagreement still exists with respect to what constitutes legitimate definitions of the word.

In the broadest sense the term "curriculum" ordinarily is used by specialists in the field in two ways: (1) to indicate, roughly, a plan for the education of learners, and (2) to identify a field of study.[1] Curriculum as a plan for the education of learners usually is referred to as *a* curriculum or *the* curriculum. At present, there is significant disagreement among curriculum specialists with regard to the ingredients of the plan. Curriculum as a plan for the education of learners is part of the subject matter of the curriculum field and is treated in this book in Chapters 13 through 16.

Curriculum as a field of study, like most specialized fields, is defined by (1) the range of subject matters with which it is concerned (the substantive struc-

---

1. Beauchamp (1968, p. 6) proposes a third meaning: "A . . . legitimate use of the term curriculum is to refer to *a curriculum system.* . . . A curriculum system in schools is the system within which decisions are made about what the curriculum will be and how it will be implemented." In this text we prefer to employ such compound terms as "curriculum development" and "curriculum implementation" to indicate the processes that Beauchamp includes in the term "curriculum system."

ture), and (2) the procedures of inquiry and practice that it follows (the syntactical structure).[2] Thus, the curriculum field, for our purposes, may be described in terms of (1) the subject matters that are treated in *all* the chapters of this book (the table of contents constitutes a general outline of the substantive structure of the curriculum field), and (2) the many processes (e.g., curriculum development and curriculum change) with which specialists are characteristically concerned. The processes and procedures of the curriculum field also are treated in this book.

Origin and Development of Curriculum as a Field of Study

Curriculum has been a consideration of writers on education for centuries. Plato (Greek philosopher, fourth century B.C.), Comenius (seventeenth-century Moravian bishop and educationist), and Froebel (nineteenth-century German educationist), for example, have all given their attention to the curriculum and its problems. But the specialized and systematic study of curriculum and curricular phenomena, and the identification of certain individuals as curriculum specialists, did not occur until the twentieth century (Kliebard 1968, p. 70).

The curriculum field had its roots in the Herbartian movement of the late nineteenth century (Seguel 1966, p. 7 ff.). Johann Friedrich Herbart (1776–1841) was a German philosopher whose educational ideas had wide acceptance in the United States in the latter half of the nineteenth century. Herbart's theories about teaching and learning required that systematic attention be given to the selection and organization of subject matter. This subject matter emphasis on the part of Herbartians led to a reawakening of interest in curriculum content in American education around the turn of the century, and as Kliebard (1968, p. 70) puts it, "curriculum became a popular issue."

During the 1890s and early 1900s, a number of significant educational events occurred that intensified interest in curricular concerns. First, the Committee of Ten, under the chairmanship of Harvard president Charles W. Eliot, issued its famous report in 1893. This report dealt with such matters as required courses, electives, college preparatory subjects, and "practical" subjects—all issues concerning curriculum. In 1895, the Herbart Society (now the National Society for the Study of Education) was formed. In the two decades that followed, members of this organization were influential in keeping alive the question of curriculum content and organization. At this same time, John Dewey was engaged in curriculum experimentation and innovation in his famous Laboratory School at the University of Chicago.

---

2. Although some writers question whether the field of curriculum is characterized by a distinctive syntactical structure, there is evidence to suggest that certain methodologies—however loosely structured—tend to recur in curriculum inquiry and practice.

Notwithstanding this concentrated attention to curriculum issues, however, no concerned individual at that time was thought of as a "curriculum specialist" and there existed no "readily identifiable field of curriculum specialization" (Kliebard 1968, p. 70). It was not until 1918 that the first book specifically devoted to the curriculum was published. Written by Franklin Bobbitt and titled simply *The Curriculum,* this volume generally is recognized as the milestone that marks the emergence of curriculum as a specialized field of study.

The 1920s usually are regarded as the formative years of the curriculum field. It was during these years, following the publication of Bobbitt's book, that volumes on curriculum began to appear which were written by educational theorists and practitioners who are thought of as curriculum specialists. W. W. Charters of The Ohio State University, for example, published *Curriculum Construction* in 1923. In the following year, *How to Make a Curriculum* appeared as Bobbitt's second major work on this subject. And in 1926, the National Society for the Study of Education (NSSE) published an exhaustive 685-page review of the curriculum movement called *The Foundations and Technique of Curriculum Construction.* This two-part yearbook of the society was prepared by a distinguished committee of "curriculum scholars" that included Franklin Bobbitt, W. W. Charters, Charles Judd, and Harold Rugg as chairman.[3]

During this period, the emergence of curriculum as a field of study manifested itself in several other ways. A number of increasingly "curriculum-conscious" school systems inaugurated programs of curriculum revision. In 1922, for example, Denver launched a systemwide curriculum improvement project, and in 1925 St. Louis attracted national attention with its comprehensive curriculum revision program involving hundreds of teachers and a large group of curriculum consultants (Caswell 1966, p. 2). Projects such as these were entirely novel to the educational community of that time.

Another manifestation of the growing interest in curriculum was the establishment of university curriculum laboratories. Following the lead of Teachers College, Columbia University, in 1926, a large number of colleges and departments of education founded curriculum laboratories as innovative but indispensable units in their professional programs.

The 1930s brought further developments that established curriculum as a field of study. State departments of education became interested in curriculum revision and improvement and started programs of implementation. Colleges and schools of education, recognizing the significance of curriculum study for education, founded departments of curriculum. The establishment of the Department of Curriculum and Teaching at Teachers College, Columbia University, in 1937 generally is considered to be a landmark in this regard. Finally, the development of the Association for Supervision and Curriculum Development as the nationally recognized organization for curriculum workers

3. An excellent critical assessment of this NSSE yearbook appears in Walker (1975).

secured for curriculum specialization the status of an acknowledged (if ill-defined) field of study.

The fact that the field of curriculum has persisted and established its legitimacy in the educational community is probably evidence that it addresses itself to a specific core of educational problems that are not treated in a systematic way by any other segment of the profession. Curriculum workers do not entirely agree as to what these problems are, except that there seems to be a reasonably large number of them. One writer in the field has concluded that during its first four decades (roughly 1895–1938) the curriculum movement was characterized by interest in four "especially persistent and significant" problems: (1) the nature of knowledge; (2) the nature of knowing; (3) the domain and limits of the new specialty, curriculum; and (4) the translation of curriculum principles and theories into educational practice (Seguel 1966, pp. 180–184). It is Seguel's further contention that since 1938 "there has been remarkably little basic change in the field" (p. 183). In the absence of any comprehensive historical investigation of the curriculum field since 1938, the contention must be viewed as an educated conjecture. If the nature of the curriculum field's central concerns are to be the index, however, there is some evidence that shifts in direction have taken place. For example, Caswell (1966, pp. 5–10) identifies three "matters of central concern" to "most or all of the curriculum movement": (1) the establishment of a consistent relationship between general goals, on the one hand, and specific objectives to guide teaching on the other; (2) the assurance of sound sequence or continuity in curriculum; and (3) the provision for balance in the curriculum.

A survey of eminent curriculum specialists would probably yield a quite disparate list of educational concerns identified as being distinctively curricular in nature, although some issues would undoubtedly emerge more prominently than others. This difficulty in defining the major interests of curriculum study testifies to the relative infancy of the field. Another indication of the developmental state of curriculum is the lack of precision in the meaning of its basic terminology. Among the most persistent difficulties in this regard is the definition of the word "curriculum" when it is used to refer to a plan for education. The following section discusses and assesses some of the variant meanings attached to the term as it is used in the curriculum literature.

Concepts of the Curriculum

The word "curriculum" comes from a Latin root meaning "racecourse," and traditionally, the school's curriculum has represented something like that—figuratively speaking, of course—to most people. Indeed, until quite recently, even the most knowledgeable professional educators regarded curriculum as the relatively standardized ground covered by students in their race toward the finish line (a diploma). It should not be a surprise, then, to find that many current concepts of the curriculum are grounded firmly in this notion that curriculum is a racecourse of subject matters to be mastered.

CURRICULUM AS THE PROGRAM OF STUDIES

When asked to describe the curriculum of a particular high school, the informed layman often recites a list of the subjects offered (or required) by the school. He is likely to answer, "The curriculum includes English, algebra, history, economics, etc." A more specific response would involve a listing of the titles of the courses offered by the school: American History, Elementary Algebra, French I, and the like. Except in a very few instances, subject matter designations convey variable and imprecise information on the content and processes of the subject. Furthermore, reflection on our own experience will serve to remind us that course titles ordinarily reveal very little with regard to learning outcomes and the experiences that students can expect to have while taking the course. For these reasons, therefore, specialists in the field prefer to use the term "program of studies" rather than curriculum to refer to a school's subjects and/or course offerings.

CURRICULUM AS COURSE CONTENT

The content of particular courses in the program often is regarded as the curriculum. For example, when asked to describe the American history curriculum, a teacher might recite the topical outline of the course: discovery and explorations before 1607, settlement of the southern colonies, colonization of New England, etc. This concept of curriculum, like the one described above, was prevalent among most professional educators before the advent of the curriculum movement. It is extremely simple and, indeed, tends toward the naive. It conceives of curriculum solely as the data or information recorded in guides or textbooks and overlooks many additional elements that need to be provided for in a learning plan. Such a conception of curriculum limits planning to the selection and organization of information that learners are to acquire. Clearly, other elements in the educational arena (e.g., the conditions under which learners are to interact with content) need to be included in the definition of curriculum.

CURRICULUM AS PLANNED LEARNING EXPERIENCES

A curriculum conceived of as planned learning experiences[4] is one of the most prevalent concepts among specialists in the field today. For example, Krug

---

4. The difficulties generated by imprecise use of the term "experiences" are dealt with in the section "Learning Activities and Learning Experiences" in Chapter 15.

(1956, p. 4) refers to curriculum as "all the means employed by the school to provide students with opportunities for desirable learning experiences," and Doll (1964, p. 15) writes: "The commonly-accepted definition of the curriculum has changed from *content of courses of study and lists of subjects and courses to all the experiences which are offered to learners under the auspices or direction of the school.*" This broader definition seems to reflect the educational state of affairs more accurately than the previous definitions. The school, after all, is established in order to educate—i.e., to develop along certain lines—the learners placed in its charge. This development is achieved through the experiences that the learners have, and so it seems reasonable to conclude that the curriculum, as a blueprint for education, consists ultimately of the experiences that it is planned for learners to have. While this definition has been criticized by a number of specialists as being far too broad to be functional (e.g., see Taba 1962; Johnson 1967; Inlow 1973), others view this rather expansive definition of curriculum as being too narrow! The latter writers would argue that the curriculum consists ultimately of all the experiences that learners *in fact do have* under the auspices of the school, whether planned for or not.

CURRICULUM AS EXPERIENCES "HAD" UNDER THE AUSPICES OF THE SCHOOL

Writers who favor the broader definition of the curriculum sometimes refer to the "invisible curriculum" or the "hidden curriculum," i.e., those aspects of the curriculum that are unplanned or unintended, and therefore overlooked. They point out that certain planned curriculum experiences are designed, for example, to teach students to read, but as a result of certain other experiences "had" by the students, they may *also* learn to dislike reading. Thus, both the experiences that teach students to read and those that teach dislike of reading must be counted as part of the curriculum, even though the latter experiences were not planned for and are unintended. Along these same lines, some critics of the schools have noted that while students experience and learn the various subject areas of the high school curriculum, they also experience the authoritarian structure of the institution and thus learn conformity to authority along with their algebra, history, and English.

The case for this wide-ranging definition of curriculum is difficult to refute if we are at all interested in the *totality* of students' experiences in school. Obviously, however, the definition is not functional at the *planning* stage of curriculum since the experiences that students actually will have as they interact with the curriculum cannot be known. At the *evaluation* stage of the curriculum construction process, however, it is difficult to refute the validity of this broader definition. Certainly, the experiences that students actually have under the auspices of the school comprise valuable data for assessing the quality and effectiveness of the *planned* curriculum.

CURRICULUM AS A STRUCTURED SERIES OF INTENDED LEARNING OUTCOMES

Among the writers who view "planned learning experiences" as too broad a definition of the curriculum is Mauritz Johnson. In a widely debated essay, this curriculum theorist points out that "there is . . . no experience until an inter-action between the individual and his environment actually occurs. Clearly, such interaction characterizes *instruction*, not curriculum." He argues that because a curriculum constitutes a guide for instruction, it must be viewed as "anticipatory, not reportorial." Curriculum "prescribes (or at least anticipates) the *results* of instruction," and "does not prescribe the *means*, i.e., the activities, materials or even the instructional content to be used in achieving the results." Thus, he maintains, the curriculum can consist only of "a structured series of intended learning outcomes" (Johnson 1967, p. 130). All else is instruction.

THE CURRICULUM-INSTRUCTION CONTROVERSY. The problem of the distinction between curriculum and instruction[5] that Johnson is dealing with above is one that has plagued curriculum specialists since the earliest days of the movement. It arose when the inadequacies of the "course of study" and "content" defini-tions were recognized and attempts were made to deal with the complexities of curriculum through the "experience" definitions.

The distinction between curriculum and instruction that Johnson draws is significant because of the far-reaching effect it has on many traditionally accepted concepts. By restricting the meaning of curriculum to a structured series of intended learning outcomes, all other planning (e.g., of content, learning activi-ties, and evaluation procedures) is viewed as *instructional*, not curriculum, planning. A live classroom situation is regarded as the implementation of the *instructional* plan, not of the curriculum. And an implemented curriculum would logically consist only of achieved learning outcomes.

Johnson's points are attractive and carry impressive logical force, but they nevertheless raise both theoretical and practical difficulties. With regard to the former, we should point out that it is simply not possible, as Johnson proposes, to divorce outcomes from the means used to achieve them.[6] Indeed, the "unin-tended consequences" generated by the "hidden" curricula discussed above dem-onstrate this point in the most graphic terms: The methods and content of reading instruction are clearly inextricably tied to a variety of curriculum out-comes. Moreover, many specialists believe that Johnson's definition of curriculum is not helpful in dealing with real school situations on a practical level. If cur-riculum specialists limit themselves only to the formulation of structured lists of intended learning outcomes, they abdicate responsibility and concern for some

5. See the section "Curriculum Learning Activities versus Instructional Learning Activi-ties" in Chapter 15 for a supplementary discussion of the curriculum-instruction issue.

6. See "The Problem of Ends and Means" in Chapter 13 for an extended discussion of ends and means.

of the most important processes that have traditionally been included in curriculum work (for example, content selection and the specification of learning activities). The semantic question of whether these processes are labeled "curriculum" or "instruction" seems less important than the persistent fact that they must be dealt with at the planning level. This being the case, it would seem that Johnson's definition is either too narrow or is acceptable only to the extent that curriculum planners change their titles to "curriculum and instruction" planners. For the present, at any rate, some broader conception of curriculum than Johnson's seems to be called for to describe the curriculum construction and development activities that are characteristic of specialists in the field.

CURRICULUM AS A (WRITTEN) PLAN FOR ACTION

The problem of the distinction between curriculum and instruction that Johnson deals with also is treated by Macdonald, another prominent curriculum theorist.[7] In the process of arriving at a solution, this specialist achieves tentative definitions not only for curriculum and instruction but for teaching and learning as well.

Macdonald (1965, p. 3) proposes that schooling be conceptualized as the interaction of four systems. The first of these, teaching, is defined as the "professionally oriented behavior of individual personality systems, called teachers. . . ." The second system, learning, consists of the "actions that students perform which teachers perceive to be task related. . . ." Combining these two systems, Macdonald defines the third, instruction, as "the action context within which formal teaching and learning behaviors take place"—in other words, the teaching-learning system. He points out that while teaching and learning taken separately are personality systems, their combination, instruction, is a social system. The fourth system of schooling is the curriculum system, which, like instruction, is a social system. The curriculum system consists of those individuals whose behaviors eventuate in *a* curriculum. Macdonald then defines *a* curriculum as a plan for action, i.e., a plan which guides instruction.

As a plan for the education of students, Macdonald's concept of curriculum is broader than Johnson's since it could contain, in addition to intended learning outcomes, other ingredients, such as content and learning activities. Like Johnson, however, Macdonald uses the principle of *action* or *implementation* of the plan as a basis for the distinction between curriculum and instruction: once the plan is acted upon, these writers say, we are in the realm of instruction.

CURRICULUM PLAN VERSUS FUNCTIONING CURRICULUM. Like the two writers above, a number of prominent curriculum theorists draw a distinction between curriculum and instruction, using the criterion of implementation. For example: "A curriculum is a written document which may contain many ingredients, but

7. See "The Scope and Function of Curriculum in Education: Macdonald's Model" in Chapter 4 for additional commentary and a graphic illustration of Macdonald's system.

basically it is a plan for the education of pupils during their enrollment in a given school" (Beauchamp 1968, p. 6). But if we observe a particular classroom in operation, are we not able to "see" the curriculum functioning? Are we not able to "see" the class move toward certain goals, employ certain content, or engage in certain activities? Furthermore, when asked to evaluate a curriculum, are we content only to examine a document? Certainly the quality of the document will be a factor in our final assessment, but who will deny that the acid test of curriculum quality really depends on how well it functions in "live" situations.

Of course, the evaluation of a functioning curriculum is far more complex and difficult than the evaluation of a curriculum document. For one thing, a curriculum functioning in a classroom situation is "filtered," so to speak, through instruction—i.e., through people in teaching-learning situations—and this condition operates to obscure curriculum-instruction distinctions. Furthermore, when it is operative in live teaching-learning situations, the curriculum is far less tangible than is the document which represents, paradoxically, only its potential. But in the last analysis, it is only when curriculum becomes a functioning component of the educational process in live classroom settings that its potential (as a document) is realized.

In the light of the points made above, this writer believes that *a* curriculum can refer either to a written plan for instruction or to the functioning curriculum that operates to guide and govern the environment and activities of live classroom situations. Consequently, when the distinction needs to be made, we will refer to the written plan as the *curriculum document* or *inert curriculum* and to the curriculum in operation in the classroom as the *functioning, live,* or *operative curriculum.* Clearly, this distinction creates as many problems and raises as many theoretical questions as other analyses of the nature of curriculum, but it does have the advantage of including under the aegis of curriculum those crucial aspects of education with which curriculum planners and workers must deal if their efforts are to affect students in any significant way.

A COMPROMISE CONCEPT OF THE CURRICULUM

Taba finds the extreme breadth of the "experience" definitions of the curriculum nonfunctional. On the other hand, she feels that "excluding from the definition of curriculum everything except the statement of objectives and content outlines and relegating anything that has to do with . . . learning experiences to 'method' might be too confining to be adequate for a modern curriculum" (Taba 1962, p. 9).

Her response to this dilemma of curriculum definition lies "somewhere in between these two extremes" and is worth quoting at length:

> *A sharp distinction between method and curriculum seems unfruitful, but some distinctions need to be drawn between aspects of learning processes and activities that are of concern in curriculum development and those that can be allocated to the realm of specific methods of teaching.*

> *Only certain objectives can be implemented by the nature of curriculum content, its selection and organization. Others can be implemented only by the nature and organization of learning experiences. Thinking, for example, is one of the latter objectives. It would appear, then, that the criteria for the decisions about learning experiences necessary to implement major objectives belong in the realm of curriculum design (Taba 1962, p. 9).*

Clearly, Taba has succeeded in drawing only a very hazy distinction between the aspects of learning processes and activities that are of concern in curriculum and those that are distinctively within the realm of teaching and instruction. The suggestion and the central thrust of Taba's conception of curriculum, however, is that the broader (i.e., more general) aspects of purposes, content, and method belong in the realm of curriculum, while the more proximate and specific aspects properly are allocated to teaching and instruction.[8] Taba's conception of curriculum, unlike Johnson's and Macdonald's, does not employ an "implementation" criterion; rather, it depends on a relatively flexible and subjective judgment as to where a dividing line is to be drawn on a continuum which is clearly ultimate-general at the "curriculum" pole and immediate-specific at the "instruction" end (see Figure 1-1).

FIGURE 1-1
Continuum along which subjective judgments are made to determine the curricular or instructional nature of educational phenomena.

Ultimate-general   Immediate-specific

←───→

CURRICULUM   INSTRUCTION

This relatively loose criterion is useful because it can be employed whether we think of curriculum as a document or as a cluster of phenomena in a live classroom situation. For example, in a curriculum document, prescribed content

---

8. Arno Bellack, another curriculum specialist, tends to agree with Taba:

> *In some quarters an attempt is made to deduce teaching methods [and learning activities] from certain generally accepted psychological principles of a high order of abstraction like the following: Learning is basically goal-seeking behavior; an individual "learns" when he is motivated to achieve goals and purposes that are meaningful and significant to him. . . . In accordance with this view, curriculum content . . . is of value to the student to the extent that it facilitates goal-setting and goal-seeking. The problem for the schools is how best to make available to oncoming generations the accumulated experiences of mankind for them to use and remake in gaining their satisfactions and meeting their needs.*
> *But these high level generalizations [curriculum directives] do not dictate specific teaching procedures; nor do they designate the precise way in which content is to be selected and organized. Of necessity, teachers must seek more explicit formulations [instructional directives] of the teaching-learning process to guide classroom practice (Bellack 1956, pp. 121–122).*

should be specific enough to provide focal thrust for the teacher, but general enough to allow for specific content and materials to be selected according to the teacher's personality and teaching style, and the students' needs and interests. A curriculum unit on prejudice in this instance might allow for a wide variety of alternative content, but certainly would reject attempts to include items from geology or analytic geometry. The same sort of distinction might be drawn in live classroom situations, although the complexities involved would make it much more difficult. Questions to be asked might include: Is the specific content being treated in the classroom consonant with general curriculum content? Are the specific activities that students are engaged in congruent with the intent and thrust of the general activities suggested in the curriculum? Are the unanticipated outcomes observed more a function of curriculum content and activities or of instructional factors?

Put in a more general way, we might say that the curriculum provides direction for classroom instruction, but it does not consist of a series of lesson plans. It is the teacher's prerogative and responsibility to interpret and translate the curriculum document in terms of her own and her students' experience.

THE NECESSITY OF MULTIPLE CONCEPTS

The concepts of curriculum discussed in the previous sections account for only a fraction of the number that have been proposed over the past five or six decades by scholars. Instead of being disturbed by this state of affairs, however, some specialists believe that the definitions of curriculum *should* be variable. Mann, for example holds that defining curriculum "is a matter of how, for the convenience of enacting a commitment," the student of curriculum "decides to imagine the in fact unsliced and unsliceable pie to be sliced" (in Mills 1971, p. 731). This definition is not as loose as it immediately appears, since it is tied to "the convenience of enacting a commitment"—in other words, to intended purposes in carrying out curricular decisions. Such a position is supported by Schwab (1969, pp. 1, 2), who asserts that the curriculum field is moribund because of its preoccupation with fine theoretical points (like the precise definition of the term "curriculum"). He insists that the curriculum field will rejuvenate itself only when it becomes concerned primarily with "the practical," a concept he views as action based on defensible decisions. Defensible decisions, of course, must involve the examination of philosophical assumptions and "theoretical" bases, and Schwab's position does not exclude theory in this sense. His contention constitutes, rather, a reaction against abstruse and often esoteric controversy in the curriculum field over such issues as the precise definition of a curriculum.

Schwab's criticism is well taken. The present state of curriculum in the public schools makes it abundantly clear that a search for *the* correct definition of the term is not a very productive enterprise and that scholars might better spend their time dealing with the realities of curriculum making in practical school situations. Beyond this, however, recent developments in the scientific community indicate that the practice of permitting only a single acceptable definition for each referent may not even be *theoretically* sound.

Since the earliest decades of the twentieth century, science has generally ceased to regard definitions (and theories) as descriptions of metaphysical reality. Rather, definitions have come to be viewed more as "policies" or "guides to action" (Conant 1952, p. 55 ff.). For example, if a layman were to ask a physicist for a definition of light, he would likely be told that light may be a wave phenomenon (wave theory) or it may be composed of particles (corpuscular theory). If the layman insisted that he wanted to know what light "really" is—i.e., if he insisted on *the* correct definition of light—the physicist would probably tell him, "That isn't a useful question; physicists have stopped asking it" (Conant 1952, p. 80). The reason that physicists no longer are interested in a "correct" definition of light is that it is irrelevant. One definition, within a limited situation, enables scientists to account for certain phenomena; the other definition, in another set of circumstances, is more useful. This concept of the function of definition is similar to that of Mann.

It seems reasonable that specialists in the curriculum field might profit from adopting this same scientific stance in their own investigations. As we have previously pointed out, for curriculum *evaluation* activities, the definition that is most useful is one that includes experiences "had" by learners, planned for or not. On the other hand, the planning stage of curriculum cannot possibly utilize a definition that includes experiences "had," but only one that includes *proposed* content and activities that will produce the planned (or rather "hoped-for") experiences. Also, at the planning stage it seems reasonable to conceptualize the curriculum as a tangible written document which can be referred to as a plan for action. But again, at the evaluation stage, curriculum unavoidably must be conceived of as a cluster of phenomena embedded in the live classroom situation.

The inference to be drawn from the foregoing observations seems to be that any definition of curriculum will necessarily vary according to the purposes which are to be accomplished. Like the physicist's concept of light, the definition of curriculum that is most useful in achieving the purposes of the situation at hand is the one that is most "correct" for that situation.

Other Aspects of the Curriculum Field

The curriculum field includes a number of concepts and processes that are related to the curriculum as it was discussed above, but which at the same time represent quite distinct areas. These areas are represented in the literature by such terms as "curriculum foundations," "curriculum design," "curriculum construction," "curriculum development," and "curriculum improvement." Unfortunately, there is little agreement among specialists in the field with respect to the precise meaning of such terms and often they are used loosely and interchangeably. The following sections attempt to clarify the distinctions among the terms, and in so doing provide the reader with some idea of the scope of curriculum study.

CURRICULUM FOUNDATIONS

Curriculum foundations are those basic forces that influence and shape the content and organization of the curriculum. Curriculum foundations often are referred to in the literature as the sources or the determinants of the curriculum.

Although the precise areas included in the term "foundations" still are disputed by specialists, most would agree that some, if not all, of the following areas should be included.

PHILOSOPHY AND THE NATURE OF KNOWLEDGE. Philosophy and philosophical assumptions, of course, undergird all of the foundational areas. However, basic assumptions about philosophy and the nature of knowledge are particularly relevant and influential in curriculum work since education's major focus *is* knowledge and learning. Curriculum objectives and content will vary considerably depending, for example, upon whether one believes that "true" knowledge exists out there in the "real world" or whether "true" knowledge is located internally, within the subjective recesses of the individual mind. In the former instance the curriculum will emphasize activities that center on objective or "scientific" studies and the learning of fixed and objective ideas and concepts. In the latter instance, the curriculum will emphasize symbolic and metaphorical studies, such as literature and art. Inquiring into the nature of knowledge is often referred to in the literature as epistemology. This foundational area and its implications for curriculum are discussed in greater detail in Chapters 5 and 6.

SOCIETY AND CULTURE. Inasmuch as schools were invented by social groups to secure the survival of the cultural heritage, it is not surprising that society and its culture exert an enormous influence on the curriculum. Traditional (and often unconscious) assumptions, values, and ideas about what is important or unimportant, good or bad, are translated into curriculum objectives, content, and learning activities. Some notion of the influence of culture on curriculum may be gained by examining and comparing British and American textbooks that deal with the American Revolution. Not only will the objectives and content of the texts differ, but the prominence and importance accorded the event itself will tend to be much greater in American texts. Chapters 7 and 8 provide an extended analysis of the relationship of society and culture to the curriculum.

THE INDIVIDUAL. The nature of the individual human organism influences the curriculum on at least two levels. First, the biopsychological nature of man places certain limits on the content and organization of the curriculum. Man is capable of learning only what his genes will allow him to learn. Thus, a curriculum intended to teach students to fly unaided by mechanical devices or to learn Chinese in a week would be doomed to failure. Second, and no less important, man's philosophical conceptions of his own nature will exert a significant influence on the curriculum. For example, notions about the innate goodness or badness of man will greatly affect the curriculum. If man is perceived as innately good, the curriculum is likely to allow learners substantial latitude in pursuing their studies. But if man is perceived as innately evil (as in the Calvinist doctrine), the curriculum will be highly prescriptive and even coercive. The individual as a foundational influence is discussed in Chapters 9 and 10.

LEARNING THEORY. Notions about *how* human beings learn will affect the shape of the curriculum. For example, the nineteenth-century theory (called "faculty psychology") that the mind was analogous to a muscle and would develop its powers through mental exercise led to curricula that emphasized drill in difficult academic subjects such as Latin and mathematics. Another popular theory of learning has held that individuals "learn by doing." This point of view eventuated in curricula that provided students with problems and "raw materials" and required them to "discover" knowledge and skills. A full discussion of the effect of learning theory on curricula appears in Chapters 11 and 12.

CURRICULUM DESIGN

Curriculum design most commonly refers to the arrangement of the components or elements of a curriculum. Often the term "curriculum organization" is used to indicate curriculum design. Ordinarily, the components or elements included in *a* curriculum are (1) aims, goals, and objectives; (2) subject matter or content; (3) learning activities; and (4) evaluation. (See Part III, "Anatomy of the Curriculum" for a detailed treatment of each of these curriculum elements.) Thus, the nature of these elements and the pattern of organization in which they are brought together as a unified curriculum constitute the curriculum design. It should be emphasized here that the term "curriculum design" identifies a substantive entity; it does not refer to a process.

More often than not, the most prominent feature of curriculum designs is their pattern of content organization. Thus, the nomenclature employed to identify various curriculum designs ordinarily refers to content organization. Some of the more familiar designs that have drawn their organizing principles from content include the subject design, the disciplines design, and the broad-fields design. A design that has not centered on content is the activities curriculum, which draws its organizing principles from the felt needs and interests of learners. The areas-of-living design centers on the social functions that learners will be required to perform as adults, and the social-problems design, as its name implies, is organized around current social problems. Chapters 17 and 18 of this text describe in detail a number of curriculum designs and discuss those problems of curriculum work that center on design.

CURRICULUM CONSTRUCTION

Curriculum construction is a term that has traditionally been employed to refer vaguely to all the processes involved in the building or making of curricula. It appears in the literature as a synonym for curriculum development and curriculum engineering. In this text we shall use the term in a more restricted sense. We define curriculum construction as the decision-making process that involves only the determination of the nature and organization of curriculum components. These decisions would involve answering such questions as the following: What is the nature of a good society? What is the nature of man? What is the good life? What is the nature of knowledge? What should the aims of education be? What curriculum design will most effectively actualize our foundational commitments? What content (knowledge) should all students learn? What activities should learners engage in as they interact with content? How should we assess the merit of educational aims, of content, and of learning activities?

Clearly, though we have sought to limit the meaning of curriculum construction, its parameters remain immense. Curriculum construction is a critical process because, more than any other aspect of the curriculum field, it determines the nature and organization of the curriculum to which learners will be exposed.

CURRICULUM DEVELOPMENT

Like curriculum construction, curriculum development refers to a process. It is intimately related to curriculum construction, but is distinguished from it by virtue of the nature of its decisions. Curriculum development is a process which determines how curriculum construction will proceed. It is concerned with the following questions: Who will be involved in curriculum construction—teachers, administrators, parents, students? What procedures will be used in curriculum construction—administrative direction, faculty committees, university consultation? If committees are to be employed, how will they be organized?[9]

In real situations curriculum development does not discretely precede curriculum construction. The processes usually overlap, with development and construction decisions being made at the same time. For example, a curriculum development decision to employ English teachers to structure the high school literature curriculum implies certain prior curriculum construction decisions regarding the nature of English (literature) and the organization of the curriculum along subject lines.

9. Curriculum development is a term that most educationists use to refer broadly to all the processes of constructing and implementing curricula. While the more restrictive definition that we propose breaks with this traditional usage and thus creates some degree of confusion, we believe that the increased precision achieved can ultimately improve communication among curriculum specialists.

Obviously, the integration of the processes of curriculum construction and curriculum development is unavoidable. The distinction is useful, however, in identifying and focusing on the nature of the decision to be made: curriculum construction is concerned with the curriculum, while curriculum development is concerned with the processes of construction.

CURRICULUM IMPLEMENTATION

Curriculum implementation is one of the few terms that is used consistently in this field. It means simply putting into effect the curriculum that was produced by the construction and development processes. It should be pointed out here that since the curriculum by definition includes an evaluation component, implementation activities will include provision for an appraisal of the effectiveness of the curriculum. Thus, curriculum implementation by definition provides evaluative feedback to the construction/development processes, in which the data are utilized for curriculum revision and improvement.

A situation in which it were possible to "implement" a "new curriculum" in toto in a "virgin" school setting might appear at first to be the ideal. Not only does such a situation rarely occur, but it may in theory be undesirable. As suggested in the previous paragraphs, the curriculum construction/development/implementation processes are not sequential. They occur both in parallel lines as well as in tandem. Construction and development are usually begun in certain curricular areas and implemented on a trial basis as an alternative to present practices. Evaluative data then are utilized in the construction/development phases to give direction to further construction/development activities and/or to modify the implemented portion of the curriculum. The entire process is highly complex and requires extremely skillful orchestration of participants and components for effective results. Further discussion of implementation-feedback problems is contained in Chapter 16.

CURRICULUM ENGINEERING

Curriculum engineering is a term of more recent vintage than the three discussed above. Beauchamp defines curriculum engineering as "all of the processes necessary to make a curriculum system functional in schools." A curriculum system "has three primary functions: (1) to produce a curriculum, (2) to implement the curriculum, and (3) to appraise the effectiveness of the curriculum and the curriculum system" (Beauchamp 1968, p. 108). Although Beauchamp has employed somewhat different language and a slightly variant division of functions, his curriculum system roughly corresponds to what we have described as the processes of curriculum construction, development, and implementation. Consequently, we would agree with Beauchamp's concept of curriculum engineering, except that we would prefer to define it as the collective processes of curriculum construction, development, and implementation.

CURRICULUM IMPROVEMENT VERSUS
CURRICULUM CHANGE

Curriculum improvement and curriculum change, as well as curriculum revision, are generally synonyms in the literature. However, Taba (1962, p. 454) has drawn a distinction that is not only interesting, but significant: "curriculum improvement means changing certain aspects of the curriculum without changing the fundamental conceptions of it or its organization." By contrast, she sees curriculum change involving transformation of the entire curriculum scheme, including design, goals, content, learning activities, scope, etc. Perhaps most important, curriculum change involves change in the value assumptions on which all the aforementioned areas of the curriculum are based.

Curriculum improvement usually is regarded favorably (and enthusiastically) by most individuals and groups concerned with schooling. Because it essentially involves only a refinement of the status quo with minimal alteration of value orientation, it is a relatively safe enterprise. But curriculum *change* is not so readily accepted. "To change a curriculum means, in a way, to change an institution" (Taba 1962, p. 454). This involves change in values, people, society and culture, and basic assumptions about what constitutes education and the good life. It is not surprising, therefore, to find that curriculum change, when it does occur, usually occurs only very gradually and in response to the pressures of historical circumstance. It is very rare that widespread, significant, and lasting curriculum change has been brought about as a result of the efforts of professional educators. Attempts to change the curriculum are almost always vehemently resisted, and individuals who engage in curriculum change should expect to assume the risks that accompany any attempt to reorder the society and its value structure.

Two final points should be made about the nature of curriculum change. First, change is inevitable; it will occur despite attempts to inhibit it. Second, change, itself, is neither good nor bad; it is the *direction* of change and the value judgment placed on it that determines its goodness or badness. It seems natural to infer from these two points that since change will occur in any case, it is preferable that it be directed by intelligent human intervention than that it be allowed to occur randomly as a result of accidental historical circumstance. Chapter 21 discusses in greater detail some personal issues connected with the area of curriculum change.

CURRICULAR VERSUS NONCURRICULAR ISSUES

We have seen in the previous sections that even curriculum specialists are not entirely clear on the parameters of their area of specialization. There is disagreement on the nature of "the curriculum," for example, and the distinction between curriculum and instruction remains a point of debate. Nevertheless, it is possible in a general way to identify certain issues as being primarily *curricular*, while others—though they affect the curriculum—are better classified as administrative, instructional, economic, political, etc.

Typically, curricular issues are those that involve curriculum foundations, curriculum design, the components or elements of the curriculum, curriculum engineering, and curriculum improvement and change. These areas represent the subject matter of curriculum study and constitute (loosely) the *substantive structure* of the curriculum field. Such issues as class scheduling, school plant design, and school finance are clearly noncurricular (though they affect the curriculum) and are rarely treated by curriculum specialists.

Most educational issues, however, are highly complex and involve subject matter that is classifiable in more than one category of specialization. For example, "nongrading" or "continuous progress schooling" could be treated either as an administrative or curriculum problem. The difference in treatment would depend upon the methods of inquiry and the contextual framework employed in dealing with it. The characteristic methodologies and approaches used in particular areas of specialization are called the *syntactical structure* of the field.

In the case cited above, nongrading may be viewed as one of several possible administrative responses to the wider issue of grouping students for instruction. The administrator, typically, would be concerned with procedures for scheduling and grouping the students on a nongraded basis. He might, in addition, be concerned with advantages and disadvantages of nongrading in terms of staff utilization, economy, and efficiency in learning. While some of his attention might be directed at considerations that are curricular in nature, on the whole his activities would be identified as administrative.

By contrast, a curriculum specialist approaching the issue of nongrading would immediately define the problem in terms of the broader issue of grouping students for effective learning. He would inevitably review foundational areas and ultimately make an assessment of the nongrading proposal in terms of the total curriculum—its aims, content, and other components. While strategies for implementing the nongrading proposal would eventually concern him, such matters as scheduling, convenience, and economy would not be central to his deliberations.

Because education involves so many interacting variables, it is impossible to indicate definitively where one domain of special inquiry ends and another begins. Nevertheless, the study of curriculum, broad as it is, clearly excludes extensive segments of the educational enterprise. In general, the areas identified in this chapter constitute what is generally understood as the curriculum field.

References

Beauchamp, George A. 1968. *Curriculum Theory*. 2d ed. Wilmette, Ill.: The Kagg Press.

Bellack, Arno A. 1956. "Selection and Organization of Curriculum Content: An Analysis." In *What Shall the High Schools Teach?* Yearbook. Washington, D.C.: The Association for Supervision and Curriculum Development, chap. IV.

Caswell, Hollis L. 1966. "Emergence of the Curriculum as a Field of Professional

Work and Study." In *Precedents and Promises in the Curriculum Field*, edited by Helen P. Robison. New York: Teachers College Press.

Conant, James B. 1952. *Modern Science and Modern Man*. Garden City, N.Y.: Doubleday Anchor Books.

Doll, Ronald C. 1964. *Curriculum Improvement: Decision-Making and Process*. Boston: Allyn and Bacon.

Inlow, Gail M. 1973. *The Emergent in Curriculum*. 2d ed. New York: John Wiley & Sons.

Johnson, Mauritz. 1967. "Definitions and Models in Curriculum Theory." *Educational Theory* (April), pp. 127–140.

Kliebard, Herbert M. 1968 "The Curriculum Field in Retrospect." In *Technology and the Curriculum*, edited by Paul F. Witt. New York: Teachers College Press.

Krug, Edward A. 1956. *Administering Curriculum Planning*. New York: Harper & Row, Publishers.

Macdonald, James B. 1965. "Educational Models for Instruction—Introduction." In *Theories of Instruction*, edited by James B. Macdonald and Robert R. Leeper. Washington, D.C.: The Association for Supervision and Curriculum Development.

Mann, John S. 1969. "The Curriculum Worker." Paper presented at ASCD Annual Conference Pre-Conference Seminar. Chicago (March), mimeographed. As quoted in Patricia Mills, "In Search of Ambiguity." *Educational Leadership* (April 1971).

Schwab, Joseph J. 1969. "The Practical: A Language for Curriculum." *School Review* (November).

Seguel, Mary Louise. 1966. *The Curriculum Field: Its Formative Years*. New York: Teachers College Press.

Taba, Hilda. 1962. *Curriculum Development: Theory and Practice*. New York: Harcourt Brace Jovanovich.

Walker, Decker F. 1975. "The Curriculum Field in Formation: A Review of the Twenty-Sixth Yearbook of the National Society for the Study of Education." *Curriculum Theory Network* (a journal from the Ontario Institute for Studies in Education). Vol. 4, No. 4.

CHAPTER 2
HISTORICAL EVOLUTION OF THE CURRICULUM: COLONIAL BEGINNINGS TO THE CIVIL WAR

Perhaps, through an evolutionary process profiting from awareness of the past and especially from strengths and weaknesses in earlier curriculum efforts, we will both produce improved curriculum materials and advance the study of curriculum. —JOHN GOODLAD

The field of curriculum, like education in general, has been prone to deal with its most complex problems in terms of fads and slogans. In recent years, for example, it has been "fashionable" to become excited about such marvelous discoveries as team teaching, programmed instruction, behavioral objectives, nongrading, discovery learning, and accountability, to mention just a few. Although most innovations fade from the scene having had little impact on the curriculum, few "reformers" seem to notice; in the curriculum game there is always a great new panacea just around the corner. The whole process, unfortunately, seems characteristic of a firmly established American operating principle: If you do not know what to do, do *something*.

Many curriculum scholars believe that the "bandwagonism" and hit-or-miss methods that characterize the curriculum field are due partly to its failure to give attention to the historical framework out of which curriculum problems arise. For example, Goodlad (1966, p. 91) notes that many curriculum reformers approach "persistent, recurring problems of curriculum construction in the naive belief that no one had looked at them before," and Kliebard (1968, p. 69), observes that the curriculum field's ahistorical stance leaves each generation "to discover anew the persistent and perplexing questions that characterize the field." As an example, the latter writer points to recent concern with curriculum for the disadvantaged. He says of this sloganized concern, "we usually fail to see it in the perspective of the larger issue of curriculum differentiation, not recognizing that our present concern is actually part of a recurring debate, with roots in our recent past" (Kliebard 1968, p. 69).

Another example of misplaced emphasis in curriculum reform is the nongrading issue mentioned in Chapter 1. Nongrading, of course, is only one response to the larger persistent issue of grouping learners for effective instruction. Furthermore, history reveals that until the grouping of children by chronological age (grading) was introduced in the early nineteenth century, American schools had *always* been "nongraded." Indeed, it was not until the time of the Civil War that the graded elementary school as we know it became an established American institution. Thus, it turns out that nongraded schools are actually more traditional than graded ones!

The characteristically ahistorical bias of planners might be due to a desire to deal afresh with curriculum, unhampered by the heavy hand of tradition, one of the most persistent influences on curriculum construction (Kliebard, 1968, p. 69). Whatever the reason, however, it seems clear that nonhistorical approaches are unwarranted and that an intimate acquaintance with the historical development of curriculum—especially American curriculum—can be an important asset in dealing with the problems of curriculum planning. More particularly, an historical perspective can "make us aware of the possibility of change, of the complexity of change, and of the carryover of the past into our present situation and future aspirations" (Charlton 1968, p. 77). With these justifications in mind, then, we turn to a brief overview of the evolution of the curriculum in American culture. It should go without saying, however, that intensive study of far more rigorous treatments than are possible in this text is essential for those students who will be significantly involved in curriculum planning.

Colonial Beginnings: Curriculum in the Seventeenth Century

It is appropriate that an account of the development of American public school curriculum begins with the New England Puritans, for these settlers, to a greater degree than their neighbors in the middle colonies and on the southern plantations, placed a high value on schools and learning. Indeed, some historians believe that it was "in the cultivation of the intellectual life that the genius of New England found its fullest expression" (Edwards and Richey 1963, p. 31).

The establishment of a utopian theocratic state was central to the Puritans' design in immigrating to America. It was the Puritans' dream, when they came to Massachusetts in 1628, to create in the wilderness a "City upon a Hill" dedicated to the glory of God and inhabited by God's "visible Saints." In order to reach this goal, strict religious orthodoxy was required of all who would aspire to membership in state and church (indivisible in the Puritan mind), and political power was exercised exclusively by an ecclesiastical aristocracy. Democracy was perceived as the worst form of government, and John Cotton, a highly esteemed minister of the day, was prompted to write: "Democracy, I do not conceyve that ever God did ordeyne as fitt government eyther for church or commonwealth. If the people be governors, who shall be governed?"

Substantial evidence points to the primarily religious focus of Puritan intellectual activity. All Puritans sought as an ultimate goal a mystical union with God that conveyed assurance of salvation. But they felt that such an experience could occur only as the culmination of an extended ordeal that included long hours of spiritual and intellectual exercises, such as church going and Bible reading. It was the learned, therefore, who were perceived as the best equipped to attain a state of grace, while the ignorant were the unregenerate ones, damned to suffer the torments of hell fire.

ELEMENTARY CURRICULUM

Since it was through the Bible that God spoke directly to man on all matters, even the most mundane, the Puritans believed that firsthand knowledge of Scripture was essential for salvation. Obviously, then, the ability to read was a vital need for every member of the community.

The Puritans' concern with religion and the ability to read is demonstrated in the well-known "Old Deluder Satan Act," passed by the General Court of Massachusetts (the Massachusetts legislature) in 1647. This law made elementary education compulsory (but by no means free) for every child living in the Bay Colony.

Given the Puritan notions of religion, government, and salvation, it is not surprising that the elementary school curriculum was restricted mainly to a blend of reading and religion. Indeed, even though the "Old Deluder Satan Act" called for instruction in writing, other laws[1] specified only that children be taught to "read and understand the principles of religion and the Capitall Laws of this country."

In addition to being narrow, the curriculum was often of meager quality due, necessarily, to the Puritans' preoccupation with the priority of wrenching a livelihood from the rugged New England country. Thus, in many schools, boys and girls were taught only to recognize the ABC's, perhaps to do some elemental reading, and, by rote, to repeat the rudiments of religious faith. In some of the better schools, however, the curriculum did include writing and arithmetic, although these subjects often were taught by a specially trained master in a separate "writing school."

The duration of the elementary course ranged from a few weeks to three years. Ordinarily, a boy who was to go on to secondary education (the Latin grammar school) would be expected to have completed the course by the age

1. For example, the Massachusetts Law of 1642 and the Connecticut Law of 1650.

of seven or eight. Indeed, entrance requirements of the Latin grammar schools usually specified that no boys be admitted to "ye learning of English Books, but such as have been before taught to spell ye letters well to begin to Read . . . to write, & Cipher for numeracion, & addicion, & no further" (quoted in Noble 1954, pp. 25, 26). Others, who were not planning to continue their educations at a higher level, might attend some form of elementary school until they were twelve, at which time, it was hoped, they had learned to read. It should be noted that the concept, as we know it, of grouping students into "grades" was unknown at this time, and that secondary and higher education were not available to females.

Text materials of the times reflect the fact that instruction in reading and religion was almost always combined (or as we would say, "integrated"). The "hornbook," for example, the chief resource for the teaching of beginning reading in seventeenth-century New England, was simply a piece of paper or parchment on which the alphabet, the Lord's Prayer, some simple syllables, and a benediction were written. The paper was attached to a paddle-shaped board and covered with a piece of transparent horn for durability.

In the last decade of the seventeenth century, the *New England Primer* was published in Boston. This first American basal reader, permeated with religious doctrine, became the most widely used textbook in the colonies for over a hundred years. Starting with the alphabet in capital and small letters, the *Primer* proceeds to syllables ("ab, eb, ib"), and then to words, almost all of which are religious and moral in nature. About half the book is taken up by the "Shorter Catechism." The somber caste of Puritan religion and morals is evident in the following selection:

> I in the Burying Place may see
>   Graves shorter there than I
> From Death's Arrest no Age is free
>   Young children too may die;
> My God, may such an awful sight,
>   Awakening be to me!
> Oh! that by early Grace I might
>   For Death prepared be.

For those children who advanced beyond the hornbook or *Primer*, the Bible, the Testament, and the Psalter became the textbooks of instruction.

SECONDARY CURRICULUM: THE LATIN GRAMMAR SCHOOLS

The "Old Deluder Satan Act" of 1647, in addition to providing for elementary reading schools, required towns numbering 100 or more families to establish secondary schools (Latin grammar schools). As already pointed out, however, Puritan New England was not a democracy. These secondary schools were not intended to provide postelementary education for the people, but rather to prepare the upper classes (and perhaps a few poor boys who might demonstrate exceptional ability) for the university.

It was quite important for the Puritan fathers "to instruct youth so far as they may be fitted for the university" because it was the university that provided the commonwealth with its elite corps—the ministers—who were best fitted to shepherd the Puritan flock. Indeed, the Puritans' intense concern for the perpetuation of an orthodox church and commonwealth is clearly demonstrated by the founding of Harvard College. In 1636, only eight years after the first Puritan set foot in the Massachusetts wilderness, that college was established principally for the purpose of training Puritan ministers.[2]

The Puritans (like most Protestants) had earlier adopted the classical heritage as part of their religious orthodoxy; thus, their view of a "learned minister" was of a man who had acquired the ability to read and study the Scriptures in their original languages—Latin, Greek, and oftentimes Hebrew. He was a man who had devoted himself to a life of scholarship and intellectual leadership in the church and community.

The first secondary school to be established in the English colonies was the Boston Latin School, founded in 1635. In the succeeding half-dozen decades this type of secondary school became highly popular, and dozens of Latin grammar schools sprang up throughout New England and even in the middle and southern colonies.

Although few courses of study which detail the exact nature of the Latin grammar school curriculum are preserved, the evidence we have leaves little doubt about the major emphasis: Latin, Greek, and more Latin. As in the case of the elementary schools, the quality of the curriculum might vary considerably from one grammar school to another; but in the better schools, the curriculum, though very narrow, was extremely rigorous.

Beginning at the age of seven or eight, the boys were required to memorize their Latin accidence and grammar, and to read and parse simple Latin sentences. When they had mastered these rudiments, they moved on to such works as *Aesop's Fables* and Erasmus' *Colloquies,* by the fourth year beginning the study of Greek. In the fifth and sixth years (by now the boys were twelve or thirteen) they wrote Latin compositions and read such works as Ovid's *Metamorphosis,* Cicero's *Letters,* and Vergil's *Aeneid.* During their seventh and final year, the scholars (as they were called) read the New Testament and

---

2. Although Harvard was founded primarily to train Puritan ministers, it would be incorrect to regard it narrowly as a vocational-training institution. It was a common seventeenth-century viewpoint that all knowledge came from God and that all education was pursued so that His ways might be made more manifest. To the Puritan mind, learning and Godliness were natural and necessary counterparts. Thus, in addition to advanced training in Puritan religious orthodoxy, the Harvard curriculum promoted a much broader aim: "to advance *Learning* and perpetuate it to Posterity. . . ." That Harvard was more than a vocational-training school for ministers is demonstrated by the fact that during the seventeenth century no more than half of its graduates actually became ministers (Miller and Johnson 1963, pp. 698–701).

a variety of classical authors, such as Horace, Juvenal, Persius, Isocrates, and Hesiod; they wrote compositions and verses in Latin, and translated Greek into Latin; they studied rhetoric and Roman history, and, if especially able, began the study of Hebrew (Miller and Johnson 1963, pp. 697, 698). Any boy who satisfactorily completed this stiff seven-year curriculum was eminently well prepared to enter the early colonial colleges.

Although apparently more secular than religious, the curriculum of the Latin grammar school in fact strongly supported the religious motive. In the first place, considerable reading from the Bible and other religious texts was required in addition to the study of classical languages and antiquity. But as we suggested in footnote 2 on Harvard College, learning per se was considered an essential counterpart of Godliness—and a requisite for salvation. "The full time of the [Latin grammar] school was devoted to the Bible and the classics, with no [secular] humanistic implications. According to [Cotton] Mather, the religious spirit infused all instruction" (Noble 1954, p. 36).

CURRICULA IN THE SCHOOLS OF THE
MIDDLE COLONIES AND THE SOUTH

For a number of geographic, political, and religious reasons, schools and education did not receive the emphasis in the other colonies that they did in New England. Nevertheless, when they did appear, their curricula were dominated by the religious motive and were very much like those of the New England schools. In most instances, the elementary schools were established by religious groups to teach children prayers, hymns, and other items of religious doctrine, and how to read from the Bible and to write. The secondary school curriculum, shaped as it was by the entrance requirements of Harvard, consisted entirely of the study of the classical languages, religion, and sometimes a little arithmetic.

CONCLUSION

This brief account of the curriculum in seventeenth-century colonial schools indicates how thoroughly a society's traditions, culture, and social philosophy influence the character of its schools' curricula. A society dominated by religion had produced a school curriculum that was religious in every aspect. In the following section, we shall see how economic, social, and cultural changes during the eighteenth century were responsible for bringing about significant modifications in the organization and curricula of American schools.

Later Colonial Developments: Curriculum in the
Eighteenth Century

During the eighteenth century, immigration to the English colonies in North America expanded dramatically. Now, in addition to the English, large numbers of Germans and Scotch-Irish arrived. Finding the areas along the eastern seaboard largely occupied, the newcomers moved westward, pushing back the frontiers, and at the same time helping to create, through their successful experiences with self-reliance and independent decision making, the democratic spirit that was to influence American schools and culture for years to come.

Among the most important economic developments of the eighteenth century was the tremendous upsurge of trade and commerce. The eastern cities became mercantile centers, and a new class of capitalist merchant-landholders accumulated vast fortunes in a wide variety of business enterprises, from land speculation and shipbuilding, to the infamous New England-based rum and slave trade. The austere, theocratic social order of seventeenth-century New England was unable to withstand the onslaught of these events, and the elected Saints of the Puritan leadership found themselves willingly transformed into an upper-middle-class capitalist Yankee aristocracy.

This spread of affluence led to a general mood of optimism and faith in the continual progress of man and society. Such an environment, of course, provided a cordial context for the growth of liberal new concepts of the nature of man and his place in the universe. Among the most important of these were the ideas of the English philosopher John Locke (1632–1704).[3] In his famous work, *An Essay Concerning Human Understanding* (1690), he wrote:

> *Let us suppose the mind to be, as we say, white paper, void of characters, without any ideas; how comes it to be furnished? . . . Whence has it all the materials of reason and knowledge? To this I answer in one word, from experience: in that all our knowledge is founded, and from that it ultimately derives itself.*

To argue that ideas are not innate, but come about from experience tended to undercut previously held notions about superiority due to inherited qualities. If men's minds were, indeed, "white paper" at birth, then men were born equal, and anyone, by virtue of self-discipline and industry might make of himself what he wished. Such a concept of the nature of the mind was being validated as a result of the frontier experience.

Another important consequence of Locke's ideas was that they shifted the focal point of man's attention from the intangible and spiritual to the empirical and secular. It is not surprising, then, to note an upsurge of interest in science during the eighteenth century. Nor is it surprising to find the wrathful and capricious despot who was the Puritans' God replaced, at least among many of the better educated, by a more reasonable and benevolent Deity.

Religion by no means ceased to be an important force during this time; but it tended to accommodate itself by taking on a form known as "Deism." The Deists (a considerable number of whom were present at the Constitutional Convention of 1787) held that God is "a wise and benevolent architect, the Designer of an intricately organized and complicated machine, nature, which

---

3. See Thayer (1965, chap. 3, "The Influence of John Locke").

operates in accordance with consistent and unchanging laws" (Thayer 1965, p. 29).

This substitution of a "natural" theology for a Bible-based one was not universal, but it does indicate the drift toward secularisim that made it possible for the school curriculum to free itself from the tight grip of religion.

ELEMENTARY CURRICULUM

The educational activities of various church denominations continued to be vigorously pressed, perhaps because of secular trends. The purpose of these activities, of course, was religious indoctrination. Interest was centered mainly at the elementary level, and the curriculum in these church-supported schools consisted mainly of reading, religion, and morals, with attention sometimes being given, for practical reasons, to writing and arithmetic. The principal textbooks of instruction continued to be the Bible, the Testament, and the Psalter.

CURRICULUM IN THE "ENGLISH SCHOOLS"

The increase in business, trade, and commerce created a need for workers trained in a variety of practical skills: surveying, gauging, and dialing; bookkeeping and accounting; letter writing; navigating; ship designing; and many others. To meet such needs, a number of private venture "English schools" or "English grammar schools" sprang up in the larger cities of the East. The curriculum of these entirely secular vocational schools included such varied subjects as writing, arithmetic, geometry, trigonometry, surveying, bookkeeping, accounting, and even foreign languages such as Italian and Portuguese for use in international trade. Some of the English schools even admitted girls, preparing them for "polite society" by teaching such courses as dancing, singing, painting, and embroidery.

Not bound by college entrance requirements, these private venture schools were able to offer a varied curriculum specifically designed to satisfy the particular demands of their clientele; as private ventures, however, they were not usually conceived of as permanent institutions, and eventually they succumbed in the competition with the more substantial *academy,* described below.

CURRICULUM IN THE LATIN GRAMMAR SCHOOLS

As families grew in wealth, they aspired to higher social standing and acceptance in "polite society." In eighteenth-century America, this required not only refined speech and gracious manners, but familiarity with the Latin and Greek tongues and the best of the classical authors. Thus, the college preparatory Latin grammar schools continued, as they had in the past, to focus on the study of the ancient languages and literatures; but now the purpose of this study became much less religious in nature and more and more oriented toward fashioning the "cultured gentleman and scholar."

But the clientele of the Latin grammar schools included many sons of the new capitalist bourgeois, a group which was well aware of the practical value of such subjects as arithmetic, accounting, and bookkeeping in the counting houses their sons would inherit. While they valued, for social reasons, the polish afforded by knowledge of the classics, they were practical enough to demand that something more useful be included in their sons' educations. Although some attempts were made to meet the demands of the times by liberalizing the curriculum, the Latin grammar schools, bound as they were by college entrance requirements and tradition, were unable and unwilling to adapt, and, as did the English schools, eventually yielded to a new kind of secondary school: the academy.

THE ACADEMY

Benjamin Franklin often is credited with establishing the first academy in Philadelphia in 1751. The first American educational institution not patterned on a European model, it became the dominant type of secondary school in America by the middle of the nineteenth century.

Typically, the academy was a private boarding school which attempted to combine in a single institution the values and content of the Latin school's classical curriculum with the values and content of the English school's practical curriculum. It did this by offering its clientele a choice of two parallel courses of study, the Latin and the English. As a private tuition school, however, the academy came increasingly to serve a college preparatory function for a middle-class clientele. When the public high school developed in the mid-nineteenth century, offering the English curriculum free to all, the academy declined. Before its demise, however, the academy's English department was responsible for significant liberalization of the secondary school curriculum. It is to these important curriculum developments that we now turn our attention.

With the urbanization of trade centers and the growth of the middle class, the practical need arose for advanced training in the vernacular, as well as the less practical desire to be "correct" and "elegant" in written and oral social discourse. The curricular response to these demands was formal English grammar, introduced principally for utilitarian reasons, but also as a source of formal culture. It quickly became the vogue, and a number of English grammar texts issued from British and American presses. For the most part, these texts were short (often less than fifty pages in length) and were patterned on the model of beginning Latin texts. Logically organized, they usually started with letters, went on to syllables, to words and parts of speech, and finally to rules and the parsing of sentences.

Although some perceptive people questioned the efficacy of formal English grammar as a method of teaching the use of language, its popularity continued to grow until it became the core of the academy's English curriculum and an almost unquestioned curricular institution. When the subject was criticized because it was "practical" rather than "cultural," its adherents defended it on the basis that its study helped one to learn the more cultural Latin. It is ironic that 150 years later, when Latin came under attack because it was *not* utilitarian, *its* adherents defended Latin's practical qualities by pointing out that the study of Latin helped one to learn English (Butts and Cremin 1953, p. 126).

Because it was widely assumed that knowledge of the rules of grammar and rhetoric automatically produced precise and elegant writers and speakers, little attention was given to actual practice in theme writing or speaking. Thus, English composition and speech as we know them were virtually absent in the eighteenth-century curriculum. Nor was English literature accorded any more attention. Although some prominent writers were urging the vernacular literature's usefulness as a medium for teaching the language, English literature did not become a prominent part of the secondary school curriculum for another hundred years.

The study of history had its beginning in the academy as an adjunct to the study of geography, Latin, or reading. Thus, as students in the Latin department might learn some ancient history concomitant with their study of Latin and Greek, students in the English department might learn some general or American history through readings contained in a work such as Noah Webster's *Grammatical Institute of the English Language* (1784), a three-part primer-speller-grammar-reader. (Part I of this work is better known as the widely used "Blue Back Speller.") As a major component of the curriculum, then, history was not to come into its own until the nineteenth century.

Mathematics was viewed primarily as a vocational subject in colonial America and, indeed, was even considered "vile" by aristocrats, who thought it necessary only for clerks and tradesmen (Noble 1954, p. 99). Thus, it was not until the second decade of the nineteenth century that the Boston Latin School introduced the subject into its curriculum. When found in the academy, mathematics was almost always taught in the English department. Arithmetic was taught in connection with its application to trade and commerce, while other branches of mathematics—geometry and trigonometry, for example—were taught in connection with surveying, dialing, gauging, astronomy, and navigation.

Some academies offered such modern languages as Spanish, Italian, and Portuguese in their curricula. These languages were taught for the practical values they afforded in international commerce. French, however, sometimes was offered to meet the demands for formal culture. In this connection, we should point out that some academies admitted young ladies to their English departments (never to the Latin), and some exclusively "female academies" were established. Music, dancing, fancy needlework, and fine arts were taught in these schools to prepare their clientele for life in the cultured circles of polite society.

CONCLUSION

Economic and social developments of the eighteenth century produced significant changes in the religion-dominated curriculum of the previous century. Growth in trade and commerce forced the introduction of such practical subjects as accounting, surveying, navigation, English grammar, and modern languages. Thus, the utilitarian motive gained prominence and the importance of the religious motive was diminished. At the same time, increased upward social mobility brought about a demand for knowledge associated with the life style of "polite society." As a result, the study of the classical languages and authors (the content of secondary and higher education) came increasingly to be associated with the acquisition of formal culture, rather than with the study of holy books, and the religious function of the Latin grammar schools declined. The study of music and fine arts served a formal culture function for girls, as did, occasionally, the study of formal English grammar. By the time of the revolution, the single-purpose curriculum of the Puritans had given way to a tripurpose curriculum for utility, culture, and religion.

The Early Years of the Republic: Curriculum from the Revolution to the Civil War

Prerevolutionary America, for all its achievements in establishing schools, was no educational panacea for the people. It has been estimated that in 1775—even in New England, where education was valued highly—not more than one out of ten children had ever attended school, and often this *one* attended only briefly or intermittently. Most Americans were still, of necessity, too occupied with making a living to be much concerned with the "luxury" of education. It was indeed a privileged few who were able to attend a Latin grammar school and qualify for admission to one of the nine select colonial colleges.

The "elementary" school of the eighteenth century, more often than not, was church supported or influenced, and it was free only to those "paupers" who could not afford to pay. It was not "graded" as we know it, and its extremely narrow curriculum could ordinarily be covered by the average student in only two or three years.

The War for Independence (1775–1781) spelled disaster for this feeble educational structure. In many cities and towns the elementary reading and writing schools continued only on a sporadic basis or shut down altogether. Latin grammar schools and academies often were forced to close for lack of students, and even the colonial colleges "were almost deserted" (Cubberley 1919, p. 51).

By 1865, however, an extraordinary transformation had taken place: The church-dominated reading and writing schools had been replaced by an eight-year graded elementary school that boasted a vastly more intensive, if only moderately expanded, curriculum.[4] Almost everywhere the principle of free, publicly supported nonsectarian schools was accepted, and it was the rule, rather than the exception, for children to attend school. Now also, over 2000 academies were serving a quarter of a million students, the public high school was well on its way to becoming the stronghold of American secondary education, and over 200 colleges and universities, many of them state institutions topping extensive state school systems, stood in place of the original 9 colonial colleges.

Of course, the potential for this vigorous educational growth was evident even in the eighteenth century: the frontier movement, the ideas of Locke, the decline of religious influence, and the growth of commercial centers were all forces that tended to encourage its development. But it was not until the nineteenth century that three additional forces—democratization, industrial development, and nationalism—converged to actualize the potential and reshape the school curriculum.

DEMOCRATIZATION

When the constitution was ratified in 1788, it is estimated that property restrictions limited voting rights to only one white male in seven. It was not long, however, before grass-roots' demands based on the frontier experience and the revolutionary doctrines of equality and "natural rights" were responsible for the removal of property and taxation qualifications as criteria for the right to vote. By 1850 twelve of the original thirteen states had abolished the property requirement, and every new state that entered the union after 1817 provided for universal (white) manhood suffrage in its constitution. The election of Andrew Jackson and the Democratic party in 1828 not only demonstrated a significant "leftward" shift in political power, but indicated the diffusion of liberal new interpretations of democracy that were already shaping the cultural ethos of the young republic.

INDUSTRIAL DEVELOPMENT

Paralleling the democratization of American politics and culture was the development of American industry. The economy of the colonies had been primarily agrarian. As the nineteenth century progressed, waterways came increasingly to be utilized as a source of power and as a medium of transportation; rapid extension of communications followed the invention of the telegraph; the development of the railroads facilitated transportation; and new

4. The eight-year graded elementary school was most characteristic of cities and towns. The one-room ungraded schoolhouse was common in many rural districts even as late as 1900. Nevertheless, the emergence of a "common school" by 1865, publicly supported and free to all, generally is viewed as a unique achievement of American democracy.

reservoirs of power became available with the invention of the steam engine. Although industrial capitalism was not to come of age until the second half of the century, its beginnings were already changing the lives of many Americans (Butts and Cremin 1953, pp. 154, 155).

NATIONALISM

Finally, the emergence of nationalism as a characteristic attitude manifested itself in a number of ways: the flag became a symbol of a common allegiance, patriotic songs were written, commemorative monuments such as the one at Bunker Hill were erected, and historic figures such as Washington were transformed into national heroes. By the middle of the nineteenth century, patriotic sentiment had created a substantial corpus of national mythology. This national feeling, we shall see, had substantial impact on the purposes and content of the school curriculum.

ELEMENTARY CURRICULUM

CURRICULUM AIMS. Although sectarian religious groups lost control over elementary education during this period, their influence far from vanished. Thus, while the elementary curriculum could be characterized as "nonsectarian," it was by no means secular. The religious motive in education came to be channeled into what was called *"moral and character development."* Even though a great many people (especially the ministers) argued to the bitter end that moral and character development could never be separated from training in a particular religious faith, the inculcation of Judeo-Christian values became the dominant aim of the common school (Butts and Cremin 1953, pp. 267, 268). The moralistic content of elementary readers of this time testifies to the prominence of this aim.

Another aim of the elementary curriculum was *universal literacy.* This aim was rooted in the democratization that occurred as a result of independence and the frontier movement. Literacy, especially in New England, had been fostered by traditional Protestant groups for religious reasons; now, it became an ideal based on the assumption that it furthered freedom for the people. Many important men of that period supported this idea in public statements, Jefferson's probably being the most familiar: "If a nation expects to be ignorant and free in a state of civilization it expects what never was and never will be. . . ."

Democratization also produced the characteristically American value of *individual success.* While individual success was promoted in much of the content utilized in the elementary school curriculum, it was more typically a curriculum aim of the secondary schools of this period, which provided for children of the common man the upward economic and social mobility that democratization promised.

Related to universal literacy is a third aim of the elementary curriculum: *citizenship.* This aim had its roots in the rise of nationalism following the

Revolution and the War of 1812. Concern for the training of loyal and responsible citizens is evident in the patriotic content of early readers and in the addition of American geography and history to the curriculum.

Allied to the aim of responsible citizenship is *vocational* or *practical competence.* Although this aim was far more evident at the secondary level, especially in the curricula of the academies, it is manifested in the greatly increased emphasis on arithmetic at the elementary level. Clearly, the aim of vocational competence had its roots in the industrial development that was characteristic of this period.

Finally, the ideal of *mental discipline* began to emerge during this period as a curriculum aim. Mainly a product of European philosophies, but somewhat allied to responsible citizenship, mental discipline was less evident in elementary than in secondary curricula. Mental discipline stressed the importance of training the mind as opposed to the acquisition of knowledge. Thus, mathematics was taught, not for any theoretical or practical value that it might have, but as an exercise that would strengthen the reasoning powers of the mind. At the elementary level, English grammar and arithmetic sometimes were employed for this purpose.

Changes in the economic, social, and political structure of a society had produced dramatic changes in its social goals and values, and consequently in its curriculum aims. At the elementary level, the curriculum stressed moral and character development, universal literacy, and responsible citizenship; at the same time it laid the groundwork for the aims that were to receive greater emphasis at the secondary level: individual success, vocational/practical competence, and mental discipline.

CURRICULUM CONTENT. Reading continued to occupy a prominent position in the elementary school curriculum. Although the popularity of the *New England Primer* was declining, it continued to be used. The Bible, also, was a prevalent resource for the teaching of reading, and if it seems to us somewhat inappropriate for beginners, we should bear in mind that most instruction in those days proceeded largely by rote and imitation, little attention being given to whether or not the content was meaningless to pupils.

Noah Webster published the *First Part of a Grammatical Institute of the English Language* in 1782. Familiarly known as "the Blue Back Speller," this volume is credited with establishing spelling as a separate subject in the elementary curriculum and with popularizing the spelling bee as an American institution. This reader-speller contained the alphabet, syllables, lists of words, moral lessons in fable form, and easy words designed to teach reading. Before Webster died in 1843, the various editions of this work had sold about 24 million copies.

It was during this period that the first of the "graded" readers appeared. The best known of these is McGuffey's, whose First and Second Readers appeared in 1836, and Third and Fourth in 1837. The purpose of the readers appears in the preface: "to insure interest in the subjects, to impart valuable information, and to exert a decided and healthful moral influence." If the Puritans infused their reading lessons with religious doctrine, McGuffey fulfilled the imperatives of his own age by filling his texts with the attitudes and ethical concepts that defined "nonsectarian moral and character development." It is estimated that for more than half a century, half the children attending school learned to read from the McGuffey series.

Writing became an increasingly important part of the elementary curriculum as the availability of materials (paper, ink, etc.) increased. In addition, the ability to write was considered more of a practical necessity than it had been in earlier days, when just the ability to read the Bible was viewed as sufficient education for common men. Reading and writing taken together gained support from the aims of universal literacy and responsible citizenship.

Arithmetic, formerly considered an academy or college subject, became firmly established in the elementary curriculum during this period. Often spoken of as "ciphering," it consisted mainly of the four fundamental processes and perhaps elementary fractions. After about 1820, however, its development was rapid, spurred by the publication of graded textbooks. During the earlier part of the period, arithmetic was taught mainly for its practical value, but as the century progressed it was increasingly valued for its mental discipline function. By the middle of the nineteenth century, arithmetic was vying with English grammar for first place in the elementary curriculum (Noble 1954, p. 252).

Formal English grammar, which became immensely popular during the second quarter of the century, was largely a matter of memorizing rules and parsing sentences. It was believed that knowledge of formal English grammar had the practical value of fostering elegant speech and writing. The myth persists in many quarters even today. Later on, formal English grammar was taught for its value in training the mind.

Geography, which entered the curriculum through various readers, became a fixed subject in the elementary curriculum by the Civil War. Although geography textbooks first were introduced in the late eighteenth century, it was not until about 1830 that their number multiplied rapidly. Many texts employed a question-and-answer format and emphasized the geography of the United States. As with most other subjects of the curriculum, memorization and drill were stressed. Learning aids such as maps were rare. Although American history did not become a separate subject in the elementary curriculum until later in the nineteenth century, a great deal of historical material appeared in geographies (and general readers). In a new nation that was experiencing a rising tide of nationalism, these readings satisfied the impulse to train loyal and patriotic citizens.

SECONDARY CURRICULUM

CURRICULUM AIMS. As one would expect, curriculum aims at the secondary level were much the same as those for the elementary level. What differences existed were primarily those of emphasis. Of course, for obvious reasons, the universal literacy aim of the elementary curriculum was not a factor in secondary curricula. But moral and character training, though not as heavy handed as in the elementary school, was a recognizable secondary-curriculum determinant. The patriotic aim—concern for training loyal and responsible citizens— had important effects on the secondary school curriculum, as did the aim of vocational/practical competence, which played a far more influential role at this level than at the elementary one. Finally, because students who were continuing their education beyond elementary school might be viewed as community leaders, the individual success motive and the mental discipline theory both operated to shape secondary curricula more significantly at this stage. In brief, the culture and utility motives of the eighteenth-century curriculum continued, while the religious motive manifested itself in moral and character training. To these continuing social goals was added the new politically motivated aim of patriotic citizenship.

CURRICULUM IN THE LATIN GRAMMAR SCHOOLS. Latin grammar schools continued to fulfill their traditional function of preparing young men to enter the university during this period. At first they taught only Latin and Greek, but when colleges began to require arithmetic for admission, this subject was added. The Boston Latin School introduced arithmetic into its curriculum sometime after 1814 (Noble 1954, p. 98). The traditional classical Latin grammar school responded only feebly to growing American demands for a broader curriculum and as a result continued to decline in importance thoughout this period.

CURRICULUM OF THE ACADEMIES. The academies, which originated about the middle of the eighteenth century, continued to grow in importance during the first half of the nineteenth century. Independent and privately controlled, these middle-class tuition schools varied considerably from one to another. Their curricula often represented imaginative responses to current demands, and on the whole it can be said that "they presented rather widespread training for any field, whether cultural, practical, classical, or purely vocational" (Edwards and Richey 1963, p. 355).

The academy was most indicative of the democratization process that was taking place in America. Unlike the Latin grammar school, which was a vestige of the old theocratic class system and which served a social elite, the academy opened opportunity for secondary education to a rapidly expanding American middle class. (Paradoxically, this same institution, because it was a private tuition school, posed a threat to democratization because for a time it represented—in opposition to the emerging public high school—an educational alternative open only to those who could afford to pay.) Because the curriculum of the academies met the varying needs of diverse constituencies, they became, by mid-century, the dominant secondary schools in America.

The academy curriculum described earlier in this chapter was representative of the offerings of most academies during the first portion of this period. As the Civil War approached, only minor adjustments were made. Most academies continued to offer the traditional college preparatory curriculum in their classical departments, where Latin, Greek, and arithmetic were the staple subjects. These subjects came increasingly to be viewed as vehicles of mental discipline. In the English department, English grammar continued to command central importance. This subject satisfied the values of practical competence (utility) and individual social success (culture) by purportedly fostering correctness and elegance in speech and writing. Although claims of mental discipline were also made for the study of formal English grammar, Latin grammar usually was viewed as far superior for this purpose.

Democratization and individual success (self-improvement) during this time gave rise to demands for training in public speaking. As a result, many academies offered courses in rhetoric and declamation. Textbooks of this period include chapters on letter writing and practical exercises in punctuation and capitalization, as well as illustrated instructions for such matters as "making the preliminary bow to the audience." The convergence of these subjects eventuated in modern-day courses in English composition.

In conjunction with the study of grammar and rhetoric, selections from the masterpieces of such English authors as Milton and Pope were read. These examples of English literature usually appeared in advanced "readers" and served the same function in the English department that the works of Caesar, Cicero, and Vergil served in the Latin. Although this content provided a source from which contemporary courses in English literature later evolved, it was not until after the Civil War that a book identifiable as an English literature text appeared.

The patriotic motive resulted in the development of geography-history in the academies along much the same lines that the subject(s) was introduced in the elementary curriculum. It has been estimated that by the second decade of the nineteenth century, 35 percent of the pupils attending academies in New York State were in schools where American history was a subject in the curriculum; and between 1801 and 1861, 107 American history texts were published (Noble 1954, p. 248). By mid-century, American history enjoyed enormous popularity as a secondary subject.

Growing nationalism and the citizenship aim were also responsible for introducing the study of American political documents, such as the Declaration of Independence and the Constitution. Although instruction in this area was usually formal, abstract, and uninspiring, it was conducted "with almost the same fervor as religious materials had received in the earlier period . . ." (Butts and Cremin 1953, p. 277). These early precursors of modern civics courses usually were associated closely with the study of history.

The role of science in the promotion of industrialization during the nineteenth century prompted the introduction of "natural philosophy" into the curriculum. Generally a potpourri of the natural sciences, natural philosophy was oriented toward the practical rather than the theoretical and emphasized useful information concerning the new machines and appliances in which everyone was interested. Sciences such as chemistry, astronomy, and botany also began to make headway in the curriculum of this period, largely as a result of their practical implications. All of these scientific subjects were taught from the textbook, and it was not until mid-century that experiments demonstrated by the teacher were being suggested. Students were not permitted to handle the apparatus. By this time, also, natural philosophy content was less centered on descriptions of engines, tools, and machines, and emphasized more the principles of mechanics, such as hydraulics and pneumatics. But it was not until after the Civil War that physics became part of the curriculum.

Arithmetic in the academy served the twofold purpose of practical competence and mental discipline. Indeed, one author of the period wrote in the preface to his arithmetic text, "the end to be sought in the study of arithmetic [is] twofold—a practical knowledge of numbers and the discipline of the mind" (quoted in Noble 1954, p. 252).

Geometry, because of its practical application in surveying, was taught in academies from an early date, but algebra did not make much headway until the nineteenth century. Undoubtedly the rising interest in science prompted by industrialization served to stimulate the growth of both of these branches of mathematics, but the mental discipline aim increasingly supported their popularity. Algebra was required for entrance to Harvard in 1820 and geometry first was required in 1844.

Modern languages, taught from an early date in academies for use in international trade, continued to be taught both for practical reasons and cultural improvement. French was exceedingly popular as a "cultural" subject and was considered a necessary accomplishment for a well-bred young lady. After about 1830, German gained in popularity as a result of interest in science and the newly published Prussian educational theories.

Among the vocational studies, almost every academy included bookkeeping in its curriculum. Such subjects as surveying and navigation also were offered, but in general vocational studies were almost invariably commercial in their emphasis. Several "commercial" or "mercantile" academies were founded during this period, and these represented the embryonic forms of what were later to develop as business colleges.

Although not dominated by sectarian religious doctrine as were the early Latin grammar schools, the academies were by no means secular. Usually nonsectarian because of the diversity of their clientele, they were vitally concerned with moral and character training and teaching the common elements of Protestant Christianity. The foundation grant of Phillips Academy at Andover, Massachusetts, makes this clear. It states, "the *first* and *principle* (*sic*) object of this Institution is the promotion of TRUE PIETY and VIRTUE . . ." (quoted in Cubberley 1919, p. 188). Thus, frequent attendance at chapel for prayers and Bible reading was an unquestioned requirement, and instruction often was pervaded by a moral-religious spirit.

CURRICULUM IN THE PUBLIC HIGH SCHOOL. The first American high school was established in Boston in 1821. Originally called "English Classical School," its name was changed to "English High School" in 1824. This high school, like the many others that followed, was intended to provide education beyond the elementary level at public expense for the children of those parents who could not afford the tuition of the academy.

As might be expected, the curriculum of the early high schools was very much like that of the academies. English grammar, arithmetic, geography, history, and bookkeeping were the basic subjects. Many early high schools also offered algebra, natural philosophy, moral philosophy, and "criticisms of English authors." Although languages other than English were not at first taught in the Boston English Classical School, high schools very early came to assume the full function of the academy and included in their offerings the college preparatory subjects of Latin and Greek. The Massachusetts Law of 1827, comparable in significance to the "Old Deluder Satan Act" of 1647, required that a high school be established in every town of 500 families or more and that these high schools offer United States history, bookkeeping, algebra, geometry, and surveying. High schools in towns having 4000 or more inhabitants were required to add to this core curriculum Greek, Latin, history, rhetoric, and logic (Cubberley 1919, pp. 193, 194).

The fundamental difference between the early high school and the academy was in their control and support. Both institutions prepared their students either for life or for college. By the time of the Civil War, some 300 high schools had been established across the United States, and by this time their curricula were becoming increasingly differentiated from those of the academy.

CONCLUSION

The period between the Revolutionary War and the Civil War witnessed the emergence of a unique experiment in public education. The forces of democratization, industrial development, and nationalism had contributed to the establishment of the nonsectarian, publicly controlled and supported common (elementary) school and public high school—a unitary ladder of opportunity specifically adapted to the needs and desires of the American people. The dual European system of education, represented by the elite Latin grammar school, had for all practical purposes been rejected.

The curriculum by the end of this era had lost its sectarian flavor, but retained a decidedly nonsectarian religious-moral cast. The eight-year course of the common (elementary) school included reading, writing, arithmetic, spelling, English grammar, geography, and "good behavior," (the name often given to moral and character development). This expansion represented a change in emphasis from single-minded religious indoctrination to education for life in a nonsectarian nationalistic democracy.

At the secondary level, nationalist sentiment and the desire to educate responsible citizens contributed to the popularization of American geography, history, and civics as important subjects in the curriculum. Industrialization fostered the vocational subjects, especially bookkeeping; the sciences, such as natural philosophy and chemistry; and mathematics. The individual success motive, which implied upward social mobility, was responsible for emphasis on "cultural" subjects, such as the classics, English grammar, and French, while mathematics and grammar were studied for the benefit of mental discipline. Clearly, the curriculum of this period was increasing in breadth and complexity in direct proportion to the increasing diversity and complexity of the society that produced it.

References

Butts, R. Freeman, and Lawrence A. Cremin. 1953. *A History of Education in American Culture*. New York: Holt, Rinehart and Winston.

Charlton, Kenneth. 1968. "The Contributions of History to the Study of the Curriculum." In *Changing the Curriculum*, edited by J. F. Kerr. London: University of London Press.

Cubberly, Ellwood P. 1919. *Public Education in the United States*. Boston: Houghton Mifflin Company.

Edwards, Newton, and Herman G. Richey. 1963. *The School in the American Social Order*. Boston: Houghton Mifflin Company.

Goodlad, John I. 1966. *The Changing School Curriculum*. New York: Fund for the Advancement of Education.

Kliebard, Herbert M. 1968. "The Curriculum Field in Retrospect." In *Technology and the Curriculum*, edited by Paul W. F. Witt. New York: Teachers College Press.

Miller, Perry, and Thomas H. Johnson. 1963. *The Puritans: A Sourcebook of Their Writings*. 2 vols. New York: Harper & Row, Publishers. (Originally published in one volume by American Book Company, 1938.)

Noble, Stuart G. 1954. *A History of American Education*. New York: Holt, Rinehart and Winston.

Thayer, V. T. 1965. *Formative Ideas in American Education: From the Colonial Period to the Present*. New York: Dodd, Mead & Co.

CHAPTER 3

HISTORICAL EVOLUTION OF THE CURRICULUM: THE CIVIL WAR TO RECENT DEVELOPMENTS

The Maturing Republic: Curriculum from 1865 to World War I

In the years following the Civil War social and economic forces, some with roots in prior periods, wrought further significant modifications in the public school and its curriculum. The process of democratization characteristic of the antebellum era continued, though imperfectly. As the ideal of equal educational opportunity became more widely accepted, the high school increasingly became a school for all adolescents. As a result, its purposes and curriculum were broadened considerably to accommodate the needs of the majority of its clientele who would not go on to college. The fervent nationalism of the post-Revolutionary War period abated somewhat, though it continued to be an influence. But the industrialization that began during the first half of the nineteenth century exploded full force after the Civil War, and in a relatively brief period of fifty years, the economic and social life of America was virtually transformed. By the second decade of the twentieth century, this transformation was reflected in the public school curriculum, whose aims, content, and methods bore only slight resemblance to the one described in Chapter 2.

THE INDUSTRIAL REVOLUTION

Enough has been written about the industrial revolution so that it is not necessary to detail its physical characteristics here. Specialization and technology by 1918 produced a host of material inventions unknown in 1865: steel-frame skyscrapers, electric elevators, automobiles, electric lights, telephones, typewriters, refrigeration, electric streetcars, the wireless, telephones, steam heating, and sanitary plumbing, to mention but a few. Equally significant, however, was the alteration in life style created by this massive industrialization. These social changes centered on two major areas: urbanization and family life.

URBANIZATION. At the beginning of this period, more than 80 percent of the population lived in rural areas and on farms. For the average farm boy or girl, life was circumscribed by the family, and the important tasks and responsibilities were learned at home. Although farm children attended school, reading and other intellectual activities were of secondary importance in their lives. In short, formal education was far from a critical necessity.

By the end of this period, industrialization had caused a dramatic shift. Now, about half the population was living in incorporated towns or cities. In contrast to the simple life of the rural farm community, life in the city was a highly complex affair. Mobility was a necessity and required literacy skills in order to locate streets and cope with vast public transportation systems. Employment meant negotiating a bewildering maze of classified advertisements, offices, factories, employment bureaus, and perhaps union halls. Furthermore, the jobs themselves were demanding increasingly complex skills: business enterprises required not only facility in reading and writing, but more than a simple knowledge of bookkeeping and accounting. Even factory employment often demanded industrial skills that could not be learned on the job without a sound basic education. Purchasing the basic necessities of food and clothing required a whole range of skills based on literacy, as well as specialized knowledge about manufactured products and marketing. Finally, participation in the community was no longer the personal, face-to-face affair of the rural setting, but often involved large and complex organizations, public meetings, and government bureaucracies. As a result of the industrial revolution and urbanization, life became so complex that formal education was indeed "more of a social and individual necessity than it had ever been before" (Butts and Cremin 1953, p. 407).

FAMILY LIFE. Family life in preindustrial agrarian America was intimate and closely knit. Frequent contact in the learning and performance of daily chores provided ample opportunity to obtain vocational, general, and moral education from older members of the family. Moreover, the child was an actual participant in family life and, indeed, in the community that usually developed among farm neighbors. As a result, he experienced very early in life a sense of purpose and belonging.

In the city, however, "home" was often a quite different experience. For a large proportion of the population, city life meant poverty, squalor, seamy tenements, and all of the degenerating influences associated with slums. Adults and even older children labored long hours in factories located in different areas of the city, and there was little opportunity for the interaction, group activities, and participation characteristic of farm life. Family ties weakened, and young people drifted into the street, where they received their educations through gangs, gambling, crime, and the other unhealthy stimuli that the city provided in abundance. Thus, the deterioration of traditional family relationships produced a new social need which contributed to the alteration of the public school curriculum.

IMMIGRATION

Until 1820, immigration to America was small and mainly from England. It increased somewhat during the antebellum period, but still averaged only between 50,000 and 100,000 people per year. During the second half of the nineteenth century, however, immigration increased dramatically and continued to increase until, by the turn of the century, the number of immigrants being admitted to the United States each year ranged from three quarters of a million to one and a quarter million people.

As immigration increased, the character of the immigrants became more and more varied. Newcomers from western, southern, and eastern Europe with divergent national, linguistic, and religious backgrounds presented the schools with an enormous problem in assimilation. Irish, German, Italian, Polish, Jewish, Greek, Slovakian, and Finnish youngsters brought to school with them a wide variety of values, customs, and traditions which could not be ignored if the society was to survive as a democratic community. Thus, the influx of large numbers of diverse immigrant children forced curricular changes that would not have otherwise occurred.

IDEAS FROM ABROAD

Up to this time most education was centered on subject matter to be learned (i.e., memorized) with little or no consideration being given to the learner. After the Civil War, certain educational theories from Europe that emphasized the nature and importance of the learner began to filter into American educational thought and practice. These ideas, mainly stemming from the writings and work of Pestalozzi, Froebel, and Herbart, in large measure constituted a stimulus for the progressive education movement of the twentieth century.

JOHANN HEINRICH PESTALOZZI (1746–1827). Pestalozzi was a Swiss educationist who conducted schools where he put his educational ideas and theories into practice. Reacting against the memorization of verbal abstractions that characterized most education of his day, he asserted that the moral, physical, and intellectual powers of the child were developed from concrete sense impressions. Thus, Pestalozzi evolved what he called "object lessons" in which plants, animals, and other objects were used to develop the child's sense of sight, touch, and sound. Emphasis also was placed on the child being actively engaged in doing, perceiving, experiencing, analyzing, and so on. Moreover, Pestalozzi held that sympathetic understanding would facilitate the achievement of educational ends far more than the harsh punishment common in most schools of that time.

FRIEDRICH FROEBEL (1782–1852). Froebel, a German educationist, originated the kindergarten—"a garden where children grow." He believed that children learn as a result of their own spontaneous activities and emphasized the self-expression of pupils through their manipulation of objects such as soft balls, building blocks, clay, paper, etc. Furthermore, group activity was viewed as a natural medium of expression. Froebel tied these educational ideas to a quasi-mystical philosophy in which the child was viewed as an agency for the realization of God's will. Although the mystical aspect of Froebel's thought had no influence in this country, his other ideas created a new respect for the individual learner among American educationists.

JOHANN FRIEDRICH HERBART (1776–1841). Herbart, a German psychologist and philosopher, held that the central aim of education was the development of moral social character. He believed that this aim could best be achieved through the study of history and literature (the record of social man) and further that these two subjects should be the core of the curriculum. Other subjects would be taught, of course, but these would be both subordinate and related to the core studies in order to maintain proper emphasis and unity in the curriculum. More important, Herbart believed that character building was an intellectual process that occurred through the development of a mass of associated ideas in the learner's mind. Thus, it was important in teaching that new ideas be presented to the learner in such a way that they were vitally related to the ideas that were already a part of the learner's experience. Out of this theory grew the famous five formal steps of Herbartian method: (1) *preparation*—the review of old ideas that are related to the new ones; (2) *presentation*—the presentation of the new material; (3) *association*—the association of the new material with the old; (4) *generalization*—the derivation of general principles from the new combination (s) of ideas; and (5) *application*—the application of new principles to specific practical situations. The five Herbartian steps became a fad and they more often than not were employed with the same formalism and rigidity that characterized traditional teaching. But before the five steps passed from the scene, Herbart's ideas had created new interest in history and literature and had provided a challenge to those traditional methods that emphasized the memorization and recitation of unrelated verbal and numerical abstractions.

INCREASE IN KNOWLEDGE

Concomitant with the industrial revolution came a dramatic increase in knowledge, particularly in the sciences. Prior to this period, the Greek and Roman classics, mathematics, theology, and philosophy constituted the major areas of learning. By the time of World War I, the physical sciences (physics and chemistry), the life sciences (botany, zoology, and physiology), and the social sciences (psychology and sociology) had all but taken center stage. Furthermore, the demands of industry, business, agriculture, and the schools had produced new stores of knowledge in areas classified as the "applied sciences," not the least important of which we might note was education. This burgeoning of "useful" knowledge was an important factor in the broadening of the secondary school curriculum.

FACULTY PSYCHOLOGY

Although its roots are to be found in the eighteenth century, faculty psychology reached its zenith during the second half of the nineteenth century. The theory variously holds that the mind consists of separate powers or faculties, among them (1) intellect or reason, (2) feelings and appetites, and (3) volition or will. These immaterial faculties are susceptible to mental cultivation or training in much the same way that a muscle is susceptible to training by physical exercise. Proponents of the theory claimed that the cultivation (discipline) of the intellect transferred to the other faculties and was necessary for the development of good moral character.

Current notions about "culture" were incorporated easily into the theory of faculty psychology. It was simple to reason, for example, that the cultured individual was the one who had cultivated and disciplined his mental faculties. Thus, mental discipline and culture during this period came to mean virtually the same thing. Furthermore, the theory could be construed to support religious othodoxy (the mind was a spiritual, God-given gift) and to combat the new materialism and scientific naturalism that were being asserted as a result of the industrial revolution and expansion of knowledge. Because mental discipline, culture, religious orthodoxy, and conservative sentiment formed an interlocking and mutually reinforcing network of ideas, faculty psychology was a widely supported theory. Indeed, it was promoted everywhere by the most prominent, best-educated, and highly respected men in the community. As a result, faculty psychology was confidently used to justify the mental discipline, moral character development, and cultural aims of the curriculum.

ELEMENTARY CURRICULUM

CURRICULUM AIMS. In spite of (or perhaps *because* of) growing challenges to the traditional curriculum, resistance to change was tenacious, and old aims continued to predominate in the elementary school during the latter half of the nineteenth century. The "good citizen" generally was viewed as a person who had learned to read and write, whose moral character had developed along orthodox lines, and whose mind had been well disciplined. Thus, literacy, moral character, and mental discipline continued to provide the focus for the elementary school curriculum until well after the turn of the century. The new or heightened economic, intellectual, and social forces mentioned above gradually made themselves felt, however, and other aims were discernible, especially toward the close of the period. The first of these was the practical vocational aim, stimulated largely by the industrial revolution. Far more important at the secondary level, the practical aim nevertheless manifested itself in the elementary curriculum in such subjects as manual training, cooking, and sewing.

The so-called twin progressive aims of individual development and democratic social competence were born during this period as a consequence of democratization and the development of liberal pedagogical theories. The experimental curriculum of John Dewey in his laboratory school at the University of Chicago is worth mentioning as an example of this curricular thrust. While not widely accepted during this period, the twin aims of individual development and democratic group participation claimed increasing attention as the twentieth century progressed. The older aim of individual success, spurred by the desire of masses of immigrants to participate in the American dream, received growing attention during the early decades of the twentieth century. Because schooling was viewed as the medium through which children gained material and social success, certain subjects of the curriculum were viewed in terms of their practical and cultural benefits. By and large, however, it was literacy, moral character development, and mental discipline, lightly supplemented by practical considerations and the embryonic progressive aims that determined the elementary curriculum at this time.

CURRICULUM CONTENT. As might be expected, the curriculum of the elementary school during the latter half of the nineteenth century reflected the three basic aims of literacy, character development, and mental discipline. For example, Butts and Cremin (1953, pp. 434, 435) note that in New York City in 1888, "reading, spelling, and grammar accounted for over 40 percent of class time, writing over 15 percent, arithmetic over 25 percent, while geography, history, music, and drawing filled out the remainder." Moreover, in spite of agitated legal controversy, the King James Protestant version of the Bible continued to be read as a source of "nonsectarian" religious training.

Reorganization of the traditional subjects as well as the addition of some new ones, however, occurred as a result of practical aims and progressive pedagogical theories. Reading instruction in some schools came to be centered more on meaning and less on rote memorization, and some arithmetic texts presented material in terms of practical problems instead of rules to be memorized. Pestalozzi's method of object lessons was sporadically adopted so that elementary science was introduced into some curricula. The object method also was influential in changing the study of geography from rote memorization of unrelated names and places to the observation of immediate surroundings and the identification of meaningful relationships between social development and geophysical conditions.

By the beginning of the twentieth century, partly as a result of Herbart's influence, history and literature were becoming important subjects in the upper grades of the elementary schools. Furthermore, the influence of Herbart's five steps tended to free these studies from the mental-discipline emphasis they had received earlier. As the twentieth century progressed, the practical, progressive, and individual success aims motivated the introduction of such subjects as manual training, physical education (formal exercises patterned after German and Swedish models), nature study, cooking, and sewing, but the three R's continued to be emphasized as the most important elements in the elementary curriculum.

SECONDARY CURRICULUM

CURRICULUM AIMS. Mental discipline more than any other aim dominated the secondary school curriculum during the second half of the nineteenth century. So unquestioned was the efficacy of mental discipline in the development of moral character and culture, that even the severest critics of the classics defended such new subjects as physics, history, and even manual training in terms of their power to discipline the mind. Around the turn of the twentieth century, however, scientific psychology, especially in the work of William James, Charles Judd, and Edward Thorndike, discredited faculty psychology, and mental discipline as an educational aim began slowly to recede. About the same time, the gathering force of the industrial revolution was making itself felt and the vocational-technical aim of education began to gain prominence. While this aim had been a factor in curriculum development since the earliest days of the academy, it was not until the end of the second decade of the twentieth century that it began to emerge as an aim of major proportions in the curriculum. Allied to this vocational-technical aim was the aim of individual success, which served to support the "cultural" subjects as a medium of upward social mobility. The theories of Pestalozzi, Froebel, and Herbart, however, had virtually no impact at the secondary level, and the progressive aims of individual development and democratic social competence did not materially affect the secondary curriculum during this period.

SPECIAL INFLUENCES ON THE SECONDARY CURRICULUM. Around the turn of the century several national committees were appointed, and their reports had a significant and lasting effect on the secondary curriculum. These reports, of course, reflected the social and political forces cited in a previous section as well as the curriculum aims described above. But their conclusions and recommendations so crystallized dominant conservative curriculum values of the time that they can be viewed as an effective direct influence on the high school curriculum of this period.

From the time of the Civil War until the last decade of the nineteenth century, the high school curriculum had "grown like Topsy." With no precedent after which to pattern itself, this entirely novel educational institution had simply retained the old subjects and added new ones as the demand arose. Most significant in number and importance of the additions were the sciences, which included botany, zoology, physiology, anatomy, physics, astronomy, and geology. But many subjects demanded by students not planning to attend college also were added, among them commercial arithmetic, business correspondence, banking, stenography, and typewriting. In short, the high school curriculum represented a disordered array of courses; students, in an attempt to cover as many as possible, were studying a large number of subjects for relatively short periods of time. The curriculum, obviously, was in need of some degree of order and standardization.

The conditions described above eventuated in 1892 in the appointment of the Committee on Secondary School Studies (commonly called the Committee of Ten) under the chairmanship of Charles Eliot, president of Harvard. In its report issued the following year, the committee acknowledged the terminal as well as the college preparatory function of the high school, but proceeded to recommend a curriculum entirely oriented toward the college-bound student. Declaring that fewer subjects should be studied over a longer period of time for "strong and effective mental training," the committee plotted out four alternative courses of study: the Classical, the Latin-Scientific, the Modern Language, and the English. In every course except one, a third of the students' time would be devoted to foreign languages, and three courses called for the study of no fewer than eight sciences. The committee recommended that terminal students be given the same program as those who were headed for college! Although the report helped to bring order out of near chaos, its domination by the conservative spirit of mental discipline was clear. By and large, the report of the Committee of Ten established college domination over the high school curriculum and "determined the course of American secondary education for a generation following its publication" (Butts and Cremin 1953, p. 390).

A few months before the report of the Committee of Ten was issued, the Committee of Fifteen on Elementary Studies was appointed, to determine among other things whether the elementary course should remain at eight years or be shortened to six. At this time, American public schools had become standardized on the eight-year elementary/four-year secondary plan. The Committee of Ten had raised questions about the feasibility of a satisfactory secondary school program limited to a period of four years, and some sentiment was expressed for beginning secondary education in the seventh instead of the ninth grade. Although the Committee of Fifteen recommended retention of the eight-four plan, it did call for closer articulation between the elementary and secondary school and the introduction of certain secondary subjects in the elementary school.

A third committee, the Committee of Thirteen on College Entrance Requirements, was concerned mainly with standardization of college entrance requirements. Traditionally, entrance into a particular college was gained by passing that college's entrance examinations. This committee, in its report issued in 1899, proposed that all candidates for college entrance be required to present evidence of having successfully completed four units of foreign language, two of mathematics, two of English, and one each of history and science in addition to a number of acceptable electives. Thus, the Committee of Thirteen established the principle of college entrance based on units of high school work rather than examination. Furthermore, this committee strongly recommended that the current eight-four organization be replaced by a six-six plan. The Committee of Thirteen influenced the secondary school curriculum by affirming the conservative curricular policies of the Committee of Ten, by furthering standardization of the secondary curriculum, and by stimulating movement toward revision of the eight-four plan.

Finally, in 1903, the National Education Association appointed a standing Committee on Economy of Time in Education. The reports of this committee, coming from 1903 to 1919, generally recommended that less time be given to elementary and more to secondary education. Thus, the committee was influential in fostering the curriculum changes that accompanied the development of the junior high school after 1910.[1]

CURRICULUM CONTENT. Having reached its peak of prominence at about the middle of the nineteenth century, the academy began to decline in importance until, by the conclusion of this period of curriculum history, it no longer constituted a significant institution on the American educational scene. The high school, by contrast, continued to grow, and subsequent to the famous Kalamazoo case in 1874, in which the Michigan supreme court affirmed the right of state and local governments to levy taxes to support high schools, its expansion was dramatic. Thus, the discussion of secondary school curriculum that follows in effect is a discussion of the public high school curriculum.

Until the time of the Civil War, the classics and mathematics dominated the secondary curriculum. During the latter half of the century, however, the modern sciences increasingly clamored for attention, and a debate was waged over which subjects were most efficacious in training the mind. Although the scientists ultimately won the argument, Latin gave ground slowly, and even after 1900, four years of Latin grammar, prose, and verse was a common denominator of many college preparatory courses.

Algebra and geometry for mental discipline remained extremely popular during this golden age of faculty psychology. These subjects were taught for the purpose of developing the power of reasoning. Thus, they were logically organized and centered on such abstruse problems as highest common factor, cube root, radicals, and simultaneous equations with more than three unknowns.

---

1. Although it was first established around 1910, the junior high school is really a product of the post World War I era, and its curriculum will be treated in the following section.

In order to compete successfully with the classics and mathematics as disciplinary subjects, the sciences, which had previously been practical in orientation, were reorganized and formalized. By 1870, natural philosophy was being replaced by physics, and more attention was being given to the abstract mathematical aspects of the subject. Thirty years later physics had become a logically organized disciplinary subject almost always taught in the last year of high school because mathematics was an essential prerequisite. Like physics, chemistry became highly theoretical, and students were required to memorize laws, hypotheses, and theories.

Concrete natural history gave way to theoretical zoology and botany after 1865. In both of these new scientific subjects, emphasis was placed on anatomical structure and classification. The subjects were logically organized, formal, and technical, and memorization played an important role in instruction.

The practical aim of teaching students the principles of health and personal hygiene resulted in the introduction of anatomy and physiology after 1870. This aim was soon subverted by the mania for mental discipline, however, and instruction consisted mainly of the memorization of the names of bones, muscles, and organs, with little attention given to their functions.

Because they had to compete with the prestigious classical languages, modern languages had difficulty in establishing themselves in the high school curriculum. Around the final quarter of the nineteenth century, however, colleges began to accept French and German for admission, and these languages came to be regarded as the equivalent of the classics for scientific courses. Of course, in order to compete successfully, the modern languages were taught for mental culture and emphasized formal grammar.

English grammar during this period tended to move in the direction of literature. It was common, for example, to extol the disciplinary benefits to be derived from the grammatical dissection of Milton's *Paradise Lost* or Pope's *Essay on Man*. The practice of "butchering literature," as Noble (1954, p. 349) so aptly phrases it, was quite in keeping with the tenor of the academic times. It is appropriate, too, to note that sentence diagraming first was introduced in 1870. It quickly became the vogue and persists even today among those who advocate its disciplinary benefits.

It was not until quite late in the nineteenth century that English literature as a study independent of grammar became more than a token gesture in secondary curricula. Around 1895 certain colleges began to list English literature entrance requirements in two groups: (1) those required for critical study, and (2) those accepted for general reading. Thus, high schools began to include in English literature courses both the intensive study of a few selections and more rapid reading of a larger number. It should be noted that traditional English authors were emphasized in these courses: American authors did not receive substantial attention until the turn of the century.

History was accorded very little attention in the high school curriculum until the final years of the nineteenth century. Chief inhibitor of history during this period was the belief that although the study of history might have some disciplinary value, other subjects, such as Latin and mathematics were far superior. During this era, subjects were not valued for the information they provided, but only for their disciplinary power.

The academic portion of the secondary curriculum described above prevailed with only minor modifications well into the twentieth century. Influential and resistant to change as they were, however, colleges and universities were not able to stem the effects of a rising tide of industrialization and immigration, and while the college preparatory function of the high school curriculum was still dominant at the time of World War I, noncollege preparatory subjects began to make noticeable inroads after the turn of the century.

Thus, the secondary curriculum came increasingly to be influenced by the practical vocational aim. Of course, the introduction of vocational subjects reignited the long-smoldering liberal education versus vocational training dispute. The conservatives condemned the new subjects as narrowly utilitarian and urged renewed vigor in promoting the liberating study of the classics and mathematics. The progressives, on the other hand, called for a fresh look at the concept of a liberal education. Writing in the *School Review* in 1911, the educational historian Ellwood P. Cubberley noted that "the high school student who has had four years of Latin, three of Greek, four of English, two of ancient and medieval history, two of mathematics and one year of mathematical physics ... is in no sense liberally educated, for he knows little about the modern world in which he lives." Indeed, Cubberley held such an education to be "narrowly technical in that it leads to but a few selected occupations."

Notwithstanding the sound and the fury of the debate, the influences of mass immigration, commercialism, and industrialism relentlessly continued to increase from 1900 to 1918. Practical subjects such as typewriting, stenography, bookkeeping, commercial law, domestic science, industrial arts, and manual training became fairly common by 1918. In addition, certain older subjects began to evidence the practical aim. In mathematics, for example, "business" arithmetic was introduced, and even general arithmetic texts included many "practical" examples of the subject taken from the real world. In addition, courses in "practical" and "commercial" English began to appear in response to the need for training in the forms of expression current in the real world of affairs. In a text published in 1916 entitled, significantly, *Practical English for High Schools*, the authors state that they have "boldly abandoned moss-grown tradition" by "stating grammatical and rhetorical theory from the point of view of function and not of classification. . . ."

Another curricular innovation of this period was the combining of several specialized subjects under a common rubric. Thus, incipient attempts were made to unify grammar, literature, and composition under the heading of "English," and courses in "science" were devised which gave attention to the elements of physics, chemistry, botany, zoology, astronomy, etc. This trend might be interpreted as a reaction against the proliferation of specialized courses that occurred during the second half of the nineteenth century. It should be noted, however, that this "dilution" of disciplinary content was resisted in many quarters, and by and large a pattern of separate courses in the specialized sciences predominated.

Although history prevailed among the social sciences as a result of college entrance requirements, the practical motive gave rise to the introduction of civics and problems of democracy courses. It was during this period, too, that fine arts and music began to appear in high school courses of study. At this early stage, however, art often was taught for its disciplinary value (coordination of head and hand in drawing), while training in music (singing) was believed to be useful in oratory and even in influencing conduct (Noble 1954, p. 359). Physical education was not included in most high school curricula during this period.

CONCLUSION

The complexity of the curriculum as well as the forces influencing it continued to increase during the period between the Civil War and World War I. Among the social, economic, and intellectual factors that proved to be the most significant were the industrial revolution and urbanization, with their accompanying effects on family life; the massive immigrations from all parts of Europe; the continuing process of democratization that fostered the ideal of equal educational opportunity; the new educational theories of Pestalozzi, Froebel, and Herbart; the expanding store of knowledge; and perhaps most important, the cult of faculty psychology.

These forces, in part, were responsible for shifting the emphasis of curriculum aims. At the elementary level, literacy (based on the three R's), orthodox moral character, and mental discipline predominated, especially during the first half of the period. Toward 1918, however, the industrial revolution, immigration, and new educational theories were responsible for greater attention to the practical vocational aim and the progressive aims of self-development and democratic social competence.

As might be expected, the elementary curriculum emphasized reading, writing, spelling, grammar, and arithmetic, with only minor consideration being given to geography, history, music, and drawing. The "nonsectarian" King James Protestant Bible continued to be used for the development of moral character. But as time passed, the new influences became more noticeable in the curriculum. Reading instruction increasingly centered on meaning and less on rote memory. Pestalozzi's object lessons were influential in introducing scientific studies and in changing geography from rote memorization of unrelated names to the identification of relationships between social development and geophysical conditions. And practical and progressive aims stimulated the introduction of such subjects as manual training, nature study, physical education, cooking, and sewing.

At the secondary level, the mental discipline and culture aims overshadowed all others during most of this period. As the twentieth century progressed, however, practical vocational considerations increasingly made themselves felt.

Neither the new educational theories nor the progressive aims of self-development or democratic social competence had much effect on the high school curriculum during this time. A series of national committees, however, exerted great influence on the secondary school curriculum during the last decade of the nineteenth century. Chief among these was the Committee of Ten. The net effect of these committee reports was to standardize the high school curriculum along conservative, college preparatory lines and to help set the stage for the development of the junior high school.

In line with the mental discipline/culture aim, the college preparatory (academic) aspect of the high school curriculum was formal, logically organized, abstract, and heavily verbal. Memorization and the solution of abstruse problems were emphasized because of the supposed benefits in mental culture. The classics, algebra, and geometry dominated the curriculum, but toward the end of the nineteenth century, these subjects were giving ground to the modern sciences of physics, chemistry, botany, zoology, physiology, and anatomy. The modern languages—German and French—also became more acceptable, but like the sciences, they were taught for mental discipline. English grammar took the form of parsing literature and diagraming sentences. It was not until the end of the century that the study of English literature, as literature, was taken seriously as a part of the curriculum. History was not highly regarded during the first part of this period because of its deficiencies in mental discipline.

After the turn of the century, forces supporting the practical vocational aim increased. Such subjects as typewriting, stenography, bookkeeping, commercial law, domestic science, and industrial arts were fairly common by 1918. In addition, traditional subjects, such as arithmetic and English often were given a practical slant. While art and music sometimes were included in the curriculum, they often were taught for their disciplinary value. Physical education was simply not a part of the curriculum in most high schools of this era.

The Corporate State: Curriculum from World War I to Mid-Century

By the end of World War I, the proponents of culture, the classics, and "liberal education"—i.e. the "conservatives"—were clearly on the defensive. In a society that had just become a world power, that had just experienced the full force of an industrial revolution, massive immigration, and an explosion of scientific knowledge, the curricular prescriptions of the conservatives seemed effete and obsolete, if not downright antique. But the "liberals" who were clamoring for curriculum reform were by no means in agreement as to the kind of curriculum that was needed. Indeed, they were divided into two camps that, interestingly enough, represented a long-standing schism in the American character and consciousness. On the one hand stood the realistic, practical, utilitarian men of action, whose philosophy rested on the tough frontier spirit that had carved a nation out of a wilderness. This wing of the liberal faction called for a practical curriculum that would make each individual a "success," i.e., an efficient, productive citizen in the emerging corporate state. On the other hand there were the "social reformers"—men of action, but visionaries as well. Their philosophy rested on the other side of the American character, the side that grew out of the dreams of liberty, equality, self-fulfillment, and social justice that had brought so many immigrants to America's shores. The curriculum proposed by this group of "liberals" was aimed at the evolution of a more humane, more democratic society through individual growth and fulfillment. Each of these liberal viewpoints eventuated in a curricular movement that persists in one form or another to this day. The former generally is known as the business-efficiency or management orientation in curriculum, and the latter as the famous (or infamous) progressive education movement. Before we discuss the impact of these two movements on the curriculum, however, we should turn to the social, political, and economic developments in the United States during this period to see how these influenced the curriculum.

THE SUCCESS OF BUSINESS

The success of American business is nowhere more graphically demonstrated than in the continuing dramatic increases in production that it brought about. With value adjusted in terms of 1926 dollars, national income grew from $4.7 billion in 1850 to $113.4 billion in 1929 (Edwards and Richey 1963, pp. 436, 437). Even during the depression decade of 1930–1940, national production increased by more than a third, and by 1950, it had reached a total of $239 billion (Butts and Cremin 1953, p. 463)! For all of its waste, inefficiency, and injustice, American business and the capitalist system had made the United States "the greatest industrial nation in the world, with a per capita income higher than that to be found anywhere else" (Edwards and Richey 1963, p. 437). It is small wonder, then, that business and business methods came to be venerated not only by rank-and-file citizens, but by large numbers of American educators.

Many factors contributed to the extravagant success of American business. Among these were an abundance of natural resources, cheap immigrant labor, and the advance of technology. However, it was the congenial climate of individual self-interest, fostered by almost universal acceptance of the economic doctrine of laissez-faire, that enabled business to exploit its opportunities and flourish.

THE DOCTRINE OF LAISSEZ-FAIRE. A laissez-faire economy is an economic system characterized by private property, free competition, the profit motive, and little or no government interference in business. The doctrine holds that the "natural" laws of supply and demand automatically regulate market forces, resulting in the most advantageous levels of production, prices, and consumption. The principles and assumptions of laissez-faire economics have become incorporated into the American tradition to such an extent that "the American free-enterprise system" often is spoken of with the reverence reserved for religious symbols.

In actual practice, however, pure laissez-faire economics has rarely, if ever, been practiced in this country. The government, to a greater or lesser degree, has always intervened in the marketplace, usually following policies that favored private enterprise business. In the past these policies have taken the form of protective tariffs, bounties to railroads, patent rights, and the disposition to private enterprises of resources in the national domain (Edwards and Richey 1963, p. 435). In spite of these deviations from the ideal, however, it can be generally claimed that until World War I, America's economy was characterized by a laissez-faire attitude on the part of government.

THE BUSINESS CORPORATION

During the industrial expansion following the Civil War, larger and larger accumulations of capital were needed for the launching of extensive business enterprises. The corporation, although it was not a new idea, presented the ideal form of organization for this purpose, since it permitted the selling of stocks and bonds to large numbers of purchasers. In many areas of the economy, partnerships and individually owned businesses steadily declined in importance to the point where whole industries were controlled by a handful of giant corporations. For example, by mid-twentieth century only three corporations owned the total of the net capital assets of the entire aluminum industry; four corporations owned over 96 percent of the linoleum industry; and four corporations owned over 88 percent of the rubber tire and tube industry (Federal Trade Commission 1949, p. 21). "The large corporation came to dominate American economic life, and it was influential in changing the very structure and operation of the economy" (Edwards and Richey 1963, p. 396).

Clearly, the growth of the giant corporation in a laissez-faire climate invalidated the free-enterprise assumptions of the system. With the elimination of competition came the elimination of "natural" controls, and the concentration of corporate power virtually made the "American free-enterprise system" a myth.

CONTRADICTIONS OF THE SYSTEM

If laissez-faire economics enabled American business to make the United States the richest country on earth, it also spawned practices and conditions that outraged the decent impulses of human beings everywhere. Cut-throat competition, secret agreements, and monopolistic practices ruined thousands of smaller businessmen. The public was abused with inflated prices and contaminated products. Perhaps most disgraceful was the cruelty of child labor. Prohibitive legislation notwithstanding, many children worked twelve to sixteen hours a day in factories and mines for abysmally low wages. And as late as 1920, the census reported 1 million children between the ages of ten and fifteen as gainfully employed. These conditions fostered the social reform movements whose visions of a better society contributed significantly to the basic philosophy of the progressive education movement.

THE GREAT DEPRESSION. While statistics had always suggested that laissez-faire economics was not the salutary system that it was claimed to be, the depression of the 1930s demonstrated its utter bankruptcy and the need for some degree of effective economic regulation. Following the crash of the stock market in 1929, all sectors of the American economy fell deeper and deeper into depression. Production slumped to between 50 and 60 percent of capacity, and 12 million people were unemployed. These debilitating conditions, along with the abject poverty that they generated, wore on year after year, and popular faith in the efficacy of the "free-enterprise system" to regulate *itself* back to a state of health ("prosperity is just around the corner") went totally unrequited.

An even more glaring indictment of laissez-faire economics was revealed in the statistics concerning the distribution of the nation's wealth. In 1935–1936, for example, 27 percent of American families received less than $750 per year, 64 percent less than $1500, and 91 percent less than $3000. In addition, the most affluent 3 percent of America's families received 21 percent of the nation's wealth—about the same amount shared by the lowest 50 percent of the population! It had become abundantly clear that not only had corporate business made free enterprise a myth, but that some form of economic regulation was necessary to correct the social injustices that arose in complex industrial societies.

THE LABOR MOVEMENT. In 1930 union membership in the United States totaled a little over 3 million persons. With the advent of the depression, however, and the election of a reform-minded liberal administration in Washington, the movement began to grow both in numbers and in power. By 1937, total union membership had increased to 7.3 million and by mid-century fully 15 million Americans belonged to unions. During this period unions, along with business, exerted significant influence in bringing about increased interest in vocational education.

MOVEMENT TOWARD A REGULATED ECONOMY

Government regulation in economic affairs was not, of course, the invention of this period of American history. The Interstate Commerce Act had been passed in 1887, and the Sherman Antitrust Act in 1890. But the policies represented in Franklin Roosevelt's New Deal and Harry Truman's Fair Deal put American society on the road to what sometimes is termed the "welfare state."

The details of the social, economic, and political revolution that took place in American society during these years cannot be given here. But even a brief summary suggests the massive reorientation just mentioned: The government loaned money, set up relief programs for the needy, established "social security," insured bank deposits, supported public electric power plants, and created jobs. It assumed responsibility for action in many areas that had previously been reserved only for the private sector—labor, agriculture, health, banking, education, and the arts. In general, its policy was to intervene where the private sector had failed or was inadequate, and to coordinate planning where it was necessary in the public interest. To do these things, the government had to establish many new agencies so that "American government began to match the 'bigness' of American industry . . ." (Butts and Cremin 1953, p. 472). While a powerful government and its potential for tyranny had traditionally been a frightening prospect for most Americans, the exercise of government control in the public interest by the democratic administrations of this period altered the attitudes of many people. The spirit of planning and cooperation in the interest of the public welfare that permeated the social thought of the depression provided a congenial intellectual environment for the growth of progressive ideas in education.

TECHNOLOGY

Technological progress, the result of advances in scientific knowledge and the industrial revolution, has affected the total pattern of twentieth-century American life, but its impact in three principal areas has had special importance for the curriculum. In the first place, technology was responsible for creating a vast number of new industries and occupations, at the same time rendering many others obsolete. In addition to necessitating a rise in the level of general education, this condition exerted a significant influence both on the pressures for, and the nature of, vocational education. For example, not only did the scope and significance of vocational education increase during this period, but older vocational subjects such as leather working, print shop, and carpentry were replaced by electronics, radio, and office-machine operation. Second, technology dramatically reduced the length of the workday, freeing many hours for recreation and other leisure-time activities. In response to this development, the curriculum incorporated subject matter and activities (such as art, music, ceramics, and dramatics) designed to actualize individual potential for living a satisfying life. Finally, technological progress resulted in an accelerating rate of cultural, economic, social, and material change. Some lag has always existed between the curriculum and social needs, but as the rate of change has accelerated, the lag has tended to widen, to become more obvious and acute. This condition led to more urgent demands for curriculum reform as well as increased experimentation with new forms of education.

ELEMENTARY CURRICULUM

During the period following World War I, the eight-year elementary school became less and less common. With the introduction of the junior high school around 1910, many school systems—especially in the cities—adopted the six-three-three plan of organization. At the same time the curriculum, in response to new and multiplying social, economic, and political forces, broadened enormously. (It should be kept in mind, however, that change always occurred quite irregularly, and during this period the one-room schoolhouse with its simple three R's curriculum remained a feature in many small rural communities at the same time that extensive experimentation was going on in sophisticated urban settings.)

Perhaps the greatest influence on the elementary curriculum during the thirty years following World War I was the philosophy of progressivism. Although only a very small proportion of public schools actually implemented progressive curricula, the "spillover" of progressive ideas was so widespread that the elementary curriculum gradually was transformed.

THE PROGRESSIVE PHILOSOPHY. An adequate exposition of the progressive philosophy, of course, is beyond the scope of this book. However, progressivism had its roots in the imported educational ideas of Pestalozzi, Froebel, and Herbart, discussed earlier. From these beginnings, a unique and characteristically American conception of education was developed, particularly by John Dewey, who became the foremost spokesman for the movement.

Progressive education is based on the ideal of a democratic society, a society, according to Dewey (1916, p. 115) "which makes provision for participation in its good of all its members on equal terms and which secures flexible readjustment of its institutions through interaction of the different forms of associated life. . . ." Among the more characteristic tenets of progressive education are the following:

Education is not preparation for life, but a social process that is life itself.

Subject matter does not consist of the logically organized data of the school subjects, but "primarily of the meanings which supply content to existing social life" (Dewey 1916, p. 126).

Learning is the reorganization of experience.

Interest is the basis of learning.

Such doctrines as these not only suggest that the learner's interests be taken into account, but that the learner and his experience assume pivotal importance in progressive curriculum making and teaching.

Dewey outlines certain other characteristics of the progressive viewpoint by making comparisons with "traditional" practices.

> *To imposition from above is opposed expression and cultivation of individuality; to external discipline is opposed free activity; to learning from texts and teachers, learning through experience; to acquisition of isolated skills and techniques by drill, is opposed acquisition of them as means of attaining ends which make direct vital appeal; to preparation for a more or less remote future is opposed making the most of the opportunities of present life; to static aims and materials is opposed acquaintance with a changing world (Dewey 1938, pp. 5, 6).*

CURRICULUM AIMS. Although the older aims of literacy and character development remained implicit in the elementary curriculum following World War I, the progressive education movement, spurred by the establishment of the Progressive Education Association in 1918, brought about a dramatic shift in focus. Literacy and character development in the progressive school were achieved through individual growth and the acquisition of democratic social skills and values. The citizenship aspect of these aims reflected the practical basis of progressive theory in contrast to the classical orientation of the conservatives. But the vocational and mental discipline influence of the former period had virtually disappeared in the newer elementary schools.

CURRICULUM CONTENT. The separate subjects of reading, writing, spelling, and arithmetic, formerly taught by drill and memorization, were learned incidentally in progressive schools through participation in a variety of activities, such as sharing experiences with storybooks, writing and participating in dramatic presentations, taking field trips, and playing games. Greater emphasis on creative expression was achieved by including drawing, painting, music, dance and rhythm, clay modeling, and craft work in the curriculum.

In many schools the range of content was expanded greatly, while the number of subjects was reduced. For example, the rubric "language arts" was used to include a wide variety of activities involving reading, writing, speaking, and listening. "Social studies" came to include the subject matters of history, geography, economics, sociology, and civics; and "science" was used to designate study in the areas of biology, geology, physics, and chemistry. In all of these subjects, of course, the achievement of the social competency aim was sought through the organization of cooperative group projects and activities. This was true even in physical education and recreation, where emphasis was placed upon organized play and team games.

As a result of progressive theories, the traditional "disciplines" or "subjects" came increasingly to be replaced by new organizations of content (and activities) which ostensibly were better attuned to the learner's interest and experience. Thus, "areas of living," "persistent life situations," and "centers of interest" were employed as organizing principles in curriculum construction. It became common for elementary pupils to study units bearing such titles as "How People Live and Work in Our Neighborhood," "Prejudice," and "Heat" (which included such topics as watching fire, making fire, friction and heat, thermometers, combustion, effects of heat, etc.). These curricula—often popularized as "unit method," "project method," or "child-centered curriculum"—shifted emphasis away from the mechanical ingestion of information to the *understanding* of information and the development of initiative, responsibility, cooperation, critical thinking, self-discipline, leadership, problem-solving skills, and the like. On the whole, curriculum developments on the elementary level tend to reflect the individual growth and social competency aims required for effective participation in the progressive's vision of a socially conscious democracy.

Unfortunately, many of the most vocal advocates of progressivism emphasized the importance of the individual learner to such a degree that the social basis of progressivism was all but forgotten. So "child-centered" were some of their schools that no prescribed curriculum was followed, the content and activities of the classroom being determined almost entirely on the basis of children's immediate interests and purposes.[2] The excesses and abuses of some progressivist educators (who really did not understand the philosophy of Dewey) contributed much to the decline of the progressive movement by mid-century. Before it passed from the educational scene, however, progressivism had done a great deal to free the elementary curriculum of its formal character, to focus attention on children's needs and interests, to call into question the pedagogical legitimacy of a solely logical organization of subject matter, and to establish the experiential nature of the learning process.

SECONDARY CURRICULUM

In 1900 only about 10 percent of all high school aged youth were in secondary schools, with 75 percent of the graduates going on to college. By 1950, some 85 percent of high school aged youth were in secondary schools, but only 25 percent of the graduates were going on to college. The story of secondary curriculum in America during the first half of the twentieth century is reflected in these data: The high school changed from a primarily college-preparatory institution for a select few to a comprehensive secondary school for all American youth.

SPECIAL INFLUENCES ON THE SECONDARY CURRICULUM. The growing trend toward vocational education before World War I received considerable impetus from the passage of the Smith-Hughes Act in 1917. This law provided federal funds for the salaries of teachers of agriculture, trades, industry, and home economics in secondary schools and stipulated in detail the vocational character of the courses to be taught. The act also provided for a federal board with broad powers of inspection and evaluation, a reflection of the management-efficiency orientation that increasingly was affecting the curriculum.

Another, perhaps even greater, impetus to the broadening of the secondary school curriculum was the report of the Commission on the Reorganization of Secondary Education issued in 1918. This report stated the commission's conception of secondary education in a democracy and identified as the "seven cardinal principles of secondary education" what, in effect, it believed the aims of the high school curriculum should be: *health, command of fundamental processes, worthy home membership, vocational efficiency, civic participation, worthy use of leisure time, and ethical character.* It is interesting to note that only one of these aims—command of fundamental processes—is connected directly with college preparation, while the other six are concerned with individ-

---

2. For a detailed description of this curriculum design, see the section "The Activity/ Experience Design" in Chapter 17.

ual development and social competence. Clearly, the seven cardinal principles of secondary education reflect the influence of both the progressive and business-efficiency movements in education and it is easy to understand why they signaled important changes in the aims and content of the high school curriculum.

CURRICULUM AIMS IN THE JUNIOR HIGH SCHOOL. Although the aims of the progressives did not affect the secondary school curriculum to the extent that they did the elementary, their mark is clear, especially at the junior high school level. The junior high school, usually encompassing grades 7, 8, and 9, developed rapidly during the 1920s. Many studies of its functions were made, and partly on the basis of these, Gruhn and Douglass have prepared a summary statement. These authors identify the following six major functions of the junior high school.

Integration: *learning experiences acquired in such a way that they are coordinated and integrated*
Exploration: *discovery and exploration of specialized interests, aptitudes, and abilities*
Guidance: *assistance in making satisfying and intelligent decisions*
Differentiation: *provision of differentiated learning opportunities suited to students' varying backgrounds*
Socialization: *preparation for effective and satisfying participation in a complex social order*
Articulation: *gradual transition from the elementary to the high school program (Gruhn and Douglass 1956, pp. 31, 32)*

Reflected in these functions are the progressive aims of individual development and democratic social competence. It was not accidental, then, that the junior high school curriculum reached maturity during the depression years of the 1930s.

CURRICULUM AIMS IN THE SENIOR HIGH SCHOOL. The picture was somewhat different at the senior high school level, however, perhaps because of the imminence of graduation and the harsh realities that this prospect sometimes represented, especially during the depression. Although some attention was given to progressive aims, success in life was heavily emphasized at this level. But success in American culture meant financial success, and increasingly, the high school diploma came to be sought for its cash value more than for any other reason. Teachers and guidance counselors urged students to "stay in school and get a better-paying job," and business and industry cooperated by requiring diplomas and degrees for employment in many categories of the corporate structure. America was on the way to becoming a "credential society."

The fact that education was being assessed in terms of its cash value encouraged the comparison of schools to business corporations. Demands for "the finest product at the lowest cost" led to efficiency studies and the adoption of pseudoscientific businesss procedures in the operation of schools. Thus, "countless educational [and curriculum] decisions were made on economic or on non-educational grounds" (Callahan 1962, p. 247).

Coincident with the growth of the business-efficiency movement in the schools was the development of empirically based psychological measurement and the field of statistical analysis. These two areas contributed substantial support to business-efficiency practices by supplying them with data that purportedly had a "scientific" basis. Unfortunately, the validity of the data and the conclusions drawn from them rarely were questioned.

BUSINESS-EFFICIENCY AND PROGRESSIVE AIMS COMPARED. Individual material success and social success, vocational competence, productive citizenship—these terms describe the general thrust of the curriculum aim *social-vocational efficiency* promoted by the business-efficiency group in education. What was needed, this group argued, was an "objective," empirical survey of the social-economic scene and a dispassionate (unromantic) determination of the knowledge and skills required for effective functioning in such a setting. A curriculum based on these data would then be constructed, and the schools, employing the best principles of scientific business management, would teach it. This, it was claimed, was the only scientific approach to education.

The business-efficiency group would have been more accurate had they described their approach to curriculum construction as empirical rather than scientific. But empiricism is not necessarily scientific or objective. Obviously, an approach that fosters education for efficient functioning in present conditions is biased insofar as it operates to inhibit change. One is tempted to label a position that supports the status quo as conservative, but such a term would probably be inappropriate in this case. The business-efficiency group was not *consciously* conservative, but rather only unreflective in considering the consequences of their approach. Indeed, the business-efficiency group quite emphatically thought of themselves—vis-à-vis the classicists—as liberals in education!

Opposed to the business-efficiency group were the progressives, who argued for the dual aims of *individual development* and *democratic social competence*. It should be pointed out that the progressives were not antivocational. Indeed, they included vocational competence within the scope of their broader aims. Their quarrel with the aim of social-vocational efficiency was its narrowness and its tendency to support the status quo. Their individual development and democratic social competence aims called for reflection on and questioning of the present state of the individual and his culture. Indeed, individual and social change figured significantly in their conception of the role of education in a democracy.

Both the progressives and the business-efficiency group were arguing for a curriculum that would help young people to function more effectively in American society. The difference was in the meaning they attached to "effective functioning." For the "visionary" progressives it meant opening up new possibilities for the development of individual human potential and more humane and democratic social structures, a highly risk-laden venture to say the least. For the "practical" business-efficiency group, effective functioning meant efficiently fulfilling the roles that were demanded by society. This included, of course, preparation for college and college attendance for those whose projected vocational roles demanded advanced training. Within this framework, then, the college-preparatory course clearly constituted vocational training, i.e., training for college admission and the vocational role that lay beyond. Although the terminology employed in stating their aims was very similar, the philosophical orientations of the progressives and business-efficiency group were fundamentally in opposition.

In the decades following World War I, the dual progressive aims came little by little to be identified with "liberal education" (although many classicists insisted that the term correctly referred only to the classical curriculum described earlier). As the liberal-vocational controversy of the pre-World War I era continued into the 1930s and 1940, it increasingly became a struggle between the progressives, who championed the new liberal education, and the business-efficiency group, whose standard of efficient functioning in the corporate state became the new vocationalism. Our review of curriculum developments during this period will show that although the progressives certainly had an effect on the curriculum, it was the new vocationalism that held sway in the schools.

CURRICULUM CONTENT IN THE JUNIOR HIGH SCHOOL. Although the social-vocational efficiency aim was influential in its development, the junior high school curriculum, as previously stated, was mainly a product of progressive theories of education. Perhaps because it was a new institutional form unbound by tradition, the junior high school became a "hotbed of experimentation" and originated a number of significant curriculum innovations. Separate subjects were correlated or fused to attain an integration of knowledge; content and activities were related to life outside school; college-preparatory and vocational studies were avoided; resource, experience, and other new types of unit organization were employed in curriculum construction; and in many classrooms, pupils shared in planning the learning activities in which they would participate.

Perhaps the most striking curriculum development at this early secondary level was the core curriculum.[3] Most often the core curriculum consisted of some combination of English (or language arts), social studies, and guidance. A block of time longer than the ordinary class period usually was allotted to the core, and the homeroom teacher, ordinarily responsible for the guidance of students in her homeroom, taught them the course.

The core curriculum was designed primarily to integrate learning outcomes. For example, language skills were emphasized in dealing with social studies and other content. In addition, the core, by providing extended time periods in

3. For a detailed description of this curriculum design, see the section "The Core Design" in Chapter 17.

which the teacher and students could work together, was supposed to improve interpersonal relations, personality development, group problem-solving skills, etc. Topics or units of study in the core curriculum carried such titles as "How Conservation Improves Daily Living," "Conservation in the Development of American Civilization," "How I Can Use My Spare Time," and "Let's Improve Our Communication with Others." Progressive aims clearly dominated the core curriculum.

Industrial arts became a feature of the junior high school curriculum, not for vocational purposes, but rather to develop interest in, and understanding of, industrial processes. It was also designed to foster self-realization by actualizing abilities in the mechanical arts and developing practical skill in the use of common tools and machines. Offerings in the industrial arts included such subjects as home mechanics, woodworking, metal working, printing, and weaving.

Home economics originally was regarded as the girls' counterpart of industrial arts for boys. By 1950, however, some schools were offering home economics for boys and industrial arts for girls. The aims of the course were individual development and social competency in the home, family, and personal areas of life. Although food and clothing were emphasized in these courses, many also gave considerable attention to problems of family relationships, child care, personal development, and group participation.

Health and physical education usually were required subjects in the junior high school curriculum. With physical fitness, health, and self-actualization through physical education as goals, the program eschewed the formal calisthenics of the previous era in favor of a developmental program of motor experiences, sports, and games. As previously mentioned, group activities and team sports were emphasized to develop social competence.

Art and music in the junior high school were almost always offered as a component of liberal general education. Painting and drawing, crafts, flower arrangement, picture framing and hanging, design and execution of school murals, and bulletin-board arrangement were some of the activities included in the art curriculum. Community art projects such as fashion shows and displays in public libraries were conducted by some art classes. These curriculum activities demonstrate the operation of the individual development and social-consciousness aims of the progressive philosophy. The music curriculum was developed along similar philosophical lines. Along with courses that taught music appreciation and the elements of notation, rhythm, and harmony, most junior high schools offered classes in instrumental and vocal music. The orchestras, bands, and choirs that resulted from these classes were often very competent, and the community performances they gave were quite impressive.

Even in the more traditional academic areas, the junior high school curriculum bore the impress of progressive aims. Grammar, rhetoric, spelling, speech, and literature frequently were combined as the "language arts." Although grammar continued to be taught in some schools, its prominence was reduced greatly, and it was justified on the basis that it fostered clarity in speech and writing, rather than mental discipline. But in most schools, the language arts curriculum was built on a number of topical or experiential units around which the skills of reading, writing, speaking, and listening were practiced. These units bore such titles as "Our Animal Friends," "Chills and Thrills," "Periodicals," and "Conservation of Resources" (Gruhn and Douglass 1956, p. 141).

The social studies in the junior high school usually combined the content of ancient, world, and United States history, civics, economics, and geography, and in some cases even vocational guidance. Emphasized in these courses were international understanding, human relationships, consumer education, critical thinking and propaganda analysis, and democratic behavior. Although some schools continued to teach separate courses such as "World History" or "Civics" under the rubrics of "Social Studies I" and "Social Studies II," the social studies curriculum came to be taught in terms of large problems or themes. For example, a grade 7 social studies course entitled "Patterns of Culture" might be composed of the following four major units: (1) How Did Early Man Develop? (2) What Were Some Contributions of Past Civilizations? (3) What Contributions Were Made by People Who Lived in Europe during the Middle Ages? (4) How Do People of the Eastern Hemisphere Live Today? (Gruhn and Douglass 1956, p. 154).

The aim of the mathematics curriculum, in addition to the general aims advocated by progressives, was to foster competence for the ordinary affairs of life. In most schools arithmetic and general mathematics were offered in the seventh and eighth grades, with some effort being made to help students understand the quantitative aspects of home, business, and community problems. Thus, banking, insurance, purchasing, and budgeting were used as vehicles for mathematics instruction. In many junior high schools, however, algebra was offered in the ninth grade for college-preparatory students, while general mathematics or no mathematics at all was offered to the noncollege group. Instances such as this indicate the influence of the vocational motive in the curriculum.

Science, like the language arts and social studies, incorporated under a single rubric material from a number of specialized areas, most notably biology, physics, and chemistry. Consonant with progressive philosophy, junior high school science aimed at an understanding of the role of science in society as well as an appreciation of its explanations of natural phenomena. The textbook emphasis of the previous periods shifted to laboratory activities that were functionally related to the learners' experience.

With the rise of the junior high school, foreign language study, formerly reserved for the senior high school grades, was often begun in the seventh grade. Most students, however, did not begin the study of a foreign language until the ninth grade. As late as the 1948–1949 school year, the most common foreign language offerings, in order of popularity, were Latin, Spanish, French, and German (Gruhn and Douglass 1956, p. 143). These data suggest the lingering influence of the pre-World War I classicists, as well as the college-preparatory motive. Some progressive junior high schools, however, treated foreign language instruction in terms of its self-realization and intercultural values by emphasizing native customs, dress, foods, art, music, and literature.

CURRICULUM CONTENT IN THE SENIOR HIGH SCHOOL. Although many of the progressive developments described above were incorporated into the senior high school curriculum, the evolution of differentiated curricula or "tracks" at this level indicated the growing influence of the social-vocational efficiency aim. Of course, differentiated curricula were characteristic of the high school in the pre-World War I period, but most of these tracks were college preparatory in aim and were believed to be suitable for all students, whether or not they planned to attend college. Among them, it will be recalled, were the Classical, Latin-Scientific, English, and Modern Language curricula. But as nonacademic and vocational subjects began to enter the curriculum, new "tracks" appeared, most often with vocational designations: commercial, industrial or manual arts, agriculture, etc. Gradually, the differentiated college preparatory curricula were replaced with a single "college prep" course, and by mid-century most high schools were operating on some variation of the tracking system that included, in addition to the college preparatory course, such differentiated curricula as business or commercial, technical, general, vocational or industrial, agriculture, home economics, and fine arts. Although the comprehensive high school democratically housed all of its students under a single roof, once they were inside, it separated them according to their social-vocational prospects. It was more than coincidence that the college-preparatory curriculum generally enrolled a middle- and upper-middle-class clientele, while the vocational and industrial tracks were composed mainly of lower- and lower-middle-class youngsters. As the United States moved in the direction of a "credential society," the secondary school curriculum assumed an increasingly important role—a role, unfortunately, in support of the status quo and social stratification.[4]

Although the social-vocational efficiency aim dominated the high school curriculum, the progressive education movement was still vigorous enough in the 1930s to believe in the ultimate triumph of a liberal secondary curriculum. After all, some high schools were implementing mainstream curricula designed for the individual and social development of all students. But one of the main barriers to progressive curricula in most high schools was college entrance requirements. Behind these requirements was the fear that "excellence" would be sacrificed if they were removed. It was argued that in an advanced technological society the nation's leaders would have to come from the best colleges and universities and that a stiff academic college preparatory curriculum was necessary for success in college. In answer to this claim, the Progressive Educa-

---

4. At the same time, it should be made quite clear that the high school underwent an extraordinary degree of democratization during this period, as the attendance figures quoted at the opening of this section testify. On balance, it was probably as democratic an educational institution as had ever been developed anywhere. Yet, it was far from perfect, and its undemocratic elements deserve to be pointed out.

tion Association launched the "Eight-Year Study."[5] During the period 1932 to 1940, the college performances of some 1475 graduates of thirty experimental secondary schools were compared with those of 1475 matched graduates of traditional college-preparatory programs. It was found that the graduates of the experimental schools did as well or better academically, socially, and psychologically as did those students who met traditional college-entrance requirements. In spite of this evidence suggesting that a traditional college-preparatory curriculum might not be the only, or even the best, way to prepare for college, the tradition persisted. For most high school students aiming at college acceptance, the curriculum allowed for only minor variations of the following theme: three or four years of English (most often a blend of grammar, composition, and literature): two to four years of mathematics (algebra, geometry, and trigonometry); two to four years of foreign language; two to three years of social studies (United States history, world history, and civics); and two to three years of science (biology, chemistry, and physics). Health and physical education usually were required, and when students had the time, art, music, home economics, personal typing, etc., might be included as electives. Noncollege-preparatory students who were enrolled in commercial, industrial, agriculture, and other curricula generally were taught English, mathematics, and science geared to their "more modest abilities" and often adapted to their projected vocations. Thus, business English and bookkeeping, for example, constituted the English and mathematics taught students in the commercial track. It was common, however, to cut across track lines to form civics and problems of democracy classes. This gesture in the direction of democratic associations, for all of its good intentions, constituted an acknowledgment of the undemocratic nature of differentiated curricula.

CONCLUSION

We have observed that the success of business and the growth of the labor movement encouraged the development of a practical vocational curriculum administered for efficiency according to business management techniques. But the intolerable social conditions created by business in a laissez-faire climate led to the development of social reform movements that climaxed in the social welfare policies of the federal government during the depression. The philosophical assumptions of these reform movements—i.e., that individual liberty, dignity, and general welfare are maximized through change brought about by planning and cooperation in the public interest—provided a climate conducive to the kind of curriculum advocated by the progressive education movement.

Both the progressives and the business-efficiency group advocated curricula designed to help young people function effectively in American society. The difference was in the meaning they attached to "effective functioning." For the

5. See Aikin (1942).

progressives it meant the aims of individual development and democratic social competence; for the business-efficiency group it meant the aim of social-vocational efficiency.

The aims of the progressives implied new frontiers in individual and social development; in other words, change. The aim of social-vocational efficiency, on the other hand, implied efficient fulfillment of the roles demanded by society; in other words, reinforcement of the status quo. As the liberal-vocational controversy of the pre-World War I era continued into the 1930s and 1940s, it increasingly became a struggle between the progressives, who championed the new liberal education, and the business-efficiency group, whose standard of efficient functioning in the corporate state became the new vocationalism.

The progressive aims had their greatest impact on the elementary and junior high school curricula. The separate elementary subjects of reading, spelling, and arithmetic, formerly taught by drill and rote, were learned incidentally in progressive schools through participation in a variety of activities, such as sharing experiences with storybooks, taking field trips, and playing games. Greater emphasis on creative expression was achieved by including painting, music, dance, and craft work in the curriculum. Thus, the range of content in the elementary curriculum was expanded greatly.

In the junior high school, the core curriculum was the most significant development resulting from progressive influences. In addition, industrial arts, home economics, health and physical education, art, and music were taught for individual development and democratic social competence. Academic subjects were correlated in order to integrate the learning experiences of students, and much experimentation was carried on with a variety of different "unit" approaches. English as a combination of grammar, composition, and literature was abandoned in favor of the language arts. This new rubric included the skills of reading, writing, speaking, and listening. Much the same kind of curriculum reorganization took place in the social studies. Mathematics and science were reorganized to make these subjects more functional in terms of the students' experience.

At the senior high school level, however, the curriculum was dominated to a far greater degree by the business-efficiency aim. Control was achieved through the device of differentiated curricula, or "tracks." The most common tracks found in high schools during this period were the college preparatory, business or commercial, industrial or manual arts, and agriculture. Although the comprehensive high school democratically housed all of its students under a single roof, once inside, it segregated them according to their social-vocational prospects. The high school and its curriculum underwent an extraordinary degree of democratization during this period, but in many respects it was so organized that it increasingly operated to support social stratification and the status quo.

Recent Developments

Following World War II, the cold war generated a great deal of anticommunist sentiment and a fear of communist world power that at times reached paranoid proportions. In this climate of international threat, the progressive aims of individual development and democratic social competence seemed highly inappropriate to many people. Progressive curricula were vigorously attacked for their "soft pedagogy" and "quackery," and a "tough, no-nonsense" curriculum that would ensure national leadership and survival in a hostile, competitive world was called for by many.

The Progressive Education Association, in a decline since the mid-1940s, finally disbanded in 1956. A year later, the Soviet Union launched Sputnik I, achieving initial victory over the United States in the race for space and challenging American supremacy on the international scene. These events effectively signaled the eclipse of progressive tendencies in American curriculum development and marked the triumph of the social-vocational motive. During the next ten years, the discipline-centered curriculum became the means employed to develop human resources to serve the threatened American corporate state.

THE DISCIPLINE-CENTERED CURRICULUM

The discipline-centered curriculum[6] of the 1950s and 1960s, while primarily an outgrowth of the social-vocational efficiency philosophy, was not a carbon copy of its prewar progenitor. Neither was it entirely a repudiation of the progressive tradition. Like the curriculum of the business-efficiency group, it was aimed at producing individuals who would perform competently in (and for) the present society. But world conditions were such that the present society was threatened by international communism and needed highly trained leaders, scientists, and technicians to meet the challenge. Thus, the emphasis in discipline-centered curriculum was on training an elite corps, and rigorous preparation for college was viewed as the first step. So intense was this conviction that even many elementary schools abandoned the progressive, self-contained classroom with a single teacher in favor of instruction by multiple teachers, each of whom was a specialist in science, mathematics, English, or social studies. Curriculum more and more came to be equated with intradiscipline organization, and "excellence" became the watchword of the new vocationalism.

The discipline-centered curriculum, as the name implies, was organized around the specialized disciplines of knowledge. Thus, science was replaced by chemistry, physics, and biology; social studies by history, economics, and sociology; English or language arts by grammar, composition, and literature. Curriculum construction proceeded by separate disciplines, and university professors dominated in the prescription of their objectives, content, and methodology.

6. For a detailed account of this curriculum design, see the section "The Disciplines Design" in Chapter 17.

This era saw the ascendancy of the "new" math and the "new" sciences, reorganized and presented according to their inherent "structure." The new curricula bore the initials of the special committees formed to develop them: in mathematics, the School Mathematic Study Group (SMSG); in physics, the Physical Science Study Committee (PSSC); in biology, the Biological Sciences Curriculum Study (BSCS); and in chemistry, the Chemical Education Material Study (CHEM study) and the Chemical Bond Approach Project (CBA). The "whole" curriculum was conceived to be simply the sum of the individual disciplines, which, it was held, represented the intellectual heritage of the race. The progressive notions of integration of knowledge, the aesthetic dimension, and the "whole child" were dismissed as unimportant or irrelevant.

But significant aspects of the progressive movement were evident in the new curricula. The disciplines were taught through discovery and problem solving. Thus, student involvement and cognitive processes (peculiar to a particular discipline) were emphasized over the passive memorization of content. Furthermore, the content itself centered on principles and concepts rather than on the factual fragments that characterized the subject-centered curriculum of the pre-World War I era. Finally, curriculum goals emphasized students *understanding* of the discipline, i.e., a sense of the mental set acquired by a scholar in the field.

As the cold war waned, however, a reaction set in against the social control and elitism represented in the discipline-centered curriculum. The characteristically American ideals that moved the progressives—i.e., liberty, equality, self-fulfillment, and social justice—reasserted themselves as a result of intensifying awareness of America's racism, poverty, pollution, and, of course, involvement in the Viet Nam war. By the mid-1960s, widespread attacks were being launched against the "irrelevance" and "immorality" of the discipline-centered curriculum. Most significantly, it was claimed that the discipline-centered curriculum was unrelated to life outside the school. "Irrelevant" became a battle cry, and critics branded the intensive study of separate disciplines as narrowly vocational. A first-rank physicist or biologist, they claimed, was not necessarily a good human being or a good citizen. Once again the struggle between liberal and vocational education was joined.

Other criticisms of the discipline approach to curriculum construction pointed to its inherent fragmentation (or lack of integration) of knowledge, its essential elitism in focusing on the college-bound students, and its overemphasis on the rational to the detriment of the aesthetic. Out of this syndrome of reaction was born (or reborn) the humanistic movement in curriculum.

THE HUMANISTIC CURRICULUM

Like all curriculum movements, the humanistic one is comprised of many factions so that it is difficult to provide a definitive statement of its principles and parameters. Moreover, its relatively recent development compounds this difficulty. A few extremists in the movement advocate the abolition of all compulsory, formal ("artificial") education in favor of the informal "curriculum" of the real world. Other radicals, while admitting the need for an institutional structure, would—à la Rousseau or A. S. Neill—allow learners total freedom within the school to determine the curriculum that they will study. Essentially, however, the best of the humanistic curriculum movement is continuous with the basic tenets of progressivism. It advocates humanization of the goals, content, and learning activities of the curriculum. Thus, it emphasizes individual development within the framework of democratic social structures, leaving open ended all conceptions of the ultimate in individual potential and social organization. Content in the humanistic curriculum focuses on man, and where desirable, utilizes social problems, human concerns, and other such principles as centers for curriculum organization. In such a framework, the disciplines become resources for content, which is related to the problem under study. In-depth study of specialized disciplines is provided for, however, when individual interest turns in such a direction. Learning activities in the humanistic curriculum take into account the cognitive, aesthetic, and personal relations dimensions of learning and recognize the essential nonseparability of these dimensions of human experience. "Realness," "dignity," "trust," and "acceptance" are words commonly employed to describe aspects of the relationships that are developed among teachers and students in teaching/learning activities. Proponents of the humanistic curriculum often sum up the humanistic position as individual integrity within a community context.

The degree to which the humanistic movement has influenced the curriculum is indicated by a survey of 270 secondary schools conducted by the National Center for Education Statistics (1971) of the U.S. Office of Education. This report indicates that many high schools, in answer to students' contentions that their studies are not relevant to their daily lives and concerns, are now offering a number of new courses intended to provide multiple curricular options: environmental studies, religious literature, psychology, anthropology, black studies, mass communications, radio/television/film, twentieth-century literature, current events, and so on. At least one secondary school has even offered a course in transcendental meditation!

At this point in time, the discipline-centered curriculum appears to be in a serious decline. However, momentum toward a more humanistic curriculum also appears to have slowed somewhat since 1970, the peak year of social-educational protest that culminated with the killings at Kent State. Since 1970, national enthusiasm for social reform has ebbed considerably, and a mood of reassessment and consolidation seems to have set in. On the curricular front, this mood may very well represent a reaction against the strident (and sometimes hysterical) attacks made on the schools by the more radical of the "humanistic" reformers.[7] In any case, it is a mood congenial to order and the status quo, and the past few years have seen a reassertion of the business-efficiency movement in curriculum. Evidence of this direction in curriculum

7. The positions of the radical school reformers are well represented in Gross and Gross (1969), and Van Til (1971).

development is indicated by recent emphasis on such particulars as behavioral objectives, accountability, national assessment, performance contracting, and performance-based curricula. Nevertheless, the humanistic-progressive thrust continues to manifest itself, mainly under the banner of "open education," or the "open classroom," curricular concepts borrowed from the British primary school. It is difficult to perceive clearly the lines along which the struggle for the curriculum presently is joined, much less to predict its future. It seems clear though that the curricular debate will continue to revolve around such issues as liberal versus vocational education, change versus the status quo, and individual dignity versus social adjustment.

This historical overview, brief as it has been, has shown that the curriculum has been determined by man, his culture, and his social institutions. To the extent that he is aware of himself, his society, and his culture, he becomes a significant force in determining through the curriculum his own nature and the quality of his existence. To the extent that he is ignorant of his heritage and his present condition, however, man forfeits control over his schools and by default relegates the future of the race to the mercies of uncontrolled events.

References

Aikin, Wilford M. 1942. *The Story of the Eight-Year Study.* New York: McGraw-Hill Book Company.

Butts, R. Freeman, and Lawrence A. Cremin. 1953. *A History of Education in American Culture.* New York: Holt, Rinehart and Winston.

Callahan, Raymond E. 1962. *Education and the Cult of Efficiency.* Chicago: University of Chicago Press.

Dewey, John. 1916. *Democracy and Education.* New York: The Macmillan Company.

————. 1938. *Experience and Education.* New York: The Macmillan Company.

Edwards, Newton, and Herman G. Richey. 1963. *The School in the American Social Order.* Boston: Houghton Mifflin Company.

Federal Trade Commission. 1949. *Report on the Concentration of Productive Facilities, 1947.* Washington, D.C.: U.S. Government Printing Office.

Gross, Ronald, and Beatrice Gross, eds. 1969. *Radical School Reform.* New York: Simon & Schuster.

Gruhn, William T., and Harl R. Douglass. 1956. *The Modern Junior High School.* 2d ed. New York: The Ronald Press Company.

National Center for Education Statistics. 1971. *Pattern of Course Offerings and Enrollments in Public Secondary Schools 1970–71.* Washington, D.C.: U.S. Government Printing Office.

Noble, Stuart G. 1954. *A History of American Education.* New York: Holt, Rinehart and Winston.

Stout, John Elbert. 1921. *The Development of High-School Curricula in the North Central States from 1860 to 1918.* Supplementary Educational Monographs, Vol. III, No. 3, June 1921. Chicago: University of Chicago Press.

Van Til, William, ed. 1971. *Curriculum: Quest for Relevance.* Boston: Houghton Mifflin Company.

CHAPTER 4
CURRICULUM THEORY

[T]heory is in the end . . . the most practical of all things. . . .

—JOHN DEWEY

In an overheard conversation on the first day of class, a graduate student remarked to a new acquaintance sitting on his right, "I hope this isn't another one of those theoretical courses. What I need are some good practical ideas to use in my classroom." This negative attitude toward theory is not uncommon among Americans, who generally regard theory and theorists with considerable skepticism, distrust, and even contempt. It reflects a rather widespread belief that theory represents an absence of sound knowledge, and that theorists usually do not know what they are talking about. Indeed, the term "egghead" often is disparagingly applied to those "intellectuals" who purportedly spin out of their heads grand theories that have little relationship to the realities of life.[1] But is this attitude justified? Or is it based mainly on misconceptions of the nature and function of theory in science, the professions, and everyday life? In a previous chapter it was argued that an historical perspective was necessary to avoid the "bandwagonism" and hit-or-miss methods that presently characterize the curriculum field. This chapter will attempt to show that a theoretical framework, judiciously conceived and utilized, is just as essential for the rational, orderly, and productive conduct of the curriculum enterprise.

Perspectives on Curriculum Theory

The totality of natural and human phenomena (reality) is so complex, interrelated, and expansive that a conceptual overview of the whole is almost certainly beyond the capacity of the human mind to comprehend. Yet man craves

---

1. See Hofstadter (1963) for a good account of this American disposition.

understanding, and imperfect partial understanding is better than none. Although reality is in fact an indivisible mass, man has found that by cutting it up into hypothetical segments and looking at it "theoretically," piece by piece, he can extract meaning from it. (He also extracts meaning by putting the pieces together again, i.e., relating the pieces to one another.) Thus, over time he has divided, subdivided, and classified his experience of reality into categories that he thinks are "reasonable" in order to come to terms with, and understand, the fantastic masses of data that impose themselves upon his senses. Roughly, this hypothesizing process has led to the development of those "theories" we call the areas, realms, or disciplines of knowledge. Seeing how these stand in relation to one another will provide us with some perspective on the place of curriculum theory in the structure of knowledge.[2]

Beauchamp (1975, pp. 3–6) develops the idea that all theories derive from those in three broad categories of knowledge: (1) the humanities, (2) the natural sciences, and (3) the social sciences (see Figure 4-1). These three categories, he proposes, encompass the "established disciplines" of knowledge. Thus, for example, the humanities include the disciplines of literature, philosophy, theology, music, etc.; the natural sciences include physics, chemistry, botany, zoology, etc.; and the social sciences include such disciplines as sociology, psychology, anthropology, and economics.

Emerging from these disciplines are theories in areas that Beauchamp identifies as the "applied areas of knowledge." The applied areas of knowledge, as Figure 4-1 shows, include such "practical arts" as architecture, engineering, law, medicine, and of course education. Although this distinction between the "pure" disciplines and the "applied areas of knowledge" is rarely explicitly argued, it is accepted by many writers. For example, O'Connor (1957, pp. 92, 93) states: "Most people would agree that education is not itself a science. It is rather a set of practical activities connected by a common aim." Theories in the applied areas of knowledge are ordinarily distinguished by the fact that they draw their authority from theory in the disciplines. Thus, many writers would agree that educational theory, for instance, consists of a unique composite of theory taken from such disciplines as philosophy (in the humanities), physiology (in the natural sciences), and psychology and sociology (in the social sciences).

Having located theories in education in relation to the disciplines, Beauchamp identifies a number of the more obvious subtheories of education—as Figure 4-1 shows, theories in administration, counseling, curriculum, instruction, and evaluation. Each of these subtheories of education can be further divided into its own constituent subtheories. Accordingly, Beauchamp identifies two such subtheories for our particular interest, curriculum: design and engineering theories. By way of expansion, we might also include among the subtheories of

---

2. The following brief discussion should not be construed as a definitive statement on the organization of knowledge. The nature and organization of knowledge is a highly complex problem about which volumes have been written by philosophers and other scholars throughout history. Although a more systematic discussion of the problem occurs in Chapter 14, "Content," even there the treatment is simplified and incomplete.

FIGURE 4-1

Curriculum theory in perspective. (Reproduced by permission from George A. Beauchamp, Curriculum Theory. *3rd ed. Wilmette, Ill.: The Kagg Press, 1975. p. 5.)*

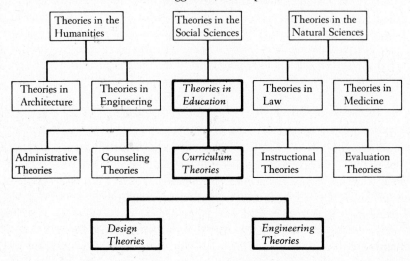

curriculum, those in such areas as curriculum foundations, curriculum development, goal determination, curriculum content, and curriculum evaluation.

Whether one accepts the assumptions and rationale underlying Beauchamp's schema for the organization of theories is less important than the fact that he has provided us with a model that functions adequately enough for our present purposes. His diagram (Figure 4-1) establishes in a rough, yet graphic way the relationship of curriculum theory to the web of theory that comprises the organization of man's accumulated knowledge.

The Nature of Theory

A precise, universally accepted definition of theory does not exist. Indeed, although the literatures of science, philosophy, and education contain numerous and extensive treatments of the nature and function of theory, of the distinction between theory and practice, and of the meaning of the word "theory" in general, many points of disagreement and even confusion persist. At the same time, however, certain recurring ideas and emphases appear in the literature so that it is possible to stake out in a rough kind of way the boundaries that circumscribe the concept.

Perhaps the best way to start is to specify what theory is *not*. In the first place, as we have suggested in the opening paragraph, theory does not represent an absence of knowledge. Nor is it, as its most extreme detractors suggest, merely a fantasy or a flight of fancy. Such explanations of everyday occurrences as the theory of gravity and the oxidation theory of combustion should easily dispel this caricature. Neither is it the opposite of practical—that is to say, the impractical. As we shall attempt to show, man could not possibly have risen much above an animal state of existence, much less erect the civilizations that he has, without theory. Other misconceptions of theory equate it, essentially, with such notions as speculation, the ideal, a dream, a philosophy, a taxonomy, or common sense (Griffiths 1964, p. 96). None of these terms characterizes the essential nature of theory.

SOME DEFINITIONS OF THEORY

The remarkable achievements of the natural sciences, generally attributed to their advanced levels of theory development, have led to the extensive utilization of scientific theory as a model for theory building in other areas of inquiry. Indeed, scientific theory has acquired so honorific a status compared with other kinds of theory that it has even come to be used as the criterion for determining the "true" nature of theory. Thus, O'Connor (1957, p. 76) tells us that theory in a scientific sense "is useful to consider here because it is a sense that gives us standards by which we can assess the value and use of any claimant to the title of 'theory.'" Whether or not we accept such a proposition at this point is less important than the fact that scientific theory, because of its past productiveness, deserves careful examination.

SCIENTIFIC THEORY. Perhaps the most frequently quoted and widely accepted definition of scientific theory is that of Feigl. He views theory as:

> *a set of assumptions from which can be derived by purely logico-mathematical procedures, a larger set of empirical laws. The theory thereby furnishes an explanation of these empirical laws and unifies the originally relatively heterogeneous areas of subject matter characterized by those empirical laws (Feigl 1951, p. 182).*

Feigl's definition attributes to theory four basic features: (1) logically connected statements, (2) generalization of particular cases, (3) explanation, and (4) unification of heterogeneous data and propositions.

Kerlinger's definition includes these features, but adds the function of prediction:

> *A theory is a set of interrelated constructs (concepts), definitions, and propositions that presents a systematic view of phenomena by specifying relations among variables, with the purposes of explaining and predicting phenomena (Kerlinger 1965, p. 11).*

Abel reinforces the notions of the generalization and unification of (heterogeneous) empirical data within a logical system.

> *A general theory is built upon the facts discovered by means of theorems and other conceptual models from empirical data and which have been*

expressed in the form of laws, correlations, or other types of generaliza-
tions. It involves synthesis and is directed to the formulation of proposi-
tions about universals (Abel 1952, p. 162).

Generalization and unification of empirical data are also emphasized by O'Connor:

the word "theory" . . . is most often used to refer (a) to a hypothesis that
has been verified by observation, and, more commonly (b) to a logically
interconnected set of such confirmed hypotheses (O'Connor 1957, p. 76).

Boring, more succinct than most writers, also emphasizes generalization and empiricism: theory "is generalizations, induced from observed particulars" (Boring 1959a, p. 45).

Pratte, on the basis of an examination of many definitions of theory, evolves his own:

we may define the nature of theory as a set of abstract propositions,
logically related to each other through assumptions, postulates, axioms,
definitions, and hypotheses; and these in turn are related by rules of
correspondence to some set of facts or data (Pratte 1971, p. 7).

This relatively small sampling of the large number of definitions of theory that abound in the literature should be sufficient to convey at least a flavor of what is meant by the term "theory" in its scientific sense. Whatever else it may consist of, it would seem that scientific theory at least must exhibit (1) a logically unified framework, (2) generality, and (3) an empirical basis.

OTHER VIEWS OF THE NATURE OF THEORY. In addition to the scientific sense in which the word "theory" is used, O'Connor (1957, pp. 75, 76) identifies three other meanings ordinarily attributed to it. The first, he notes, occurs in areas such as philosophy, where theory may mean "no more than 'a body of related problems.'" In this sense, he says, philosophers may talk about "the theory of knowledge" or "the theory of value."

A second sense in which the word "theory" is used occurs in fields like mathematics, where it refers to "a very highly organized and unified conceptual framework with little or no relation to any practical activity" (O'Connor 1957, p. 75). Thus, mathematicians may refer to the "theory of numbers" or "set theory."

In everyday affairs, theory often is used in a third sense—to "refer to a set or system of rules . . . which guide or control actions of various kinds" (O'Connor 1957, p. 75). Relatively modest crafts such as plumbing and carpentry may be guided by "theory" in this sense. In these cases, however, the "theory" would be fairly simple, and "would probably amount to little more than a set of rules of thumb" (O'Connor 1957, p. 75). More significantly, however, such practitioners as doctors and engineers commonly use theory in the sense noted above in order to diagnose and solve rather complex and sophisticated problems in their respective fields. The theories employed by these practitioners, however, are far more complex, unified, and systematic than the rules of thumb followed by craftsmen.

It should be noted that theory defined as "a system of rules which guide or control action" implies a prescriptive dimension not present in scientific definitions of theory. Prescription tells us what we *ought* to do, and many educationists object to this view of theory, calling it philosophy, ideology, or doctrine, but in any case, a misconception of what theory really is. Almost all who take this position argue on the basis of what is commonly called the "is-ought" dichotomy. In the field of educational administration, for example:

> some writers have used this term (theory) in the sense of "value theory," to refer not to how administrators do behave, but to how they ought to behave. . . . No one will deny that we need normative standards—in the ethical meaning of the term—for how administrators ought to behave, but these prescriptions do not constitute theory (Halpin, 1958, p. 6).

Other writers disagree, however. For example, Scheffler (1960, p. 75) states: "The aim of inquiry is to construct theories adequate to all of the facts, theories that may thus be taken as our best estimates of the truths of nature and *as guides to action*." (Italics added.) And Maccia (1962, p. 165) notes that theory should establish "relationships between knowledge of teaching-learning behavior (means) and *knowledge of oughts of teaching-learning behavior* (ends)." (Italics added.)

This basic "is-ought" disagreement about the nature of theory constitutes a long-standing issue in the curriculum field. Ordinarily, those who advocate the "is-ness" conception of theory characterize themselves as "objective" and "scientific" in their approach, while those who opt for the "ought-ness" conception tend to be classed as "ideological" or "unscientific." The issue is a crucial one for the curriculum field, however, for two reasons: first, because curriculum work must ultimately concern itself with curriculum *practice*, and second, because effective practice cannot avoid involvement with considerations of the *relationship* of theory and practice. The next section of this chapter argues in favor of the "ought-ness" conception of theory and suggests that this conception is not in conflict with what generally is meant by "scientific theory." The following section, "Scientific Theory and Curriculum Theory," attempts a detailed demonstration of the essential "ought-ness" of all scientific theories.

The Functions of Theory

O'Connor (1957, p. 81) and many other writers have ascribed three functions to theory taken in its most technically "scientific" sense: (1) description, (2) prediction, and (3) explanation. Although disputes have developed over which of the three is the primary function of theory, it seems clear that all are important and closely related.

The first function, description, is particularly characteristic of lower forms of theory. It involves careful and precise definition of the terms employed in the theory. For example, "molecule" in chemistry and "reliability" in measurement are terms that are consistently used in exactly the same way in discourse within these two fields.

Description may also involve the classification of data. Thus,

> as a classification, it [theory] provides a set of pidgeonholes, a filing cabinet, in which fact can accumulate. For nothing is more lost than a loose fact. The empty folders of the file demand filling. In time the accumulation makes necessary a more economical filing sytsem, with more cross references, and a new theory is born (Homans 1950, p. 5).

Finally, description often involves giving an account of events. Boyle's law, for example, describes the behavior of gases under varying conditions of pressure with constant temperature. This kind of description is particularly significant because it enables us to *predict*—in this case, the behavior of gases under given conditions of temperature and pressure.

Prediction, the second function of scientific theory, is plain enough in meaning to require no elaboration here. Its significance, however, should not be underestimated. Many writers contend that the ultimate test of a theory is its predictive efficacy. What they are saying, in other words, is that the best summary of past experience (read "the best theory") is that which guarantees future experience.

The third function ascribed to theory, explanation, is somewhat more nebulous than the previous two because differences of opinion exist as to what constitutes an explanation. Some writers equate explanation with prediction (e.g., see Beauchamp 1975, p. 18). They argue that explaining means "accounting for something," and accounting for something means "establishing predictable relationships." This conception of explanation is satisfactory, however, only in a narrowly behavioral sense. Its argument runs something like this: "To explain means to render understandable. Genuine understanding of what-is-to-be-explained (e.g., water, a geranium, a five-year-old male child) can be demonstrated only by predicting its behavior under a variety of conditions. If one is unable to predict how it will behave, one does not really understand it, and thus it cannot be explained.

O'Connor (1957, pp. 81–91) presents a somewhat broader concept of explanation. This writer defines explanation as the establishment of a relationship between what-is-to-be-explained and present knowledge. To put it another way, we might say that an explanation removes the puzzlement connected with what-is-to-be-explained by fitting it in with our present understood experience. With this definition, it follows that an explanation cannot be given to any person whose present knowledge is insufficient or faulty in relation to the phenomena to be explained. It is for this reason, for example, that the theory of relativity cannot be explained to the average layman.

Happily, O'Connor's definition also provides us with a criterion for judging the adequacy of explanations. The best explanations, he points out (1957, p. 84), will be those that relate to what we *know* as opposed to what we may mistakenly *believe*. For example, we would find an explanation of a smallpox epidemic in terms of witchcraft and evil spirits less adequate than one involving bacterial infection, even though certain primitive populations would prefer the former. The witchcraft theory is rendered inadequate for *us* by our present store of knowledge. On the other hand, the primitives' ignorance of relevant concepts and data would make the bacterial infection theory incomprehensible to them; that is to say, no explanation at all.

These three functions of theory—description, prediction, and explanation— are emphasized by those who insist on the "is-ness" nature of theory. For them, science and scientific theory are totally "objective" and should not be contaminated with values, preferences, or prescriptions. Scientific theory, they hold, simply describes and explains the nature and relationships of things.

As Gowin points out, however, objectivity in such an absolute sense may be an illusion. If we "turn theory around and point it toward the person using the theory," an entirely different set of functions emerges (Gowin 1963, p. 8). From this standpoint, we find that theory can help the researcher to choose data for analysis and to make economical summaries of them. Perhaps most important, theory can guide the researcher in further studies. These heuristic functions, especially the last, are regarded by many scientists to be the principal job of scientific theory!

The heuristic functions of theory noted above are clearly value loaded since they suggest, guide, direct, and even prescribe the behavior (actions) of scientists. Furthermore, from this point of view even the so-called objective functions of description, prediction, and explanation are value loaded in a certain sense because they are "guided" by the researcher. What is to be described, for example, is determined by what the (partially developed) theory *says* needs to be described. "Begin by collecting facts? Aye, but what facts?" (Cohen 1931, p. 76). Cohen's point is that without theoretical direction (or at least suggestions) we should not know what facts to gather. Theory not only tells us which facts are relevant, but gives meaning to the facts by illuminating the relationships among them. In doing so, it suggests how researchers *ought* to act if they desire to bring about further heuristic consequences. It seems clear that while scientific theory may be distinguishable by virtue of its precision and/or refinement in the areas of description, prediction, and explanation, it is by no means unique or different in principle. In the last analysis, scientific theory distills to O'Connor's (1957) more general definition: "a set of rules which guide or control actions."

Thus, theory describes, predicts, and explains phenomena, and it *guides the practice of those who use the theory*. In the case of research scientists, the "guided practice" will be the pursuit of new knowledge—the collection, analysis, and synthesis of new data, which activity comprises the practice of empirical research and theory building. In other cases, the guided practice will involve a variety of different activities. It will center, for example, in medicine on the prevention and cure of disease, and in engineering, on the construction of roads, bridges, and buildings.

Scientific Theory and Curriculum Theory

Our discussions of the nature and function of theory have indicated that many writers attribute to scientific theory the quality of "objectivity." Theory describes and explains what *is,* they claim, but it cannot tell us what we *ought* to do. Griffiths (1964, p. 16), an advocate of the "is-ness" conception of theory, provides us with a vivid concrete example of this distinction. He says that if a person were to jump out of a thirtieth-story window, theory would enable us to predict with remarkable accuracy both the speed at which his body would hit the sidewalk below and the force of the impact. Theory would also enable us to predict with a high degree of probability that the person would die. Thus, the statement, "If a person leaps from the thirtieth story of a building, he will die" represents a descriptive, predictive theoretical proposition. The proposition does not tell us whether we ought or ought not to jump out of thirtieth-story windows. It contains no values and no directives.

Of course, we might object that the statement *does* contain a value component since, if a person did not *wish* to die, the theoretical proposition would clearly direct him to refrain from jumping out of thirtieth-story windows. Our objection, however, would be countered by the assertion that the "wish" is obviously an assumption that does not appear in the proposition.[3] It is, so to speak, "excess baggage" that is imposed upon the theory. To press our point further, however, we might argue that it would certainly be "logically odd" not to infer from the proposition the reasonableness of refraining from jumping out of thirtieth-story windows. But it turns out that the logic is odd only because jumping out of thirtieth-story windows is inconsistent with one's wish to stay alive—that is to say, inconsistent with a prior assumption. If a person wished to commit suicide, for example, there would certainly be nothing "logically odd" about jumping from a thirtieth-story window. In summary, the "is-ness" proponent would say that the theory has simply rendered certain phenomena more intelligible. It does not contain, in any logically necessary sense, implications for action one way or another.

The logical force of these arguments for the "is-ness" nature of theory is indeed impressive. Clearly, they call into serious question the arguments in the previous section purporting to show that scientific theory functions as a guide to scientific research. Yet, oddly enough, many natural scientists continue to insist that their theories are *not* objective. "The activities of scientists in their laboratories are shot through with value judgments" (Conant 1952, p. 107).

---

3. This argument for the "is-ness" of theory, as well as the ones that follow, are based on Newsome (1964, p. 37).

What, then, are the arguments that the scientists themselves make in defense of the "ought-ness" concept of scientific theory?[4]

In presenting the scientists' case we shall lean heavily on the analysis of modern science made by James B. Conant, best known as a college president (Harvard), critic of American education, and ambassador, but also a highly regarded scientist in the field of chemistry. Conant begins with an historically oriented explication of the basis of the "is-ness" conception of theory. He notes that until the twentieth century, or more accurately until the advent of the revolution in modern physics, scientific theories generally were regarded as discovered, objective explanations of extant reality. Matter and phenomena were seen as existing "out there" in a substantially "real" sense, and scientific theories, to the extent that they were good, described and explained the "true" unchanging principles underlying the world. Thus, theory building was viewed as a process of accumulation. As new theories were discovered (rather than developed) or as old (less accurate) ones were altered in the light of new discoveries, man came to have a truer, more accurate picture of what the world was really like. Furthermore, the nineteenth-century scientist believed that *in principle*, the totality of nature's secrets would eventually be discovered, at which point man would have in his possession a description and explanation of what the entire world was like—in other words, a clear conception of the nature of ultimate reality. It is not surprising, then, that scientific theory was regarded widely as a kind of absolute knowledge.

Conant clarifies the import of this objective conception of theory by applying the analogy of a map.

> *Those who said they were investigating the structure of the universe imagined themselves as the equivalent of the early explorers and map makers . . . by a series of successive approximations, so to speak, maps and descriptions of distant lands were becoming closer and closer to accurate accounts of reality. Why would not the labors of those who worked in laboratories have the same outcome? . . . one could doubt any particular map or description, of course, but given time and patience, it was assumed the truth would be ascertained. By the same token there must be a truth about the nature of heat, light, and matter (Conant 1952, pp. 93, 94).*

The conception of scientific theory as a map is substantially the conception advocated by the proponents of the "is-ness" position on theory in education and curriculum. Indeed, they sometimes use the analogy to make their point: A theory is like a map, they say; it describes the landscape, but it cannot tell you where you ought to travel (Gowin 1963, p. 9). As we have previously stated, however, modern natural scientists no longer view scientific theory in this way.

---

4. On this note, it is interesting to observe that the "is-ness" position on theory is embraced most ardently by those social scientists and educationists who seem to be striving to "legitimize" their fields as authentic sciences by patterning them on what they believe to be "objective scientific theory" as it is conceived by natural scientists.

Indeed, Conant (1952, pp. 97, 98) contends that in view of the revolution in physics, "the whole analogy between a map and a scientific theory is without a basis."

A grasp of the dramatic change wrought in the way that many natural scientists now view the nature and function of scientific theory depends to a large extent on an understanding of the revolution in physics itself. Of course, deficiencies in our scientific backgrounds preclude our complete understanding of the full import of this revolution. Nevertheless, considerable insight is possible as a result of Conant's lucid, simplified explanations of a number of significant scientific occurrences.

The first of these was alluded to briefly in Chapter 1 and has to do with the nature of light. Conant (1952, p. 69) relates that at the end of the nineteenth century, experiments seemed conclusively to have established that light was undulatory—i.e., a wave phenomenon. The older theory that light was a stream of particles—i.e., corpuscular—seemed to be unequivocally "disproved." But by 1910, certain experimental phenomena were observed indicating that light sometimes behaved like a wave, and sometimes like a stream of particles. "To the scientists of [those days] this was the equivalent of saying a box was both full and empty; it was impossible, so they maintained, for light to be both undulatory and corpuscular" (Conant 1952, p. 70). We might observe at this point that the "map theory" of theory was being sorely tested.

Let us put aside this disturbing dilemma of the dual nature of light for a moment and consider another of Conant's explanations, this one having to do with the nature of heat. In the first half of the nineteenth century heat was presumed to consist of a weightless, colorless, odorless substance called "caloric" that flowed from hot bodies to cooler ones. Then certain phenomena were observed that could not be accounted for in terms of the caloric theory (e.g., the generation of heat by friction), but which suggested that heat was associated with the motion of particles. This new "molecular motion" theory of heat turned out to be extremely useful in a vast number of situations and it seemed that the caloric theory of heat was disproved. But though "disproved," the caloric theory of heat persisted:

> We still talk of the flow of heat and even set up mathematical expressions to formulate this flow as though there were a caloric fluid. Within a limited range of experimental facts in physics and chemistry, the caloric theory of heat is still the most convenient way of ordering these facts (Conant 1952, p. 68).

Like light, then, heat is differentially. defined in modern science by two apparently incompatible theories.

One more example can be given before we consider Conant's interpretation of these perplexing developments in modern science. With the splitting of the atom, the nineteenth-century principles of conservation of both mass and energy were unified, so to speak, in the conservation of mass-energy theory. The new theory held that all matter and all energy could be accounted for in mass-to-energy transformations. In most cases, of course, this was true; but as Conant (1952, p. 73) points out, in certain situations the conservation of mass-energy theory "failed": the mass-energy ledger, so to speak, did not balance. Scientists had the choice of assuming that the conservation of mass-energy theory had been "disproved" or of postulating the existence of an hypothetical particle—the *neutrino*—to balance the equation in certain situations. Since the conservation of mass-energy theory worked so well in most situations, they chose the latter option, even though it was incompatible with the conservation theory. It is, incidentally, entirely unlikely that any experiment can ever be devised that will either prove or disprove the existence of a "neutrino."

How can a rational scientist accept contradictory and incompatible theories of light, heat, and the conservation of mass-energy? The answer is "that he has discovered how general is the paradox and by what mathematical manipulations of experimental data he can get forward with all manner of undertakings because of the paradox" (Conant 1952, p. 80).

This statement gives us a clue to the modern scientist's conception of theory. Scientific theory should not be regarded as an objective map that describes and explains reality, but rather, as "a policy—an economical and fruitful guide to action by scientific investigators" (Conant 1952, p. 97). But a policy, or guide, implies value; policies and guides tell us what we ought to do. Conant's view of theory, of course, is quite similar to the "ought-ness" conception that was branded "unscientific" by those writers advocating strict objectivity in theory. How ironic that the modernist partisans of science and "objective" *scientific* theory appear in the end to have been the defenders of an obsolete and quasi-scientific position in the debate! In missing the revolution in physics, they missed a metaphysical shift of major proportions. Scientific, empirical-rational methods had revealed the meaninglessness of "objectivity" and established the principle of relativity. Scientific, empirical-rational methods had shown that scientific theory was not, as had been thought, a value-free, objective description of reality, but a construct invented to advance human endeavors. And empirical-rational methods had demonstrated that the "map" concept of theory was itself a value orientation that seemed not to be supported by the evidence.

At this point, a few brief observations concerning the two competing conceptions of theory will help our understanding of the implications of each. Theory regarded as a map, as mentioned earlier, purports to tell us what the world is really like. It implies *discovered* knowledge, which literally represents an uncovering of the nature of reality. By contrast, modern scientific theory—that is, theory regarded as a policy for action—claims only to tell us what are the best *representations* of the world in terms of present experience. Knowledge from this point of view is regarded as *constructed*,[5] that is, fabricated on the basis of human experience for particular ends-in-view. By fabrication, of course, we do not mean inventing something false by the exercise of imagination or

5. I am indebted to Professor I. N. Thut for these uses of the words "discovered" and "constructed." See Chapters 5 and 6 a more detailed account of these theories of knowledge.

fancy; rather, we mean uniting the fragmented parts of experience into a coherent (for us, now) pattern. We should also note that the theory may vary accordingly as purposes for which it is constructed may vary. For example, in many research situations a chemist will obtain the most fruitful consequences by employing the molecular-motion theory of heat. On the other hand, an engineer designing a heating system for a building will find the molecular-motion theory almost worthless. For him, the only theory likely to get the desired results is the caloric theory of heat. To generalize these specific cases we may say that researchers use scientific theory for purposes that generally center on the direction of further scientific research. Engineers, on the other hand, use scientific theory to guide whatever activities (e.g., designing heating systems) are most central to their sphere of activity.

As we noted in a previous paragraph, all of the evidence available seems to indicate that the revolution in modern physics has rendered the "map" concept of scientific theory both an illusion and a presumption. Scientific theory not only *does* not describe the nature of reality, but it *cannot*. The reason, some physicists contend, is that theory is a product of human thought processes, and modern physics suggests that human thought processes may not correspond sufficiently to the structure of nature to permit us to think about it at all (Bridgman 1952, pp. 86, 87). Put another way, the nature of reality and the concept of existence are meaningless, not because of the nature of the world, but because of the construction of the human organism. It is simply impossible for man to transcend the human reference point. "We cannot even express this in the way we would like. . . . It is literally true that the only way of reacting to this is to shut up" (Bridgman 1952, p. 87).

CURRICULUM THEORY

Because scientific theory has been so widely accepted as an objective map of reality, many writers in education and curriculum who have favored the "ought-ness" concept of theory have felt compelled to draw a distinction in principle between scientific and educational (or curriculum) theory. For example, Pratte (1971, p. 10) states: "That there is a *prima facie* difference between scientific and educational theory is undeniable." These writers generally ascribe to scientific theory the role of "end product of knowledge," while they view curriculum theory as a "guide to activity." Our analysis of modern scientific theory, however, has shown that many scientists view scientific theory in virtually the same terms that these educationists view curriculum theory, i.e., as a policy for action. The only difference between the two kinds of theory, it turns out, is in the arena in which the action takes place. A research scientist, as we have noted, employs theory as a policy that suggests, stimulates, and generates further scientific research and experimentation. (There exists a moral dimension to this activity insofar as the scientist must bear the responsibility for the consequences of his activity.) But a curriculum theorist-researcher employs curriculum theory in much the same way—as a policy productive of further research and theory building (also within a moral context). By contrast, an electrical engineer employs scientific theory, not as a policy to advance research and theory building, but as a guide, for example, in the construction of generators for an electrical power plant. (Again, decisions in this arena have moral consequences.) Finally, the curriculum planner (engineer?) employs curriculum theory to construct and implement curricula in the schools (obviously a heavily moral undertaking). Nowhere is it implied that the theory employed in any of these undertakings should not coincide with the best representations that our experience affords us up to the present time. What is denied is that the theory is a value-free representation of reality that comprises immutable knowledge. But this, not even science claims. Thus, happily, it turns out that we need not feel "unscientific" when we acknowledge and advocate the value dimension of theory. Indeed, curriculum theorists would be unscientific were they to deny its presence.

In the light of these observations, then, we can summarize our lengthy discussion by proposing an eclectic concept of curriculum theory. We view curriculum theory as a generalized set of logically interrelated definitions, concepts, propositions, and other constructs that represents a systematic view of curricular phenomena. The function of curriculum theory is to describe, predict, and explain curricular phenomena and to serve as a policy for the guidance of curriculum activities.

Theory into Practice

Accepting the proposition that curriculum theory functions as a guide to activity, we are presented with the problem of how—i.e., in what sense—theory guides practice. For example, a recipe guides the practice of a cook; a handbook on gardening directs the activity of a gardener; and the directions in a do-it-yourself kit prescribe the actions necessary for the assembly of a ship model. Yet these instances rarely are regarded as the application of theory. Theory, clearly, constitutes something more complex than a recipe or a set of directions.

A common conception of the relationship between theory and practice assumes that theory and practice are in opposition. The introductory paragraph of this chapter touched on this either/or point of view. The question usually posed takes some such form as "Should curriculum planners be theoreticians or practitioners?" Unfortunately for education, a great deal of time and energy has been expended in debating this issue. But, framing the question in this way presents a "dilemma or false disjuncture; [it] presumes that the alternatives are mutually exclusive when they are not" (Pratte 1971, p. 21). It seems eminently preferable to avoid the limitations of either/or propositions and, as do most writers on the subject, admit the necessity of both theory and practice. It is no exaggeration to state that theory without practice is idle speculation, while practice without theory constitutes little more than blind or random groping.

Another view of the theory-practice nexus has it that the question really is not *how* theory guides practice since it inevitably *does*. The problem is how to make theory explicit so that we are conscious of the theories that are in fact guiding our practice. Writing about theory in educational administration, Getzels argues this point of view: "the question of whether we should use theory in our administrative behavior is in a sense as meaningless as the question of whether we should use motivation in our behavior. Our actions are inevitably founded in our motives and steered toward goals by the relevant explicit or implicit theories that we hold" (Getzels 1960, p. 42). He seems to be including in his conception of theory all manner of conscious and unconscious principles, values, and assumptions that individuals carry with them as a consequence of the enculturation process.[6] And, of course, these do function as variables in the translation of theory into practice. But it is doubtful that theory in its more formal sense—i.e., as a generalized system of logically interrelated constructs—can really operate on an unconscious level to direct practice: "it is difficult to see how a set of verified hypotheses could ever be implicit in one's behavior" (Gowin 1963, p. 9).

A clue to the functional relationship between theory and practice inheres in our conception of the nature of theory. Among other things, we viewed theory as a coherent *generalization* of particular, diverse phenomena. We may elaborate this point now by saying that the more general a theory is, the more useful it is because its explanatory scope is more inclusive. To put it another way, we could say that the more general theory is the more useful one because it makes intelligible to our minds a wider range of apparently diverse phenomena. Einstein's theory of relativity, for example, is more powerful than Newton's laws of motion because it *includes* Newton's laws and places them in perspective in the wider scheme of things.

Obviously, theory as an explanatory generalization cannot function to prescribe activity in a one-to-one deductive relationship. The variability of particular situations render such direct correspondence of theory and practice impossible. For example, in diagnosing a case of malaria, a doctor does not expect to find in a particular patient the classic or ideal syndrome of symptoms generalized "in theory" as malaria in his medical books. But the theory or generalization functions as a guide, along with other theories, to the thought processes in which the doctor engages to reach his conclusion. Gowin (1963, p. 10), among others, supports this conception of the theory-practice connection: "theory turns out to be a guide to thought; it is a screen, a way to think about fundamental problems, a way to reach a decision." Pratte (1971, p. 17) agrees with this analysis: "a theory is an instrument, a guide to thought, not necessarily a guide to direct practice." Thus, he points out that theory is not prescriptive in the sense that it functions as "a command, a pure imperative, whose force resides in the authority or power of the speaker" (Pratte 1971, pp. 13, 14). (It does not command, for example, "If teachers want children to learn, they must apply positive reinforcement.") Rather, theory is directive in the sense that it requires the user of the theory to employ reasonableness with respect to the propositions of the theory in particular situations. (It gives teachers a basis for deciding on

6. See the section "Culture and Values" in Chapter 7 for an extended discussion of the role of unconscious values in human behavior.

the applicability, role, and function of positive reinforcement in a particular learning situation.) To put it another way, theory provides direction for inquiry into particular situations. It suggests what is worthwhile to take note of and provides criteria for judging the adequacy and implications of proposed practices. In short, it provides a basis for reasoned inquiry into practice.

In closing this section, it is appropriate to note that the conception of the theory-practice relationship advocated here implies a reciprocal relationship. That is to say, theory guides practice *and vice versa*. Clearly, the data provided by practice (in other words, experience) inevitably alter our conceptions and hence the theoretical representations of reality that we construct. Thus, theory is viewed as an evolutionary phenomenon. This last point is nowhere more strikingly illustrated than in the transformation wrought by the revolution in physics on our conception of the very nature of theory.

Theory Building

Theory building encompasses an extremely wide range of activities. In addition, theory-building activities tend to be dictated by choice, rather than any particular set of rules (Beauchamp 1975, p. 19). (One might even say that one's choice of theorizing activities depends on one's theory of theory.) Some notion of what theory building involves, however, is contained in Homans' list of six rules of theory building:

1. *Look first at the obvious, the familiar, the common. In a science that has not established its foundations, these are the things that best repay study.*
2. *State the obvious in its full generality. Science is an economy of thought only if its hypotheses sum up in a simple form a large number of facts.*
3. *Talk about one thing at a time. That is, in choosing your words (or, more pedantically, concepts) see that they refer not to several classes of fact at the same time but to one and one only. Corollary: Once you have chosen your words, always use the same words when referring to the same things.*
4. *Cut down as far as you dare the number of things you are talking about. "As few as you may; as many as you must," is the rule governing the number of classes of fact you take into account.*
5. *Once you have started to talk, do not stop until you have finished. That is, describe systematically the relationships between the facts designated by your words.*
6. *Recognize that your analysis must be abstract, because it deals with only a few elements of the concrete situation. Admit the dangers of abstraction, especially when action is required, but do not be afraid of abstraction (Homans 1950, pp. 16, 17).*

Obviously, Homans' rules for theory building are suggestive and should not be followed slavishly.

"THEORIES FOR . . ." AND "THEORIES OF . . ."

"Theories for . . ." are those that are proposed for testing: "trial balloons of systematization presented falteringly, without a secure basis . . ." (Boring 1959a, p. 45). Such theories are also commonly referred to as a priori theories or hypotheses. In this sense, we may speak of a "theory for curriculum" or a "theory for motivation."

"Theories of . . . ," by contrast, are those that summarize (i.e., economically describe and explain) observed phenomena with varying degrees of adequacy. These theories tend to be offered rather more confidently and often are referred to as a posteriori theories or generalizations. Thus, we may speak of a "theory of gravity" or a "theory of matter."

Figure 4-2 graphically shows "theories for . . ." and "theories of . . ." as extremes at opposite ends of a continuum characterized by degrees of confirmation through experience. Thus, a "theory for . . ." at the extreme left of the continuum moves toward "theory of . . ." status as it is found increasingly to correspond with experience. At what point on the continuum a "theory for . . ." becomes a "theory of . . ." is, of course, a matter of judgment and impossible to prescribe.

FIGURE 4-2
"Theories for . . ." and "Theories of . . ."

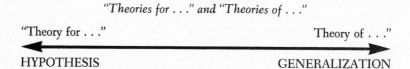

"Theory for . . ."   Theory of . . ."

HYPOTHESIS   GENERALIZATION

Developing "theories for . . ." and confirming "theories of . . ." are both important activities of theory building. "Theories for . . ." are generally the fruit of thought, reflection, insight, and that often nebulous creative mental activity we call intuition. "Theories of . . . ," on the other hand, develop out of the arduous task of empirically testing and checking the constructs of "theories for . . . ," often under experimental conditions. It should not be inferred from these statements that constructing "theories for . . ." comprises pure speculation with no basis in experience and empirical phenomena, or that confirming "theories of . . ." does not involve thought and imagination.

THE STATUS OF "THEORIES OF. . . ." It often is assumed that "theories of . . . ," because they have been more or less "confirmed," are to be accorded a different (higher) status than "theories for. . . ." In a certain sense this is true. "Theories of . . ." have, by definition, been confirmed in present experience to constitute useful policies for the conduct of our affairs. This claim, of course, cannot be made for "theories for. . . ." But if what is meant by a "confirmed status" is a "factually confirmed" degree of absolute truth, then, as a previous section showed, no theory—"of . . . or for . . ."—can qualify. "Theories of . . ." deserve a different status than "theories for . . ." not because they have been proven true, but because they are meaningful representations of present experience and have stood the test of usefulness.

When "theories of . . ." cease to be useful, they are often said to be false or wrong. For example, Boring (1959a, p. 45) says that "the history of science is partly the story of [a posteriori] theories' being wrong. . . ." This is a good point to make because it sweeps away a lot of nonsense about the infallibility of "proven theories." At the same time, however, talking about theories being "wrong" tends to perpetuate by implication the fiction of "right" theories—i.e., theories taken to be "right" in the sense that they represent absolute truth. "Theories of . . ." that do not coincide with new experience might, of course, be called "wrong" in the sense that they are inadequate explanations or poor policies, but it would probably be better to use some such terminology as "inadequate," "deficient," or "obsolete" to refer to them.

THE STATUS OF "THEORIES FOR. . . ." There is little disagreement over the point that science has developed an impressive repertoire of reliable techniques for the confirmation or rejection of "theories for. . . ." Indeed, these techniques are largely credited with being responsible for the rapid advance of science over the past seventy years. Yet many writers believe that emphasis on scientific techniques for theory *testing* has been excessive (due, partly, to the "practical" orientation of American culture), and that the creative generation of "theories for . . ." has suffered commensurately.

The significance of the creative generation of "theories for . . ." is noted by Conant. "The history of science demonstrates beyond a doubt that the really revolutionary and significant advances come not from empiricism but from new theories" (Conant 1952, p. 53). Copernicus' theory of a heliocentric universe first published in the sixteenth century and Einstein's more recent theory of relativity are two obvious cases in point. Neither theory was "confirmed" until well after it was first proposed, but each in its own way was "earth shaking" in its significance.

How a narrow focus on theory testing can impede the development of new directions in theory development is explained below:

> The matter of rushing into a procedure to test hypotheses may reduce rather than extend meanings. This would suggest that the most productive activity . . . may be to ask questions in terms of the thinking that gave rise to the hypotheses (Pritzkau 1970, p. 130).

From these points we may conclude that theorizing activities focused on "theories for . . ." are as important, if not more important, than those which involve the confirmation of hypotheses.

MODELS

Generally speaking, models are miniature representations that summarize data and/or phenomena and thus act as an aid to comprehension. In other words, "models in science act like metaphors in language; they enlighten us by suggesting arguments by analogy from known resemblances to resemblances so far unnoticed" (O'Connor 1957, p. 90). Although the term "model" sometimes is used as a synonym for "theory," it more properly connotes a representation of only a portion of a theory. One of the main functions of models is to aid in theory building.

TYPES OF MODELS. Models can take on a variety of forms depending on the nature and complexity of what they represent, as well as the purpose to which they are put. Perhaps the most familiar type of model is the physical or working model, usually a three-dimensional device that shows how something works. A common example is the three-dimensional cluster of colored balls used in chemistry classes to show the structure of molecules. Miniature airfoils for testing plane designs are also physical models, as are the models of the solar system exhibited by some museums to demonstrate the motion of the planets around the sun. Physical models are probably the simplest of the model types.

A second kind is the conceptual or verbal model. Here, a verbalized concept or metaphor is imposed on phenomena as an aid to comprehension. The "systems" and "games" metaphors, used to describe and explain certain sociological phenomena, are examples of conceptual models. Another conceptual model in wide use is the familiar "business" or "industrial" model of schooling, in which students are likened to raw material that is "manufactured" by the school (factory) into a finished product. It is appropriate to note here that models significantly affect the nature of the theories to which they contribute and hence constitute an influence on the policies for action that evolve from them.

Another kind of model is the mathematical one. Common mainly in the physical sciences, this most sophisticated of the model types reduces complex phenomena to the regularity of mathematical expressions. Chemical equations which describe and predict the compounds that are formed by combining certain elements and/or other compounds are examples of mathematical models. Ohm's law in electricity (amperes = volts/ohms), which describes the relationship of three constructs in electricity, is another example of a mathematical model. Probably the most widely known mathematical model is the famous $E = mc^2$ equation in physics. So highly developed has the discipline of physics become that theory building in this field consists mainly of the manipulation of mathematical models of physical phenomena.

A fourth kind of model is the graphic representation. Probably the most common of the model types, graphic models are usually drawings or diagrams of some kind that attempt by visual means to describe the components of the thing being modeled and to explain the relationships among its parts. The diagram in Figure 4-2 of the relationship between "theories for . . ." and "theories of . . ." is an example of a very simple graphic model. Maps constitute models in this sense, as do the grammatical diagrams of sentences that are such a familiar staple in many English classes. Curriculum theory has been characterized by the proposal of a large number of graphic models of the curriculum and curriculum processes. Three of these are presented and discussed in a following section, "Theory in Curriculum."

THE USES AND LIMITATIONS OF MODELS. It should be emphasized that models are devices that *represent* phenomena and their relationships, but they are not reproductions of the phenomena or relationships *themselves.* Analogously speaking, models are like paintings of the real world—that is to say, interpretive; they are not, like photographs, reproductions of reality. Put another way, models are piecemeal approaches to meaning which reduce the bewildering complexity of direct experience to the more limited scope of human comprehension by *selecting* relevant features. In this sense, they are "as-if" hypotheses (Boring 1959b, p. 385) which may be relied on in proportion as they are confirmed in experience and function effectively as guides to action.

Although models are clearly useful devices, their disadvantages should not go unnoted. Chapanis (cited in Good 1963, p. 8) lists six:

1. *Models invite overgeneralization.*
2. *Models entice us into committing a logical fallacy.*
3. *The relationships between variables may be incorrect.*
4. *The constants assumed in the model may be incorrect.*
5. *Models are too often not validated.*
6. *Model building diverts useful energy into nonproductive activity.*

Obviously, most of these limitations can be minimized by taking them into account in the model-building process. Indeed, most writers concede the general utility of models in theory building in spite of their shortcomings.

Models are useful in theory building because they economically summarize and explain limited areas of the total theoretical domain. In curriculum work, this is especially true of graphic models, which enable planners to visualize curriculum components, their relationships, and the processes of development and implementation. Furthermore, models aid theory building by suggesting questions that need to be asked of data and by providing clues to possible answers. Finally, models can be used as tools with which to think about curriculum, thus stimulating research and the formulation of new theoretical constructs.

Theory in Curriculum

Clearly, the complexity of the curriculum field, as well as the nature of the theories upon which it must draw (i.e., theories from psychology, sociology, anthropology, philosophy, etc.) make the development of a logically coherent theory of curriculum an awesome undertaking. It is not surprising, then, to find that at the present time there does not exist any well-developed theory of (or even *for*) curriculum. Even in the relatively more modest area of model building, the picture is not very encouraging. Curriculum models have generally been limited to the conceptual and graphic types which, as Fattu (1965,

p. 64) points out have provided only general or gross representations of reality—"e.g., organization charts, diagrams of classroom interaction, or simple geometric figures upon which an outline has been imposed." Consequently, models in curriculum, although useful in summarizing enormously complex clusters of phenomena, have never developed the precision or detail needed to constitute a reliable basis for curriculum planning.

As has been previously suggested, however, without theory, curriculum practice proceeds at best by trial and error, and at worst on a totally random basis.[7] Reason demands that some sense be made of curricular phenomena, and fortunately, enough theorizing has been done to provide us with at least a beginning. As a point of departure, three curriculum models are presented in the following sections for the reader's consideration. They are not directly competing models in that each represents a somewhat different aspect of the curriculum enterprise. It should be noted that some of the territory encompassed by the models was treated verbally in the previous chapter. Thus, the reader may find it interesting to compare his response to the verbal material with his response to the same material presented in the form of a graphic model. In any case, the three models will provide a point of departure for thinking about the scope, nature, and processes of the curriculum enterprise.

THE SCOPE AND FUNCTION OF CURRICULUM IN EDUCATION: MACDONALD'S MODEL

Macdonald's model (Figure 4-3) shows curriculum as one of four interacting systems. Reference to Macdonald's conception of each of these systems was made in the previous chapter where, it will be recalled, *teaching* was defined as a personality system (the teacher) acting in a professional role; *learning* was defined as a personality system (the student) performing task-related (learning) behaviors; *instruction* was defined as the social system within which formal teaching and learning take place; and *curriculum* was defined as the social system which eventuates in a plan for instruction.

Macdonald, commenting on his model, writes:

> The small shadowed spot represents that point of congruence where curriculum goals are operative in the instructional setting through the agency of effective teaching activity as evidenced by the changed behavior or learning of the students. . . .
> . . . Space (V) is illustrated dramatically by the phenomena of concomitant learning. Space (VI) would include teacher modification of behavior in response to the immediate feedback of the instructional situation. Space (VII) could be described as in-service experiences. Space (VIII) could include supervision experiences. Although few ready examples

7. Students interested in an alternative view of the role of theory in curriculum should see Schwab (1969). Three excellent articles which analyze Professor Schwab's position appear in *Curriculum Theory Network* (1972).

come to mind, Spaces IX and X might deal with pupil-teacher planning experiences (Macdonald 1965, p. 5).

Unquestionably, Macdonald's model clarifies a number of points having to do with the nature of teaching, learning, instruction, and curriculum by dealing with them as discrete systems. At the same time, however, the model leaves unresolved a wide range of problems involving the scope and nature of curriculum, and indeed even presents us with new problems, e.g., the meaning of such intersections as Spaces IX and X. Obviously, Macdonald's model is helpful in clarifying certain relationships among the four areas that it represents, but it is not adequate to deal with the enormous complexity of phenomena included in the curriculum-instruction domain.

FIGURE 4-3

Macdonald's model. (Reproduced by permission from James B. Macdonald, "Educational Models for Instruction." In Theories of Instruction *edited by James B. Macdonald and Robert R. Leeper. Washington, D.C. Association for Supervision and Curriculum Development, 1965).*

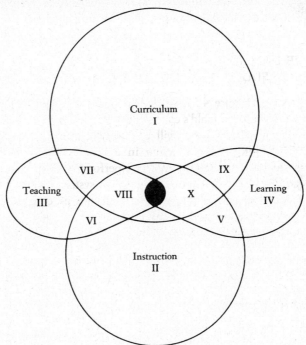

THE DYNAMICS OF CURRICULUM AND INSTRUCTION SYSTEMS: JOHNSON'S MODEL

Johnson's model (Figure 4-4) shows the curriculum as the output of a curriculum-development system. The curriculum (defined as a structured series

FIGURE 4-4
*Johnson's model. (Reproduced by permission from Mauritz Johnson.
"Definitions and Models in Curriculum Theory." Educational Theory,
April 1967).*

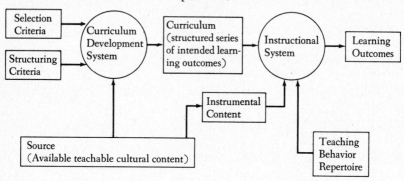

of intended learning outcomes) subsequently becomes input for the instructional system. Guided by the curriculum, the instructional system employs instrumental content and teachers' behavior to actualize learning outcomes.

Although Macdonald and Johnson appear to agree on the *role* of curriculum in instruction (i.e., it is a plan or document that *guides* instruction), only Johnson's model clearly indicates the dynamics of the process of curriculum construction, development, and implementation. In this respect it is superior to Macdonald's model, which, although it purports to deal with processes, is essentially a static representation. Although Johnson's model is helpful in enabling us to conceptualize processes in sequential terms, it does not, as does Macdonald's model, attempt to grapple with the complex relationships that in fact exist among teaching, learning, instruction, and curriculum.

THE FOUNDATIONS AND NATURE OF THE CURRICULUM: AN ECLECTIC MODEL

Figure 4-5 is a simple eclectic model that attempts to portray in static terms the components of the curriculum and the principal forces that affect its substance and design. It is not concerned with processes—either of curriculum construction, development, or implementation—or even with design per se. Its purpose is to portray graphically the principal variables, and their relationships, that planners need to consider in curriculum construction.

The curriculum is shown in the model as a somewhat formless entity girdled by a double line. This indicates that the curriculum, although its boundaries (as we presently understand them) are somewhat ill defined, is essentially an integrated unity. Within the double line the model shows the four components that make up the curriculum (aims, goals, objectives; content; learning activities; and evaluation) separated by jagged lines. This manner of representation is

FIGURE 4-5
An eclectic model of the curriculum and its foundations.

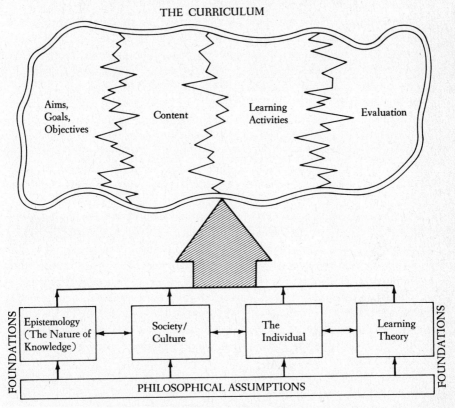

meant to emphasize the relatedness of each component to all of the others and to suggest that, as in a jigsaw puzzle, all of the pieces should fit precisely to produce a coherent picture.

The large shaded arrowhead that joins the four foundations blocks to the curriculum indicates the influence of curriculum foundations on the content and organization of curriculum components (i.e., the curriculum design). In analogical terms, we might say that the foundations blocks represent the soil and climate which determine the nature of the curriculum "plant." Each of the foundations blocks are joined to the others by double-headed arrows, suggesting the interrelatedness of all of the areas. Although intimately connected, however, they do not, as do the curriculum components, form a unified whole. Undergirding each of the four foundational areas is the broad area of philosophical assumptions. This aspect of the model indicates that, consciously or unconsciously, basic philosophical assumptions influence value judgments made about the foundational areas.

The eclectic model in Figure 4-5, insofar as it deals only with the static nature of a portion of the curriculum enterprise, is quite modest. Yet it is highly significant because it deals with what are probably the most crucial aspects of the curriculum field: the nature of the curriculum and the forces that determine its content and organization. It is interesting to note in this regard that far more attention has been paid in the literature to prescribing *processes* of curriculum development and change than to developing *understanding* of the bases and nature of the curriculum itself. This typically American emphasis on activity and "how-to-do-it," however, does not seem to have borne much fruit. Experience shows that in spite of a surfeit of instruction and activity in the processes of curriculum improvement and change, the curriculum remains controlled for the most part by the forces and events of historical accident, to say nothing of the influences of fashion and fad. The suggestion here is that superficial understanding has apparently generated superficial strategies that get superficial results.

The present condition of the curriculum field seems to call for serious study of the basic nature of the curriculum and its foundations, for only by understanding these phenomena can we influence them in any significant way. This is not to say that the processes of development and change are unimportant. Nothing could be further from the truth. But it seems clear that the processes of curriculum development and change can only be determined in the light of knowledge about the existing curriculum and the one toward which we would change. Put in more general terms, we might say that the essential relatedness of ends and means suggests the necessity for determining procedures in the light of ends-in-view.

Because of these considerations, a substantial portion of this text has been given over to an examination of curriculum foundations and the curriculum itself. Part II (Chapters 5–12) deals with the four foundational areas depicted in the eclectic model, while Part III (Chapters 13–16) deals with the four basic components of the curriculum. A thorough grounding in the nature of the curriculum and its foundations, by illuminating many otherwise invisible problems, will demonstrate the awesome complexity of the curriculum-construction task. At the same time, however, it will help to render curriculum-construction activities more significant and productive.

References

Abel, Theodore. 1952. "The Present Status of Social Theory." *American Sociological Review* (April).

Beauchamp, George A. 1975. *Curriculum Theory*. 3d ed. Wilmette, Ill.: The Kagg Press.

Boring, Edwin G. 1959a. "Theory." *Contemporary Psychology* (February).

———. 1959b. "The Model," *Contemporary Psychology* (December).

Bridgman, P. W. 1950. "Philosophical Implications of Physics." *American Academy of Arts and Sciences Bulletin* (February). Quoted in James B. Conant. 1952. *Modern Science and Modern Man*. New York: Columbia University Press. Reprinted by Doubleday Anchor Books, New York.

Cohen, Morris R. 1931. *Reason and Nature*. New York: Harcourt Brace Jovanovich.

Conant, James B. 1952. *Modern Science and Modern Man*. New York: Columbia University Press. Reprinted by Doubleday Anchor Books.

Curriculum Theory Network. 1972. Publication of the Ontario [Canada] Institute for Studies in Education, No. 10 (Fall).

Fattu, N. A. 1965 "A Model of Teaching as Problem Solving." In *Theories of Instruction*, edited by James B. Macdonald and Robert R. Leeper. Washington, D.C.: Association for Supervision and Curriculum Development.

Feigl, Herbert. 1951. "Principles and Problems of Theory Construction in Psychology." In *Current Trends of Psychological Theory*, edited by W. Dennis. Pittsburgh, Pa.: University of Pittsburgh Press.

Getzels, Jacob W. 1960. "Theory and Practice in Educational Administration: An Old Question Revisited." In *Administrative Theory as a Guide to Action*, edited by Roald F. Campbell and James M. Lipham. Chicago: Midwest Administration Center, University of Chicago.

Good, Carter V. 1963. *Introduction to Educational Research*. 2d ed. New York: Appleton-Century-Crofts.

Gowin, D. B. 1963. "Can Educational Theory Guide Practice?" *Educational Theory* (January).

Griffiths, Daniel E. 1964. "The Nature and Meaning of Theory." In *Behavioral Science and Educational Administration*, edited by Daniel E. Griffiths. Sixty-third Yearbook of the National Society for the Study of Education. Chicago: University of Chicago Press.

Halpin, Andrew W. 1958. "The Development of Theory in Educational Administration." In *Administrative Theory in Education*, edited by Andrew W. Halpin. Chicago: Midwest Administration Center, University of Chicago.

Hofstadter, Richard. 1963. *Anti-Intellectualism in American Life*. New York: Alfred A. Knopf.

Homans, George C. 1950. *The Human Group*. New York: Harcourt Brace Jovanovich.

Johnson, Mauritz. 1967. "Definitions and Models in Curriculum Theory." *Educational Theory* (April).

Kerlinger, Fred N. 1965. *Foundations of Behavioral Research*. New York: Holt, Rinehart and Winston.

Maccia, Elizabeth Steiner. 1962. "The Separation of Philosophy from Theory of Education." *Studies in Philosophy and Education* (Spring).

Macdonald James B. 1965. "Educational Models for Instruction." In *Theories of Instruction*, edited by James B. Macdonald and Robert R. Leeper. Washington, D.C.: Association for Supervision and Curriculum Development.

Newsome, George L., Jr. 1964. "In What Sense Is Theory a Guide to Practice in Education?" *Educational Theory* (January).

O'Connor, D. J. 1957. *An Introduction to the Philosophy of Education*. New York: Philosophical Library.

Pratte, Richard. 1971. *Contemporary Theories of Education.* New York: Thomas Y. Crowell Company.

Pritzkau, Philo T. 1970. *On Education for the Authentic.* New York: Thomas Y. Crowell Company.

Scheffler, Israel. 1960. *The Language of Education.* Springfield, Ill.: Charles C Thomas, Publisher, 1960.

Schwab, Joseph J. 1969. "The Practical: A Language for Curriculum." *School Review* (November), 1–23.

II

FOUNDATIONS OF THE CURRICULUM

As noted in Chapter 1, curriculum foundations generally are acknowledged to consist of four basic areas: Epistemology, Society/Culture, the Individual, and Learning Theories. Ideas, attitudes, and beliefs in each of these four areas constitute the primary forces that influence, and indeed control, the content and organization of the curriculum. Chapters 5 and 6 deal with the philosophical foundations of the curriculum and present an extended discussion of epistemology—the nature of knowledge. Knowledge, after all, is the stock-in-trade of schools and their curricula. Chapters 7 and 8 center on society and culture, whose perpetuation, in a very real sense, is the curriculum's primary raison d'être. Chapters 9 and 10 explore the nature of the individual, that single human being who is the ultimate subject and recipient of the curriculum. And finally, Chapters 11 and 12 survey the field of learning theory—formulations of the processes by which learning occurs in the interaction of student and curriculum.

CHAPTER 5

PHILOSOPHY: BASIC CONSIDERATIONS

If we are willing to conceive education as the process of forming fundamental dispositions, intellectual and emotional, toward nature and fellow men, philosophy may even be defined as the general theory of education. —JOHN DEWEY

In Chapter 4 it was noted that basic philosophical assumptions influence value judgments made about all of the foundational areas. It is appropriate, then, that we examine briefly the nature and scope of philosophical inquiry in general before proceeding to epistemology, that area of philosophy which is of special concern to curriculum specialists.

What Philosophy Is

Defined literally, philosophy means "love of wisdom." Unfortunately, this definition conveys the impression that philosophy is a somewhat abtruse and esoteric enterprise engaged in for its own sake by scholars who are only in tenuous touch with the world of practical affairs. In reality, however, all of us engage in philosophizing (in an informal way) as we make the decisions on which the courses of our lives depend. For example, a philosophical disposition to place a higher value on material welfare than on spiritual renewal has caused us to spend more of our time in productive work activities than in reflective meditation. Assumptions about the essential equality of men have led us to prefer decisions arrived at in a democratic manner over those mandated by authority. Implicit in these dispositions and assumptions, of course, is the notion that, when acted upon, they yield a life experience that is generally superior in quality to the one we would have if we acted on alternative dispositions and assumptions. It is no exaggeration, then, to state that philosophical assumptions about the nature of the good life play a significant role in determining how we live.

Philosophy, moreover, is not an activity of very recent origin. Man, it should be noted, has always been faced with the necessity of making crucial decisions whose consequences have far-reaching effects on his future comfort and happiness. The problem was finding the knowledge that would enable the *best* possible decisions to be made. In primitive times, for example, a recurring problem must have been that of a neighboring tribe menacing community safety. How was man to deal with this threat? Should the belligerency of the neighboring tribe be met with massive retaliation? Or should they be paid the tribute they demanded? Perhaps an alliance with other neighboring tribes ought to be attempted. But such a course held inherent obligations, even dangers, of its own. How was it possible to know which decision was the right one? What knowledge could be brought to bear to increase the probability of a wise choice? We can see that in a very real sense philosophy had its beginnings when men first recognized the need to accumulate knowledge that would enable them to make wise, or good, decisions.

Of course, the need for knowledge as a guide to wise decision making led many of our forebears to search for it from prophets, oracles, or soothsayers who purportedly had access to knowledge not available to ordinary men. In these instances, the source of true knowledge was believed to be a world beyond man's natural world of sense and feeling. As time has passed, however, other ways of knowing and other forms of knowledge have evolved. Aided by the sciences, for example, man has built for himself a vast store of knowledge concerning the operation of natural phenomena. Helpful as this knowledge has been in certain areas of decision making, however, it has not solved the persistent dilemma of the *wise decision* in most areas of life. The fact that, in times of crisis in particular, people are inevitably forced to fall back on values and beliefs of a moral or religious nature, or on their own "inner resources," amply testifies to the limited usefulness of scientific knowledge. Take, for example, a situation in which a prisoner of war is told that if he does not reveal his regiment's position, his fellow prisoners will be tortured to death one by one. Should he tell or not? Should he attempt to lie? How viable a solution is suicide? Empirical (or "scientific") knowledge enable the POW to predict quite reliably the *factual* outcome of his decision, whatever that may be; but it does not solve for him the concomitant issues of morality, responsibility, and guilt, and certainly provides no clue as to what a *good decision* might be.

It seems clear, then, that philosophy is a very practical enterprise inasmuch as it provides the knowledge that helps us to make wise decisions. A wise decision, of course, implies a *desirable* outcome—that is, an outcome that is *good* or *ought to be*. Indeed, many philosophers define philosophy simply as "the search for knowledge of the good," taking the *good* to include "any or all principles, acts, arrangements, concepts, and purposes which enhance the quality of our subsequent experience" (Thut 1957, pp. 22–27). Thus, any coherent body of knowledge that represents a "master plan," so to speak, for wise decision making in life may qualify as a philosophy; and the individual who adopts such a "master plan" is said to have acquired a "philosophy of life." We can now see more clearly what is meant by the term "wisdom" as it is used in the literal definition of philosophy cited at the beginning of this section: it means, simply, "knowledge of the good."

Most laymen "adopt" a philosophy of life—as it were, by "osmosis"—from family, school, peer group, church, and other components of the culture. Frequently, this philosophy of life is unexamined and operates at an unconscious level. As a result, it often is found to contain irrational elements, incomplete ideas, and inconsistent beliefs. Implicit and irrational as it may be, however, the philosophy represents a deeply felt commitment and is a powerful determinant in the decision-making processes of every individual, as well as of the society as a whole.

Contrasted with the "homely" philosophies generated by cultures are the studied and systematic philosophies developed by philosophers, theologians, scientists, educators, and other thinkers who are concerned with the bases for decision making in matters concerning the good life. Their consciously developed philosophies aim at being coherent, unified, and complete; i.e., they attempt in a single rational structure to provide an understanding of life and a set of guides (the knowledge) by which the good life can be lived. Among other features, it is these latter characteristics of *unity* and *completeness* that distinguish the philosophical enterprise from other theoretical endeavors. For all their rationality and completeness, however, *all* philosophies, homely or formal, can ultimately be pushed back to a set of fundamental assumptions about the nature of existence. It is these assumptions, often comprising little more than an act of faith, that need to be explicitly articulated, for they can control the curriculum in powerful but subtle ways.

Philosophy and Curriculum

Every society is held together by a common faith or "philosophy" which serves its members as a guide for living the good life. It is natural, then, for the adults in the society to want to pass this philosophy—or "knowledge of the good"—on to their children, so that in the years to come their lives will be more secure and satisfying. In primitive societies knowledge of the good life is ordinarily passed on informally, from father to son and from mother to daughter. But in more highly developed societies, schools are established to induct the young into the ways of living that adults consider good. Thus, the curriculum of the schools, whatever else it may do, is first and foremost designed to win the hearts and minds of the young to those principles and ideals that will direct them to wise decisions—i.e., decisions whose consequences lead to the adult conception of the good life. Indeed, the curriculum is so thoroughly permeated with the culture's philosophy of life that one philosopher of education has been prompted to write, "What a man really believes . . . is frequently more clearly revealed in what he teaches his children than in what he professes in his public statements" (Thut 1957, p. 16).

Besides this de facto connection between philosophy and curriculum, however, we can point to a higher, and perhaps more positive one. Philosophy and curriculum in a very real sense are variant approaches to the same problem. Both are concerned with the central question: What can man become? The only difference is that philosophy asks the question "in macrocosm—'Man,'" while curriculum asks it "in microcosm—'men'" (Morris 1961, p. 224). Seen in this perspective, curriculum work, among other things, is simply a special aspect of philosophy, while philosophy is really a "general theory of education" (Dewey 1916, p. 383).

It seems self-evident from the above that before undertaking any aspect of curriculum work, the curriculum specialist must first attempt to determine and understand the basic assumptions and commitments of his own philosophy. To do this, it will be necessary, in addition to inspecting his innermost thoughts and feelings, to examine the articles of faith supported by his culture and to compare these with alternatives proposed at other times and in other places. A challenging and arduous task at best, this process of philosophical self-discovery can, nevertheless, be somewhat simplified by attacking it in a systematic way. To this end, the curriculum specialist will find himself greatly aided by the pattern of philosophical inquiry that has been developed over the years by a large number of professional philosophers. These scholars have organized philosophical inquiry into a relatively limited number of critical categories[1] that represent the problems to which all philosophies and all philosophers must eventually give their attention. By organizing our own inquiry around only three of these basic problems, we can at least begin to understand the philosophical bases of our own curricular preferences and, alternately, to extrapolate the practical curricular implications of these newly examined and consciously held philosophical assumptions. Bearing in mind, then, that our discussion in the following section represents only a very simplified introduction to the organization of philosophical inquiry, we may now turn our attention to the three philosophical categories that have particular relevance for curriculum decision making: *ontology* (the nature of reality), *epistemology* (the nature of knowledge), and *axiology* (the nature of value).

The Organization of Philosophical Inquiry

ONTOLOGY

Ontology is the philosophical problem that deals with the nature of reality. It asks the question: "What is real?" If the question seems foolish and a waste

1. Among these categories are metaphysics (the nature of the cosmos, the nature of reality), epistemology (the nature of knowledge, the process of knowing), logic (the systematic treatment of the relation of ideas), and axiology (the nature of good and evil, the principles governing the creation and appreciation of beauty).

of time because the answer is so obvious, we need only compare our assumptions about what is real with those of a different age to see that (1) what we accept as "real" seems so "obvious" only because in matters of fundamental philosophy we implicitly believe whatever our culture tells us to believe, and (2) our lives are in fact significantly affected by our assumed notions of reality. For example, the medieval ethos had it that reality existed in another world and in another life—that this earthly life was merely a transitory sojourn in a domain of superficial appearances. Thus, the most important questions asked about life had reference to other realms of existence: heaven, hell, and purgatory. When, with the advent of the Renaissance, an ontological shift in the culture occurred and the location of reality was transferred from heaven to earth, questions about the meaning of life centered on the nature and quality of earthly existence, making possible certain technological exploits that radically altered man's material life style. Steam engines and jet planes, to say nothing of such inventions as the atom bomb and space travel, became possible because "we changed our ontology, i.e., changed our theories of what the world, at its most fundamental and basic level, consists of" (Morris 1961, p. 28).

"Very well," you may respond. "Granted that the question is an important one. The answer is *still* obvious even if we concede that reality *is* what the culture says it is. Reality consists of this objective world."

Unfortunately, a little reflection reveals that the answer to the problem of reality and its character is not as simple as the culture would have it appear. Take, for example, the question of what it means *to be*—i.e., *to exist* in a "real" sense. When we say that the apple exists, do we mean that it exists spatially, taking up "cubic territory in the cosmos"?(Morris 1961, p. 30). If so, how do we determine this fact? If the answer is "through the senses," then the question arises, "if there are no sensations of the apple, does it exist?" (Morris 1961, p. 31). The ordinary response, "Of course it does," however, is simply a throwback to the original question, since it repudiates the claimed criterion of sensation.

A more complex problem is raised if we consider the question of *human* existence. If I say that "I am," do I mean only that I take up three-dimensional space? Or do I mean that I exist, more significantly, as a psychic consciousness —a "self" that is aware of its own existence? If the latter is the case, did I exist from conception, or from birth, or only from the "existential moment" that I became self-conscious? Which of these "realities," in short, is the "real" me? Whatever the case, the meaning of my existence is far from clear (Morris 1961, p. 31).

Another problem of the nature of existence has to do with the status of ideas. Is it possible to say, for example, that justice, loyalty, democracy, or love exist in any real sense? If the answer is "yes," then the criterion of their existence cannot be our perception (as with the apple). In other words, ideas, if they exist, must exist in a different mode from physical things like apples. How, then, can we determine the reality (or spuriousness) of such things as ideas?

Finally, and of particular concern to educationists, is the question of the ontological status of symbols. For example, we have just discussed a familiar physical entity, an apple, without the necessity of producing one. We have been able to do this by employing five little marks—a p p l e—made of black ink on white paper. Clearly, an "apple" was not "present" in our discussion in the way we would expect if we were able to point out a "real" apple. Yet it was present in *some* sense. No such question, however, can be raised about the presence (or existence) of the little black marks "a p p l e." We were able to see them with our eyes.[2] But the problem is that we do not attend to the little black marks on paper in the same way that we attend to the physical existence of the apple. That is, it is not the existence of the five-letter ink mark per se that is important to us. What *is* important is that a five-letter *symbol* introduces into our experience something which is neither the apple itself nor the little black marks, but something that stands for the apple and makes possible the experience of "apple" even though no apple is present (Morris 1961, pp. 33, 34). This suggests a reality whose nature is different from that of physical entities (or, for that matter, of ideas or human selves).

Digressive as this discussion may appear, it has a direct, practical bearing on man, society, and curriculum. In the first place, symbols and their manipulation are the principal means by which human beings gain their present understanding of the world and the universe. Furthermore, symbols make possible the enormous amount of communication of information and ideas required in technological societies. This obvious importance of symbols in the affairs of men has led some educationists to conclude that the reality of symbols (whatever it may be) is existentially superior to that of the *things* they represent. As a result, the curriculum they advocate tends to emphasize the abstract study of such wholly symbolic subjects as English and Latin grammar, geometry, algebra, trigonometry and calculus, with little or no allusion to the connection these symbols may have with possible referents in the world of *empirical* reality. In addition, the learning activities of such a curriculum almost exclusively center on the paper-and-pencil manipulation of symbols.

By contrast, an educationist who places a higher ontological value on things rather than on symbols tends to advocate a curriculum that stresses such subjects as laboratory physics/biology/chemistry, physical geography, geology, practical English, bookkeeping, woodworking, and sewing. The learning activities of this curriculum tend to place students in direct contact with the tangible environment and include field trips, demonstrations with physical objects, and projects involving the manipulation of all sorts of tangible materials.

While the above demonstrates the connection between our ontological commitments and the curriculum we advocate, it does not settle the essential problem of the existential nature of symbols. Are they "real" entities? Do they exist in the same way as the things they represent? How can their reality (or spuriousness) be determined?

---

2. The following line of reasoning can be used, *mutatis mutandis*, with the spoken word (i.e., symbols in the form of sounds).

Even from the brief discussion above, it should be obvious that there is no simple answer to the question of reality or what it means "to be."

> *Perhaps, as some say, things that are said to exist actually exist in differ-*
> *ent ways; there are different classifications, as it were, of existence. Apples*
> *may exist in one way; feelings, like hunger, for instance, may exist in*
> *another; ideas, like love or Communism, exist in another, and perhaps*
> *human selves in yet another (Morris 1961, p. 31).*

THE REAL VERSUS THE APPARENT. Especially because the ontology of twentieth-century culture is an empirical one based on the senses, we are faced with the problem of distinguishing that which is "genuinely" real from that which is only "apparently" real, or spurious. Anyone who has had the least experience with so-called optical illusions is well aware of the tricks that our senses can play on us. But beyond these cases in which the obvious falsity of our perceptual reports is made clear to us, many instances can be cited of the profound problems generated when the senses are employed as the basic criterion for determining the nature of reality. For example, my senses tell me that a wooden table exists in reality as a hard, rectangular object. Indeed, it resists my corporeal existence so adamantly that I must avoid attempting to walk *through* it in order to escape the sensation of pain. To a *chemist*, however, the table exists as a cluster of hydrocarbons joined in a specific arrangement so as to behave in a particular way under certain conditions of temperature, moisture, and so on. But the table exists for a *physicist* in yet another mode of reality: as the atomic behavior of given arrangements of electrons, neutrons, protons, etc. So full of motion are these submicroscopic clusters of potential energy, and so distant from one another are they in proportion to their "size,"[3] that it is remarkable that I am not, in fact, able to actually walk "through" the table.

In the light of these "appearances" of the table proposed in the above discussion, it seems justifiable to ask which is the most "real." Clearly, the answer proposed by our culture (i.e., "a table is a hard object, and that is that") is a bit too facile, perhaps even naive. Most thinking people are either very cautious and tentative about their statements concerning the nature of reality or are not prepared to draw a conclusion at all. Indeed, it seems appropriate at this point to recall the comment on reality made by the physicist P. W. Bridgman in the preceding chapter: it may be that the nature of reality and the concept of existence are meaningless because it is impossible for man to transcend the human point of reference.

For the curriculum worker, however, the question of the nature of reality, although unsolvable, may be unavoidable. Obviously, whatever we teach in

---

3. It has been estimated that "the electron moves in an orbit about the proton at a distance so great that if the atom were enlarged until the proton became the size of the head of a pin the diameter of the electron's orbit would be roughly equivalent to the height of a sixty-story skyscraper." (L. W. Chubb, *The World within the Atom*, Westinghouse Little Science Series Booklet, 1946, cited in Thut 1957, pp. 304, 305.)

schools we would like to have a real rather than a spurious or counterfeit basis. For example, consider the status of literature as a segment of the curriculum. Is literature (the novel, drama, poetry) "real," or is it simply an entertaining fiction? If the former, then literature's stock-in-trade—that is to say, human ideas like love, loyalty, and justice—must be established by some criterion as having a basis in reality. If literature is merely a counterfeit *appearance* of reality, however, it must go, to be replaced by something more "real"—perhaps chemistry or biology. In short, the nature of the curriculum will depend in large measure upon what we believe is real and what is fictional or deceptive.

Another illustration can be taken from the field of history. Certainly we want to teach a type of history that is "real," that represents events as they actually occurred. Unfortunately, however, an inspection of a number of history texts reveals that different historians "see" things differently. It seems that the "facts" of history are uncomfortably dependent on the perceptions of those through whom they get filtered. Yet, it can be argued that on some issues historians *do* agree. Suppose 90 percent of the historians see a particular event in the same way? Would that mean we are close to the reality of the event? Suppose *all* agreed. Would that situation be a *certain* warrant for the discovery of the "really real"? To answer in the affirmative amounts to basing the nature of reality on an opinion poll. What if the poll eventuates in 51-to-49 percent result? Do we conclude that the reality claimed by the 49 percent is false?

Simplified as this discussion has been, we can see that ascertaining the location and character of that which really exists is a far more complex and perplexing task than it immediately appears to be. At the same time, however, experience indicates that few of us can psychologically tolerate the uncertainty inherent in the proposition that the location of reality and its nature are un-knowable. We seem to require the assurance that the basis of our beliefs is real rather than apparent—i.e., a *reality* rather than a pretense. Consequently, we *assume* an ontological commitment which we use as an anchor for our belief-superstructure or *Weltanschauung* (world view).

THREE ONTOLOGICAL POSITIONS: THREE PHILOSOPHICAL FAMILIES. Over the course of recorded history, man has developed a multiplicity of belief-super-structures or *Weltanschauungs*, often informally referred to as philosophies. Fortunately, these numerous philosophies can be grouped into three broad cate-gories or families based on their ontological anchors, i.e., their sources of reality. For example, we can observe that although the *Weltanschauungs* of early civ-ilizations varied considerably according to specific religious beliefs, almost all were anchored in an ontology that placed the locus of reality in a supernatural realm (e.g., the spiritual domain of the gods or the "idea" world proposed by Plato). Thus, in certain basic respects these civilizations all viewed man, nature, knowledge, and the good life in substantially similar terms. Philosophies based on supernatural ontologies are still prevalent among a number of contemporary social groups and exert considerable influence on many important curriculum decisions made in America today. This group of philosophies and their curricular significance are discussed in Chapter 6, in the section titled "The Nature of Knowledge: Other-Worldly Philosophies."

A second group of philosophies is predicated on the assumption that reality is inherent or indwelling in the present, external, natural world. That is to say, it is assumed that the "really" real consists of the matter out of which the universe is made. Although this philosophical tradition dates back to Aristotle (Greek philosopher, fourth century B.C.), it has become increasingly prevalent with the development of modern science. Philosophies anchored in the "naturalistic" tradition have been extremely influential in determining contemporary American curricular policy. This family of philosophies is examined more closely in Chapter 6, in the section titled "The Nature of Knowledge: Earth-Centered Philosophies."

The third, and the most recent, family of philosophies has developed around the notion that reality can reside only in human experience. In other words, it is claimed that talking about the location and nature of an external reality is meaningless since man cannot know it directly (see Bridgman, 1950) and that ultimate and final reality must reside within the individual self. A number of twentieth-century philosophies are based on some version of this "man-made" ontology, and although they clearly have not constituted a dominant influence on curriculum decision making, they have made their mark felt, particularly within the last fifty years. The section in Chapter 6 titled "The Nature of Knowledge: Man-Centered Philosophies" examines in more detail the bases of these twentieth-century contributions to philosophy as well as their potential for affecting the curriculum.

Before turning our attention to the three philosophical families, however, we must continue our present discussion with an examination of the second category of philosophical inquiry: epistemology. We shall see that while epistemology represents a distinct set of philosophical problems, it is intimately related to ontology, which functions as a kind of logical rudder for epistemological thought.

EPISTEMOLOGY

Epistemology is the philosophical problem that deals with the nature of knowledge and the nature of knowing. It asks the questions: What is true? How do we know the truth? And how do we *know* that we know? As we mentioned earlier, it is the epistemological question—of all the philosophical questions—that is of most concern to curriculum specialists since, after all, knowledge is what the curriculum is all about. A good illustration of the centrality of epistemology in contemporary curriculum work appears in the persistent dispute over whether it is the biblical or the Darwinian version of the origin of man that belongs in the curriculum. Which version is the authentic one (i.e., the "truth")? How can we know? It is quite important, after all, that the knowledge we pass on to our children be genuine, not false or deceptive.

Opting for the biblical version of man's origin, of course, suggests the belief that ultimately, truth is revealed to us by supernatural powers residing in an *other-worldly* reality. On the other hand, a position favoring the Darwinian version implies that truth is discovered by "scientifically" examining the reality inherent in *this world*. Although the position a person takes on this curriculum issue will depend directly upon his epistemological commitment, it will derive more basically from his most fundamental (i.e., ontological) beliefs.[4]

The paragraph above demonstrates the very close relationship that exists between ontology and epistemology, a relationship that we cannot emphasize too strongly. Clearly, in our illustration the assumption of an other-worldly ontology led to a supernatural or mystical epistemology, while an earth-centerd ontology produced an empirical one. But the relationship is actually more complex than the biblical-Darwinian dispute reveals. For example, how do we come to *know* the ontology that we assume in the first place? How can we ascertain its truth or falsity? Can there be more than one true ontology? These questions suggest that for all practical purposes our epistemology will tend to warrant our ontology; that is, it will determine to a large degree what we can know and say about reality. Reciprocally, of course, our ontology (as we have seen) will circumscribe the nature of our epistemology; i.e., it will suggest the nature of knowledge and the procedures that are used to obtain it. While this interdependence may suggest a degree of circularity,[5] the necessary coherence of ontologies and epistemologies is not surprising when we consider that philosophy is by definition a rational enterprise.

To continue our inquiry into the epistemological/ontological problem, we find that knowledge of reality may very well be impossible because, as Bridgman (1950) says, our minds do not correspond sufficiently to the cosmos to permit us to know it at all. If this is the case, then authentic (true) knowledge is simply unavailable to us, and we are forced to recognize that our present "knowledge" of the world (and ourselves) consists of nothing but groundless visions and fantasies. Clearly, this is a "dead-end" position. On the other hand, if we hold that knowledge of reality *is* possible, we are faced with the prospect that it might, as reality might, present itself to us in different ways or modes. For example, most mystics would be quite willing to accept the soundness of knowledge acquired through the senses, even though they would also insist on the authenticity of the insights (knowledge) they received during a contemplative trance. But a world containing different kinds of knowledge can pose many problems. For example, what if the mystical insight and the sense perception do not agree—i.e., what if different kinds of knowledge turn out to be contradictory? Which is to be relied on as the truth? Or, to put it another way,

---

4. There is some disagreement among philosophers of education on this point. For a summary of their positions see Brubacher (1962, p. 20 ff).

5. As was pointed out on our earlier discussion of "What Philosophy Is," all belief systems can ultimately be pushed back to those fundamental assumptions that constitute little more than an act of faith.

which procedures for obtaining knowledge produce knowledge in which we can place the greatest confidence?

The question of confidence, taken to its logical extreme, raises the possibility of knowledge so certain and so true that we are simply obligated to believe it. Is there a type of knowledge somewhere in the cosmos that is so universally and eternally true that it applies to all men at all times in all places?[6] Such knowledge, obviously, would be extremely valuable to us in solving the enormous problems of life. It is precisely the kind of knowledge that we would like to include in the curriculum, inasmuch as it virtually assures those who know it of the ability to make wise decisions. Indeed, we could even say that such knowledge represents a curriculum worker's dream since it constitutes the material needed to fashion the *ideal* curriculum.

However, "The great difficulty with this type of truth (often spelled with a capital *T*: *Truth*) is that men are, generally speaking, not agreed on what it is" (Morris 1961, p. 115). Even in cases where agreement is apparent, conditions and reservations are always turning up to becloud the issue and generate dispute. To illustrate the difficulties inherent in absolute propositions, Morris (1961, pp. 115, 116) cites Jefferson's declaration that "all men are created equal." Although Jefferson elevated the principle to the status of absolute truth by proclaiming it "self-evident," King George did not see it that way. As often happens, one man's "self-evidence" turned out to be another man's heresy. But even if we grant general agreement among Americans on the proposition, we still are faced with the problem of the precise *meaning* of it. Obviously, Jefferson's declaration does not mean that all men are created physically and intellectually equal, but rather equal before the law. Thus, the contemporary interpretation of Jefferson's Truth generally is taken, as Morris notes, to be something like, "All men are equal before man-made institutions." But it is not difficult to see that even *this* proposition is subject to qualifications and reservations, and, "only one reservation is required to repeal the absoluteness of a statement" (Morris 1961, p. 116). It seems clear, then, that much as we would like to believe our knowledge to be unquestionably true, we had best be extremely cautious about attributing to it universal and eternal characteristics.

WAYS OF KNOWING. If, as we have noted above, there is a close relationship between ontology and epistemology, we should expect to find that certain ways of knowing are associated with, or characteristic of, certain ontologies. Although this indeed turns out to be the case, we must be careful throughout the following section not to view our classification in too rigid terms. Most often, a way of knowing is neither discrete—i.e., without reference to other ways of knowing—nor is it exclusively attributable to a single ontology.

With these caveats in mind, then, we may begin by observing that other-worldly ontologies usually hold that knowledge of the good is received (Thut

6. The term "absolute truth" often is employed to designate this kind of knowledge.

1957, p. 39 ff.)[7] That is, man is viewed as the passive receptor of knowledge that originates in another world, whether it be the supernatural domain of a god, the "idea" region of Plato's cosmos, or the human soul hypothesized by Jean Jacques Rousseau (eighteenth-century French philosopher). Receiving knowledge from a supernatural source, however, can take place in a number of ways, and those ways will depend, to a large degree, on the nature of the other-worldly reality that the ontology assumes. The most commonly cited method, of course, is the process of revelation, a significant way of knowing for most of the world's religions. The Bible, for example, is said to consist of knowledge directly revealed to its writers, who received it from God. But many times since the writing of the Bible, and even in our own time, people have made claims to direct contact with a supernatural world during which they received knowledge through revelation. Such knowledge is almost always viewed by its receivers as highly valuable and authentic, and often as *absolutely true.*

In contemporary speech, the term "intuition" usually is employed to indicate "revealed" insights that have no apparent empirical basis, and the word commonly carries with it a mystical connotation (e.g., in the expression "women's intuition"). Some psychologists, however, entirely eschew any mystical explanation of intuition, preferring to interpret such immediate apprehension of new knowledge as a kind of step-skipping intellectual leap which is in fact based on sound, although sometimes unconscious, prior knowledge. This scientific analysis of the intuiting process is not, of course, based on an epistemology of received knowledge.

Because revelation is not a common experience, other-worldly ontologies are compelled to turn to alternative methods of knowing to disseminate knowledge of the good. As pointed out above, revealed knowledge usually is preserved in written form (e.g., in the Bible) so that those who have not had the good fortune to receive it directly are yet able to have access to it. Thus, the written body of revealed knowledge, certified as authentic, is taken *on authority* to be valid knowledge of the good by those who would know it. We should hasten to point out that the method of *knowing by authority* is probably our most common way of knowing, even in the sciences, and should not be regarded as necessarily inferior to other methods. After all, how many of us are content to take it on authority, for example, that the earth is a sphere? And how many of us have checked out this knowledge by other methods of knowing?

Even from the incomplete account provided above, it is easy to see that the curriculum worker who adopts an other-worldly ontology will have no great difficulty in determining what content should be included in the curriculum: obviously, the knowledge of the good (whatever it may be) that has been received from the other world of ultimate reality!

---

7. I am indebted to I. N. Thut for many of the concepts and much of the terminology of this chapter. This is particularly the case with regard to the threefold classification of epistemologies that appears in this section.

We must now move on to the ways of knowing that are characteristic of earth-centered ontologies. Clearly, for those who view this material world as the locus of ultimate reality, sense data will be favored as the most reliable route to knowledge. After all, it is through our senses that this material world is disclosed to us. Of course, all ontologies must to some degree accept the knowledge to which we have access through our five senses, but those who believe that ultimate reality is indwelling in the material universe are wont to accept nothing else! Indeed, so convinced are they that the senses yield knowledge of this world's inherent ultimate reality that they have defined their epistemology as a process of *discovery*—literally the *un-covering* of this world's reality.

No one can deny, of course, that our senses provide us with a good deal of authentic information: we see the desks that fill the classroom, hear the students' chatter, feel the hardness of the chalk, taste the coffee in the cafeteria, and smell the cigarette smoke in the teachers' lounge. Yet experience (and substantial psychological research) indicates that our perceptions are not nearly as reliable as we sometimes think they are. Our sensory equipment, for example, is far less acute than that of many animals. Dogs can hear and smell far better that we, and the eagle's sense of sight is much keener than ours. But the undependability of our senses is never clearer than in those situations where several witnesses are required to describe the circumstances of an event such as an accident. The widely acknowledged difficulty in arriving at what "really" occurred in such instances testifies to the "unnumbered hazards of error [involved] in relating what actually happened" (Morris 1961, p. 122).

Even if our senses *were* completely dependable, however, the question remains as to whether they can account for *all* of the knowledge we acquire. To assume that the full range of human knowing is encompassed in sensory perception is a grandiose presumption indeed! Certainly knowledge gained through the senses qualifies as a beginning in the knowing process, but it is highly doubtful that it can "cover all the territory."

The undependability of individual perception has fostered the acceptance of another way of knowing by the proponents of earth-centered ontologies—a way that scientists call "intersubjective verification" and that the layman calls "collective perception" or "common sense." Through the use of symbols men are able to communicate with one another and thus to share their experience. Consequently, it is possible for them to "check up on" each other's sense perceptions and determine what "most" people perceive, that is, determine what knowledge is most authentic and hence will be most dependable to use in arriving at wise decisions. This method of employing the *common* sense to verify the authenticity of knowledge has significant advantages. If your eyes or ears have a tendency to betray you on occasion, you can determine the "truth" by checking your peers' sensory evidence. (Does this milk taste as though it is getting sour? Perhaps; but you can be much surer by confirming—or refuting—your suspicions with the taste sensations that Bill and Jane and Ted report having with it.)

Although the method of common sense has been shown to be exceedingly fruitful, it is by no means an infallible route to knowledge. It is subject to the same kind of criticism that we leveled against popularity polls in the previous section on ontology. And it *is* ultimately, based on the admittedly undependable perceptions of individuals. (Remember the incompatible reports of the accident witnesses!) Lest the maxim "Fifty million Frenchmen can't be wrong" be taken literally, we are obliged to observe that seventy million Nazi Fascists *were* (Morris 1961, p. 123)!

We cannot close this section on earth-centered epistemologies without some attention to the method of logic. Clearly, logic, or the systematic treatment of ideas, is contained in the epistemological repertoire of a variety of ontologies. It is an important adjunct of the senses, for example, among those proponents of earth-centered ontologies who view the external material world as the source of reality. Scientists, for example, find logic an indispensable tool in dealing with sense data. By contrast, however, logic *itself* is the *central* epistemology for those who locate reality in what they view as the most significant existent of this present world: the human intellect. Although they readily admit that sensory data can function in a subordinate role, they hold that logic is superior because it can greatly extend knowledge gained through sensory experience, and can even function without it!

The well-known syllogism is a good example of how logic can produce knowledge which is unavailable to the senses by using sensory data. Consider this familiar pattern of argument:

> All women are mortal. (Premise)
> Miss America is a woman. (Premise)
> Therefore, Miss America is mortal. (Conclusion)

The first two statements (premises), of course, are established in sensory experience. But Miss America is presently alive and well; we have no way of knowing *through sensory experience* if she is mortal until such time as we are able to verify her death through sensation. The conclusion of the syllogism, produces knowledge that goes beyond that which is available only through our senses.

More impressive than the syllogism, however, is the logicians' alleged access to knowledge that is not in any way based on sensory experience. Beginning with a "self-evident" proposition or truth, he is able to build up bodies of knowledge exclusively through the use of logic. The most common example of this process comes from mathematics, especially geometry, where a "self-evident" axiom like "Two things equal to the same thing are equal to each other" can be expanded through logic into a whole system of mathematical theorems (principles that can be proved). Indeed, mathematics often is referred to as the "pure" science because it consists of knowledge that is not based in any way on sense data.

As noted above, "pure" knowledge always begins with a "self-evident" truth. This is knowledge that is directly and immediately apprehended as true by the intellect. It is true in and of itself and is totally independent of sensory experience. Oftentimes alluded to as "intuitive knowledge," it is said by its proponents to demonstrate, along with logic, the preeminence of the intellect in epistemological affairs.

It is worthwhile to point out here that both the *discovering* and *receiving* processes imply epistemologies that yield "absolute" or immediately true knowledge. One cannot impute the possibility of error, for example, to knowledge that has been received from an other-worldly or supernatural source. Nor can one doubt that, having unveiled (discovered) the *real* nature of something, its nature is spurious or will change. But the methods of discovering and receiving knowledge contrast significantly in another dimension. Whereas the former (discovery) suggests an active role for the knower (sensing, reasoning, seeking self-evident truths), the latter (receiving) implies a passive role (accepting a revelation, accepting knowledge on authority).

In terms of curriculum content, an epistemology of discovery will emphasize the external world of physical reality: Students will attend to physics, chemistry, and biology in order to learn the indwelling and immutable "laws of nature" that govern inanimate and living reality; and they will study sociology, psychology, and anthropology in order to discover the equally indwelling and immutable laws that govern individual and collective human behavior. Thus, through the active pursuit of discovery, the human intellect is able to apprehend the ultimate reality of this universe.

We conclude this section with a brief description of the methods preferred by proponents of *man-centered* ontologies. In many respects, these are similar to ones described in the paragraphs dealing with earth-centered epistemologies, but with a very big difference: no claim is made for the absolute or immutable truth of the knowledge that the methods yield. Thus, while the proponents of man-centered epistemologies would include sense perception and logic in their repertoire of ways-to-know, they would hasten to add that all they can really know as a result of these processes is their *experience*. The fact of the matter, they point out, is that human beings simply cannot know the environment directly (as claimed, for example, by proponents of the discovery method); knowledge is always filtered through the screen of experience. It follows that, in fact, experience is the "stuff" out of which we "build" our conceptions of the world, our environment. And this suggests that acquiring knowledge is a process of construction, rather than discovering or receiving. Indeed, proponents of man-centered ontologies hold that knowledge of the good is constructed out of human experience.

One extremely important method of constructing knowledge has been designated variously as "the scientific method," "the complete act of thought," and "reflective" or "critical thinking." It usually is presented as a five-step process:

1. *Awareness of an undetermined difficulty or problem*
2. *Definition or statement of the problem*
3. *Catalogue of all possible solutions*
4. *Catalogue of projected consequences*
5. *Testing of consequences in experience*

The "scientific method," of course, is not a rigorously defined procedure. It can (and should) be modified to meet the demands of the particular problem to be solved (e.g., research-scientific, social, moral, etc.). Nevertheless, it represents a way of arriving at knowledge for decision-making purposes that is distinctive and unique in human history. Far from proclaiming the absolute truth of the knowledge produced by the "scientific method," its proponents attribute to it two important (but quite unpretentious) advantages:

1. *An open and public character; i.e., the validity of the knowledge can be verified (or refuted) by anyone who is willing to employ the same method (on this point, see the method of revelation, which requires special status for participation)*
2. *The temporary and tentative nature of the knowledge; since the knowledge is founded in experience (as opposed to an ontologically ultimate reality), it is subject to revision, modification, or even outright rejection as a consequence of altered experience*

Although this knowledge does not provide the certainty claimed for received and discovered truth, it has the distinct advantage of being open ended. It allows not only for the correction of error (something the absolute epistemologies cannot tolerate, lest their entire basis be called into question), but revision of previously valid knowledge when required by changed conditions of life.

A curriculum based on an epistemology of constructed knowledge will tend to be somewhat flexible with regard to content. After all, if knowledge (in a substantive sense) is tentative and changing, it may be less important to "know *that*" than it is to know *how*" (e.g., to generate knowledge). Consequently, the curriculum will generally place increased emphasis on *process*—i.e., on learning those proficiencies required to construct knowledge.[8] Reading, writing, doing, adding, thinking, and similar activities will occupy students' time, and skills will take precedence over knowledge when the time comes to evaluate curricular effectiveness. Indeed, the name "activity curriculum" has been given to one curriculum that has grown directly out of the epistemology of constructed knowledge, and another (more society oriented) has come to be known as the social problems curriculum. In the latter design the focus is learning *how* to solve social problems.

Although the examples we have used in the preceding discussions of *received, discovered,* and *constructed* knowledge tend to focus mainly on curriculum content, they demonstrate that epistemological assumptions can affect the curriculum in many complex ways. Moreover, we saw that epistemological positions make sense only insofar as they dovetail with other components (e.g., the ontology) of the philosophical "master plan." It seems reasonable, then, to conclude that curriculum construction requires not only the maintenance of an

---

8. It should be noted that content and process are never, in actuality, separable. This problem is treated more fully in the section "Process as Content" in Chapter 14.

explicit, consistent relationship between epistemology and curriculum, but congruent positions on what is real and what is true.

AXIOLOGY

Axiology is the branch of philosophy that deals with problems of value. It poses the question: What is good? What should man prefer? What is really desirable? The importance of values in our lives is so obvious that it seems fatuous even to broach the subject. We shall content ourselves, therefore, with the simple observation that virtually every moment of our lives is taken up with valuing, that is, with choosing one alternative over many other possibilities in the expectation that our collective choices will eventuate in what we assume to be the good life.

Axiological questions customarily are divided into two main categories: ethics and aesthetics. Ethics is concerned with concepts of right and wrong, good and bad, as they apply to human conduct. Aesthetics, on the other hand, deals with the qualities of beauty and enjoyment in human experience. Both of these categories of value questions, obviously, have a direct bearing on the curriculum.

ETHICS. The central question posed by ethical inquiry is, What should I do? (Morris 1961, p. 225). Given a particular situation, what is the "right" or "good" course of action to take? So seriously do men view the question of ethics that they often refuse to condone "legally" sanctioned conduct if, in their judgment, it is not "moral." Thus, a businessman may be condemned by the community for ruining another businessman even though he employed legal competitive means to do it. Matters of fairness, honesty, deception, cruelty, charity, etc., are seen as moral issues because they involve the quality of relationships between human beings.

The larger question of what constitutes moral conduct is obviously beyond the scope of this chapter. Nevertheless, it is vital to curriculum decision making. It involves, among other things, being aware of discrepancies between professed values and those that in fact govern conduct.[9] It requires a consideration of ends and means.[10] And most importantly, it includes an inquiry into the nature of the human condition.

In spite of a good deal of talk about "objectivity" in the classroom, it seems eminently clear that the curriculum enterprise cannot escape its distinctly moral character. Education, after all, is a process of deliberately influencing children and youth in such a way that they become what they would not otherwise become. And the curriculum is the master plan by which this purpose is accomplished. Thus, for example, we encourage children to learn their numbers, tell nouns from verbs, know the presidents, and understand why the free-enterprise

9. See Chapter 7, "The Structure of Culture" and "Culture and Values" for an exposition of this problem.

10. See the discussion, "The Problem of Ends and Means," in Chapter 13.

system works so well. Perhaps more significantly, however, we urge them to mind the teacher, share their crayons, take turns, get along, and follow directions. In short, we make curricular decisions that foster those dispositions and values we believe young people need most if they are going to live the good life, and we ignore, discourage, and suppress those we think will inhibit it (e.g., free love and communism). In so doing, we obviously incur a heavy responsibility, for we cannot escape being held accountable for deliberately altering the individual and social lives of human beings.

AESTHETICS. The central question posed by aesthetics is, What should I like? (Morris, 1961, p. 234). What are those sensations of sight, hearing, smell, touch, and taste that yield the highest quality of enjoyment? Or in the more familiar terms of formal aesthetics: What is beautiful?

Obviously, men develop a liking for a wide range of experiences (just as they develop preferences for a wide variety of behaviors). Some prefer to spend their leisure hours listening to serious music; others enjoy TV football; still others choose an X-rated movie; while yet others are happy with a few beers at the corner bar. But just as all conduct is not equally moral, so all aesthetic experience is not equally enjoyable.[11] That is, certain aesthetic experiences are to be preferred over others because they yield a "higher order" of enjoyment. The elusive basis of this "higher" order of enjoyment is the standard used to determine what we *ought* to like and constitutes the focus of inquiry in aesthetics.

Among the problems that beset aesthetic inquiry is the nature of the aesthetic experience. What, for example, is its character? We know that it has something to do with the stimulation of one or more of the five senses, but what? Further, we know that the nature of the stimulus is a crucial factor governing the quality of the experience. Can *any* stimulus trigger an aesthetic response? With respect to this last question we may ask whether enjoying sunsets (as opposed, for example, to enjoying paintings) qualifies as an aesthetic experience. If we admit the enjoyment of sunsets to the category of aesthetic experience (as many philosophers do) we then are obliged to consider as "aesthetic" all manner of enjoyments taken from the "natural realm." Thus, not only sunsets, but the sight of seascapes and grazing deer; the smell of flowers and mountain air; the taste of cool fresh water and just-picked cherries; and the feel of a warm spring shower must all qualify as aesthetic experiences. Indeed, Morris (1961, p. 236) even raises the question of whether or not the tactual sensations of sexual play and intercourse qualify as aesthetic experience.

The difficulties noted above do not evaporate, unfortunately, even if we arbitrarily decide to confine our aesthetic inquiry to artificial or man-made aesthetic stimuli (the arts). Most of our popularly recognized art forms (e.g., music, dance, painting, sculpture, literature) traditionally appeal to the senses of sight and/or hearing. But man, we know, is also capable of responding with enjoyment and appreciation to the stimulation of his senses of taste, smell, and feel-

---

11. This position would not be accepted by the total relativist.

ing. Thus, we are confronted with the problem of deciding whether to include in our repertoire of aesthetic experience the appreciation of fine wines, savory roasts, exquisite perfumes, euphoric massages, and galvanizing skydives. If we attribute to such experiences the quality of aesthetic, we are, of course, obliged to raise to the status of "artist" the winegrower, chef, perfume maker, masseur, and inventor of skydiving. These problems, obviously, have no easy solution, mainly because the distinction between the genuine aesthetic experience and the merely sensory one has never been clearly made (Morris 1961, p. 236). Nevertheless, they are problems of value that the curriculum specialist can ignore only at the peril of falling into the genteel snobbishness that limits aesthetic legitimacy to traditional upper-middle-class art forms.

Even if we were able to establish the exact nature of aesthetic experience, however, we would still be faced with the problem of selecting preferred experiences. Most of us will admit that, for one reason or another, we do not always like or appreciate what we *ought* to like. For example, we *should* want to hear the symphony, but prefer, and in fact do watch, the TV wrestling matches instead. In a situation such as this—where we do not like what we ought to like—we are said to lack taste, or to exhibit bad taste. On the other hand, when we really like what we ought to like, e.g., the symphony, we are said to have good taste.

Unquestionably, the "tastes" that an individual develops affect the quality of his life. If there are some tastes that yield a superior quality of experience than do others (and we are assuming that there are), it is important to know what they are. True, men have never agreed on what constitutes "good taste" and perhaps never will (this is nowhere clearer than in the writings of art, music, and literary critics). Nevertheless, aesthetic inquiry has produced general principles for judging aesthetic merit, and it generally is conceded that in many areas agreement does exist on what we ought to like.

Insofar as the curriculum is concerned with the development of preferences and dispositions that eventuate in the good life, it will clearly be interested in the promotion of good (aesthetic) taste.[12] That is, it will endeavor to enrich learners' lives by producing dispositions to like and appreciate what *ought* to be appreciated. But, as was the case with ethics, it is an awesome responsibility to undertake the alteration of human lives; let us hope that the task will be approached with both knowledge and humility.

THE COHERENCE OF AXIOLOGIES AND ONTOLOGIES. The relationship between epistemology and ontology that we pointed out in the previous section holds true for axiology as well. Given a particular ontological commitment, we can infer likely axiological imperatives. For example, an other-worldly ontology suggests that what is good or desirable is what God wills. The Ten Command-

12. "We are beginning to appreciate the fact that children who go to dingy, dirty schools . . . will grow up with different tastes in architecture, art, and interior design from those of children who go to bright, colorful, attractive schools . . ." (Morris 1961, p. 10).

ments are probably the best example of this position, although it has often been pointed out that they invoke as many "should nots" as they do "shoulds." On the other hand, a commitment to a reality inherent in *this* world implies that we ought to "follow nature" in matters of conduct and taste. Alexander Pope (eighteenth-century English poet) expressed this axiological position quite succinctly when he wrote, "Whatever is, is right." What he meant was that the extant reality of this world, whatever form it might take, was an *absolute* and therefore an unimpeachable value standard. Finally, man-centered ontologies suggest that values are man made and evolve out of human experience. Thus, what is good is relative and depends on what value we place on the consequences of our choices.

But the relationship of ontology and axiology (like that of ontology and epistemology) is reciprocal. To ask which ontology we prefer is an axiological question—i.e., a value question. And in answering it we are simply expressing a view of what we would like the cosmos to be. Although we usually assume that the position we take is "well-founded," "logical," and "sound," we should be aware that at bottom our wishes may in fact be "prior to and therefore more ontologically real, more existentially authentic, than the reality which we are presumably speaking of" (Morris 1961, p. 249).

Being aware that philosophical commitments are ultimately founded on an "act of faith" does not necessarily, as many suggest, discredit philosophical inquiry. As a meaning-creating animal, man seems instinctively to resist the notion that life is meaningless. Indeed, with the possible exception of one branch of existentialism, all of the ontologies proposed over recorded history hypothesize a cosmos that supports meaning and purpose in human life. And while there is certainly the possibility that man's existence is in fact absurd, it seems so much better, in the absence of any real knowledge to the contrary, to hypothesize that life does have meaning, and to engage in the search for that meaning.

THE ORGANIZATION OF PHILOSOPHICAL POSITIONS

In the previous sections our discussions have suggested a "three-by-three" division of philosophical thought: Each of the three main philosophical positions (other-worldly, earth-centered, and man-centered) was divided into the three basic problem areas of philosophical inquiry (ontology, epistemology, and axiology). Chapter 6 will examine the three main philosophical positions and draw conclusions about their curricular applications. As an aid to visualizing the "big picture," a summary of our three-by-three organizational scheme is reproduced in Table 5-1. We should be aware, of course, that man's philosophical thought is far too complex to be so simply classified and that our schema undoubtedly does violence to philosophy's more subtle aspects. Nevertheless, it is a basically reliable schema and hopefully will prove helpful as a conceptual guide to contrasting philosophical systems.

TABLE 5-1
The Organization of Philosophical Positions

Problem Area / Philosophical Position	(1) Ontology	(2) Epistemology	(3) Axiology	Representative Philosophical Schools
Other-worldly (1)	Absolute reality exists in another *supernatural world*	Absolute knowledge is *recieved* (by revelation or other mystical means)	The absolute good is *God* or the *ideal*	The world's religions Idealism Transcendentalism
Earth-centered (2)	Absolute reality is inherent in *this world* (the cosmos)	Absolute knowledge is *discovered* (through the senses or reason)	The absolute good is the *law of nature*	Rational realism Empirical realism Positivism Naturalism Logical empiricism Dialectical materialism
Man-centered (3)	Relative reality is human *experience*	Relative knowledge is *constructed* (out of experience)	The relative good is the *preferred consequence*	Pragmatism Instrumentalism Experimentalism Existentialism Phenomenology

Philosophy and Linguistic Analysis

We cannot close this chapter without commenting at least briefly on an important new movement in philosophy: linguistic analysis. This school of philosophy holds that practically speaking, ideas do not exist independently of language. That is, in order to conceive or communicate an idea it is necessary to formulate it into the words and sentences that carry its meaning. Obviously, then, before anything can be said about the truth or falsity of an idea, it is first necessary to examine the language in which it is couched to determine its *meaning*. Since philosophy is essentially the expression of ideas, then, meaning has come to be the focus of the linguistic analysts' philosophical inquiry.

Linguistic analysts begin their exposition of meaning by pointing out that our language is essentially dyadic. That is to say, our basic meaning-structure, the sentence, is divisible into two main components—subject and predicate. The subject stands as a substantive *thing* (an object, idea, or event), while the predicate supplies a characteristic, or describes an action, of the subject. It is through this basic device of the subject-predicate relationship, say the analysts, that our language conveys meaning.

An examination of the semantics of sentence structure has led linguistic analysts to the conclusion that meaning is conveyed only by two basic kinds of subject-predicate relationships, the *analytic* and the *synthetic*. Analytic sentences are those whose predicate is contained in the meaning of its subject. For example, "Half a dozen equals six" is a *true* (analytic) statement because six by definition (or "legislation") is one of the meanings of half a dozen. Conversely, "Half a dozen equals five" is a *false* (analytic) statement. Both statements convey meaning, but the meaning of the first is true, while that of the second is false. Other examples of analytic statements are: "A circle contains 360 degrees," "Four is less than five," and "One plus one make two." Each of these statements conveys absolutely true meaning, says the analytic philosopher, because what the predicate tells us about the subject is inherent in the subject *by definition*. Obviously, we could expand our stock of analytic statements almost indefinitely simply by elaborating on the meanings inherent in the expressed subjects.

Traditional philosophers, as we have seen, hold analytic statements to be *absolutely true* because they are "self-evident"—i.e., capable of being "immediately apprehended" by the intellect as true. Indeed, they frequently view the ideas inherent in analytic statements as the purest kind of authentic knowledge. Analysts, however, refer to such statements as *tautologies*—i.e., statements that are "absolutely true," but that tell us nothing that we did not know beforehand.[13] Thus, although analytic statements are quite useful insofar as they convey meaning "by definition," they cannot, according to the analysts, *produce knowledge*.

Synthetic statements, the analysts' second classification of meaning-producing linguistic structures, are those whose predicates depend upon empirical evidence for their verification. For example, "Maine is larger than Massachusetts," "John weighs more than Henry," and "My uncle took his car to the garage" are meaningful because they can be demonstrated to be true or false by the use of sense experience. The analysts claim that *only* synthetic propositions are capable of producing knowledge.

We can conclude from the foregoing that the main argument of linguistic analysis is that the meaning of a sentence is inherent in its method of verification. Thus, as we have seen above, analytic sentences are verified *by definition* and synthetic ones by *empirical observation*. But if a statement is not susceptible of verification by one of these methods, analytic philosophy maintains that it is

---

13. Bertrand Russell (twentieth-century mathematician-philosopher) has expressed the belief that mathematics is essentially an empty tautology (Russell 1959).

neither true *nor* false; it simply has *no meaning*—to be emphatic, it is literally *senseless*. Examples of this latter type of statement are: "God loves us all," "Truth is the spirit that moves the world," and "The universe is infinite." Since there is no evidence that we could possibly obtain to prove or disprove these propositions, say the analysts, they are simply meaningless.

We are now prepared to make a connection between philosophy as linguistic analysis and the extensive discussion of philosophy and the nature of knowledge that we have conducted over the many pages of this chapter. The linguistic analysts claim that virtually the entire literature of philosophy that has developed from the beginning of recorded history is essentially nonsense! It is nonsense, they say, because it is based on propositions that are incapable of being verified. For example, "Reality is an other-world of ideas," "Truth is discoverable in the laws of nature," and "Experience is all that we can know" are crucial propositions, respectively, to the philosophies of idealism, realism, and pragmatism. Yet, they are incapable of verification; and being so, they are neither true nor false, but meaningless. This being the case, say the analysts, it is no wonder that philosophers have been unable to reach any agreement in their philosophical disputes. How could they? The only possible conclusion to draw, then, is that philosophy insofar as it concerns itself with ontology, epistemology, and axiology is a waste of time. Indeed, claim the analysts, if it is to contribute anything at all to improving the conditions of life, philosophy must abandon attempts to build comprehensive thought systems that purport to explain the meaning of existence and concentrate on the more modest, scientific, but fruitful task of analyzing language to determine its effect on our thought and behavior patterns.

This is not the place for a detailed exegesis of the relative merits of the analytic and the older philosophical positions. Suffice it to say that linguistic analysis has made a significant contribution to the literature of philosophy by identifying and clarifying a great deal of muddle that has passed as philosophical thought. On the other hand, we should point out that the arguments of the analysts hold only if we accept their ontological and epistemological assumptions, which in spite of their protests to the contrary, they have not been able to escape. Pushed to the ultimate limit of their position, the analysts are forced logically to "take on faith" that *only* logical empirical procedures produce knowledge.

> At this point the [linguistic analyst] commits the "nothing but" or reductive error. He takes a good thing—namely, the scientist's way of knowing, his convincing criteria of testability—and insists that these criteria provide the only valid approach to knowledge (Royce 1964, p. 60).

The tenuousness of the analysts' position is exposed further by Alfred North Whitehead (twentieth-century mathematician-philosopher):

> In the study of ideas, it is necessary to remember that insistence on hard-headed clarity issues from a sentimental feeling, as it were a mist,

*cloaking the perplexities of fact. Insistence on clarity at all costs is based
on sheer superstition as to the mode in which human intelligence functions (Whitehead 1933, p. 79).*

While we are quite willing to accept what we find useful in linguistic analysis, therefore, we are at the same time reluctant to reject as nonsense the intense concern with problems of ontology, epistemology, and axiology that has occupied countless numbers of highly intelligent and scholarly individuals over a period of more than twenty-five centuries.

References

Bridgman, P. W. 1950. "Philosophical Implications of Physics." *American Academy of Arts and Sciences Bulletin* (February). Quoted in James B. Conant. 1952. *Modern Science and Modern Man.* New York: Columbia University Press. Reprinted by Doubleday Anchor Books, New York.

Brubacher, John S. 1962. *Modern Philosophies of Education.* New York: McGraw-Hill Book Company.

Dewey, John. 1916. *Democracy and Education.* New York: The Macmillan Company.

Morris, Van Cleve. 1961. *Philosophy and the American School.* Boston: Houghton Mifflin Company.

Royce, Joseph R. 1964. *The Encapsulated Man.* New York: D. Van Nostrand Company.

Russell, Bertrand. 1959. *My Philosophical Development.* New York: Simon & Schuster.

Thut, I. N. 1957. *The Story of Education.* New York: McGraw-Hill Book Company.

Whitehead, Alfred North. 1933. *Adventures of Ideas.* New York: The Macmillan Company. Mentor Book Edition of The New American Library.

CHAPTER 6
PHILOSOPHY: THE NATURE OF KNOWLEDGE

The Nature of Knowledge: Other-Worldly Philosophies

The appeal to a supernatural realm for knowledge of the good has constituted a long-standing and virtually universal tradition among men. Indeed, one group of other-worldly "philosophies," the religions created by man, has its roots deep in the prehistoric past. The ontology of these religious "philosophies," of course, is predicated on a supernatural other-world of the gods. Another, more recent, group of other-worldly philosophies had its beginnings in ancient Athens and is predicated on a supernatural other-world of ideas. The history of Western civilization shows that these two conceptions of other-worldly realities (ontologies) have profoundly influenced our culture and our curriculum.

THE OTHER-WORLD OF THE GODS

In primitive times tribal chiefs and medicine men were looked to for special knowledge of the good because it was believed that they had established lines of communication with a superior god-world beyond the senses. In much the same vein the pharaohs of Egypt, the prophets of the Hebrews, the oracles of early Greece, the emperors of Imperial Rome, the popes of Christendom, and the kings of postmedieval Europe all claimed special status by virtue of their access to knowledge not available in the realm of earthly existence.

This other-world of the gods was, of course, thought to be vastly superior to the world in which ordinary mortals lived. It was said to be inhabited by beings endowed with superhuman power and consummate intelligence. (Often, too, it was viewed as the ultimate habitation of especially virtuous mortals, whose reward after death was eternal association with the sublime residents of the other-world.) Obviously, knowledge that superbeings deigned to transmit to earthlings was regarded as far more valuable than any that might originate in this world. Thus, when it was believed that such knowledge *had* been communicated, it was highly prized, and great care was taken to ensure its preservation for future generations.

The rise of monotheistic religions enhanced the status of both the other-worldly place and its chief inhabitant. The Hebrews in particular developed the concept of heaven as the ultimate and perfect reality and the concept of one God as the all-knowing, all-powerful, and all-good supreme being. It is not surprising, then, that knowledge of the good and knowledge of the will of God were taken to be one and the same by the Hebrews (Thut 1957, pp. 74, 76).

God revealed his will to the Hebrews over a rather substantial period of time. He communicated with Adam and Eve, Abraham, Isaac, Noah, Joseph, Moses, the prophets, and other specially chosen agents. The written account of these communications, of course, is what constitutes the Old Testament. This substantial body of revealed knowledge is what the Jewish people have generally come to regard as the full and final word of God. And while it is believed that God maintains an active interest in His people (His assistance still is required in coping with human weakness and the demands of daily existence), intimate knowledge of God's will is nevertheless held to be the surest path to the good life.

In principle, the Christian tradition is essentially similar to the Judaic. In fact, Christians readily accept the Old Testament, but not as the full and final word of God. They believe that Jesus, the last true prophet and Son of God, was sent by God to reveal additional knowledge, without which the good life is not possible. This additional knowledge, of course, is recorded in the New Testament, which like the Old, is to be accepted on faith as the only sure guide to salvation. As Thut (1957, p. 80) points out, the validity of these bodies of revealed knowledge is not to be questioned. It "is guaranteed by its source. Its author is God in heaven, the All-Good, All Powerful, All-Knowing."

Because the Christian tradition, of all God-centered traditions, is the one that has most affected the curriculum of the Western world, we shall focus our discussion on *its* curriculum ramifications. We should be aware, however, that in spite of doctrinal differences regarding the specifics of revealed knowledge that exist between Jews, Christians, Moslems, "pagans," etc., in all cases agreement is firm on the real source of knowledge [another-world of God(s)] and the true method for acquiring it (revelation).

With the development of the Christian church, an increasing volume of doctrine was amassed. Not only the record of Jesus' teachings, but the Epistles of the Apostles and the writings of the church fathers came to be regarded as divinely inspired knowledge of the good. The assimilation of so formidable a body of knowledge obviously requires substantial time and study. But in the relatively underdeveloped societies that existed in Europe during the first and much of the second millenia after Christ, such a luxury was impossible, and indeed almost all of the common people were illiterate.[1] It was thus that oral communication and interpretation of knowledge of the good became the rule for educating the masses. Curriculum content consisted of a series of questions and answers relating to the primary articles of Christian faith, and curriculum learning activities were restricted to memorizing the answers to the questions. In short, for the common man the curriculum consisted of the catechism, and the catechetical method was the means for learning it.

In such times, obviously, important decisions affecting the society were not made democratically by the masses, but rather by ecclesiastical leaders and secular rulers. It was this select group that had most need of knowledge of the good, since it was they who were ordained by divine decree to lead the society toward the good life. It is easy to see how the assumption of an other-worldly source of truth (absolute knowledge) can easily (though not necessarily) eventuate in the development of an elite social class. An account of the formal training required for membership in such a class, then, not only becomes an account of the truths *received* from the other-world of God, but an account of a curriculum for educating an elite.

THE TRIVIUM. In the early days of the church virtually the entire revealed word of God was written down in Latin. Consequently, this ancient language (which by association with the "highest of all knowledge" in time acquired a special status of its own) became an important aspect of the curriculum. Because most prospective scholars were older boys and men, it seemed natural and reasonable to teach Latin grammatically, i.e., in accordance with the rules and precepts of its inflection and syntax. Thus, this first branch of the trivium came to be called *grammar*.

Once the rudiments of Latin grammar had been mastered, readings from various segments of orthodox Christian literature were introduced. This literary branch of the trivium was designated *rhetoric*.

At a more advanced level, students were rigorously exercised in the principles of orthodox theology. It was the privileged class, after all, who were charged with the preservation of church doctrine in its purest form and whose responsibility it was to protect it from error and heresy. This third branch of the trivium was called *dialectic*.

Although elements of such subjects as arithmetic, geometry, astronomy, and music (the quadrivium of the Platonic curriculum) might be included in a minor way in the education of a cleric, the trivium of grammar, rhetoric, and dialectic constituted virtually the entire curriculum.

CONTEMPORARY CURRICULAR APPLICATIONS. The trivium represents an excellent example of a curriculum based on the assumption that knowledge is revealed

---

1. As a matter of fact, when Charlemagne became emperor of the West in 800 A.D., "neither he nor his nobles nor even the vast majority of the clergy of whom he had knowledge were what we would today call functionally literate" (Thut 1957, p. 109).

from an other-worldly source, and from it we can generalize the characteristics of curricula so based, whatever the specific contemporary orthodoxy they represent. In the first place, such curricula tend to focus attention on revealed or "higher" knowledge since knowledge based on the experience of this world generally is regarded as untrustworthy or at best inferior. Physics and geography, for example, to say nothing of driver education and home economics would be minimized, if not entirely absent, in a curriculum based on an other-worldly ontology.

Second, since revealed knowledge ordinarily is preserved in written form, other-worldly-based curricula inevitably take on a distinctly literary caste, usually with heavy emphasis on a foreign or ancient language, specifically the one in which the revealed word is preserved. The revealed body of knowledge, as well as scholars' commentaries on it, are read, studied, discussed, and written about. Words as symbols become central to the educational process, as is clearly demonstrated in the trivium. This is especially true of the curriculum intended for the priest class, since they in particular have the need to know the truth as it was set down in the original tongue. Third (and it is worth repeating here), curricula based on revealed knowledge almost always require a dual system of education with dual curricula—one for the decision makers (leaders and priests) charged with the preservation and interpretation of the revealed word, and one for the masses (followers and laymen).

Due to the doctrine of the separation of church and state, the curriculum of contemporary American public schools does not manifest the influence of God-centered philosophies as obviously as do those of most sectarian, privately supported Bible, parochial, and religious schools. Nevertheless, the God-centered tradition is operative in many subtle (and a few not so subtle) ways. In many schools and classrooms atheisim, both explicitly and by innuendo, is disparaged as grossly evil. Further, a concern for "spiritual values" and certain varieties of "character development" is a prominent feature of many public school curricula. Indeed, these curricula often draw heavily upon the revealed literatures of the Judeo-Christian tradition for their content, as well as the values that they advocate. More significantly, they certify the authenticity of this material by appeal to its other-worldly source! Many school communities, in spite of Supreme Court decisions to the contrary, still include prayer and Bible reading in the curriculum. Finally, the ongoing creation-evolution dispute mentioned in a previous section provides an excellent example of the power that other-worldly philosophies still exercise over the curriculum.

Since Western civilization has been so deeply affected by philosophy based on God-centered ontologies, it is not surprising to find that education (and curriculum construction) until very recent times has been almost exclusively an ecclesiastical function. We are indebted to the various religious denominations for much of the educational development that has taken place over the years. But except for several Protestant sects of Christianity (e.g., the Puritans of colonial America), little inclination has been shown by ecclesiastical authority to foster literacy among the masses. It has largely been a convergence of Protestant theology and technological progress that has produced the curriculum for mass education as we know it today.

THE OTHER-WORLD OF IDEAS

Probably no single philosopher has had a more extensive and enduring effect on the curricula of the Western world than has Plato (Greek philosopher, fourth century B.C.). In *The Republic*, the first fully developed statement on the role of education in society, Plato spells out the ontological and epistemological bases of his philosophy and details the curriculum that derives from his assumptions. So influential was this pre-Christian thinker that both Catholic and Protestant authorities incorporated significant elements of his theory into their religious curricula, and even today the philosophy of idealism (more accurately "idea-ism"), which rests on Platonic metaphysics, affects many contemporary curriculum practices.

Observing the crass materialism that prevailed in the Athens of his day, Plato decried the life style and motivations of what he called "belly-men."[2] He proposed that the truly great and good society cannot be built by people whose greatest concern is their own material well-being, but only by those who aspire to the emulation of lofty "abstractions" such as justice, virtue, and truth— entities (or ideas) that exist only in a realm of being that transcends sense. Thus, Plato holds that the real world is not the one inhabited by our physical bodies, but a nonmaterial domain in which

> the various goods exist as ideas, perfect in every detail and unchanging for all times. These ideas . . . have a real existence. They are "things," even though they cannot be seen by the eye or held in the hand. And they are the only perfect things that exist anywhere (Thut 1957, p. 46).

To illustrate his notion of the hierarchy of reality and value, Plato uses the example of a bed. A bed, he says, has three modes of existence: First, it exists in nonmaterial form in the idea realm beyond our senses. This is its most perfect and absolutely real state of being. Second, a bed exists in material form as, for example, the wooden object made by a carpenter. The wooden bed, obviously, is merely an imitation of the carpenter's conception of the idea bed, and is consequently inferior in perfection and reality. Finally, the bed can exist as a picture painted by an artist. This state of being of the bed is the most inferior of all, since it is only an imitation of the carpenter's bed, that is, an imitation of an imitation.

Plato extends this line of reasoning to all ideas, whether their imitation in this world takes the form of wood, stone, cloth, personality traits, social arrange-

2. A remarkable parallel between ancient Athens and modern America is seen by many observers of the contemporary scene.

ments, laws, or institutions. Thus, he holds that not only the absolutely real and perfect bed, but the absolutely real and perfect courage, school, teacher, political system, man, and society exist in idea form in the other-world. Obviously, then, one would be foolish to look to *this* world for knowledge of the good. Here, he will find only imitation, inferiority, and imperfection—considerations and conceptions that lead to error and misfortune, to say nothing of villainy and evil. Knowledge (qua immaterial perfection), clearly, cannot be appropriated through the physical senses. Rather, one must look to the other-world of *ideas* for knowledge of the good, for only there will he find the perfect knowledge required for decisions that lead to virtuous conduct and the good life. Indeed, for Plato, knowledge and virtue are so intimately linked that he was prepared to write: "you are aware . . . that [most people] cannot explain what they mean by knowledge, but after all are obliged to say knowledge of the good?" (Plato, *The Republic,* I, in Jowett 1899, p. 255).

Plato hypothesized that every human being is endowed with an eternal immaterial *psyche* (soul or mind).[3] This mind, before implantation in a physical body at its birth, has spent various periods of time in the nonmaterial other-world directly exposed to the brilliance and perfection of absolute ideas. Knowledge of these ideas is retained by the mind, but unfortunately, on leaving the idea realm, they are lost to consciousness. Thus, the educational problem, according to Plato, is simply getting the mind to *recall* the knowledge that it presently possesses. This process, and the content required to achieve it, constitute the curriculum of Plato's *Republic.*

PLATO'S CURRICULUM. According to Plato, there are three processes by which the mind's latent knowledge can be brought to consciousness. First, it can be recalled by chance sensory stimulation. This is obviously not a very dependable or promising possibility. Second, it can be recalled by a skillful teacher asking probing questions. This technique is what constitutes the famous Socratic method[4] of questioning that is so highly regarded as a pedagogical technique by many teachers even today. Even this method has its limitations, however, since knowledge to be recalled is restricted to that already in the possession of the teacher. While the Socratic method may represent a useful pedagogical device, it obviously falls short as a generator of new knowledge.

But Plato suggested a third method, *contemplation,* by which the mind can reach into its own subconscious and recall knowledge of the good. Although contemplation is effective for recalling new knowledge—i.e., knowledge never before recalled—it is an activity that requires a "liberated" mind. To bring minds

---

3. The Greek *psyche* (meaning "soul") does not carry the religious connotation that the word later acquired during the Christian era. The Greek "soul" represents something closer to the meaning conveyed by our word "mind."

4. Plato wrote in dialogue form, and many of his ideas are presented as originating with his teacher Socrates (Athenian philosopher, fifth century B.C.). Thus, the appellation "Socratic method."

to a state of liberation, a state conducive to contemplation, is the central aim of Plato's preparatory curriculum.[5]

Plato's preparatory curriculum consists of four areas of study: arithmetic, geometry, astronomy, and music. These designations do not necessarily signify the same studies we associate with them today. Arithmetic (the science of numbers) was to be studied in its most abstract form in order to compel the mind to use "pure intelligence" to see the nature of numbers in their most perfect state of being (Thut 1957, p. 63). Any "practical" (i.e., material) connection between numbers and, for example, construction or trade, was to be rigorously avoided, since preoccupation with the concerns of this world turns the mind from the apprehension of pure truth. Geometry, both plane and solid, was to be studied for essentially similar reasons. Just as pure numbers do not exist in nature, so point, line, angle, circle, and so on, are nowhere to be found. Geometry, therefore, leads the mind away from imperfect and inferior objects of sense toward ideas of pure being. Clearly, the contemplative aspects of arithmetic and geometry are designed to develop a feeling of harmony and love for pure truth.

Astronomy, the third subject of Plato's curriculum, was to be studied not for its value in navigation or the measurement of time, but rather as a pattern to assist in the apprehension of a higher knowledge—knowledge of "the true motions of absolute swiftness and absolute slowness, which we use relative to each other, and carry with them that which is contained in them, in the true number and in every true figure" (Plato, *The Republic*, VII, in Jowett 1899, p. 287). Astronomy, then, though it begins with the senses, should be studied with an eye to the contemplation of the harmony and perfection of pure motion.

By including music in the curriculum, Plato did not intend his students to become professional musicians; in his opinion, that profession was suitable only for slaves and other inferior people. Rather, he expected that music (or more properly, *harmony*) would be studied on an intellectual plane so that the mind might apprehend "the natural harmonies of number, or reflect why some numbers are harmonious and others not" (Plato, *The Republic*, VII, in Jowett 1899, p. 290). In short, the subject of music in Plato's curriculum would closely parallel modern courses in harmonic theory.

These four subjects, then, constitute what Plato called the "sciences" that prepare for (but do not directly foster) the contemplation of pure idea, i.e., knowledge of the good. Knowledge of the good, he held, can be attained only through the systematic study of "dialectic" or philosophy. Thus, Plato viewed philosophy not only as the queen of all the sciences, but as the entire curriculum of higher education.

It is only a select few, Plato believed, whose minds (in another existence) have had the benefit of significant exposure to the other-world of ideas, who can profit from higher education. But it is only those fewer still who are able to *complete* the higher learning who are capable of *applied* dialectic, i.e.,

---

5. It is in this sense that the curriculum we presently know as the "liberal arts" curriculum was conceived.

deliberate contemplation for the recall of knowledge. This tiny elite represents the group that Plato believed should rule the state—the "men of gold" whose minds have gazed upon the good, the true, the beautiful. This tiny elite, in short, comprise Plato's celebrated philosopher kings.

CONTEMPORARY CURRICULAR APPLICATIONS. The Platonic system has undergone substantial modification as it has been integrated into latter-day philosophies whose ontologies rest on another-world of ideas. Although we cannot go into the details of these modifications here, it is significant to note that Plato's influence remains clearly evident in all of them, as the term "idealism," the name by which this group of philosophies is known, amply testifies. Although the influence of idealism appears to be on the wane in America today, idealist assumptions are still apparent in many of our current curricular predilections. A good example of this is the disposition of most contemporary American communities to view the subjects of the curriculum in terms of a hierarchy, with the "idea" subjects (like history and English) considered much more important than the "practical" subjects (like bookkeeping and auto mechanics). Indeed, the "college prep" idea subjects generally continue to be regarded as important for the elite class of leaders who will go on to college, while the "practical" or "vocational" subjects are deemed "good enough" for working-class youth.

We should bear in mind that idealists do not advocate the study of abstract ideas merely for the sake of intellectual exercise or social-economic advancement. What they are after, ultimately (and what will foster decisions that lead to the good life), is a grasp of the idea of man in the universe. In the language of the idealists, we might say that the goal is a transcendent sense of cosmic-human existence, that is, an understanding at the most profound level of the *idea* of the cosmos and the meaning of human existence. (If this sounds somehow quasi-mystical, says the idealist, no apologies need be made; truth, after all, is to be found in idea form in a transcendent other-world.)

In order to achieve this understanding of the cosmic-human idea, idealists advocate a curriculum centered on subject matters that deal with distinctively human concerns. It is not surprising, then, that history holds a preeminent position in their schools. It is this subject, the idealists claim, that best provides students with a sense of man's role in the universe. Students, of course, must go beyond the mere facts and dates of history and attempt to discern in them the trends and currents of historical movement; for here lies the answer to the question of meaning. But as students begin to grasp the meaning of history, they start to penetrate the riddle of the cosmic-human enterprise.

Important as history is, though, it cannot make up the entire curriculum. There are a number of other "man-centered" idea subjects, idealists say, that help us to sense the meaning of our existence in the universe. Among the more important of these is literature, a subject that explores the eternal questions of life and provides insights into our human condition. It is this concern with the enduring ideas of human "being" that makes Dante, Shakespeare, and Milton, for example, as illuminating and meaningful today as they ever were.

Additional facets of existence are revealed to students as they study the other subjects of the idealist curriculum: art, music, philosophy, theology, etc. These subjects, like history and literature, are valued for the ideas they convey. It should be apparent by now that the group of subjects which form the un-equivocal core of the idealist curriculum are those that we ordinarily classify as the *humanities*; and although idealists certainly have no monopoly on them, they are the subjects most often associated with the other-world of ideas.

In order to deal with the other-world of ideas in *this* world, idealists are forced to employ symbols: i.e., words and numbers. As a result, they place a premium (as do many of our public schools) on a symbol-permeated curriculum: reading books, writing compositions, debating propositions, conjugating verbs, and solving equations. This emphasis on symbols is not at all surprising when we consider that symbols, for the idealist, "are the medium through which the mind works," and hence, "are the keys to truth and reality" (Morris 1961, pp. 182, 183).

The idealist's curriculum will not (as do some of our public school curricula) make provisions for learning by direct experience on field trips to parks, banks, stores, offices, factories, and so on. Rather, it will center on the vicarious symbol-activities of the library and classroom, both viewed as sanctuaries for ideas (such is the situation in many of our schools today). Nor is the term "sanctuary" an ill-considered choice of words. As the idealist sees it, it is only in a retreat removed from the distractions and confusion of everyday material existence that one can contemplate the nonmaterial ideas that constitute the good life. "But this makes the university an 'ivory tower'!" we complain. "Exactly what it *should* be," the idealist retorts.

The idealist's preoccupation with symbols should not be mistaken for advoc-acy of the mechanistic absorption of facts and information. As we noted earlier, he is pursuing the broadest, deepest understanding of cosmic-human existence possible. In order to achieve this understanding of self in relation to man and cosmos, he must not only steep himself in the humanities, but also "identify" —i.e., establish relationship—with the larger community of minds. Given this condition, it is clear that the psychological climate of the school takes on con-siderable importance. The curriculum must be administered in such a way that students "respond" to one another and the teacher in communitarian terms. A school, then, is not just a library, classrooms, and books; it is an esprit that binds students and teachers together as a "community of scholars." The partic-ular communitarian ethos nurtured in the essentially idealist "public schools" of England is an example of such an esprit. Whether or not we accept the values inherent in that type of community, we cannot dismiss as an empty boast the claim that "Britain's battles are won on the playing fields of Eton." True knowledge for the idealist is indeed a spiritual affair.

In summary, this section on other-worldly philosophies has shown that whether the other-world of reality is viewed as a world of gods or ideas, it is always regarded as a nonmaterial realm of absolute good. Thus, the knowledge it contains is supernatural and absolutely good and true. Furthermore, this nonmaterial realm is separated from the world of sense by a chasm so great that it can be bridged only with the assistance of supernatural processes. The best that ordinary men can do to reach knowledge of the good is to prepare themselves by appropriate discipline (education) to receive the knowledge that other-worldly powers might bestow on them. Such preparation could include a curriculum of prayer, study of the revealed word, or intellectual exercises with pure ideas; in any case, however, attention to the data of the temporal world is eschewed as an impediment to the reception of true (i.e., spiritual) knowledge.

In addition to preparing individuals to receive knowledge from the other-world, the other-worldly curriculum usually serves a selective function, for as we have seen in the previous sections, only a specially endowed class of people is capable of communion with the supernatural realm. It is this select group, equipped by training to acquire knowledge from the other-world, that is charged with making the decisions for all. Only by following the lead of this erudite group can the life that is good to live be achieved.

The Nature of Knowledge: Earth-Centered Philosophies

The philosophies dealt with in the previous section are said to be *dualistic* because they postulate two realms of being: the nonmaterial, supernatural, but *real* world, and the physical, temporal, but *spurious* world. Earth-centered philosophies, by contrast, are often classified as *monistic* philosophies because they are interested only in *this physical universe* as an object of inquiry. Although certain "materialistic" earth-centered philosophies are, by virtue of their monism, based on an atheistic position, many others are not. These latter usually argue that God is the author of the universe and that He makes His will known to man through the workings of this physical world (the philosophy-religion of Deism is the best example of this position). Thus, whether theistic or atheistic, earth-centered philosophies locate ultimate reality in this physical universe and hold that true knowledge of the good is indwelling or immanent in it. Obviously, then, if man is to make the kinds of decisions that lead to the good life, he had best look around him; he had best use his senses and his reason to discover the knowledge that this physical reality holds. In contrast to the other-worldly philosophers, who regard this world of sense as an imperfect imitation worthy only of suspicion and distrust, the earth-centered philosophers picture it "as a friendly place, a place that is worth knowing and cultivating for our own good" (Thut 1957, p. 160).

Although not as old as the God-centered tradition, earth-centered philosophies are far from recent arrivals on the philosophical scene. They trace their origin to ancient Athens and the theories of Aristotle (Greek philosopher, fourth century B.C.), Plato's most celebrated student. Whereas Plato taught that this physical universe is merely an imitation of reality (just as a picture of a bed is an imitation of the real thing), Aristotle believed that *this world* constitutes the genuine realm of existence.

Aristotle held that the physical universe is made up of two basic ingredients: *matter*—a primary, but shapeless substance, and *form*—the principle which gives purpose and meaning to matter. These two basic ingredients, matter and form, are combined in a variety of ways to produce entities that we experience in our daily lives. Air, water, and sand, for example, represent combinations of matter and form containing only slight traces of the latter. On the other hand, with the addition of more form, matter can assume a variety of properties and becomes highly purposeful, as when it takes the shape of paper, books, trees, houses, and even men. Since the nature of the world that we experience depends upon the principle of form, it follows that form is an indwelling attribute of each and every physical entity.

Because form gives meaning and purpose to unformed matter, it constitutes the principle upon which the nature of reality is based. Thus, for Aristotle, knowledge of form is equivalent to knowledge of the real, and hence, knowledge of the good. Further, as we have seen, traces of form permeate all aspects of the physical universe; it follows, thus, that the search for knowledge of the good must center on the particular objects and forms that inhabit this world.

Given these foundations, the search for knowledge, obviously, becomes an inductive one. It begins with the senses and the observation of particulars, and proceeds by the use of reason to the discovery of generalizations. These generalizations, we should hasten to say, should not be construed as hypotheses or constructs invented by the intellect. Rather, they comprise the conscious intellectual appropriation of the very nature of reality—that is, the conception of pure form. In culminating the discovery process, then, the intellect is said to have laid hold of true and absolute knowledge. This, from the earth-centered philosopher's point of view, is the reward of active, persistent inquiry, and it is the only certain basis for sound decision making.

Simplified and incomplete as the foregoing account has been, it reveals the debt that modern science owes to Aristotelian thought. Of course, with the advent of the dark ages, Aristotelian, and for that matter, all Greco-Roman, thought was either lost or suppressed, and for many centuries the other-worldly ontology of the Christian church dominated philosophical thought. Eventually, however, Aristotle was rediscovered, and when the Renaissance dawned, earth-centered philosophy[6] appeared in the first rumblings of what was to become one of the major achievements of man: the scientific revolution. From that time forward, as science repeatedly demonstrated the advantages of *this*-worldly inquiries, other-worldly philosophies were increasingly forced to go on the defensive.

Ultimately, however, in what some scholars view as a consummate act of hubris, science claimed dominion over the true answer to the riddle of exist-

6. Science, especially what we presently know as chemistry and physics, was known as natural philosophy until the late nineteenth century.

ence. It insisted that *only* scientific inquiry into the nature of the physical world brings forth knowledge of what really is, and, therefore, knowledge of the good. And it maintained that *only* trained scientists willing to strive and labor in the scientific quest are capable of discovering the truth embedded in nature.

With the emergence of man-centered ontologies in the twentieth century, many scientists abandoned the absolutist stance for a more relativistic position. But that is another story and will be dealt with in a following section. For the present, we are interested in the two branches of earth-centered philosophy that have had a significant effect on school curricula. The first of these developed earlier and postulates reality as an *immutable* physical universe. The second branch, which did not mature until the nineteenth century, views reality as an *evolving* physical universe.

A STATIC UNIVERSE

As early as the thirteenth century A.D., Roger Bacon, an English monk and philosopher, was arguing that in many matters knowledge gained from personal experience and observation should be relied on more heavily than authority purportedly founded in an other-worldly source (Thut 1957, p. 209). But not until the seventeenth century and the discoveries of Leonardo da Vinci (fifteenth-century scientist), Nicolaus Copernicus (sixteenth-century astronomer), Galileo Galilei (seventeenth-century astronomer), and Isaac Newton (seventeenth-century scientist) did a system of philosophical thought based on the ontological reality of an immutable physical universe reach full development. It was at this juncture that Newton, on the basis of his scientific work in astronomy, hypothesized that the physical universe is composed of minute, indestructable building blocks or atoms having fixed and identifiable properties. These atoms, he maintained, are joined in distinctive combinations to form the various substances that make up the physical *mass* of the universe. Newton believed that mass (atoms and their combinations) is inert, so that the formation and disassembly of mass structures (that is, the molecules of chemical compounds), as well as motion of mass itself, are the result of the influence of some *force* (e.g., oxidation, fermentation, gravity, etc.).

Newton studied a variety of physical phenomena and generalized the regularities of his observations in terms of mathematical formulas. These formulas, expressions of what Newton viewed as the immanent and immutable "laws of nature," were said to describe the effects "of *force* operating on *mass* within the limits of *time* and *space*" (Thut 1957, p. 218). These studies, of course, resulted in the mathematical equations that we presently know as Newton's famous "Principles of Motion."

The inference that Newton drew from his scientific investigations was that the universe is a great machine whose workings are controlled by mechanical principles or laws. Further, he reasoned that man, being a part of the machine, is subject to its laws of operation. Such doctrines, of course, raised havoc among other-worldly philosophers, that is, among orthodox theologians, many of whom saw them as sacrilegious and atheistic. Obviously, if it were granted that all phenomena (including human behavior) are, in principle, explainable and predictable from knowledge of the "laws of nature," God would appear to be redundant. The theological solution to the dilemma posed by Newton came in a form known as *Deism*. Deism, as we saw in a previous chapter, postulates "God as the Great Clockmaker, who, having created this machine universe, wound it up, set it in motion, and promptly turned to other matters" (Thut 1957, p. 218). This reconciliation of science and religion made it possible for intellectuals to accept an earth-centered approach to decision making and at the same time to avoid an atheistic world view.

Atheistic or not, however, acceptance of the foregoing earth-centered ontology suggests that knowledge of the good can be achieved only by discovering the workings of the machine universe: From the atheist's point of view, the laws of nature are a reality that man is powerless to change; consequently, the good life can be achieved only by accommodating his decision making to the known reality of nature's immutable laws—in other words, by conforming to the natural order. The theistic argument is remarkably similar: Since God created the universe and set it in motion according to fixed principles, the future of man already is determined according to His plan. Indeed, one might say that the will of God and the laws of nature are one and the same. Obviously, then, the good life (i.e., the life intended for man by God the All-Good) can be achieved only by discovering the laws of nature and utilizing this knowledge in the decision-making processes; in short, by conforming to the natural order.

CONTEMPORARY CURRICULAR APPLICATIONS. The introduction of the physical sciences into the American public school curriculum beginning in the latter nineteenth century owes much to the efforts of individuals disposed to an earth-centered curriculum. Indeed, many of these individuals argued strenu- ously[7] that since the good life depends on knowledge of the laws of nature, the scientific subjects are the ones that should be accorded centrality in the curric- ulum. Thus, biology, chemistry, physics, geology, astronomy, and their com- binations and subdivisions are viewed as the subjects that best prepare students to come to grips with the "realities" of life. While the humanities of the ideal- ists, it is admitted, may sometimes provide pleasant diversions, they are rather vague and fanciful, and are certainly not useful in coping with daily affairs. This fundamentally "realist"[8] attitude is often the basis of present-day attacks on art, music, and literature as "frills" in the curriculum.

If the humanities are regarded as ethereal, vague, and fanciful, the sciences by contrast are seen as concrete, specific, and exact. Idealists, it is claimed, are

7. For example, Herbert Spencer, in his famous essay, "What Knowledge Is of Most Worth?" wrote in answer to that question: "the uniform reply is—Science."

8. Empirical realism is the name most often associated with the school of philosophy that is based on a static, earth-centered ontology.

interminably speculating on the "meaning" of an historical movement or the "controlling idea" behind a moral question, while the scientist is establishing with precision the law governing some specific natural phenomenon. Thus, when students study science, they acquire *certain* knowledge of what *is*, knowledge that has been incontrovertibly established as true. It is quite reasonable, then, for teachers following an earth-centered curriculum to expect their students to "know the facts": Boyle's law, Ohm's law, or the molecular structure of sugar, for example, are not matters of opinion or subjects for discussion; they are positive facts that are either known or not known.

Mathematics has always played an important role in science, and so it is natural that it play an important role in the earth-centered scientific curriculum. But whereas the idealists might employ this symbolic study for its own sake as a manifestation of pure idea, the realists view it as a vehicle for rendering the absolute essence of physical reality into precise, quantitative, symbolic form. Thus, such subjects as arithmetic, algebra, trigonometry, and calculus are highly regarded in the earth-centered curriculum as the *basic tool subjects*, and often constitute prerequisites for the study of the physical sciences.

This penchant for mathematics and science in the curriculum reflects the view that measurement of reality is the key to knowledge. Such a position was succinctly expressed by the educational psychologist E. L. Thorndike when he wrote, "Whatever exists exists in some amount." The comment was made in defense of his efforts to measure intelligence (a quality of *mind* that idealists regard as a nonmaterial, and therefore nonquantifiable, reality). The number that we commonly use to refer to an individual's IQ, therefore, in a sense represents the quintessence of an earth-centered view of knowledge.

The previous paragraph suggests the belief that certain members of society are better qualified than others to discover knowledge of the good and thus to make the important policy decisions that will direct society toward the good life. Indeed, this is the thinking of most empirical realists. It is their firm conviction that *only* those individuals endowed by *nature* with superior intelligence *who are highly trained in the sciences and the techniques of scientific discovery* are suited to making the right decisions for society. Such an attitude appears in B. F. Skinner's *Walden II,* where it is suggested that the important policy decisions regarding the aims of education be made by scientists trained in the methods of empirical inquiry.

A curriculum based on the assumption of a static, earth-centered reality will generally take a hard-line position on skills, content, and knowledge. That is, it will insist that there are positive things to be known and that the student's task in school is to learn them. During the early grades when students are acquiring skills in the tool subjects of reading and mathematics, the curriculum will prescribe reading, lectures, and other symbolic activities that efficiently get the content to the students. Care, of course, will be taken to maintain a connection between the symbolic skills learned and the real world; unlike the idealist, the realist finds no value in the study of symbols for their own sake. As students progress through school and begin the serious study of the physical sciences, they will spend increasing amounts of time in laboratories or field settings in direct contact with the real, physical world. The library and class-room are important resources, of course, for efficient transfer of the large amounts of information that students need to learn, but substantial sensory contact with reality is essential if students are to get beyond the symbolic world of words. This propensity for reality (or audiovisual aids when the real thing is not available) contrasts sharply with the exclusively symbolic orienta-tion of the idealist curriculum.

Finally, we may point out that that the esprit that idealists hope to generate among students and teachers in their schools usually is rejected as spiritual foolishness by the hardheaded realists. Just as science discovers and measures the nature of the world's reality, it can discover and measure the degree to which students have acquired the skills and information that make up knowl-edge of the good. Each one is on his own; and we have in our possession the tools needed to determine with relative precision who knows and who does not.

AN EVOLVING UNIVERSE

The assumption of a static, earth-centered reality implies a totally deterministic view of life. It follows from this assumption that given sufficient information and the necessary tools, it is in principle possible to reconstruct the entirety of the past and to predict the totality of the future. Indeed, at one time, this monumental achievement was perceived as the ultimate goal of science.

But during the nineteenth century certain discoveries were made that seri-ously eroded confidence in the concept of an immutable world order. Jean de Monet, Chevalier de Lamarck (nineteenth-century zoologist), Thomas Robert Malthus (nineteenth-century political economist), and finally Charles Darwin (nineteenth-century naturalist) published books that either suggested or pro-posed a struggle for existence that is survived only by those organisms able to adapt to the conditions of the immediate environment. Darwin in particular developed the "theory of evolution" with which he is associated so closely today. In effect, the theory holds that:

> *many more individuals of each species are born than can possibly survive . . . consequently, there is a frequently recurring struggle for existence . . . any being, if it vary however slightly in any manner profitable to itself, under the complex and sometimes varying conditions of life, will have a better chance of surviving, and thus be naturally selected. From the strong principle of inheritance, any selected variety will tend to propagate its new and modified form (Darwin 1915 vol. 1, p. 5).*

The publication of Darwin's theory, of course, provoked a maelstrom of con-troversy. Even today, it continues to be the target of bitter attacks and recurring efforts at suppression. Nevertheless, the substance of the theory has been incor-porated into the *Weltanschauung* of Western civilization and is accepted by most educated people.

Unfortunately, we do not have the space here to accord Darwin's theory the extended discussion it deserves and can only comment on some of the theory's most significant implications for curriculum thought. Perhaps the most important of these is that *survival* becomes the criterion by which we judge the good. What this means is that

> *forms and arrangements may be judged good or bad only in relation to the environmental conditions, both physical and social, in which they are to be used. In brief, the good is no longer to be considered as absolute but merely as relative to conditions which nature provides. . . . (Thut 1957, p. 258).*[9]

A second important implication of the theory of evolution for curriculum is that *nature* determines what is good. Like the empirical realists of the previous section, evolutionists maintain that man can experience the good life only insofar as he conforms to the conditions that nature prescribes.[10] Conforming to natural necessity for the evolutionist is very much like conforming to the natural order for the realist.

Finally, we must note that the Darwinians' theory of evolution was adopted by many social scientists, who collectively developed a political philosophy which has come to be known as social Darwinism. This adaptation of the theory of evolution maintains that human society itself constitutes a form of struggle for survival and that our present social institutions are a manifestation of that struggle. Thus, as social conditions evolve, those individuals best suited to cope with them will succeed in society, while those who are less fit will fail.

The most crucial principle to be derived from the doctrine of social Darwinism is that man does not have the power to shape social conditions according to his (arbitrary) wishes; to attempt it is to invite disaster. Rather, he must accept the fact of natural necessity and align his behavior with the thrust of evolution. This, incidently, is the philosophical principle that underlies laissez-faire economics, the doctrine that the *natural* laws of supply and demand automatically regulate market forces, resulting in *optimal* levels of production, prices, and consumption (note the juxtaposition of *natural* and *good*).

A second important principle to be derived from social Darwinism is that personal and social traits of individuals and groups that are "successful"[11] are the ones that nature has obviously chosen to reward. It follows then, that their values and practices are the ones that society should strive to perpetuate. These two principles in particular have a significant impact on the curriculum advocated by the social evolutionists.

9. But still absolute in terms of the reality immanent in nature.

10. We should keep in mind that although the empirical realists and the evolutionists differ on the nature of earth-centered reality, they are in agreement with respect to the theory that reality is immanent or indwelling in this physical universe.

11. Success usually is interpreted to mean material wealth, social status, and personal influence or power.

CONTEMPORARY CURRICULAR APPLICATIONS. We should expect to find many similarities between the curriculum advocated by the empirical realists and that of the evolutionists inasmuch as both are founded in an earth-centered ontology. There are a number of differences in emphasis, however, that are well worth noting.

In discovering the knowledge of the good that should be taught to the young, the evolutionist will, of course, look to the laws of nature, but he will be especially disposed to look at those evolutionary laws that manifest themselves in successful patterns of individual and social behavior. Thus, curriculum content will center on the skills and knowledge that statistical research has found to "pay off" in the real world of (evolutionary) affairs. The justification for this method of determining curriculum content is argued in a book published in 1918 by Charles Judd, one of the more prominent advocates of social evolution. In a chapter division entitled "Systematic Studies as Devices for Facilitating Evolution of the Curriculum," he writes:

> The curriculum is to be modified and improved, with every new accession of knowledge and with every new evolution in life. . . .
>
> The purpose of scientific studies here, as in every other sphere, is to facilitate natural evolution and to give it rational guidance (Judd 1918, p. 200).

Thus, the elementary curriculum of the evolutionists emphasizes reading and spelling exercises based on words shown by statistical research to be in current use by successful adults; arithmetic problems applied to the practical aspects of successful everyday life; and speaking and writing instruction in the "correct" forms employed by the first citizens of the community. Present thrusts toward "career education" in the early elementary years which are designed to help children find their appropriate niche in the evolving social order are a manifestation of basically evolutionist assumptions.

At the secondary level, the curriculum will also emphasize the "practical" in terms of evolutionary survival in society. Practical English, business math, auto mechanics, stenography, office management, good grooming, personal budgets, family life, and the like are offered for those whose "natural abilities" suit them for survival in lower- and middle-echelon social roles. For those whose talents indicate leadership potential, the secondary curriculum offers the preprofessional training needed for survival in upper-echelon social roles. The "survival panic" triggered by the Soviets' successful launching of Sputnik in 1957 eventuated in curriculum reform that closely followed these classical evolutionist lines. Scientific and technological talent was viewed as the key to success in the evolving struggle for national survival; consequently, the early 1960s saw the development of dozens of specialized scientific curricula[12] designed to provide the talented few with the knowledge and skills America's elite needed to ensure

12. For example, SMSG, PSSC, BSCS, CHEM, etc. See "The Disciplines Design" in Chapter 17 for an extended description of the disciplines curriculum design.

national survival. Although this particular thrust has diminished somewhat with the ebbing of the cold war, other curricular developments have occurred which reflect the continuing potency of evolutionist assumptions. Now, for example, the customary single-stream "college prep" program is being divided into a number of preprofessional programs: premedicine, preteaching, preengineering, prenursing, prebusiness, and the like.[13] In these differentiated programs, students acquire relatively early the skills and knowledge needed to survive not only in their academic careers, but in the struggle for survival that is the American evolution.

The foregoing discussion suggests that earth-centered curricula, like the other-worldly ones, demonstrate intense concern for the training of an elite class, and this, of course, is the case. Since some individuals are *naturally* better endowed to survive as leaders, while others are *naturally* more suited to be followers, it seems clear that the society as a whole will benefit—i.e., experience positive and fruitful evolution—if everyone plays his *natural* role. To oppose nature in this respect only invites disaster for the society. Consequently, the aptitudes of students are of particular concern in evolutionist earth-centered curricula, and homogeneous grouping on the basis of ability (e.g., by IQ score and grade-point average) often is unequivocally specified. In addition, special programs for the "gifted," particularly accelerated curricula, often are given priority in the allocation of resources. The justification for these programs in the most simple terms is that the gifted not only become the leaders of their own generation but also, because of their superior adaptive abilities, pioneer the new values and practices that will bring society to its next higher level of social evolution.

Obviously, space limitations have made it necessary to omit a great deal from this account of the nature of knowledge and contemporary curriculum applications of earth-centered philosophies. Nevertheless, certain basic concepts treated in this section provide an essentially sound orientation to the position. In summary, we may note that earth-centered knowledge, whether based on the ontology of a static or an evolving world, is regarded as *absolute* insofar as it is derived from the indwelling reality of *this physical universe*. Thus, knowledge can be discovered by men through the use of their senses and their reason. For those who view the universe as *static*, discovered knowledge is absolute, immutable, and necessarily true for all times. For those who view the universe as *evolving*, discovered knowledge is absolute (i.e., necessarily true) within the framework of the total evolutionary process, even though it may not be valid for a particular temporal period. Thus, knowledge discovered fifty years ago would be considered absolute both for that time and for all time in terms of the totality of evolution; however, while the knowledge might not be relevant to changed conditions fifty years later, it would still be considered a necessary and unavoidable truth that had had its day during the relentless course of historical mutation.

13. This secondary curriculum design is not a speculation, but a fact. With substantial funding from state and federal sources, it is presently operative on a pilot basis in many schools.

Because reality inheres in this physical universe, and because the knowledge discovered in that source is necessarily true, man is, obviously, powerless to change it. It follows, then, that the good life can be attained only by conforming to the reality of this physical world. Knowledge of the good is equated with knowledge of nature, and wise decisions are the ones that employ discovered knowledge to bring man into the closest possible alignment with the natural order.

Finally, we should point out that earth-centered curricula, like other-worldly ones, are ordinarily differentiated so as to provide one kind of education for an elite class of leaders and another kind of education for the mass of followers. This is true whether the curriculum is based on realist or evolutionist assumptions, but it is especially true of the latter. The curriculum prescribed for the elite class of leaders generally is oriented toward the skills and knowledge needed in the discovery/decision-making process (mathematics, science, and related technological fields), while the curriculum for the masses usually is oriented toward the lower-echelon vocational-civic areas needed to produce happy and acquiescent followers.

When the humanities are included in earth-centered curricula at all, they are included for the sake of students' "cultural development" and are relegated to a peripheral position. Never are they allowed to interfere with the activities of the "regular" subjects, those subjects that deal with *reality*.

The Nature of Knowledge: Man-Centered Philosophies

Man-centered philosophies are relative newcomers to the philosophical scene. Whereas other-worldly philosophies reach back to prehistoric times, and earth-centered philosophies are rooted in pre-Christian Greece, man-centered philosophies are products of late nineteenth-century and early twentieth-century Western thought. The origin of one important branch of man-centered philosophy, pragmatism,[14] usually is attributed to two American philosophers, Charles Sanders Pierce (1839–1914) and William James (1842–1910). The source of another important man-centered philosophy, existentialism, generally is held to be a nineteenth-century Danish philosopher, Søren Kierkegaard (1813–1855). Pragmatism and existentialism are discussed individually in following sections.

Before the advent of man-centered philosophy, all philosophers, whatever their ontological preference, viewed ideas as descriptions of things that have an existence independent of human knowledge of them. Thus it was (and still is) customary among other-worldly and earth-centered philosophers to talk about the *antecedent reality* of ideas. Even today, theologians, for example, consider an idea significant or true to the extent that it corresponds to its non-

14. Pragmatism, it will be recalled, also is known by the names experimentalism and instrumentalism.

material referent in the other-world of God. Empirical realists, likewise accept the validity of an idea only to the degree that it constitutes an accurate description of a reality embedded in this physical universe. In other words, the validity of ideas in traditional philosophies (i.e., other-worldly and earth-centered philosophies) is determined principally on the basis of their *source*.

Almost as important as *source* in determining the authenticity of ideas are the *procedures employed* to arrive at them. Thus, whether knowledge is believed to be received or discovered, traditional philosophies maintain that only approved epistemological methods can produce true and valid ideas. For example, a theologian will have confidence in an idea only if it is derived by a clergyman who has spent considerable time and effort studying the sacred literature and church orthodoxy, and who, by prayer and life style, represents a reasonable candidate for received knowledge. In the same way, an empirical realist will judge an idea true and significant only if it is discovered by a trained scientist using the canons of inquiry approved by the community of leading scientists.

Thus, the philosophies we have discussed so far are, by their natures, *authoritarian*. In all cases they hold that access to knowledge of the good, and consequently the capacity to make wise decisions, is out of reach of the common man. Only the select few—that is, the *authorities*—by virtue of their special gifts for knowing, are able to make wise decisions. It follows, then, that the authorities are the ones who are best suited to design the social, political, and economic arrangements that will eventuate in the good life for all.

Man-centered philosophies break sharply with traditional ones on the philosophical issue of the antecedent validity of ideas. Pierce and James, for example, proposed that an idea should not be regarded as the description of a reality hidden from direct observation, but rather as a plan for action. The validity or truth of the idea could then be certified or repudiated depending on whether the consequences following upon the action were what they were predicted to be. Thus, as Thut (1957, p. 313) notes, ideas "would have *future* rather than *past* reference."[15] As an example, suppose that I consult a consumer guide for information regarding the quality of vacuum cleaners and find that Brand X is described as having the weight, maneuverability, and suction power that I prefer. The validity or truth of this information does not reside in its *source* (the reliability of the publisher) or in epistemological *procedures* (how the firm procured the information it published); rather, it resides in my own experience as I use the machine. In the last analysis, it is the consequences for *me* that determine whether the ideas (the information in the consumer guide) are good (true) or bad (false). This is another way of saying that knowledge of the good is constructed from experience.

We shall discuss man-centered ontologies and epistemologies in greater detail in the following sections. For the time being, however, we need only point out

15. On this point, compare the conception of scientific theory held by nineteenth-century scientists with that of contemporary scientists (such as James B. Conant) whose thought incorporates the findings of modern nuclear physics. (See "Scientific Theory and Curriculum Theory" in Chapter 4.)

that the man-centered epistemology outlined above suggests that, ultimately, the final judge of knowledge of the good is each individual human being as he experiences the consequences of ideas put into action. In short, unlike the traditional philosophies, man-centered philosophies hold that every individual is an "authority" who, through his own experience, has access to knowledge of the good. It follows from this, then, that every one of us has the capacity to make wise decisions.

PRAGMATISM

In terms of ontology, man-centered philosophies are rather close to their earth-centered cousins. At least they start out from the same point. Both agree that an other-world, whatever its nature is presumed to be, is vague and inaccessible. In the last analysis, all we really have to go on is *this* world, the physical world in which we live. But whereas the realists and evolutionists claim objective knowledge of the inherent reality of this universe, the pragmatists stop short. It is impossible, the latter claim, to extract an objective account of reality from this universe because all we really have of it, or can ever hope to have is experience: the sensations, thoughts, feelings, and actions that it evokes in us.

Because all we can ever hope to know firsthand is raw experience, we must, say the pragmatists, be satisfied with *it* as the stuff of reality. Since the transcendent realms of other-worldly philosophies are unknowable, we really cannot say whether they exist or not. Likewise, the "real" world of earth-centered philosophies is out of reach, and unknowable. Undoubtedly, something *is* "out there," but its true essence is forever beyond us because we are condemned by our very natures to "know" it only as appearances filtered through experiences. In short, "our *conception* of reality, resulting from careful inquiry, is as close to reality as we can ever hope to get. Let us call it reality and be done" (Morris 1961, p. 71). In the pragmatist ontology, then, reality is neither an other-world nor this world; it is human experience.

Although pragmatists propose human experience as the ultimate in ontological reality, they are somewhat uncomfortable about ontological discussions, and if given a choice, would probably prefer to avoid them. This is easy to understand when we consider that experience, even though the word is a *noun,* is not a substantive noun. That is, it is not a "thing," like an *other-world* or a *physical universe,* but rather a process or activity. Experience really means something that is more like an active "experience-*ing,*" and it is probably wrong to try to conceptualize it in terms of an existential substance.

The basic structure of our language is at least partly to blame for this problem because it teaches us to expect nouns to be "things" and verbs to be "actions."[16] For this reason, nouns that are really "actions" give us trouble. The best we can do at this point, then, is simply to observe that traditional

16. See the section "Language" in Chapter 7 for a discussion of the limitations of language on thought processes.

philosophies tend to view reality as *noun* or *subject*, while pragmatism assigns it *verb* or *predicate* status (Morris, 1961, p. 72). Given this fluid, moving, ongoing, process ontology, the philosophy of pragmatism probably is best argued on epistemological grounds, where the *process* of knowing (i.e., experiencing) becomes a primary consideration.

PRAGMATIST EPISTEMOLOGY. Pragmatist epistemology is built on the concept of *transaction*. Essentially, a transaction is a reciprocal exchange in which an individual does something to the environment and the environment responds by doing something back to him. For example, an individual may plant some seeds, and the environment "responds" by growing flowers; or he may turn up the thermostat, and the environment "responds" by raising the room temperature. In short, a transaction involves phenomena in which the individual *acts* and then undergoes the *consequences* of his action. Where it all starts (i.e., who actually initiates the transaction) we need not go into here. For example, a prior environment of cold air was probably responsible for the action (or "reaction") noted above of turning the thermostat up.[17] Suffice it to say that, for the pragmatist, the process of everyday living constitutes an ongoing stream of transactions between individual and environment.

Transactions, clearly, are occurring for all of us every minute of our lives. Even an involuntary sneeze to which the environment responds by removing a tickle in the nose may be considered a transaction of sorts. But the transactions of primary interest to pragmatists are those in which individuals associate their intentional actions with particular *wanted* consequences. In other words, pragmatist epistemology is concerned with actions deliberately taken because certain wanted consequences can reasonably be anticipated to follow. It is in transactions such as these that *intelligence* is said to operate. In fact, pragmatists *define* intelligence as the degree to which individuals comprehend at increasingly sophisticated levels the connections that exist between their actions and the environment's response (i.e., the *consequences* of the action). The systematic application of intelligence as it is defined above is clearly desirable because it minimizes the unwanted random effects of unintended chance transactions and maximizes the control we have over our lives.

So far so good. But what, you may ask, is the criterion by which pragmatists judge the *desirability* of "wanted" consequences? Which consequences, in other words, represent knowledge of the good? In all fairness, it must be noted that this question strikes at a critical weakness of pragmatist epistemology.

The pragmatist is most likely to respond to the above question with: "The most desirable consequence is the one that works best at a particular point in time." But if experience serves us at all, we know that there is likely to be substantial disagreement among individuals over "what works best," and therefore which of many alternatives is the "good" consequence. For pragmatists, the

17. See "The Problems of Ends and Means" in Chapter 13 for a discussion of cause-effect relationships.

only reasonable response to this problem is the democratic one. At any given point in time, a consensus of informed opinion is most likely to produce a good choice as to which consequence is the most desirable. But as we have previously seen, "popularity polls" are often bad bases for decision making. Overwhelming majorities have often been dead wrong! Of course, the pragmatists would argue that considering the human condition and the nature of our existence, it is the best method we have. And in a way, the pragmatists are right. Man-centered ontologies cannot logically be expected to produce *absolute* criteria for judging knowledge of the good, and it should not surprise us, therefore, that pragmatism is as *relativistic* as it is in the establishment of criteria.

The foregoing discussion points up three other important characteristics of pragmatism's version of knowledge of the good. In the first place, pragmatist knowledge is held to be only *tentatively* true. The phrase "at a particular point in time" in the preceding paragraph indicates this quality. Because knowledge is founded in experience, it is always subject to revision and even rejection in the light of subsequent experience. Second, pragmatist knowledge generally has a social reference. Because democratic consensus is the basic criterion for truth, it is in the social arena that the validity of pragmatic knowledge is established. Finally, pragmatist knowledge is neither *received* nor *discovered*, but rather *constructed*. It is constructed because it is derived from human experience. When we select one idea (i.e., plan of action) over another because it produces preferred consequences in experience, we are in effect constructing certain environmental conditions which would not have been produced had we acted otherwise. This implies that the universe (as it is appropriated through experience) is not the determined absolutely final affair that it is in otherworldly and earth-centered philosophies. Rather, it is not yet finished; it is an open-ended enterprise that within limits can become whatever we want it to become. Through reflective thought—the application of intelligence—man has it within his power to construct the conditions of his future life. Obviously, then, the major task of the curriculum is to develop intelligence.

CONTEMPORARY CURRICULAR APPLICATIONS. Historically, the progressive movement of the post-World War I era best represents the curricular applications of pragmatist philosophy. "The Corporate State: Curriculum from World War I to Mid-Century," a section of Chapter 3, describes a large number of curriculum practices which, in the light of our present discussion, can be directly tied to pragmatist principles. For example, it was noted in Chapter 3 that the curriculum aims of individual growth coupled with democratic social competence were high on the progressive's list. These aims, of course, reflect the emphasis on individual experience and democratic decision making that characterize pragmatist epistemology. In the following paragraphs we shall highlight only a few of the most important curricular applications that most obviously reflect the principles and assumptions of pragmatism.

If knowledge of the good is constructed out of intelligent transactions with the environment, we should expect to find the "learning of truth" that character-ized traditional curricula supplanted by "learning intelligent transacting" in the pragmatist curriculum. And indeed, it turns out that for the pragmatist, the cur-riculum does not focus on a body of subject matter to be learned, but rather on a series of activities through which the student "experiences," and thus is led to construct his own "reality" of the world.[18]

The above position suggests that *process* is most important in pragmatist curricula, and therefore, subject matters that are most fluid (i.e., least "estab-lished" and "still in the making") will be emphasized. Given a choice, for example, between chemistry and economics, the pragmatist would undoubtedly choose the latter. It is not that he scorns highly warranted knowledge; but he believes that students need to be impressed with (1) the *process* of making knowledge and (2) the *tentative* nature of *all* knowledge. The trouble with traditional curricula, he holds, is that knowledge is taught as though it were absolutely certain, true, and final.

If we add to this bent for *process* the pragmatist's preference for a *social* reference, it is not surprising that the *social studies* by far and away constitute the most important "subject" of the pragmatist curriculum. Indeed, "social studies" (a plastic blend of history, economics, sociology, anthropology, political science, ethics, psychology, etc.) are in a sense the hallmark of the pragmatist curriculum. Such unification of diverse subjects into a single study is particu-larly characteristic of more radical pragmatist pedagogy. Theoretically, all of the disciplines simply constitute special resources for the study of the single most important "subject": living. Thus, education for pragmatists is not a preparation for life, but life itself.

Although the pragmatist might develop a social studies curriculum around such courses as Civics, Problems of Democracy, Adolescent Problems, and Social Living, often the single rubric "Social Studies" is employed to designate a fluid course which deals with a variety of relevant individual/social problems. Sub-ject matter is a very important aspect of the course work, but it is never included simply to be learned for its own sake. Data, information, concepts, facts, etc., are important only insofar as they contribute to intelligence, *i.e.*, the ability to think reflectively about ideas and their consequences. Thus, students are en-couraged to use subject matter in school projects which focus on social problems in need of solution (e.g., crime, poverty, delinquency, women's rights, and war). Indeed, a pragmatist curriculum often is composed mainly of an inven-tory of relevant topical social problems along with suggestions for projects which will actively involve students in practicing the skills needed to arrive at solu-tions. Among the skills that interest the pragmatist most are those on which intelligent transacting depends: reading, writing, personal relations, listening

18. This emphasis has led to the criticism that pragmatist curricula are weak in terms of "solid content." Content is extremely important in pragmatist curriculum making, but it is utilized in reorganized (i.e., nondisciplinary) forms that are intended to coincide with learners' experience.

(and hearing), speaking, computation, question asking, problem formulating, data gathering, data selection, inference drawing, etc.

In many instances, problems to be studied will not be prescribed in advance. Rather, they will be determined by the students themselves. That is, the problems, in accord with pragmatist epistemological assumptions, will grow out of the experience (i.e., the "reality") of the particular group to be educated.

While social studies constitutes the core of the curriculum, science is also an important subject for pragmatists. Indeed, it is viewed as a critical resource for the study of many social problems (e.g., pollution, natural ecology, energy crisis, space priorities, etc.). But the conviction that *all* knowledge is tentative leads pragmatists to avoid teaching the "facts" of science as established truths (see, for example, the realists on this point), and to emphasize the *process* of constructing scientific knowledge.

Art and music also are included in the pragmatists' curriculum. In line with their epistemological assumptions, they emphasize not only the aesthetic experience to be gained from these subjects, but the public airing of the quality of that experience in the interest of establishing, by democratic consensus, reasonable canons of taste. Chronological history, Latin, abstract algebra, and other "dead" subjects generally are omitted from the pragmatist curriculum unless requested by students for whom they may be of particular interest.

In summary, we may say that the pragmatist curriculum is "learner centered," process oriented, and emphasizes student activities in the core subject of the social studies. Subject matter ordinarily is selected on the criteria of (1) students' capacity to derive meaning from it (i.e., incorporate it into their experience), and (2) its usefulness in problem-solving projects. Finally the pragmatist curriculum is the vehicle which fosters students' growth in intelligence—i.e., the capacity to construct knowledge of the good for wise decision making in life.

EXISTENTIALISM

The significance of existentialism for curriculum is problematical, first because it is so recent an arrival on the philosophical scene, and second because it is primarily concerned with the *individual*, while education is essentially a *social* process. Moreover, it has been suggested that, strictly speaking, existentialism does not even qualify as a philosophy, but is rather merely an "attitude toward life." The doctrines of existentialism, however, are no less intriguing for these reasons, and we shall find its basic assumptions highly suggestive of radically new directions in curriculum construction.

Traditional philosophies for centuries have been concerned with the question: "What is the nature of man?" Finding an answer to the question of man's essence would obviously shed a great deal of light on what properly constitutes the good life. But for the existentialist, this is the wrong question to ask. If Descartes (seventeenth-century rationalist philosopher) based his philosophy on the irreducible premise, *"Cogito ergo sum"* (I think, therefore I am), the existentialist begins with the premise, "I am, therefore I think." This is the existentialist's way of saying that man does not have a prior nature. Rather, his primary property is *existence*. First, the existentialist declares, man *is*; only afterward, over the course of his life, by virtue of how he chooses to live it, does his essence evolve. In short, for the existentialist, existence precedes essence; man is "thrown into existence," and then defines himself through the choices that he makes.

Ultimately, existentialism holds, man cannot relieve himself of the responsibility for choosing, and in so choosing, defining himself. Even a rejection of this position constitutes a choice. For example, if an individual claims that he is not free to choose because his life is "determined" by a large number of external factors such as social class, geographical location, economic status, etc., the existentialist would respond: "You are free whether you think you are or not. You have freely chosen to deny your freedom. And this says something about your nature as a human being." This argument, it should be noted, is remarkably similar to the point previously made with respect to the basic assumption of all beliefs and philosophies: ultimately, they reflect an "act of faith": a freely taken, arbitrary choice.

Thus, existentialist ontology places ultimate reality "within the self of the individual human person" (Morris 1961, p. 76). In the last analysis, whether we act on reason or emotion is a matter of individual choice; whether we act on principle or expediency is a matter of individual choice; and whether we make judgments on the basis of other-worldly, earth-centered, or man-centered assumptions is a matter of individual choice. In short, when all of the baggage of "civilization"—law, morality, science, religion, education, etc.—"have been stripped away, there stand you and I, our choosing selves naked before a cosmos of alternatives, trying . . . to give . . . essence to the Idea of Man" (Morris 1961, p. 76).

The notion that ultimate reality is *self* places a terrible burden on every individual. Not only is he "alone" in the universe, the only "reality" with which he is in complete touch, but he has sole responsibility for the nature of that reality. He *is* and he is *becoming* at one and the same time. Morris expresses this predicament probingly and succinctly: "Reality in Existential language is 'self-operating-in-cosmos-of choice' or simply 'self-choosing.' There is a sly double-entendre here. For not only is the self choosing, but it is choosing *itself*; that is, it is choosing . . . what a human being is . . ." (Morris 1961, p. 77). Clearly, existentialist choice is not a matter to be lightly taken; it is always a heavily *moral* enterprise.

In opting for an ontology of self-choosing, existentialism, like pragmatism, clearly rejects traditional philosophy's concept that the cosmos is a finished and final reality. Rather, it views man and the world as an open-ended, becoming enterprise. Furthermore, existential philosophy rejects the authoritarianism of other-worldly and earth-centered philosophies and places decision-making power directly in the hands of every individual. This power, however, is accompanied in existentialism with strong and insistent warnings that every individual is personally responsible for the decisions he makes.[19]

If reality resides within the individual self, existential knowledge of the good obviously will be something very close to self-knowledge. As a result, a good deal of existential literature deals with this complicated, special kind of subjective personal knowledge. Although we cannot hope to do justice to it here, the following brief discussion should provide some basis for understanding existential epistemology.

Existentialism posits two basic modes of knowing: *objective* and *subjective*. In most instances we are involved with the first, a knowing, awareness, or consciousness of the external world. For example, we are aware of a book, an automobile, the law of gravity, or H_2O existing "out there." These "facts" simply *are*, and our consciousness of them is essentially separate from *ourselves*. That is to say, we know them in a "scientific" sense. On the other hand, during those relatively less frequent periods when we become conscious of our own *consciousness* of these "facts," we are suddenly aware of our own being, our feeling, our knowing. This knowledge, according to existential epistemology, is personal and *subjective*, that is, it puts the individual in touch with himself and his nature or essence. In a word, it constitutes his awareness of his own being.

While *objective* or scientific knowledge is "public" and can be understood by anyone who possesses the necessary "qualifications" (e.g., that H_2O is the chemical composition of water), *subjective* knowledge is unique to each knowing individual. Only John, for example, can know what the fact of H_2O means *subjectively* to him, just as only John can know what it means to be John.

As the foregoing discussion unquestionably demonstrates, the meaning of existential subjective knowing is difficult to communicate. One might even claim with justification that it is by definition undefinable (in rational-objective terms). Perhaps it is possible only to *suggest* its meaning: "[It] is *awareness*, a kind of total feeling-tone which is simply had by the individual" (Morris 1961, p. 170). Or: "Existential knowledge is 'intuitive.' It is 'humane.' It originates in, and is composed of, what exists in the individual's consciousness and feelings as a result of his experiences . . ." (Kneller 1958, p. 59). These observations indicate that existential knowledge, whatever else it may be, at least can be characterized as affective-intuitive and highly moral in nature.

Given an ontology of self and an epistemology of subjective self-knowledge, it follows that the criterion for validity of knowledge can only be the individual self, i.e., personal choice: "the validity of knowledge is determined by its value to the individual. The teacher therefore . . . should cultivate in himself the awareness that all human situations are different . . ." (Kneller 1958, p. 59).

Although existentialism warrants a far more extensive discussion than we have been able to provide here, we must now turn to the curricular applications

19. While pragmatists would certainly hold individuals responsible for decisions, their criterion of social-group consensus can substantially mitigate the grinding weight of *sole* responsibility that existentialists insist upon.

of this most individual and personal of all philosophies with the expectation that they will represent radical departures from the familiar practices of present-day schools.

CONTEMPORARY CURRICULAR APPLICATIONS. The existential attitude has manifested itself in actual curriculum practice only very recently, and quite sporadically at that, although it appears to be gaining supporters in education as time goes on. "Mini-courses" (especially in the arts), sensitivity training, and transcendental meditation[20] are examples of contemporary public school curriculum reform efforts that have existential overtones. Moreover, existential tendencies are evident in the curriculum of such movements as the British infant school, the so-called free schools and universities, and what currently is passing for "open education" and "the open classroom."

Although it would be a presumption to infer a total curriculum solely on the basis of existential principles as we presently understand them, it *is* possible to document some of the important features that such a curriculum would probably evidence. Since existentialism is a philosophy of self, we should not be surprised to find its curriculum intensively focused on the individual, his self-knowledge, and his self-choosing. The subject matters best suited to this emphasis, of course, are the arts. Thus, painting, music, sculpture, literature, poetry, dance, drama, and the like, are given a central position in the existentialist curriculum because they foster human introspection and the expression of the innermost consciousness of self. Too, it is these subjects that encourage choice based on private judgments of value and meaning. The curriculum will *not* be concerned with the study of artistic masterpieces in these areas, but rather with students' own creation of paintings, sculptures, poems, stories, essays, plays, songs, dances, etc. Nor will the students' artistic products be subject to evaluation. Viewed as the public expression of private consciousness, their function is to put the students in touch with their selves, and evaluation, of course, would destroy this intent.

The existential curriculum will have particular significance at the secondary level. It is at this level, we know, that learners ordinarily reach puberty and the so-called adolescent stage of development. Adolescence, viewed as a psycho-social phenomenon, often is defined as *"the period during which a young person learns who he is, and what he really feels"* (Friedenberg 1959, p. 29). Student needs and interests during this period of development, therefore, would seem to coincide perfectly with existential curriculum aims. Thus, the existential curriculum maker properly will look to his adolescent charges for substantial guidance in his professional task.

We saw that choosing and the responsibility for choices were important aspects of existential philosophy. Consequently, the existential curriculum will not only *allow* learners a plethora of choices, but *insist* on their being made, and students will be given virtually free rein in the selection of curriculum content and activities. Although this principle can very easily lead to a laissez-

20. See Driscoll (1972).

faire, "anything goes" climate in the school, the strict existentialist would claim that the corollary of free choice—moral responsibility—will, if insisted upon, prevent the eventuality of chaos.

Choices involving self, of course, are choices involving real life. It follows, then, that the existentialist curriculum will attempt to involve students in real-life choice situations, particularly those concerned with the moral aspects of existence. Moreover, because existential choices are intuitive, choices based on a rational analysis of the situation will be discouraged in favor of choices based on affect or feelings. Of course, as the student makes his choices he is engaging in the process of defining himself, i.e., determining his own nature as a human being. A typical "involving" existential curriculum might include the study of each individual's responsibility for such conditions as: the spending of billions on military armaments while millions of people are literally starving to death; support of corrupt neofascist regimes on the political justification that it inhibits the spread of communism; the desecration of millions of acres by strip mining for "industrial progress"; and billions spent on cosmetics, deodorants, and electrical gadgets, while schools, libraries, museums, and the performing arts exist in poverty and manage only the most precarious survival.

It should be noted that a rational analysis of these topics often leads to a "practical" conclusion that is diametrically opposed to the conclusion which is based on intuition or emotion. For the existentialist, of course, it is the latter conclusion that is to be trusted, since it is the one that is based on knowledge of the good. This final observation is an appropriate one with which to close this section on man-centered philosophies, for it clearly demonstrates the conviction that decisions based on knowledge *constructed* by individuals are the wise ones that ultimately lead to the good life.

References

Darwin, Charles. 1915. *The Origin of Species*. New York: Appleton-Century-Crofts.

Driscoll, Francis. 1972. "T[ranscendental] M[editation] as a Secondary School Subject." *Phi Delta Kappan* (December).

Friedenberg, Edgar Z. 1959. *The Vanishing Adolescent*. New York: Dell Publishing Company.

Jowett, B., trans. 1899. *The Works of Plato*. New York: The Dial Press.

Judd, Charles Hubbard. 1918. *Introduction to the Scientific Study of Education*. Boston: Ginn & Company.

Kneller, George F. 1958. *Existentialism and Education*. New York: John Wiley & Sons.

Morris, Van Cleve. 1961. *Philosophy and the American School*. Boston: Houghton Mifflin Company.

Spencer, Herbert. 1885. *Education: Intellectual, Moral and Physical*. New York: John B. Alden, Publisher.

Thut, I. N. 1957. *The Story of Education*. New York: McGraw-Hill Book Company.

CHAPTER 7
SOCIETY AND CULTURE:
BASIC CONSIDERATIONS

Environments are not passive wrappings, but are, rather, active processes which are invisible. The groundrules, pervasive structure, and over-all patterns of environments elude easy perception.

—MARSHALL MCLUHAN

As we saw in Chapters 2 and 3, which dealt with the historical evolution of the curriculum, schools do not exist in a vacuum. The character of the culture that provides their context influences to an extremely high degree the nature and organization of curriculum objectives, content, learning activities, and evaluation. Indeed, Mauritz Johnson (1967, pp. 131, 132), even though he has restricted his conception of curriculum to include only "a structured series of intended learning outcomes," notes that "the source of curriculum—the *only possible source*—is the *total available culture*." (italics added).

The importance of culture in the study of curriculum is underlined further when we note the consistency with which writers on curriculum (and on many other aspects of education) have raised what has become a perennial, if somewhat fruitless, question: "Should the curriculum be designed primarily to transmit the culture to the young or to foster their individual development?" Without commenting either on the meaning or the validity of this question now (we will do so in a later chapter), we may point out that its prevalence in one form or another in the literature demonstrates that the study of curriculum *implies* the study of society and culture.

Society and Culture Distinguished

A society is a collection of individuals who have organized themselves into a distinct group. To be a society, however, a *distinct group* and not just a collection of individuals, the members of the group must perceive themselves as "having things in common" which enable them to "belong." These "things in common" are the stuff of which culture is made. Culture, then, may roughly be viewed as a kind of social cement that consists of the characteristic habits, ideals, attitudes, beliefs, and ways of thinking of a particular group of people. Even from these sketchy definitions it is clear that while society and culture are certainly not the same thing, "without a culture there could be no society, and without a society there could be no culture" (Smith, Stanley, and Shores 1957, p. 4).

Complexity of the Concept "Culture"

Culture is a highly complex concept that requires a great deal more consideration and study than we are able to allow for here; it is similar to such concepts as "democracy," "morality," and "love," which have a multiplicity of meanings and connotations that go well beyond any definitions that dictionaries are able to provide. However, some generalizations, while somewhat oversimplified, can be made.

In relatively broad terms we might say that culture defines an accepted way of life: it includes a vast array of easily observed facets of living, such as material products, political and social organizations, characteristic vocations, modes of dress, foods, games, music, child-rearing practices, and religious and patriotic rituals. But such visible factors as these represent only the top of an immense iceberg. The most powerful controlling aspects of a culture tend to be submerged and not easily brought to view for examination, especially by members of the culture under examination. This submerged or hidden aspect of a culture (what has been called the "psychology" of a society) consists of an interlocking fabric of ideas, ideals, beliefs, values, assumptions, and modes of thought that individuals in the social group adhere to at the "gut level." It is these visceral, and largely unconscious, dispositions that govern not only behavior, but the very *Weltansicht* (world view) of members of the social group. While this notion of unconscious culturally induced bias is not new, its enormous power to control human behavior has become increasingly evident over the past few decades. The well-known anthropologist Ruth Benedict, for example, was well aware of the power of culture as an invisible controlling force when she wrote:

> No man ever looks at the world with pristine eyes. He sees it edited by a definite set of customs and ways of thinking. Even in his philosophical probings he cannot go beyond these stereotypes; his very concepts of the true and the false will still have reference to his particular traditional

customs. John Dewey has said in all seriousness that the part played by custom in shaping the behaviour of the individual as over against any way in which he can affect traditional custom, is as the proportion of the total vocabulary of his mother tongue over against those words of his own baby talk that are taken up into the vernacular of his family (Benedict 1934, p. 2).

Culture, then is clearly much more than the sum of a set of institutions, customs, and beliefs. In a very real sense it comprises a significant—perhaps the *most* significant—part of an individual's environment, impinging upon and limiting his behavior even as the physical force of gravity or the lack of a set of wings limits his ability to fly. And while differences in beliefs and/or conflicting beliefs may tend, to a greater or a lesser degree, to produce multiple subgroupings within a society, the dominant culture functions to preserve social order by delimiting the range of possibilities for individual behavior and development.

But a culture is a ruthlessly deterministic and limiting force only to the degree that individuals and social groups are unaware of its operation. To the degree that education illuminates the culture, that is, reveals to us the submerged bases of our beliefs, to that degree we are freer to shape that culture—and our lives. "There is absolutely no inevitability as long as there is a willingness to contemplate what is happening" (McLuhan and Fiore 1967, p. 25). Clearly, then, the best curriculum designer will be the one who best understands the complex ways in which culture shapes ideas.

The Structure of Culture

In Chapter 4, a structural framework was proposed for the purpose of facilitating the study of curriculum. This theoretical model was based upon a classification of the total curricular phenomenon into a complex of eight interrelated factors.[1] In much the same way, the study of culture will be facilitated if we are able to proceed upon the basis of an hypothetical structural framework. One useful framework, proposed by Ralph Linton (1936), is presented here because of its simplicity and its congruence with the theoretical constructs of society and culture that we have been developing.

Linton has proposed that all elements of culture can be classified into three principal categories: (1) Universals, (2) Specialities, and (3) Alternatives.

The *Universals*, he says, comprise those values, beliefs, and customs that are generally held by the entire adult population. For example, in a wide variety of instances, behavior in such areas as language, foods, religion, and economics tend to be rather circumscribed in our society. We speak English (not French or Hindi), eat beef (not horse meat or lizard), believe in *some* God (not atheism), and champion free-enterprise capitalism (not socialism). Of course,

1. Epistemology, Society/Culture, The Individual, Learning Theory, Aims, Content, Learning Activities, and Evaluation.

some variation within the broad categories is sanctioned, but in most specific instances taboos are extremely explicit, and sometimes brutal social sanctions are imposed upon those who deviate from Universals. Universals, of course, are only necessarily universal within the context of a given culture; between cultures, Universals can be quite different. In our culture, for example, inges- tion can be, and in most instances is, considered a social function (we are sympathetic with the person who must dine alone). Excretion, however, is never so viewed among Americans today, but in ancient Rome the exercise of this biological function was commonly regarded as a fine opportunity for socializing.

Specialties, the second category identified by Linton, includes those elements of the culture to be found only within subgroups of the society. Among the most common of these are the vocational subgroups; in our society certain be- haviors are expected of professors, for example, that are quite different from those expected of businessmen. Thus, professors are expected to be shabbily dressed *thinkers*, leftish in their politics, absentminded, and impossibly imprac- tical in worldly affairs; businessmen, by contrast, tend to be viewed as smartly dressed *doers*, conservative in their politics, mentally alert, well organized, efficient, and practical.

The relatively large number of vocational Specialties in our society has gen- erated a wide variety of behavioral expectations, values, and beliefs that are characteristic of individals within each Specialty.

Another important basis for classification according to Specialty is social class. Clearly, the beliefs and behavior repertoire of the extremely wealthy—the socio- economic elite—are quite different from those peculiar to the middle, lower middle, or lower social classes. Each class, even allowing for the inevitable overlapping that occurs between them, tends to have ways of thinking, valuing, and behaving that we all "know" are typical of the group.

These two categories, vocation and social class, by no means exhaust all of the bases on which Specialties are maintained by subgroups of a society,[2] but they do demonstrate Linton's rationale for the existence of beliefs and attitudes that are held only by the individuals of certain subgroups of society.

Linton's third grouping of cultural elements, the *Alternatives*, are those beliefs and practices that violate culturally accepted norms (Universals and Specialties) in their attempt to fill a need, solve a problem, or simply to allow a more con- gruent perception of reality. Alternatives are like Specialties in that they are not shared by all members of the society; unlike Specialties, however, they may not be shared by *any* recognized subgroup. A simple, tangible example of an Alternative might be the introduction of pizza in place of the traditional ham- burger as an after-movie snack. Of course, while pizza after the movies may have been an Alternative twenty years ago, today it shares with the hamburger the dignity of very nearly being a Universal.

On a more serious, intangible, and global level is a cluster of attitudes and values commonly associated with a certain subgroup of young people, a charac-

---

2. Some other bases for cultural Specialties are religion, sex, age, and ethnic background.

teristic point of view called the "counterculture" or "the new morality" (more fully discussed below). This cluster of attitudes would represent a group of Alternatives that collectively constitute an entirely new *Weltansicht*.

One important point to be made about Alternatives is that they are distinguished from Universals and Specialties by virtue of the fact that they offer the members of society a choice. In relation to the previous section, which examined the notion of unconscious culturally induced bias, we may note here that if a choice between a Universal and an Alternative is to be made intelligently, both options will have to be made explicit and examined in the full light of consciousness. As we shall see, this is by no means as easy as it appears.

Since curriculum workers and teachers are in the business of intervening in the lives of young people for the purpose of making them something that they would not otherwise become, it is necessary not only that they have full and conscious knowledge of cultural Universals and Specialities, but that they evaluate these and compare them with all manner of Alternatives. Current practice, however, consists mainly of accepting cultural directives and transmitting them through the curriculum as efficiently as possible. This procedure, of course, constitutes little more than mindless indoctrination. To *educate*, on the other hand, calls for a curriculum that promotes the illumination, examination, and evaluation of cultural Universals and Specialties in the light of projected desirable Alternatives. As we shall see in the following sections, breaking out of the cultural trap is a long, demanding process requiring substantial quantities of both wisdom and courage.

Culture and Values

We have noted that culture defines an accepted way of life. One implication of this statement, of course, is that the "accepted" way of life is the preferred way; that is, the "accepted" way of life has more "value" than other, alternative ways. If, as we have noted in Chapter 5, philosophy inquires into the question "What is the good life?" culture, it would seem, purports to provide the Answer—with a capital *A*.

Thus, we can see that culture is a "value-loaded" enterprise, so to speak. It provides the members of society with the "goods" and the "bads," the "beautifuls" and the "uglies," the "shoulds" and the "should nots."

Like the concept of "culture," "value" is a deceptively complex notion. One of the greatest difficulties with this idea lies in the area of interpreting with accuracy the nature of the values held by an individual or a society. Van Cleve Morris (1961, p. 220) for example, raises the question, "How do you tell what a person values—from what he says or from what he does?" Charles Morris (1956) attempts to deal with the difficulty by proposing a distinction between *conceived* values, (the values that people *say* or *think* they believe in), and *operative* values (those values that are implicit in the way they behave). But even this distinction has its difficulties. Many people, for example, *really believe* what they say their values are, and when discrepancies in observable conduct are pointed out, beg pardon for behaving in a way "that was not intended." Thus, we often excuse a person for an act if he can convince us that he did not mean to do it.

> *A Catholic priest in confession can excuse sinful acts if the suppliant can prove that his intentions were good. We sometimes say, in other connections, that such-and-such a person is mean, greedy, or rude, but that "his heart is in the right place" or "he means well." What this suggests is that what he does is not so reliable a measure of his values as what he believes "down deep inside" (Morris 1961, p. 221).*

In spite of this disposition to treat an individual charitably on the basis of "good intentions," the force of the old adage "Actions speak louder than words" is difficult to avoid, especially when we are dealing in a collective way with the values of a culture. Thus, when a society like our own proclaims "liberty and justice for all" over a history of more than 200 years, we cannot help questioning the culture's *real* value commitment when we observe the long-term abuse to which some 200 millions of its black- and red-skinned citizens have been subjected.

Raymond Muessig has documented what he perceives as significant and persistent incongruities between what Americans *say* and how they *behave* in conducting their secondary schools. His essay deals with three conceived American democratic values: (1) the dignity and worth of the individual human personality, (2) faith in intelligence and the rational capacity of man, and (3) freedom with responsibility. We need cite only a short excerpt from the section on the dignity and worth of the individual to make our point:

> *for a significant number of our students a feeling of dignity and worth in a school milieu is an unknown or rare experience. Standing and esteem have been withheld from . . . youth who are from low income situations; who are "culturally deprived"; who are members of identifiable minority groups; who are "slow learners"; who are not "properly motivated"; who have emotional or "adjustment" problems; or who are "different" in other ways (Muessig 1968, p. 27).*

And yet, ironically, practically every curriculum includes a statement of philosophy that professes in glowing terms its earnest concern for the dignity and worth of each and every student.

In another place,[3] the conceived-operative discrepancy is expressed somewhat more succinctly and picturesquely: In this article Edgar Friedenberg is said to have noted that school personnel have not yet absorbed the basic lesson taught to the staff of every decent hotel: "Don't insult the clientele." It is interesting that the *Times* article goes on to observe, "This may not be entirely fair; none of the teachers and administrators *mean* to insult the children . . ." (italics added).

---

3. *The New York Times*, March 23, 1969.

It might be pointed out at this juncture that the notion of conceived versus operative values is congruent with the theoretical construct of culture developed in the preceding section. We noted there that some of the most forceful aspects of culture were submerged, so to speak, and we characterized these as a complex of values called "unconscious culturally induced bias." Thus, those operative values that are implied by overt behavior and are different from the conceived values professed by the behaver may be viewed within the framework of unconscious culturally induced bias. While such an analysis is certainly not the case in all instances of individual behavior, the relationship of conceived-operative values and unconscious cultural bias will provide us with a very useful tool in the analysis of culture.

Aspects of Culturally Induced Bias

In a previous section we observed that culture comprises a significant portion of our environment and therefore serves, to a remarkable degree, to define the terms on which individuals are permitted to deal with the activities of daily life. In this section we shall examine in more detail some concepts that may help us to better understand the complexities of the total phenomenon of culture.

"NORMAL" PERSONALITY AND CULTURAL RELATIVITY

To say that culture defines an acceptable way of life is to imply that culture is the shaper of personality; for is it not the case that the life style followed by an individual is the basis we use to draw conclusions about his character and his personality? Thus, each culture aims at producing in every member of the society an "ideal type"—that is, the adult who theoretically reflects a culturally perfect configuration of values, characteristics, attitudes, and behaviors in his personality. A curriculum usually is judged "good," then, to the extent that it produces large numbers of individuals whose personalities enable them to fit into and function well in the existing society; it is judged "bad," on the other hand, to the extent that it develops individuals whose personalities deviate significantly enough from the norm to generate "problems" for the society.

While the "ideal type" never is found in any society (because of the existence of "individual differences"), cultural standardization of personality occurs frequently enough so that we are easily able to identify the "normal" personality, that configuration of personality traits that is shared by most members of the society. Indeed, a number of anthropologists and social psychologists have established the practice of empirically studying "national character structures"—that is, the characteristic personalities of such national social groups as the British, German, and Japanese; and students of culture and personality are careful to make the distinction between "social character" (those personality traits shared in common by members of a society), and "individual personality" (those personality traits that distinguish members of a society from one another). Of course, as we noted in our discussion of the concept of Universals, "ideal" and "normal" as we are using the terms here, have meaning only within the context of a particular society. Furthermore, we should bear in mind that this anthropological concept of "normal" personality is only one way of dealing with the problem of personality and provides an interesting contrast to the individualistic theories of human nature and personality development that underlie the psychologies discussed in Chapters 9 and 10.

In her classic study of cultural relativity, Benedict writes:

> *It is in cultural life as it is in speech; selection is the prime necessity. The numbers of sounds that can be produced by our vocal chords and our oral and nasal cavities are practically unlimited.*
>
> *In a culture too we must imagine a great arc on which are ranged the possible interests provided either by the human age-cycle or by the environment or by man's various activities. A culture that capitalized even a considerable proportion of these would be as unintelligible as a language that used all the clicks, all the glottal stops, all the labials, dentals, sibilants, and gutterals from voiceless to voiced and from oral to nasal (Benedict 1934, pp. 21, 22).*

Thus, Benedict lays the foundation for her comparison of three primitive cultures, each as different from the other as it is from our own; and her study shows how, by selecting for approval only a limited number of an almost infinite range of possible behaviors, various cultures produce dramatically dissimilar "normal" personalities. To help us to understand the conditions of this phenomenon we will briefly examine the cultures of two societies described by Benedict: the Pueblos of New Mexico, and the Dobuans of the South Pacific.

Benedict describes the Pueblo Indians of New Mexico as a people who are mild, nonviolent, unemotional, moderate, self-effacing, cooperative, and community—rather than individualistically—centered. In the Pueblo society, personal ambition and individual achievement are disparaged. Even in games or contests, if a man wins consistently, he is barred from further participation; the Pueblos are interested only in activities in which many can participate with an equal chance.

This disapproval of the assertion of personal authority is manifested in a number of ways: the phrase "a leader of his people" is attributed scornfully to individuals who seek power; folktales tell of "good men" who were unwilling to take office; and even in domestic situations, the culture does not recognize authority as vested in the father, who would never think of disciplining his children. Occasions that call for the exercise of authority are simply not allowed to arise.

The absence of the exercise of personal authority is complemented in this culture by the submergence of the individual in the group. Responsibility and power are always distributed, and the individual looks to the constituted forms of society, the formal structure, for the filling of his needs. Groups of men jointly cultivate the fields and store the harvest in collective storerooms. And if a man is worried about the harvest, he does not offer a prayer for rain, but joins in the community rain dances. This society's approach to life is so oriented to group action that Benedict (1934, p. 96) has felt it necessary to comment, "their whole orientation of personal activity is unfamiliar to us."

The effect of this culture has been to produce a "normal" individual who is self-effacing and cooperative; he avoids office, conflict, and violence, and never manifests a trace of arrogance or strong emotion. How would this culture deal with a personality that deviated from such a norm? How would it respond, for example, to an individual who, in the American tradition, was ambitious, a "go-getter," an individual who manifested so many of the traits that we admire in a "leader"? Of course, he would receive censure, but more significantly he would very likely be persecuted for sorcery, and indeed such a personality often *has* been treated in this way. It is interesting to note here that historically the charge of witchcraft is the basis on which less "sophisticated" societies deal with the condition of personality deviance that we more familiarly identify as neurosis, psychosis, or insanity.

Let us now examine the culture of the inhabitants of Dobu, an island off the southern shore of eastern New Guinea. Life on these south sea islands provides a great contrast with the commitment to cooperation and moderation found among the Pueblos.

> *Life in Dobu fosters extreme forms of animosity and malignancy. . . . The Dobuan lives out without repression man's worst nightmares of the ill-will of the universe, and according to his view of life virtue consists in selecting a victim upon whom he can vent the malignancy he attributes alike to human society and to the powers of nature. All existence appears to him as a cut-throat struggle in which deadly antagonists are pitted against one another in a contest for each one of the goods of life. Suspicion and cruelty are his trusted weapons in the strife and he gives no mercy, as he asks none (Benedict 1934, p. 159).*

The self-interest, suspicion, ill will, and hostility of Dobuan culture are evident even in the relationships engendered in marriage. Quarrels between husband and wife recur constantly, obscene abuse is mutual, and faithlessness is an expected condition of matrimony. Since adultery is a favorite pastime, the atmosphere is rife with tension and suspicion. The offended partner is likely to bribe his own, or any other, children for information. If it is the husband who is the victim, he breaks his wife's cooking pots; if the wife, she abuses her husband's dog. They quarrel violently, and when the situation reaches intolerable proportions one or another attempts suicide. Although the attempt is rarely successful, it serves to ameliorate the dispute—not as the result of love-induced regret or remorse, but out of fear of what the attempted suicide's outraged family might do to avenge itself on the one responsible for driving a relation to do away with himself or herself. The partners in the marriage now are angrily and sullenly reconciled. Needless to say, broken marriages are common on Dobu.

The malevolence of Dobuans is nowhere more evident than in the character of their magical incantations, which play an enormous role in their lives. Every Dobuan "owns" at least one, and as many as five, "charms," which are designed to bring disease or death to his enemies. "Whoever has elephantiasis or scrofula knows at whose door to lay it. The charms make the owner powerful and are greatly coveted" (Benedict 1934, p. 137).

But murder is not restricted to magical means. Suspicion of poison is widespread, and "no woman leaves her cooking pot untended lest someone gain access to it" (Benedict 1934, p. 153). Thus, Dobuans try out poisons as they do their incantations. Benedict relates the story of a young man who gave an account of his experiments with a poison his father had told him about. He tried it on a child, who died. The child was his cousin, the orphaned daughter of his father's sister, whom his father had earlier poisoned in the same way. Asked why his father had poisoned his own sister, the young man replied, "She bewitched my father. He felt weak. He killed her and his body grew strong again" (Benedict 1934, p. 153).

It is not surprising in the light of the culture, then, that the "normal" Dobuan tends to exhibit an extreme dourness. He is consumed with jealousy, suspicion, resentment. He feels himself "good" insofar as he is able to survive his encounter with a malicious world and at the same time attain some degree of prosperity. It is assumed, of course, that in order to do this he has been successful as a cheat, a thief, or worse. He feels himself "bad," by contrast, insofar as it is he who has been injured, whether physically or in fortune, in his conflicts with other people, since they have been able to gain the advantage over him. Finally, our "normal" Dobuan is treacherous. He does not invite disaster by challenging or insulting his adversaries. He is polite and unctuous. "If we wish to kill a man we approach him, we eat, drink, sleep, work and rest with him, it may be for several moons. We bide our time. We call him friend" (Benedict 1934, p. 157).

In contrast to the "normal" personality projected by the assumptions and values underlying Pueblo culture, the "normal" Dobuan is quite another kind of person. The "normal" Dobuan, however, would certainly not be considered at all "normal" by the Pueblos in New Mexico. Indeed, he would be considered mentally ill—psychopathological in the extreme. Of course, the Pueblos would be using "normal" in a value-loaded sense that Benedict and the cultural anthropologists never intended. For the Pueblos, in this instance, "normal" would be equated with "desirable" or "good," while "abnormal," or mentally ill would be equated with "undesirable" or "bad." For Benedict, however, "normal" simply means "according to a type or pattern," and carries no connotation of worth.

What, then, does this suggest about people whom we consider either "normal" or "mentally ill" in our own culture? Is it possible for us to take the anthropologists' relatively value-free position? Or are we forced to make a value judgment? Is it impossible to say that anyone, in an absolute, not relativistic sense, is mentally ill? Or can we judge such-and-such a syndrome of character traits to represent psychopathology regardless of the culture? And do these questions not imply value judgments applied to the culture as a whole?

Erich Fromm has dealt with this difficult issue of normal personality and cultural relativity in his essay "The Sick Individual and the Sick Society." Fromm (1969, p. 134) points out that for the psychoanalyst Freud, mental illness was an individual pathology, an imbalance of id and ego. In most cases we know that our society deals with mental illness in much the same way—that is, as an individual condition. The standards for behavior set by our society are rarely questioned; usually, only the degree to which an individual patient is well adjusted to cultural demands is considered. (As we noted earlier in this section, this individualistic viewpoint provides an important additional dimension to our understanding of the relationship of the individual to society and is discussed in Chapters 9 and 10.)

But Fromm (1969, p. 134) goes on to point out that for the social philosopher Marx, the essential psychological illness was a pathology common to society and resulting from the institutions of that society. Thus, Marx raises the point that the criteria for "normal" or "healthy" personality go *beyond* the culture. He might ask, for example: How "normal" or "healthy" is a personality that is well adjusted to, and functions well in, a fascist society like Nazi Germany of the 1930s?

It would seem that it is simply not enough to be aware of cultural relativity and the relationship of culture to "normal" personality. We find that, in fact, we cannot avoid the value questions that many students of comparative cultures have consciously refused to ask. What is the preferred "normal" personality? Or, since anthropology has demonstrated that "normal" personality and culture are reciprocal, what is the preferred culture?

These are indeed crucial questions for designers of curriculum, for unless one is willing to take refuge in the position that curriculum should simply function as the transmitter of the existent culture, he is forced to launch an intensive inquiry into the basis of cultural values. This is no easy task. "There is no royal road to social understanding . . . . There is only the way of hard work, intensive study, thinking to the bottom of things" (Rugg 1939, p. 7). At the same time, there is no more crucial job in the entire educational enterprise, for in a very real sense a school curriculum is the shaper of human destiny.

LANGUAGE

We have already pointed out that culture consists of the entire fabric of characteristic ideas, habits, customs, values, and ways of thinking of a particular group of people and that these factors not only delimit the behaviors permissible in dealing with the environment, but indeed operate as the shaper of individuals' perception of the nature of reality (*Weltansicht*). Research in linguistic science over the past several decades has shown that language is a particularly significant aspect of culture, not so much because it operates as a vehicle for the expression of cultural ideas, but because it operates in extremely subtle and powerful ways as the very shaper of those ideas. This point is particularly significant in view of the fact that there exist in the world more than 2000 language systems. To see how language functions in this regard, we shall take a look at some of the work of Benjamin Lee Whorf, an articulate writer in the area of cultural linguistics.

Whorf (1956) begins by pointing out that if a rule has no exceptions, it is not recognized as a rule at all; that is, if it is impossible to contrast a given condition with an interruption of its regularity, we are not apt to isolate and thereby consciously experience the condition. It is somewhat like not realizing the existence of air until we are somehow prevented from breathing it.

In much the same way, we might note that the law of gravity could not have been formulated until astronomy and other sciences had discovered that bodies did not always fall, but moved in orbits, or in other ways. (This principle, it will be noted, is quite analogous to the one suggested in the section on cultural relativity: People tend to view their culture as representing a "natural" or "universal" way of life until they experience interruptions of that mode, that is, until they become aware of other cultures and those cultures' ways of dealing with social existence.)

But in most cultures (even sophisticated ones like our own, which concede the principle of cultural relativity), the phenomenon of language is unperceived and beyond the critical consciousness of the ordinary speaker. If the fact of language is brought to his attention, it is viewed as functioning primarily in a background capacity, that is, as a passive vehicle for expressing "pure" or "universal" thoughts that occur prior to, and independent of, their expressed forms. But could it be that our thoughts—our ideas, philosophies, and logics—are to a large degree an extension of the language we speak? Could it be that our very *Weltansicht* is conditioned by the structure (grammar) of our language?

Whorf is very illuminating along these lines when he compares basic structures in English with those of some unrelated languages. He notes that in English most words are divided into two basic classes: nouns (like "house" and "man") and verbs (like "hit" and "run"). Such a structure, he points out, yields an essentially bipolar division of nature; that is, a division of nature into long-lasting or stable events (nouns) and short-term or temporary events (verbs). But is nature really so polarized?

> If it be said that "strike, turn, run," are verbs because they denote temporary or short-lasting events, i.e., actions, why then is "fist" a noun? It also is a temporary event. Why are "lightening, spark, wave, eddy, pulsation, flame, storm, phase, cycle, spasm, noise, emotion" nouns? They are temporary events. If "man" and "house" are nouns because they are long-lasting and stable events, i.e., things, what then are "keep, adhere, extend, project, continue, persist, grow, dwell," and so on doing among the verbs? If it be objected that "possess, adhere" are verbs because they are

stable relationships rather than stable percepts, why then should "equilib-rium, pressure, current, peace, group, nation, society, tribe, sister," or any kinship term be among the nouns? (Whorf 1956, p. 215).

Thus, he concludes that it is not possible to define such words as "event," "thing," "object," or "relationship" from nature, but that the definition of such terms always involves a "circuitous return to the grammatical categories of the definer's language" (Whorf 1956, p. 215). Our dissection of reality into "sub-stantives" in "action" is essentially a linguistic process!

In contrast to this dualistic analysis of nature into "things" and "events" im-posed by English and the Indo-European languages, Nootka, a language of Vancouver Island, has only one class of words, which seem to us to be verbs, but which are really not analogous to any category of our language. To say "house" in Nootka translates something like "a house occurs" or "it houses"; and suffixes of the word denoting the "house event" allows expressions for "long-lasting house, temporary house, future house, house that used to be, what started out to be a house," and so on (Whorf 1956, p. 216). Thus, the one-class structure of words in this language yields a monistic view of the world.

In a similar way, the language of the Hopi Indians imposes a strikingly dif-ferent interpretation of certain aspects of experience than does English. For example, English verbs are inflected so that they convey essentially three prin-cipal divisions of temporal meaning: past, present, and future. And speakers of English (as well as other similar Indo-European languages) project a meta-physics of "time" that is one dimensional (linear) and that flows perpetually and uniformly from the future, into the present, and back into the past.

Hopi verbs, by contrast, have no tenses. (They have, rather, such categories as "assertion," "mode," and "status," which we need not, for our purposes, go into here.) Indeed, the Hopi language contains "no word, grammatical forms, constructions or expressions that refer directly to what we call 'time,' or to past, present, or future . . ." (Whorf 1956, p. 57). Thus, the Hopi, *approxi-mately,* sees "time" as circular rather than linear in nature, and views tomorrow as the return of light in a light/dark cycle. In fact, however, it would be im-possible for the Hopi to translate our notion of time into Hopi consciousness, just as it is impossible for us to conceive of the "time"-less metaphysic of Hopi without some understanding of his language forms.

What does this mean for curriculum designers? It means, in short, that we are now in a position where we can at least *concede* the relativistic basis of our viewpoint, even though we may not be able really to *conceive* the viewpoint of the other culture (unless, of course, we understand its language). But this in itself is quite an important step, for there now exists the possibility of over-coming in some degree those unperceived but inexorable patterns of language that channel our thoughts and mold our consciousness.

The analysis of culture is an important prior (and concomitant) activity of the curriculum designer. If the analysis is to be sophisticated and rigorous, it will have to take into account the biases imposed by the language of the culture.

This means that students of curriculum need to be conversant with the linguistic processes of their own language and have access to contemporary discoveries in cultural linguistics.

MEDIA

Media, defined as the technology employed to move information, generally are recognized as being crucial to the functioning of all societies. Most commonly thought of as radio, motion pictures, and television, media also include such technology as print, telephones, phonographs, photographs, bicycles, automobiles, and airplanes.

Until recently, it has been widely assumed that media were neutral conveyors of information, that is, that the medium and the message were two quite separate and distinct entities. But about a decade ago a professor named Marshall McLuhan gained international prominence when he proclaimed to the world that "the medium is the message."

Startling and perceptive as this alliterative slogan appears, however, we are in a position to note that its insight is not entirely original. What McLuhan was saying about media was the same thing that linguists and anthropologists had already observed about language and culture (two forms of media in their own right): that is, that many aspects of our environment—like language, media, and culture—are composed partly of pervasive invisible forces that shape and control human ideas and behavior.

As McLuhan puts it, media "massages" us, works us over by altering the environment and evoking in us unique ratios of sense perceptions (McLuhan and Fiore 1967, p. 41). For example:

> The dominant organ of sensory and social orientation in pre-alphabet socities was the ear—"hearing was believing." . . .
>
> Until writing was invented, man lived in acoustic space: boundless, directionless, horizonless, in the dark of the mind, in the world of emotion, by primordial intuition, by terror. . . .
>
> The phonetic alphabet forced the magic world of the ear to yield to the neutral world of the eye. . . .
>
> The goose quill put an end to talk. It abolished mystery . . . [it] fostered and encouraged the habit of perceiving all environment in visual and spatial terms—particularly in terms of a space and of a time that are uniform,
>
> c,o,n,t,i,n,u,o,u,s
and
c-o-n-n-e-c-t-e-d
>
> (McLuhan and Fiore 1967, pp. 44–48).

Perhaps most important for students of curriculum is McLuhan's comparative analysis of the effects of print and electronic media, for our society is clearly in the midst of a revolution in communications technology.

According to McLuhan, the print medium is a "ditto device" which confirms the visual stress of written language. Like writing, it fragments wholes into sequential, linear, mechanical representations (for example, compare the totality of perceiving a flower concurrently through the senses of sight, touch, and smell with reading a description of these sensations in a book). So thoroughly has this print-oriented analysis of reality permeated our consciousness that we have based our entire *Weltansicht* on it. Indeed, McLuhan claims, logic has come to depend so heavily on the visual representation that we equate "rational" with "uniform, continuous, and sequential."

Another effect of print technology is that it brought into common use the conveniently portable book, which is ordinarily read in isolation from others. Thus, print encouraged detachment, individualism, and the private point of view; it created a "public" of "separate individuals walking around with separate, fixed points of view" (McLuhan and Fiore 1967, p. 68).

By contrast, McLuhan says that the media of electric circuitry have created a "mass"—a world of interdependent participants, a world that he calls "the global village." This condition has been brought about largely by television, which "demands participation and involvement in depth of the whole being" (McLuhan and Fiore 1967, p. 125). This involvement is not limited to the visual, but draws upon a wide range of senses and emotions. It recognizes the fact, lost to the print-oriented response, that much of conscious experience has little "visuality" in it. McLuhan cites the TV broadcast of President Kennedy's funeral as the event that demonstrated the power of this medium to draw an entire world population into total participation in a common experience.

Although the full effect of television is impossible for us to grasp at this time, the medium clearly presents us with stimuli that are beyond anything we have experienced before.

If print media project a fragmented, linear, and sequential image of reality, television offers "mosaic" *gestalt* states. Thus, "story lines" lose their importance, and "linear" TV programming (for example, old movies) proves unacceptable to young audiences weaned on the mosaic zooms and flashes that make up commercials and antilinear shows such as "Rowan and Martin's Laugh In" and "Monty Python's Flying Circus." Also, instantaneous electronic media have the effect of pouring out upon us such vast quantities of information that it is impossible to classify and structure them block upon block as we have been used to doing with print-fed information. This condition has led to the observation that today's television children, who are accustomed to processing (in novel ways) mosaic masses of adult information, are bewildered when they enter the print-centered culture of the school "where information is scarce but ordered and structured by fragmented, classified patterns, subjects, and schedules" (McLuhan and Fiore 1967, p. 18).

Incomplete as this account of McLuhan's thesis is, it provides us with additional insight into the way in which we structure meanings from the data that flow in upon our senses. According to McLuhan, many of us are perceiving our electric age through a "rear-view mirror"—that is, in terms of the sense balance and assumptions of print-culture perception. We are "numb, deaf, blind, and mute" about the encounter of instantaneous electric circuitry with the Gutenberg technology (McLuhan 1964, p. 32).

Many of our young people and students, however, born into the world of electronic media, may literally "see" things differently. They have "naturally imbibed an urge toward involvement in depth . . . the total involvement in all-inclusive *nowness* that occurs in young lives via TV's mosaic image" (McLuhan 1964, p. 292). Adequate understanding of this condition and of its relevance for education can only occur if curriculum workers open themselves to experience alternatives and embark on the imaginative reorganization of their perceptual equipment.

SOCIAL-PSYCHOLOGICAL FACTORS THAT RESULT IN CULTURALLY INDUCED BIAS

The research of social psychologists has demonstrated that there are a number of conditions in the interplay of man and his culture that result in his receiving a distorted impression of many of the situations that he encounters in daily life. These situations are perceived in such a way that they are "worked over," so to speak, so that they will take on the configuration that we think they ought to have. Of course, man has long been aware of the fact that he often perceives his world inaccurately, especially in situations where egocentric motivations like pride play a role. A perfect example of this realization occurs in Robert Burns's famous lines:

> O wad some power the giftie gie us
> To see oursel's as ithers see us!

However, most of us are under the impression that we view situations in a reasonably accurate way. This may not be the case at all.

In an important study of the cultural basis of human perception, Klineberg (1964, pp. 90–99) reviews some of the factors that contribute to our inability to view our environment accurately. For example, he points out that *we perceive according to our training and previous experience.* Thus, the auto mechanic is able to detect irregularities in the sound of an engine that simply are not heard by the average layman; and the orchestra conductor agitatedly halts a rehearsal for errors in tone or rhythm that are undetectable to the casual listener. On a more significant level, this factor operates in the value arena. For example, our past experience leads us to reject horses as acceptable food, while pigs, utterly repugnant to some societies, are quite suitable for even the most delicate of dining situations. Odors regarded as pleasant in some societies are disagreeable in others. Our current fetishization of deodorants is an example of recent training in the unpleasantness of the human scent. And finally, we may note that European men have not been taught by experience or training that underarm or leg hair on women is unsightly; thus, unlike their American sisters, European women need not subject themselves to the additional cosmetic chore of shaving.

Klineberg also notes that *we perceive according to our expectations.* Everyone is familiar with errors in proofreading that occur because we expect to see a word spelled correctly, even though it is not. In a similar way, a mother often "hears" her baby cry when it does not; or, because she expects it to wake soon, hears its cry, though everyone else, preoccupied with reading or conversation, hears nothing. The "halo effect" in the grading of themes is a perennially bothersome instance of this phenomenon, and our expectations with regard to the behavior of people whom we have stereotyped leads us to perceive in them traits that they never possessed.

Related to "expecting" is *"wanting,"* and Klineberg points out that many errors in perception are due to this phenomenon of wish fulfillment. A recent experience of mine clearly demonstrates this phenomenon. After some fourteen hours of driving on a superhighway, my wife and I were quite anxious to arrive at the "Kent Exit" and home. On two separate occasions both of us misperceived road signs that read "Next Exit 5 Miles" as "Kent Exit 5 Miles." Klineberg (1964, p. 91) reports abundant psychological research that demonstrates the influence of wishes in distorting perception. One experiment involved ambiguous drawings that were presented both to a group of hungry college students and to a group that had just eaten. The hungry students tended to perceive the drawings as such food objects as sandwiches, salads, and roasts; no such effect was found among the other students. In another experiment school children were asked to judge how well some of their classmates performed certain exercises. Often, classmates whom they liked were reported to be superior, even when the opposite was true. Finally, we are all aware of the honest errors in perception that occur among the supporters of one or another of competing baseball teams. This effect of wishes, of course, is the reason that we need umpires.

A fourth factor that alters our perception is *the influence of other people.* A number of experiments have been done that demonstrate that individuals will deny the evidence of their own senses in order to bring their judgment of relatively simple data, such as the length of a line, into agreement with that of the group. Of course, as we noted in our previous discussion of culture, the pressure for conformity is always present, and most of us, because of the desire to "belong" or to be "accepted," tend to hold beliefs that coincide with those of the group. A dangerous situation occurs, however, when the group consumes its constitutent members, as in the case of a witchhunt or a lynch mob. The important points to be made here, however, are that (1) the tendency toward conformity can, and often does, result in major distortion of perception; and (2) only to the degree that we are *aware* of its operation can we correct for it. The same points, of course, should be made for training, expectations, and wishes, the other social-psychological phenomena discussed above. Thus, if unconscious culturally induced bias is to be mitigated, we will need to be aware not only of its existence, but of the ways in which it operates.

At least two other concepts related to the problem we have been dealing with are worth mentioning: egocentric perception and the self-fulfilling prophesy.

Egocentric perception is the tendency to perceive situations in terms of one's own personal ethnic, vocational, socioeconomic, or national identification—that is, in terms of one's own particular set of needs, values, beliefs, expectations, and ideals. Such a point of view, of course, is what makes it possible for a forty-five-year-old teacher and a sixteen-year-old student to look at the same set of circumstances and see things so differently.

What are the possibilities of avoiding such situations? Osgood (in Klineberg 1964, p. 96) has proposed a hierarchy of three levels of social thinking:

1. We unconsciously project our own frame of reference onto others (as when the individual with beard, long hair, and guitar berates the crew-cut "straight" person as being "unliberated").

2. We recognize the relativistic nature of the other person's frame of reference, but not our own. (The essence of this stage of social thinking is revealed in the story of the Christian missionary who headed a group of workers sent to the Orient to proselytize the Buddhists there. At one of their first meetings he told his workers that they must not become impatient with the Buddhists if they did not accept the true religion without resistance; after all, they were all born and brought up in the Buddhist tradition. The irony, of course, is that the missionary saw quite clearly the cultural basis of the Buddhists' belief, but viewed his own as somehow *naturally* true and valid.)

3. We recognize the equally relativistic nature of all frames of reference, including our own. (This point of view is an extremely difficult one to achieve, but unless some general progress in this direction is made among people and cultures, no curriculum that transcends the parochialism of enculturation is possible).

The other related concept, that of the self-fulfilling prophecy, suggests a process that is particularly insidious because it results in the creation and validation of situations that are *believed* to exist, but which never, in fact, did exist. Thus, the way in which people *define* a situation is in many instances more important than the "real" nature of existent conditions since the action that follows is based upon perception rather than the fact.

The remarkable degree to which the self-fulfilling prophesy operates in all spheres of human activity has been well documented in the literatures of the social and behavioral sciences. Rosenthal and Jacobson (1968) report a number that are worth recounting here.

In one study involving the effects of placebos, the female subjects participating in the experiment were divided into three groups. One group of women was given the contraceptive pill and warned that they might expect some unpleasant side effects with its use. A second group was given a placebo with the same warning. (Both groups were asked to continue using their usual method of contraception during the experiment.) The third group was given the oral contraceptive, but without the warning of unpleasant side effects. About 6 percent of the women in this "unwarned" group reported side reactions such as nausea, vomiting, and headache. But *three times* as many women in each of the first two "warned" groups reported such effects. It did not make any difference that one group did not take the real contraceptive. The women who received the placebo with a warning reported unpleasant side effects as often as those who were administered the real pill with the warning.

In another study, conducted by Rosenthal and Fode, two groups of psychology students were each assigned thirty laboratory rats and asked to teach these rats to run the darker of two arms of an elevated T-shaped maze. The students were told that maze brightness and maze dullness could be genetically developed by successively inbreeding generations of well-performing and poorly- performing rats. One group of students was told they had been assigned thirty "bright" rats, the other group thirty "dull" rats. In fact, sixty ordinary laboratory rats had been randomly divided among the two groups.

The results were remarkable. The rats believed to be "gifted" consistently performed better than those thought by their teachers to be "disadvantaged," in most cases at a statistically significant level. Furthermore, the teachers who believed that they were working with "bright" rats rated their animals as "brighter, more pleasant, and more likeable." These same teachers also reported that they felt "more relaxed in their contacts with the animals" and described their behavior toward them as "more pleasant, friendly, and enthusiastic" (Rosenthal and Jacobson 1968, p. 38).

Finally, *Pygmalion in the Classroom*, Rosenthal and Jacobson's major study of teacher expectations makes a great contribution to the literature dealing with the phenomenon of the self-fulfilling prophesy.[4] This study, conducted in a south San Francisco public elementary school, has special relevance for curriculum theory and practice because it deals with the effects of the self-fulfilling prophesy on intelligence and learning. The authors began by administering an ordinary, relatively nonverbal standardized intelligence test to all students from kindergarten through grade 5. They then told the school's teachers that what they had given the students was the new "Harvard Test of Inflected Acquisition," an instrument that was designed to predict academic "blooming" or "spurting." They further informed the teachers that on the basis of this new test, about 20 percent of the students in their classes could be expected to show significant gains in intellectual ability during the school year. Each teacher was

---

4. While this study has generally received favorable response in the popular press (e.g., *San Francisco Chronicle, Saturday Review,* and *Time*) and in some professional publications (e.g., *Personnel and Guidance Journal,* February 1969), the research has been subjected to substantial criticism in the professional literature. Indeed, Thorndike (1968, p. 708) has written, "it is so defective technically that one can only regret that it ever got beyond the eyes of the original investigator!" Taken as a whole, however, the criticism does not so much refute the central conclusions drawn in the study as to suggest that "the expectancy factor subsumed in the experimenter bias effect is not as pervasive as the earlier work of Rosenthal and the *Pygmalion* manuscript would have us believe" (Gephart and Antonoplos 1969). Despite its technical defects, therefore, the study may be accepted as supporting the theory of the self-fulfilling prophesy, though not in the magnitude to which its authors suggest. In addition to the citations noted above, other sources critical of the *Pygmalion* study include: Barber et al. (1969) (the issue includes a rebuttal by Rosenthal and answer to the rebuttal by Barber); and Buckley (1968).

given the names of those children who were "identified by the test" as academic "spurters." In fact, the names given to the teachers had been selected by means of a table of random numbers, so that as the authors point out, "The difference between the children earmarked for intellectual growth and the undesignated control children was in the mind of the teacher" (Rosenthal and Jacobson 1968, p. 70).

About eight months after the teachers had been told they could expect certain of their students to be "spurters," the same intelligence test that was initially administered to all the students was given again. Children in both the experimental and control groups scored higher, but, especially in the first and second grades, "spurters" scored significantly higher than the "ordinary" students.

Table 7-1 shows that while only 5 percent of the "ordinary" children gained at least 30 IQ points, four times as many—or 21 percent—of those believed to be "spurters" gained this many points. Such a difference could occur by chance alone in only four cases out of a hundred. The results obtained with lower levels of IQ gain are less startling, but no less significant. More than twice as many of the "spurters" as ordinary children gained at least 20 IQ points and 30 percent more of the "spurters" than "ordinary" children gained at least 10 IQ points.

TABLE 7-1
*Percentages of First and Second Graders Gaining at Least
10, 20, or 30 Total IQ Points*

IQ Gain at Least	"Ordinary" Group	"Spurters"	Probability
30	5%	21%	.04
20	19	47	.01
10	49	79	.02

Source: Adapted from Rosenthal and Jacobson (1968, p. 76).

The design of the study, of course, is more complex than is indicated in this account, and the data far more extensive than we can report here. Nevertheless, while the findings associated with other aspects of the study are sometimes less dramatic than those which are reported above, they still tend to confirm the theory of the self-fulfilling prophesy.

What are the possible explanations for this phenomenon? The authors, of course, can only speculate:

> *we may say that by what she said, by how and when she said it, by her facial expressions, postures, and perhaps her touch, the teacher may have communicated to the children of the experimental group that she expected improved intellectual performance. Such communications together with possible changes in teaching techniques may have helped the child learn by changing his self-concept, his expectations of his own behavior,*

and his motivation, as well as his cognitive style and skills (Rosenthal and Jacobson 1968, p. 180).

The significance of *belief* in the shaping of human destiny is nowhere more startlingly demonstrated than in the functioning of the self-fulfilling prophesy. And since, as we have seen is often the case, belief results from unconscious culturally induced bias, we become more convinced than ever that without an increasingly intensified study of culture, we can never hope that school curriculum will be more than a cultural rubber stamp.

Values, Culturally Induced Bias, and the Curriculum

The previous sections have sought to demonstrate that societies perpetuate themselves by implanting values in a variety of subtle psychological ways that result in unconscious culturally induced bias. The effects of this bias on school curriculum are revealed, however, only when the curriculum is examined reflectively by individuals who are to some degree aware of the "massaging" nature of cultural processes. A few examples of the connection between cultural bias and curriculum practice will demonstrate this point.

Sex roles sanctioned by American society have long held that "the woman's place is in the home" and that woman's work be limited to cooking, housekeeping, child rearing, and other domestic tasks. Women doctors might be tolerated oddities if they specialized in gynecology or pediatrics, but a female surgeon was almost unthinkable; and women as engineers, airline pilots, business executives, or school superintendents were virtually beyond consideration. This unconscious (and rationally unwarranted) bias concerning sex roles has become clear on a broad scale, however, only as social change has induced a reexamination of traditional attitudes. As a result, the role of curriculum in supporting and perpetuating the bias has just recently been disclosed. Studies have shown that school texts, almost without exception, portray females as wives concerned mainly with the mundane tasks of homemaking, while their male counterparts occupy themselves with a wide variety of socially constructive, and often glamorous, activities. In terms of program, home economics has traditionally been a "girl's subject," while industrial arts was reserved for boys, even after the male/female division of labor was no longer a functional arrangement in our rapidly expanding technological society. It now seems clear to most people, however, that males need to know how to shop for food and clothing and how to prepare meals, just as females need to know how to replace a light switch and use a hammer. Many other instances of how the curriculum reinforces cultural bias as it relates to sex roles could be cited and explored at some length.[5] The important point, however, is that, even though some change

5. For example, in physical education, English for girls/science for boys, career counseling, etc. It is also interesting to note instances of reverse discrimination: boys have systematically been discouraged from pursuing careers in nursing.

presently is taking place, the school curriculum has been deeply implicated in the uncritical perpetuation of unconscious cultural bias; it has changed only in response to forceful legal pressures; and, even today, curriculum personnel resist change proposed on the basis of sound cultural analysis, mindlessly citing unexamined cultural directives to justify the status quo.

Another example of the presence of unconscious cultural bias in the curriculum has to do with the role of blacks in American society. Before the advent of the civil rights movement of the 1960s, blacks were generally an "invisible" subgroup in the society. Mainstream America knew that they were present, of course, but they were regarded as less than human, somewhat akin to animated fixtures—washing floors, working the cotton fields, shining shoes, tap dancing, or occasionally achieving notoriety in a bizarre profession, such as Joe Louis as the heavyweight boxing champion. Rarely were blacks thought of as thinking, feeling, human personalities who had mothers and fathers, who fell in love, got married, and reared families in home environments similar to those of whites. (It was a time when the armed services were strictly segregated and big league baseball was lily white.)

As has long since been pointed out, school texts of his period supported total black invisibility. With the possible exception of a brief statement in high school history texts to the effect that George Washington Carver made peanut butter (an interesting curiosity), the existence of the black minority virtually was ignored. In the critical early elementary grades, not only was the content of reading texts exclusively white, but geography materials further dehumanized blacks by citing the unimportance and backwardness of their African origins. Far from constituting a deliberate and malicious policy. of repression (as is sometimes claimed), this condition merely represented the curricular manifestation of unexamined cultural bias. Substantial change has taken place over the past two decades, of course; but it is worthwhile to point out that it has occurred in response to often violent social change rather than to the reasoned examination of submerged cultural attitudes.

Our final example of unconscious cultural bias in the curriculum has to do with nationalist sentiment. Of course, we live in a world of nation-states, and the virtual universality of this present-day world-political arrangement makes it appear "natural" and desirable, indeed beyond question. But the tensions and wars propagated by nationalism, the threat of nuclear war, the relative success of such nonnational systems as the feudal order of the Middle Ages, and some of the alternative international systems[6] proposed in recent decades suggest that other, unconsidered systems of world organization may be preferable (if not necessary). The fact that alternatives to the present arrangement all seem so impractical, idealistic, and utopian is probably a tribute to the enculturating power of national societies and their schools. As we have demonstrated in the previous section, *belief* plays a startlingly powerful role in the

6. See Falk and Mendlovitz (1966).

shaping of human destiny. Thus, belief supports system, which conditions belief, which maintains system, which supports belief, ad infinitum.

In what ways do school curricula reinforce the belief that nationalism is the natural and preferred system of world government? First of all (and chiefly), by their admitted cultivation (or inculcation) of "patriotism." Now it is very difficult to argue against patriotism since doing so casts one in the role of "traitor," or at least of subversive. Patriotism, after all, involves loyalty to one's own group and this value often brings out the best in us. But there are various ways of perceiving patriotism, and the argument being made here is that, unfortunately, school curricula, reflecting unconscious national cultural bias, presents the concept meanly—as blind attachment to national cultural values, uncritical conformity to prevailing social mores, and, most importantly, rejection of other nations as outgroups. In fact, our schools do not teach patriotism (in its best sense) so much as they teach chauvinistic nationalism.

The teaching of nationalism begins in the early elementary grades with lessons on the flag, perhaps a pledge of allegiance, national heroes (e.g., Washington and Lincoln), early national mythology (in American schools, for example, stories about the Pilgrims, the Revolution, and "the winning of the West"), and so on. In the later elementary grades we find that nationalism permeates a great deal of the curriculum in reading, history, geography, and literature. Indeed, a number of studies based on the content of school texts show not only the cultivation of noncritical patriotism, but the perpetuation of national stereotypes. For example, Walworth (1938) examined the treatment of the same wars and battles by American writers and by those of certain former enemy countries (e.g., Britain, Spain, Mexico, and Germany). He found that the authors in all countries generally agree that the leaders of their own countries were honorable and their soldiers noble and courageous. When they were defeated, it was the result of the overwhelming force of the enemy. The enemy, on the other hand, was pictured as treacherous and cowardly. Such stereotyping, obviously, reinforces an extremely narrow nationalist point of view and helps to render the consideration of an international stance virtually unthinkable.

Of course, changes in cultural attitudes toward international cooperation have occurred in recent years. American-Soviet détente is one of the most tangible indications of this change. Some schools have reflected these new attitudes by implementing programs of international and cross-cultural education. But the nationalistic structure of world cultures is still such that the delegation of even the most inconsequential national prerogatives to a multinational governing body is presently beyond serious consideration.

References

Barber, Theodore X., et al. 1969. "Five Attempts to Replicate the Experimental Bias Effect." *Journal of Consulting and Clinical Psychology,* Vol. 33, No. 1.

Benedict, Ruth. 1934. *Patterns of Culture.* Boston: Houghton Mifflin Company. Reprinted by Mentor Books, 1950.

Buckley, James J. 1968. "Who Is Pygmalion, Which Is Galatea." *Phi Delta Kappan* (October).

Falk, Richard, and Saul Mendlovitz, eds. 1966. *A Strategy of World Order*. New York: World Law Fund.

Fromm, Erich. 1969. "The Sick Individual and the Sick Society." In *Selected Educational Heresies*, edited by William F. O'Neill. Glenview, Ill.: Scott, Foresman and Company.

Gephart, William J., and Daniel P. Antonoplos. 1969. "The Effects of Expectancy and Other Research-Biasing Factors." *Phi Delta Kappan* (June).

Johnson, Mauritz. 1967. "Definitions and Models in Curriculum Theory." *Educational Theory* (April).

Klineberg, Otto. 1964. *The Human Dimension in International Relations*. New York: Holt, Rinehart and Winston.

Linton, Ralph. 1936. *The Study of Man*. New York: Appleton-Century-Crofts.

McLuhan, Marshall. 1954. *Understanding Media*. New York: Signet Books.

———, and Quentin Fiore. 1967. *The Medium is the Massage*. New York: Bantam Books.

Morris, Charles W. 1956. *Varieties of Human Value*. Chicago: University of Chicago Press.

Morris, Van Cleve. 1961. *Philosophy and the American School*. Boston: Houghton Mifflin Company.

Muessig, Raymond H. 1968. "Youth Education: A Social-Philosophical Perspective." In *Youth Education: Problems/Perspectives/Promises*, edited by Raymond H. Muessig. Yearbook. Washington, D. C.: The Association for Supervision and Curriculum Development.

Rosenthal, Robert, and Lenore Jacobson. 1968. *Pygmalion in the Classroom*. New York: Holt, Rinehart and Winston.

Rugg, Harold. 1939. "The Culture and the Curriculum." In *Democracy and the Curriculum. The Life and Program of the American School*, edited by Harold Rugg. Third Yearbook of the John Dewey Society. New York: Appleton-Century-Crofts, chap. 1.

Smith, B. Othanel, William O. Stanley, and J. Harlan Shores. 1957. *Fundamentals of Curriculum Development*. Rev. ed. New York: Harcourt Brace Jovanovich.

Thorndike, Robert. 1968. Book Review. *American Educational Research Journal* (November).

Walworth, A. 1938. *School Histories at War*. Cambridge, Mass.: Harvard University Press.

Whorf, Benjamin Lee. 1956. *Language, Thought, and Reality. Selected Writings of Benjamin Lee Whorf*. Edited by John B. Carroll. Cambridge, Mass.: The M.I.T. Press.

CHAPTER 8
SOCIETY AND CULTURE: CONTEMPORARY AMERICAN PATTERNS AND PROBLEMS

From the dictum that the life and program of the new school must be designed from the culture, it follows directly that the curriculum-designer must become a thorough student of that culture. To build a stream of dynamic educative activities for young Americans, then, he must know his America—the modes of living of the people, their achievements and their deficiencies, their liabilities as well as their assets. He must know not only its material civilization but its basic institutions and its directive psychology. He must be dynamically aware of its crucial issues and problems. He must be sensitive to the values and ideals which the people hold, their taboos as well as their objects of allegiance. But to know all of this he must understand the psychological basis of their institutions, their unique outlook and tradition together with the mechanism they have conconstructed for carrying those out. Moreover, he must really understand the parent European culture that gave birth to American life . . . In short, to be a competent curriculum-designer he must be a competent student of the new industrial culture.[1]

Rugg, in the above quotation, has given us, as he admits, "an absurdly large order." Thus, what we are able to say in this section can at best only scratch

---

1. Reproduced by permission from Harold Rugg, "The Culture and the Curriculum." In *Democracy and the Curriculum. The Life and Program of the American School*, edited by Harold Rugg. Third Yearbook of the John Dewey Society. New York: Appleton-Century-Crofts, 1939, pp. 7, 8.

the surface. But perhaps we can gain some insight that will illuminate certain aspects of American culture and give us direction for further exploration.

American "Normal" Personality

In a previous chapter we say that Ruth Benedict was able to describe in some detail three quite distinct "normal" personalities that had been produced by three different cultures. Her analysis, it should be noted, was aided greatly by the fact that the cultures under study were rather primitive, simple, and therefore relatively homogeneous, that is, comprised mainly of Universal elements. Subgroups embracing habits and values classifiable as Specialties were quite small in number, and these did not significantly influence the mainstream of the culture. In addition, these relatively homogeneous cultures were static, changing little from generation to generation; consequently, few, if any, individuals or groups would consider Alternatives as appropriate directives for behavior. It is easy to understand, then, why the normal personality produced by each of these cultures tended to be relatively uniform so that we could speak with little reservation about the "normal" Pueblo personality, or the "typical" Dobuan character structure.

American culture, however, is considerably more heterogeneous than the ones that Benedict described. Because of the high degree of specialization that exists in advanced technological societies, twentieth-century American society is marked by a wide range of subgroups which are easily identified because of their association with particular Specialties. Furthermore, since change takes place very rapidly in American society, we find many individuals and groups experimenting with and adopting Alternatives as determiners of life style. Because of this diversity within the culture, we find that Americans tend to be less like one another than do members of more primitive societies; and this is what makes it so difficult to delineate *the* "normal" American personality in the fairly precise way that Benedict has done for the primitive cultures. Nevertheless, it would be hard to deny that there *are* clusters of traits that, taken together, suggest personalities that people agree are characteristically American, and indeed, a number of writers have published studies that attempt to delineate American social character. An examination of some of these characteristic American personality types can assist us greatly in discovering many aspects of the submerged part of the American cultural iceberg. These descriptions of personality types, however, should be regarded as suggestive probes toward further understanding, rather than as definitive representations of American types.

A "NORMAL" AMERICAN TYPE:
THE FRONTIER PERSONALITY

A "normal" American character structure that has been suggested by a number of writers is the one that, for convenience we shall call the frontier personality, a character type variously designated as the "inner-directed" or "Consciousness I" man (Riesman 1969; Reich 1970; Whyte 1956). Most writers agree that, although this type is still very common in America today, he is more characteristically a product of eighteenth- and nineteenth-century American culture.

The principal characteristic of the frontier personality is that his behavior is directed by an inner core of generalized values or principles which he regards as moral imperatives—for example, "honesty is the best policy." Such a generalized source of direction would be particularly well suited to life in eighteenth- and nineteenth-century America because in that place and time an entirely new way of life was being evolved. Traditions and social class structures of the parent European cultures, which had always dictated prescribed patterns of behavior, had been swept away; and the individual found himself a new freeman, seeking opportunity and happiness under a radically new form of government that could not exercise arbitrary control over his life.

This inner source of direction is likened by Riesman (1969) to a "psychological gyroscope" which keeps the individual "on course" even when novel situations arise for which tradition has provided no directive pattern of response. It should be noted that, although the frontier character structure we are depicting here in a certain sense suggests a high degree of individual freedom from the culture, independence is by no means as predominant as it might appear. The "inner" direction, the cluster of directive principles, "is implanted early in life by the elders," and although the principles are generalized, they are "nonetheless inescapably destined goals" (Riesman 1969, p. 21). Thus, the inner-directed frontier man goes through life in a cultural association with many other inner-directed personalities, all of whom have adopted a similar inner core of principles; and getting off course, that is, violating the inner principles, often leads to feelings of *guilt*. Thus, we can see that the mechanism of inner direction operates as a kind of cultural cement that holds the society together.

What is the nature of the gyroscope that pilots the frontier personality? Reich provides some answers in a description of what he calls Consciousness I as it emerged in the early years of the Republic:

> *America would prosper if people proved energetic and hard-working. The crucial thing was to release the individual energy so long held back by rigid social customs and hierarchical forms. Each newly sovereign individual could be the source of his own achievement and fulfillment. One worked for himself, not for society. But enough individual hard work made the wheels turn (Reich 1970, p. 21).*

As part of the American dream, the emphasis on the equality of individuals was a high watermark in American thought, for it endowed the frontier personality with a sense of inviolable human dignity. But in the struggle for material well being, this broad humanistic vision became deeply colored by the Darwinian notion of "survival of the fittest." Thus, competitive self-interest turned out to be an unlikely (though dominant) overlay of individual equality and dignity in shaping the psyche of the inner-directed man.

Consonant with this general framework of competitive individual self-reliance are a number of other beliefs that govern the behavior of the frontier personality. For example, he believes that, since material success depends on hard work and self-denial, wealth demonstrates moral rectitude. Conversely, poverty is almost *prima facie* evidence of indolence and/or immorality. He believes that being "practical" gets results and that at best, "thinkers" are unproductive dreamers, or worse. It is this emphasis on material well being that has led some writers to characterize the frontier personality type as "anti-intellectual" and "shallow" (e.g., Hofstadter 1963; Reich 1970).

It may be that the frontier personality is represented best by Sinclair Lewis' Babbitt; however, Reich (1970, p. 25) proposes a number of American sub-group types as models for the frontier (Consciousness I) man: "farmers, owners of small businesses, immigrants who retain their sense of nationality, AMA-type doctors, many members of Congress, gangsters, Republicans, and 'just plain folks.' "

Perhaps the most important point to be made with regard to the goals and principles that guide the frontier personality is that they are regarded as absolute: they can be depended upon to serve as beacons for guiding right action because they are eternal verities—never-changing Truths. It is this belief that provides the frontier man with the fortitude required to stand alone, if necessary, and, meeting the slings and arrows of a hostile and threatening world, survive intact.

This sketchily drawn profile of one American personality is, of course, vastly oversimplified; it is offered with many reservations only as a vehicle for further inquiry. Nevertheless, it does suggest a certain syndrome of values and attitudes that are generally characteristic of at least one segment of American culture.

FRONTIER PERSONALITY AND THE CURRICULUM. In Chapter 7 we noted that, from society's point of view, the function of the curriculum is to develop individuals whose character structures closely resemble the ideal social type, that is, to develop individuals who conform to the culture's definition of the "normal" personality. Consequently, as this section will reveal, it is possible to draw numerous parallels between features of the fontier personality and certain traditional American curriculum practices.

Since the development of the frontier personality depends upon the individual internalization of certain absolute values—chiefly self-reliance for social/ economic success—the traditional American curriculum, not surprisingly, emphasizes intellectual (academic) achievement within the context of appropriate social and personal decorum. Such an emphasis, of course, obviates the necessity for personalization in the curriculum, or for the consideration of pupils' needs, interests, or emotional problems. Roles are clearly defined, and every individual is personally responsible, on pain of well-understood penalties for failure, for meeting the requirements of the school and for achieving academic success.

The impersonality that runs through the frontier curriculum is reflected in the physical environment of the school. Decorations consist mainly of representations from the dead and distant past; on the walls are sepia prints of the Parthenon and the ruins of Pompeii, and in the corner is the perennial plaster bust of Caesar on an ionic pedestal. Pupils' desks, of course, are arranged in regular rows, and all face front. Often, alphabetical seating is the rule, and sometimes the sexes are segregated.

The teacher's job is to see that students learn the curriculum, not to make it "relevant" or enjoyable; and the students, in turn, understand that only brains and hard work will enable them to demonstrate their skills and competencies on written examinations. *We,* of course, are aware of the class biases built into this individualistic academic system, but the frontier school, citing unequivocal and unalterable standards for success, does not recognize them. As a result, the curriculum bears harshly on those (usually lower-class) students who cannot make the grade. But although they are psychologically broken by their failure, in the end they usually accept and internalize the frontier standards. Indeed, just enough of their class, by dint of effort and fortune, succeed to support the belief that "anyone can do it if he tries."

As already suggested, the frontier curriculum does not attempt to be "relevant" to life. Since it is designed to inculcate the basic values of "normal" personality—hard work, self-reliance, self-interest, competition, survival, and material/social success—the content of "real life" is inappropriate except insofar as it might contribute to the decorum demanded in upper-middle-class society. Thus, the teacher may enforce certain standards of diction, honesty, truthfulness, or modesty of dress, but his main energies will focus on the impersonal direction of formal academic learning: reading, writing, and arithmetic in the lower grades; geometry, algebra, literature, science, and foreign language in the upper. This emphasis on intellectual ability is profoundly important in shaping the frontier personality because it affirms to the student that what really matters is what he, individually, can accomplish, not how nice is his smile or how cooperative is his attitude (Riesman 1969, p. 29).

A "NORMAL" AMERICAN TYPE: THE CORPORATE PERSONALITY

If the frontier personality is a product of open-ended opportunity and laissez-faire economics, the corporate personality is validated in the managed institutionalism of the technological-industrial state. Whyte has described this "normal" American character structure most succinctly as the "organization man," and Riesman and Reich, respectively, have dubbed him the "other-directed" personality and "Consciousness II."

In order to respond appropriately to the cultural stimuli presented to him, the corporate personality must know his role. But in large measure, he cannot be taught the role as a child because, in a rapidly changing technological society, his adult role is not known, or is changing. Furthermore, the absolute principles that governed the individualistic frontier personality are not valid because they simply do not work in most situations. What *will* work, however, is getting along in one's peer group, for the individual is simply part of a larger hierarchical organization. If the frontier personality's motto was, "What's good for the individual is good for society," the corporate man's creed is, "What's good for the organization is good for the individual."

Thus, the source of direction of the corporate personality is not an inner, constant principle, but the approval of his peers, or those contemporaries who "count." And though he cannot be taught as a child precisely how to behave in unknown situations, the corporate personality can, and is, taught the importance of being sensitive to his contemporaries' points of view and to align his behavior with that of the group. In a word, he is taught to be socially reflexive—to "get along."

If the analogy of the gyroscope suits the modus operandi of the frontier (inner-directed) personality, the metaphor of radar seems most appropriate for the corporate (other-directed) man (Riesman 1969, p. 26). Thus, the corporate personality navigates his way through life with his antennae out, receiving signals from his peers. And when some inner impulse or conviction leads him to deviate from what is "acceptable," he is beset with *anxiety* (Riesman 1969, p. 26).

This quality of response (anxiety) to one's own deviation is in itself an interesting contrast to the frontier personality's feeling of *guilt* in situations where he has committed some violation of an internalized principle. But it also provides us with an insight into recent attitudes toward the treatment of violators of normative behavior. Guilt, of course, is a proper feeling to have if one is "guilty" of violating an absolute principle of right or wrong; after all, the principle is regarded as a consecrated Truth. It is not surprising, then, that the frontier personality responds to violations of the code in harsh, punitive terms, for something regarded as sacred has been profaned. People who do evil should be punished.

For the corporate personality, however, violation simply means deviation from the norm (thus, *anxiety* rather than *guilt*). The deviator has not violated an eternal principle, he is simply "out of step"; punishment, then, is neither appropriate nor "civilized"; what is required is "counseling," "rehabilitation," or some other humane and civilized procedure to get the deviator back into step—"better adjusted to the group," as the jargon goes.

As he did for the frontier (Consciousness I) model of "normal" American personality, Reich proposes a number of occupational and social subgroup types that fit the corporate (Consciousness II) character structure. Included are "businessmen (new type), liberal intellectuals, the educated professionals and technicians, middle-class suburbanites, labor union leaders, Gene McCarthy supporters, blue-collar workers with newly purchased homes, old-line leaftists, and members of the Communist Party, U.S.A." (Reich 1970, pp. 67, 70).

What brought about the social and cultural changes that produced the corporate personality? It became clear by the end of the nineteenth century and the years prior to World War I that the fierce individualism that was the basis of inner direction had led to a host of grotesque consequences: cut-throat competition had impoverished and degraded masses of the weak or unfortunate; boys and girls of eleven and twelve were paid a pittance in return for a twelve-hour workday in sweatshop or coal mine; the so-called robber barons had amassed fantastic fortunes which were spent in lavishly ostentatious display (Cornelius Vanderbilt's "summer cottage" in Newport, in which he spent only the two summer months, was a seventy-room Italian palazza built at a cost of some 2 million dollars—at a time when carpenters and bricklayers were receiving two dollars for a ten-hour workday); and recurrent scandals, instigated by the "muckrakers," were showing that fortunes were made on defective products, contaminated and adulterated foods, and false advertising. It seemed that the promise of dignity inherent in the individualism of eighteenth-century America had, incredibly, spawned an American life style governed by P. T. Barnum's twisted creed: There's a sucker born every minute.

What had gone wrong? What had happened to the dream? Something that no one had counted on: Events had caught up with and passed by the directive psychology of the culture; the industrial revolution had made local rural America a mass industrial society. But a mass industrial society governed by individualistic self-interest can only result in chaos, a jungle in which the individual is powerless, except as he exercises the bludgeon in a brutal (and brutalizing) struggle to survive. A number of perceptive people saw what had happened, and some valiant efforts at reform were attempted in the early decades of the century. But it took events again—the great depression of the 1930s—to move the culture into better alignment with social and economic reality.

Since the 1930s, coordination and management, hierarchy and organization, have become the hallmarks of the American corporate-industrial state. No longer does the office boy by virtue of individual honesty and hard work, Horatio Alger fashion, work his way to the presidency of the company. Rather, the large corporation selects (often by standardized test) likely college graduates for top management and executive positions. It then proceeds to "train" these junior executives in the protocols of the "profession." This reliance on, and indeed *faith* in, the competence of "specialists" or "professionals" has permeated almost all aspects not only of business, but of government, labor, and even the academic world. Thus, the corporate personality, the "organization man," becomes a role, a standard set of behaviors appropriate to a position in the culture.

It should be noted here that, while the frontier personality was by no means independent or nonconformist, he at least was provided with the inner reserve to stand alone, if need be, for the eternal principles which had early been implanted in his psyche. By contrast, the creed of the other-directed social character tends toward "adjustment" to the extent that the very act of standing alone for the sake of what is perceived as "a matter of principle" is almost inconceivable. It is this shift in the directive psychology of American "normal" personality that has resulted in "conformity" replacing "independence" as a core value in American culture.

CORPORATE PERSONALITY AND THE CURRICULUM. A curriculum designed to produce the corporate personality can be found in many "modern" American schools. Typically, these schools are located in upper-middle-class suburban communities inhabited by young, well-educated professionals and rising corporation executives.

If the frontier curriculum is impersonal and emphasizes academics and decorum, its corporate counterpart is highly personalized and stresses cooperation and easy informality. Since the corporate personality is "other-directed" and must be sensitive to the cues broadcast by peers, it is not surprising that in modern schools students' social and psychological adjustment are of greater concern than their academic progress. Indeed, as Riesman (1969, p. 30) notes, it is not unusual for outstanding intellectual performance to be regarded with suspicion, as a sign of social maladjustment.

Even the school's physical environment reflects the social emphasis of the curriculum. Gone are the dead forms of classical Greece and Rome. The walls are covered, rather, with the students' social studies projects, art work, and "creative" compositions. Although this personalization of decor appears to be a salute to individual "creativity," closer inspection reveals that in many cases it simply constitutes "the socialization of taste" (Riesman 1969, p. 31) by which imagination and creativity are channeled into stylized norms. Students know that they must *not* copy or imitate the work of a recognized master, nor even repeat an earlier work of their own.

Seating arrangements, too, are personalized and informalized. The sexes always are mixed and seats are clustered into "small groups." A sociogram or other sociometric device, *not* the alphabet, is used to determine group composition and even the teacher joins in their activities, eschewing his aloof former place at the front of the class.

The studied dismantling of formality and decorum facilitates the rapid circulation of tastes, an important condition of corporate personality development. Whereas the keeping of a diary is a private, noncurricular activity for a student in the impersonal traditional school, the "sharing" of "self"—in stories, paintings, feelings, etc.—is encouraged in the modern school as a serious and important part of the curriculum. With regard to the academic component of the curriculum, it is not permitted to interfere with the socialization process; it merely serves as a vehicle for "small group projects," whose real purpose is the learning of group relations and other corporate social skills. Indeed, in the modern school the cardinal sin is not academic failure (which usually does not exist), but uncooperativeness.

Not surprisingly, the corporate teacher does not consider himself so much a subject matter expert as a specialist in human relations. Generally, he is far more concerned with the needs, interests, and emotional problems of his students than he is with their IQ's or their intellectual attainments. Like his frontier counterpart, however, the corporate teacher sees that the pupils learn the curriculum. As opinion leader, he supports the canons of taste emanating from the best upper-middle-class culture and conveys to students the importance of cooperation, adjustment, and (carefully regulated and delimited) initiative and leadership. He is really an authority, but in the corporate mode, he hides it, employing "reason," "counseling," and other methods of manipulation to enforce cultural directives. When students' behavior consistently violates norms, it is not *their* fault, as the frontier teacher would insist; rather, it is the *teacher's* failure; it is the result of poor management on his part. This role of the teacher in the modern corporate school can be compared with the role of the industrial relations department in a modern factory (Riesman 1969, p. 32).

A RECENT AMERICAN TYPE:
THE LIBERATED PERSONALITY

It seems clear that for all its complexity and diversity, American culture of the 1950s and early 1960s was at least regular enough to yield, upon analysis, some comprehensible notion of what life in the United States was really like. Since Berkeley and Columbia, the ghetto riots and Viet Nam, marijuana and Woodstock, Nixon, inflation and recession, it seems that American culture is in such a state of flux as to make analysis almost impossible. Nevertheless, the effort continues to be maintained, and most observers are convinced that if we are to gain any understanding of the cultural turmoil that we presently are experiencing, at least one focal point of our inquiry will have to be directed at the "new generation." On this score Reich has painted an attractive though controversial portrait of the liberated psyche and dubbed it "Consciousness III."

Like the previous two American social characters, the liberated personality has its roots in the social and cultural conditions that brought it about. Unlike their parents who were involved in inventing and building the technology, affluence, and promise of the new corporate state, the liberated youth were born into it, were weaned on it, and accepted its possibilities for real alternatives in life style. Thus, unlike their parents, who accept the bounty of technology within the framework of the old culture, with its workweek, status relationships, and success goals, the liberated personality type views his options as totally open, so much so that Reich (1970, p. 235) is able to write of him, "a life of surfing *is* possible, not as an escape from work, a recreation or a phase, but as a *life*—if one chooses."

But it is not only the promise held forth by the corporate-technological society that has generated this totally new *Weltansicht*; it is (perhaps even more so) revulsion from the corruption, ugliness, and cyncism that are persistent facts of existence in America today: riots and war, racism, poverty, political corruption, nuclear threat, pollution, and the violent plunder of nature in the name of progress and production. Furthermore, this profane juxtaposition of promise and corruption in American society is seen by youth as a projection of the hypocrisy of the older generation. The young do not reject their parents' ideals; they only feel betrayed by their parents' failure to live by them.

According to Reich (1970, pp. 241–244), the liberated personality (Consciousness III) lives by three commandments: (1) be true to oneself; (2) never judge anyone else; and (3) be wholly honest with others, use no other person as a means.

Consciousness III postulates the self and its integrity as inviolable. Thus, the liberated personality rejects goals proposed for it by society and does not allow itself to become the instrumentality by which public or social ends are achieved. Reich warns, however, that this centering on self does not constitute selfishness or an "ego trip"; rather it is "a radical subjectivity designed to find genuine values in a world whose official values are false and distorted" (Reich 1970, p. 242).

Never to judge anyone else translates as total acceptance of all human beings for themselves. Thus, competition in life situations is eliminated, and disparagement of any kind is taboo. In this regard:

> *A boy who was odd in some way used to suffer derision all through his school days. Today there would be no persecution; one might hear one boy speak, with affection, of "my freaky friend." Instead of insisting that everyone be measured by given standards, the new generation values what is unique and different in each self . . . (Reich 1970, p. 243).*

This quality of nonjudgment in personal relationships defines a totally new (for American culture) concept of community, according to Reich. It is predicated on the brotherhood of man and contrasts starkly with the frontier man's notion of community as jungle, with every man for himself, and the corporate man's notion of community as a corporate hierarchy of roles, with highly defined relationships drawn on the basis of signals received and transmitted.

Closely related, and a logical extension of the first two commandments is the third: Be honest with others, use no other as an instrument. Being honest with others, being one's own real self, of course, is equivalent to leaving oneself vulnerable, something beyond possibility for the frontier or corporate man. But presenting oneself in this way precludes what happens so often in society today: "manipulation of others, forcing anyone to do anything against his wish, using others for one's own purposes, irony and sarcasm, defensive standoffishness" (Reich 1970, pp. 244, 245).

Thus, no liberated personality allows himself to take part in role relationships, to give commands, or to relate to another human being in any way that is impersonal. This involved sense of community that Reich sees in the liberated personality is startlingly congruent with McLuhan's notion of participational mass man.

Reich, of course, warns that he is describing an idealized character structure, not a personality as it exists in any single individual. The same caveat, to be sure, is appropriately delivered with respect to our descriptions of the frontier and the corporate personality types. Nonetheless, the latter two social characters, along with their share of sharp, critical commentary, have received substantial recognition as basic American character types. And in spite of Reich's belief that "there is a revolution coming," both the makeup of the liberated character and the extent of its diffusion, even among the new generation, are highly problematical. At the same time, it is clear that new "normal" personality types are forming in response to the rapid movement of American culture, and undoubtedly many of the elements that Reich includes in Consciousness III are diffused among them. Will American culture produce a new synthesis of frontier and liberated, or of corporate and liberated? And to what degree will the new personality shape American culture? To play a useful and meaningful role in building a better human society, curriculum designers will have to keep their fingers on the pulse of American culture and character.

LIBERATED PERSONALITY AND THE CURRICULUM. The relatively recent (as well as tenuous) delineation of the liberated personality has, of course, precluded its institutionalization as a curriculum form in American public schools. Nevertheless, many writers (generally known as the "compassionate" or "radical" school reformers)[2] have described curricula that they claim will foster character traits similar to those of the liberated personality. In addition, a number of "open," "free," and "alternative" schools have been established to implement these "humanizing" curricula. But the currency of the radical school reformers seems now to be on the wane, and many of the alternative schools that their writings inspired have not endured. This is not to imply that the cause lies in defective curriculum theory or in faulty implementation, although it very well may. It merely suggests that cultural support for the development through education of a liberated personality type is not yet vigorous enough to sustain the movement. Be that as it may, we can still draw upon the writings of the radical reformers and the curriculum practices of alternative schools to understand the curricular implications of developing the liberated personality.

Since the liberated personality holds the integrity of self inviolable and abjures the imposition on it of any (social) goals or requirements, the curricula of alternative schools tend to be extremely permissive, allowing virtually total freedom for students to learn what they wish. Further freedom is provided by including in the curriculum opportunities to experience all manner of extra-school settings: city streets, farms, stores, factories, and the open country. Textbooks and other materials associated with conventional curricula generally are rejected as being coercive and overstructured. Although teachers sometimes suggest learning activities in order to multiply students' options, they would never think of employing a preplanned curriculum in the usual sense. Indeed, teachers make a point of being "nondirective" with their students, perceiving themselves as resources who will be brought into play as the need arises.

Acceptance without judgment, another commitment of the liberated per-

2. See the section "The Humanistic Curriculum" in Chapter 3 for further perspectives on the "humanistic" movement in curriculum.

sonality, translates as the absence of evaluation and grading in the alternative schools. Because tests of any kind are taboo, competition is minimized, and the activities and products of *all* students simply are accepted as worthwhile. As a result, it is not unusual for individual students to occupy their school time with such diverse pursuits as making pottery, growing flowers and vegetables, writing poetry, reading magazines, talking with friends, or just strolling about the school grounds.

Finally, the stricture that the liberated personality be totally honest with others allows for the free and open expression of feelings among students and teachers. Language and topics ordinarily regarded as inappropriate in the main culture are (often self-consciously) given full play in alternative schools. Outbursts of temper are "understood" and accepted with empathy. Thus, the curriculum aims at building a community of "authentic selves" who are able to relate to one another as "real" human beings rather than as roles.

Although this brief sketch does some violence to the complexities of curricula based on the liberated personality, it suggests why "free" and "alternative" schools have generally not been successful. Not only is the "good" (e.g., be true to self, do not judge others) defined in highly abstract, and therefore unclear, terms, but absolute faith is invested in the notion that a virtually laissez-faire environment in which everyone is permitted to do his own thing will "naturally" develop the "good," liberated man. Experience, however, has shown that the central problem of society—man's relationship with his fellow man—is far too complex and involved to be solved with a prescription of absolute freedom governed by a simple homily: Be wholly honest wtih others, use no other person as a means. In his relations with others, man cannot escape either choice or responsibility for choice, and his choice in each specific instance will be "good" only to the extent that he *evaluates* and *judges* (according to some consciously adopted value system) as many situational variables as possible. The development of such decision-making skills clearly requires much more in both planning and substance than is offered by the curricula of most alternative and free schools.

The decline of America's romance with what was thought to be the pristine integrity of the youth movement (the source of the liberated personality) has accelerated since 1970 with the discovery that the youth culture is capable of most of the nasty habits of the adult culture, as well as some of its own invention. Most curriculum specialists are now of the opinion that it will take more than a do-your-own-thing curriculum to produce a personality type capable of developing and supporting the good society.

The American Value System

A comprehensive exposition of the value system of so diverse a society as ours is, of course, beyond the scope of this text. However, some notion as to the value configuration generally considered to be typically American can be gained in this limited space if we focus our discussion on core values—those broad value orientations which generate many of our culture's specific values and directives.

TRADITIONAL AMERICAN VALUES

For our purposes, "traditional American values" means those values adopted by the dominant middle class. Although we are talking about a total value system that is characteristically American, it should be recognized that many single "American" values are held in common by a number of other societies, especially those. that are the products of the Western European tradition. Even values which are characteristically American, however, can often be shown to rest on assumptions that are basic to Western culture in general. An example of one such assumption is what DuBois (1969, p. 10) calls "the oppositional mode." Partly a product of the structure of Indo-European languages (one is reminded here of B. L. Whorf's analysis), the oppositional mode dichotomizes experience in terms of contradictories. This process, which pervades Western thought patterns, is seen in such propositions as male-female, good-bad, kind-cruel, subject-predicate, mind-body, rational-emotional. Although, as DuBois points out, many of these dichotomies are "poorly conceived contradictories," the opposition is perceived as an uncomfortable dilemma that strains for consistency. This bipolar condition has generated two values highly prized in our culture: (1) *compromise,* a notion basic to the operation of the realities of the democratic process, and (2) the penchant for *change,* a value which manifests itself in Americans' disposition toward upward mobility and "progress."

With regard to the prizing of compromise, the characteristic American expression "splitting the difference" "reveals particularly an appreciation of the spurious quality of the oppositions, since it implies that neither oppositional term represents 'truth' . . ." (DuBois 1969, p. 10). While this may be the case, one cannot help but point out that, compromise notwithstanding, *defining the situation* in terms of the oppositional mode operates to limit possible alternatives to a one-dimensional linear spectrum. For example, when the school environment is defined in terms of a "strict-permissive" polarity, the "compromise" is simple and obvious: not too strict, not too permissive; but to define the situation in these terms is to mask many components of the school environment that may be far more relevant to the school's purposes than "strictness" or "permissiveness."

The prizing of change in American culture is connected with a complex core value which, for convenience, has been designated *effort-optimism* (DuBois 1969, p. 11). Effort-optimism manifests itself in the high value Americans place on work. Work becomes an end in itself and, as DuBois points out, Americans even tend to work very hard at their recreation. Thus, America has traditionally been a society marked by palpable activity, movement, and change, and those individuals who "get things done" have always been the most highly regarded and richly rewarded.

This optimistic disposition toward work and the activity that it generates has resulted in great value being placed on vigor and, subsequently, youth. Frequently commented on by foreign observers, America's fetishization of youth has manifested itself in clothing, cosmetics, television, sports, and sex. In contrast with many other societies, which have revered their elders, America's preoccupation with youth is a unique, but natural, outgrowth of the effort-optimism orientation.

Another core value that controls many specifics of the American value structure is *material well-being* (DuBois 1969, p. 12). The regard in which this value is held is demonstrated amply both by the American standard of living and the heavy criticism "American materialism" has sustained from domestic and foreign sources. One should be careful to note, however, that what on the surface seems to be raw materialism must be tempered by an understanding of the Puritan-Protestant ethic out of which the value of material well-being emerged. As far back as the seventeenth century, the earliest settlers regarded material success as tangible evidence of God's reward for moral and spiritual rectitude. Thus, Americans, who regard work as an intrinsic good, associate material well-being with "the moral connotation of 'rightness' . . ." (DuBois 1969, p. 13).

The association of morality and material well-being has resulted in some interesting and peculiarly American attitudes. For example, Americans prefer to win their wars by providing the military with massive quantities of war matériel, rather than depending on ingenius strategy or personal heroism. They generally are untouched by the misery of the poor, yet at Christmas time are ebulliently energetic in providing for the "needy." They find repugnant the condition of disaster victims, yet draw generously on the wealth of the nation to send them aid. These examples suggest the ambivalence created in Americans by the moral dimension attributed to the value of material well-being.

A core value that seems to be gaining increasing currency in American culture is *conformity*. This is interesting inasmuch as Americans tend to pride themselves on their independence.

In fact, the values of independence, self-reliance, initiative, and liberty *were* a part of the American value structure and manifested themselves in a wide variety of ways during the early years of the Republic. However, these are now largely "conceived" values and are not effectively operative in the American value structure. Nor has the demise of these values been as recent as we might like to believe. The remarkably complete assimilation of diverse immigrant groups to traditional middle-class values is testimony to the effective operation of the conformity value. This assimilative process began in the early nineteenth century and constantly gained momentum until it reached its peak during the first decades of the twentieth century.

The adoption by the culture of conformity as a core value has resulted in a number of attitudes characteristic of the corporate personality discussed in a previous section. Cooperation becomes an important value; one must " get along" and be a "well-liked" member of the group. The effort-optimism value that allows for material and social success can be served, but in moving upward, the individual must not exceed his bounds; the need to be liked ensures "moderation" and orthodoxy in the climb to success.

Although American hostility toward figures in authority is almost legendary and has been duly noted in the literature, this hostility has tended to be directed at figures characterized as aristocratic, haughty, or arrogant. Recent research tends to suggest that Americans, consonant with their affinity for conformity, are becoming increasingly acquiescent to authority.

It is interesting to note that DuBois' analysis of the dominant value profile of American culture addresses itself to values that are *operational* in that culture. Thus, we are struck by the absence of many values that Americans traditionally claim to hold. To what degree, for example, are such widely proclaimed values as freedom, individual worth and dignity, and democratic decision making inoperative in American culture? It seems legitimate to ask whether America's *conceived* values are significantly different from its *operative* values; and if it turns out that, indeed they are, we may be forced to admit that the hypocrisy our youth sees in society is really there.

EMERGING ALTERNATIVES

It is extremely difficult, if not impossible, to determine to what degree, if at all, emerging alternative values are significantly operative. Indeed, a good deal of what is said about emerging alternatives to the present value system exists only on the spoken or conceived level. Clearly, however, traditional American values are under attack and change is taking place. We shall attempt here to suggest directions that have been recently proposed and to supply as best we can any evidence that these new values are being practiced.

Variously characterized as "the new morality," "the counterculture," and "the greening of America," the new value structure appears to place an uncompromising primacy on *self*. This new orientation holds that whatever the individual may be, he is a human being first, and by virtue of that fact, inviolate. Three concomitant propositions follow from this value: (1) The individual should accept himself, a human being, as he is, for whatever he is; therefore, (2) he should be real and genuine, not putting on airs, playing roles, or pretending to be what he is not; and finally, (3) each self should be accorded absolute personal freedom of action as long as that action does not impede the same freedom in others.

In its best sense, this new value structure is not, as it might appear to be, egocentric and hedonistic.[3] Among the nonself-centered values devolving from this orientation are the following: (1) the equality of selves; (2) an accepting, nonjudging attitude toward other individuals; (3) an absolute honesty in one's relations with others, so that the possibility of "using" another to achieve one's

---

3. Despite this disclaimer, some analysts view the new morality as little more than a rationalization of self-indulgence.

goals is precluded; (4) the rejection of competition among individuals; (5) high regard for town-meeting type participatory democracy; (6) the rejection of materialism; and (7) the notion that all people, whether they have met or not, are members of the same family—in short, brotherhood and community.

The seriousness that some people attach to these values has manifested itself in a number of ways: massive antiwar demonstrations, marches for the poor, civil rights protests, and the ecology movement, among many others. Also, however, violent outbreaks that have included burnings and bombings demonstrate the anger, frustration, and loss of control experienced by some adherents of the new morality, whose destructive responses to the "corrupt values" of the culture constitute, ironically, a grisly perversion of the principles for which they purportedly stand. A more characteristic expression of the counterculture, though, is evidenced by the large number of communes that have been established across the United States. Here, young people say, they are able to live close to nature and in harmony with the human values that have been corrupted in the manufactured artificiality of the dominant culture. Additionally, a number of youth groups on college campuses have formed living units which enable them to evolve life styles more attuned to the new morality. It should be pointed out, however, that self-interest and materialism (e.g., in the form of sports cars and stereos) are still widely accepted values among the young.

The value tendencies of the new morality are not without precedent in the Western tradition. Indeed, the work and life of Henry David Thoreau, as well as the numerous utopian settlements attempted in the nineteenth century, demonstrate that the new directions in values have their roots deep in an American tradition. But it is also true that the mainstream of American culture has not followed this tradition; rather, it has focused on the external aspects of life, exalting the empirical, the practical, and the rational. In contrast, the new morality, following the subordinate "romantic" tradition, focuses on the inner life of the individual, emphasizing the spiritual, the aesthetic, and the intuitive. Clearly, the liberated personality's affinity for perception-expanding agents like marijuana, mysticism, Eastern religions, and the aesthetics of sex all testify to the operative status of the new value system.

The emergence of this new value system and the alternative life styles that it has generated have undoubtedly been a response to events and conditions of modern life that, it is claimed, are the result of the "false values" of the dominant culture. The most commonly cited of these conditions, of course, are war, the bomb, poverty, racism, and human devastation of the ecosystem—including pollution, the population explosion, and commercial ravaging of natural resources. Other, more subtle conditions that have generated dissent against the "system" are the erosion of liberty; the manipulation of democratic processes by power elites (e.g., business, labor, government); the rise of the bureaucracy with its accompanying dehumanization; and the superficiality of a jaded society, whose central concerns are sexual titillation and the accumulation of electric mechanical gadgets.

But protest against these conditions—so vocal in the 1960s—has recently subsided, giving way to a mood of reassessment, resignation, and passivity. Some observers see in this new mood the ascendency of an old and unsavory value: cynical self-interest.

What seems to be behind this turning away from alternatives preferred by the new morality? First of all, the advent of the twin economic calamities of inflation and recession have, understandably, led many Americans to subordinate their involvement with larger social issues to increased concern for personal and family well-being. At the same time the growth of bureaucratization has made accountability increasingly difficult to maintain. Not only do individuals feel powerless to cope with mass organizations, but, conversely, institutional indifference toward personal responsibility for excellent performance has tended to undermine pride of achievement. As a result, it is not unusual to hear Americans complain bitterly about shoddy products and slipshod services. Finally, the national disgrace of the Nixon scandals has dealt a devastating blow to the concept of personal moral responsibility. As evidence, we may note that virtually every subcultural group—i.e., coal miners, truckers, teachers, doctors, merchants, blacks, women, ethnics, farmers, industrialists, and not the least, oil companies— has at some time in recent years callously rejected its obligations to society at large, while it has cynically employed every available expedient to attain its own selfish ends. In such a climate it is not surprising to find personal honor and unselfish moral conduct disparaged. But one cannot help questioning the viability of a society that makes cynical, expedient self-interest a condition of survival for its members.

The values inherent in the new morality provide an attractive alternative to the ones that make up the traditional American configuration. Nevertheless, the fulfillment of the new morality in the back-to-nature movement appears to be totally inadequate to deal with the alarming conditions of modern society noted above. The facts of technology, instantaneous electric communication, and population cannot be ignored. This fact seems to be recognized, however, by the numbers of young people who have recently become politically and socially involved. Nader's Raiders, the National Organization for Women, and Common Cause are excellent examples of this kind of activism.

Whether the fledgling values of the new morality discussed here accurately reflect the direction our society is taking is highly problematical. Will the new orientation overthrow the traditional values? Will cynical self-interest prevail? Will we become more driven, materialistic, and conformist? Will a new synthesis emerge? Or will some, as yet unforeseen, value commitment sweep our culture?

Whatever direction is taken, it is essential that it occur as a result of intelligent, conscious, human action. To the extent that it does not, we will be helplessly swept up by events—directed and determined by forces beyond our control. To prevent such a disaster (and it has occurred frequently in history) is the job of education, and of the curriculum designer. Only to the degree that curriculum helps men to understand the forces that affect their lives will they have freedom of choice necessary to determine their destiny.

Social Issues in Contemporary American Culture

We have already commented on the need for curriculum planners to be dynamically aware of the crucial social issues and problems that face not only the United States, but the world. These problems are legion and in a constant state of flux. Because they often result from the clash of conflicting cultural values, they pose monumental problems in analysis, to say nothing of resolution. How an individual perceives the nature and relative importance of a social issue depends, of course, on the configuration of his conceived and operative value commitments.

Examples of conflict and variation in the perception of social issues can be seen in the results of public opinion polls taken by Samuel Lubell during the 1972 presidential campaign (*Akron Beacon Journal*, September 17 and 18, 1972). In one example, Lubell (1972a) reports that interviews with former supporters of Hubert Humphrey indicate that their shift to Nixon was motivated by the belief that he would halt government pressures on behalf of blacks, even to the extent of pushing some racial issues such as busing and job preferences out of national politics. This seems to indicate that many former supporters of racial equality, for reasons that we need not go into here, no longer view racism and discrimination as a social problem; the issue, as these people now seem to view it, is preferential treatment for blacks. In another example, Lubell (1972b) reports, "my interviews indicate that for many voters, 'welfare' has built up into the issue that stirs the most intense emotional agitation in some families, even overshadowing concern over the [Viet Nam] war." That antiwelfare feeling in 1972 agitated voters more than any other "social issue," even the Viet Nam war, is an interesting commentary on priorities in the American value system.

Despite problems of perception, however, most observers of the culture tend to agree on the general identification of our principal social issues, if not on their analysis, priorities, or solutions. Of course, an adequate discussion of these issues would require far more space than we can allow here. We shall have to content ourselves, therefore, with only a brief identification, in no particular order of priority, of a few of the current social issues with which curriculum workers and teachers ought to be conversant.

DISCRIMINATION, RASCISM, MINORITY RIGHTS, AND INTEGRATION. Although the issue of racism has always been with us, it received preeminent attention in the 1960s with the demands of blacks for an end to discrimination. Since then, Indians, Chicanos, Puerto Ricans, and other racial and cultural minorities have been recognized as victims of social and economic bias. School curricula were affected as integration (often as a result of busing) changed the character of school populations. Curricular responses have included courses in black history and culture, more emphasis on minorities in text materials, bilingual programs, and multicultural programs.

POVERTY. Closely connected with discrimination against minority groups is the poverty that they suffer as a result. However, extremely large numbers of white

Americans also experience abject poverty in inaccessible rural areas in all parts of the United States. The moral questions raised by the fact of poverty in a land of plenty are precisely the kinds of questions that deserve intensive consideration in contemporary curricula.

POLLUTION AND THE ENVIRONMENT. Although conservation of natural resources has long been given lip service in the curriculum, recent attention to the devastating consequences of pollution (air, water, land, and noise) has resulted in redoubled efforts to provide more effective (and truthful) content in curriculum materials. In curricular terms, the issue of pollution and environment usually is treated in four dimensions: biochemical, sociological, economic, and moral.

URBANIZATION AND METROPOLITANISM. Mid-twentieth-century America has seen the centers of its large cities turn into vast (usually black) slums as the middle-class white population fled to the suburbs. This separation of central city from suburb is both a socioeconomic and racial problem. It resulted in pleasant but culture-void suburbs existing alongside central cities whose rich cultural resources were being strangled by decay, crime, and violence. The answer most often proposed is metropolitanism, but the problem of integration is almost overwhelming. A first step for curriculum planners seems to be providing inner-city minorities with an education that will enable them not only to break the poverty cycle, but to appreciate the richly diverse advantages of the cities.

WAR AND PEACE. Nothing is more horrible nor needlessly destructive than war. If our children are to live in a peaceful world, they will need the attitudes and skills to create it. Curriculum initiatives that focus on education for peace have already been made,[4] but much in our culture (e.g., its preference for nationalism) militates against it. Existing conflicts between patriotic and internationalist values will make curriculum work in this area difficult for many years to come.

WOMEN'S RIGHTS. We have just recently discovered the depth of the unconscious cultural bias that has relegated women to the position of second-class citizens in our society. The number of books that have illuminated this bias has been large and of uneven quality, but one of the best is by Millet (1969). The curriculum, as noted in an earlier section, has been deeply implicated in teaching the subjection of women, but changes in curriculum materials are now occurring. Moreover, litigation is forcing schools to discontinue policies that exclude girls from participation in classes and other school activities that the culture has traditionally considered "unfeminine."

OTHER SOCIAL ISSUES. It has not been our intent to imply that the half-dozen social issues just discussed are the six most important facing American society

---

4. See, for example, Henderson (1973).

today. Indeed, the number of important problems facing Americans is so large as to preclude even the brief commentary provided for each of the above. Because of the limitations of this text, then, we present only a list of crucial contemporary social issues (each of which impinges in many ways on the curriculum) for the reader's consideration and further study.

The energy crisis in oil, coal, uranium, and other finite fuels
The world population problem
The world food crisis
Crime and violence
New attitudes toward sexual latitude
The use of drugs (including alcohol) and drug abuse
Moral integrity, honesty in government, the American "moral crisis"
The right to privacy (dangers inherent in electronic surveillance, credit company dossiers, etc.)
Growth of technology (computers, television, and other technology that alters modes of living)
The role of religion in mass technological society
The increasing influence of bureaucracies
The "youth culture"
Individual (including students') rights
The rise of multinational corporate industry

References

DuBois, Cora. 1969. "The Dominant Value Profile of American Culture." In *Selected Educational Heresies,* edited by William F. O'Neill. Glenview, Ill.: Scott, Foresman and Company.

Henderson, George, ed. 1973. *Education for Peace.* Yearbook. Washington, D. C.: Association for Supervision and Curriculum Development.

Hofstadter, Richard. 1963. *Anti-Intellectualism in American Life.* New York: Alfred A. Knopf.

Lubell, Samuel. 1972a. "Voter Resentments Pay off for Nixon." *Akron Beacon Journal* (July 17).

———. 1972b. "Welfare Agitates Voters More than Vietnam War." *Akron Beacon Journal* (July 18).

Millet, Kate. 1969. *Sexual Politics.* New York: Doubleday & Company.

Reich, Charles. 1970. *The Greening of America.* New York: Random House. Bantam Books edition, 1971.

Riesman, David. 1969. (With Nathan Glazer and Reuel Denney.) "Tradition-Direction, Inner-Direction, and Other-Direction." In *Selected Educational Heresies,* edited by William F. O'Neill. Glenview, Ill.: Scott, Foresman and Company.

Rugg, Harold. 1939. "The Culture and the Curriculum." In *Democracy and the Curriculum. The Life and Program of the American School,* edited by Harold Rugg. Third Yearbook of the John Dewey Society. New York: Appleton-Century-Crofts, chap. I.

Whyte, William. 1956. *The Organization Man.* New York: Simon & Schuster.

CHAPTER 9

THE INDIVIDUAL:
BASIC CONSIDERATIONS

*A machine can be built to perform any function that a man can per-
form in terms of behavior, computation, or discrimination. Shall we
ever know, however, what components to add or what complexity of
circuitry to introduce in order to make it feel?* —SEYMOUR KETY

The essential interrelatedness of the four foundational areas was pointed out in
Chapter 4. It is not surprising, therefore, to find that our conception of the
nature of man is conditioned both by our philosophical assumptions and by the
society in which we live. For example, idealists tend to view man as a creature
uniquely endowed with a nonmaterial mind or intellect, while realists view
him as a "master machine" in a machine-universe, and pragmatists see him as
a social actor who constructs meaning by transacting with the environment.
Furthermore, we saw in the previous chapter that American culture has generated certain "personality types" that serve to define the nature of the individual human being. Thus man often is viewed in our culture essentially as an
independent "frontier-type" individualist, as a conforming "other-directed" social
type, or as the liberated ideal of an "authentic" human being. Helpful as these
conceptions are in understanding the nature of man, however, they tend to
gloss over and simplify what all of us "feel in our bones" to be an enormously
complex and confusing entity: our individual selves. Thus, it is necessary to
inquire specifically and extensively into what some thinkers have called "the
supreme mystery of the universe." Nor is our inquiry born in this instance of
casual, vain, or idle motivations; it is a crucial prerequisite for curriculum work
because "It is important to know what men are in order intelligently to determine what they should become" (Hook 1946, p. 23). We should unnecessarily

belabor this point by dwelling on the fact that ultimately, a curriculum's principal *raison d'être* is the shaping of individual selves, i.e., determining what men become.

The Nature of Human Nature: Some Basic Considerations

The age-old question, "What is man?" has been asked at one time or another by all thinking human beings, but it has been a special concern of theologians, philosophers, and scientists. Often, attempts at a definition have centered on identifying in man the single quality that allegedly sets him apart from all other living organisms. As a consequence, man has at one time or another been classified as "the rational animal," "the tool-making animal," the "self-conscious animal," and the "meaning-creating animal." Such thumbnail sketches, however, generally leave out too much that is important if we are to grasp in any comprehensive way the essence of what it means to exist as a human being.

Few will dispute the contention that the most impressive contributions to the study of human nature in recent years have come from the sciences, notably biology, psychology, and anthropology. By subjecting the human organism to the empirical methods of scientific inquiry, many myths about man have been dispelled and many startling (and often unpleasant) characteristics have been brought to light. Unfortunately, however, the success of science in the study of man has often led to the conclusion that purely empirical methods are sufficient in themselves for discovering the nature of human nature. For example, behavioral psychologists, in order to be rigorously scientific, insist that only observable *overt behavior* qualifies as valid data for describing human nature and functioning. They hold that evidence derived from personal awareness of internal states of consciousness is far too subjective to be taken seriously. Thus, such concepts as will, purpose, and consciousness are dismissed as "unresearchable" because they are not susceptible to scientific (empirical) study. This position is difficult to dispute, however, only if one accepts the assumption that empiricism is the only valid route to knowledge. But are we not guilty of denying highly significant nonempirical data if we ignore insights derived from personal introspection? The role of self-conscious purpose in motivating behavior is as good an example as any of nonempirical evidence generated in this way. Who has not, on any number of occasions, been conscious of the self-willed origin of his acts? It would seem almost perverse to reject such conscious experience as invalid on the grounds that it is not subject to empirical verification. Thus, while many students of human nature are quite willing to accept the validity of the scientific mode, they insist that it addresses itself only to certain aspects of human nature and that other kinds of data are needed to produce a comprehensive conception of man. By way of approaching such a conception, we shall now explore four basic considerations on which much of the debate on the nature of human nature has turned.

MAN: MIND AND/OR BODY?

Recalling the discussions of Chapter 5, we immediately recognize that the question of whether man is essentially spirit or flesh, or both, is basically an ontological one. Its answer, in effect, aims to establish the essential reality of man. Our cultural heritage, especially in its religious aspects, teaches that man is both material flesh and spiritual "soul," and for all practical purposes we tend to operate on this dualistic assumption about the nature of man. In addition, we tend to view man's mental/spiritual nature as a force for good struggling to overcome the base (and even evil) impulses that originate in his physical body. But certain logical problems arise if we begin to think about the relationship between a purportedly coexisting material body and nonmaterial mind/spirit. For example, how can a nonmaterial entity (which does not take up space) be contained in a material body (which occupies space)? Furthermore, how can a nonmaterial mind interact with and direct the behavior of a physical body (Brubacher 1962, p. 46)? Notwithstanding such problems, the assumption that man is comprised of a union of mind and body is widely held and has affected curriculum policy in certain distinctive ways: Since it is the mind that activates the body, the curriculum aims primarily at training the individual's nonmaterial being. Thus, content and activities center on the intellectual (and spiritual), with scant attention being paid to physical, practical, or "bodily" concerns. Indeed, impulses originating in the body are ordinarily suppressed, and mental/spiritual *discipline* becomes an important consideration in the curriculum and its implementation.

The problems inherent in a body-mind view of the nature of man are avoided by those who conclude that man is either entirely mind or entirely body. The former take the position that all matter is ultimately reducible to nonmaterial mind, while the latter hold that man is a totally material organism entirely explainable in physical terms.

Some partisans of the *all-mind* concept of man view the mind in much the same way as the proponents of the *body-mind* concept. Although the former dismiss the corporal aspect of man as superfluous, they (like their body *and* mind counterparts) conceive of mind as a nonmaterial entity that generates thoughts and ideas by perceiving, conceiving, analyzing, synthesizing, etc. But another group of all-mind proponents denies that mind exists as a thought-producing entity, either material or nonmaterial. These mentalists point out that however hard the mind tries to think about itself—to become conscious of its own being—it cannot do so because it is unable to avoid preoccupation with ideas of external origin. That is, it never seems able to catch itself not thinking about something other than itself. They conclude, therefore, that since the mind seems incapable of achieving a state of self-perception, or even self-contemplation, it is unlikely that it has any independent existential status. The result is that mind is conceived as nothing more than a succession of conscious states.

The theory that man is a succession of conscious mental states suggests a curriculum which enables learners to correlate and integrate their ideas (mental states) into coherent wholes for comprehensive understanding. Thus, considerable attention is accorded the sequence and organization of subject matter to ensure the proper association of ideas. The educational theories of such "associationists" as Herbart (discussed in Chapters 1 and 3) were founded in this mentalistic view of human nature.

Opposed to the mentalists are the physicalists, who view the individual human being as a totally material organism. Even so-called mental states are held to be neurologically based and reducible to physical terms. Indeed, human nature is defined as "essentially an electron-proton aggregate which is identical in nature with inorganic substances except for the presence of . . . life . . . [which] is believed to be due to 'organizational properties' inherent in organic tissue" (Thorpe, quoted in Brubacher 1962, p. 49).

The physicalist position, as suggested in the introduction to this section, is most clearly associated with such scientific (or more appropriately, "scientistic") movements as behaviorism. Because of their materialistic-mechanistic view of human nature, behaviorists' inquiries into the nature of man are limited to the observation of overt physical behavior in the context of presumed naturalistic cause-effect relationships. Curriculum based on this view of human nature, then, consists essentially of proposed stimulus-response sequences accompanied by prescribed reinforcement schedules. Programmed instruction is probably the best contemporary example of curriculum based on a physicalist view of man.

The ontological questions addressed in the paragraphs above may have the effect of oversimplifying the mind-body problem by setting up three discrete options for defining the essence of man. If we do not insist on an *ontological* analysis, however, and allow ourselves the more flexible option of a *functional* one, we may in the long run make much more headway in understanding human nature. For example, we can observe, as has Dubos (1962, p. 3 ff.),[1] that man's behavior has at various times exhibited profoundly contrasting characteristics. It has ranged from greed and cruelty to asceticism and self-sacrifice, from earthy sensuality to high idealism, from practical dealing to aesthetic ecstasy. These contrasts suggest that, while human nature certainly evidences an animal or "bestial" side, its "most interesting and significant aspects . . . are derived from traits which do not exist or are barely noticeable outside of mankind" (Dubos 1962, p. 9). Thus, Dubos suggests that the individual human organism is a highly complex integrated structure that, to a far greater degree than other forms of life, is capable of responding to its environment in either of two contrasting modes. The "beast" in man consists of behavior originating in the animal nature he shares with other forms of life, while the "angel" in him is a manifestation of more complex structures.[2] Mind, then, is not defined in existential terms,

1. René Dubos is a prominent microbiologist and pathologist. He was the first scientist to demonstrate the feasibility of obtaining antibiotics from microbes.

2. Man has long recognized the "beast" and the "angel" in his nature, as works such as *Everyman*, Goethe's *Faust*, Stevenson's *Dr. Jekyll and Mr. Hyde*, and Wilde's *The Picture of Dorian Gray* so aptly testify.

either material or nonmaterial, but as

> *a manner of response by the living organism to the total environment—
> a response which is more or less elaborate, depending upon the complex-
> ity of the organism and perhaps even upon its history (Dubos 1962, p.
> 11).*

Although all living organisms manifest mind in some degree, it is most prominent in man.

Dubos goes on to explain that the complex structures associated with man's
spiritual/mental nature are responsible for his "richer and more subtle perception of the cosmos" and the wider range of his responses to stimuli. Thus,
consciously or unconsciously man "is linked to cosmic influences which include
not only the present, but also what he remembers of the past, and the manner
in which he visualizes the future" (Dubos 1962, p. 11).

Dubos' position is supported by C. H. Waddington, a British biologist.
Waddington (1961, p. 27) proposes that it is the *biological nature* of the
human individual to become an "ethicizing being," to formulate a "particular
system of ethical beliefs," and to criticize "those beliefs by some supra-ethical
criterion of wisdom." Waddington, of course, is cognizant of the complex system of social teaching and learning that man has developed and of its importance
in shaping human nature. Because of this, he eschews the "either-or" trap of so
many writers who argue the "nature-nurture" dichotomy, and he insists on
what he calls a "socio-genetic" view of human evolution. Indeed, Waddington
employs the term "human evolution" to refer to the *cultural* changes that differentiate contemporary men from their Stone-Age ancestors.

The arguments of these biologists avoid the ontological mind-body problems
by proposing that man's "higher" motivations are the result of highly developed,
complex, uniquely human psychophysiological structures. It thus becomes possible to argue that whether man's behavior is *human* (a manifestation of "mind")
or *bestial* (a manifestion of "body") depends essentially on whether it is controlled by complex, distinctively human, psychobiological structures or by the
less complex structures that man shares with other forms of life. Seen in this
light, man is both mind *and* body. The curricular implications of this view of
human nature are obvious: the development of uniquely human attributes in
learners and the subordination (not suppression) of their animal instincts. The
criterion for judging the humanness of particular attributes, at least for Waddington, is the degree to which those attributes foster the *ethical evolution of the
human species*. As we shall see in the next chapter, this analysis of the mind-
body nature of man has significant implications for a contemporary, scientifically
based conception of human nature.

MAN: A CONSTANT OR A MUTABLE NATURE?

Perhaps the most prominent contemporary proponent of the view that human
nature is constant is Robert Maynard Hutchins. This philosopher-educator
writes: "We must insist that no matter how environments differ, human nature

is, always has been, and always will be the same everywhere" (quoted in Hook 1946, p. 19). Such a position on the nature of human nature inevitably leads to the conclusion that the curriculum must everywhere and at all times be the same for every individual to be educated.

Dissenting from this position is the educational philosopher Sidney Hook, who views the denial that human nature can change as "the sheerest dogmatism." He cites not only the microcosmic plasticity of the individual human organism in response to specific environmental conditions (such as education), but the macrocosmic plasticity of the human race under conditions of genetic-environmental evolution. In large measure, whether men change or not "depends upon whether they choose to retain or transform their culture" (Hook 1946, p. 24). And, of course, he is quick to point out that "Human history is an eloquent record of cultural change, of continuities and discontinuities, in social institutions, language, values and ideas" (Hook 1946, p. 26). Thus, Hook argues for an evolving curriculum that reflects this evolutionary pattern of man's development.

Few writers argue for the unlimited variability of human nature just as few argue its total immutability. In general, a position is taken somewhere in between, with mutability *within limits* being granted. However, some scholars regard these limits as far more indefinite than others, so that the argument usually takes the form of *how much* of human nature is attributable to genetics (and, therefore, is fixed) and how much is due to environmental influence (and, therefore, is variable). Obviously one's position on this issue has significant implications for curriculum.

The trait of human nature that has been subject to the most widespread "constant-or-mutable" debate in education is intelligence. As measured by IQ tests, human "intelligence" has been shown to vary extensively from one individual to the next. Indeed, obtained IQ scores (which average around 100) may range from below 30 to above 170.[3] While admitting that individual IQ scores can vary up to 15 points due to error and other accidental circumstances, many psychologists maintain that intelligence is essentially a genetically based constant in human nature. It is fundamentally viewed as the fixed and innate "capacity to learn."

The assumption that intelligence is a fixed, genetic trait which is *expressed* through education almost always leads to elitist curriculum policies: an intellectually rigorous curriculum for high-intelligence individuals (society's leaders) and manual-vocational curricula for low-intelligence workers (society's followers). Since a high correlation has been found to exist between social class and "intelligence," the schools become an instrument for maintaining the socioeconomic status quo. Even more tragic, perhaps, is the fact that the genetic assumption is used to protect inferior curricula and ineffective teaching: some students just *cannot* learn, it is claimed, because "they do not have the ability."

Critics of the view that intelligence is essentially a genetically based constant

---

3. See the section "Indirect Nature of Measurement" in Chapter 16 for an exposition of the assumptions and theoretical bases of IQ tests.

maintain that it is much more heavily dependent on environment and is, therefore, modifiable. While admitting the existence of a genetic component (apes, for example, cannot learn quadratic equations), they see the line between nature and nurture as being very broad and quite unclear. The question of whether or not genetically based intellectual potential of individuals is equal is really irrelevant, say the environmentalists, because whatever individual potential may be, it far exceeds any demand level likely to be placed on it by society. In other words, genetically based intellectual potential is so great in comparison to its actualization under most conditions of life that innate differences, if they do exist, just do not matter.

This view of the nature-nurture relationship has led environmentalists to take the position that IQ scores are not an index of fixed innate intellectual capacity, but rather of its level of actualization. That is, IQ scores are viewed essentially as the *effect* of environment (learning) on genetic potential. This being the case, substantial opportunity is seen for raising intelligence levels through environmental management. The curricular application of such a position is not difficult to derive: Since intelligence is something that is created and developed, all learners are exposed to enriched curricula designed to actualize intellectual potentials and to overcome whatever intellectual deprivation may have resulted from prior environmental poverty. We might say that in terms of social policy, the curricular challenge is to raise the intelligence of the masses to, and beyond, the levels heretofore attained only by the elite.

The mountain of research done on intelligence over the years has failed to settle conclusively whether the trait of intelligence is grounded essentially in genetics or environment. Moreover, whether intelligence is regarded as fixed or mutable depends to a large degree on how the concept is defined. It should be pointed out, however, that Western European culture has traditionally supported the notion of a hierarchy of fixed intellectual ability among individuals. And as we have seen in previous chapters, culture can permeate our values and thought processes in ways that completely escape conscious reflection. The question these points raise is simply this: To what degree is one's position on the intelligence issue the effect of rational assessment of available evidence and to what degree is it the result of unconscious culturally induced bias?

Notwithstanding the indecisiveness of the research evidence and the overwhelming tendency of American curriculum to be based on the genetic-elitist ideology, a disposition to favor the environmentalist position seems to be warranted. Since scientific research has provided us with virtually no definitive conclusions regarding human intellectual potential, it seems morally incumbent upon us to declare in favor of the most optimistic view of man. To do otherwise, we run the risk of unjustly condemning millions of human beings to inferior, shriveled lives, not only socioeconomically, but also in terms of the satisfactions to be derived from the maximal actualization of individual potentials, talents, and capacities—all on the presumption that they "do not have the ability." The ideal of equal opportunity in fact rests upon the open-ended assumption of the mutability of human nature.

The arguments above respecting intelligence can be generalized to broader aspects of human nature. Man's moral sense, for example, as it was discussed in the previous section on mind, can be viewed either in constant or evolutionary terms. (While Darwin admitted that a high standard of morality gives "a slight or no advantage" to individuals in their struggle for survival, he did maintain that it gives "an immense advantage" to one social group over another.) So, too, with self-consciousness, ideal formulation, future awareness, conscious purpose, and many other distinctly human traits that separate man from all other forms of life. Like intelligence, these aspects of human nature can be viewed genetically as vast reservoirs of potential only scantly actualized by present environmental conditions. Thus, human nature, within rather broad genetic limits, would appear to be susceptible to a wide range of possible modifications.[4]

Is science able to shed any light on the general question of whether human nature is constant or mutable? The evidence of the past hundred years seems overwhelmingly to indicate not only that man is capable of changing his nature, but that he in fact is presently the subject of significant evolutionary processes. Sir Julian Huxley, the celebrated British biologist, has stated that almost all scientists "now believe with confidence, that the whole of reality is one gigantic process of evolution [which] produces increased novelty and variety, and ever higher types of organization . . ." (cited by Dubos 1962, p. 84). Huxley elaborates this position by pointing out that the evolutionary process of the cosmos can be classified into three phases: (1) the lifeless or inorganic phase that characterizes most of the universe, (2) the organic or biological phase that characterizes the Earth and perhaps some planets of other suns, and (3) the human or psychosocial phase that characterizes man on Earth and perhaps a few organisms elsewhere in the universe. This latter phase, according to Huxley, is based on

> the accumulation of knowledge and the organization of experience. It works chiefly by a conscious selection of ideas and aims, and produces extremely rapid change. Evolution in this phase is mainly cultural, not genetic; it is no longer focussed solely on survival, but is increasingly directed towards fulfillment and towards quality of achievement (quoted in Dubos 1962, pp. 84, 85).

This view of human nature closely parallels that of the environmentalists in education, especially insofar as it attaches much more importance to environmental conditions than it does to biological antecedents. Moreover, it is highly compatible with Waddington's concept of sociogenetic evolution. Perhaps most importantly, it provides us with an optimistic, as well as practically useful, con-

---

4. The emphasis on variability as a result of environmental forces in the foregoing paragraphs is not intended to suggest the absolute immutability of genetically based traits. The genetic basis of human nature, of course, is susceptible to change as a result of evolutionary processes; this change takes place so slowly, however, that it is scarcely perceptible. Thus, for all practical purposes genetic traits usually are treated *as if* they are constants.

ception of human nature. Its importance for curriculum becomes apparent when we draw together all the strands of its arguments and state them in something like the following terms: Evolution has endowed man with the sophisticated biological structures that provide the raw material for his distinctly human characteristics (nature). Just as biological evolution involves "the continuous invention of self-reproducing matter" (Dubos 1962, p. 85), the evolution of human nature involves continuous invention in self-reproducing human traits, such as mind, consciousness, and a moral sense. The evolution of these traits (like intelligence) depends on those psychosocial factors in the environment that represent the accumulated experience of man—i.e., the culture. Hence, the evolution of more *human* human beings will be fostered by a curriculum that selects from the culture those factors that provide developmental experiences with the distinctively human aspects of man's collective life. It is such a curriculum, perhaps, that most appropriately is designated "humanistic."

MAN: FREE OR DETERMINED?

For centuries the debate has raged: Does human nature include the capacity to choose and act freely or, as with inorganic matter, is it so aligned with the rest of nature that it permits man only passively to react to external forces? The position for absolute freedom is ordinarily argued either from an old or a relatively new viewpoint. Traditionally, free will has been regarded as a transcendent faculty possessed by all human beings. The doctrine holds that the individual, as "an originating source of energy," is "self-directive" and "self-determining." Being a free agent, man may intervene in the natural stream of cause-effect events and thus determine his destiny. This is so because freedom "is a primary quality of reality. It is God-given" (Brubacher 1962, p. 66). More recently, it has been the existentialists who have most vigorously championed man's freedom to choose.[5] The existentialists maintain that man does not *possess* freedom, he *is* his freedom (Kneller 1958, p. 25). Man not only *can* choose, he *must*. Whether an individual believes himself to be free or determined is evidence that he has made a choice; indeed, even refusing to choose represents a free choice, say the existentialists.[6]

Contrasted with these free-will positions are those—old and new—which view human beings as essentially determined creatures. The older viewpoint has a religious basis and is best represented, perhaps, in traditional Calvinist theology. This school of thought teaches (at least in the abstract) that everything is determined by the will of God. Since the eighteenth century, however, and the rise of scientific materialism,[7] the determinist position has had increasing sup-

5. See the section "Existentialism" in Chapter 6.

6. In a sense, the existentialists are saying that man, by his nature, is *determined* to be a free choosing being. It may therefore be argued that since man cannot choose *not* to be free, he in fact is not.

7. See the section on Earth-centered philosophies in Chapter 6.

port from the scientific community. As a matter of fact, determinism today is regarded almost exclusively as a "scientific" position. Those who advocate determinism base their argument on the chain of cause-effect relationships observable in everyday life. Isolate any event or action in the natural world, they say, and we are able to identify its immediate past cause or causes. These past causes, in their turn, are the results of immediate prior causes, and so on into the indefinite past. Thus, all present actions, events, and conditions are explainable in terms of their antecedents. Since man is simply one factor in this gigantic system of cause-effect processes that we know as the "world machine," his behavior, like that of all the other factors, is inextricably bound by the cause-effect laws of the system. Far from being free to introduce novelty in the system, human beings and their behavior are determined by the necessity of preceding conditions.

The question of man's freedom, as well as the conditions under which it does or does not exist, has important implications for curriculum planners. For example, if the individual is in fact totally free to choose or reject in all circumstances, we cannot be sure of the influence (and hence the effectiveness) of *any* curriculum. The individual student may choose to learn or not, but since it is entirely his prerogative (free will), there is no way that curriculum planners can be held responsible if he does not learn. Furthermore, this position on human nature suggests that the curriculum should consist of as great a "smorgasbord" of experiences as possible in order to maximize free-choice possibilities.[8] Since every individual is free, he is responsible for choosing the nature of his own educated self. With no goal other than "maximized free choice" possible, education becomes virtually nondirective, a sort of random, leave-it-to-chance (i.e., free-will) enterprise.

The curriculum suggested by scientific determinism contrasts markedly with the one described above. It consists of a carefully controlled sequence of cause-effect events intended to mold students' individual natures into a desired configuration. In effect, the aims, goals, and objectives of the determinist curriculum describe (and prescribe) the ultimate nature of the educated human being. As the behavioral sciences discover more and more about the cause-effect relationships governing human behavior, of course, the curriculum will become an increasingly efficient instrument for controlling the nature of man.[9] The account of education given by B. F. Skinner in his utopian novel *Walden II* provides many specific examples of what an ideal deterministic curriculum is like.

The issues involved in the free-will/determinism controversy are by no means as clear and discrete as the extreme positions outlined above might indicate. Reality is rarely an either/or proposition; and the truth in this case, as in most others, probably lies in the massive gray area somewhere between total freedom

8. Many existentially based "free schools" have developed curriculum policies that allow virtually *anything* to be included in the curriculum.

9. See the section "Perspectives on Training and Education" in Chapter 13 for a comprehensive discussion of training and the "technical model" of curriculum planning.

and ironclad determinism. At this point, we need to explore some of the things we know about ourselves and the world not only to illuminate the real basis of the human condition with regard to this problem, but to establish for ourselves what we *mean* when we talk about free will.

Observation clearly indicates that whether or not people *believe* in determinism, they almost always *behave* as if they were free. For example, even though differences exist in the degree to which individuals assert themselves in determining the direction of their lives, they are rarely so passive as to suggest that they are the totally helpless (determined) pawns of biological-environmental forces. Furthermore, we are all wont to hold people responsible for their actions, a habit that implies belief in at least some degree of free will, since people whose behavior is determined can hardly be held accountable for their actions. If these common-sense observations on human freedom are convincing, however, they do not strike the depths of our experience nearly as certainly as do the words of the American physicist Arthur Compton: "One's ability to move his hand at will is more directly and certainly known than are Newton's laws. If these laws deny one's ability to move his hand at will, the preferable conclusion is that Newton's laws require modification" (quoted in Dubos 1962, p. 19).

Notwithstanding the apparent freedom inherent in these accustomed ways of dealing with life, the contradictory regularity of cause-effect conditions that govern so much of our experience is difficult to ignore. We know that matter, both inorganic and organic, *is* subject to natural laws, and science has demonstrated that in many, many respects, men *are* the products of natural and environmental forces. How, then, can we reconcile the great paradox? How can we synthesize the apparent power of free will with the cause-effect regularity of material existence?

Science, i.e., that branch of twentieth-century physics called "quantum mechanics," provides us with an illuminating and helpful perspective. Until the development of quantum mechanics, scientists believed that *in principle* the motion of all particles could be calculated *in advance* if all the data and all the physical laws involved in the situation were known. "Now they are convinced that this is true only within certain limits defined by a mathematical equation" (Conant 1952, p. 85). In order words, it is possible to treat a large number of particles mathematically (and thereby determine their positions within certain limits of probability), but it is not possible to predict the precise behavior or position of any individual particle. This condition of the behavior of matter (e.g., molecules and electrons) commonly is referred to as the "indeterminacy principle."

The promulgation of the indeterminacy principle by physicists confirmed what for many scientists and philosophers had been a long-held conviction: that unpredictability is a general characteristic of the evolving universe. For example, Conant (1952, pp. 108, 109) expressed this view when he wrote: "The common-sense world is one of partial uniformity only. There are areas of experience where we know that uncertainty is the certainty. . . ." This extrapolation of the indeterminacy principle is really not a novel concept in modern education, where statistical data are commonly used to predict, for example, the *probability* of success in school of given individuals. On the basis of group data and statistical treatment we can determine the probability of an individual succeeding, but because of the indeterminacy principle (involving, among other things, individual free choice within limits), it is *impossible to predict with certainty* his success or failure. It should be emphasized that our inability to predict with certainty is only partly due to ignorance of *all* of the factors governing the situation; no matter how many data are available or how much is known about the "natural laws" governing behavior, certainty of prediction is obviated by the operation of the indeterminacy principle, involving, among other factors, the operation of free human choice.

The foregoing discussion is important because it highlights three factors that are critical to human nature: (1) the future orientation of man, (2) the future of logical necessity, and (3) the indeterminacy principle. The future orientation of man is significant because it explains his distinctively human concern for prediction and decision making:

> The main reason for which men desire to know whence they came, and how they are what they are, is that they would so much like to know whither they are going. Concern about the future is the most powerful motivation of man . . . (Dubos 1962, pp. 20, 21; emphasis added).

If the curriculum is to be at all relevant, of course, it must take into account man's concern for his individual future and for the future of the race. The second factor—the future of logical necessity—refers to the preordained future. If man is going to have any control over his future, he must be able to count on a certain regularity in the flow of cause-effect sequences. Thus, the fact that nature, including all living things, even man, is subject in some degree to the operation of natural laws must be regarded as a congenial factor in decision making for the future. In this regard, the curriculum is bound to include and transmit what is known about the operation of the physical universe and its inhabitants (the physical, natural, and behavioral sciences).

Finally, the indeterminacy principle frees man (and the rest of the universe) from what might appear to be the determined future of natural necessity. It is this characteristic of human nature, working through distinctively human biological structures, that differentiates man (in degree) from other forms of life and matter. Of course, indeterminacy, as we have seen, is an operative principle in all forms of life and, indeed, in inorganic matter as well. It is the comparatively greater degree of its operation in man, via sophisticated human biological structures, that enables man to achieve his relatively greater degree of freedom.

How, specifically, does the indeterminacy principle operate in man? In the historical past man's choices tended to be fairly predictable because they were dependent on traditional conceptions of life handed down from generation to generation. That is, cultural evolution was so slow, and tradition so deep rooted, that change was almost imperceptible. Relatively speaking, determinism held sway. Every now and then, however, extreme novelty was introduced by a person or persons who saw things quite differently. Thus, Christ, Galileo, Luther, and Marx introduced *ideas* that radically altered man's conception of himself and his world, and thus radically altered his decision-making process and the future. These "great moments in human history," as Dubos (1962, p. 89) calls them, represent the indeterminacy of human intervention—the revolutionary *willed* departures which correspond to new ideas and attitudes toward life. During the past half-century man's accumulated knowledge and technology have reached a level that makes possible, and indeed generates, significant willed departures at an extremely accelerated rate, affecting "a wider and wider range of human activities" (Dubos 1962, p. 89). Man and his culture have multiplied opportunities for choice (and its consequences) at such an exponential rate that, in effect, the indeterminacy of human choice has gained ascendency over the relative determinism of the past. Change has become so much a fact of life that, "Whether deliberately or not, we are in the process of *creating tomorrow*" (Dubos 1962, p. 90).

Because of their importance it is worthwhile to elaborate on the above points. As we noted in a previous chapter, men have always been faced with the need to make choices and reach decisions. In the distant past these choices tended to be determined by antecedent forces operating according to natural laws. This was so because man was not aware of the forces that were shaping his decisions; the vast potential of his distinctively human biological structures had scarcely been actualized. In short, man was not a significant factor in determining the flow of cause-effect events.

As man evolved toward increasingly advanced phases of the psychosocial stage of development, however, actualization of the potential in his sophisticated biological structures enabled him to reduce his subjection to natural forces and to increase his control over his future and the world. Awareness and knowledge of himself and his environment enabled him to become a more significant factor in determining the direction and quality of evolution. Thus, human ideas, purposes, opinions, tastes, manners, interests, etc., became increasingly influential determinants in directing the course of events. These determinants (rooted in the psychosocial actualization of human biological structures) operate in such independent ways that they make the future to a large degree unpredictable, or at best predictable only in a statistical sense. It is these self-conscious factors in human activity (perhaps best summarized by the term "human *ideas*") that represent the indeterminacy principle working in man. The characteristic of human nature that we call "free will," then, becomes maximally actualized insofar as the forces operating in a given situation (and this includes man and human nature) are known, understood, and taken into account in the decision-making process.

In view of the foregoing discussion, it seems clear that the future of the world and the very nature of man are today more dependent than ever on the choices that human beings make. Physiologically speaking, man has the capacity to be aware that his decisions have both immediate and long-term consequences. In other words, biological structures enable him to choose responsibly. Unfortunately, however, biological structures cannot guarantee responsible choosing, for this characteristically human behavior rests on the psychosocial actualization of the biological potential.

One reading of history leads to the conclusion that man's animal impulses (those governed by deterministic necessity) dominate his human faculties (those grounded in self-conscious thought and ideas). A more optimistic reading of human evolution maintains that man's human capacities are increasingly gaining dominance over impulses he shares with lower forms of life. We should bear in mind that whichever of these two views of man we choose to accept will itself have consequences for our future.

The material wealth and creature comforts made possible by human knowledge and technology are, of course, important for human happiness. But the future of the world and the nature of man are ultimately dependent upon human choices concerned with the kind of world that *should* be created in the future. The future, therefore, depends on the ideas that men entertain and the questions that they ask. What criteria will man select to judge the future as it *should* be? What ideas and concepts of human existence will govern his choices? What, in short, will be the ideas that lead him to a judgment of the good life?

To conclude this section we can observe that the question "Is man free or determined?" is probably the wrong one to ask. Man is free, but within the limits of the facts and laws of human and cosmic existence. The way we have described it, freedom as a characteristic of human nature is a matter of the aggregate influence man is able to exert on the future by way of conscious, purposeful intervention in the flow of events. It follows from this that human freedom is maximized by increased awareness of and knowledge about the forces directing the evolution of events.

The curriculum suggested by this view of man is not difficult to infer. Its major aim would be the development of humanness through the maximization of human freedom. Since freedom depends upon knowledge of the forces operating in the universe, the curriculum would give some attention to the physical and biological sciences. But human freedom also depends both on knowledge of man(kind), and perhaps more crucially, on self (or individual) knowledge. Knowledge of mankind would be gained through such content as human physiology and the social and behavioral sciences, while self-knowledge, though gained in part through this same content, would also depend on the affective insights provided by literature and the arts.

Because human freedom is today far more constrained by social conventions and other man-based institutions than it is by natural forces, the curriculum would center its greatest efforts on the study of man and his institutions. Furthermore, because freedom depends so crucially not only on *what* is known, but on how it is utilized in the decision-making process, the curriculum will place great emphasis in its learning activities on developing skill in analysis, synthesis, problem solving, and other aspects of reflective and self-critical thinking. If this sounds remarkably similar to the curriculum advocated by the pragmatists, we should not be too surprised. Their concept of "intelligent transacting" in many ways is the same as the concept of "free will" described in the discussion above. Finally, because man (and his decision making) is future oriented, the curriculum would be intimately concerned with society and the conditions of life that it supports. Curriculum "relevance" would in large measure be determined by the degree to which it enabled students to transact intelligently now to bring about desired futures.

MAN: GOOD OR EVIL?

Jean Jacques Rousseau (eighteenth-century philosopher and educational theorist) believed that man is *naturally* good. He reasoned that all things created by God come into existence in an uncorrupted, perfect state. Furthermore, he argued that before the establishment of organized social systems, man lived happily and in harmony with nature. It seemed plain to Rousseau that it is society and its institutions—especially its private property claims that make laws, police, and punishments necessary—that corrupt the original goodness of human nature. This assumption about the nature of man (held even today by many educationists) leads to definite conclusions regarding curriculum theory and practice. For example, since an inherently good nature implies naturally good growth impulses, it follows that the central aim of the curriculum is to foster children's growth along lines revealed by their "naturally good" impulses. Curriculum content and learning activities, therefore, will be selected on the basis of the natural propensities and interests of students. Furthermore, if children are active and boisterous, the teacher must avoid suppressing them for fear of deflecting and distorting good tendencies. In short, a curriculum growing out of the assumption that human nature is naturally good will be highly "student centered" and "permissive." Some offshoots of progressive curricula of the 1930s represent this tendency in curriculum as do, for example, the contemporary proposals of such educators as Holt (1967), Postman and Weingartner (1969), and Neill (1960).

The opposite of this view of human nature is probably most unequivocally stated by Jonathan Swift in *Gulliver's Travels*. Here, Swift pronounces mankind to be "the most pernicious Race of little odious Vermin that Nature ever suffered to crawl upon the Surface of the Earth." Although not quite so unequivocally, perhaps, most Western religions, especially Christianity, take much the same view of man. Their position is grounded in the doctrine of original sin (which Rousseau, incidentally, rejected): when Adam rebelled against God in the Garden of Eden, he forfeited his pristine nature and fell from grace into corruption. Religious education (and all of modern Western education traces its roots to church-controlled systems) tends, therefore, to be founded on a curriculum whose central aim is to suppress man's "naturally evil" tendencies and thereby enable him to attain a state of grace. A curriculum designed for this purpose will clearly contrast markedly with one designed to foster the unfolding of assumed good tendencies. Its content, for example, will be drawn from the storehouse of knowledge accumulated by the race and certified to be good by clerical authorities. Furthermore, since children's interests "naturally" tend to be perverse, they cannot possibly be employed as curriculum-selection criteria. Moreover, since the learner's natural behavioral tendencies are born of wicked motivations, they are to be suppressed—brutally, if need be—so that he can learn the behaviors that lead to salvation and grace.[10]

Although rooted in the religious tradition, the view that human nature is evil has been adapted to the more secular *Weltanschauung* of contemporary civilization. Modern scientists who have studied human nature in exclusively Darwinian terms, i.e., in terms of the evolution of animal instincts (e.g., aggression, sex, territoriality, etc.), see man in much the same way as their more religious counterparts. They agree that man's naturally evil (animal) instincts need to be suppressed and if possible extinguished by appropriate conditioning so that the more rational and civilized behaviors certified by the educated elite can be learned.

It is interesting to speculate on how an assumed conception of human nature can affect a curriculum and by extension, the product of that curriculum. If we view human nature as bestial, will we be prone to construct curricula designed to control and train beasts? And what consequences will such a curriculum have for its students? On the other hand, if we view human nature as angelic, will our curricula encourage the unfolding of the saintly man? What is suggested here is that our assumptions, at least in part, may operate as self-fulfilling prophesies. To the extent that they do, we must make every effort to subject them to careful and enlightened examination. But there is another reason for examining this question of the inherent goodness or evil of human nature. Even granting the partial operation of the self-fulfilling prophecy, we find that it oversimplifies the case by assuming the overriding importance of perceptions and neglecting the fact of external existence. Important as our assumptions may be, attention must be paid to a reality "out there." Can we determine whether human nature is "really" good or evil? It is to this inquiry that we now turn our attention.

To ask whether man is good or evil elicits the type of response briefly discussed above, i.e., that man is *either* basically good or basically evil. But as we have noted before, the either/or type of question might not be the right one to ask. With regard to man's good or evil nature, are there other possibilities to consider? A minimum of reflection, of course, indicates that there are.

One possibility that warrants our attention is that man may be both good *and* evil. Dubos (1962, p. 3 ff.) takes this position and, it will be recalled, passing reference was made to it in an earlier section (Man: Mind and/or Body). There we noted that man's behavior has at various times exhibited pro-

10. When seventeenth-century Puritan schoolmasters said that they "beat the devil" out of their pupils, they meant it, literally.

foundly contrasting characteristics of good and evil: from rank avarice to selfless generosity, for example, and from vicious cruelty to altruistic self-sacrifice. This Jekyll-and-Hyde schizophrenia, Dubos suggests, represents what may seem to be a condition of contradiction and paradox, but which in fact may reflect a characteristic of existence called "complementarity." Complementarity "denotes the logical relation between two concepts which appear mutually exclusive, both of which, nevertheless, have to be used in order to achieve a complete description of reality" (Dubos 1962, p. 4). Examples of complementarity, although not so noted, have already appeared in this text. For example, the decision of physicists to conceptualize light as both a corpuscle and a wave (see Chapter 4) constitutes complementarity because it produces a more comprehensive description of light. In the same way, physicists invoke complementarity when they contrast matter with "antimatter." And we have employed complementarity in previous sections of this chapter when we argued that human nature is characteristically both mind *and* body, free *and* determined. With regard to the problem at hand:

> *the most common determinants of human behavior are today, as they always have been, crude material appetites and selfish ambitions; but even the most ordinary events of life lead me to believe that the performance of mankind is far more exciting and inspiring than could ever have been expected from the trivial and selfish motivation of the apelike creatures which constitute the human species (Dubos 1962, p. 6).*

Thus, Dubos concludes, "Ever since man has emerged from his brutish origin, the beast and the angel have coexisted in him" (p. 10).

Related to the theory that man is both good *and* evil, but perhaps more useful because its emphasis is behavioral/functional rather than ontological, is the view that man is essentially neutral. According to this position, man is an energy-converting and purposive organism that seeks maximization of his own being and his own sense of self (Becker 1969, p. 641). When the environment permits self-maximization only in ways that have evil consequences, man's behavior is "evil"; but when environments are so arranged that channels for self-maximization lead to creative, socially beneficial consequences, his behavior is "good." As we noted earlier, evolution has reached a state that permits more extensive control over the conditions of man's environment. It follows from this that to a large degree man is the producer of his own good or evil nature.

While the foregoing discussion outlines very broadly the basic tenets of the theory that man is neutral, it omits many critical considerations with which a complete exposition of the theory must deal. For example, what are the criteria by which good and evil consequences are judged? What are the conditions under which good and evil environments are generated? And what are the characteristics of good and evil men and environments?

Because the proposition that man is essentially neutral is a part of the synoptic view of man to be argued in Chapter 10, we shall not attempt a more detailed presentation here. We shall only note that a conception of human nature incorporating neutrality, freedom, and mutability takes the future of man out of the realm of ontological necessity and places it in human hands. As Maslow (1962, p. 14) has noted, "man has his future within him, dynamically active at this present moment." Any curriculum that does not take this open-ended concept into account can never educate; it can only train.

References

Becker, Ernest. 1969. "The Evaded Question: Science and Human Nature." *Commonweal* (February 21).

Brubacher, John S. 1962. *Modern Philosophies of Education*. New York: McGraw-Hill Book Company.

Conant, James B. 1952. *Modern Science and Modern Man*. New York: Columbia University Press. Reprinted by Doubleday Anchor Books.

Dubos, René. 1962. *The Torch of Life*. New York: Pocket Books.

Holt, John. 1967. *How Children Learn*. New York: Pitman Publishing Corp.

Hook, Sidney. 1946. *Education for Modern Man*. New York: The Dial Press.

Kneller, George F. 1958. *Existentialism and Education*. New York: John Wiley & Sons.

Maslow, Abraham H. 1962. *Toward a Psychology of Being*. New York: D. Van Nostrand Company.

Neill, A. S. 1960. *Summerhill*. New York: Hart.

Postman, Neil, and Charles Weingartner. 1969. *Teaching as a Subversive Activity*. New York: Delacorte.

Waddington, C. H. 1961. *The Ethical Animal*. New York: Atheneum Publishers.

CHAPTER 10
THE INDIVIDUAL:
A SYNOPTIC VIEW OF MAN

We are now in a position (1) to sketch, if only in outline form, a portrait of human nature, and (2) to suggest the directions that man must take in order to develop his characteristically human potentials—that is, in order to evolve as a more *human* being. Moreover, our portrait will be firmly grounded in the broadest scientific tradition, including not only objective-mechanistic science, but subjective science, which understands that "man is immersed *in* nature, is part of nature, and so can never hope to know the inner secret of things" (Becker 1967, p. 19). The awesome implications of this observation presage a philosophical dimension to our portrait of human nature, and as we shall see, this is the unavoidable case. The science on which our portrait is based avoids the hubris of objective-mechanistic science because it fully appreciates what Dewey knew so long ago: that ultimately, "scientific fact" is merely "cosmos examined by a speck of cosmos."

The Concept of Encapsulation

In a previous chapter a condition of human existence that we called "unconscious culturally induced bias" was discussed. This condition, it will be recalled, consists essentially of an unconscious "gut-level" adherence to an interlocking fabric of ideas, ideals, beliefs, values, assumptions, and modes of thought that have been implanted by cultural forces into the individual's psyche. Language, media, child-rearing practices, customs, and a variety of other social-psychological factors contribute to this condition. It will further be recalled that the unconscious and unexamined dispositions that comprise culturally induced bias not only influence the individual's behavior but may in many respects contribute to the shape of his world view or reality image (*Weltanschauung*). This is an extremely significant concept, since, as we have seen, individuals tend to act in terms of their definition of the situation.

Unconscious culturally induced bias, however, represents only one facet of a more encompassing and pervasive state of unconsciousness that occurs with the interaction of the individual human organism and his total natural/social environment. This larger unconsciousness, which is viewed by many as a significant determinant of human nature, has been treated by various writers under the designations "adjustment," "alienation," "out-of-awareness," "encrustation," and "encapsulation."[1]

Encapsulation (as well as the variant terms noted above) refers to a general condition in which the individual believes that he has an accurate perception of reality when in fact, because of various limitations, he has only a partial and distorted image of what is really "out there." In addition to its external cultural basis, this condition has roots in both the physiology and internal psychology of man.

PHYSIOLOGICAL LIMITATIONS OF HUMAN NATURE

At the most elemental level, we may point out the obvious, but commonly overlooked, fact that all men are encapsulated simply because they exist as *homo sapiens*. Genetically and physiologically, man is constrained to see the world from a uniquely "human point of view." The limitations on an individual's ability to "know" what is "really" out there become clear when we consider, for example, that man cannot hear sound frequencies outside the 20 to 20,000 cycles-per-second range. This means, of course, that there is a whole world of sound "out there" that is simply unavailable to his senses. Further, man is able to see only one-seventieth of the total range of light wavelengths. How presumptuous the dictum "Seeing is believing" appears when we consider this physiological datum! Indeed, the inherent deficiencies of our native visual equipment become all too clear when we think of the teaming worlds of life that exist unseen around, upon, and within our bodies. The foregoing observations, of course, can be extended to man's other physiological means for deriving his interpretation of reality: his ability to discriminate scores of smells and tastes is extremely poor, and his tactual sense has often been cited as one of his feeblest (Royce 1964, pp. 36, 37). In short, man views the world through a set of physiological sensory "goggles" that he believes conveys an accurate image

1. "Adjustment" is a term routinely used to convey unexamined psychological alignment with the environment. "Alienation" is Becker's (1967) word. Pritzkau (1970) employs the terms "out-of-awareness" and "encrustation." "Encapsulation," Royce's (1964) name for the concept, is the one which, for the sake of consistency, we have somewhat arbitrarily chosen to use in this chapter.

of "what is," but which in fact present him with a highly edited and uniquely human point of view.

PSYCHOLOGICAL LIMITATIONS OF HUMAN NATURE

The psychological factors that contribute to human encapsulation are so numerous, complex, and interrelated that volumes would be required to treat them adequately. For our purposes, however, it will be necessary only to touch on a few of the most important to make our point. As Royce (1964, p. 37) notes, men are limited in their ability to learn and think. For example, man's memory (both short and long term) is highly restricted. Most people cannot repeat ten digits that have just been recited to them, and even fewer are able, five years afterward, to pass the twelfth-grade history exam that was graded "A" when it was first taken. Indeed, we know that "forgetting is much more rapid than learning" (Royce 1964, p. 37).

The ability to conceptualize abstract ideas and relationships is another area of man's psychological limitation. The metaphorical images conveyed by literature and poetry seem to be beyond the understanding of some individuals, and the abstract concepts of higher mathematics baffle many others. Even man's imagination (commonly believed to be highly creative) has obvious and significant limitations. Before Copernicus, it was virtually impossible to imagine the earth as anything but flat, and before Freud, who could imagine human beings moved by any motivation other than conscious will? Today, we all *concede* infinity, but who among us actually possesses the imagination to *conceive* it? The prospect of the boundless universe, outer space, and the meaning of its existence simply staggers all human imagination (Royce 1964, p. 38).

Finally, it is ironic to note that man's rationality, his one-time most cherished characteristic, is limited extensively by his irrationality. Since Freud and the psychoanalysts, it has become clear that emotional and *unconscious* processes frequently divest man of his capacity for rational thought; indeed, the enormous role that unconscious psychological processes have been found to play in man's motivations could legitimately lead to the conclusion that man is the *irrational* animal.

UNCONSCIOUS PSYCHOLOGICAL DRIVES AND MASLOW'S THEORY OF MOTIVATION. There are a number of theories of motivation (and of human nature) that effectively develop the concept of unconscious drives as determinants of human behavior. Among the most powerful is that of Maslow,[2] who notes that every human physical body has certain basic nutrient needs, such as protein, vitamin C, calcium, and so on. When the body is deprived of these basic needs, disease results. By the same token, he hypothesizes, man requires certain basic psychological satisfactions, and when he is deprived of these, mental illness, or neurosis,

2. The following paragraphs are based essentially on Maslow (1962, chap. 3, "Deficiency Motivation and Growth Motivation").

results. On the basis of data gathered over many years of study and research, Maslow identifies man's basic psychological needs, in order of prepotency, as: (1) safety, (2) love and belongingness, and (3) respect and self-esteem. It should be emphasized that these basic needs are essentially unconscious, and when they are not filled, man's behavior is more or less dominated by the drive to fill them. Maslow calls this behavior *deficiency-motivated* (or coping) behavior. To the extent that the environment does not permit basic needs to be filled, psychopathology occurs: The individual becomes "starved" for safety, love, or esteem; he perceives himself and the world around him from an extremely limited, narrow, and distorted perspective; and he behaves (to a greater or lesser degree) neurotically. At the risk of great oversimplification, we might say that according to this theory, paranoia, for example, results from extreme deprivation of the safety need.

In contrast to the neurotics described above, psychologically healthy people have more or less gratified their basic needs for safety, love, and esteem. When these needs are satisfied, Maslow hypothesizes that individuals tend to be motivated

> *primarily by trends to self-actualization (defined as ongoing actualization of potentials, capacities and talents, as fulfillment of mission (or call, fate, destiny, or vocation), as a fuller knowledge of, and acceptance of, the person's own intrinsic nature, as an unceasing trend toward unity, integration or synergy within the person) (Maslow 1962, p. 23).*

This behavior of self-actualizing individuals is called *growth-motivated* (or expressive) behavior. Because growth-motivated individuals are less encapsulated (by unconscious basic needs), they interpret environmental situations in more objective terms.

We should hasten to point out that self-actualization should not be viewed as a static state of *being* (something like nirvana) that is reached as the culmination of basic needs satisfaction. As Figure 10-1 indicates, self-actualization is more properly conceived as a complex and dynamic *becoming*: A psychologically healthy person matures *through* the satisfaction of recurring deficiency needs *toward* longer and more consistent episodes of growth motivation. Thus, individuals do not become "self-actualiz*ed*"; rather, they tend to become "self-actualiz*ing*" more (or less) often than others.

Between the extremes of neurosis and self-actualizing, there lies a wide spectrum of degrees of psychological health. While the number of psychological cripples in our society is probably not overly large, it is certain that the number of really healthy (self-actualizing) individuals is far smaller. This means that most of us, though not incapacitated, are to one degree or another the victims of unconscious drives, distorted perceptions, and decision making based on partial and misleading data. In short, most of us are encapsulated, and our unfulfilled basic needs make a significant contribution to that condition.

To help us to understand the dynamics of deficiency- and growth-motivated behaviors, Maslow contrasts their differences on some thirteen points. Although

FIGURE 10-1

Graphic representation of the development of a self-actualizing person.

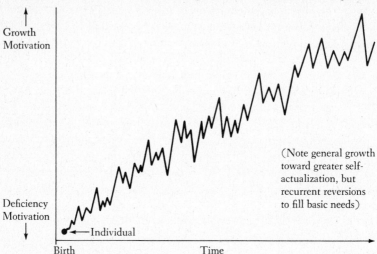

(Note general growth toward greater self-actualization, but recurrent reversions to fill basic needs)

space does not allow so extensive an exposition here, a brief discussion of five of the areas that have special relevance for our concept of escapsulation is in order.

1. *Dependence on versus Independence from the Environment.* Maslow notes that unfulfilled basic needs for safety, love, etc., can only be satisfied by other people. Thus, at the deficiency-motivated level the individual is considerably *dependent on the environment.* He is subject to the wishes and demands of others; he must be sensitive to their approval, desires, good will, etc. In short, he is like the "other-directed" personality discussed in Chapter 8. Placed in this predicament, the deficiency-motivated person must fear his environment, since "there is always the possibility that it may fail or disappoint him" (Maslow 1962, p. 32). Such dependence, we know, generates anxiety and breeds hostility. With such unconscious forces channeling behavior, the individual can hardly be said to be free (i.e., choosing his actions in the light of a clear perception of the reality within and about him).

In contrast, self-actualizing (or less encapsulated) individuals are

> *far less dependent, far less beholden, far more autonomous and self-directed . . . . The determinants which govern their behavior are now primarily inner ones, rather than social or environmental . . . . Since they depend less on other people, they are less ambivalent about them, less anxious and also less hostile, less needful of their praise and their affection. They are less anxious for honors, prestige and rewards* (Maslow 1962, p. 32).

This independence from the environment translates into psychological freedom. While deficiency-motivated people are determined by the unconscious forces that "drive" them, self-actualizing (or less encapsulated) people tend to determine their own behavior on the basis of a more or less accurate perception of reality.

2. *Self-Interested versus Self-Disinterested Interpersonal Relations.* The deficiency-motivated person's perception is colored and limited by his dependence on the environment. Other people are not viewed as complex, idiosyncratic, whole individuals, but rather in terms of their usefulness as sources of supply. They are classified—waiter, mailman, administrator, teacher, etc.—and dealt with in terms of role or function: food bringer, mail deliverer, disciplinarian, and grade giver. Children can become sources of esteem ("My Carol was valedictorian and got accepted at twelve colleges, but she chose Vassar") and parents can be sources of approval ("I'm working for a B average first semester so my father will buy me a sports car"). In interpersonal relationships such as these, the participants play out their games unaware of the realities of self-interest that manipulate their behavior.

In contrast, the self-disinterested (growth-motivated) individual does not categorize others. Because he needs nothing from other people, he perceives them in "desireless, objective, and holistic" terms (Maslow 1962, pp. 33, 34). Furthermore, people are valued (or not) for what they *are*, not for what they can *supply*. An individual is admired because he is worthy of love, not because he can fill a love need. Perception of others in this self-disinterested, unrewarded, desireless way is increasingly difficult as basic need deficits increase.

3. *Ego Centering versus Ego Transcendence.* Ego centering in deficiency-motivated people is related to the self-interest in personal relations noted above. It involves excessive self-consciousness and the definition of reality in terms intended to cope with unmet basic needs. Paradoxically, however, it is the individual whose ego strength is at its height who is most able to forget or transcend his self, "who can be most problem-centered, most self-forgetful, most spontaneous in his activities, most homonomous . . ." (Maslow 1962, p. 34). Freed from the gratification-orientation characteristic of the deficiency-motivated person, this self-actualizer is able to overcome his egocentricity and thereby perceive the world *and himself* as it (and he) really is.

4. *Instrumental Learning versus Personality Change.* Maslow (1962, p. 36) claims that our "so-called learning theory" is a relatively "limited body of knowledge" useful "only in small areas of life" because it is based "almost entirely on deficit-motivation with goal objects usually external to the organism."[3] He views the "learning" that takes place as the result of such deficit motivation as the acquisition of new habits, concepts, etc., added or tacked on one by one in the manner of new external possessions. By contrast, he characterizes growth-motivated learning as "the increase of insight and understanding

3. What Maslow has in mind here is the particular learning theory developed in behavioral psychology. This theory (which has probably been more influential than any other in education) defines learning as the conditioning or behavior modification brought about by the application of an external system of rewards (and sometimes punishments).

. . . knowledge of self and . . . the steady growth of personality, i.e., increased synergy, integration and inner consistency." Although such learnings occur commonly enough through growth-motivated explorations of self-actualizing, our most important learning experiences are often "single life experiences such as deaths, traumata, conversions, and sudden insights, which [force] change in the life-outlook of the person and consequently in everything he [does]" (Maslow 1962, p. 36). This kind of learning might also be described as "the discovery of personal meaning" that results, to a greater or lesser degree, in an altered *Weltanschauung*. While instrumental learning may be adequate for the acquisition of certain skills associated with vocational and professional training, it would seem that the personality change suggested by Maslow's growth-motivated learning should be the aim of the curriculum intended to develop the human potentials of man.

5. *Deficiency-Motivated versus Growth-Motivated Perception.* This contrast is probably the one that is most directly applicable to the concept of encapsulation. The deficiency-motivated, need-interested individual tends to perceive in abstract and mutually exclusive categories: good-bad, kind-cruel, male-female, adult-child, etc. His unmet needs force him to ignore or reject data that are incompatible with or not related to their fulfillment. Starved for safety, for example, the threatened and insecure individual, because he requires a tangible object to justify his unconsciously based fears, fabricates a rubricized figure of Jew, Negro, or other "different" minority.[4] These figures are perceived in stereotypical terms: clearly and unequivocally avaricious, deceitful, predatory, violent, or otherwise evil and dangerous.

In contrast, the growth-motivated person, because he is need disinterested, can view the world much less selectively. Less prone to classify and categorize, he perceives more accurately the complex reality of what is "out there," whether it be object or person: "he can perceive the intrinsic nature of the percept . . . the opposites, the dichotomies, the polarities, the contradictions and the incompatibles . . ." (Maslow 1962, p. 37).

The contrast in deficiency- and growth-motivated perception can be seen clearly by taking the concrete example of a hungry person and an apple. As a result of his unmet hunger need, the deficiency-motivated individual perceives the apple solely as food. While he may be incidentally aware of its color, shape, etc., his perception will be taken up mainly by "apple" classified as a juicy, sweet, or otherwise hunger-satisfying fruit. A growth-motivated nonhungry individual, on the other hand, has a much more insightful and subtle perception of the apple. Of course, he is aware of its nature *qua* sweet and delicious food, but he also can see it aesthetically, as a sculptured spheroid of a particular shape, color, and texture. Still-life paintings of apples (e.g., those by the nineteenth-century French painter Paul Cézanne) reflect this kind of aesthetic perception of apples. In addition, the growth-motivated individual might perceive the

---

4. These figures also constitute the objects against which he vents his hostility and thereby aberrantly "fulfills" his safety need.

paradox of *this* apple's utter uniqueness and individuality and the sameness that it concomitantly shares with all others of its kind—past, present, and future. Further, the openness of his perception might lead the growth-motivated individual to reflect on the apple's existence as the biological seed of a rather wonderful form of plant life, the lovely blossom that last spring was the apple's miraculous beginning, its relationship to the tree that bore it, the marvel of its cellular structure, the chemical elements of which it is composed but which it so far transcends, and any of a virtually unlimited number of ways of perceiving and knowing what an apple is. Clearly, such profound and variegated appreciations of the nature of "apple" foster the actualization of human potential for richness in understanding, both of self and environment.

Deficiency-motivated perception, of course, is severely restricting, but it is particularly insidious and destructive when, as it often does, it operates in social or interpersonal relationships. Unfortunately, as Maslow (1962, pp. 37, 38) notes, we are seldom conscious that we are perceiving others in a colored, distorted, need-interested way; but we are usually (if at all sensitive) acutely aware when we ourselves are perceived in this way, "as a money-giver, a food-supplier, a safety-giver, someone to depend on, or as a waiter or other anonymous servant or means-object." One feels a glow of appreciation and satisfaction, for example, when a supervisor or principal engages him in the corridor with: "You're doing a great job with that 'Problems of Democracy' course; from reports I've heard, the students are involved and excited with the course. You seem to have a rare gift for teaching." But one gets a sick feeling in the pit of his stomach when this seemingly sincere encomium is followed with: "I wonder if you'd be the faculty advisor to the student government. They only meet twice a week after school from 3:00 to 5:00."

> We want to be taken for ourselves, as complete and whole individuals. We dislike being perceived as useful objects or as tools. We dislike being "used" (Maslow 1962, p. 38).

Even on the basis of the abbreviated account given above, it should be clear that Maslow's theory of motivation has made a significant contribution to our understanding of human nature. More specifically, his theory of unconscious basic needs explains a great deal about the internal sources of encapsulation. But we would neglect an important dimension of our study of the individual if we omitted any reference at all to the work of the celebrated psychoanalyst Sigmund Freud. Although few people today subscribe to *all* of the psychological principles that he developed, most would agree that his contributions to human thought rank in importance with those of Einstein, Darwin, and Marx.

FREUD'S THEORY OF UNCONSCIOUS PSYCHOLOGICAL MECHANISMS. Many psychologists identify three psychoanalytic ideas as representing the clearly outstanding contributions of Freudian thought to our understanding of human nature (Klineberg 1964, pp. 82, 83): (1) the prominence of early childhood experience as a determiner of adult personality; (2) the role of the unconscious in human motivation; and (3) the postulation of numerous "unconscious mechanisms" as significant influences on thought processes and, consequently, on behavior. The latter two ideas, of course, are the ones that relate most directly to our own concept of encapsulation. The following paragraphs provide a brief (and sometimes oversimplified) discussion of a few Freudian unconscious mechanisms; even so, we shall be able to see how completely they trap us into unawareness of the psychological forces that direct our thoughts and actions, and thereby limit our freedom.

1. *Rationalization*. Briefly defined, rationalization means justifying beliefs or behavior with *good reasons* instead of *real reasons* (because the *real* reasons are rarely *good* ones). Probably the most widely acknowledged of the unconscious mechanisms, rationalization has become a part of most laymen's *Weltanschauung*. Although conceded cognitively, however, its operation in self and others is seldom recognized.

The truth is that few of us really take the trouble to study the origin of our beliefs and convictions. We feel most comfortable continuing to believe what we have become accustomed to believing. As a result, most of what we regard as so-called reasoning really amounts to finding arguments to justify our presently held beliefs. What are the reasons that one is a Catholic or Protestant, a Moslem or Jew? Why is a person for or against abortion, legalization of marijuana, sex education, the new school levy, or corporal punishment? Just as an aborigine can give all sorts of good reasons for his belief in evil spirits, the "America-firsters" can find a host of reasonable arguments for purging communists from the schools. Little does either one realize, however, the real basis of his position.

As we noted in Chapter 7, we grow up in an environment in which ideas about family, community, nation, religion, marriage, private property, business, freedom, etc., are ever so subtly piped into our brains. It is the "obvious truth" of ideas such as these that seems to be beyond question. And so we accept these ideas without thought until a challenge arises, at which time we eagerly seek reasons to justify them. Indeed, ordinarily we regard the few who presume to question basic beliefs as intellectual carpers carrying skepticism to an absurd degree.

Rationalizations, of course, take on a myriad of forms. A large number, however, can be reduced to two general categories: "they deserve it" and "it is good for them." Thus, in schools, teachers often justify failing students with "He *never* did his homework." "He failed *all* of the tests," "He *never* pays attention in class," or some other form of the "he deserved it" rationalization. But how often does the rationalization mask a latent hostility born of the student's personal appearance, religion, color, socioeconomic class, lack of "proper humility," or any number of other factors unconsciously perceived by the teacher either as a threat or as some deficiency in the student's worth, propriety, or goodness? In the same way, teachers who, for unconscious reasons of habit, security, etc., cling to such superannuated curricula as formal English grammar usually justify their positions with "it is good for them" statements like: "They'll never learn to write unless they know their grammar," "Grammar helps them to think straight," and "The 'lower group' especially need grammar because they speak so badly." Often, these rationalizations may even conceal intense malice and an unconscious desire to inflict punishment on students by assigning distasteful tasks. But the insidiousness and pervasiveness of the rationalization's mechanism is nowhere more incisively articulated than in Horton:

> *Man incessantly seeks to compromise with his conscience or with his innate humanitarianism, by rationalizing his predatory behavior. He must convince himself that the act of grabbing is somehow noble or beautiful, that he can rape in righteousness and murder in magnanimity. He insists upon playing the game, not only with an ace up his sleeve, but with the smug conviction that God has put it there (quoted in Klineberg 1964, p. 83).*

2. *Projection.* The unconscious mechanism of projection operates when an individual attributes (i.e., projects) his own feelings to others. For example, an individual feels hatred for another. But it is wrong to hate, so he unconsciously projects his hatred to the other person. Now, it is the other person who hates him, and he is therefore justified in taking whatever action is necessary to protect himself from the other's hostility and possible aggression. Thus, projection provides us with an excuse for expressing feelings which we regard as undesirable.

Projection is often the basis of scapegoating. Particularly when things are not going well, when our lives are unsatisfactory, we tend to project the blame onto others rather than accept the responsibility for our own failure. For example, a student's justifiably poor grades in school may generate hatred for the teacher. This hatred is projected onto the teacher who, because it is now *he* who hates the student, "gives unfair tests full of obscure or 'trick' questions." Projection thus makes it possible for the student to justify cheating on tests to protect himself from the scapegoat-teacher's unfair hostility. Sometimes, in very disturbed individuals, projection makes possible the justification of quite severe retaliation against a scapegoat-teacher, who, to the amazement of the entire community, suffers a gunshot wound or a knife attack at the hands of a heretofore model student. On a broader scale, prejudice—racial, religious, ethnic, or national—is a form of scapegoating which enables frustrated, dissatisfied, or threatened people to focus the blame for personal failure on an external source and to justify aggressive behavior against that source.

By functioning at an unconscious level, projection prevents us from dealing honestly, openly, and rationally with the forces that are influencing our feelings, thoughts, and behavior. Like rationalization and the other mechanisms, the entire process is nothing more than an elaborate psychological subterfuge.

3. *Displacement.* The mechanism of displacement allows disapproved feelings to be expressed, but toward a substitute figure. For example, a teacher

who feels obliged to meet submissively the unreasonable demands of an over-bearing and authoritarian principal may very well vent his stored-up hostility toward the principal against his own wife and children. Often, too, students become the victims of displacement when teachers (and other elders) use them as substitute objects for pent-up aggression which they are unable to vent against its real source. Unfortunately, displacement of hostility and aggression is least restrained when substitute figures are most helpless. Indeed, many writers regard displacement as an important factor in the abuse to which children, the retarded, the elderly, and even incarcerated convicts are subjected.

4. *Repression.* The unconscious mechanism of repression involves the selective proscription of unhappy past experiences from conscious memory so that only the pleasant ones are recalled. To a large degree, repression operates in "the good old days" syndrome, when, for example, we fondly recall the five-cent cigar and hot dog, but conveniently forget (repress) unpleasant memories of thirty-five cents an hour wage rates and the sixty-hour week. In the same manner, the businessman who has reached the pinnacle of financial success remembers (and relates in minute detail) the long hours of grueling work that were responsible for his ascent, but forgets (represses) the unsavory "deals" that also contributed to it. To the extent that repression operates to eradicate important aspects of our past behavior, it promotes fictionalized self-concepts of who and what we are. And to the extent that we unconsciously engage in such subterfuges, our decisions will not be freely and openly made, but directed and determined by forces beyond our awareness.

Many other unconscious mechanisms could be cited and discussed,[5] but for present purposes enough has been said to demonstrate how these mechanisms interfere with our perception of the external world and thereby contribute to encapsulation. Before leaving this topic, however, we should point out for clarity's sake that unconscious mechanisms are not discrete, but rather interdependent and interacting. Furthermore, they are not necessarily entirely negative in their effects. For example, repression of certain monstrous, traumatic experiences (such as being raped or seeing one's child murdered) may be necessary for the maintenance of sanity. It is only when these mechanisms are employed habitually to mask the unpleasantness of one's own thoughts, motives, and behaviors that they distort perceptions of reality and thereby undermine mental health.

To summarize and conclude this section on encapsulation as an important factor in our synoptic view of human nature, we should emphasize first that the sources of encapsulation are physiological, psychological, and as we saw in Chapter 7, cultural. A second point is that totally unedited, undistorted, "pure" knowledge of ourselves and the world is impossible. We are constrained by our psychobiological equipment to view the world from the viewpoint of our individual senses and minds, the existence of which represents a barrier, as it were,

---

5. The interested student should consult Monroe (1955) for a more detailed discussion of Freudian mechanisms.

between us and the ultimate truth.[6] But within these boundaries a tremendous range of encapsulation can exist. At the biological level, for example, we know that some individuals' physical senses are far more sensitive and perceptive to what is "out there" than are others'. More importantly, at the psychological level the "open attitude" toward experience that some people have produces a more accurate perception of situations than a paranoid view, for example, that (unconsciously) colors situations with threat and persecution. Finally, at the cultural level, an individual who is aware of the effects of unconscious cultural bias is in a far better position to perceive situations as they are than is an individual "crippled," so to speak, by the unconscious, unexamined prejudices, opinions, and ideas that the culture has stamped into him. When we consider that our decisions and actions depend so much on our analysis of situations, it is easy to see why awareness of encapsulation and its sources is so important.

A third point has to do with the argument that since we can never reach absolute truth, the struggle to know it is a vain one and not worth the bother. But there is no reason to believe that even if man could attain "pure" truth (knowledge of ultimate reality), he would achieve a state of nirvana. Rather:

> the great adventure in life resides in the search for ultimates, but not the attainment of them. Our history books are filled with the testimony of what happens to a people when they become convinced they have the truth. They perish. And they perish because their reality image becomes frozen (Royce 1964, p. 43).

Such a view of life is tantamount to saying that the search for knowledge of reality is part of what it means to be human. If man is to attain a world view that approaches what is really "out there" (and "in here") it will be necessary for him to begin to cut away the unconscious psychological crust that obscures his perception. The first step, of course, is to recognize the existence of the biological, psychological, and cultural limitations that constitute encapsulation.

What Man Is

Armed with our scientifically rooted concept of encapsulation, we are now prepared to develop, if only in the most general terms, the essential (for education and curriculum) characteristics of the nature of man.

MAN: THE MEANING–CREATING ANIMAL

Earlier in this chapter we learned that man is a highly complex integrated organism capable of responding to his environment in either of two contrasting modes: (1) with behavior originating in the psychobiological structures he shares

---

6. Not to be so constrained would imply the possibility of a state approximating God-like omniscience.

with lower forms of life (e.g., drives, instincts), or (2) with behavior originating in the more elaborate and highly developed psychobiological structures that are characteristic only of the human species (e.g., self-consciousness and reflection). The former (animal) structures generate specific, relatively predictable, reflexive behavior. But the latter (human) structures generate conscious *ideas meanings*. And if psychology has taught anything at all, it has taught that human (unlike animal) behavior is governed chiefly by ideas, beliefs, and attitudes—in a word, *meanings*.

But meaning does more than just govern ·behavior in man. It draws together the strands of his experience and makes his life comprehensible. It "satisfies" the need generated by man's most characteristically human psychobiological structures. Indeed, we may say that beyond the urge to gratify his most basic physiological needs, man's greatest need is for the creation of meaning.[7] These points lead us to the conclusion that constitutes the basis of our theory of human nature: man is "an *energy-converting and purposive organism* [who] seeks the maximization of his own sense of self . . . [i.e.,] who seeks to expand his experience [meanings] in composite ways" (Becker 1969, p. 641).

In general, the maximization of human selves is accomplished by meanings generated in two fundamentally contrasting modes. At the lowest levels of human functioning, meanings are "stamped" in, so to speak, by parents, teachers, peers, mass media, and other sources of culture, and are accepted uncritically and literally *unconsciously* by the "good" citizens of the society. Uncritical acceptance is rewarded with the filling of basic psychological needs: safety, belongingness, and self-esteem. *Encapsulated* man maximizes himself (and fills his basic needs) by celebrating the unexamined "social fiction" (as Becker calls it) of his society. It is this condition that makes possible, for example, what Becker (1967, p. 156) has called the "fetishism of commodities" in contemporary American society. We might say that an unexamined "consumer mentality" has promoted the creation of meaning and self-maximization through the accumulation of consumer goods. "Everyone thrust[s] his hands into the great grab bag of the new consumer society, [draws] out a handful of gadgets and trinkets, and [hurries] home to fondle and admire them" (Becker 1967, p. 156).

But science has shown us that fully (authentic) human meanings can result only from the actualization of the highest levels of distinctively human potential: critical intelligence, self- and other-consciousness, ethical sensibility, etc. What we are claiming is that at higher (distinctively human) levels, self-maximization occurs as a result of meanings generated out of enlarged present awareness of self in relation to environment. For the human being functioning on this level of meaning-creation, it requires critical examination of all data involved in a given situation including basic assumptions underlying self and environment. In short, it means grappling with one's own condition of encapsulation.

7. See Maslow's theory on this point: After meeting certain basic physiological and psychological needs, man's energies are invested in striving for self-actualization, which in most respects is essentially synonymous with striving for (authentic) meanings.

In summary, man is an energy-converting organism that seeks maximization of itself through the creation of meanings. Whether those meanings foster the organism's humanity or not will depend on whether they derive from the unexamined fiction of encapsulation or from the authenticity of critical awareness.

MAN: A NEUTRAL ORGANISM

The essentially neutral nature of the human organism was briefly alluded to in the section, "Man: Good or Evil?" There, we promised a more definitive treatment of this position, and it is appropriate that it be provided now. If the human organism is really "neutral," argues the critic of this position, how can we explain such "nasty" instincts and drives, such as aggression, acquisitiveness, and territoriality? One reading of history (and certain scientific research) suggests that wars and the ills of society are directly traceable to such "innate and instinctual drives." Could it not be the case, horrible as it may seem, that man "maximizes" himself by satisfying such ugly drives?

This could be the case, of course; but the fact is that in spite of mountains of research on the subject, no conclusive evidence exists to demonstrate that man's "nasty" traits are innate—"that man has specific antisocial drives that are modifiable only with difficulty . . ." (Becker 1969, p. 648). Why, then, so strong a tendency to explain man's historical career in terms of a few dominant and innate "nasty" drives? One reason is the *simplicity* of the explanation: "The popular imagination takes refuge in an image of man that shows him to be [innately] mean and vicious because such an image easily explains all the world ills at one swoop" (Becker 1969, p. 640). Furthermore, such an explanation "protects" us (in much the same way that the genetic explanation of intelligence protects poor teaching): We prefer the narrow and the inevitable (i.e., the *genetic* explanation) because it excuses us from bearing the responsibility for our ills. In addition, comprehensive and thoroughgoing explanations are complex and require extensive knowledge of history, politics, economics, social theory, psychology, and—not the least important—knowledge of self. Few of us can bring such knowledge to bear as we attempt to understand our situations, but more importantly (as we have suggested above), few of us really *want* to (*see* "Freudian mechanisms," *supra*). Better to lay the blame for war on an innate aggressive drive than to consider the possibility that it follows from our unexamined attachment to such ugly social determinants as nationalistic ideology, the military-industrial complex, power elites, mass identification with charismatic leaders, and rapacious economic motivations. The safety and comfort of encapsulation—constricted, narrow meanings—is preferred over the psychological distress incurred by independent and honest inquiry.

But to return to our original point: If no conclusive evidence exists to demonstrate that man's "nasty" traits are innate (or acquired), are we not obligated (as we suggested we were in our argument involving claims of an inherited hierarchy of intelligence) to assume the most generous and optimistic posture in dealing with the situation? If we consider the behavioral consequences that will probably follow from the assumption that human beings are innately aggressive, we are immediately cautioned by the uncomfortable prospect of invoking the self-fulfilling prophecy. Treat men *as if* they are aggressive, and they may very well *become* aggressive! It all raises the question of how many of our social ills are due to the evil characteristics we *presume* to be inherent in man, and how many are elicited by the presumption itself.

Mitigate the world's ills by changing our assumptions about man! The argument is attractive, and valid, too; but it really is not adequate. It does not completely satisfy us because it does not answer the persistent question of a well-founded, empirically based portrait of man. Science and reality cannot be ignored. And happily, we can be much more definite and enlightening in sketching our portrait of the authentic human being than is suggested in the previous paragraph—if we are willing to grapple with some of the complexities of the interaction between human psychobiological equipment and environmental conditions.

To begin with, it seems clear that human beings *are* determined by certain innate, biologically based drives (e.g., hunger, thirst, and sex). But these drives represent *potentials*, whose actualization is determined to a greater or lesser degree not only by the environment, but by certain elaborate psychological structures found only in homo sapiens. For example, the sex drive represents a potential that can be actualized in a variety of ways, ranging from sadomasochistic orgies and rape/murder to the tenderest expressions of altruistic love. In addition, the drive can also be sublimated, as Freud knew, by diverting energies into a wide range of activities not specifically related to glandular satisfactions (e.g., creative art, gymnastics, etc.). This example points up the principal difference between man and animals and suggests the reason that research and questions relating to the nature-nurture debate may be quite unimportant and a misdirection of our energies: animal behavior is restricted by the relatively simple, *specific* drives and instincts that govern it. For example, the sex drive in animals eventuates in relatively limited patterns of behavior compared with the variegated sexual conduct of man. In contrast, man's "innate drives" are not only far less specific, but are diminished in importance to the degree that culture and complex, characteristically human psychostructures, operate to increase the organism's flexibility of response. Apply to the sex drive self-consciousness, cultural imperatives, ethical beliefs, rational reflection, and the myriad other complex, distinctively human psychocultural determinants of man's behavior, and the drive becomes as malleable as putty.

Certainly, human beings have the potential for aggression; that is obvious enough in the trait's actualization. But human beings have many potentials, including the potential for generosity, kindness, love, and self-sacrifice. The point is that innate human drives and instincts are so nonspecific[8] and unim-

---

8. Relatively speaking, basic human drives such as hunger, thirst, need for sleep, etc., are fairly specific; however, they do not weaken our argument "for the simple reason that they do not make for disharmony in social life except under unusual crisis conditions " (Becker 1969, p. 648).

portant (when measured over against the enormous potential for flexibility and variety inherent in elaborate, distinctively human psychobiological structures interacting with the environment) that for all practical purposes the human organism may be regarded as essentially *neutral* ground.

But the critic of our position presses his objection: If the human organism is essentially neutral, how are we to account for the copious evil we find in the world? Evil is not, we insist, the result of insidious forces inherent in man (*or* his environment, *or* the supernatural). Rather, it is only the result of uncritical human behavior, behavior directed by unconscious internal needs and uncritical (sometimes unconscious) attachment to cultural values and meanings. This is the reason that evil is not (as it was so long thought to be) an exciting force with which man must do battle, but only a banal blunder, a humanly created meaning gone tragically awry.

The banality of evil is easy to see in our everyday lives. It is apparent in our abuse of children (because "they must be taught to behave") and in our segregation of blacks (because "those people are really racially inferior to whites"). The reasons for such behavior (and its resultant human suffering) are the unexamined cultural meanings (assumptions) by which we live our lives.

But what about really shocking evil, like the Nazis' methodical annihilation of 6 million Jews? Can such a frightful enormity as this seeming apotheosis of human evil really be regarded as *banal?* Seen from the perspective of our synoptic portrait of man, it can be nothing else.

In her analysis of Adolph Eichmann, one of the principal instruments of the Holocaust,[9] Hannah Arendt shows that "evil is a function of the impersonality of bureaucracy, of the giving and taking of orders, of the smooth functioning of organization, of the unquestioned daily duty of basically decent men, who ask only to be rewarded by praise for a job well done" (quoted in Becker 1967, p. 145). Eichmann was not a villain in the traditional sense at all; he was not a fiend lusting for the diabolical. He was merely a commonplace actor, uncritically fulfilling the requirements of the role set out for him by the culture that shaped his *Weltanshauung.* "Evil is banal because evil is merely the toll of the *game* of society, and not of any basic iniquity of man" (Becker 1967, p. 145). Evil is man become agent, the mindless functionary carrying on the social fiction whatever its toll of human suffering might be.[10]

It is difficult to resist the mass social ideology, whatever it may be, because it seems so "natural" to the uncritical, encapsulated masses for whom it represents vital life meanings. In the 1930s, Hitler "became a drum major, trans-

9. The name ordinarily used to describe Hitler's annihilation of 6 million Jews.

10. The enormity of bureaucratic evil is reflected in the story of a man who rushed into a government agency shouting, "Quick! Phone for an ambulance. A man just collapsed with a heart attack!" only to be met with, "Sorry, our phones can be used for official business only." Also consider the absurdity of the American position on Viet Nam: "We'll keep the South Vietnamese free from Communism even if we have to kill every one of them to do it."

lated the 'Rah, rah, rah' into 'Sieg Heil,' [and] hypnotized the German masses into one great hysterical national drama which drew them together with a frenzy of conviction" (Becker 1967, p. 145). In the 1970s, industrial-commercial interests translate the "rah, rah, rah" into "buy, buy, buy," and a hypnotized American people, emptied of reason, ideals, and all values except consumer self-interest, frantically celebrate the great national potlatch, which draws them together in a frenzy of conviction.

We can see more clearly now what man is: a neutral, meaning-creating organism whose development as an authentic human being is hobbled by encapsulation, a condition that produces involuntary life styles based on constricted, distorted, and destructive meanings. The question now becomes: How can man overcome the constraints of encapsulation and realize his most human potentials? Or, to put it another way: How can we solve the problem of ordered society without taking a toll of individual human life and potential?

What Man Should Become: The Authentic Human Being

Having developed a synoptic view of the nature of the human organism, we turn to the task that is probably the most significant of all for curriculum construction: considering what is possible and most desirable for man to become.

AUTHENTIC MAN AND RESPONSIBLE FREEDOM

The matter of human freedom was discussed at length in the previous chapter, and there is no need for a detailed reiteration of that discussion here. Suffice it to say that human freedom is essentially a function of behavior originating in the elaborate and highly developed psychobiological structures that are most characteristic of the human species (e.g., structures engendering self-consciousness, ideal formation, reflection, future orientation, etc.). Since these structures permit a far greater range of possible responses to the environment than the simple structures man shares with other animals, they enable him to become a much more important determinant in the course of events. This is another way of saying that characteristically human psychobiological structures provide man with diverse meanings, allowing him relatively greater freedom than is possible in other forms of life.

But, as we also pointed out in the previous chapter, man's potential for freedom (i.e., decision making based on the relatively full functioning of his human psychobiological equipment), while immense, has been only scantly actualized in present environmental conditions. Although part of the problem has been (and still is) human inability to discover, understand, and take into account the multitude of environmental forces operating in given situations, we now know that the overwhelmingly significant problem of human freedom is one of encapsulation—i.e., simple unawareness. Science has shown us how factors involving the social psychology of perception, unconscious culturally induced bias, basic internal psychological needs, unconscious Freudian mechanisms, and a host of other encapsulating agents channel human thought and behavior away from the self- and social-critical assessments upon which human freedom depends, toward the conditioned, reflexive, and instinctual response. However, now possessing scientific knowledge about the operation of encapsulating forces, man is in a position, as he has never before been, to break out of his unawareness and, by actualizing human potential for self- and social-criticism, expand his flexibility of response (freedom) to a magnitude never before possible. Moreover, as man's freedom expands, it opens ever wider the question "What can man become?" both by multiplying possibilities and facilitating change. The psychosocial evolution of man through the self-choosing actualization of characteristically human potential shifts organismic energies from specific, chiefly survival-directed behavior (the animal level) increasingly toward flexible, personal-social fulfillment (the human level).

The foregoing conception of human freedom has particular appeal because it links freedom to responsibility. The humanly free act, we have seen, is the act that is based on a maximally unencapsulated consideration of (1) all factors operating in a given situation and (2) all consequences likely to issue from feasible alternative courses of action. But would such an act not also be the most responsible? What better definition of "responsible behavior" than "behavior based on a full and critical consideration of its own consequences"?

The preceding paragraphs suggest an intimate relationship between the exercise of responsible freedom and man's striving for meaning. Indeed, in the exercise of responsible freedom, we observe that man creates his truest, richest, most significant meanings because such meanings are based on maximal awareness (unencapsulation) and the broadest possible range of data. We may therefore conclude from our scientifically established portrait of what man is, not only that it is *possible* for man to exercise responsible freedom, but that it is *humanly desirable* for him to do so. The *empirical-logical* justification for this claim is obvious: man's welfare will best be served if his transactions with the environment are based on meanings that most accurately reflect situational conditions—i.e., meanings which are least partial and least distorted. But we can also make our argument on *naturalistic* grounds: Man *should* exercise responsible freedom to the greatest degree possible because to do so represents the actualization of distinctly human psychological potential, in other words, the actualization of authentically human characteristics.

To summarize, human behavior not only can be increasingly governed by critical knowledge, concepts, and ideas, it should be, to the greatest extent possible. Thus, the authentic human being is the individual who maximizes his self by striving to exercise responsible freedom.

AUTHENTIC MAN: SELF-RELIANCE AND COMMUNITY

What is self-reliance? It is authentic man fulfilling his individual human potential through the exercise of responsible freedom. He is no longer the uncritical conformist, the encapsulated herd animal unconsciously dependent on and responding to the ready-made meanings served up by the controlling culture. By dealing consciously and honestly with all men, by turning a critical eye on the cultural beliefs that shape society's (and his own) *Weltanshauung*, self-reliant man assumes responsibility for his own autonomous meanings and their applicability to his own life and times. His existence is at once a response to the Socratic enjoinder, "Know thyself," and a model of the democratic ideal.

Can there be a society of self-reliant men? Certainly this is a contradiction! How can society be possible without common cultural meanings, beliefs, and ideals? And as soon as men depend for their meanings on these, where is self-reliance? Our problem is compounded further when we consider that although man is a creature who actualizes his best human potentials through the exercise of individual freedom, he is at the same time a social animal who needs the support of his fellow men. This is the tragic paradox of the human condition, and it underlines the critical question raised earlier: How can we solve the problem of ordered society without taking a toll of individual human freedom and life? This question, of course, is the one that goes to the very heart of the curriculum-construction enterprise.

Whatever response we make to the question, we should note that to be adequate it must be at once *ideal* and *general*. It must be ideal because only ideals are adequate as criteria to judge men's very best capabilities. Without an ideal against which to measure individual and social conduct, we can never hope to rise above the convenient and expedient. But our answer must also be a general one, because the ideal-question of what man can become must be left open ended. Direction we must have—and the ideal provides this—but to fill in the details is to close off possibility, to settle the future, to create the new encapsulation.

It should come as no surprise that our response to the paradox of the simultaneous human need for self-reliance and community is to be found in the scientific-moral *Weltanschauung* we have been describing as "a synoptic view of man."[11] What we are proposing is a community held together by the view that man is a neutral, meaning-creating organism who, hobbled by internal and external encapsulation, produces meanings that take a terrible toll in human suffering. But the hope of this community—its ideal—is a vision of man who progressively overcomes encapsulation, who actualizes his potential for responsible freedom and self-reliance, and in so doing fosters the freedom and self-reliance of others in the community. As knowledge increasingly begets further

---

11. This *Weltanschauung* is scientific because it is based on the best research currently available on the nature of man. It is moral because it provides us with an ideal of what man should be.

knowledge, as awareness leads to greater awareness, self-reliance and community integration grow together.

This is a community that fits the democratic ideal, one that fosters the creation of self-critical and social-critical meanings. If the claim is made that it encapsulates by insisting on the belief that knowing is better than not knowing, we can only point out that under critical examination knowing has been *shown* to be generally preferable to not knowing.[12] And herein lies the vital center of a society of self-reliant men: an openness to experience such that knowledge is held to be tentative and *all* beliefs are *always* subject to examination.

It is not very difficult to intellectualize about one's openness to experience and willingness to examine all beliefs, but it is quite another matter to engage actively in the process. The difficulties are easily seen, however, if we ask even the best-educated Americans what meanings about human existence are generated, for example, by their apparent support of the commercial professional sports industry? What are the consequences of the social fictions that it celebrates? What toll of human life does it take, not only of its star performers, but of the millions of minds that it consumes in its daily rituals? In what ways does it enrich, and impoverish, its participants and spectators? These are difficult enough questions for the impartial observer, but they demand the ultimate in self-reliance from Americans, who have been steeped from early childhood in the wholesomeness of sports, even to the extent that opposition to them is viewed as unpatriotic and un-American.

Our generalized ideal, the synoptic view of man, does not resolve the paradox[13] of self-reliance and community. But it does provide us with a reasonably satisfactory concept for dealing with it. It shows us where and how to start, by illuminating the internal and cultural constraints on human development; but by *not* supplying us with a blueprint of the final product, it provides a man-centered *Weltanschauung* that is general enough to keep open the question, "What can man become?" At the same time, our *Weltanschauung* supplies a scientific-moral ideal against which we can judge the evolution of the authentic man and his meanings: Are his ideas based on the best self- and social-critical knowledge available? And what is the toll they take in human suffering?

We should further note that the ideal—authentic man, completely self-reliant in a fully integrated community—is impossible to achieve. But without ideals life is absurd. Without them man has nothing but his finite transitory self, "his dazzling and diverting little consumer objects; his few closely huddled loved

12. The unencapsulated man would admit that in certain situations not knowing could be preferable to knowing.

13. Finite man is faced with many paradoxes, e.g., the simultaneous needs for independence and dependence, change and permanence, striving and repose, reason and sentiment, and, of course, the one we are concerned with above, individual diversity and social unity. The question is not "How can these be resolved?" for they are unresolvable. Rather, the question is "How can they be dealt with in a humanly satisfactory and meaningful way?"

ones; his life-span; his life-insurance; his place in a merely biological and finan-cial chain of things" (Becker 1967, p. 213). Though he can never hope to attain his ideals, man needs them in order to transcend the absurdity of his finite self, to extend his striving toward meanings at the highest possible levels of significance and seriousness.[14] The ideal democracy, for example, will always elude us; yet without the vision our social-political lives lack significance.

Finally, we must point out that the ideal, unhappily, is subject to change. Because it is based on the most critical assessment of the best knowledge cur-rently available, it is the finest vision we are presently capable of projecting. But we are certain to learn more tomorrow, and still more the day after tomor-row. And that knowledge may dictate a modification of the ideal.

This is certainly an irrational position. Ideals subject to change are no ideals at all! Hypotheses, perhaps, but not the unchanging, steady lights we need for guiding our lives. Again we face the paradox: we need an anchor, a cer-tainty. And yet to invest our ideals with absolute and unchanging permanence is to submit ourselves to encapsulation. We cannot really afford ideals, and yet we cannot live without them!

The ideal-problem, particularly as it relates to the authentic human being, merits volumes on its own. Enough has been said here, however, to demonstrate the importance of a well-founded concept of the authentic (ideal) human being—the "educated man," if you will—for curriculum construction. Without such an ideal, the curriculum could develop as a foundationless, random, shift-ing superstructure, lacking in integration and susceptible to the most whimsical of influences. Even worse, however, is what it in fact most often turns out to be: a plan for education based on implicit, unexamined, ideological, and un-conscious assumptions about the nature and (ideal) future of man. In other words, without a thoroughgoing inquiry into the nature of human nature and its humanly desirable potentials, submerged prejudices control the education of youth.

Curricular Applications of the Synoptic View of Man

We can only hope to suggest in the most abbreviated and general terms what a curriculum design based on the ideal of the authentic human being would be. This should be enough, however, to demonstrate the direct and vital link that exists between the "individual" foundational area and curriculum aims, content, learning activities, and evaluation.

It is necessary at the outset to stipulate that our synoptic view of the individ-ual calls unequivocally for a curriculum for general liberal education, as opposed to a curriculum designed for special, vocational, or professional educa-

14. For a sophisticated treatment of this problem, especially as it relates to the need for a self-transcending cause, see Becker (1967, chap. 7, "The Theological Dimension").

tion. That is, the ideal of the authentic man generates concerns related to the *basis on which men live,* rather than how they make a living or what individual talents they may wish to develop. The latter concerns, clearly, are dependent on the judgments we make about the former.

The general aim of the curriculum is to develop individuals along lines consonant with our ideal of the authentic human being. But since our authentic human being is a responsibly free, self-reliant person living in a community of self-reliant men, we may alternately phrase our major aim as "self-knowledge for every student."[15] Goals, therefore, will include (among others) enabling students (1) to become aware of the interior basis of their encapsulation, (2) to become conscious of the enculturating effects of society, (3) to assess the relationship of themselves to their environment in self- and social-critical terms, and (4) to develop an openness to experience. Each of these goals summarizes an immensely complex attainment and therefore may appear deceptively simple. It should be clear, however, that implicit in each one is a multitude of subgoals and, in terms of translation to the activities of daily classroom work, literally thousands of possible objectives. The first goal, for example, might include (among others) such subgoals and objectives as the following: (1) understanding of human physiology, (2) understanding of human growth and development, (3) awareness of the effect of psychological needs on personal feelings and behavior; more specifically, (1) the ability to recognize anxiety (or fear, jealousy, or need for affection) when it is present in one's interior, (2) the ability to recognize these same feelings in others, and (3) the ability to deal consciously and rationally with these factors in assessing situations and determining courses of action.

Content selection and organization for a curriculum designed to educate the authentic human being will generally depend on two criteria: (1) effectiveness in fostering present awareness of self in society, and (2) growth toward the increasing exercise of responsible freedom. Generally speaking, the content will consist of those ideas, concepts, facts, observations, and hypotheses that reveal how encapsulation occurs and how it constricts human striving for self-reliant meanings. More specifically, child-rearing practices, family relationships, human psychological needs, and other content from psychology, physiology, anthropology, etc., will provide students with a history of their own personal encapsulation. War, scapegoating, industrial economics, revolution, governments, and other topics from sociology, history, economics, anthropology, and political science will reveal to students the nature of the social fiction and its role in cultural encapsulation. In short, curriculum content will be organized into a personal social account of encapsulation.

The content of this curriculum will, of course, be much more wide ranging and flexible than the above paragraph might suggest. The important thing is its self- and social-critical character. To illustrate this point we may take Pritzkau's

15. Self-knowledge for communitarian man, of course, includes study involving the basic question, "What is man?"

marvelous example of *food* used as a topic to develop present awareness of self-in-society with elementary children. Although the study of food often occurs in elementary schools, it is ordinarily restricted to the establishment of certain concepts "relative to its origin, where it is found, how it is distributed and so on" (Pritzkau 1970, p. 117). This "separate" treatment of the subject is "constricted" because it does not relate to extended value meanings of most concern to man (what we have called the self- and social-critical meanings). He proposes a much expanded treatment of the topic of food:

> *children might secure simple data about behavior of people in selecting food in a supermarket and possible reasons for this behavior . . . .*
>
> *More searching questions relative to the topic of food would relate to the problems of adequate supply to all people. It has been suggested . . . that man possesses great ability to produce food in abundance and to distribute it. Does this mean then that no one remains hungry? Obviously the question needs no answer. There are millions of people throughout the world who are literally starving—in the United States as well as in other nations. The question might be phrased, In a world where abundance is prevalent, why does hunger still exist? This question, of course, poses a paradoxical situation—abundance and hunger existing virtually side by side . . . .*
>
> *In approaching this question, there must develop some real confrontation with present realities. These evoke the whole question of man's inhumanity to man. The problems of the economy must come under more severe scrutiny. The values basic to this problem must be laid bare. Why do individuals and systems permit a condition where children grow up unhealthy because of hunger? Isn't this a form of violence? Doesn't the continuation of this condition among many other people suggest a callous indifference to the birthright of human beings? How are we part of this problem? (Pritzkau 1970, pp. 117, 118; emphasis added).*

The content that Pritzkau describes is obviously highly self- and social critical and places students themselves at the very center of the inquiry. The questions encourage student involvement with their own behavior (including acts of omission) and their ultimate responsibility for it. The questions also link individual students to the totality of the human drama. In this context content is more than information set out to be learned; it is internalized as critical meanings that breach encapsulation and foster self-knowledge, self-reliance, and community.

The content questions that Pritzkau presents suggest a general policy for curriculum learning activities: whatever form they take, they must arouse inquiry and questioning. But not *any* kind of questioning will do. It has been said that in many of our schools today students spend a great deal of time finding the right answers to questions that do not matter. In a curriculum for educating the authentic human being, emphasis will be placed on activities that generate self- and social-critical questions, like the ones raised in Pritzkau's account of an inquiry on food.

Questions that probe personal encapsulation are inherent in all sorts of activities. As students read books and newspapers, view films and television; write papers; visit fire stations, museums, or factories; or simply sit quietly and meditate, questions of all sorts relating to the condition of their existence and the realities inherent in it can arise. Perhaps the most promising learning activity for the kind of curriculum we are describing, however, is what Pritzkau calls the *dialogue*. He defines this activity as:

> *conversation between two or more persons in which each transcends his solitude and accepts his aloneness and that of the other persons, thereby seeking a form of transaction which maintains the maximum freedom of each (Pritzkau 1970, p. 10).*

Pritzkau warns that dialogue should not be construed as simple communication. It is not merely the movement of information from one to another. In dialogue,

> *there exists an attitude of "trust of the mind" in seeking meanings . . . a condition of "openness to experience." This means that the individual has opened himself to receive messages from others as well as all types of media, with no priority necessarily placed upon one over another . . . .*
> *Finally, in dialogue every effort is directed by individuals to liberate each other in the quest for meanings and to approach an integrity with surrounding phenomena (Pritzkau 1970 pp. 11, 12, passim).*

Obviously, the dialogue is akin *in form* to what we usually refer to as "discussion." Also obvious, however, is that what ordinarily passes for discussion in classrooms is totally inadequate to the demands of educating the self-reliant student. At its best, discussion is exchange of views, debate, or clarification. At its worst, it is merely role playing. In any case, it is rarely self-critical.

These points underline a central problem in the "implementation" of curriculum learning activities based on our synoptic view of man: they can be "implemented" (for that matter *understood*) only by teachers who are themselves moving toward authenticity. That is, implementation is not so much an organizational or replicative task as it is a task of *being* with others.

For example, one does not "learn the skills" of carrying on a dialogue; as one becomes more authentic, he simply *is* more dialogic.

The issue here under consideration is a specific example of the problem of encapsulation that we have spent so long discussing. The normative perspective on the conduct of learning activities is the technical perspective of American culture: overt procedures specified and carried out by actors in the process. But to grasp the character of dialogue from that point of view—that *Weltanschauung,* so to speak—is impossible. What is required is a leap into another world view. In the words of Pritzkau, "You can't get there from here."

The previous paragraphs suggest some of the alterations we will have to make in our present conceptions of curriculum evaluation. Not that paper-and-pencil tests of student achievement will tell us nothing about the effectiveness of our curriculum; only that what they tell us will not be sufficient. Measures of language competency, for example, will not be irrelevant to the curriculum goals we have set, but we shall want to know things about the curriculum that go far beyond students' level of language development, for example, the degree to which students' questions affect the evolution of the curriculum itself. Indeed, this suggests what might be one of the most significant aspects of an evaluation of a self-critical curriculum: the ongoing reappraisal of curriculum goals themselves.

In the light of his own evolution toward authenticity and the interactions he has with all people concerned with education, the authentic curriculum evaluator asks whether curriculum goals are consonant with the self- and social-critical orientation he has set for himself. Or are these areas in which he has become so settled with his *Weltanschauung* that points of "closure" or "out-of-awareness" are developing? After all, the greatest danger to any curriculum, however "open" it may be at the outset, is that it can very easily establish itself as the new encapsulation.

Another aspect of critical importance to an evaluation of the self-critical curriculum is the evaluation procedures themselves. Are these self-critical? Or are they unconsciously built into the curriculum design so that they constitute a "blind spot" that controls aims, content, and learning activities? Although it may begin to appear surrealistic to talk about "evaluating the evaluation," we do know that the kinds of questions we ask and the performance demands we make of curricula have a far-reaching effect on their design and outcomes.

Of course, many of the evaluation procedures currently in use may be quite appropriate for this curriculum if a critical perspective is maintained. It is only when standardized tests, college-entrance requirements, "competency" assessment, and other such "practical" devices are allowed to obscure the realities of human existence that the curriculum assumes an encapsulating function. Unfortunately, this is often the case because of the high priority our culture places on quantification.

The general thrust of a curriculum for unencapsulated self-reliance can be summed up quite nicely using Pritzkau's distinction between the *real* and the *realistic*. The realistic represents the familiar—a coming to rest with surrounding conditions (Pritzkau 1970, p. 51). The realistic individual has the situation well in hand and pursues a course which, for its time and place, is considered "normal," "regular," "practical." Question his conduct of affairs, and he replies, "I know, but we must be realistic." Because the "realistic" is accepted uncritically, or at best assessed within an encapsulated framework, chances are that it has little grounding in reality. Indeed, at its worst, it may even be absurd, bizarre, grotesque (e.g., Adolf Eichmann being "realistic").

The real, by contrast, represents the enquiring, the reflective, and the self and social critical. The real individual places himself in a "dialogic and inter-probing condition" with himself and his environment (Pritzkau 1970, p. 55). He is our synoptic man moving toward awareness, responsible freedom, self-reliance, community, authenticity—in short, a more human existence.

The "realistic" curriculum is one that most of us have known, the curriculum that historically has served the purposes of church and state. The "real" curriculum is an ideal based on an ideal. To the extent that we can move significantly in its direction, we can look forward to more *human* human beings and more humane societies.

References

Becker, Ernest. 1967. *Beyond Alienation*. New York: George Braziller.

————. 1969. "The Evaded Question: Science and Human Nature." *Commonweal* (February 21).

————. 1971. *The Lost Science of Man*. New York: George Braziller.

Klineberg, Otto. 1964. *The Human Dimension in International Relations*. New York: Holt, Rinehart and Winston.

Maslow, Abraham H. 1962. *Toward a Psychology of Being*. New York: D. Van Nostrand Company.

Monroe, R. L. 1955. *Schools of Psychoanalytic Thought*. New York: Holt, Rinehart and Winston.

Pritzkau, Philo T. 1970. *On Education for the Authentic*. New York: Thomas Y. Crowell (Chandler Publishing Company).

Royce, Joseph, R. 1964. *The Encapsulated Man*. New York: D. Van Nostrand Company.

CHAPTER 11
LEARNING THEORIES:
AN OVERVIEW

A teacher will never succeed in giving proper guidance to a child if he doesn't learn to understand the psychological world in which that individual child lives. —KURT LEWIN

Introduction

How do human beings learn? Under what conditions is learning facilitated? Under what conditions is it inhibited?

Whether conscious or subconscious, ideas about the nature of the learning process always influence the curriculum. For example, a curriculum built on a step-by-step accretion of specific learnings (as evidenced in programmed textbooks) suggests the theory that learning is an incremental acquisition of simple behaviors which, added together, comprise our more complex skills and concepts. On the other hand, a curriculum that presents students with masses of data accompanied by problems to be solved implies the theory that learning occurs by "insight," and that complex skills and concepts are indivisible wholes comprising something more—and more significant—than the simple sum of their related parts. Clearly, a sound and effective curriculum depends heavily on a well-founded theory of learning.

It is less than a hundred years that the nature of the learning process has been scientifically investigated by psychologists.[1] Even in this relatively short time, however, a prodigious body of research has been accumulated which, because of its direct bearing on the curriculum-construction task, constitutes an important resource for workers in the field. Unfortunately, this research also

---

1. Hilgard and Bower (1966, p. 1) date the scientific study of the psychology of learning from 1885, when H. Ebbinghaus published his research on memory.

presents us with a serious problem: Although an overwhelming majority of learning psychologists accept the data findings of virtually all researchers in the field as valid, they disagree considerably with respect to the conclusions that can be properly drawn from them. As a result, conflicting theories of learning have emerged which serve to complicate the curriculum worker's task. Of course, a single, well-integrated learning theory may some day be developed,[2] but for the time being, we are faced with the necessity of identifying, understanding, and assessing the various theories of learning generated by research and psychologists, and selecting from these the components that best serve our curricular purposes.

One may legitimately ask the reason for the existence of conflicting learning theories among psychologists. "Theories of learning (like much else in psychology) rest on the investigator's conception of the *nature of man* . . . psychologists who investigate (and theorize about) learning start with some preconceived view of the nature of human motivation" (Allport 1961, p. 84). This point may be generalized to include not only assumptions about the nature of man (the individual), but assumptions in the other foundational areas as well. We have previously emphasized this interrelationship of the foundational areas, so that it should be no surprise to find that, in spite of the "objective-scientific" aura that surrounds the field of learning psychology, preferences for particular learning theories in the last analysis are heavily dependent on the theorists' basic assumptions about knowledge, society, and man.[3]

Two examples will illustrate the interrelationships noted above: First, a propensity (either conscious or unconscious) toward philosophical realism and a conception of man as "master machine" will tend to stimulate research studies that show learning to be an aggregate of objective, reinforced, molecular behaviors acquired in response to external stimuli. In contrast, an inherent disposition toward pragmatism and a conception of man as social transactor generally favors a type of research that shows learning to consist of holistic insights achieved through the internal reorganization of perceptions. These two examples grossly oversimplify highly complex situations, of course; but they do point up the need for (1) awareness of one's basic assumptions and predispositions and (2) consistency in orientation.

Besides the problem of conflicting theories, a paucity of research on higher-level learning, such as ideational thinking and interest formation, hampers the work of curriculum theorists and planners. As Bruner (1960, p. 4) points out, the psychology of learning has tended to be chiefly concerned with the precise details of short-term learning in highly simplified laboratory situations. (In fact, much of this research involves learning in animals, rather than in human beings.) Psychologists have neglected, to a large extent, research into the sophisticated, long-term learning that is the principal concern of the schools.

2. Hill (1971), among others, perceives an ongoing convergence of learning theories.

3. Hilgard (1964, p. 58) suggests that the current decline of interest in gestalt and field psychologies is due to an unfavorable *Zeitgeist*.

Indeed, it would not be an exaggeration to say that although investigations into the psychology of learning have contributed a great deal to our understanding of how people learn specific behaviors in controlled situations, little progress has been made in explaining the complex, long-term cognitions and affects that are learned in the context of the individual's psychophysical ecosystem.

Conceptions of Learning

No universally accepted nor entirely satisfactory definition of learning exists. However, a feeling for the general dimensions of the learning process, as well as some of the problems associated with the study of learning, can be had by surveying a few of the provisional definitions offered by learning theorists.

Saylor and Alexander (1966, p. 195) favor the definitions of (1) Hilgard, Marquis, and Kimble (1961, p. 481), who define learning as "A relatively permanent change in response potentiality which occurs as a result of reinforced practice"; and (2) Gagné (1965, p. 5), who states that *"learning is a change in human disposition or capability, which can be retained, and which is not simply ascribable to the process of growth."*

The advantage of these definitions, as Saylor and Alexander point out, is that they do not insist on overt, observable behavior as evidence that learning has taken place. Rather, by using the terms "response potentiality" and "disposition" they suggest that learning can consist of an internal reorganization that will manifest itself as a change in overt behavior when an appropriate situation occurs. Needless to say, strict behaviorists reject this definition on the grounds that it is impossible to verify the presence of learning in the absence of a change in observable behavior.[4]

The criterion of "reinforced practice" stipulated in the first definition is one which is accepted mainly by learning theorists in the associationist tradition. Although it appears to be clearly applicable in situations involving the acquisition of a skill (such as typewriting), its usefulness is called into question (especially by psychologists of a gestalt persuasion) when learning that involves problem solving, attitude formation, or "creative thinking" is under consideration.

An important point emphasized in the second definition is that a change in capability, to qualify as learning, must not be ascribable simply to the process of growth. Clearly, considerable change in human behavior potential is due to maturation rather than to learning. For example, a child's ability to walk and talk is highly dependent on his level of neuromuscular development. Likewise, his ability to engage in higher-level, abstract thinking is precluded until he has attained a required level of chronological maturity. The research of the Swiss psychologist Jean Piaget, for example, has shown that until children reach the

---

4. This dispute actually reduces to a definition of behavior. For behaviorists, the meaning of the word is confined to the organism's physicalistic responses. Nonbehaviorists also include such "interior responses" as thoughts and feelings in their definition.

age of eleven or twelve, they are incapable of abstract reasoning, i.e., reasoning without the aid of material objects or "directly representable realities" (Piaget 1970, p. 33). In addition to behavior changes brought about by maturation, psychologists ordinarily exclude from "learning" changes resulting from fatigue, drugs, and other "temporary" conditions.

On the basis of the foregoing observations we can see that even though psychologists have attempted to circumscribe the meaning of the term "learning," they are still forced to include in the concept a wide variety of acquired behaviors not commonly associated with its vernacular meaning. Thus, besides such ordinarily accepted activities as reading, writing, swimming, and skating, we must also account in our definition for such acquisitions as "prejudices . . . preferences and other social attitudes and ideals, including many skills involved in social interplay with other people . . . [and] . . . tics, mannerisms, and autistic gestures" (Hilgard and Bower 1966, p. 2). This is a rather large order, and as Beckner and Cornett (1972, pp. 123, 124) point out, an adequate, single definition of learning may very well be precluded by the existence of too wide a variety of types of learning. Whatever the case may be, a final determination is presently out of reach. We close this section, then, with the definition proposed by Hilgard and Bower, who acknowledge that, although it is "not formally satisfactory because of the many undefined terms in it," it does "call attention to the problems involved in any definition of learning." These authors provisionally define learning as:

> the process by which an activity originates or is changed through reacting to an encountered situation, provided that the characteristics of the change in activity cannot be explained on the basis of native response tendencies, maturation, or temporary states of the organism (e.g., fatigue, drugs, etc.) (Hilgard and Bower 1966, p. 2).

Differential Characteristics of Learning

The previous section suggested that learning is not only complex, but that it is differentiable. A minimum of reflection will confirm this contention: There seems to be little similarity, for example, in situations which involve (1) a very young child learning to speak, (2) a student memorizing the pledge of allegiance, (3) an apprentice acquiring skill with a jigsaw, (4) a graduate student understanding a sophisticated logical proposition, (5) a dilettante learning to like electronic music, and (6) a scientist acquiring understanding by initiating his own original research. The situation becomes even more complex if we acknowledge a distinction between process and product. Gagné (1967, pp. 296–300), for example, identifies such differential performances as "trial-and-error learning," "discrimination learning," "paired associate learning," "concept learning," and "conditioned response learning," and notes that these differential performances imply differential capabilities, and hence different kinds of learning. Taba (1962, p. 78) suggests a variety of learning types: "mastering motor skills, memorizing information, learning feelings, concepts, and intellectual skills, such as generalizing, scientific inquiry, and problem solving." Such variety suggests not only the dubiousness of a unitary definition of learning, but the futility of searching for a single, integrated theory of learning.

A survey of the research literature reveals that particular learning theories emphasize particular kinds of learning and learning environments, while they neglect others. For example, associationist theories are based mainly on investigations dealing with habit formation and the acquisition of motor skills; they almost entirely ignore learning situations that call for the conceptualization of interrelated wholes. Field theories, on the other hand, tend to emphasize problem-solving situations in which perception, ideation, and insight are important elements; learning under practice and reinforcement conditions is almost entirely neglected. Disputes, of course, develop when one theory or another is employed (as it usually is by its proponents) to explain all kinds of learning. It is this kind of theoretical overextension that not only inhibits openness in research, but has quite harmful effects when employed to direct the total curricular diet of learners.

The curriculum worker would do well, then, not only to become familiar with various learning theories, but to differentiate the kinds of learning that are called for in his proposed curriculum. It may very well be that different kinds of learning are best achieved under conditions obtained with differentiated, but appropriately matched, learning theories.

Prescientific Learning Theories

As we saw in Chapter 6, Plato developed a learning theory of sorts when he proposed his ideal curriculum in *The Republic* 400 years before the birth of Christ. He believed that learning occurred when the *psyche* or mind recalled ideas that it had assimilated in another existence. Since that time many learning theories have been proposed, but most of them (like Plato's) have little correspondence to contemporary psychological thought. In the more recent past, however, two distinct and contrasting schools developed whose principles are still influential among both laymen and professionals. The first of these is *faculty psychology* (briefly discussed in Chapter 3); the second is *classical associationism*.

FACULTY PSYCHOLOGY

Although contemporary learning theorists repudiate the theory of faculty psychology virtually without qualification, we are obliged to give it some consideration here because its principles linger, somehow, in the practice of many school personnel. A product of the eighteenth century, the theory was expounded by the German philosopher Christian von Wolff in 1734 and again in a related version by the Scottish philosopher Thomas Reid in 1785 (Stephens

1956, p. 240). Faculty psychology progressively grew in acceptance as an explanation of learning until the late nineteenth century, when, as we noted in Chapter 3, it reached its zenith and became a predominant force in the shaping of the American secondary school curriculum.

The theory of faculty psychology holds that the mind, although unitary, consists of separate powers or faculties. The most significant of these powers are the intellect, feeling, and will. Many theorists, however, declared the mind to consist of a larger number of faculties, and included among them sense perception, observation, consciousness, noumenal perception, memory, fantasy, imagination, conception, judgment, and reason (Thut 1957 p. 231). Faculty theorists further held that each of these faculties, which reside in a specific area of the brain, can be strengthened with training, and that "formal" or "mental discipline" is the best vehicle for accomplishing this purpose.

According to the theory, formal training of the mental faculties is best achieved through the activity of drill. For example, memorizing poems, multiplication tables, Latin declensions, etc., constitutes excellent training for the memory. Of equal importance, however, is that the material to be memorized be difficult and unrelated to the learner's interests (and therefore unpleasant for him). If these conditions are met, not only will the learner's memory be trained but his power of will will be strengthened. In the same manner, heavy doses of logical-mathematical subjects, like algebra, geometry, and trigonometry train the faculty of reason, and generous quantities of classical literature (especially the Greek and Roman) develop the power of imagination.

The relationship of these activities and subject matters to the real world of affairs is of little concern to the proponent of faculty psychology, for he insists that a well-developed intellect, will, judgment, imagination, etc., is the best preparation for *all* life situations. In other words, he believes that transfer of training is general—applicable to all situations: algebraic and geometric exercises train the power to reason and enable one to decide competently and rationally which car to buy, which foreign policy to support, or which candidate to support. Likewise, consistent application to the distasteful drills and recitations required by the curriculum develops the will power needed to hold steadfastly to a morally correct life style and to overcome the temptations of the flesh, such as drink, drugs, and sex. It is little wonder, then, that whether a student's prospects indicate a future in law, medicine, engineering, insurance, farming, factory work, or rubbish collecting, the faculty psychologist prescribes the same curriculum: Latin, grammar, mathematics, and literature.

Although the foregoing description of faculty psychology is somewhat oversimplified, it does preserve the thrust advocated by the faculty theorist. That similar views are held by many educationists today is evident when we consider the learning theory implicit in the following commonly expressed statements:

Interesting or not, they need this material.
Math teaches reasoning.

Everyone should take a foreign language.
Memorize the Gettysburg Address.
We need more solid subjects and fewer frills.

CLASSICAL ASSOCIATIONISM

Unlike faculty psychology, classical associationism represents a germinal source for the learning theory advocated by the associationist school of scientific psychologists. Of course, the association of ideas in human consciousness has always been apparent to man, but it was the English philosophers Thomas Hobbes (1583–1679), David Hume (1711–1776), James Mill (1773–1836), and his son John Stuart Mill (1806–1873) who contributed most to the development of prescientific associationism.

Generally speaking, classical associationism holds that the human mind is simply an aggregate of a large number of minute percepts, ideas, and feelings held together by patterns of association. For example, if I see a large dog, I not only experience a perception of the animal, but, because of association, may recall a past experience in which a dog bite necessitated a trip to the doctor. The ideas of dog bite and doctor elicited by the dog are in turn connected with many other ideas, which may be drawn into my awareness by other bonds of association. According to Hume, associations are fostered by the presence of one or more of three situational qualities: (1) resemblance, (2) contiguity of time or place, and (3) cause and effect. The process of drawing ideas into consciousness by means of association defines the meaning of mind in associationist theory.

This tradition of classical associationism was the basis on which Herbart, some of whose ideas were discussed briefly in Chapters 1 and 3, developed his own associationist-learning theory. Herbart believed that sensations originating in the sense organs are transmitted to the *conscious* area of the mind, where they are somehow converted into percepts or ideas. Subsequently, these ideas pass into the *subconscious* area of the mind, where they join with similar ideas to form clusters of related percepts, or, as Herbart called them, "apperceptive masses." The ideas of the apperceptive masses may be recalled to consciousness when needed or when appropriate stimuli are presented to the individual.[5] Herbart and his followers, of course, expended great effort to determine the manner in which associations are established, and as a result laid the foundations for the beginnings of scientific associationism (Thut 1957, pp. 236–238).

---

5. In the light of this theory, we can understand more clearly why Herbart stressed that in teaching, ideas must be presented to the learner in such a way that they are vitally related to his experience—i.e., to the percepts that comprise his apperceptive masses. Herbart's carefully formulated five formal steps reflect this concern. We can also see more clearly now how Herbart's learning theory contributed to the development of the curriculum movement by requiring a reexamination of content and of content organization.

Associationist versus Field Theories

Most contemporary learning theories can be classified into one of two broad categories: associationist theories and field theories. Some psychologists would object to such a classification as being too simple, and in certain respects they would be right. Careful study of learning theories shows that the two-category classification tends to conceal or blur the exceptional features of theories within each category. Associationist theories often disagree with one another. on significant points while agreeing on others with certain field theories; the same, of course, can be said for certain field theories. Moreover, many psychologists believe that the sharp distinction between associationist and field theories is progressively diminishing and that the two orientations are converging in the direction of a unitary learning theory. Nevertheless, the contrast between associationist and field theories continues to represent the most fundamental cleavage in the psychology of learning. The obvious reason for this cleavage is that the basic philosophical assumptions on which the two schools of psychological thought are predicated are quite different. Associationist theories draw mainly on the assumptions of earth-centered philosophies, while field theories draw mainly on the man-centered tradition (see Chapter 6). In view of these basic differences, therefore, it does not appear inappropriate, especially in an introductory exposition, to utilize this simple two-class system.

ASSOCIATIONIST THEORIES

Scientific associationist theories sometimes are referred to in the literature as connectionist, stimulus-response, or reinforcement theories. They began to develop in the late nineteenth century when experimental psychologists questioned the classical associationist notion of "immaterial" mental ideas held together by bonds of association. These scientifically minded researchers preferred the more physiological explanation that mental experience is really neurological activity resulting either from external stimuli or associations established in the nervous system by prior contacts with stimuli. In other words, they believed that human activity is governed by associations between stimuli and responses.

This stimulus-response form of associationism views organismic activity in terms of three basic components: (1) the *stimulus situation*, (2) the organism's *response* to the situation, and (3) the *connection* between stimulus and response. The connection, called the S-R *bond*, refers to the tendency of the organism to respond in a particular way to a given stimulus. Its strength is a function of the *probability* that, given a certain situation, the organism will make a particular response. Thus, an S-R bond is said to be strong when this probability is high and weak when it is low (Kingsley and Garry 1957, pp. 84, 85).

Most contemporary associationists believe that the formation of S-R bonds takes place gradually through a process of *trial and error*. Given an unfamiliar and problematic situation (stimulus), the organism attempts to respond in a way that results in satisfaction for itself. The process ordinarily involves a number of unsuccessful or unsatisfactory responses that are eliminated gradually in favor of the response that the organism eventually recognizes as the "right" one. Thus, associationists think of learning as essentially a trial-and-error process.

In general, contemporary associationists view individual behavior, personality, knowledge, etc., as systems of S-R bonds. For example, learning a complex skill like playing the piano is a process of developing a very large number of small, contributory S-R bonds. Likewise, learning American history is a process of acquiring a large number of appropriately related bonds which, taken together, constitute "knowledge of American history." When a student is presented with "1776," he responds with, "Declaration of Independence." Asked about "unalienable rights," he answers, "life, liberty, and the pursuit of happiness." Basic bonds such as these build into more complex concepts, such as the libertarian spirit of the eighteenth century and its influence on the American Revolution. Each time a teacher makes an assignment or asks a question, therefore, his purpose is to build or strengthen a desired S-R bond and thereby contribute to the learning of a more complex totality. Illustrated here is one of the basic tenets of associationist theory: learning is a process of building simple units into complex wholes; it is analogous to constructing a brick building.

Most associationists would agree that habit formation, i.e., the development of strong S-R bonds, occurs as a consequence of *conditioning*. The Russian psychologist Ivan Petrovich Pavlov (1849–1936) first performed the now classic experiments demonstrating the operation of this phenomenon. Upon placing meat powder in a dog's mouth, Pavlov observed that a marked increase in salivation took place. In this "natural" situation, the meat powder constitutes an *unconditioned stimulus* and the increased salivation an *unconditioned response*. Pavlov then introduced an arbitrary stimulus (a tap on a tuning fork) just prior to presenting the food to the dog. After a number of repetitions of this procedure, Pavlov found that the sound of the tuning fork alone evoked the salivation response in the dog. In this instance, the sound of the tuning fork constitutes the *conditioned stimulus*, and the increased salivation the *conditioned response*. In effect, Pavlov's dog had been taught (conditioned) to respond to the tuning fork with increased salivation by the repeated application of a positive reinforcer (the meat powder).

Pavlov's influence on American psychology has been considerable, and though his "classical conditioning" has been subject to many variations, its basic principles are applied widely in both laboratory and classroom. In the laboratory, for example, the reinforcement of a food pellet is used to strengthen the "turn to the right" bond for laboratory rats and in the classroom a gold star or other reward is employed to strengthen the "accurately spelled word" bond for elementary school pupils. (Aversive stimuli—i.e., punishments—behave somewhat more complexly, researchers have found, so that it is not possible to say the punishment weakens or extinguishes bonds in all cases.) In any event, conditioning (by application of appropriate reinforcers when "correct" responses to presented stimuli are made) is the associationists' generally accepted means for promoting learning.[6]

BEHAVIORISM. Until the twentieth century S-R psychology consisted of the study of both mental and physical situations and responses. But around the time of World War I, John B. Watson (1878–1958) observed that internal mental events are really available only to the individual who experiences them. If a psychologist wishes to study another person's thought processes, it is necessary that the person translate his interior experience into physical terms—whether speech, writing, or other observable signals. These, clearly, are not mental events at all, but rather overt behavior. Thus, Watson held that psychologists deceive themselves if they imagine they can really study mental processes, and he urged that they abandon inferential speculation about mental states (which is subjective) and attend exclusively to the objective and scientific study of *behavior*.

Because of his adamance on the issue of behaviorism, Watson generated a maelstrom of controversy that continued into the 1930s. Since then extreme positions have softened somewhat, the debate has cooled, and psychology has incorporated in one form or another a great deal of Watsonian doctrine. Even so, it is probably fair to say that while many learning theorists evidence distinctly behaviorist leanings, the position continues to be challenged by a variety of nonbehaviorists, especially those with preferences for field or perceptual analyses of learning.[7]

Generally speaking, associationism has had overwhelming acceptance among learning theorists in the United States. Moreover, in spite of the fact that most associationist principles are based chiefly on research involving simple trial and error learning in animals, associationism has probably exerted a greater influence on education and curriculum than any other school of psychological thought. The fact that associationist principles emanate from "scientific research" has apparently lent them extraordinary credence among school personnel, who quasi-automatically transfer them, often quite inappropriately, to classroom situations. As a matter of fact, however, the higher human mental functions have been given very little attention by associationist theorists, who have consistently rejected as "unresearchable" such important aspects of learning as purpose, thinking, and insight.

6. Some associationists (e.g., Guthrie, whose learning theory is discussed in the following chapter) do not subscribe to reinforcement as a factor in learning. They argue, rather, that S-R bonds are formed merely by the contiguity of stimulus and response.

7. The "behaviorist" dispute in psychology is essentially analogous to the philosophical debate between the realists and the pragmatists; the issues involved are also the same as those in the so-called behavioral objctives controversy (see the section "Behavioral Objectives" in Chapter 13).

FIELD THEORIES

Sometimes referred to in the literature as cognitive, organismic or *gestalt* (meaning "pattern" or "configuration") theories, field theories are relative new-comers to the psychology of learning. Their origin and early development generally is credited to three German psychologists, all of whom later emigrated to the United States: Max Wertheimer (1880–1943), the official founder of the school, who first published the theory in 1912; Kurt Koffka (1886–1941), whose book *Growth of the Mind* (1924) attacked associationist trial-and-error learning; and Wolfgang Köhler (b. 1887), whose now classic experiments with apes introduced to psychology the rather obvious, but at the time scientifically unrespectable, notion of learning by insight (Hilgard and Bower 1966, pp. 229–232, passim).

For twenty-five years after the turn of the century, associationist learning theories were virtually unchallenged in the United States. Disputes occurred among associationist theorists, of course—e.g., between behaviorists and non-behaviorists—but the basic tenets of associationism described in the previous section were generally held to be reliable and undisputable descriptions of how learning occurs. In the mid-1920s, however, English translations of books by Koffka and Köhler were published, and for the first time, a radical alternative to associationism was given serious attention in this country.

Perhaps the best place to begin a general description of field orientation is with Köhler's experiments with apes, conducted during World War I (1913–1917) on the island of Tenerife off the coast of Africa. In one experiment Köhler hung from the top of his apes' cage a banana which could be reached only by standing on a box that had been placed in a distant part of the cage. After unsuccessful attempts to reach the banana by jumping up under it, one ape solved the problem without assistance by moving the box under the fruit. Other apes, after watching the solution take place, were able to master the problem. A variation of this experiment involved a banana set beyond reach outside the apes' cage and a stick for raking it in placed inside the cage. After a period of time and a number of unsuccessful attempts, Köhler's primates "got the idea" and used the stick to reach the banana. Subsequently, Köhler made the problem more difficult by requiring the joining of two shorter sticks (the end of one fitting into the end of the other) to reach the banana. Only his most intelligent ape was able to solve this problem unassisted.

From Köhler's point of view, experiments such as these indicated not only that animals can reason and use tools, but that learning is not a piecemeal, trial-and-error progression. Because the apes frequently solved problems suddenly, and after periods of time during which they were not actively seeking the banana, Köhler concluded that a perceptual restructuring had taken place. In the first experiment, for example, the ape suddenly saw the box not as just a plaything, but in relation to the banana and his problem. This analysis reflects one of the basic principles of field theory: learning is the sudden restructuring of integrated wholes—in other words, *insight*.

Emphasizing the role of perception in learning, field theorists maintain that we see things as organized and structured wholes rather than as masses of separate details. A photograph, for example, has a center of interest and a background: a ship against a vague expanse of sky and sea, or a skier against an indefinite mass of snow, trees, and sky. Even when no structure is obvious, we tend to interpret our experience in structural terms. The mass of dots appearing in Figure 11-1, for example, may be seen as a vertical pattern, or as groupings of squares. Although the pattern we see tends to vary because there is no grouping inherent in the figure, we "see" groupings because we tend to experience "organizationally," as it were.

FIGURE 11-1
Uniform array of dots stimulates the perception of variable patterns.

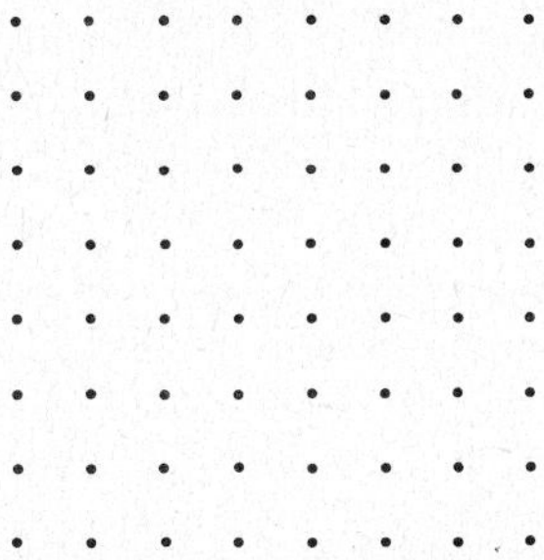

The importance of perceptual organization for learning can be seen clearly in the following example: A group of students is asked to memorize within a period of *ten seconds* the arbitrary code signs for the first nine letters of the alphabet as shown in Figure 11-2.

FIGURE 11-2
Code signs for the first nine letters of the alphabet.

A = ⌐	F = ⊏
B = ⊔	G = ⌐
C = ∟	H = ⊓
D = ⊐	I = ⌐
E = ☐	

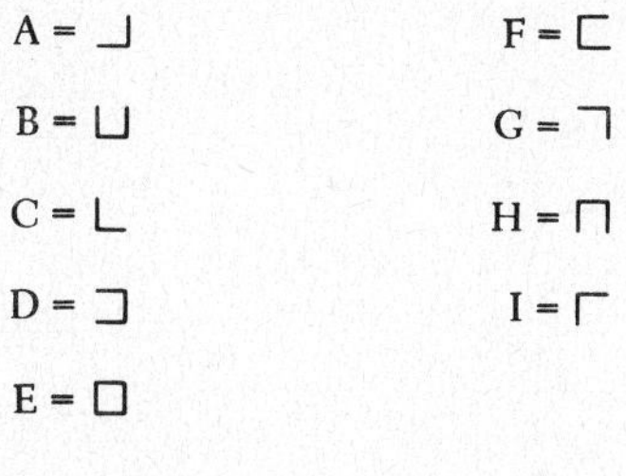

It is a rare individual indeed who can "learn" the nine code signs in the allotted period of time. However, if the "code" is represented as an organized configuration as it is in Figure 11-3, the task becomes absurdly simple. The "code" can be learned at a glance.

FIGURE 11-3

Code signs presented as an organized whole.

A	B	C
D	E	F
G	H	I

For the field psychologists, therefore, learning is not a process of building small, simple units into more complex wholes, but the occurrence of insights by which wholes are "seen" antecedently. "Seeing" wholes, of course, necessitates a grasp of the relationships that exist among the parts, for it is these relationships that endow the whole with its distinctive qualities. For example, a bicycle is not just the sum of two wheels, a frame, and a set of handle bars; it is these components *placed in a particular relationship.* In the same way, the tic-tac-toe design of Figure 11-3 is a quite different unity from the mere list of code equivalents shown in Figure 11-2. Consequently, field psychologists maintain that the whole is more than the sum of its parts and, in contradiction to the associationists, that it *precedes* the parts, knowledge of which is derived from the whole.

THE CONCEPT OF FIELDS. Perhaps because he had extensive training in physics, Köhler rejected the associationist notion that the elements of psychological situations were connected mechanically in fixed and objective ways (e.g., responses connected to stimuli by S-R bonds).[8] He preferred an interpretation analogous to the concept of energy fields employed by modern physicists (Thut 1957, pp. 337, 338).

Using a single drop of water as an example, Köhler noted that if it could retain its identity within a much larger volume of moving water, it would shift about considerably, exposed as it would be to pressures from every direction. There would be no linear and mechanical cause-effect relationship by which the drop's path could be predicted; rather, its path "at any given moment would depend upon the 'dynamical situation it encounters at each stage,' and the direction would change whenever the situation itself changed" (Thut 1957, p. 338).

Köhler's point is that just as the path of the drop of water is determined by its interaction with all the other moving drops in the larger volume of water, human behavior is determined by dynamic interaction with environmental forces. Stimulus does not elicit response in a linear, mechanical operation. Rather, "stimulus" and "response" interact as force fields, altering a total situation.

8. The fundamental assumptions underlying the associationist and field positions in the following discussion are the same as those, respectively, underlying the "map" and the "policy" positions on theory discussed in the section "Scientific Theory and Curriculum Theory" in Chapter 4.

The essence of field theory can be illustrated with the familiar elementary science experiment in which a magnet is placed beneath a sheet of paper on which iron filings have been sprinkled (see Figure 11-4). In situation 1 of Figure 11-4, the iron filings arrange themselves into a pattern representing the "N" force field of magnet A. In situation 2, the "N" force field of magnet B is shown. Situation 3 indicates how the introduction of magnet B (the stimulus?) alters the force field of magnet A (the response?). But the "response" of magnet A has also altered the force field of the "stimulus" magnet B, resulting in an entirely new and different total situation![9] In the same way, say the field psychologists, our "responses" affect the total environment (including the "stimulus") and so produce new total field configurations. This way of viewing individual human behavior has much in common with the recently developed concept of the world as a vast ecosystem.

Granting this analysis of the stimulus-response situation, how do the field psychologists explain habit formation? It will be recalled that in the previous section, the associationists were said to view habit formation as the development of strong S-R bonds resulting from conditioning. Thus, when an S-R bond is established firmly, we can predict that the presentation of stimulus x will almost always elicit response y. The field theorists, however, maintain that, although in the ongoing interaction of the individual and his total environment similar situations may elicit similar individual behaviors, no two responses to what appear to be the same stimuli are ever identical. This tendency to view habit as similar, but not identical, behavior indicates the nonmechanistic character of field theory (Thut 1957, p. 340).

The behavior of the needle in a magnetic compass provides an excellent illustration of the field concept of habit. The needle's tendency to point in a northerly direction may be described as a "habit." But the needle's behavior is not mechanical, invariable, and precisely predictable. The presence of a knife or other steel object "in the total situation" will affect the behavior of the needle. Furthermore, since the earth's magnetic pole is not constant, periodic corrections to "true north" are needed to adjust for the pole's variation. Actually, then, each reading of the compass, while it may produce similar results, is in fact a distinct occurrence. In the same way, the field theorists argue, apparently repetitive human "responses," no matter how similar the situations in which they occur, are distinctive (and to a degree even unique) behaviors (Thut 1957, pp. 340, 341).

The view that human behavior is a consequence of dynamically interacting fields clearly obviates the possibility, in principle, of precise prediction. This should not lead us to conclude, however, that field systems are entirely lacking in order. Sufficient organization and regularity inhere in field systems to permit prediction, but only in a statistical sense. This position on human behavior incorporates the scientific principle of indeterminacy described in Chapter 9.

A curriculum based on field principles will, of course, differ markedly from

9. If the "S" pole of magnet B were the "stimulus," a different situation 3 would result.

FIGURE 11-4
Field theory illustrated with magnets.

Situation 1: Magnet A

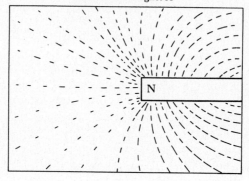

Situation 2: Magnet B

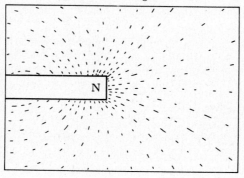

Situation 3: Magnets A and B in "stimulus-response" situation

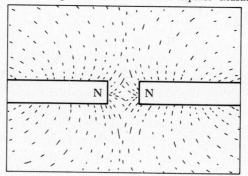

one based on associationist theory. In contrast to the associationist practice of dividing curriculum content into its simplest components and "programming" it so that the learner gradually acquires the simple units making up complex behaviors, the field theorist begins with major themes, concepts, ideas, and problems. He attempts to illuminate the structure of these wholes so that by a leap of insight the learner grasps the whole and its organizational principles. From that point on, it is possible to determine the character of the parts and to study more closely the details of their relationships. Nor does the field theorist expect learning to occur in the gradual, step-by-step manner assumed in the associationist's programmed curriculum; rather, he assumes it will occur quite irregularly—as periodic leaps of insight separated by a series of plateaus.

Field theorists maintain that the "joy of discovery" inherent in periodic flashes of insight is internally satisfying and therefore operates as intrinsic motivation for learning. This analysis contrasts sharply with the associationists' position that extrinsic reinforcers (rewards) are needed in order to motivate learners to acquire desired S-R bonds. We might note incidentally that the so-called discovery learning popularized among curriculum workers in the 1960s is rooted in this field-theory approach to learning.

We conclude this chapter with a brief summary of the basic characteristics of associationist and field approaches to learning. Associationists view learning as a process of trial and error. Learning is judged to have occurred when strong S-R bonds have been established as a result of conditioning. Complex skills and habits are learned by the gradual acquisition through reinforcement of the many simple S-R units that comprise the whole. Thus, for associationists the whole is equal to the sum of its parts. Behavioral associationists stress the importance of overt responses to external stimuli while rejecting as inaccessible internal mediating variables such as ideas and perceptions. In general, associationists view behavior and learning in terms of the mechanical relationships among discrete variables.

In contrast, field theorists view learning as a process of insight. Learning is judged to have occurred when the organism has experienced a restructuring of perception of the total situation. Because field theorists stress the importance of relationships inhering in organized wholes, they maintain that the whole is greater than the sum of its parts. Interior perceptions and cognitions, as well as overt behaviors, are regarded as very important in field theory because of the role they play in insight. In general, field theorists view behavior and learning in terms of the dynamic interaction of energy fields.

References

Allport, Gordon W. 1961. *Pattern and Growth in Personality*. New York: Holt, Rinehart and Winston.

Beckner, Weldon, and Joe D. Cornett. 1972. *The Secondary School Curriculum: Content and Structure*. New York: Thomas Y. Crowell Company.

Bruner, Jerome. 1960. *The Process of Education.* Cambridge, Mass.: Harvard University Press.

Gagné, Robert M. 1965. *The Conditions of Learning.* New York: Holt, Rinehart and Winston.

———. 1967. "Instruction and the Conditions of Learning." *Instruction: Some Contemporary Viewpoints,* edited by L. Siegel. New York: Thomas Y. Crowell Company.

Hilgard, Ernest R. 1964. "The Place of Gestalt Psychology and Field Theories in Contemporary Learning Theory." In *Theories of Learning and Instruction,* Sixty-third Yearbook of the National Society for the Study of Education. Chicago: University of Chicago Press, chap. III.

———, and Gordon H. Bower. 1966. *Theories of Learning.* 3d ed. New York: Appleton-Century-Crofts.

———, and Donald G. Marquis (revised by Gregory A. Kimble). 1961. *Conditioning and Learning.* New York: Appleton-Century-Crofts.

Hill, Winfred F. 1971. *Learning: A Survey of Psychological Interpretations.* Rev. ed. New York: Thomas Y. Crowell Company.

Kingsley, Howard L., and Ralph Garry. 1957. *The Nature and Conditions of Learning.* 2d ed. Englewood Cliffs, N. J.: Prentice-Hall.

Köhler, Wolfgang. 1929. *Gestalt Psychology.* New York: Liverwright.

Piaget, Jean. 1970. *Science of Education and the Psychology of the Child.* Translated by Derek Coltman. New York: The Viking Press.

Saylor, J. Galen, and William M. Alexander. 1966. *Curriculum Planning for Modern Schools.* New York: Holt, Rinehart and Winston.

Stephens, J. M. 1956. *Educational Psychology.* Rev. ed. New York: Holt, Rinehart and Winston.

Taba, Hilda. 1962. *Curriculum Development: Theory and Practice.* New York: Harcourt Brace Jovanovich.

Thut, I. N. 1957. *The Story of Education.* New York: McGraw-Hill Book Company.

CHAPTER 12
LEARNING THEORIES: SOME REPRESENTATIVE POSITIONS

Associationist Approaches to Learning Theory

EDWARD L. THORNDIKE'S CONNECTIONISM

Generally regarded as the originator of stimulus-response or S-R psychology, Edward L. Thorndike (1874–1944) is a central figure in the development of associationist learning theories. Indeed, Hilgard and Bower (1966, p. 15) note that Thorndike's connectionism dominated all other theories for nearly half a century and even today continues to influence a great deal of experimentation. The theory is of particular interest to curriculum specialists because of the marked effect it has had on educational practice, an effect which in no little respect is due to Thorndike's prodigious volume of writing, not only on the theoretical aspects of laboratory learning, but on the application of his theory to classroom situations (Kingsley and Garry 1957, p. 96).

Thorndike viewed learning as essentially a trial-and-error process. Trial-and-error learning begins when a motive of some sort—e.g., a need, problem, goal, or discomfort—disturbs the equilibrium of the organism. The organism then makes a variety of responses to the new situation in hopes of meeting its need, solving its problem, reaching its goal, etc. Unsuccessful, superfluous, and other wrong forms of activity are abandoned progressively until finally, the response or responses by which the goal is achieved gradually is integrated and established (Kingsley and Garry 1957, pp. 92, 93). The association between the established response and the motivating stimulus (i.e., the S-R bond) is what Thorndike conventionally refers to as a *connection*.

This four-step trial-and-error process (which Thorndike preferred to call "selecting and connecting") is demonstrated in Thorndike's earliest experiments with cats. The typical experiment involves a hungry cat, which is placed in a slatted cage. Outside the cage, beyond the reach of the cat's paw, is an aromatic dish of salmon. To get the salmon, the cat must depress a lever that springs a latch opening the cage door. The first trials of the experiment cover long periods of time because the cat engages in a wide variety of behaviors—clawing, biting, mewing, reaching out of the cage, etc.—before accidentally depressing the lever that opens the door. Succeeding trials become progressively shorter, but very slowly and irregularly, as the cat gradually abandons useless and superfluous responses. Over a period of 60 or so trials, a gradual discovery of the relationship between depressing the lever and opening the door takes place, and as the number of trials approaches 100, the cat learns to walk directly to the lever and without any useless activity, to depress it with his paw.

The irregularity and gradualness with which the cat learns suggested to Thorndike that it really did not "get the idea" in the sense that it understood the relationship of lever depressing and door opening (cf. Köhler's experiments with apes). He believed that understanding in animals is extremely rare and that their learning consists in the "stamping in" of correct responses (connections) and the "stamping out" of incorrect or useless ones. While Thorndike did not deny the existence of human insight and understanding, he believed that even in man it occurred only infrequently and that when it did, it was rooted in an acquired structure of appropriately organized connections and habits.

THORNDIKE'S LAWS OF LEARNING. Experiments such as the one described above led Thorndike to formulate the three basic laws which, he believed, govern learning in both animals and man. These are the laws of readiness, exercise, and effect.

The *law of readiness* states that when an organism is prepared to respond, making the response is satisfying, and being prevented from doing so is annoying. By readiness, Thorndike did not mean *maturational* readiness, the sense in which the term is used when teachers speak, for example, of reading readiness. Rather, he meant the arousal of a tendency to act as a result of prior attitudes, sets, adjustments, etc. For example, the sight of an attractive toy would arouse in a child a readiness to approach it, grasp it, and play with it.

Thorndike's *law of exercise* states that connections are strengthened with practice (exercise) and weakened when practice is discontinued. This law later was withdrawn by Thorndike when experiments showed that exercise alone did not lead to strengthened connections. The revised form of this law (which relates it to Thorndike's third law) states that weakening or strengthening of connections by exercise depends on whether satisfaction or annoyance results from making the response.

Thorndike's *law of effect* is by far his primary law of learning. It states that the stamping in of connections depends not only on stimulus and response occurring in temporal proximity, but on the *effects that follow the response*. If a stimulus is followed by a response which then is followed by a satisfying state of affairs, the S-R connection will be strengthened. On the other hand, if the S-R sequence is followed by an annoying state of affairs, the connection will be weakened. This law clearly categorizes Thorndike as a reinforcement learning theorist.

Although Thorndike was criticized by behaviorists for using such subjective terms as satisfaction and annoyance, he had in fact defined these two words in behavioral terms. In his two-volume *Educational Psychology*, published in 1913, he wrote:

> By a satisfying state of affairs is meant one which the animal does nothing to avoid, often doing things which maintain or renew it. By an annoying state of affairs is meant one which the animal does nothing to preserve, often doing things which put an end to it (quoted in Hilgard and Bower 1966, p. 20).

In view of his propensity for "objectivity," then, we may say that, in addition to being a stimulus-response reinforcement theorist, Thorndike is, in a broad sense, a behavioral psychologist.

After 1930, Thorndike's research led him to modify his law of effect. He found that while satisfyers (positive reinforcers, rewards) effectively strengthen connections, annoyers (punishments) do not directly weaken them. Although he probably underestimated the importance of punishment, he was essentially correct in assigning preeminence to reward. His revised law of effect simply states that rewarding consequences strengthens stimulus-response connections.

Thorndike's connectionism, coming as it did in the first quarter of the twentieth century, had at least three important effects on the curriculum. First, through the laws of readiness and effect, it focused attention on the importance of motivation in learning. Heretofore, the curriculum, in the grip of faculty psychology, had totally ignored motivation in its drive to train the learner's mind. Second, Thorndike's theory that learning consists of building specific S-R connections challenged the faculty psychology notion that learning could be *generally* transferred from any one (school) situation to any other (life) situation. Although Thorndike's belief that transfer is almost entirely specific has since been revised, his work generally is credited with demolishing the myth of mental discipline. Finally, Thorndike's emphasis on scientific verification at long last helped to bring the learning aspects of curriculum out of the realm of philosophic speculation and into the arena of empirical science.

CURRICULAR APPLICATIONS. Because Thorndike's connectionism is in the mainstream of associationist theories, many of the curricular characteristics described in the preceding chapter's section on associationism hold for this particular theory. Thorndikian connectionists would advocate subdividing curriculum content and activities into their most elementary components and arranging them in a sequence that allows for complex learning to be acquired by the additive process of stamping in contributory S-R connections. In addition, connectionists advocate the study of learners because knowledge about them is needed in order to (1) develop their readiness for learning tasks, and (2) ensure that they are capable (e.g., by virtue of prior connections) of making the desired responses. The process of bringing curriculum and learner together involves the presentation of stimuli, the observation of responses, and the stamping in of S-R connections by ensuring that rewards (satisfactions) quickly follow upon desired responses. When appropriate, stimulus-response-reward sequences are repeated in order to strengthen desired S-R connections.

Although a connectionist curriculum makes little or no allowance for "understanding" (and this is its chief weakness), it does not, as sometimes is claimed, foster rote learning. The students' interest and enthusiasm is enlisted by appropriate attention to the factor of readiness, and their learning is made joyful, or at least satisfying, through the operation of the law of effect. While Thorndike's conception of learning (as the stamping in of S-R connections) has been condemned by many educators as dehumanizing, his theory generally is credited with having had the opposite effect by providing an alternative to the stultifying rote procedures of early twentieth-century schools.

EDWIN R. GUTHRIE'S CONTIGUITY THEORY

Like Thorndike, Edwin R. Guthrie (1886–1959) is a stimulus-response behaviorist who views learning as a process of conditioning. However, he denies that Thorndike's principles of effect and exercise are factors in learning (conditioning), and in so doing, places himself in opposition to the mainstream of modern associationism, which generally regards reinforcement and repetition as pivotal theoretical elements.

Guthrie's learning theory is based on a single, elegantly simple law of learning: the law of association by contiguity. This is stated as: "A combination of stimuli which has accompanied a movement will on its occurrence tend to be followed by that movement" (Guthrie 1935, p. 26). According to this law the only condition necessary for learning is that the stimuli and response occur together (contiguously); there is no need for rewards, punishment, or practice. To make his position on this point absolutely clear, Guthrie later presented a supplementary statement that elaborates on his primary law: "A stimulus pattern gains its full associative strength on the occasion of its first pairing with a response" (Guthrie 1942, p. 30).

The great appeal of Guthrie's theory is its simplicity. It can even be summed up, without doing it violence, in a single vernacular sentence: "In any given situation we learn what we do and in similar situations repeat what we have learned." Yet on closer examination we find that the theory is really "so maddeningly complex" that it "stands as a challenge to students of learning" (Hill 1971, p. 41).

One difficulty with Guthrie's contiguity theory has to do with the interpretation to be placed on the word "contiguity." For example, in most stimulus situations we respond by doing a number of different things. Since all of our responses are "contiguous" in the sense that they occur in the stimulus situation, which will be the one that is learned and repeated? For Guthrie, the answer is *the last one*. By "the last one" Guthrie means the response just prior to, and presumably the cause of, the removal of the stimulus that has activated the organism. The principle that the last (most recent) response to a stimulus combination is the one that is learned has come to be known as the *recency principle*.

Guthrie's recency principle is well illustrated by the example of a person struggling to solve a mechanical puzzle (Hill 1971, p. 42). In the process he makes many responses before he finally solves it. It is this last, puzzle-solving (and stimulus-removing) response, according to Guthrie, which is learned and which will be repeated when the puzzle is presented again. This would seem to settle the matter satisfactorily. But what happens if the person cannot solve the puzzle and puts it aside. What, then, is the learned response? Guthrie would say that although the person has not learned to solve the puzzle, he *has learned*. He has learned to "give up," so to speak (this was his last and stimulus-removing response), and upon again being presented with the puzzle would tend simply to lay it aside. Unlike most observers, Guthrie does not classify the former response as learning "success" and the latter as learning "failure." To him, both are simply examples of learning by the process of contiguous conditioning.

Guthrie's contention that all learning takes place in a single contiguous pairing of stimulus and response is another source of difficulty. If we learn completely in a single trial, how can the improvement of performance with practice (repetition) be explained? Improvement with practice is supported not only by certain widely held laws of learning, but by our own experience: most of us can easily identify a large number of complex learnings (e.g., playing a musical instrument, driving a car, or skiing) that almost certainly are not capable of being learned in a single trial.

In response, Guthrie points out that the reason practice appears to improve performance is that improvement is defined in terms of total acts or achievements rather than in terms of specific muscular movements. He reminds us, however, that every complete act is composed of a multitude of minute, specific muscular movements learned in the variety of different circumstances under which the act is performed. Therefore, learning an act involves learning each of the many specific S-R connections that constitute the act. What appears to be "improvement with practice," Guthrie notes, is really the one-trial learning of increasing numbers of correct S-R movement connections on successive trials of the total act.

A common illustration of Guthrie's explanation of so-called improvement with practice is a boy learning to shoot a basketball. This act, according to Guthrie, consists of a large number of responses that become associated with the multitude of stimuli present in the situation—for example, the position of the boy's body, hands, and feet; the feel and weight of the ball; the boy's position and distance from the basket; different sounds occurring at the time. All these, and many more stimuli become associated with the act, which is performed with a greater or lesser degree of success. On the second trial, stimuli which are identical with those in the first trial will elicit identical responses (complete learning having occurred). But the boy will tend to substitute correct responses for some of the incorrect ones made in trial one. Furthermore, slightly different stimuli will also be present—a modified angle, different noises, etc.—and these will affect total performance. Improved total performance will not result from the strengthening of correct responses made on trial one, but rather from an increase in the proportion of correct responses made on trial two. The increase in the proportion of correct responses is due to (1) substitution of correct for incorrect responses to stimuli which are identical in both trials, and/or (2) the addition of the correct responses made to the new stimuli in trial two. Ultimately, a perfect performance results when correct responses are made to all of the specific stimuli in the situation.

If practice does not strengthen S-R bonds, then it follows that lack of practice cannot weaken them. We forget, or perform less well, says Guthrie, not because S-R connections weaken from disuse (learning occurs at full strength in a single trial), but because the responses of the old habit are being replaced by responses of new habits. For example, if our skill in basket shooting declines, it is because we have been playing volleyball; i.e., we have learned a number of new and competing responses to stimuli similar to those in the basket-shooting situation. Likewise, if we forget all of that American history we learned in high school, it is because many of the stimuli occurring in the American history situation have subsequently gotten connected with responses other than the American history ones. The general rule may be formulated, then, that new learnings tend to interfere with previous ones. Although Guthrie's explanation of the gradual improvement of performance is not necessarily correct, it is plausible and supports the basic postulate of his theory.

Since the substitution of correct for incorrect responses is central to Guthrie's learning theory, procedures for breaking undesirable habits should logically occupy a good deal of his attention, and this, indeed, turns out to be the case. In fact, Guthrie proposes three methods for the breaking of habits: the threshold, fatigue, and incompatible stimuli methods. Each of these methods constitutes a procedure for causing a new (wanted) response to replace the old (unwanted) one in the presence of stimuli that evoke the bad habit.

The *threshold* method involves presenting stimuli in a form too faint to arouse the undesirable response (a substitute response is always made, however, even if it is only "doing nothing"). On successive presentations, the stimuli are increased very slowly in strength. Each graduated presentation of the stimuli evokes the substitute response, consequently raising the threshold of the undesirable one. Eventually, the stimuli are presented full strength without eliciting the undesirable response because a new connection has been formed. Guthrie uses the old cavalry method of training horses to illustrate the threshold method of breaking habits. The untrained horses's response to a saddle and rider (substantial weight) is violent bucking. But if a blanket is placed on the horse's back, the stimulus (minimal weight) is too weak to elicit the bucking response.

Rather, the weak stimulus elicits the response of standing still. Over a period of time weight is gradually added to the horse's back, and the "standing still" response is learned for each successive increase in weight. Eventually, saddle and rider can be placed on the horse's back without eliciting the bucking response.

The *fatigue* method of breaking a habit calls for repeated presentations of the stimuli so that the undesirable response is given again and again. Finally, the subject becomes so tired that he stops giving the undesirable response and substitutes another—often one of doing nothing. The "bronco-busting" technique of riding untrained horses until they are "played out" is an example of how this method works. Another example given by Guthrie involves a young child who was an habitual match lighter. In order to break this danger-ous habit, her mother presented her with a box of matches and made her light match after match in rapid succession. The child became tired and complained, but her mother insisted she continue. Finally, exhausted the child threw down the box and pushed it away. Having learned, in a single trial, to respond to the matches by pushing them away, the child showed no inclination to light matches when presented with the match-box stimulus on future occasions. The fatigue method emphatically reveals Guthrie's rejection of laws of repetition (exercise) and his total reliance on the recency principle. If practice were an important factor in the situation, the child should have been more inclined than ever to light matches after her repetitive match-lighting experience. Rather, she learned the *last thing* that she did in the presence of the match-box stimulus: pushing the matches away (Hill 1971, pp. 48, 49).

The *incompatible stimuli* method requires that the stimuli evoking the unde-sirable response be presented when other factors in the situation inhibit the undesirable response. Guthrie's example of this method is the college student who could not concentrate on her textbooks because of distracting noises. By switching for a time to fascinating mystery stories, she found that she became so absorbed in her reading that she was able to ignore the noise. When she returned to her textbooks, she was able to study without being distracted by the noises because they had become connected with reading responses rather than with listening responses.

CURRICULAR APPLICATIONS. Guthrie's analysis of complex acts and achievements into their component muscular *movements* leaves little doubt that even more than many associationists, he would advocate the subdivision of the curriculum into its most elemental parts. This characteristic part-to-whole orientation facili-tates contiguous conditioning of the multitude of S-R connections that constitute complex learning. But Guthrie, unike many of his associationist colleagues, would ignore (as irrelevant) the factors of motivation, repetition, punishment, and reward. The main curricular task, he would claim, is simply to arrange for the desired response to occur in the presence of the appropriate stimuli.

Because the observed response—Guthrie's criterion for learning—is specifically connected with particular stimuli, the curriculum will consist essentially of cues or stimuli that elicit desired behavior patterns. This means that students learn by doing: they learn to read by reading and to write by writing; and if curriculum goals call for skill in adjusting carburetors, then carburetors must be available for students to adjust. In terms of the learning tasks to be mastered, the curriculum must be as realistic as possible.

In addition to being realistic, a curriculum predicated on contiguous conditioning will include substantial quantities of practice and drill. Practice and drill are necessary so that incorrect specific connections can be replaced by the correct ones making up competent performance. In these learning situations every attempt will be made to reduce extraneous stimuli to a minimum so that fortuitous learning will not interfere with the fixing of desired S-R connections.

Finally, faulty learning or "bad habits" will be eliminated by one of the three methods described above. Because students, for whatever reasons, have developed so many negative learnings in the presence of school and classroom stimuli, we may presume that the role of these methods in Guthrie's curriculum would not be inconsequential.

We may summarize Guthrie's contiguity theory by emphasizing its fundamental opposition to associationist theories in the reinforcement tradition. While it rejects the operation of reward or practice in learning, however, it is a true associationist theory in that it defines learning in terms of the conditioning of S-R connections. Moreover, it is a highly mechanistic and behavioristic theory.

The difficulty in evaluating Guthrie's theory lies in the limited amount of research that has been done to test its hypotheses. Indeed, the theory is chiefly a logically, rather than experimentally, based formulation. Guthrie's main contribution to curriculum work lies in his many practical suggestions for facilitating and inhibiting learning (e.g., the three methods for breaking habits).

B. F. SKINNER'S OPERANT CONDITIONING

Burrhus F. Skinner (b. 1904) has probably had a greater impact on American curriculum than any other living psychologist. Such educational developments as programmed instruction, teaching machines, computer-assisted instruction (CAI), behavior modification, and individually prescribed instruction (IPI) are all traceable to Skinnerian principles of learning. Although Skinner denies that he is a learning theorist at all (he thinks of himself mainly as an empirical, descriptive, scientific investigator), his work is quite generally recognized as a formidable contribution to associationist-reinforcement learning theory. Indeed, W. S. Verplanck, a psychologist who has studied Skinner's work very closely, maintains that Skinner's is "a highly formal, but not a highly formalized, theory" (quoted in Hilgard and Bower 1966, p. 143).

Like Thorndike, Skinner is a behaviorist who emphasizes reinforcement as an important factor in learning. Unlike Thorndike, however, he generally is not considered a stimulus-response psychologist because of his opinion that specific S-R connections account for only a small portion of all learning. Rather, Skinner maintains that most learning results from the immediate reinforcing of responses, whatever stimuli may have elicited them.

This position, of course, places him almost totally at odds with Guthrie, who attaches great importance to specific S-R connections and denies that reinforcers have any effect on learning at all. About all that Skinner shares with Guthrie is a behaviorist orientation and an interest in practical (as opposed to theoretical) learning situations.

The basis of Skinner's theory is the predication of two different types of behavior. The first, called *respondents,* refers to behavior *elicited* by specific stimuli. Examples of respondents are the constriction of the pupil in response to intense light and the knee-jerk reflex in response to a blow on the patellar tendon. The second class of behavior, called *operants,* refers to behavior that "operates" in the environment to produce certain effects. Operants are said to be *emitted* by the organism because they are not called forth or associated with any particular stimuli; that is, "there is no particular stimulus that will consistently elicit an operant response" (Hill 1971, p. 61). Examples of operants are walking, driving a car, playing tennis, talking, etc. S-R psychologists conventionally assume that operants are really respondents connected with unknown stimuli. Skinner does not deny this, but he holds that whatever the stimuli may be, they are irrelevant to the response because "its strength cannot be measured according to the usual laws of the reflex, which are all stated as functions of stimuli" (Hilgard and Bower 1966, p. 108). According to Skinner, operants, i.e., emitted behavior, constitute by far the greatest proportion of human behavior.

Each of these two types of behavior is associated with a particular kind of learning (conditioning). Learning *respondent* behavior follows the pattern of Pavlov's classical conditioning (described in the previous chapter): A new (conditioned) stimulus is presented together with the old (unconditioned) stimulus that elicits the "natural" (unconditioned) response. After a number of presentations of both the old and new stimuli, the subject learns (is conditioned) to give the old response when presented with the new stimulus alone. Learning takes place because the old (unconditioned) stimulus functions as a reinforcer during the conditioning procedure.[1] Because so little human behavior is *respondent* in nature, Skinner attaches relatively little importance to classical conditioning.

Because operants comprise so large a proportion of human behavior, Skinner has given most of his attention to operant learning or conditioning. Indeed, Skinner's contribution to the psychology of learning may be said to consist

---

1. Some psychologists deny the existence of classical conditioning. Others hold that it does occur, but not in a pure form. See Hilgard and Bower (1966, p. 109), for a discussion of this issue.

almost entirely of the development of the concept of operant conditioning and the determination of circumstances under which it occurs.

The basic law of operant conditioning is quite simple: *"If the occurrence of an operant is followed by presentation of a reinforcing stimulus, the strength is increased"* (Skinner 1938, p. 21). It is significant to note that as stated, this law emphasizes two factors: the operant and the reinforcer. No mention is made of the stimuli that originally elicited the operant response.[2] What gets strengthened is not an S-R connection, but *the probability of the operant occurring again.* Operant strength, therefore, is assessed in terms of the *rate* at which an operant is emitted. An increase in the frequency of emissions is an index of increased probability, which in turn is an index of strength. This represents a significant contrast to the way in which the strength of S-R connections are measured. These, it will be recalled, are assessed in terms of the probability that a particular stimulus will elicit a particular response.

In consequence of the foregoing, it seems clear that operant behavior takes on its identifiable character not so much because it is elicited by particular prior stimuli, but because its emission upon the environment will produce a particular reinforcing agent. Thus, with conditioning, the operant needs no stimulus; it will occur again because it depends upon the posterior reinforcer.

The most common laboratory example of operant conditioning involves a rat placed in a box containing a small metal lever. When the lever is pressed, a pellet of food is delivered. Lever pressing is the operant and the food pellet is the reinforcer. The lever-pressing response is strengthened each time it is followed by the food-pellet reinforcer. This mechanical system in which the response of the organism produces a reinforcing stimulus constitutes the essential character of operant conditioning.

DRIVES. In the foregoing example, the question may be raised as to whether or not hunger (food deprivation) constitutes a stimulus in an S-R situation. After all, the rat "emits" the lever-pressing response when deprived of food, but ceases to do so on becoming well fed.

Skinner denies that variables such as food deprivation are stimuli (in the sense that they elicit respondents); rather, he classifies them as *drives.* Characteristically, he views drives not as physiological or psychological states, but *operationally*—e.g., as "hours without food." Thus, the word "drive" refers to a certain category of operations that affects behavior in ways other than the ways in which reinforcement affect it. In support of Skinner's position, research has shown operant strength (e.g., lever pressing) to correlate *not* with the level of food deprivation, but with the number of prior reinforcements (Strassburger, cited by Hilgard and Bower 1966, p. 123).

---

2. Even though stimuli for operants are unknown and considered irrelevant, Skinner conventionally refers to operants as responses.

DISCRIMINATION. Skinner acknowledges that, although stimuli do not elicit operants in the same way that they elicit respondents, they may affect the conditions under which an operant will occur. For example, if an operant is reinforced in the presence of one stimulus, but not when it occurs in the presence of a second, the tendency for the operant behavior to occur when the second stimulus is present disappears. Because the organism, in effect, learns to distinguish between two different situations, the process is known as *discrimination*. A rat, for example, can be taught to emit a lever-pressing response when the lever is white, but to ignore it when it is black, by reinforcing white-lever pressing with a food pellet and not reinforcing black-lever pressing. It is important to note that the white lever is not a stimulus in the sense that it elicits white-lever pressing (white lever or not, the rat will not emit the conditioned response when it is satiated with food). Rather, it is reinforcement in the presence of the white lever that produces the operant. Although the white-lever stimulus does not *elicit* the rat's pressing response, it is an important *determiner* of it. In situations like the one described above, the operant is said to be under stimulus control (Hill 1971, p. 65).

POSITIVE AND NEGATIVE REINFORCERS. Skinner recognizes two classes of reinforcers: positive and negative. He defines a *positive reinforcer* as "a stimulus which, when added to a situation, strengthens the probability of an operant response. Food, water, sexual contact, classify as positive reinforcers" (Skinner 1953, p. 73). In contrast, he defines a *negative reinforcer* as "a stimulus which, when removed from a situation, strengthens the probability of an operant response. A loud noise, a very bright light, extreme heat or cold, electric shock, classify as negative reinforcers" (Skinner 1953, p. 73). It is clear from the foregoing definitions that a reinforcer, whether positive or negative, *increases* the probability of an operant response. In other words, both positive and negative reinforcers can be considered "rewards."

PUNISHMENT. Negative reinforcement (reward) involves the removal of aversive stimuli. Punishment, in contrast, involves either the *presentation* of a negative reinforcer or the *removal* of a positive one. Punishment defined as the presentation of aversive stimuli is of particular interest to educationists because the conventional wisdom has long held that its application eliminates unwanted behavior. Thus, "paddling," "detentions," "extra homework," and other aversive stimuli have commonly been employed to extinguish such pupil misbehavior as talking, fighting, swearing, and smoking. The assumption is that since reinforcement (reward) *produces* behavior, its opposite (punishment) will have the opposite effect of *eliminating* it. Psychologists acknowledge that the nature and consequences of punishment are far from clear (limited empirical research having been done in the area), but it is virtually certain that the single oppositional relationship proposed in the above layman's assumption does not hold.

While research indicates that punishment is not a uniformly reliable way to prevent responses from occurring, "experience" (and certain other research)[3] tells us that it appears to "work" in many situations. Does this constitute evidence in favor of punishment as a deterrent to behavior? Probably so, although in any given situation where reduction in the probability of a response follows the presentation of aversive stimuli, the reduction may be only temporary and/or it may be accompanied by other unwanted consequences. Hill (1971, pp. 63, 64) presents three possible explanations of why this is so.

First, it seems clear that punishment is likely to produce emotional side effects. The appearance of these emotional responses, being incompatible with the punished behavior, reduces the probability of its occurrence. For example, a child who is severely scolded for eating candy becomes very fearful and bursts into tears. Since crying and eating candy at the same time is difficult, the candy eating is terminated, apparently as a result of the scolding. With the removal of the aversive stimuli, however, the emotional effects (crying) dissipate and candy eating is quite likely to recur, often, according to Hill, at an increased rate. While punishment is effective in temporarily terminating undesired behavior, in many cases it does not prevent it from recurring at a later time.

A second reason that punishment may tend to eliminate behavior is that it conditions an accompanying neutral stimulus to the emotional response that punishment elicits. The presence of the neutral stimulus in future situations, therefore, elicits the emotional response that prevents the unwanted behavior. For example, the candy in the situation cited above becomes conditioned to the emotional response of fear. As a consequence, the child becomes fearful on approaching the forbidden sweets, and his candy eating tends to be inhibited. This effect of punishment appears to be longer lasting than the first.

The third reason that punishment may eliminate behavior is connected with the second. When the child, on being scolded, puts back or otherwise turns

3. An excellent review of this research is presented in Tullock (1974). Tullock's review of research on the deterrent effect of punishment indicates not only that punishment *does* deter crime, but that (1) the severity of the punishment and (2) the probability that punishment will be imposed are extremely important deterrent variables. He notes that many educated people recoil from the use of sure and severe punishment as a deterrent to unwanted behavior because of its unpleasant, primitive, and inhumane overtones; rather, they prefer more "civilized" methods, such as education and rehabilitation. But as Tullock notes (and recent crime statistics appear to demonstrate) these widely employed "humane" methods have "(at least so far) never . . . worked."

Although our intention here is not to draw parallels between criminal behavior and undesirable classroom conduct, the principle of punishment is applicable in both cases. The general rejection of punishment as a teaching device among most competent professionals has left its use in the hands of marginal teachers and administrators, who apply it unevenly, clumsily, and even brutally. This, in turn, has made its use even more repugnant. But it may be that popular negative attitudes toward punishment need reexamination. Much research is needed, of course, to determine the conditions under which punishment might have salutary consequences; but the moderate, just, and intelligent use of punishment as a deterrent to antisocial behavior may some day represent an acceptable recourse in education.

away from the candy, punishment is ordinarily withdrawn, thus providing negative reinforcement for the act of avoiding the candy. The child, therefore, tends
to be conditioned to avoid an aversive stimulus (candy). Although this is the
effect that disciplinarians hope to achieve, "like the second one, [it] lasts only
until the conditioned aversiveness of the stimuli extinguishes" (Hill 1971,
p. 64). Further punishments ordinarily are required to maintain the new
behavior.

These three explanations of the effects of punishment in eliminating
unwanted behavior reveal why Skinner generally regards it as a poor method
of control. First, while punishment may appear to be dramatically successful,
its results, as demonstrated in the first example,' are often only temporary.
Second, the emotional responses it produces are almost always undesirable:
"Replacing misbehavior with crying or anger is seldom a good solution" (Hill
1971, p. 64). Finally, as shown in the second and third examples, emotional
responses can become conditioned to a variety of unintended stimuli, including
the stimulus of the punisher himself. Not only is punishment an unreliable
method for controlling behavior, then, but it is quite likely to produce undesirable side effects (Hill 1971, p. 64).

REINFORCEMENT SCHEDULES. Although free operant behavior is related to a
number of factors (e.g., drives, emotions, discriminated stimuli), Skinner's primary interest has been the relationship of operants to reinforcers—particularly
the pattern according to which reinforcers are presented. As a result, Skinner
and his followers have defined and classified several patterns of reinforcement
delivery which they call schedules of reinforcement.

The simplest schedule, *continuous reinforcement,* calls for the delivery of a
reinforcer each time the operant to be conditioned is emitted. Continuous reinforcement ordinarily is used in the "basic training" of laboratory subjects.

Skinner's most extensive work, however, has revolved around two other categories of reinforcement schedules: ratio reinforcement and interval reinforcement. *Ratio reinforcement* calls for the delivery of a reinforcer after a certain
number of responses have been emitted. Ratio reinforcement, then, is based
on the *rate* at which responses are emitted. In contrast, *interval reinforcement*
calls for the delivery of a reinforcer after a specified period of time has elapsed
(assuming, of course, that the operant has been emitted during the time period).
Interval reinforcement, then, is contingent upon the passage of *time intervals.*

Both ratio and interval reinforcement schedules can be further subdivided
into two classes: fixed and variable. A *fixed-ratio* schedule delivers a reinforcer
after a standard number of responses—e.g., after every third, seventh, or tenth
response. A *variable ratio* schedule, in contrast, delivers a reinforcer after different numbers of responses, but according to a specified *average* number of
responses per reinforcer. Thus, variable ratio five reinforcement calls for a reinforcer to be delivered on the average of once every five responses, but reinforcement might occur after the fifth, sixth, eleventh, and twentieth responses.

A fixed-interval schedule delivers a reinforcer after a fixed period of time has elapsed (e.g., every 30, 60, or 240 seconds). On the other hand, a variable-interval schedule substitutes an average time interval for the fixed one so that a reinforcer may follow immediately on a previous one, while a third might be delayed for a considerable period of time. The possibilities for varying reinforcement schedules within the framework of the ratio-interval fixed-variable factors are virtually limitless. Indeed, a book called *Schedules of Reinforcement* (Ferster and Skinner 1957) reports the results of research employing an overwhelming variety of reinforcement schedules.[4]

Research indicates that patterns of operant response are significantly related to the type of reinforcement schedule used in conditioning. For example, ratio schedules generally produce higher rates of responding than interval schedules. This result is what one would logically expect since ratio schedules deliver an increased number of reinforcers for rapid responding, while interval schedules deliver only a standard number of reinforcers regardless of how rapid the response is. Also, the rate of responding immediately following the delivery of a reinforcer tends to decline for most schedules. The reason appears to be that the subject "learns" that additional reinforcement rarely occurs immediately after a reinforcer has been delivered. This pause after reinforcement, however, can be eliminated by using a variable-ratio schedule (i.e., a schedule which delivers a reinforcer after varying numbers of responses). Since the probability of reinforcement is equivalent at any given point in a sequence of responses, the rate of response is fairly constant. Finally, it has been found that intermittent schedules of all kinds produce more responses per reinforcer than a continuous schedule. In addition, when reinforcement is discontinued, subjects retain the operant behavior conditioned on intermittent schedules to a far greater degree than subjects conditioned on continuous schedules.

EXTINCTION. As suggested in the previous sentence, extinction of operant behavior following the cessation of reinforcement is a reliable index of operant strength. Two measures of operant strength commonly are used during extinction: (1) rate of responding, and (2) total number of responses before responding declines to its preconditioning rate. Research on the extinction of conditioned operants indicates that operant strength is not directly proportional to the number of reinforcements presented. Indeed, it has been found that a single reinforcement has considerable influence and that additional reinforcements

---

4. The variety possible is illustrated by a reinforcement schedule which Ferster and Skinner call "Tandem." This schedule calls for the following procedure: "A simple reinforcement is contingent upon the successive completion of two units, each of which would have been reinforced according to a single schedule. Thus in FI 10 [Fixed Interval Ten] FR 5 [Fixed Ratio Five], reinforcement depends upon a response after 10 minutes have passed, followed by 5 additional responses, whatever their spacing" (quoted in Hilgard and Bower 1966, p. 118). The variations of Tandem schedules alone are overwhelming.

only increase the number of responses during extinction very slowly. In general, resistance to extinction is greatest when a variable-ratio reinforcement schedule is used.

SHAPING. Shaping is the term that Skinner uses to describe his procedure for teaching complex behaviors through a series of approximations. By selectively reinforcing certain operants and disregarding others, Skinner gradually builds a cluster of simple constituent responses into a more complex end behavior. For example, a rat can be taught to pull a string to obtain a marble from a rack, pick up the marble with its forepaws, carry it to a tube projecting from the floor of the cage, and drop it into the tube (Skinner 1938, pp. 339, 340). In brief, the procedure used to accomplish this rather remarkable pedagogical feat would begin with teaching the rat to obtain food from the rack by pulling the string. At first, a food pellet would be delivered if the rat merely touched the string. When it had learned to acquire food by touching the string, the reinforcer would be withheld until, after several touches, the rat (perhaps by chance or through frustration) tugged on the string. At the point that the rat had learned to pull the string to obtain its food pellet, a marble would be introduced, and the rat would be taught to obtain food by pulling the string and then touching the marble. This having been learned, food would be delivered only if the string were pulled and the marble removed from the rack. The foregoing process of *shaping by successive approximations* would continue until the rat had learned to perform the full, complex sequence of behaviors. Skinnerians maintain that shaping has significant implications for human learning and education. Indeed, programmed instruction, which is discussed in the section below, is predicated on this principle.

CURRICULAR APPLICATIONS. Because of the actual curriculum-construction work done by Skinner and his followers since 1954, there is no need to speculate on the curricular applications of operant conditioning. In fact, many programs that condition desired operants by the process of shaping are presently in use in some schools today.

From Skinner's point of view, our present custom of having a single teacher guide twenty-five or thirty students through the curriculum at the same time is highly inefficient. In the first place, students learn at varying rates so that the teacher's pace may be too slow for some and too rapid for others. Then, too, the group situation provides extremely limited opportunity for individual responses. Even where responses occur, they are not likely to be adequately reinforced by a teacher responsible for the concurrent learning of so many students. Obviously, for learning to be efficient, each student, like each laboratory animal, must be *individually* conducted through the curriculum.

Skinner's solution to the practical problem of individual conditioning is the *teaching machine*. A teaching machine may be a very simple mechanical device, such as a window-box arrangement involving two knobs that move a paper scroll, or it may be a highly sophisticated computer. In any case its basic component is always the *program,* the importance of which is reflected in the term *programmed instruction.*[5]

The character of programmed instruction is illustrated in an early program that teaches arithmetic by presenting number combinations to be added. The student punches his answer into a kind of adding-machine keyboard, and if the answer is correct, he is "reinforced" by the presentation of the next problem. Of course, many more sophisticated programs have been developed since this early one, but the conditioning principles are the same: the problems proceed gradually from the simple and familiar to the more difficult and less familiar, with each correct response being conditioned by positive reinforcement. It it worth noting that in accordance with his emphasis on positive reinforcement, Skinner believes that very gradual shaping (which avoids mistakes and thus punishment) is the best pattern for learning.

The foregoing description of programmed instruction indicates that curriculum construction based on operant conditioning is concerned with three basic procedures: (1) identification (in behavioral terms, of course) of the operants to be conditioned, (2) meticulous sequencing of curriculum elements from simple to complex in order to facilitate shaping, and (3) the identification of reinforcers required to strengthen and maintain the desired operants. Except for Skinner's disposition to reject stimuli as irrelevant, his *system* (he would object to the term "theory") is rooted squarely in the associationist tradition.

Aside from the direct application of Skinner's system to teaching machines and programmed instruction, it seems fair to ask about the system's application (1) to "real life" and (2) to its implications for the foundational, or value, aspects of curriculum. Although the picture is far from clear, there is some evidence to suggest that principles of operant conditioning operate in many real-life situations. The fact, for example, that fishermen continue to fish even though they do not always catch fish, or that gardeners continue to plant even though their efforts are not always rewarded, suggests that responses may be optimally strengthened and maintained by *intermittent* reinforcement (Hilgard and Bower 1966, p. 114). Further, the commonly observed behavior pattern involving a student who finishes a term paper in a burst of effort and speed and then procrastinates at length before beginning his next assignment suggests the same kind of response decline that occurs under a fixed-ratio reinforcement schedule (Hilgard and Bower 1966, p. 117).

Skinner has gone far beyond these real-life analogies, however, to suggest the relevance and efficacy of operant conditioning for education in society. In a book called *Walden II* (Skinner 1948), he describes a utopian society in which operant conditioning is employed beginning at birth to channel indivi-

---

5. It is the program, or curriculum, and not the machine that ultimately determines the character and quality of learning. In a certain sense, even books are "teaching machines" whose character and quality are determined by the "program" they contain. Indeed, the currency of "programmed texts" tends to bear out this claim. It is unquestionably an irony that many programmed texts turn out to be far poorer teachers than ordinary books that are simply well written.

dual human behavior into socially productive directions. Operants such as reason, tolerance, and cooperation are reinforced, while others like aggression, envy, and greed are extinguished. A critique of Skinner's proposal is, of course, beyond the scope of this book. We should note, however, that attractive as *Walden II* appears to be, it has been the subject of severe criticism. Some psychologists, for example, ask why the arch-behaviorist Skinner, while refusing to make inferences from how a rat behaves to what is going on inside the rat, is quite ready to make inferences from how a rat behaves to what the operation of human social organization ought to be like (Hill 1971, p. 76). Others point out that Skinner's concentration on a few principles of behavior (e.g., the rate of emission of simple, free operants) is far too narrow a base from which to speculate on the complexities of human learning. The most telling criticism, however, is not connected with the *feasibility* of creating a "Walden II," but with the *values* and *assumptions* that underlie it. Skinner's utopia, and the curriculum that shapes it, are based chiefly on a philosophy of empirical (scientific) realism and the view that man is nothing more than a sophisticated biological mechanism that functions according to the laws of nature. Reacting against this orientation, one social psychologist assesses *Walden II* as:

> *a vision of the future in which man is controlled by science, made happy by technique,* rendered well-adjusted *by the manipulation of others. Emerson's vision? Only the* hubris *of science could take Thoreau's* Walden, *and dare to appropriate a word with such noble connotations, for such a vile vision (Becker 1967, pp. 243, 244).*[6]

Notwithstanding these criticisms, however, Skinner's contributions to the psychology of learning (and thus to the curriculum field) are considerable. Operant behavior, reinforcement schedules, shaping, teaching machines, and programmed instruction have all had a significant impact on contemporary curriculum.[7] For better or for worse, it is unlikely that Skinner's influence on the curriculum will diminish very rapidly in the forseeable future.

Representative Field Approaches to Learning Theory
CLASSICAL GESTALT THEORY

Classical gestalt theory generally is considered to be the product of the German psychologists Wertheimer, Koffka, and Köhler, and insofar as their general orientation was treated in the previous chapter, we need not repeat it here. Certain important concepts and laws of classical gestalt theory were omitted or

---

6. Students interested in Skinner's defense of his philosophical position should see his most recent popular book (Skinner 1971).

7. A distinction is made in the section "Training versus Education" in Chapter 13 between *education* and *training*. Skinner's system has had its greatest influence on training.

abbreviated in that general discussion, however, and it is to these that we now turn our attention.

The key term in this learning theory is *gestalt,* a German word meaning "pattern" or "configuration." Gestaltists point out that we perceive (and learn) in terms of dynamic structured wholes. For example, when listening to a musical performance, we do not hear separate tones, but rather a melody, which is a total configuration of tones that depends for its character on the relationships among its individual notes. When the key is changed we hear a totally different set of tones, yet the gestalt—the melody—is still the same (Hill 1971, p. 95). Similarly, when three round dots are presented so ∴., we tend to see a triangle rather than three separate dots. Changing the dots to open squares (⬚⬚⬚) presents an entirely different set of visual components, yet the essential characater of the gestalt is not altered. These examples point up the centrality of organized wholes in classical gestalt theory.

Although gestaltists concede that it is possible to analyze a gestalt into its component parts, they point out that this activity normally *follows* perception of the whole. Moreover, they insist that even when an analysis is made, it does not ordinarily reveal the essential character of the whole. In the examples given above, for instance, it is not the particular notes or dots or squares that are significant about what we hear or see, but the relationships that exist among them. This observation is the basis of a fundamental principle of classical gestalt theory: The whole is more than the sum of its parts.

The concept of figure-on-ground (briefly touched on in the section on field theories) is another important idea in gestalt theory. The *figure* constitutes the gestalt that we perceive, while the *ground* is the rather vague undifferentiated background on which the figure appears. Figures and grounds can alter according to our past experience or focus of attention. For example, a melody may at one moment be a figure against a backdrop of other sensory experiences (e.g., accompaniment, record player, group of friends, etc.) and at the next moment recede into ground when we direct our attention away from the music toward a friend's comments, which now constitute the figure in a new total situation. "Such changes in figure-ground relationships play a part not only in perception but in learning and thinking as well" (Hill 1971, p. 95).

GESTALT LAWS OF LEARNING. The laws of learning in gestalt theory derive from a single general principle called the law of *Prägnanz.* The German word *Prägnanz* can be translated as "pregnancy," but its real meaning is more adequately conveyed by the phrase "compact but significant" (Hilgard and Bower 1966, p. 233). The law of *Prägnanz* states that gestalts tend toward the "compact but significant," that is, toward regularity, simplicity, stability, etc.—general characteristics of the "good" gestalt. In other words, gestalts tend to be perceived in ways that generate organized meaning for the perceiver.

Although as we have noted above, gestalts can be influenced by individual past experience or a particular focus of attention, gestalt theorists have identified in "good" gestalts certain specific properties that promote learning and facilitate remembering. Some of these properties are described in four laws of learning developed by Koffka.

1. *The law of similarity.* Analogous to the connectionists' principle of association, the law of similarity asserts that "good" gestalts are composed of like or similar elements. Köhler, for example, showed that pairs of nonsense syllables, two-place numbers, and two-dimensional figures were learned more readily when members of the pairs were similar than when they were dissimilar. He reasoned that the similarity of the members resulted in an "interaction" which produced a unitary gestalt and thereby facilitated learning. This explanation, of course, contrasts with the associationist one, which would explain such learning in terms of connection between similar elements.

2. *The law of proximity.* This law states that gestalts tend to be composed of elements that are closest to one another—either in space or time. For example, if a number of circles is drawn across a page with alternately wide and narrow spaces between them, the circles that are closest together will be seen as groups or gestalts (see Figure 12–1). Recall, retention, and learning will be facilitated by the formation of these gestalts and will follow their particular organization. This principle is analogous to the associationist position that learning occurs through association by contiguity.

FIGURE 12-1
Illustration of the law of proximity.

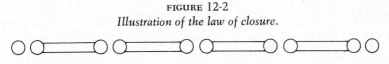

When the law of proximity is applied to temporal situations, gestalts are said to consist of those elements that occur closest in time. In terms of learning theory, this principle is analogous to the associationist law of recency. In contrast to associationists, however, gestalt theorists maintain that recent events are more easily remembered because they are more readily related to elements of the present in the structuring of gestalts.

3. *The law of closure.* This law specifies that closed areas more readily tend to form gestalts. If the most distant pairs of circles in Figure 12–1 are joined by a pair of parallel lines to form a closed area (see Figure 12–2), the gestalts composed of proximate pairs of circles are dissolved, and the more distant circles are seen to form four "long" gestalts with an "extra" circle appended to either side of the figure. Recall, retention, and learning will now occur in terms of the revised gestalts.

FIGURE 12-2
Illustration of the law of closure.

When gestalt theorists apply the law of closure to learning situations, they refer to a sense of completion (or closure) that occurs when a learner has attained a goal or achieved a condition which, for him, represents an end situation. This interpretation of closure is analogous to Thordike's law of effect in the sense that closure represents the reward that comes with successful completion of the learning task. However, as Hill (1971, p. 100) so aptly points out, this interpretation of closure and closure in the visual sense noted above "is somewhat forced." Indeed, it is Hill's opinion that two different laws, one concerning perception (visual closure) and one concerning learning (closure as end-condition), have somewhat inappropriately been given the same name.

4. *The law of good continuation.*   Allied to the law of closure, the law of good continuation states that perceptions are formed on a pattern that tends to continue the pattern perceived in incomplete gestalts. For example, a straight line appears to continue as a straight line, a partial circle is perceived as a complete circle, and a partial star (e.g., ⵥ) is seen as a completed figure, even though other perceptual structurings are possible. Thus, the law of good continuation suggests that learning is maximized when stimuli or cues are appropriate, or fit well with, gestalts to be learned.

As the law of *Prägnanz* and its four derivative laws imply, gestalt theory emphasizes perception in its explanation of learning. Unlike associationists, who are likely to ask "What has the individual learned how to do?" gestalt theorists ask "How has the individual learned to perceive the situation?" (Hill 1971, p. 96). Because of this emphasis, some associationists regard gestaltists (and other field theorists) more as perceptual psychologists than as learning theorists. Insofar as perception and learning are inextricably related, however, the nature of the label one carries is probably less important than the fact that the study of perception be recognized as an important aspect of the psychology of learning.

MEMORY TRACES AND FORGETTING. In contrast to the S-R bonds that associationists use to explain the phenomenon of memory, gestalt theorists employ the concept of *memory traces*. The trace theory is highly complex, but its essential features can be summarized as follows:

> *(1) a trace is assumed which persists from a prior experience, so that it represents the past in the present; (2) a present process is also posited, one which can select, reactivate, or in some manner communicate with the trace; and (3) there is a resulting new process of recall or recognition . . . . The trace system is organized according to the same laws applying to other fields, and the communication process and trace follows these laws* (Hilgard and Bower 1966, p. 237).

From this summary, it is clear that, unlike S-R bonds, memory traces are not separate elements, but organized wholes—gestalts; and learning is not a matter of adding new traces to the present store, but of reorganizing old traces into new gestalts (Hill, 1971, pp. 96, 97).

The gestalt theory of forgetting follows logically from the memory-trace theory and the law of *Prägnanz*: Forgetting occurs when memory traces change with time to form "better" gestalts. Thus, forgetting is not simply the decay of a memory trace, but its reorganization to form a gestalt that is more consonant with the inherent properties of a "good" gestalt and/or with the familiar, meaningful gestalts that inhere in individual past experience.

LEARNING AS INSIGHT. Insofar as learning by insight is concerned, we need only elaborate briefly on the discussion of insight found in Chapter 11. Since insight is a process of restructuring integrated wholes, gestalt theorists tend to be concerned with such qualities in learning as originality, creativity, and understanding—or, as Wertheimer (1945) terms it, "productive thinking." This contrasts sharply with the associationist view that learning is a rather mechanical process of stamping in S-R bonds or forming habits.

Wertheimer conducted a series of studies to demonstrate the superiority of insightful understanding over the rote memorization that in his view constitutes too great a proportion of children's school learning. The most celebrated of his experiments involves finding the area of a parallelogram. Wertheimer initiated the experiment by teaching his subjects how to find the area of a *rectangle* (area of a rectangle equals base times height). But he went beyond just teaching the formula. As part of the lesson he divided the rectangle into a number of small squares so that his subjects might "understand" that "base times height" means "the number of squares in a row times the number of rows" (see Figure 12-3). He then presented his subjects with a parallelogram (see Figure 12-4) and instructed them to find the area. Some subjects objected that the figure was a new one and they could therefore not be expected to find its area. Others blindly repeated the rectangle formula, multipling side A by side B and,

FIGURE 12-3

Wertheimer's explanation of the formula for the area of a rectangle.

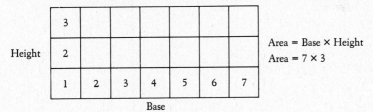

Height

3						
2						
1	2	3	4	5	6	7

Base

Area = Base × Height
Area = 7 × 3

FIGURE 12-4

Wertheimer's parallelogram problem.

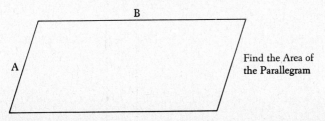

B

A

Find the Area of
the Parallegram

of course, getting the wrong answer. Still others were simply perplexed, being unable to see a relationship between the rectangle problem and the new one. A few subjects, however, on the basis of understanding, originality, and productive thinking, came up with novel solutions. One mused, "It is troublesome, here and there," and pointed to the protruding ends of the parallelogram. After hesistating for a moment, she suddenly cried, "May I have a scissors? What is bad there is just what is needed here." She proceeded to cut off the left end and place it on the right, making a rectangle out of the parallelogram, the area of which she could now obtain with the base-times-height formula (see Figure 12-5) (Wertheimer 1945, p. 48). Another subject, remarking that the middle was all right but the ends were not, bent the parallelogram into a ring and declared that a vertical cut anywhere would produce a rectangle, the area of which could easily be calculated (see Figure 12-6).

It is possible, of course, that the area of the parallelogram might be calculated by the base-times-height (i.e., altitude) formula, but doing so would not neces-sarily indicate *understanding*. Indeed, it would probably reflect little more than the blind application of the rectangle formula. The two subjects who achieved novel solutions, in contrast, demonstrated their understanding by restructuring the new unfamiliar gestalt into a "better" one, i.e., a more familiar one in terms of their experience. As Hill (1971, p. 103) points out, "The important thing about the [novel] solutions was the insight by which the new problem situation was restructured."

FIGURE 12-5
Solution to the parallelogram problem.

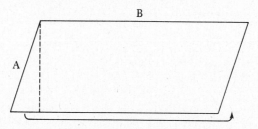

FIGURE 12-6
Second solution to the parallelogram problem.

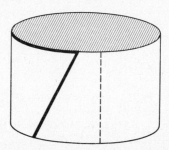

CURRICULAR APPLICATIONS. A curriculum based on classical gestalt theory will of course incorporate those general characteristics noted in the section on field theories (see Chapter 11). It will feature wholes (e.g., the theme, "prejudice in human existence"), relationships (e.g., of prejudice to poverty, scapegoating, need for esteem, etc.), and regard for the perceptions of learners. Since "understanding" is a central goal, the curriculum will be designed to help learners see significant relationships and organize their experiences into functional and effective patterns. To accomplish this, instruction will necessarily begin with the familiar, and great care will be taken to ensure that content and learning activities are organized into meaningful patterns. Essential generalizations will be emphasized, while supporting details and data will receive subordinate status.

The gestalt spirit is reflected in the procedures recommended for reading a book. First, the dustcover flaps, table of contents, etc., are surveyed so that a global impression of the book's subject matter is obtained. Then, as each chapter is read, its relationship to the whole (and to the other chapters) is understood more clearly. The process may be likened to "seeing" the whole situation and gaining an increasingly deeper understanding of it as one examines more closely the relationships among its component parts. Of course, the reading of a single chapter follows the pattern set for reading the book: chapter title, main headings, and subheadings are surveyed first in order to grasp the structure of the whole chapter, after which the chapter itself is read for in-depth understanding.

Just as it is necessary for each subject to be treated as an integrated whole in a gestalt-based curriculum, so all the subjects of the curriculum need to be related in order that the learner's educational experiences result in a coherent and meaningful gestalt. Wherever it is possible to do so, therefore, courses should bring skills and content into relationships that reflect the gestalts of functional experience: not the separate and isolated study of mathematics, chemistry, biology, history, sociology, economics, government, reading, writing, and oral expression, but projects and activities that integrate these subjects—as they would be integrated, for example, in a course or unit on the problems of pollution or the nature and function of prejudice. Considering the gestalt emphasis on perception and the understanding of relationships, it is not difficult to see how gestalt learning theory gives rise to curriculum designs that reorganize the formal disciplinary structure of knowledge into gestalts corresponding to the categories of meaning encountered in experience.[8]

LEWIN'S TOPOLOGICAL THEORY

An associate of Wertheimer, Koffka, and Köhler, Kurt Lewin (1890–1947) developed his topological theory along lines that coincide with basic gestalt

8. This is not to suggest that the disciplines organization of knowledge is not logical or meaningful. Indeed, the disciplines organization is probably the most effective for (1) specialized study of a particular discipline, or (2) retrieval of information needed to deepen understanding of the functional gestalts of daily life.

principles. Like his gestaltist colleagues, Lewin contends that experience (and learning) is determined by the overall pattern or *field* of events that inheres in given situations. But whereas gestaltists are interested chiefly in perception, learning, and thinking, Lewin emphasizes personality, social psychology, and especially *motivation*. It is not surprising, then, that many purists among the fraternity of learning theorists regard Lewin as even less of a psychologist of learning than they do his classical gestalt colleagues.[9]

Lewin does not claim to be a learning theorist per se. His argument, rather, is that we cannot have a clear understanding of learning unless we take into account the entire, complex, psychological world—he calls it the "life space"—of the individual learner. Indeed, Lewin is highly critical of the tendency of learning theorists, especially associationists, to treat learning as a unitary phenomenon explainable by a single law (association). On the contrary, he contends "the term *learning* refers to a multitude of different phenomena," and he asks, "Have we any right to classify the learning to high-jump, to get along without alcohol, and to be friendly with other people under the same term, and to expect identical laws to hold for any of these processes?" (Lewin 1942, pp. 219, 220). The response to this rhetorical question is, of course, "no," and Lewin proceeds to distinguish "at least" four classes of learning: "(1) learning as a change in cognitive structure (knowledge), (2) learning as a change in motivation (learning to like or to dislike), (3) learning as a change in group belongingness or ideology . . . , [and] (4) learning in the meaning of voluntary control of the body musculature (. . . skills, such as speech and self-control)" (Lewin 1942, p. 220).

It seems clear from the foregoing that learning, from Lewin's point of view, cannot be considered a specialized or isolated problem in psychology. Rather, it is something that can be dealt with only within the broader context of changes in the individual's total life space. If we can gain an understanding of the principles governing the structures of the life space, then, we will have answered the basic questions of psychology including, of course, those of its subdivision, learning. This must certainly constitute the gestalt view carried to its ultimate degree—to the field of psychology itself!

THE LIFE SPACE. As suggested above, the life space is an important concept in Lewin's theoretical system. It may briefly be defined as the total field of forces within which the individual operates. In addition to certain internal forces such as the basic physiological drives for food, water, sex, etc., the life space includes the external environment with which the individual transacts: the people he

9. Kurt Lewin was dropped from the 1966 edition of Hilgard and Bower's *Theories of Learning* because "his views on learning have not been sufficiently influential in recent years . . ." (p. v). At the same time, however, it is conceded that "Lewin's views are currently very much alive in social psychology and in relation to some aspects of human motivation (p. vi). Insofar as learning occurs in the context of social situations governed by individual motivation, Lewin's work will have relevance for curriculum planners.

meets, the objects he manipulates, the geographical space in which he ma-
neuvers, and so on. We must hasten to add, however, that it is not these
elements as *objective physical factors* that constitute the life space. Rather, it is
these elements *as perceived by the individual* that define it. Hence, a physical
object of which the individual is unaware is not part of his life space, while one
that is only imagined to be present (like the proverbial pink elephant) constitutes a bona fide life-space component. Likewise, a tiny, harmless mouse may
constitute an overwhelmingly horrible threat to one housewife's life space, while
a ferocious tiger may represent an object of challenge to an experienced animal
trainer. A final example from everyday life will provide a more routine illustration of the psychological basis of life space: If I am planning to spend the day
working in my study, I will most likely be only peripherally concerned about
the sudden drop in temperature outside and the blizzard conditions that are
rapidly developing. The snow storm is little noticed and is not a significant part
of my life space. But if I know that in three hours I must meet a plane at the
airport twenty miles away, the storm becomes a central element in my life space,
affecting my behavior in a number of important ways. Although the objective
existence of the snow storm is exactly the same in both instances, the way in
which it was perceived made the difference in determining my life space.

In short, life space refers to the *psychological*, rather than the physical/
geographical, environment of the individual. It includes the goals that he seeks
to attain, undesirable elements that he tries to avoid, barriers that limit his
movement, and available avenues leading to his goals. And it is the interaction
of these forces—*as perceived*—that determines individual behavior.

As an aid to understanding his system, Lewin has developed a two-dimensional schema for diagraming the life space (see Figure 12-7). The chief elements of these diagrams are what Lewin considers the basic components of any
life space: (1) goals sought, (2) threats to be avoided, and (3) barriers that
restrict movement. Any goal (object, state, psychological condition, geographical
location, etc.) that an individual desires to move toward is said to have a *positive
valence* and is indicated on the diagram with a "plus" sign. Any threat that an
individual wants to avoid is said to have a *negative valence* and is marked with

FIGURE 12-7
Simple Lewinian diagram of a life space.

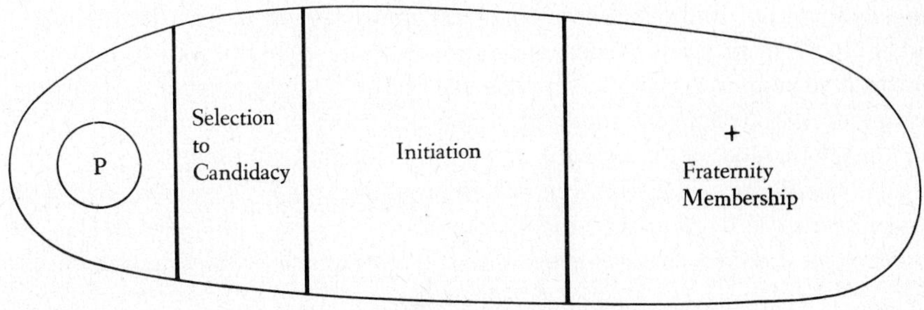

a minus sign. Barriers to movement are indicated by heavy lines separating areas of the life space. In Figure 12-7, for example, the person (P) is represented as being motivated by a single force (positive valence)—the desire to become a member of the fraternity. Before he can reach this goal, however, he must first pass through the areas of selection and initiation. These areas represent barriers between him and fraternity membership. Whether or not the person acts to become a fraternity member will depend on the dynamic interaction of the forces (person, goal, and barriers) diagramed in Figure 12-7. This diagram would, of course, be made more sophisticated by including more goals and forces in the person's life space. The essential relationships would remain the same, however, and his behavior would ultimately depend on the pattern of forces in operation.

In Lewin's life-space diagrams neither the shape nor size of the component areas, nor the physical distance between person and goal has any particular meaning. This is why they are called *topological* diagrams and why his system is called a topological theory. Lewin held that physical distance and shape were inappropriate indicators of psychological "space," and he was therefore led to adopt a branch of geometry called topology as a vehicle for representing life space. In topological geometry physical distance, direction, size, and shape are unimportant; only the boundaries between regions have significance. Thus, if the life space diagramed in Figure 12-7 were to be drawn on a sheet of rubber, it could be stretched and distorted in an infinite number of ways, increasing distance here, changing shapes there, etc. But the number of areas to be crossed, and the sequence in which they must be crossed, would remain the same. In a topological (and psychological) sense, then, all that really matters is what areas separate one point from another. For this reason, it is possible to diagram the life space shown in Figure 12-7 in a number of different ways, all of which mean exactly the same thing (see Figure 12-8).

Topological diagrams can be used to depict a wide variety of elements, both physical and psychological, in the individual's life space. For example, a motor-bike, an "A" in algebra, political power, or peer admiration may all be represented as positive valences. In the same way, a speeding ticket, a spanking, guilt feelings, or fear of humiliation constitute negative valences. Barriers, too, may be physical or psychological: a locked door, a college degree, a warning from the teacher, or a fear of height. Formerly neutral barriers, such as a locked door, may acquire a negative valence, and become an object of attack (breaking down the door). Too, formerly neutral barriers may take on a positive valence, as when a college degree (needed to acquire teaching credentials) becomes a goal in itself. These examples demonstrate the variety of meanings that individuals attach to the physical environment. They also point up the *changing* meanings that make for a constant restructuring of the individual's life space.

The significance of Lewin's insistence on a *psychological* analysis of the life space is caught by Stephens (1956, pp. 253, 254) when he says of it: "The psychological world changes even in the face of a relatively constant physical

FIGURE 12-8
Three equivalent topological diagrams.

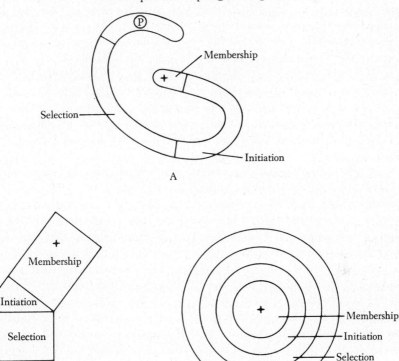

world, just as, conversely, the psychological world may remain constant in spite of extensive changes in the physical world."

LEARNING AS A CHANGE IN COGNITIVE STRUCTURE. As a field psychologist, Lewin places great importance on learning as a change in cognitive structure, identifying at least three aspects of such change. The first type of change he calls the *differentiation of unstructured areas* (Lewin 1942, pp. 224–227). When a freshman first arrives on a college campus and is settled in his dormitory room, his college life space is likely to consist of person-in-dormitory-room surrounded by a vast undifferentiated campus area. As he begins to take his meals at the refectory, view orientation presentations, and attend classes, however, distances, directions, and other relational data among points on campus slowly become differentiated so that the previously vague unstructured mass surrounding person-in-dormitory-room becomes organized and specific. The rate and manner of differentiation is, of course, significantly affected by the individual's particular valences. In the same way, the freshman's life space in terms of social relation changes from a vague mass to a specific structure: group memberships, roles, status positions, etc., become clearer to the freshman, enabling him to know what behavior to assume with which people in order to move toward goals and avoid negative valences.

Lewin describes a second aspect of cognitive restructuring as *restructurization, psychological directions, and meaning* (Lewin 1942, pp. 227–229). This category of learning is the equivalent of classical gestalt "insight" and does not involve any increase in differentiation. The learning of Köhler's apes is as good an example as any of this type of cognitive restructuring. Another interesting example is provided by Lewin and involves a reference to Mark Twain's *Life on the Mississippi*. Here, the beautiful waves in the middle of the river which are admired by riverboat passengers have been restructured in the life space of the pilot to mean "dangerous rocks." Motivation, of course, plays as important a role in insight as it does in differentiation.

Lewin's final aspect of cognitive restructuring is treated under the heading *time perspective, psychological reality and irreality* (Lewin 1942, pp. 229–231). Here, Lewin points out that the behavior of the individual does not depend entirely on the present situation, but is significantly influenced by his views of his own past[10] and future, and his hopes and wishes with regard to this time perspective. A discrepancy between an individual's wish level and the reality level of his psychological past may produce feelings such as guilt. For example, wanting to be a good student and perceiving the immediate past as a time spent in frivolous activities can produce guilt feelings in the present life space that can significantly affect future behavior. A similar discrepancy with regard to one's wishes regarding his psychological future is a decisive factor in determining the level of "hope" (Lewin 1942, p. 230). Commenting on the significance of time perspective and reality, he notes:

> *Teachers and educators have been aware of the importance of time perspective as one of the fundamental aspects of development. "Broadening the pupil's view" has always been considered one of the main purposes of education. Such an increase in time perspective can be viewed as one type of change in cognitive structure (Lewin 1942, p. 230).*

LEARNING AS CHANGE IN VALENCES AND VALUES. Learning as change in valences and values refers to learning in what is commonly called the affective domain. Although it is related to cognitive structures, it is essentially concerned with likes and dislikes.

Lewin points out that "learning" to like or dislike anything ordinarily involves a long-range change in needs. Repetition of a positively valenced activity in the short term tends to result in satiation. For example, if an individual is strongly attracted (has a positive valence) toward singing, playing checkers, or bird watching, a high level of participation in the activity will produce a change in

---

10. Some learning theorists erroneously attribute to Lewin a lack of concern with past experience.

valence: "the psychological 'consumption' of the activity satiates the underlying need" (Lewin 1942, p. 234). Indeed, oversatiation may even result in a permanent dislike for the activity. This is the reason that "the method of writing and reading by learning sentences or words [which introduce variety] is superior to the older method of learning letters [which emphasizes repetition]" (Lewin 1942, p. 234).

Because the valence of an activity depends partly on its meaning, it is related to the cognitive structure of the life space. For example, I may "learn" to detest lillies because of the role they played in a good friend's funeral, or I may genuinely relish the straight bourbon—unpalatable at home—which is served at the dean's reception for distinguished faculty. More often than not, school efforts to change the valences of students are grounded in cognitive restructuring of their life space. For example, black students may be told about the scientific breakthroughs of such-and-such black scientists in hopes of producing a positive valence toward high school science; or kindergarten children may be told that "good boys do not throw things" in order to develop a negative valence toward flinging objects about the classroom. In the same way, Lewin (1942, p. 235) points out, much advertising and propaganda is not aimed at changing values and attitudes as such, but at changing the cognitive structure in such a way that the advertised product or activity appears to be part of, or a means to, a positively valenced area in the individual's life space. This, of course, is what makes it possible to create a demand for a particular toothpaste, deodorant, or hairspray by associating it with sex.

MOTIVATION. As noted earlier in this section, Lewin is much more sensitive to the role of motivation in learning (and to the factors affecting motivation) than any of the learning theorists we have considered. His theory of the life space, which centers on positive and negative valences, bears this out. Moreover, his descriptions of learning both as cognitive change and as change in valences reflects this emphasis. With respect to the former, we have seen that in any cognitive change (i.e., intellectual learning, change in knowledge, etc.), individual needs, valences, values, hopes, etc., play an important role. With respect to the latter—learning as a change in valence (i.e., motivation)—no further comment is needed.

Because of his interest in motivation and perception, many psychologists of learning claim that Lewin's work leaves much to be desired in terms of its direct application to the problems of learning.[11] However, it may be that Lewin's greatest strength is that he has placed the special problems of learning in their proper perspective: rooted in the field of forces that constitute the total psychological personality.

CURRICULAR APPLICATIONS. Earlier remarks concerning the curricular applications of field and gestalt psychologies will, of course, be generally true for

11. See Hill (1971, pp. 110–115) for an extended statement of this point of view.

Lewin's topological theory. Lewin would probably go somewhat further, however, in emphasizing the need to understand the learner's life space, particularly with regard to the relationships prevailing among self, motives, environment, and behavior.

Since knowledge of the learner is so important in implementing a curriculum based on a topological theory, small classes and extended class periods will probably be specified in the curriculum plan. Also, where possible, time for extensive interpersonal exchange on a one-to-one basis between teacher and learner will be recommended.

Given the perceptual-psychological basis of the life space, it is particularly important that curriculum planners and teachers keep clear the distinction between curriculum goals and the learner's psychological goals. When significant discrepancies are observed, activities that stimulate valence changes in appropriate directions are indicated. (Such occasions may also signal the need to reappraise curriculum goals.) For learning to occur, it is essential that students pursue goals that are their own, rather than artificial goals set by the curriculum. Given a reasonable consonance of individual and curricular goals, however, curriculum content and activities will be designed to remove barriers between the learner and positively valenced areas in his life space. Reasonable as this procedure sounds, it is commonly violated in a large number of public schools, where all kinds of barriers to learning are erected in the name of "quiet," "order," "decorum," "standards," and other presumed characteristics of an "environment conducive to learning."[12]

In view of Lewin's emphasis on perception and meaning in terms of the individual life space, curriculum planners will need to give careful attention to the probable meaning of content and activities as they relate to the learner's perspective. One thinks here of the progressive's call for a "psychological organization" of content (as opposed to a logical one), and of Bruner's (1960, p. 33) dictum that the task of teaching a child is one of representing the subject "in terms of the child's way of viewing things." Thus, curriculum reorganization based on topological theory will need to take special account of the psychology of child and adolescent development.

To summarize, a curriculum grounded in topological theory will reflect the characteristics of any field-oriented curriculum, but will still be distinctive in many respects. In content, it will emphasize wholes and relationships, both within and among wholes. In activities, it will avoid repetition and drill and center on problem solving, discovery, and other devices that stimulate insight, cognitive restructuring, valence change, and so on. It will clarify the distinction between curriculum goals and learner goals and make provisions for their accommodation. In recognizing the validity of the learner's psychological world, it

12. One of the most blatant barriers observed by this writer was the requirement in one high school that special permission be granted to obtain a "library pass." The pass was punched each time the student visited the library, and ten punches per semester was the maximum allowed.

will take the life space into account in curriculum planning, particularly insofar as motivation is concerned. And finally, the topological curriculum will provide for the removal of barriers (as perceived by learners) that interfere with movement toward goal achievement.

Learning Theories and Curriculum Practice

Chapter 11 has presented an introduction to the psychology of learning, and this chapter has treated in some detail a limited number of representative theorists.[13] We have seen that learning is a highly complex aspect of human mental functioning about which psychologists are by no means in agreement. It seems natural, then, to ask, "Which is the best theory to follow in curriculum work?" Such a question, of course, misses the point. In the first place, as we have previously noted, whether an individual favors theories in the associationist tradition or in the field tradition will depend on his basic philosophical assumptions about the nature of reality and man. This is essentially a value question, and although we have argued in favor of the field tradition in this book, we admit that associationism has certain merits that cannot be denied. This brings us to our second point. Some principles of learning appear to apply in all situations, while others are germane only in particular (or specially defined) circumstances. This implies that curriculum planners may have to be eclectic in their stance toward learning theories. In addition, Hilgard and Bower (1966, pp. 562–564) have developed a list of learning principles that seem to hold rather widely and that are generally acceptable to most psychologists of learning, whether associationist or field oriented. These generalizations provide the curriculum worker with a body of information about learning that he can be reasonably sure is sound and which he can use as a basis for curriculum planning. With the warning that broad agreement on these principles does not dispel the real differences that exist among learning theories, we present the following summary of Hilgard and Bower's commonly accepted principles of learning.

1. *The learner should be active, rather than a passive listener or viewer.*
2. *Frequency of repetition is important in acquiring a skill such as typing, playing the piano, or speaking a foreign language.*

13. Some important contributors to learning theory with whom serious students of curriculum should be acquainted have necessarily been omitted from this introductory chapter. Among these we should mention Clark L. Hull, Neal Miller, Edward C. Tolman, O. Hobart Mowrer, and William K. Estes. Although often not regarded as learning theorists per se, the following psychologists have made contributions that directly apply to learning and deserve the close attention of curriculum planners: Jean Piaget, Sigmund Freud, Abraham Maslow, and Carl Rogers. In addition, some recent developments in the learning-theory field that curriculum planners should be aware of are (1) mathematical models of learning, (2) cybernetics, or feedback theory, and (3) the neurophysiology of learning. Both Hill (1971) and Hilgard and Bower (1966) provide good introductory statements on these topics.

3. *Repetition should take place under conditions in which correct responses are rewarded (reinforcement).*

4. *Motivational conditions are important for learning.*

5. *Conflicts and frustrations in learning situations must be recognized and provision must be made for their resolution or accommodation.*

6. *Learning problems should be presented in a way that their structure (e.g., figure-ground relations, organic interrelatedness etc.) is clear to the learner.*

7. *The organization of content is an important factor in learning and is an essential concern of the curriculum planner.*

8. *Learning with understanding is more permanent and more transferable than rote learning.*

9. *Goal setting by the learner is important as motivation for learning.*

10. *The learner's abilities are important, and provisions should be made for differential abilities.*

11. *The learner should be understood in terms of the influences that have shaped his development.*

12. *The anxiety level of the individual learner is a factor affecting learning. With some kinds of tasks high-anxiety learners perform better if not reminded of how well or poorly they are doing, while low-anxiety learners do better when interrupted with comments on their progress.*

13. *The organization of motives within the individual is a factor that influences learning.*

14. *The group atmosphere of learning (competition versus cooperation, authoritarianism versus democracy, etc.) will affect satisfaction in learning as well as the products of learning.*

References

Becker, Ernest. 1967. *Beyond Alienation.* New York: George Braziller.

Bruner, Jerome. 1960. *The Process of Education.* Cambridge, Mass.: Harvard University Press.

Ferster, Charles S., and B. F. Skinner. 1957. *Schedules of Reinforcement.* New York: Appleton-Century-Crofts.

Guthrie, Edwin R. 1935. *The Psychology of Learning.* New York: Harper & Row.

———. 1942. "Conditioning: A Theory of Learning in Terms of Stimulus, Response and Association." In *The Psychology of Learning.* Forty-first Yearbook of the National Society for the Study of Education. Chicago: University of Chicago Press, chap. I.

Hilgard, Ernest R., and Gordon H. Bower. 1966. *Theories of Learning.* 3d ed. New York: Appleton-Century-Crofts.

Hill, Winfred F. 1971. *Learning: A Survey of Psychological Interpretations.* Rev. ed. New York: Thomas Y. Crowell Company.

Kingsley, Howard L., and Ralph Gary. 1957. *The Nature and Conditions of Learning.* 2d ed. Englewood Cliffs, N.J.: Prentice-Hall.

Lewin, Kurt. 1942. "Field Theory of Learning." In *The Psychology of Learning.*

Forty-first Yearbook of the National Society for the Study of Education. Chicago: University of Chicago Press, chap. VI.

Skinner, B. F. 1938. *The Behavior of Organisms: An Experimental Analysis.* New York: Appleton-Century-Crofts.

———. 1948. *Walden II.* New York: The Macmillan Company.

———. 1953. *Science and Human Behavior.* New York: Macmillan Company.

———. 1971. *Beyond Freedom and Dignity.* New York: Alfred A. Knopf.

Stephens, J. M. 1956. *Educational Psychology.* Rev. ed. New York: Holt, Rinehart and Winston.

Tullock, Gordon. 1974. "Does Punishment Deter Crime?" *The Public Interest* (Summer).

Wertheimer, Max. 1945. *Productive Thinking.* Harper & Row.

III

ANATOMY OF THE CURRICULUM

Part III continues our discussion of the curriculum-construction process begun in Part II. It shifts its focus, however, from curriculum foundations to the constituent parts of the curriculum itself, both as a written document and as a functioning element in classroom instruction. In accordance with the model proposed in Chapter 4, we conceptualize the curriculum as consisting of four basic components: (1) aims, goals, and objectives; (2) content; (3) learning activities; and (4) evaluation. Each of the four chapters of Part III explores curriculum-construction problems as they relate to one of these elements.

CHAPTER 13
AIMS, GOALS, AND OBJECTIVES

"Death is the only terminal behavior."   —W. KENNETH RICHMOND

We have seen in previous chapters that societies tend to produce curricula that are consonant with their philosophies, cultures, notions about the nature of man, and theories about how people learn. Aims, goals, and objectives—collectively—as a component of curriculum, are particularly sensitive to these fundamental forces, since desired curricular outcomes not only influence the very shape of the curriculum, but provide direction and focus for the entire educational program. The importance of curricular purposes is reflected in the fact that no other aspect of education has received more serious consideration or provoked as much heated controversy as has the question of aims. In this chapter we will examine in some detail, not only the nature, function, and organization of curricular aims, goals, and objectives, but some of the assumptions built into the very concept evoked by the word "goal." These discussions will provide us with an opportunity to examine some assumptions about goal setting and goal seeking that tend to limit the curriculum worker's capacity to keep the curriculum enterprise open ended.

The Problem of Ends and Means

Whether we use the word "ends," "purposes," "aims," "goals," or "objectives," we understand that reference is being made to some terminal point toward which we are moving, working, or traveling. Having created a terminal point in our minds, we ordinarily set about identifying the process or processes of getting there, employing the word "means" to name the way(s) by which we reach this terminal point. For example, in curriculum work it is not uncommon for planners to identify an end—something like the objective: Students will be able to write a coherent, well-organized paragraph—and then to prescribe the content and learning activities that will most effectively move students toward acquiring this skill. But is this the way things really are? Can we really divide our activities and experience into ends and means?

Suppose that my "aim" is to buy a loaf of bread at the market. What "means" do I employ to reach this "end"? I open the closet door and put on my coat. I could not have put on my coat (an end) without opening the closet door (the means). Further, turning the knob on the closet door can be termed the "means" by which the "end" of opening the door was achieved. If you perceive all of this as "splitting hairs," we can proceed forthwith to the "real aim" of all of this prior activity (i.e., buying the loaf of bread). The argument can be made, however, that this aim, in turn, becomes a "means" to some further "end"—the act of eating the bread. But eating bread is not an end in itself (i.e., a terminal proposition). The end of eating the bread becomes a means to some further activity—satisfying hunger, which in its turn becomes a "means" for the "end" of sustaining health, which becomes the "means" for attaining a virtual infinity "of ends."

This rather superficial but intriguing example suggests that "ends" are not at all terminal points, but rather "terminals of deliberation, and so turning points *in* activity" (Dewey 1964, p. 70). Dewey points out that our present conceptions of ends and means are the result of philosophical assumptions originating with Aristotle and handed down in our Western European cultural heritage; and that these assumptions have led us to regard ends as things outside of human action, "as fixed limits and conclusions" toward which human action is directed. Such "ideals" as happiness, self-realization, honesty, and godliness are examples of ultimate ends that have been (and still are) regarded as intrinsically valuable and as existing outside of the realm of human action.

If, as Dewey has done, we reject the notion of aims as things lying outside of human activity, how are we to regard the familiar dichotomy of ends and means that we have inherited from our cultural tradition?

> *Ends are foreseen consequences which arise in the course of activity and which are employed to give activity added meaning and to direct its further course. They are in no sense ends of action. In being ends of deliberation they are redirecting pivots in action (Dewey 1964, p. 72).*

Thus, we see that Dewey regards the ends-means dichotomy as a spurious description of reality. For him, reality is simply a ceaseless flow of events in cause-effect relationships, and ends and means are just two ways of regarding the same actuality. The value of Dewey's perspective lies in his analysis of this reality and his explanation of the human response to it. In order to give meaning and direction to human activities, men *hypothesize* the consequences of certain courses of action. These hypothesized consequences are called ends (Dewey prefers "ends-in-view"), and they constitute "redirecting pivots" in a constant flow of action.

If ends and means are simply two ways of regarding the same event in a stream of events connected in a cause-effect relationship, it follows that "ends" and "means" are inextricably related. Logically speaking, then, it is not possible to give consideration to one without the other.

One example of the fallacy of separating ends and means is provided by the proposition that "the end justifies the means," that is, that the "end-in-itself" has *intrinsic* value such that *any* means employed to attain it are justified. By separating an end from the flow of human activity, the proposition implicitly relieves itself, not only of surveying the *other possible consequences* produced by action leading to the desired end, but of surveying the *further consequences produced* by the desired end. In other words, a *fragment* of possible consequences has been arbitrarily selected for actualization without consideration of the other ends which will be brought to actualization along with it. Such a proposition is not immoral; it is stupid.

What are some of the problems generated by our traditional way of perceiving ends as terminal points rather than as "directive stimuli to present choice" (Dewey 1964, p. 73)? In the first place, the traditional conception of ends discourages the examination of consequences and therefore the intelligent generation of alternate purposes. For example, curriculum workers in English have become relatively fixed upon achieving the "obviously proper goal" of understanding English grammar. The result has been an enormous expenditure of energy on developing the "means" to reach it, with very little attention paid to the possible disastrous consequences of the enterprise. Indeed, little attention has even been given to the consequences of *reaching* the goal. As Patricia Mills (1971, p. 733) has put it, "Could they become so expert at building more and more intricate cuckoo clocks that they fail to realize that cuckoo clocks have become anachronisms?" Clearly, the traditional conception of ends can result in narrowness and rigidity.

A second difficulty with the traditional conception of ends is that it "renders men careless in their inspection of existing conditions (Dewey 1964, p. 77). Macdonald (1967, p. 168) was aware of this problem when he wrote that preoccupation with the efficient meeting of fixed objectives can cause us to lose touch with reality. Our history is replete with horrifying examples of this condition, the most recent one being the Viet Nam holocaust—the "means" for achieving the "aim" of liberating the South Vietnamese. This disposition of the traditional conception of ends and means to inhibit inquiry into present conditions has been shown to reside in the very nature of the language we have adopted. Huebner (1966, p. 12 ff.), for example, has shown that the word "objectives," which has become so much a part of the conventional wisdom of curriculum discourse, can actually restrict the kinds of questions curriculum workers ask.

Finally, fixing upon goals as terminal points outside the flow of human activity can, in extreme cases, result in arrogance and fanaticism. The narrow singlemindedness and intolerance of religious zealots, superpatriots, and otherwise highly logical scientistic scientists are good examples of the restricted perception of people who view religious, patriotic, or scientific ends as intrinsically the most desirable terminal goals of human action.

What are the benefits to curriculum workers who maintain a tentative "ends-in-view" stance toward curriculum aims and goals? By regarding aims as hypothetical consequences—"directive stimuli to present choice" (Dewey 1964, p. 73)—curriculum workers will be more apt to consider ends-in-view in terms of their further consequences. For example, the aim of teaching children to read will be assessed in terms of its further consequences (i.e., what ensues from reading capability?). In addition, because the curriculum worker regards ends and means only as two different ways of perceiving the same actuality, he will be more prone to assess (1) present conditions and (2) the possible *other* consequences of means proposed to achieve the intended outcome. With respect to the specific aim of teaching children to read that was just proposed, the curriculum worker would have a tendency to proceed somewhat as follows:

1. *What kind of reading skills seem likely to be needed in the child's school and postschool life? (What is the reading to be used for? What should it be used for?)*
2. *An assessment of the present situation indicates that a great deal of time is spent viewing TV. Should we expend less time than planned on reaching the reading goal and include in the curriculum a "critical viewing" goal? Are there other goals, such as "social responsibility" that, on examination of the present situation, seem to be more important than either of the former?*
3. *What are all of the consequences of following a particular strategy of reading instruction? That is, what impact will the proposed reading curriculum have on the child's emotional development, on his interests in reading, and on his disposition to read?*
4. *Reading does not occur in a vacuum. Some content is read. What are the likely consequences of utilizing certain reading materials in the curriculum over others?*

This questioning, hypothesizing, and examining of conditions could be greatly extended. Enough has been presented here, however, to suggest the magnitude of the problem and the vast number of variables that require consideration.

The objection often is brought against this process of determining purpose that, with ends endlessly becoming means in the stream of activity, "finalizing" goals is a hopelessly infinite quest. Of course, ends-in-view goals are not final or ultimate in the sense that they are independently validated and stand outside the conditions of the specific situation; but they do carry the quality of "finality" in the sense that they represent the *last* warranted conclusions for *this* situation; in this pivotal sense they do provide direction for activity.

True, the process is difficult and requires extensive intellectual energy to pursue. But the result of it is the generation of goals based on an analysis of all the variables operating in a specific situation. The logical force carried by such goals stands in sharp contrast to the arbitrariness of criteria that confer value on ends independently of their contexts.

Sources of Aims, Goals, and Objectives

As we view the plethora of curriculum purposes that have been advocated by one proponent or another, we find that it is possible to place the sources from which they are derived into three principal groups: empirical, philosophical, and subject matter sources.

By organizing curriculum purposes according to their sources, we shall be able to clarify what has turned out to be a bewildering array of diverse aims, goals, and objectives. In addition, inquiring into the sources will help us to gain some insight into the *processes* by which aims, goals, and objectives are formulated. Thus, we shall be provided with one more basis for assessing their usefulness in curriculum construction.

EMPIRICAL SOURCES

STUDIES OF THE SOCIETY. The requirements of contemporary life have always provided, at least informally, a standard source from which curriculum purposes have been derived. But the procedure of empirically studying society as a direction-giving source of curriculum purposes has only become current within the last hundred years.

The movement may be said to have begun in 1859, when Herbert Spencer (the nineteenth-century English social philosopher) published his now famous essay, "What Knowledge Is of Most Worth?" Spencer's informal observations of contemporary society led him to conclude that in order to lead successful lives, students needed preparation in a fivefold hierarchy of activities: (1) direct self-preservation, (2) indirect self-preservation (e.g., securing food, shelter, etc.), (3) parenthood, (4) citizenship, and (5) leisure activities. (Incidentally, he proposed that *science* is the most valuable study in achieving all of these purposes.)

Since the publication of Spencer's essay, literally thousands of empirical studies of all aspects of social life have been conducted and utilized in the framing of curriculum aims, goals, and objectives. Some of these have been broadly based comprehensive surveys of many facets of contemporary life. Havighurst's (1962) and the Lynds' (1929) studies are examples of general sociological surveys that have suggested curriculum purposes. More specific in nature have been surveys in such areas as employment opportunities; the demands of citizenship, parenthood, and family life; and the ways in which people spend their leisure time. Such studies have been responsible for including in the curriculum many new "subjects" such as woodworking, electronics, home economics, courtship and marriage, and driver training. More recently, the recognition of certain social problems such as pollution, racism, and war has generated curricular purposes involving ecology, black studies, and peace.

Whatever form the societal studies take, however—general survey or specific study, formal research or informal observation—the logic is similar: the curriculum should aim at educating in those areas required for successful functioning in life outside the school. This position, its proponents assert, has the very great advantage of keeping curricular aims, goals, and objectives "relevant." On the other hand, it should be pointed out that the practice of deriving purposes from the condition of contemporary society raises several problematic questions. For example, since, in the latter half of the twentieth century, the contemporary scene is changing so rapidly, will the situations for which we are educating be superseded by others by the time students move out into the society? Second, does educating for contemporary activities foster a kind of "presentism" which slights aims that transcend temporal considerations and that foster enduring (though not necessarily fashionable) skills, knowledge, and attitudes? Finally, and perhaps most seriously, does educating the young to fit into existing conditions tend to perpetuate the status quo?

STUDIES OF LEARNERS. Empirical studies of children and adolescents for the purpose of determining their "needs" has long provided educators with a source of curriculum purposes. However, the nature of the purposes derived from such a source critically hinges on the interpretation one gives to the word "need." Tyler (1950, pp. 5–6) points out that needs can be defined in two distinct ways. The predominant meaning defines "need" as a gap that exists between some predetermined norm and the actual status of the individual. Thus, children are observed in order to determine their "needs" in terms of a criterion that might be established, for example, philosophically or culturally. Purposes derived from this definition of need, although depending in part on an empirical examination of the learner, do not really grow out of the learners' needs in the strict sense. In fact, it is the norm or criterion, however it is arrived at, that provides directing force to the purpose. Thus, the objective of teaching children "good eating habits," based on a study to assess the degree of their need to know these, is in fact grounded in normative ideas about what constitute good eating habits. Indeed, most of our so-called studies of learners' needs are simply aimed at determining the *status* of students in terms of generally accepted or desirable norms.

Another way of interpreting needs places the criterion squarely within the individual. Some psychologists point out that the human being is a dynamic organism which can maintain itself in a state of either health or sickness. Health involves the satisfying of the basic types of needs: (1) physiological needs, such as food, water, and sexual gratification; (2) social needs, such as affection, belongingness, and esteem; and (3) self-integrative needs, such as the need for meaning or for self-realization in one's life. This position on needs, it will be recalled, was developed more fully in Chapter 10 in the discussion of Maslow's hierarchy of needs.

Utilizing the inherent needs of the individual provides a very attractive basis on which to develop curriculum aims, since (1) the individual is assumed to be naturally and inherently good, and (2) the individual becomes the center of the educational activity. Deriving curriculum purposes from this source, however, presents at least two serious problems. First, individuals do not exist outside the context of society. Even though hunger, for example, is a universal need among human beings, the ways in which this want of food can be filled are virtually infinite. Should schools aim at producing gourmets who "live to eat" or Spartans who "eat to live"? *What* we eat and *how* we eat it are *learned* behaviors and tied to the values of society. On the psychological level, we find that satisfying a need—for example, for "belongingness"—is probably even more relative a process than satisfying the hunger need.

What *kind* of groups individuals need to belong to, and the procedures used to induct them, can vary among and within cultures even more than the ways of satisfying hunger. How would we evaluate the curriculum outcome, for example, that filled youths' need for belonging by fostering their induction into the Boy Scouts, or into the "jet set," or into the Ku Klux Klan? Clearly, even if it is established that "belongingess" is a universal natural human need, the value questions involving the *kind* of groups that acceptably fill the need are not answered.

A second problem associated with aims derived from the needs of individuals involves the separation of the "natural" from the "learned." It seems fairly certain that the needs for food, water, and sexual gratification are inherent in the organism. Beyond certain basic physiological needs, however, it is extremely difficult, if not virtually impossible, to distinguish the genetic from the cultural. How can we say for certain that men are born with an innate need for love? One might legitimately ask to what degree our Western cultural heritage has influenced our perception on this point. Does man also have an innate need to hate? One reading of history would provide an affirmative answer to this question. Should we then build the hate need into our statement of curriculum aims? If we are to be faithful to empirical data, it would seem the logical thing to do if individual needs are to provide directing force for curriculum purposes.

The problems we have raised with respect to utilizing society and the individual as sources of educational purposes seem almost insurmountable. And yet, common sense tells us that we dare not ignore these empirical sources of data if curriculum aims are to be at all relevant to human life. An examination of the philosophical source of curriculum purposes may shed some light on this apparent dilemma.

PHILOSOPHICAL SOURCES

Curriculum aims, goals, and objectives imply directions that we *ought* to take in educating the young. An empirical study of society (or the individual), provided it is carefully conducted, can yield a reasonably accurate picture of the *state* of society (or the individual), but it cannot tell us, as we have suggested in the previous section, the kind of society (or individual) that we ought to value. For example, even if an empirical study indicates that competitiveness is highly prized and extremely important for success in our society, the question persists: Should the curriculum seek to foster a competitive attitude in youth, or should it aim at suppressing competitive tendencies? This question has to do with our notions of the *value* of competition, irrespective of its predominance in the society. In short, empirical sources have told us what *is*, but a philosophical inquiry is necessary to help us decide what *ought* to be.[1]

Although, clearly, the justification of *all* curriculum purposes is ultimately a philosophical matter, the empirical data cannot be ignored. If competition is present in a society, a judgment as to its desirability will be wiser if it is based on an inquiry into the meaning of competition and the operation and consequences of competitiveness in the society. This procedure, of course, involves empirical examination; but it also involves philosophical reflection (analysis and judgment) on the situation observed.

If philosophy concerns itself with the question: "What is the good life?" the source matter of part of its inquiry must consist of human experience. So it is with the aims, goals, and objectives of the curriculum: decisions regarding the desired life outcomes affected by the school are most effectively determined by bringing philosophical reflection to bear on existing conditions.

SUBJECT MATTER SOURCES

Probably the most commonly used source of aims, goals, and objectives in public school curricula is subject matter (or more accurately, subject matter specialists). Despite its currency as a source of objectives, however, subject matter is open to rather serious criticism on the grounds that the objectives it generates tend to be exceedingly specialized, narrow, and technical. The reason for this is that when subject matter constitutes the source of curriculum goals, it is difficult, if not impossible, to avoid the assumption that the long-range aim is professional expertise in the subject. Thus, when mathematicians, for example, set out to develop objectives from the subject matter of mathematics, their central consideration is usually the elementary, intermediate, and advanced skills and knowledge (objectives) that characterize the professional mathematician. Clearly, within the context of vocational or professional *training*, subject matter is a quite legitimate source of curriculum goals.

But as Tyler (1950, p. 26) points out, the *educational* question is rather different and runs somewhat like this: What can a particular subject contribute to the education of young people who are *not* going to be specialists in the field? That is, what can the subject contribute to the general education of the lay citizen?

The subject matter specialist who can provide unbiased answers to the above questions can make an important contribution to curriculum goal formulation. It is important to recognize, however, that to provide enlightened and unencapsulating answers to these questions, the subject matter specialist will have to be much more than just an expert in his field; he will have to be a liberally educated (authentic) individual who can transcend the constricting effects not only of his culture, but of his area of specialization. Indeed, providing unen-

1. See Chapter 5 for a more detailed account of the nature and method of philosophy.

capsulating answers to the above questions will make far greater demands on the specialist's general knowledge than it will on his professional expertise. It is for these reasons that subject matter in most instances can serve only as a source of subordinate goals and objectives.

Levels of Objectives

In the previous sections we have drawn no distinctions between such terms as aims, goals, objectives, purposes, and ends, treating them very much as approximate synonyms. In this section, however, we will select three for more precise definition: aims, goals, and objectives.

Unfortunately, no universal agreement as to the precise meaning of these words exists among curriculum writers; therefore, although the meanings we assign to them will not be uncommon, they will, of necessity, be somewhat arbitrary. In any case, using these three words in this restricted way will help to clarify our discourse on curriculum.

PURPOSES AND THE ANALOGY OF THE TARGET

Purposes are somewhat like targets; the closer they are, the easier they are to hit. For example, relatively immediate purposes, such as teaching a student to add 2+2, are not very difficult to achieve. The target is fairly close and easily seen. We propose that the term "objective" be used to refer to such specific and immediate purposes.

But why should a school want to achieve such an objective? "Perhaps," it is answered, "in order to provide the student with insight into quantitative relationships." This statement, in comparison to the objective of adding 2+2, represents a target that is still plainly visible, but somewhat more distant, and consequently a bit more difficult to hit. We propose that the term "goal" be used to refer to such relatively intermediate purposes. Obviously, goals are more general and remote, and involve the achievement of a relatively large number of objectives for their attainment. But *which* objectives? Therein lies a substantial margin for error and a significant curriculum problem.

The problem expands enormously, however, when we ask: "Why should the student have insight into quantitative relationships?" On hearing the answer: "So that he can achieve self-realization," we feel overwhelmed. Our target has become so distant that it is a virtual pinpoint on the horizon. Such distant and long-range targets we propose calling "aims." How can we help students achieve so ultimate an aim as self-realization? *How*, indeed, represents the long-range problem of the entire educational enterprise.

The metaphor of the target provides us with a rough analogy for three levels of curriculum purposes (a term we will henceforth employ when no particular level is intended). It suggests that as stated purposes tend to be broader (rather than narrower), they tend to be more significant; and as they tend to be more significant, they will usual. be more remote (rather than proximate). With these rough distinctions in mind, we turn to a discussion of each of the three levels of curriculum purposes.

CURRICULUM AIMS

In general, curriculum aims are statements that describe expected *life* outcomes based on some value schema either consciously or unconsciously borrowed from philosophy (Broudy 1971, p. 13). Their distinctive quality (in contrast with curriculum goals and objectives) is that they do not relate directly to school or classroom outcomes. That is, as targets, they are so far removed from the school situation that the degree of their achievement is determinable (if at all) only in that part of life well after the completion of school. "Self-realization," "ethical character," and "civic responsibility" are examples of curriculum aims that have been proposed at one time or another. Clearly, a major problem for curriculum workers is the translation of these remote aims into the more immediate and specific school outcomes to be reached if the aims are to be achieved.

CURRICULUM GOALS

For our purposes curriculum goals will refer to *school* outcomes. While goals *may* refer to outcomes specified at the individual school level (for example, "Bishop Elementary School" or "Davis Junior High School"), they will more often reflect goals of a school system. Curriculum goals will vary as to their degree of specificity, but in general will tend to be long range in nature and, as targets, somewhat removed from what ordinarily is considered immediate classroom assessment. Examples of curriculum goals might be: "appreciation of literature," "ability to think (or read) critically," "knowledge of the American heritage," and "interest in civic affairs."

CURRICULUM OBJECTIVES

Curriculum objectives are defined here as the most immediate specific outcomes of classroom instruction. In general, they refer to the everyday business of the operative curriculum, and the degree to which they have been achieved is assessable, at least theoretically, at any given point in time. As targets, curriculum objectives are close and quite visible. Examples of curriculum objectives might be:

The student will be able to solve correctly four out of five quadratic equations.
Given a social problem, the student will take an informed position on each of the issues.
The student will master the principles of chemistry.

Clearly, some of these objectives are far less immediate than others, involve implied subsumed objectives, and require much more time to achieve. Nevertheless, they all refer to the immediate classroom curriculum at its most specific level.

RELATIONSHIP OF AIMS, GOALS, AND OBJECTIVES

At precisely what point on the continuum an objective becomes a goal, or a goal an aim, is impossible to specify. In some cases, fuzziness and/or overlap will make classification dubious. The important consideration, however, is that recognition of the broad hierarchy of curriculum purposes suggested in this section can be of considerable help in organizing a curriculum into a logical and coherent structure.

In most cases the distance between a curriculum objective and a curriculum goal is great; between an objective and an aim, it is enormous. The greatest problem for the curriculum worker once he has committed himself to a program of curriculum aims, is to maintain a justifiable congruence from aims through goals to objectives. He has an obligation, when called upon, to demonstrate the relationship of the required school tasks (objectives and goals) and the desired life tasks (aims). The establishment of such a relationship requires intimate knowledge of both educational philosophy and the logical and psychological bases of learning and teaching. Such extensive topics as these, of course, are beyond the scope of this book. Nevertheless, the task of justifying the school's programs in terms of desired *life* outcomes (aims) is a responsibility curriculum workers cannot avoid.

Classification of Aims, Goals, and Objectives

In the previous section, we structured curriculum purposes into a vertical hierarchy of three broad categories: aims, goals, and objectives. Several writers have, in addition, proposed horizontal organizations within these categories. In this section we shall examine some representative classifications of curriculum puposes.

AIMS

Broudy (1971, pp. 13–23) examined statements of curriculum aims and found that aims are generally classifiable into four related categories. The first of these takes the form of a central *value pattern*. Aims in this category virtually represent a philosophical position and function as the controlling mechanism to determine the character of the aims in the other three categories. For example, if the focal point of one's perception of the "good life" were individual self-realization (rather than, for example, service to God) all of the aims in the other categories would center on the development of that value.

The remaining three types of aims are classified as those proposing a preferred *social organization*; an explication of preferred *social roles*; and a preferred *life style*. Thus, if the central value pattern were self-realization, aims of social organization would most likely specify democratic social outcomes. Further, aims specifying preferred social roles would delineate the particular qualities desirable in workers, family members, citizens, etc., consonant with the individualist/democratic ideology. Finally, aims that identify the desired life style by specifying models of character that ought to be initiated are included. Perhaps the most persistent life style promoted in American curriculum aims has been Horation Alger's "work-hard-and-succeed" character type, but as Broudy points out, other models, such as Jackie (Kennedy) Onassis and the Beatles, are educationally influential, even though their life styles were never proposed in formal statements of curriculum aims.

One statement of aims that has been extremely influential in shaping the curriculum of American schools is the "Cardinal Principles of Secondary Education" (see Chapter 3). Following Herbert Spencer's lead, the Commission on the Reorganization of Secondary Education (1918, pp. 11–16) utilized the organizational principle of important life activities to identify curriculum aims in seven major areas:

1. *Health*
2. *Command of fundamental processes*
3. *Worthy home membership*
4. *Vocational education*
5. *Civic education*
6. *Worthy use of leisure*
7. *Ethical character*

Other influential statements, too numerous to review here, have reflected a variety of organizational principles, but many appear not to have incorporated any organizational logic at all.

GOALS AND OBJECTIVES

A lack of organizational coherence seems especially to plague many statements of curriculum goals and objectives. In most cases, immediacy, generality, and importance (the vertical organization) have not been considered, so that the goal of "developing an understanding of self" for example, appears on a parallel with "developing an understanding of the effects of alcohol and drugs on the body." Confusion also arises, however, because goals of a clearly differential nature have been indiscriminately grouped together. Thus, it is possible to find a goal like "has a favorable attitude toward school" in the same grouping as "has the ability to write complete sentences." Because of this confusion, it is difficult to determine how the statement of goals and/or objectives as a whole relates in a coherent way to the broader aims of the total curriculum.

FACTS, SKILLS, AND ATTITUDES. For many years, a simple three-category classification scheme was the predominant device employed to organize curriculum goals and objectives. The system is losing some currency, but is still widely recognized. Under it, curriculum outcomes are classified in terms of the learning of facts, skills, and attitudes. *Facts*, as generally interpreted, refer to the assimilation of information, whether that information is classifiable as units of data, opinions, or complex concepts. *Skills*—the ability to perform—include such processes as reading, writing, critical thinking, communicating, and a host of other functions. *Attitudes* in this schema involve those outcomes that point to desired dispositions or feelings toward a variety of stimuli, including such tendencies as liking or disliking, interest or disinterest, and wanting or not wanting. It should be noted that facts, skills, and attitudes are really inseparable. The learning of facts involves a variety of skills; the learning of any skill involves knowledge of many facts; and the learning of both facts and skills takes place within the context of a complex of attitudinal dispositions. Thus, as is the case in most analytical procedures, the classification of objectives *helps* us to understand and deal with experience, but does not present us with an accurate representation of reality—that interrelated whole which is something more than (and qualitatively different from) the sum of its parts.

TAXONOMY OF EDUCATIONAL OBJECTIVES. A more sophisticated and complex classification of objectives has recently been developed by Bloom (1956) and by Krathwohl, Bloom, and Masia (1964). This schema, known as the Taxonomy of Educational Objectives, divides objectives into three principal domains: cognitive, affective and psychomotor.

The *cognitive domain* includes those objectives which involve intellectual tasks, such as naming the presidents of the United States, writing expository compositions, and solving problems in algebra. The cognitive domain is divided into a hierarchy of six intellectual functions. From the lowest to the highest level, these six mental abilities are:

1. *Knowledge: the simple recall of specifics, methods, structures, etc.*
2. *Comprehension: understanding of a type which does not include the ability to see its fullest implications*
3. *Application: the ability to use generalizations or rules in specific situations*
4. *Analysis: the ability to divide a communication into a hierarchically arranged organization of its component ideas*
5. *Synthesis: the ability to arrange and combine a number of unstructured elements into an organized whole*
6. *Evaluation: the assessment of material, methods, etc., using selected criteria.*

A detailed explanation of this domain is available in Bloom (1956).

The *affective domain* of the taxonomy includes those objectives which deal with the feeling, attitudinal, or valuing dimension. Affective objectives include such outcomes as voluntarily reading novels, developing an appreciation of impressionistic painting, and preferring neatness to sloppiness.

This domain is divided into a five-part hierarchial classification which places the internalization of feeling on a continuum from simple awareness to a condition in which the feelings significantly operate to control behavior. The five categories of the affective domain, from lowest to highest, are as follows:

1. *Receiving: sensitivity to the existence of certain phenomena*
2. *Responding: active attention to phenomena, reflecting interest but not commitment*
3. *Valuing: perception of worth or value in phenomena*
4. *Organization: arrangement of values into an organized system*
5. *Characterization: the development and internalization of the "organization" level to the extent of representing a philosophy of life*

A detailed explanation of the affective domain is available in Krathwohl, Bloom, and Masia (1964).

The psychomotor domain deals with the curriculum goals and objectives intended to develop manipulative and motor skills, such as correctly operating a band saw, typing ninety words per minute, or shooting at least eight baskets in ten tries.

The psychomotor domain is divided into four ascending levels of manipulative skill as follows:

1. *Observing: attending to the performance of a more experienced person*
2. *Imitating: basic rudiments of the skill acquired*
3. *Practicing: repetition of the sequence of phenomena as conscious effort decreases*
4. *Adapting: perfection of the skill, although further improvement is possible*

Perhaps because few psychomotor objectives are found in the literature, this domain has not received the concentrated development of the other two. Furthermore, some question has been raised about the adequacy of the distinctions made among the categories of this domain. Interested readers may refer to Simpson (1966–67) and Harrow (1972) for a more extensive discussion of classification problems in the psychomotor domain.

OTHER CLASSIFICATIONS. Classifications of goals and objectives that utilize many other organizational principles have been suggested. Among these we may mention in passing content/process, tangible/intangible, and general/specific categories. Many of these dimensions, however, are incorporated in one way or another into the classifications discussed in this section.

As was the case in the relationship of facts, skills, and attitudes, the domains of the taxonomy are not, in reality, discrete entities. For example, learning to write one's name (a psychomotor skill) is intimately connected with knowledge of the letters (the cognitive domain) and attitudinal dispositions toward the task (the affective domain). Indeed, Krathwohl, Bloom, and Masia (1964, p.

62) note that "an objective in one domain has a counterpart in the opposite domain, although often we do not take cognizance of it. . . ."

THE USE OF TAXONOMIES. Taxonomies of objectives have contributed most significantly to the refinement of measurement techniques and thus to the evaluation of curriculum outcomes. In this respect they constitute an extremely useful device in curriculum work. Furthermore, analyses provided by the taxonomies help curriculum workers to maintain a logical consistency from general aims to specific objectives and to effect a balance in the curriculum with respect to intellectual, attitudinal, and motor outcomes. However, "the knowledge problem has been with us for more than 2,500 years. It has not been solved by the 'taxonomies' " (Stoops 1972, p. 200). Indeed, we may well question the usefulness of classifications of objectives in dealing with many of the perennial and overarching problems of curriculum, such as value and insight. To the extent that classifications provide a framework that inhibits "breakthrough" thought on major curriculum issues, they may even be harmful (Stoops 1972, p. 200). The caveat implicit in the use of taxonomies of objectives is that curriculum workers should avoid infatuation with neat and attractively ordered structures and maintain a reflective and inquiring stance toward the totality of the curriculum enterprise.

Behavioral Objectives

The educational community has experienced a rapidly increasing interest in behavioral objectives over the past twenty years. During this period, as might be expected, debate has quickened. At one extreme, behavioral objectives are vehemently condemned as mechanistic and dehumanizing, while at the other they are perceived as a virtual educational renaissance. The situation, of course, is nowhere nearly as clearly defined as the extreme contenders would have it. In this section we shall attempt to clarify the basis and nature of behavioral objectives and explore some of their uses and limitations.

THE NATURE OF BEHAVIORAL OBJECTIVES

Despite their relatively recent arrival on the educational scene, behavioral objectives are fundamentally neither new nor a creation of the educational establishment. The theoretical basis and much of the substance of behavioral objectives have been borrowed from physics and other disciplines of the scientific community from a long-established concept called "operationalism."

OPERATIONALISM. In our daily activities, we very often refer to qualities that do not "really" exist, at least not in the sense that they can be perceived through the senses. For example, we may call John "strong" or Jane "beautiful." No one, in fact, has ever seen (or heard, smelled, touched, or tasted) pure "strength" or "beauty," but we create these (intangible) *constructs* to enable us to organize experience and so to deal with everyday affairs.

If we are asked why we think, for example, that John is "strong," and we say that John has great "force" or "power," our answer is likely to be regarded as unsatisfactory. What we have done is to fall back on a definition of strength as it appears in the dictionary—i.e., in more or less synonymous, and hence circular, terms.

If, however, our friend's question about John's strength leads us to answer: "John can do 200 consecutive push-ups," our friend is apt to feel more satisfied. What we have given him is a (tangible) *operational* definition, i.e., an unambiguous index in terms of observable conditions that can be verified or refuted.

Our friend may not, however, agree with the operational meaning we have given to the construct "strength." He may propose, and argue the validity of, another criterion—e.g., lifting a 150-pound barbell over one's head. We may argue with him, and together decide that *both* operational criteria need to be present to indicate strength. This process constitutes a progressive refinement of the meaning of the "strength" construct in operational terms.

It is important to emphasize here that the construct of strength has been *inferred* from the two observable behaviors which we have chosen to associate with strength. In other words, "strength" is an intangible idea, *created* by people to give meaning to an otherwise unorganized cluster of observable phenomena. Logically speaking, we have made the argument: *If* "200 push-ups" plus "lifts 150-pound barbell," *then* strength. (The weakness of this logic when applied to behavioral objectives will be discussed in the following section.)

In our daily affairs, operationalism permeates thinking, but at an unconscious level. When we attribute strength to John, beauty to Jane, intelligence to Dick, or competence in mathematics to Liz, we are usually making judgments on the basis of sense impressions unconsciously internalized during encounters with these people. In other words, our constructs are based on inexplicit and unanalyzed, but nevertheless empirical, data. As a result, it often turns out that our conclusions, although empirically based, are unwarranted. Operationalism, then, is the process of consciously specifying those unambiguous observable indices that we agree *imply* the existence of the construct we wish to identify.

BEHAVIORIZING OBJECTIVES. The principle of operationalism comprises the theoretical basis for the concept of behavioral objectives. Thus, behavioral objectives are simply objectives stated in terms of the observable behavior expected of students after instruction. As an example of the advantages to be gained by behaviorizing objectives, let us take a familiar curriculum goal such as "appreciation of literature." How many people would agree on its precise meaning? How could one determine whether, or to what degree, such a goal had been achieved? The problem with such a nonoperationally stated goal is that, being an intangible construct like strength and beauty, its meaning can vary according to subjective impressions. In addition, the goal suggests no reasonable means for evaluating its attainment. For example, one teacher may be satisfied that the goal "appreciation of literature" has been achieved if students were able to write an acceptable critical essay on the themes of *Paradise Lost,* while another might view its attainment as more visibly represented by students' rhapsodizing over the beauty of Milton's poetry. It would appear, then, that if curriculum workers are to agree on the *meaning* of the objectives that students are to achieve, they need to agree on the *operational criteria* that represent those objectives.

Behaviorists avoid the use of verbs such as "appreciate," "understand," and "know," because these words stand for vague, unobservable, internal constructs. They prefer to use verbs that signify *observable behaviors,* such as "name," "describe," and "solve," in the formulation of objectives. For example, the behaviorist would complain that an objective like "The learner will understand the American system of government," is neither clear nor specific and is open to so many interpretations that "no one has the slightest idea of the intent of the person who selected the objective" (Mager 1962, p. 15). While he would not deprecate the *value* of such an outcome, he would prefer any of the following as clear and precise statements of what is to be achieved:

1. *The learner will write a 1500-word essay explaining the relationships among the legislative, executive, and judicial branches of American government.*
2. *The learner will answer correctly at least eighty questions of a ninety-question multiple-choice test on the American system of government.*
3. *Given the constitutional questions involved in a previously unencountered Supreme Court case, the learner will write an analysis of the issues and determine the outcome in concordance with the majority decision of the court.*

USES AND LIMITATIONS OF BEHAVIORAL OBJECTIVES. Unquestionably the greatest advantage of framing curricular objectives in behavioral terms is the clarity of communication that ensues (see, e.g., Gagné 1972, pp. 394–396). The discussions in the previous section made this clear; everyone concerned knows *precisely* what a given behavioral objective means and is able to determine the extent to which it has been attained. Such clarity in direction is a necessity in the development of curriculum.

The objection often is made, however, that although they clarify meanings, behavioral objectives are useful in specifying only the lowest levels of learning, and hence the more trivial outcomes of the curriculum (e.g., adding numbers, spelling words, or memorizing facts). When it comes to higher-order tasks (e.g., analytic or synthetic thinking, internalizing of value systems, or appreciation of art and literature), it is argued that behavioral objectives cannot be applied since these complex constructs are manifested in such a vast number of ways that specifying all possible observable behavior(s) would involve a listing of literally thousands of specific objectives and simply be impracticable. More importantly, it is argued that these higher-order goals are intended to be open ended in character, and deal with the actualization of the idiosyncratic and unknown potentials of human beings. Even if a listing of behavioral indices of these broad intangible outcomes could be accomplished and made operative, such a practice would, in principle, make education a closed-end enterprise. In other words, specifying and teaching for behavioral objectives precludes taking into account the possible, but presently unknown, behaviors that have the potential for enlarging and enriching human existence. The human organism, behavioral critics claim, is not a finished product, and to define him in terms of prescribed behaviors is to ignore the most significant question that the curriculum poses: What can man become?

Behavioral objectives also are criticized because they do not take into account what the philosopher Michael Polanyi has called "tacit knowing." Tacit knowing consists of having "a knowledge that we may not be able to tell" (Polanyi 1966, p. 10). One common example of tacit knowing is the ability to identify the face of a friend from a crowd of hundreds, yet not be able to describe clearly the particulars of the face either in words or pictures. Indeed, Polanyi points out that concentrating one's attention on the particulars (e.g., the individual features of a face) so as to bring them into consciousness, makes it difficult, if not impossible, to recognize the gestalt. Thus, Polanyi's findings call into question the validity of organizing all statements of curriculum purposes around the accretion of observable behaviors, since concentrating on these objectives may obliterate the more significant gestalts that depend for their existence on the nonbehavioral, tacit state of particular knowledge.

Another criticism of behavioral objectives is centered in the inherent weakness of the logic of operationalism when the concept is utilized as a means of behaviorizing objectives. In a previous section, it will be recalled that an operational definition of "strength" was cited which involved the logic: *If* "200 push-ups" plus "lifts 150-pound barbell," *then* strength. As a definition of strength for, say, research purposes, such a statement might, because of its restrictedness and precision, be quite useful. It *implies*: if—*and only if*—"200 push-ups" plus "lifts 150-pound barbell," then—*and only then*—"strength." (See Smith 1972, pp. 429–431 for a detailed explication of this argument.) But are curriculum workers willing thus to restrict the meaning of their objectives for learners? May we infer the attainment of the objective "strength" if—*and only if*—we observe the two specified behaviors? To do so is to fall into the delusion that the two behaviors *are* strength, and that the construct is being directly measured.

In order to avoid the obvious absurdity of so narrowly defining intangible, higher-order curriculum goals, some behaviorists favor the development of comprehensive lists of behavioral indices. While some of the objectives in these lists are stated in terms that are more general than others, behavioral purists maintain that maximum specificity is necessary for ultimate clarity. Thus, Mager (1962, p. 49) presents as models such precisely formulated statements as the following:

Given a list of 35 chemical elements, the learner must be able to recall and write the valances of at least 30.

Given a human skeleton, the student must be able to correctly identify by labeling at least 40 of the following bones; there will be no penalty for guessing (list of bones inserted here).

Curriculum construction based on behavioral objectives at this level of specificity would require the cataloging of literally millions of such outcomes. Thus, the if—*and only if*—fallacy of behavioral objectives forces proponents to buy clarity of purpose at the expense of extremely restricted definition on the one hand, or unmanageable proliferation of highly specific objectives on the other.

It may be worthwhile at this point to reemphasize that the concept of operationalism originated with sciences and was developed to meet the need for precision in research. For those educationists whose interests center on the science of learning (i.e., training), it may be an extremely useful instrument. But learning should not be equated with education (Stoops 1972, pp. 175–176), and the aims and goals of education (as opposed to the more immediate objectives of learning) involve statements of value founded in philosophical assessments of the meaning of human existence. The behavioral view is only one way of perceiving a portion of the curriculum; it does not constitute a comprehensive model for the education of youth.

Even conceding the not insignificant advantage of clarity of purpose, it would seem that, in the light of the criticisms that have been leveled against behavioral objectives, they may be more harmful than beneficial. But it is important to point out that most of the criticism of behavioral objectives is based on what turns out to be a dogmatic application of the operational principle to a pre-Deweyan notion of "ends"—i.e., objectives viewed as independently validated terminal points toward which action is directed. This view invests the objective with an ontological existence, the consequences of which are the problems pointed out in the preceding paragraphs. In the following paragraphs we shall try to show that the principle of operationalism, more liberally construed as empirical method, can be a very useful tool in thinking about curriculum aims, goals, and objectives.

It has already been mentioned that the judgments we make in everyday life about the presence or absence of abstract qualities (like strength and beauty, intelligence and appreciation of literature) in fact are based on an informal process of drawing inferences from the observation of empirical data. Although imprecise and often open to a degree of error, these judgments, made on the basis of observable evidence, usually turn out to be more reliable than those made on other bases, such as visions and tea leaves. Thus, we appear to be on fairly solid ground when we infer than an individual "appreciates good music" if we observe that he has spent $500 for stereo equipment and has accumulated over the years a library of 400 serious recordings ranging from Vivaldi to Vaughan Williams.

Of course, the possibility *does* exist that he is a pseudointellectual who has money, cares nothing for music, and is simply projecting a fashionable image.

Awareness of this alternate possibility reminds us of the tenuousness of our inferences and emphasizes the prudence of bearing in mind that the observed data are not to be *equated* with the inferred construct. After all, we are only human beings *inferring* (and defining) an intangible construct from sense impressions. To be more certain about the validity of our conclusion, of course, we can seek further observable clues that (we hypothesize) are other reasonable manifestations of the presumed construct.

The substance of this process is quite like the substance of behavioral objectives: We are resorting to empirical data—that is, observable behavior—for evidence of the existence of the hypothesized construct. The difference between this process and that employed by most behavioral objectivists, however, is that we are openendedly entertaining *behavioral clues*[2] that we hypothesize are probable indices of the construct, rather than stipulating behaviors in advance and then rigorously attempting to elicit these behaviors in order to prove that we have reached the goal.

To define the issue as a choice between behavioral and nonbehavioral objectives is a fallacy that may have been propagated by the very language inherent in the term "behavioral objectives." The term implies (1) that the observed behavior is *equated with* (as opposed to *a hypothesized manifestation of*) some level of a learner's attainment, and (2) that the objective (behavior) is an external fixed terminal point at which action is to be directed. This interpretation invites all of the criticisms of behavioral objectives raised in the preceding paragraphs. On the other hand, utilizing operationalism as a liberally construed empirical method—i.e., in terms of the generation of behavioral clues—enables curriculum workers to retain the advantages of the empirical method while at the same time escaping the trap of rigid scientism. As curricular dogma, both behavioral *and* nonbehavioral objectives deserve rejection.

Training versus Education

The issues discussed in the previous section are intricately related to the training-education dichotomy. In broad philosophical terms, the aims of the former are represented by prescribed terminal points, while those of the latter involve the open-ended possibilities connected with such questions as: What can man become? Training often is referred to as the *technical model* in curriculum construction, while (liberal) education sometimes is called the *humanistic model*.

Although the training-education dichotomy is spurious in that actual school situations always fall somewhere on the line between the two extremes, the distinction is important to make since curricula, while never purely one or the other, can emphasize either the training or the education model. The follow-

2. I am indebted to my colleague, Professor George Harrison, for this terminology with reference to behavioral objectives.

ing two sections will describe the hypothetical extremes by way of bringing into broader relief the characteristics of these two curriculum models.

TRAINING: THE TECHNICAL MODEL

Briefly stated, training is a process by which teachers, employing the validated discoveries of the behavioral sciences, manipulate learners and their environments in such a way that the learners efficiently acquire prescribed behaviors. In this paradigm learners are viewed as the raw material to be processed under certain curricular and instructional treatments for the purpose of producing a desired finished product. This empirically based technical model may be described as essentially a four-step process:

1. *Specify objectives (preferably in behavioral terms).*
2. *Preassess learners (to determine prerequisite skills and/or their status with respect to the prescribed objectives).*
3. *Apply instruction (designed to teach the prescribed behaviors).*
4. *Evaluate outcome (the degree to which objectives have been achieved).*

A curriculum based on the training paradigm would include a hierarchical, highly organized statement of outcomes framed in behavioral terms. Since the focus of training is efficient behavior modification, behavioral psychology, including all that is known about positive and negative reinforcement schedules, would be prescribed. The "motivation" and behavior change of learners would be extrinsically managed, and the teachers would function in the role of skilled technicians. The training model, skillfully executed and employing the best of educational technology, has met with remarkable success in a variety of settings, especially in many of the schools of the armed forces.

EDUCATION: THE HUMANISTIC MODEL

A concept that defies precise definition, education is probably most succinctly described as the process of actualizing human potentials. As previously stated, it poses the question: What can man become? A notion of what education is may be best conveyed in metaphoric terms. Thus, the educated man often is viewed as a person who has transcended the psychological contraints of the culture, yet who retains membership in the human community. At the same time he is able to grapple with the open endedness of existence in the search for meaning.

Some describe education as the process of expanding awareness and extending one's existence to an ever greater sense of Being. Others propose that education is the process of defining and redefining oneself in terms of successive reassessments of one's transactions with others and the environment. Still others maintain that education concerns itself with the "big" questions of human existence: What is real? What is man? What is good? Implicit in all these statements is the notion of "liberation" (embodied in the term "liberal education") and the position that the specific outcomes of education are always in question.

A curriculum based on the humanistic model then, would be structured around "openness." Outcomes would tend to be stated in humanistic rather than behavioral terms, and the behavioral psychology of the training paradigm would be supplanted by the "self" or "existential" psychology of Abraham Maslow or Carl Rogers. Rather than specifying the psychological principles which would govern teachers' manipulation of learners, the education curriculum would call for "authentic" interpersonal relationships among learners and between teacher and learners. The "motivation" and behavior change of learners would be intrinsically stimulated, and teachers would function in the role of "sensitive" and "responsive" whole human beings.

PERSPECTIVES ON TRAINING AND EDUCATION

Training has alternately been condemned as horribly mechanistic, dehumanizing, and manipulative on the one hand, and lauded as the only rational, responsible, and accountable way of teaching on the other. It is neither of these, of course, and deserves serious consideration for use in some curriculum situations for which it is appropriate.

Training, as previously stated, assumes that the objectives to be achieved are understood clearly and not open to question. There are many learning situations in which this condition, for all practical purposes, must exist if society is to function in anywhere near a reasonably smooth way. For example, certain clearly defined terminal professional behaviors are expected of airline pilots, nurses, computer programmers, teachers, electricians, and typists. Obviously, the curriculum and teaching procedures involved in producing the terminal behaviors associated with the above roles should be designed so that the behaviors are thoroughly learned in the shortest possible time. Thus, because of its characteristics of clarity and efficiency, the training model appears to be particularly suitable to vocational-professional curriculum designs. Indeed, so closely tied is "vocational training" to the training paradigm that many educationists object to the often-employed designation "vocational education" as being a contradiction in terms.

But the training model, while viewed as appropriate in vocational situations, often is rejected in the public school setting where the "education of individuals" is the major concern. A closer look, however, reveals that many of the skills subsumed in general liberal education can also be construed as falling with the scope of the training model. Among these we might mention handwriting, reading, computing, and speaking foreign languages. Certainly, given agreement on the desirability of developing clearly defined curriculum outcomes such as these, the training paradigm, judiciously executed, can contribute significantly to the development of effective curricular and instructional strategies. Many curriculum outcomes in the area of reading, for example, need to be stated in precise behavioral terms to be useful, and the four-step training paradigm can be employed to get efficient results. However, curriculum workers should be careful to maintain a long-range perspective on the place of training in the larger enterprise of education. If the chief mission of the public schools (kindergarten through grade 12) is the liberal education of the members of society,[3] then the training model will operate only as one of the tools employed to bring about the larger aims of education. Thus, the appropriateness of the behavioral objectives of reading mentioned above might in many instances be questioned because of the hypothesized effect their attainment might have on other areas of the educational development of certain learners.

To champion the training model to the exclusion of other curricular forms, as some behavioral objectivists have done, is to sacrifice education to learning efficiency. On the other hand, to advocate a nonempirical "feeling-based" model of education to the exclusion of behavioral methodologies, as some "humanistic" educationists have done, is to sacrifice demonstrable competence to a questionable form of laissez-faire psychotherapy.

How Aims, Goals, and Objectives Function in the Determination of Curriculum

CONCEIVED AND OPERATIVE PURPOSES

Anyone having a passing acquaintance with curriculum documents is probably aware that, whatever else they may contain, a section on goals and objectives is seldom missing. Teachers using such documents are painfully aware that these statements of goals and objectives rarely are reflected in the curriculum as it becomes operative in the classroom. And yet, we have made the claim that the curriculum (and by implication, the curriculum *goals*) reflects the foundational commitments of the society. Is this situation not contradictory?

The resolution of the apparent contradiction has to do with an important distinction in curriculum goals: (1) goals which schools *in fact* attempt to achieve, and (2) goals at which schools think they *ought* to be aiming. (The situation here is similar to the problem of conceived versus operative values discussed in Chapter 7.) For the curriculum worker this distinction between. *is* and *ought* in curriculum goals presents two problems with which he must wrestle: First, he must ensure that the *goals* of his curriculum document are consonant with all of its other components: its content, learning activities, and evaluation. It is inconsistent, for example, for a school to entertain the goal, "understands the process of scientific inquiry," and then to design the evaluation component in terms of learners' ability to name the five steps of the "scientific method." Second, the curriculum worker must be aware that in the process of implementation, curriculum goals which may represent the "ought" are easily subverted in the direction of the "is." This is especially the case when the

3. See Broudy, Smith, and Burnett (1964) for a statement on this position.

"ought" represents a significant change over the "is." The experiences of many supervisors have indicated, for example, that new science curricula aimed at developing students' inductive reasoning skills (the "ought") were subverted, so that although the science *content* taught was different, it was taught in a way that achieved the established ("is") objective of deduction and memorization.

INTENDED AND UNINTENDED OUTCOMES

Curriculum evaluation in America is based almost exclusively on determining the degree to which stated curriculum purposes have been achieved. If we recall Dewey's caveat with respect to treating ends as fixed terminal points outside the flow of activity, we immediately become aware that this procedure can be not only misleading, but dangerous. By concerning ourselves only with determining the degree to which *stated* purposes have been achieved, we leave ourselves entirely in the dark with respect to a whole range of consequences unshered in by the implementation of our curriculum.

For example, suppose that one stated goal of a curriculum is a specified level of reading proficiency. When a curriculum evaluation indicates that we have been highly successful in attaining the goal, the curriculum is judged to be effective. Unknown to us, however (because we evaluated only for *intended* outcomes), might be an *unintended* (and undesired) consequence of the curriculum: aversion to reading!

While the evaluative problems generated by this situation will be treated more fully in Chapter 16, it is appropriate to point out here that stated curriculum purposes can operate to limit effective evaluation. Just as the selection of certain curriculum outcomes influences the character of curriculum content and learning activities, it also has a tendency to determine the character of evaluation. Since every curriculum involves intended and unintended outcomes, curriculum workers need to design evaluations that can provide a reasonably accurate representation of all curriculum outcomes—unintended as well as intended.

References

Bloom, Benjamin S., ed. 1956. *Taxonomy of Educational Objectives*, Handbook I: *Cognitive Domain*. New York: David McKay Co.

Broudy, Harry S. 1961. *Building a Philosophy of Education*. Englewood Cliffs, N.J.: Prentice-Hall.

————. 1971. "The Philosophical Foundations of Educational Objectives." In *Curriculum: Readings in the Philosophy of Education*, edited by Martin Levit. Urbana: University of Illinois Press.

————, B. Othanel Smith, and Joe R. Burnett. 1964. *Democracy and Excellence in American Secondary Education*. Chicago: Rand McNally & Company.

Commission on the Reorganization of Secondary Education. 1918. "Cardinal Principles of Secondary Education." Bureau of Education Bulletin 1918, No. 35. Washington, D.C.: U.S. Government Printing Office.

Dewey, John. 1964. *John Dewey on Education: Selected Writings*. Edited by Reginald D. Archambault. New York: Random House.

Gagné, Robert M. 1972. "Behavioral Objectives? Yes!" *Educational Leadership* (February).

Harrow, Anita. 1972. *A Taxonomy of the Psychomotor Domain: A Guide for Developing Behavioral Objectives*. New York: David McKay Co.

Havighurst, Robert J., Paul H. Bowman, Gordon P. Liddle, Charles V. Matthews, and James V. Pierce. 1962. *Growing Up in River City*. John Wiley & Sons.

Huebner, Dwayne. 1966. "Curricular Language and Classroom Meanings." In *Language and Meaning*, edited by James B. Macdonald and Robert R. Leeper. Washington, D.C.: The Association for Supervision and Curriculum Development.

Krathwohl, David R., Benjamin S. Bloom, and Bertram B. Masia et al. *Taxonomy of Educational Objectives, Handbook II: Affective Domain*. New York: David McKay Co.

Lynd, Robert S., and Helen Lynd. 1929. *Middletown*. New York: Harcourt Brace Jovanovich.

Macdonald, James B. 1967. "An Example of Disciplined Curriuculum Thinking." *Theory into Practice* (October).

Mager, Robert F. 1962. *Preparing Instructional Objectives*. Belmont, Calif.: Fearon Publishers.

Mills, Patricia. 1971. "In Search of Ambiguity." *Educational Leadership* (April).

Polanyi, Michael. 1966. *The Tacit Dimension*. New York: Doubleday Anchor Books.

Raths, James D. 1971. "Teaching without Specific Objectives." *Educational Leadership* (April).

Richmond, W. Kenneth. 1971. *The School Curriculum*. London: Methuen & Co.

Saylor, J. Galen, and William M. Alexander. 1966. *Curriculum Planning for Modern Schools*. New York: Holt, Rinehart & Winston.

Simpson, Elizabeth Jane. 1966–67. "The Classification of Educational Objectives, Psychomotor Domain." *Illinois Teacher of Home Economics* (Winter).

Smith, Philip G. 1972. "On the Logic of Behavioral Objectives." *Phi Delta Kappan* (March).

Spencer, Herbert. 1885. "What Knowledge Is of Most Worth?" In *Herbert Spencer, Education: Intellectual, Moral and Physical*. New York: John B. Alden, Publisher.

Stoops, John A. 1972. "Current Approaches to Accountability: A Dissent." *Pennsylvania School Journal* (April).

Taba, Hilda. 1962. *Curriculum Development: Theory and Practice*. New York: Harcourt Brace Jovanovich.

Tyler, Ralph W. 1950. *Basic Principles of Curriculum and Instruction*. Chicago: University of Chicago Press.

CHAPTER 14
CONTENT

Only in education, never in the life of farmer, sailor, merchant, physician, or laboratory experimenter, does knowledge mean primarily a store of information aloof from doing. —JOHN DEWEY

Massive quantities of content (information, data, subject matter) constantly bombard individuals, particularly in advanced technological societies, as they carry on the ordinary pursuits of life. Television, radio, motion pictures, newspapers, magazines, speeches, conversations, and directly perceived objects and events comprise some of the many sources of content that converge on the individual's senses. Under such conditions, the individual internalizes, integrates, ignores, or rejects particular content in a somewhat haphazard way according to his experience, proclivities, interests, goals, and so on. Thus, a great deal of "informal learning" takes place in what has commonly been referred to as the "school of daily experience."

The curriculum of the "school of daily experience," however, is obviously not adequate to the needs of education in civilized societies. Such informal education leaves too much to chance. It is the special function of the curriculum of formal education to select and arrange *content* (the second component of the curriculum) so that the desired curriculum aims, goals, and objectives are most effectively achieved and so that the most important and desirable knowledge of the race is effectively transmitted. This task is far more complex and difficult than it immediately appears. While the aims, goals, and objectives of the curriculum do provide some direction in the task, many nagging questions remain, such as the following:

What is content? Does all content constitute "knowledge"?
Which content (from the overwhelming store that has been amassed by man over the centuries of recorded history) should be included in the curriculum? What criteria are the most valid ones to use in the selection process?

Are there some things that everyone *should know? Some things that only* some
students *need to know?*

*In what sequence should the selected content be presented? What criteria
should be used in determining sequence?*

We shall see that the character and organization of content in a curriculum
will depend to a large extent on how these and other questions are answered.

Importance of Content

Until the curriculum reform movement of the 1960s (generally known as the
disciplines-centered movement), probably no aspect of schooling received as
little attention among professional educationists as did the subject matter of
the curriculum. While volumes of material appeared on such topics as educational objectives, the learner, the teacher, the learning environment, methodology, and evaluation, content was assumed to require little comment, to be the
given variable, "familiar, fixed, and at hand when wanted" (Schwab, 1964a,
p. 4). As Schwab reminds us, while teachers were fully prepared to accommodate themselves to new *methods* of teaching mathematics, for example, they
were totally unprepared—indeed "speechless"—when new mathematics content
was introduced. Thus, whatever were the other consequences of the disciplines
movement, it at least had the beneficial effect of renewing educationists' interest
in the long-neglected topic of curriculum content.

It is a truism to state that all school curriculum (indeed all human experience) has content. Obvious as this statement appears to be, however, many
instances can be cited in which curriculum planners seem to have lost sight of
the ubiquity and efficacy of content. For example, much discussion today is devoted to the problems of teaching students *how* to read with only incidental
attention given to the critical consideration of *what* is to be read. By the same
token, we hear teachers discuss students learning *how* to add or subtract with
little or no consideration given to the *content* being manipulated, whether apples, angels, dimes, or abstract numbers. Similarly, much discourse centers on
the significance of learning *how* to think, *how* to learn, etc., often accompanied
by disparaging comments on the relative unimportance of the "facts" or content
in the curriculum. This current tendency to separate and elevate "knowing how"
from "knowing what" appears to be unjustified. Obviously *every* learning
activity must involve some content "whether we think of the activities of
kindergarten children in making a model of terrain in a sandbox or a class in
physics studying the structure of the atom" (Saylor and Alexander 1966, p.
161). The importance of content is nowhere more forcefully demonstrated than
in the religious content of the Puritan colonial reading schools: many students
learned to read there, of course; but of far greater consequence was the effect
of the religious content on the total life style of the students.

It would thus appear that an inquiry into the nature and structure of content
is a necessary activity for curriculum planners. Because curriculum content will

be present in *any* case, it seems far more desirable that its character and organization be the product of inquiry and design rather than oversight and accident.

Conceptions of Content

For purposes of general understanding, it is probably best that we interpret content rather broadly; otherwise we are apt to exclude one or another category of material that clearly ought to be included as "content," but which does not fit within the parameters of our definition. On the other hand, we had best be careful not to include too much in our definition, or we shall not be able to handle our inquiry with adequate coherence and rigor.

Saylor and Alexander propose a definition which seems to be adequately broad, but at the same time well delineated. They define curriculum content as:

> those facts, observations, data, perceptions, discernments, sensibilities, designs, and solutions drawn from what the minds of men have comprehended from experience and those constructs of the mind that reorganize and rearrange these products of experience into lore, ideas, concepts, generalizations, principles, plans, and solutions (Saylor and Alexander 1966, p. 160).

It is worthwhile noting that this definition, while broad, omits mention of *skills* (processes) and *affects* (values). Many curriculum scholars, however, include these elements as content. For example, Hyman (1973, p. 4) defines content as:

> knowledge (*i.e., facts, explanations, principles, definitions*), skills and processes (*i.e., reading, writing, calculating, dancing, critical thinking decision making, communicating*), and values (*i.e., the beliefs about matters concerned with good and bad, right and wrong, beautiful and ugly*).

While strictly speaking, curriculum content *does* include the three elements identified above, it does so because they are not, in reality, separable. The operative curriculum (and learning) always consists of knowledge, process, and value. Thus, it is incumbent upon curriculum planners consciously to account for each of these elements in curriculum construction. But for purposes of inquiry and analysis, we shall generally find it far more productive to restrict the meaning of the term "content" as Saylor and Alexander have done—to such substantives as information, ideas, concepts, generalizations, principles, and the like. Even holding to this broad, but well-delineated, definition, our inquiry will be no simple task.

CONTENT AND KNOWLEDGE

Although some curriculum writers prefer not to make a distinction between content and knowledge (e.g., Saylor and Alexander 1966, pp. 160–161), others (e.g., Dewey 1916, Richmond 1971) see the distinction as critical to effective curriculum planning. For those who do make the distinction, content generally is defined as the *record* of knowledge (symbols, graphics, recorded sounds), independent of its potential for interaction with the human organism; knowledge, on the other hand, is viewed as the increased and deepened meaning that accrues to the individual as a consequence of his transaction with content. Pritzkau (1970, p. 9) makes the point somewhat more colorfully: "Knowledge is not 'over there,' ready-made and waiting to be appropriated. It is encountered . . . ."

Is this distinction just another example of academic hair-splitting, or does it have some real significance for curriculum planners? We may begin by pointing out that, whatever other criteria are used, a curriculum planner who selects certain content for inclusion in the curriculum selects it on the basis of *what it means to him*—i.e., on the basis of content translated into *his* knowledge. The point is that content is never really selected as content per se, but always as knowledge. For example, the concept that "all men are mortal" would appear to be legitimate curriculum content since it represents a highly warranted assertion. But as Richmond (1971, p. 205) points out, this content means quite different things to the healthy man and to the chronic cardiac case. The former carries on his daily life "as if he only partly believed it" while the latter "knows and believes it literally, in his heart." What a difference in the significance that would be accorded this particular curriculum content by two such curriculum planners! This same translation process (of content into knowledge) is also what makes it possible, for example, for one history curriculum to dwell for eight weeks on the Civil War while another spends only two weeks on this period and devotes eight weeks to the New Deal. Thus, *awareness* that content tends to be selected in terms of its *meaning as knowledge for the curriculum planner* provides him with an additional critical perspective, and consequently a less distorted and more intelligent basis, on which to make his selection. But this is only half the case for making the distinction between content and knowledge.

Dewey (1916, p. 182 ff.) makes the point that the immature experience of the learner is remote from the far more comprehensive experience of the adult so that the same content is viewed by the two in quite dissimilar ways. The curriculum planner, unaware of the problem of *knowledge* generated by the adult child experience gap, selects content on the basis of his own internalization of content, i.e., within the sophisticated framework of his own larger experience. The learner's encounter with the same content may generate quite different knowledge, if indeed it generates anything worthwhile at all. The latter possibility (or rather probability) constitutes what in fact has turned out to be a disaster area in curriculum content selection that is directly attributable to the failure to make the distinction between content and knowledge: Most students' school learning is "verbal learning."

VERBAL LEARNING. Curriculum content selected only from the point of view of its meaning to the adult curriculum planner may be very well "learned" by students; and the learning may be certified as effective on the basis of good examination results. But this content, although it represents knowledge to the curriculum planner, is merely information (other men's knowledge, second-hand knowledge) to the learner. *His* learning is verbal learning, learning "for school purposes, for purposes of recitations and promotions . . ." (Dewey 1916, p. 187). Is it any wonder, then, that so much of what students "learn" in school so little affects their character or conduct? The selection of content in terms of its meaning to curriculum planners and without reference to its potential for knowledge in the experience frame of learners is what makes it possible for English grammar, for example, to be taught and retaught throughout all of school life, for students to pass their grammar examinations, and then to graduate from high school knowing no grammar. But it is significant to note that while preservice English teachers know little if any grammar as a result of their public school experience, they internalize its intricacies well enough—indeed, are often fascinated and intrigued by it—when they "learn" it for a meaningful professional purpose: teaching it.

THE PRIMACY OF MEANING. Dewey (1916, p. 186) makes the point that content becomes more than information to be learned for school purposes only when two conditions exist: First, the content must have a relationship to "some question with which the learner is concerned," and second, it must "fit into his more direct acquaintance so as to increase its efficacy and deepen its meaning." Clearly then, unless the curriculum planner takes into account the *potential* for content (i.e., content *qua* knowledge or meaning in terms of the learner's experience) he is more apt than not to develop curriculum content that may very well be "learned," but which will *not* be educative in the sense that it has not been transformed into knowledge—i.e., it has no meaning for the learner.

This point, of course, is the crux of the argument for making the distinction between content and knowledge. Curriculum planners can justify their content-selection activities only in terms of its potential for generating knowledge. That is, the end-in-view of curriculum planning is to turn content into meanings or knowledge for learners. Thus, a sound basis for content selection cannot avoid (1) awareness of one's own state of knowledge with respect to the content and (2) awareness of the potential for knowledge that inheres in the content in terms of the learners and *their* experience.

PROCESS AS CONTENT

As indicated in the section on the importance of content, curriculum writers have recently given a great deal of attention to the significance (and preeminence) of *process,* in contradistinction to *content,* in curriculum construction. Most of these writers correctly point out that where the emphasis has traditionally been put upon content (generally defined as information to be transferred to students), rote or verbal learning ensues. They point out that while this content is often soon forgotten, certain processes (memorization, submission to authority, uncritical acceptance of ideas, etc.) are learned that in fact operate to affect behavior and character. As a result, they describe the learned processes as the real content of the curriculum.

Proponents of the process-as-content position (e.g., Parker and Rubin) define process as the diverse operations associated with the handling and creating of knowledge. There are processes "for utilizing knowledge and for communicating it. Processes are involved in arriving at decisions, in evaluating consequences, and in accommodating new insights . . . . [Process] exists in an infinite variety of shapes and forms" (Parker and Rubin 1968, p. 131). Because of their position on process, these authors would attach more importance to methods of acquisition and utilization of content than to the content itself. For them "knowledge becomes the vehicle rather than the distination" (Parker and Rubin 1968, p. 131).

Certainly we would agree with these authors insofar as they conceive of content as a tool rather than an end in itself. Certainly, too, the processes that surround the acquisition, utilization, and communication of knowledge deserve far more consideration than they have heretofore received. But to infer from these propositions that the data, concepts, principles, and generalizations to be manipulated somehow are less important appears to be an overreaction against the preeminence that content has traditionally been given in the curriculum. It matters a great deal whether the history one studies is American or ancient, political-military or social-intellectual; as a consequence, the residual ideas by which the learner defines his existence will vary even if the learned intellectual processes are the same. Furthermore, the logic or modes of thought employed in dealing with history may be far different from those appropriate to a problem in physics. Thus the content itself may very well have directive force on the processes that come into play.

In reality, content and process constitute an indivisible blend, even though it is convenient to make a distinction for purposes of analysis. But we disagree with those authors who equate content and process. They are *not* the same thing, and curriculum planners must not only make the distinction, but face the hard decisions involved in content *and* process selection.[1]

It should be pointed out that there is a special sense in which process might legitimately be viewed as content. As an example, take a four-year-old child who has learned the grammatical processes necessary for him to generate quite competent original sentences. Asked to explain the processes, the child is at a loss. In effect, he has been conditioned to behave with language in a particular way, but he does not understand (indeed, is not even aware of) the processes he has learned to use. These processes can become content, though, when they are treated as the subject matter of inquiry—i.e., when the (unconscious) processes are made explicit by studying them as the content of a curriculum (e.g.,

---

1. "Process selection" is treated in Chapter 15, "Learning Activities." Processes are learned from the *activities* that students engage in as they interact with content.

the study of transformational grammar or psycholinguistics). It is in this sense, we think, that process as the content of curriculum may very well be an extremely valuable focus for content selection. And it is on this point that we believe the proponents of process have generally fallen short. The ingestion of processes, however rational, useful, or laudable they may be, is no different in principle from the conditioning of learners that occurs with content; what makes the difference is examination of the processes themselves, as the subject matter under study. When people (teachers and learners) reflect upon, make explicit, and study the processes by which their thoughts, feelings, and behaviors operate, intelligent human functioning may become the rule rather than the exception. At any rate, it would seem that in the sense proposed above, process could very well be the most valuable content for the attention and consideration of curriculum planners.

The foregoing paragraph suggests the artificiality of separating content from process. When grammatical processes are made the content of the curriculum, they are necessarily, in their turn, subjected to other processes—conscious and critical reflection, inquiry, study, analysis, etc. Thus, content is always in reality merged with some process. But also suggested in the foregoing paragraph is the importance of distinguishing content from process, especially if we are interested in the conscious development of processes such as reflection, critical thinking, reasoned inquiry, and problem solving. But this aspect of curriculum work is better dealt with in Chapter 15.

The Architectonics of Content

When faced with the bewildering array of content that is available for inclusion in the curriculum, we quite naturally seek to develop some organizational scheme that will enable us to select in an orderly and rational way the content that is most important for learners. If we are bound by the traditions of our culture, we will probably fall back on such comfortable and seemingly discrete categories as mathematics, history, geography, and English, giving little thought to the meaning inherent in these conventionally accepted "labels." On the other hand, we can launch an inquiry into the nature and organization of knowledge[2] before engaging in content decision making. While we are likely to become somewhat disconcerted by the complexities and problems that emerge from this inquiry, we are almost certain to be wiser in our decisions about content (as well as less dogmatic about their "obvious correctness"). Such is the justification for this section on the architectonics of content, the area of study having to do with "the principles of ordering knowledge into systematic categories" (Phenix 1964, p. 44).

2. Because so much of the literature in this area does not make a distinction between content and knowledge, we will use the two terms interchangeably in this section.

THE NATURE OF CLASSIFICATION

The basic reason for classifying anything, of course, is to render our experience intelligible. "Without categories there could be no thought and no understanding. Experience would consist of a profusion of unrelated impressions" (Phenix 1964, p. 45). But it is important to bear in mind that classification schemes are not necessarily inherent in the nature of the objects being classified; our classification schemes, in large measure, are functions of the purposes for which we classify. For example, we may classify postage stamps according to country of origin, color, shape, date of issue, monetary value, or any number of other criteria. Likewise, we can classify students according to their age, sex, socioeconomic status, interests, IQ, etc. The categories into which we place them are dependent upon our purposes. It would seem to follow, then, that whatever the criteria used in the process of structuring the universe of knowledge from which we select our curriculum content, our ultimate purposes should be kept clearly in the foreground. These purposes, singularly curricular in nature, generally are conceived to be utility and learnability. This means that the content and its organization which we finally settle on should (1) be the most useful to the learner as an educated human being in his encounter with life and (2) be readily learnable.

Such purposes, obviously, are quite different from those that a philosopher or other scholar might have in mind in his effort to classify knowledge, and we need to be aware of these differences in our evaluation of various classification schemes. On the other hand, it may very well be that the categorization of knowledge on bases other than utility and learnability may prove to be valuable *resources* for curriculum planners (Phenix 1964, p. 45). Thus, we should be careful not to dismiss out of hand a scheme that is not based entirely on criteria that reflect our own specific purposes.

ORIGIN AND NATURE OF THE DISCIPLINES

A number of roughly synonymous terms, such as subject matter, knowledge, and information, commonly is employed to refer to curriculum content. Whatever the term used, however, what is usually meant are the data, concepts, generalizations, and principles of school "subjects"—i.e., mathematics, history, chemistry, etc.—rationally or logically organized into "bodies of knowledge" sometimes called "disciplines." Furthermore, the assumption generally is made that the interconnected data, concepts, generalizations, and principles that constitute these bodies of knowledge or disciplines have been validated in one sense or another to be "true." In what sense is the curriculum worker to view this "content"? That is, is its status different from the "content" of everyday experience, such as the "facts" that apples are usually red, that ten dimes make a dollar, or that insurance policies provide protection against possible future calamities?

In a very real sense, the disciplines, the traditional "subjects" of the school curriculum, are "the perfected outcome of learning—its consummation" (Dewey 1916, p. 188). Historically they are the result of seeking practical social ends. Dewey makes this clear when he writes:

> *It is pertinent to note that in the history of the race the sciences grew gradually out from useful social occupations. Physics developed slowly out of the use of tools and machines . . . chemistry grew out of processes of dying, bleaching, metal working, etc. . . . geometry . . . means literally earth-measuring: the practical use of numbers in counting to keep track of things and in measuring is even more important today than in times when it was invented for these purposes (Dewey 1916, p. 201).*

But while the stores of knowledge known as the disciplines have grown out of useful social occupations, their present data and organization are based rather on "the successful conduct of the enterprise of discovery [and] knowing as a specialized undertaking" (Dewey 1916, p. 190). Thus, for Dewey, the subject matter disciplines as we know them assume a special status as bodies of rigorously validated information organized to promote further discovery.

This point of view is shared by Phenix, who maintains that the discipline is a unit "definite and significant enough to serve as the basis for the organization of knowledge." He makes his argument on empirical and pragmatic grounds:

> *disciplines prove themselves by their productiveness. They are the visible evidences of ways of thinking that have proven fruitful. They have arisen by the use of concepts and methods that have generative power (Phenix 1964, p. 48).*

For Phenix and Dewey, then, a discipline is an organization of concepts and methods whose chief characteristic is their power to generate new knowledge.

Others, however, have proposed different conceptions of the discipline. Probably the most common is the position that a discipline is simply a defined area of study (e.g., history, chemistry, or zoology). More complex is Broudy's (1961, p. 29) conception, which involves the identification of four aspects of a discipline:

1. *Terminology or concepts that are short-hand names for very complex and abstract processes, e.g., oxidation . . . and the superego.*
2. *A whole network of data, facts, rules, generalizations and theories that have been more or less satisfactorily proved in the history of the discipline.*
3. *A method of investigation in some sense peculiar to itself.*
4. *Rules for evaluating evidence.*

An apparently precise definition has been proposed by Wheeler (1967, p. 178): "A research discipline or subject is taken to be a coherent and consistent body of knowledge which relates to some particular area of man's concern and which gains its unity from its own inherent logic, in most cases the logic of explanation or exposition."

Similar to Dewey's and Phenix's conceptions is that of Foshay (1968, p. 65): "A discipline is a way of making knowledge. A discipline may be characterized by the phenomena it purports to deal with, its domain; by the rules it uses for asserting generalizations as truth; and by its history." Finally, King and Brownell (1966, p. 68) conceive of the term "discipline" as meaning a community, "the corps of human beings with a common intellectual commitment who make a contribution to human thought and to human affairs."

We might continue this litany of definitions almost indefinitely since the effort to define the significant characteristics of disciplines has occupied thinkers for many centuries. Plato, Aristotle, Descartes, Kant, among the greatest minds, have all grappled with the complexities of the ordering of and the relationships among the disciplines. It is significant to note, however, that no definition or combination of definitions has adequately solved the riddle of the structure of man's knowledge.

PROBLEMS IN THE CLASSIFICATION OF KNOWLEDGE

Three central issues which define the problem of the disciplines have been identified by Schwab (1964a and 1964b) as (1) the structure of the disciplines, (2) the syntactical structure of each discipline, and (3) the substantive structure of each discipline. The first issue, the *problem of the structure of the disciplines,* is defined as "the problem of determining the membership and organization of the disciplines, of identifying the significantly different disciplines, and of locating their relations to one another" (Schwab 1964b, p. 11). Such questions as the following are treated in this area: Is the knowledge of mathematics significantly different from the knowledge of "things" (e.g., as in physics or chemistry)? Is there a difference in kind between "practical" and "theoretical" knowledge? Or is "practical knowledge simply the application of theoretical knowledge? Does individual behavior and group behavior differ in such a way that psychology and sociology constitute *different* disciplines, or are individual and group behavior so related that psychology and sociology constitute branches of the same science? It is worth repeating for emphasis here that these questions address themselves to the organization of the *collective disciplines* into the *total architecture* of knowledge.

In contrast, the second problem that Schwab identifies has to do with the *syntactical structure of each discipline.* The syntactical structure concerns itself "with concrete descriptions of the *kinds* of evidence required by the discipline, how far the kinds of data required are actually obtainable, what sorts of second-best substitutes may be employed, what problems of interpretation are posed, and how these problems are overcome" (Schwab 1964a, p. 28). In short, the syntax of a discipline deals with its modus operandi, but it is important to point out that modus operandi is not reduceable to an abstracted "method of inquiry" —e.g., a conception like the popular version of the "five-step scientific method."

The complexity of syntax as modus operandi is made clear by Schwab (1964a, p. 31): "a syntax cannot be described except through reference to the concrete subject matter involved in concrete inquiries." For example, while science seeks the most generalized forms of knowledge (e.g., physics attempts to generate broad comprehensive theories that explain vast ranges of physical phenomena), history deals in particular details. Thus each enterprise generates problems of inquiry peculiar to itself which give direction to the kinds of questions it asks, the kinds of data it seeks, its canons of evidence, and its verification procedures. Because of the number and variety of the fields of inquiry and the sometimes intricate differences among them, there exists, according to Schwab, a wide variety of syntaxes and combinations of syntaxes. This intricate relationship between the context (meanings generated by a discipline) and the syntax (modes of thought employed to handle meanings) is, in principle, the same kind of interconnectedness claimed in a previous section for content and process. The necessity of this connection will be made clearer in the following paragraphs, which deal with the third major issue that defines the architectonics of content: the problem of the substantive structure of each discipline.

The *substantive structures* of the disciplines addresses itself to questions inherent in the nature of the data and conceptions that identify the powers and limits of a particular field of inquiry. For example, the concepts of "element" and "compound" constitute substantive structures peculiar to the discipline of chemistry, while "id," "ego," and "superego" represent substantive structures of (Freudian) psychology. The substantive structures of each discipline function to guide inquiry in the discipline and to render comprehensible the disparate data that constitute its subject matter. Moreover, the structures take on meaning and are understood in terms of their relationships to one another. For example, in physics "it is impossible to discuss work without discussing force; and force cannot be discussed without concern for momentum. Further, not one of these can be defined by mere pointing. Pushing, pulling, or lifting are ways of applying force but do not correspond to 'force' as this conception appears in classical mechanics" (Schwab 1964b, p. 36). Thus, the substantive *structures* (plural) of a discipline are interrelated in such a way that they may collectively be said to represent the substantive *structure* (singular) of the discipline.

It is important to point out that the substantive structure(s) of a given discipline never constitute a literal and finished description of a fixed reality. For example, we are aware that the naive concepts developed by fledgling disciplines are later abandoned or revised in favor of more sophisticated structures as the discipline matures (e.g., the concept of oxidation supplanting the phlogiston theory in chemistry). At the same time, some disciplines entertain and accommodate competing substantive structures all of which have their own usefulness and generative power (e.g., psychoanalytic, behavioral, and perceptual structures in psychology). Situations such as these point up the inventive, tentative, and revisionary character of knowledge, an important concept of which curriculum planners should be aware.

Jerome Bruner, a prominent proponent of the structural viewpoint, explains why knowledge cannot be conceived of in terms of absolute truth:

> *Knowledge is a model we construct to give meaning and structure to regularities in experience. The organizing ideas of any body of knowledge are inventions for rendering experience economical and connected. We invent concepts such as force in physics, the bond in chemistry, motives in psychology, style in literature as means to the end of comprehension (Bruner 1963, p. 120).*

What is the significance of these three problem areas to the task of content selection? The implications are numerous, of course; however, we will mention only a few of the most important. With respect to the first problem area (the organization of the disciplines) we quote Schwab:

> *To identify the disciplines that constitute contemporary knowledge and mastery of the world, is to identify the subject matter of education. . . . To locate the relations of these disciplines to one another is to determine what may be joined together for purposes of instruction and what should be held apart . . . (Schwab 1964b, p. 11).*

With respect to the second and third problem areas (the syntactical and substantive structures of each discipline), we may note the important implication that curriculum planners need to consider the relationship of content and process in developing curriculum content. Furthermore, "to know what structures underlie a given body of knowledge is to know what problems we shall face in imparting this knowledge" (Schwab 1964b, p. 13). Finally, and perhaps most importantly, we should note the revisionary and plural character of substantive and syntactical structures; the tentative nature of the disciplines points up the need to avoid the dogmatic and inculcative approach to content (an approach which, unfortunately, now characterizes most curricula). To inculcate a particular version of history, a particular literature, or a particular view of science (i.e., to treat selected content as absolute fact or truth) not only does violence to the nature of the content, but promotes narrowness and divisiveness, the very opposite of openness and community which are the desiderata of education.

THE DISCIPLINES: UNITY OR DIVERSITY?

Are the disciplines each part of an interrelated totality which we can point to as constituting man's knowledge? Or is each discipline an autonomous body of substantive and syntactic structures that deal independently with a particular vector of reality? King and Brownell (1966) argue that man's age-old fascination with the idea of oneness and the traditional domination of philosophy (the "queen of disciplines") are mainly responsible for the repeated (but unsuccessful) attempts to bring all the domains of knowledge into a unified, coherent system. They point out, for example, that Aristotle (Greek philosopher, 384–322 B.C.), using the principle of "final causes," attempted to organize all the disciplines into just three classes: the theoretical (e.g., physics and mathematics), the practical (e.g., ethics and politics), and the productive (e.g., art and engineering). Centuries later, René Descartes (French philosopher, 1596–1650) tried to unify the disciplines under the umbrella of a universal logic—a deductive method resting on self-evident first principles. Thus, he viewed the disciplines as a philosophical unity, a system in which "philosophy as a whole is like a tree whose roots are metaphysics, whose trunk is physics, and whose branches . . . are all the other sciences." Later, Auguste Compte (French philosopher, 1798–1857) attempted to unify the sciences using the organizational principle of subject matter. He constructed a hierarchy in which each discipline was classified according to the complexity of the substances that were its subject of study. Thus physics, because it was concerned with the simplest physical structures preceded chemistry, which was concerned with combinations of physical structures, then came biology (combinations of chemicals), and finally at the top, sociology (combinations of biologicals). It is interesting that some curricular prerequisites (e.g., physics before chemistry and chemistry before biology) that are based on this organization of the disciplines persist even today in many schools. Of course, none of these efforts to build a unified system of knowledge has been successful, and the more knowledge we acquire, the clearer it becomes that

> There is an imperative in the indispensable distinctions among the various disciplines of knowledge. . . . We conclude that no imposed, monolithic unity can presently account for . . . [the] . . . distinctive aspects of the modern disciplines. . . . With respect to the curriculum and the schools, only a pluralism of knowledge seems plausible (King and Brownell 1966, pp. 60, 61).

Although these authors define pluralism as "diversity-in-unity," they emphasize the "autonomy and diversity of the various disciplines of knowledge" and view the school as "a microcosm of the realm of knowledge" (King and Brownell 1966, pp. 62, 63). Thus, they advocate the use of the separate disciplines as the content of the curriculum.

But another view of the disciplines, one advocating the relatedness of knowledge, would argue that King and Brownell's conclusions are not warranted. Even if the possibility of a "monolithic unity" of knowledge could be disproved (the authors have shown only that "monolithic unity" has not yet been demonstrated), it by no means follows that a highly significant network of relationships does not exist among many of the disciplines or that awareness of these relationships is not vital to an understanding of the disciplines. Levit argues for the existence of interdisciplinary relationships:

> over many centuries of human existence, extremely varied relations among things . . . have been found or established. . . . Stated in terms of subject matter, these developments have been reflected in the revolutionizing of those disciplines which are open to inquiry in extensions, modifications, and intertwinings of their concepts, procedures, and objects of study . . . [for example,] the phenomena and principles of physiology continue to be reinterpreted as they are brought into expanding theoretical and practical relations with the materials and principles of physics and biophysics, chemistry, anatomy, embryology, genetics, ecology, psychology, and many other areas of inquiry (Levit 1971, pp. 175–177).

On the basis of Levit's argument, it almost seems that the direct opposite of King and Brownell's conclusion is warranted: The more knowledge we acquire, the clearer the interrelationships between the disciplines become! Of course, Levit does not make this claim. He admits that "there are discontinuities; not everything is related to everything else in every possible way" (Levit 1971, p. 176). Nevertheless, it seems clear that relationships between disciplines must be a factor to consider as curriculum planners select and organize content.

CURRICULUM CONTENT: UNITY OR DIVERSITY?

Just a glance at the offerings of a modern multiversity ("university" seems so inappropriate a word today) suggests that the proposals of King and Brownell are widely accepted. A fantastic diversity of specialized offerings emanate from a profusion of specialized schools, departments, centers, and institutes. Much the same condition ensues in modern secondary schools, which include in their curricula content ranging from cosmology to cosmetology. But that the diversity approach to content is adequate to the educational needs of individuals and societies is a highly arguable proposition. In fact, many schools' curricula have sustained considerable criticism precisely *because* of the fragmentation (and irrelevance to life) deriving from the "pluralistic" disciplines approach.

If there is any substance at all to the argument that people in societies need to make sense out of their existence, it would appear that an integration of knowledge is a necessary condition. This does not mean that the "integrity" of the "disciplines" is at stake; it does mean that, in the general education (as opposed to professional training) of human beings, the disciplines function most often as *resources* for content (not as *the* content) in the development of an educated *Weltanschauung*. As Foshay (1970, p. 351) so aptly notes: to teach subjects separately leaves the problem of integration of knowledge to the student himself to carry out, more or less unaided." Our confidence that unaided integration can take place is bolstered neither by experience nor by the plea of King and Brownell (1966, p. 142) for "some faith that in the plurality of knowledge freedom will lead to order."

Harking back to the points made on the nature of classification: classification criteria may vary according to the purposes of classifying; they are not necessarily inherent in the objects being classified. Exacting delineation and separation of the disciplines may be necessary in order to meet the demands of research or professional training; but developing the constructs that enable one to build viable conceptions of the meaning of one's existence in the cosmos may demand organizational patterns based on different criteria, e.g., "social problems" in general, and "pollution" in particular. In this instance, the relevant materials from chemistry, biology, psychology, ethics, anthropology, history, and other disciplines might be organized (and interrelated) to fulfill this particular purpose.

Obviously, the alternatives available are not limited to a choice between the disciplines as a monolithic unity and the disciplines as unrelated segments of knowledge. But moving away from the highly discipline-centered organization of content (that we know results in fragmentation and irrelevance to life) will require a radical rethinking of traditional categories of knowledge. Curriculum workers will have to be acutely aware, for example, that the record of man's knowledge appears in disciplines form for purposes of retrieval, research, professional training, or other reasons that may have little to do with its organization *qua* knowledge for the liberally educated individual. Just as there are many ways of classifying postage stamps and students, there are many ways of categorizing content. Some of the other alternatives to the disciplines organization of content are discussed in detail in Chapter 17.

LOGICAL AND PSYCHOLOGICAL CONTENT ORGANIZATION

The issue involved in the distinction between the logical and psychological organizations of subject matter[3] is similar to that involved in the previously discussed distinction between content and knowledge. We are concerned here with the meanings that accrue to learners as a consequence of their transactions with content *arranged in particular organizational* patterns that have been identified as *logical* and *psychological*. A logical organization of subject matter in large measure corresponds to what we have been defining as a "discipline." Put another way, it is "an artificial arrangement of the fruits or results of racial experience" (Bode 1927, p. 47). In a logical organization, principles, propositions, and conceptions are organized rationally so that one follows from another and leads to yet others in a mutually supporting fashion (Dewey 1916, p. 190). Thus, a logical exposition of physics, for example, might begin with definitions of matter, force, and energy from which would be deduced other more complex explanations of the operations of the physical world. This arrangement of content ordinarily bears no relation to the (psychological) sequence or order by which the experiments, trials, hypotheses, and errors of physicists in the past brought the network of interrelated concepts into being. A logical arrangement of content obviously is extremely useful in a number of instances, not the least of which is the propagation of further knowledge. But as Bode (1927, p. 54) notes, "Life is more than scholarship," and we may well ask whether the logical arrangement is the optimal one for purposes of general education.

On this point we might observe that a logical organization of subject matter is impersonal, detached, objective. It represents a "catalogue of results . . . with a marshaling of data to show that the inferences are sound" (Bode 1927, p. 47). A psychological organization, in contrast, takes as its organizing principle the learner, and hence assumes a distinctly human dimension. To illustrate what this might mean in a concrete situation let us adapt an example from Dewey (1916, pp. 183–184). The average child is most likely not particularly concerned with geography as it is organized for its own sake by geographers. Introduced

3. For a contrasting view of this issue, see Goodlad (1968, p. 318).

to the subject through a globe, the poles, continents, oceans, seas, etc., all of which have names to be learned, the student will probably respond, at best, with what we have called verbal learning because the data, abstractions, and nomenclature of the logically organized subject are entirely unconnected with his understanding, interest, and restricted experience. On the other hand, the starting point of the study of geography might consist of identifying the locations of various pupils' homes relative to the location of the school; at this juncture, the introduction of the points of the compass becomes a natural consequence, from which, in turn, might evolve the construction of a map of the school district based upon the gathering of all manner of empirical geographical data. Because the content of the learning experience has grown out of a consideration of the learners' psychological location in space and time, the learning is much more apt to reflect the appropriation of personal meaning and, in effect, enlarge and deepen the learner's experience. From this enlarged experience it is possible for the learner to move from the materials of his own concrete world toward increasing use of the communicated content and information of books and other materials. The farthest-reaching outcome of this process occurs when the content "is enlarged and worked over into rationally or logically organized material—that of the one who, relatively speaking, is expert in the subject" (Dewey, 1916, p. 184).

This final point is an important one to make. A psychological organization of content is not "illogical"; nor does it imply sacrificing the authority of knowledge to the superficiality of content that resides in organizations based on extreme attachment to pupils' "needs," "interests," or "activities." Psychological organization of content in general means taking into account the concrete, empirical basis on which learning begins and only then moving toward the deductive and abstract. Its aim is the transformation of the learner's present experience.

THE DISCIPLINES AND INFORMAL CONTENT

Even if inquiries into the nature and organization of the formal content of the "disciplines" were to yield a satisfactory answer to the problem of the nature and organization of this knowledge, we are still left with the uncomfortable fact that the data and ideas included in the organized disciplines by no means encompass anywhere near the total record of information produced and used by man.

Knowledge about consumer products, from foods to appliances; the operations of local government; media and its effects; current social problems; and such topics as sex, war, love, crime, and the future, are critical concerns of all people, young and old alike. This less organized (and often less rigorously validated) information—what we are calling "informal content"—may derive in part from some of the disciplines, but it often cuts across discipline lines and includes much that is not included in the disciplines. Some curriculum writers (e.g., Phenix, Broudy, and King and Brownell) argue that only the disciplines, organized as disciplines, are proper content for inclusion in the curriculum; others (e.g.,

Bode, Dewey, and Richmond) would hold that curriculum content be selected from the total store of information available and be organized according to curricular purposes. Both of these positions on content, obviously, have far-reaching implications for the nature of the finished curriculum.

SCOPE OF CURRICULUM CONTENT

Scope is the term generally employed in the field to refer to the breadth and depth of the content of a curriculum.[4] The word refers not only to the range of content areas represented, but to the depth of treatment each area is accorded. The previous section has raised one of the more prevalent questions concerning scope: Should the curriculum include content from both the disciplines and informal sources? Other important questions of scope include: What content should *all* students be required to learn? (English, history, and arithmetic are now common.) What content should be included in an elective mode? (Music and art usually are offered on this basis.) And what content is outside the province of the school and should be entirely excluded? (In most public schools, religion is excluded.)

It will be recalled from Chapter 2 that the scope of the seventeenth-century curriculum was extremely narrow, consisting mainly of reading and religion in elementary school, and Latin and Greek in the secondary school. All students were required to study *all* of the content in the curriculum. Since that time, as we have already noted, the addition of a profusion of school subjects has greatly expanded the scope of curriculum content in the contemporary public school, making it impossible for any learner to take all the subjects offered. As a result, it has become customary to treat the question of scope as two related sub-problems: (1) required or common content and (2) elective or special content.

COMMON CONTENT. General education tends to suggest the desirability of a shared corpus of content through which members of a social group come to distinguish themselves as a community with a common culture. This concept may be narrowly interpreted as raw indoctrination into a parochial social unit (a nation may be a parochial social unit) or broadly interpreted as a shared corpus of content by which people transcend parochial considerations of time and geography and gain membership into the worldwide community of civilized human beings. A preference for the broader interpretation, of course, seems the more reasonable and it is on this basis (rather than the narrow one) that the argument for the inclusion of common content in the general education curriculum is made.

Friedenberg (1959, p. 72 ff.) addresses himself to this issue when he discusses the "Americanization" (or general education) function of the public school. At its worst, he believes that the school turns students "into an article sufficiently standardized to fit efficiently into a productive system . . . and

4. See Chapter 18 for a comprehensive discussion of scope and sequence in curriculum design.

trusted not to raise questions about that . . . [system] . . . in the universe of values" (Friedenberg 1959, pp. 77, 78). But what he believes "Americanization" (general education) ought to be doing, is developing a community of learners "with a fairly tough and firmly fixed philosophical apparatus for making a certain kind of sense out of their lives, and communicating with other people who may be assumed to have a basically similar apparatus" (Friedenberg 1959, pp. 75, 76). Part of the curriculum planner's task, then, would appear to be the identification of the common content with which it is essential for all learners to interact if they are to develop the categories of thought and feeling, and the approaches to understanding, that define membership in the human community. This "common" or "required" aspect of the content should not be construed as the advocation of conformity or the rejection of autonomy for individuals. Nevertheless, it is clear that individuals (not including, of course, recluses) exist in a community context and that the quality of the community (including its allowances for individual autonomy) will depend upon common ideals regarding human relationships.

It has been noted that a unique characteristic of American society and culture is its lack of community (e.g., see Packard 1972). If there is any validity in this analysis, there is certainly urgent cause to examine the meanings inherent in the traditional American ideal of "individuality"; it may turn out, as we have suggested earlier, that the word is nothing more than a euphemism for "self-interest."

The common content of traditional curricula has consisted mainly of subjects such as reading, writing, arithmetic, American history, and English. Chapter 17 presents in some detail a number of curriculum designs that embody various other formulations of common content for general education.

SPECIAL CONTENT. Curriculum content which is experienced by only a portion of the learners may be aimed either at vocational training or liberal education. Content aimed at vocational training usually is determined by specialists in the area who make their decisions on the basis of (1) prior policy commitments which establish the training program, and (2) the settled goals and objectives to be achieved in a particular program. Thus, special content for vocational training will not concern us to any degree here. But special content for liberal education raises some highly problematic issues (most of which are yet unresolved), and these deserve our closest attention.

Some curriculum writers (e.g., Becker 1967) would advocate a common curriculum for *all* of general/liberal education. Others, however, would argue that the "knowledge explosion," coupled with the variety of human potentials inherent in "individual differences" dictates the desirability of a "smorgasbord" of elective offerings with no required content. Our notion of a liberally educated individual as one who is actualizing his individual potentials while retaining membership in the human community leads us to conclude that a curriculum for a *liberal*/general education ought to contain both common and special content. Reasons for the inclusion of common content were presented in the previous section. Special content, we believe, should be part of the curriculum so that learners have an opportunity to develop those idiosyncratic qualities which will distinguish them as unique personalities. Thus, whatever special areas of the curriculum are offered will depend upon students' interests, social context, or both. For example, offerings in black history or literature, fire-escape gardening, urban architecture, public transportation, or ecology might characterize special content in an urban school, while horsemanship, farming as an industry, animal husbandry, dried flower art, or ecology might be included in a rural school curriculum.

Special content often takes the form of in-depth treatment of certain areas. Thus, advanced study of the novel, analytic geometry, and Roosevelt's New Deal might be offered on a special-content basis for those interested students who had already studied the basic content of corresponding areas (i.e., English, mathematics, and American history).

Time, of course, is a constraint in determining the scope of curriculum content. Thus, breadth of content is always bought at the expense of depth, and vice versa. In addition, the proportions of common and special content to be included in the curiculum is a problem for those planners who advocate both kinds.

SEQUENCE OF CURRICULUM CONTENT

Sequence is defined as the order in which curriculum content is presented. The concept includes the consideration of at least three key questions (Leonard 1950, p. 70): What criteria should determine the order of succession of the materials of instruction? What follows what and why? What is the most desirable time for learners to acquire certain content? Sequence often is referred to as the "vertical" organization of content to distinguish it from the "horizontal" organization, which concerns the arrangement of content at a given level of instruction (e.g., the integration of tenth-grade English, art, and music into a "humanities" course).

Determining the sequence of content, like all other specific curriculum tasks, is intimately connected with basic assumptions in the foundational areas. Thus, how closely one adheres to a particular sequence of content will depend upon one's disposition toward such matters as the structure of the subject matter or the psychological theories that govern human learning.

With respect to the structure or "logic" of the subject matter, sequence will vary according to the organizational principles that one perceives as governing the discipline. Smith, Stanley, and Shores (1957, p. 233) identify four such principles: simple to complex, prerequisite learnings, whole to part, and chronology.

Sequences governed by the *simple-to-complex* principle are found most often in areas such as biology, chemistry, and grammar. Here, sequence is defined as progression from simple subordinate components to complex structures, which are composed of combinations of the subordinates. Thus, content in biology frequently begins with one-celled animals and proceeds through simple, but multi-cellular, organisms to human physiology; chemistry begins with elements and moves toward complex organic compounds; and grammar typically starts with the study of elementary parts of speech (e.g., noun, verb, adjective) as the foundation for later analyses of the syntax of compound and complex sentences.

Determining sequence according to *prerequisite learnings* is common to subjects that depend for their exposition on laws and principles, such as geometry and physics. The nature of the interdependency of the principles of the subject determines which is to be learned first—as, for example, the logical relationships of geometric theorems determines the sequence of their presentation.

The *whole-to-part* principle of sequence is most common to geography, whose study frequently begins with the globe. The rationale here is that understanding of the whole—i.e., the earth as globe—makes possible the understanding of partial phenomena, such as differences in time and seasons.

Finally, *chronological* sequence is utilized as the "natural" organization in a subject like history, which has traditionally been perceived as a structure of chronologically recorded events (the recital of "one damned thing after another," to quote the historian Arnold Toynbee). Chronological sequence often is defended on the basis that understanding of the causal relationship of earlier to later events is enhanced when learners are acquainted with events in the order of their occurrence. Reverse chronology, however, has been utilized in history courses on the grounds that learning begins with the present experience of students and that inquiry into the causes of present consequences is a more rational approach to sequence. Many literature courses also are arranged chronologically because of the belief that literary appreciation is enhanced by an understanding of the cultural eras that produced the works to be studied.

Learning theory, as previously noted, can also influence one's position on the sequence of curriculum content. For example, the work of the French psychologist Jean Piaget (1950, pp. 87–158) suggests that the development of children is characterized, roughly, by four intellectual stages. The first, the sensory-motor stage, involves the control of perception and motor responses in dealing with objects and language, and occurs during the first two years of life. The second, the preoperational stage, consists principally of establishing relationships between experience and action and lasts until the child is five or six years old. The third, the stage of concrete operations, involves the ability to internalize instinctive symbolic systems (e.g., the concept of "reversibility," which the child uses to understand that a divided collection of marbles can be restored by adding the subgroups together again); this stage lasts until ages ten to fourteen. The fourth, the stage of formal operations, enables the young person to go beyond his experience or immediate present reality and to formulate hypothetical propositions (e.g., the notion of probability as a fraction of certainty). Obviously, this theory of the stages of intellectual development implies that the sequence of curriculum content be carefully coordinated with the learner's stages of development.

By contrast, some interpretations of Bruner's (1960, p. 33) widely quoted dictum that "any subject can be taught effectively in some intellectually honest form to any child at any stage of development" has led to the virtual rejection of sequence as an important aspect of structuring curriculum content. Indeed,

> *In some schools two- and three-year-olds were being taught to read and write; first graders were being asked to deal with fundamentals of economics and algebra . . . fourth and fifth graders were encouraged to "discover" set thory in mathematics . . . and high school students studied physics and literature courses formerly taught only in college (Keppel 1966, pp. 113, 114).*

Richmond's reaction to such fatuous applications of the Brunerian hypothesis is worth quoting at length.

> *All very gratifying, no doubt. But what would John Dewey have made of these marvels, one wonders? Come to think of it, what is so unprecedented—or so desirable—about these* jeunes professeurs? *By all accounts, seven-year-olds were translating and commenting on Cicero's* Verrine orations *in Sturm's Academy at Strasbourg as long ago as the early sixteenth century, yet few educationists nowadays would regard this as a cause for congratulation, still less for emulation . . . and may it not be timely to remind ourselves of Pestalozzi's wry comment on the well-drilled pupils in the schools of Geneoa: "Se Kennen wiel und wissen nichts"? [They are acquainted with so much and know so little?] (Richmond 1971, p. 195).*

Richmond's point is that curriculum planners, in determining sequence, have been asking the wrong question; and the results, while startling, have seldom been educative. Rather than centering on what children are *capable* of "learning" at a given stage of development, curriculum planners ought to ask: What *should* children be internalizing at a given stage of development? Of course, children's capabilities are a factor in sequence, but when they become the *central* factor, the consequences are more often than not the verbal learning discussed in the previous section.

Yet Bruner's assumption is helpful inasmuch as it sweeps away a good deal of mythology about "readiness" and the need for a carefully calibrated and closely followed sequence in curriculum content. The most judicious conclusion would seem to be that sequence can be an important factor, but should not be a fetish, in curriculum planning.

Criteria for Selecting Content

Because they establish ultimate direction, curriculum aims operate as the final arbiters of content selection. Thus, the primary basis for content selection must always be the stated aims, goals, and objectives of the curriculum.

Curriculum planners, however, will want to select the content that is *most effective and efficient* in bringing about the realization of curriculum aims.

Thus, a problem of translation (aims-to-content) is generated whereby it becomes necessary to make judgments about content *priorities*. Consequently, the application of intermediate and/or auxiliary criteria comes into play.

Curriculum writers have identified a large number of such criteria—far too many to enumerate and discuss here. Four of these, however, recur often enough in the literature for us to identify as commonly accepted standards for selection. They are (1) significance, (2) utility, (3) interest, and (4) human development.

SIGNIFICANCE

The criterion of significance most often is applied in situations where a particular area of study (e.g., mathematics or history) has already been assumed to be worth including in the curriculum. Rarely is the significance of a total field questioned. Thus, the significance of content usually is judged in terms of how essential or basic it is to the discipline under study. For example, Broudy, Smith, and Burnett (1964, p. 132) state that "other things being equal, basic concepts [and principles] should be emphasized." According to these authors, basic concepts are (1) those which are most "basic to the behavior of an individual" and (2) those which are "logically basic to a given field of study."

Concepts which meet the first criterion usually are found "in the fields of mathematics and languages—the symbols of information—although other subjects do contribute to their development (Broudy, Smith, and Burnett 1964, p. 132). The concept of direct proportion is given as an example which meets the first criterion. To illustrate, if the price of apples is ten cents apiece, then the total amount paid for apples is directly proportional to the number of apples purchased. Clearly, the concept embodied in this illustration is broadly applicable in most of the disciplines as well as in everyday life.

Concepts that are logically basic to particular disciplines are those which "include other ideas," those which "have greater explanatory power than others," or those from which "other propositions making up the field of knowledge are derivable. . . ." For example, in physics, the molecular theory of matter is more basic than Boyle's law because it has greater explanatory power, while in geography, conceptualizing the earth as globe is more important than conceptualizing Italy as a boot because more important data "can be interpreted by the idea of the earth's roundness than by the concept of Italy's shape" (Broudy, Smith, and Burnett 1964, pp. 115, 116).

The criterion of significance became highly prominent in content selection with the advent of the disciplines-centered curricula of the 1960s. Bruner popularized the criterion by noting that knowledge of the "fundamental structure" of a discipline makes the discipline more comprehensible. This is true, he claimed, not only in the highly structured disciplines of mathematics and physics, but in social studies and literature as well.

> Once one has grasped the fundamental idea that a nation must trade in order to live, then such a presumably special phenomenon as the triangu-

lar trade of the American colonies becomes altogether simpler to understand as something more than commerce in molasses, sugar cane, rum, and slaves in an atmosphere of violation of British trade regulations (Bruner 1960, p. 23).

The criterion of significance is most relevant to content perceived as a logical structure and finds its widest application in curriculum development situations that involve experts and scholars in those disciplines which the curriculum includes. While the criterion, judiciously applied, can result in the selection of the most significant concepts of the cultural heritage, it tends to foster specialized competence and to ignore the needs and problems of learners and society.

UTILITY

The criterion of utility as applied to curriculum content generally is restricted to mean useful in the performance of adult activities. For example, adult activities involving personal health, citizenship, family living, courtship and marriage, vocations, etc., would provide guides for the selection of appropriate curriculum content. Herbert Spencer's essay "What Knowledge Is of Most Worth" (cited in Chapters 6 and 13) is an example of the application of the utilitarian criterion.

The utilitarian criterion often is claimed to be the most "scientific" one to use since it is based on empirical studies of what people need to know in order to function effectively in society. Thus, the criterion (sometimes called the criterion of social efficiency) is most compatible with those curriculum development situations in which aims, goals, and objectives are derived from empirical studies of society.

Broadly applied, the criterion can be instrumental in maintaining a relevant connection between curriculum content and the real world "out there." For example, an examination of the kinds of language activities that people engage in when they communicate effectively with one another can provide highly useful data in selecting content for the language arts curriculum. However, narrowly applied (as has most often been the case), the criterion becomes a mechanistic straight jacket that perpetuates the status quo. Such is the case, for example, when a study is conducted to determine the kind of arithmetic problems that adults encounter, and the results are used to select the content of the arithmetic curriculum.

Utility was a widely applied criterion for content selection during the early decades of the twentieth century. It was instrumental in breaking the stranglehold that the classics had on the curriculum and in making curriculum content more "relevant" to students and to society. But several dangers are inherent in this criterion when it is employed as the central device for content selection. First, because it is centered on adult activities, it gives little consideration to the lives of children and the meanings inherent in their experience. Second, it implies an uncritical acceptance of all adult activities. Clearly, not all adult activities are either desirable or educationally significant; thus, content that teaches featherbedding, deceptive business practice, income tax evasion, or plane reservation making is certainly utilitarian in terms of adult activity, but hardly desirable as curriculum content. Finally, the most telling criticism of content selection on the basis of utility is that it supports the status quo. Because the criterion is based on the *present* situation, it gives no direction for (indeed, no recognition of) change that is taking place in society. Thus, the curriculum, by virtue of its role as the *reflector* of society, actually operates to inhibit social change.

INTEREST

With respect to learners' interests as a criterion for content selection, many relevant points have already been made in the discussions relating to the psychological organization of content and the section in Chapter 13 relating to studies of learners and their needs. The following paragraphs will review and expand some of these points and introduce some new material on the function of interest as a criterion for content selection.

One implication of interest as a criterion for content selection is that whatever interests the learner becomes the content of the curriculum. Clearly, such a supposition precludes any possibility of determining curriculum content in advance since students must be consulted in order to determine their interests. Although this position has rarely been acted upon, it is manifested to some degree in the "teacher-pupil planning" procedures of the 1930s and 1940s, by which learners and their teachers jointly planned the curriculum to be studied.[5]

Interest as a criterion for content selection has generated a whole literature of research on students' interests. Research in reading interests is a good example. Consisting of over 300 studies conducted during a period more than seventy-five years, the research identifies normative student interest in reading as related to sex, age and grade, intelligence, reading achievement, personality, and maturity. Two generally accepted conclusions that have resulted from this research are (1) that sex is "conspicuously more important than age or intelligence as a determiner of reported interest pattern" (Thorndike 1941, p. 36), and (2) that girls tend to prefer fiction, while boys tend to prefer nonfiction (Terman and Lima 1925, p. 71). Although interests, of course, will vary from individual to individual, such normative findings as these make it possible to select curriculum content in advance for certain categories of students. Indeed, these particular findings have been widely employed as criteria for content selection in language arts and literature.

Learner interest as a criterion for content selection, however, is often (and justifiably) criticized on the grounds that normative interests are largely culturally induced phenomena (rather than innate qualities) and that using them as criteria for content selection contributes to the support of unconscious cul-

5. A good description of the process of teacher-pupil planning may be found in Hoover (1968, chap. 10).

turally induced bias. In the case of the reading interests research reported above, for example, findings, from the modern feminist viewpoint, reflect sex stereotyping in American culture. Thus, their use in curriculum construction merely serves to confirm and perpetuate sex-role biases.

The criterion of learner interest has also been (justifiably) criticized on the basis that, since students are immature, their interests hardly constitute a sound basis on which to select content. But this criterion holds only in those situations in which *all* content is based on students' interests. The point is similar to the one made in the section on logical and psychological organization of content: psychological organization of content means taking into account the basis on which learning begins and only then moving toward logically organized content. This point is reinforced by Dewey (1902, pp. 99, 100) in his comments on the nature of interest:

> Interests in reality are but attitudes toward possible experiences; they are not achievements; their worth is in the leverage they afford, not in the accomplishment they represent.

To approach content selection entirely on the basis of student interests is "inevitably to result in indulgence and spoiling" (Dewey 1902, p. 100).

Beyond the selection of content on the basis of interest is the use of subject matter "in direction or guidance" (Dewey, 1916, p. 100). In this realm content selection is aimed at determining what subject matter is needed to move the crude impulses of interest toward the order and clarity of logically developed content.

Clearly, interest as a criterion for content selection finds its justification in the laws of educational psychology. To ignore the principle that learning begins with "wherever the child is" is to risk verbal learning at best, and mental or physical dropping out at worst.

One final criticism of the criterion of interest bears mentioning. Even where the criterion is not permitted to the point of "indulgence and spoiling," it tends to result in content that is most appropriate for individual self-development. Because of this individualistic emphasis, Smith, Stanley, and Shores (1957, p. 146) note that this criterion fails to take into account content important to social ends that need to be collectively achieved. In other words, larger community interests tend to be neglected when this criterion is applied.

HUMAN DEVELOPMENT

The criterion of human development often appears in the literature under the nomenclature of "democratic value orientation," "social worth," or "social development." It assumes that the schools operate not merely as the reflectors of society, but as an instrument for the intelligent direction of social change (and, of course, concomitant individual change). We are calling this fourth criterion "the criterion of *human* development" because the term reflects both the *individual and collective* aspects of *humanity* that grow out of the intimate relationship of individual character and social context. It is important to note that the criterion does not imply that the school, as a social institution, should function as the architect of a new social order; certainly other institutions (economic, political, religious, and social) have responsibility (and prerogative) for influence in this regard. But in view of its purported role as gatekeeper for knowledge and intelligence, it would seem that the school's unique responsibility (and prerogative) is to see that knowledge and intelligence are brought to bear in the society's decision-making process. It discharges this responsibility through the education of its students.

Dewey's position is similar. He believes that content selection based on the criterion of human development (he calls it the criterion of social worth)

> *must take account of the adaptation of studies to the needs of the existing community life; it must select with the intention of improving the life we live in common so that the future shall be better than the past. . . . Democracy cannot flourish where the chief influence in selecting subject matter of instruction are utilitarian ends . . . (Dewey 1916, p. 225).*

In general, content selected on the basis of human development centers on inquiry into moral values and ideals, social problems, human emotions, effective thinking processes, controversial issues, etc. This does not mean, for example, that history is not part of the curriculum. While it will probably not be chronologically organized, a great deal of historical data may be used, but in an *adapted* form so as to be relevant to the social problem or other issue under study.

It often is argued that a curriculum built on the criterion of human development is excessively social-studies oriented because it includes mainly content from history, sociology, economics, political science, etc. Critics note that subjects such as biology and chemistry, because they are socially neutral or value free, are slighted.

In the first place, this argument simply misses the tremendous value load inherent in the sciences, perhaps because the social values attached to the sciences have been ignored in most schools. Closer examination, however, reveals that value orientation not only directs the kinds of questions that scientists ask and the nature of the inquiries they engage in, but, taken beyond the laboratory, directs the use to which scientific knowledge is put. It seems somewhat less than intelligent, for example, to claim that research in nuclear fission has been a value-free enterprise.

Nor need the study of the sciences be slighted when the criterion of human development is applied. In one article Tanner (1970, pp. 353–356) makes a plea for recognition of the values inherent in the scientific enterprise and for an examination of those values. He suggests three themes for science content development that are good examples of human development criteria for content selection:

1. *Will man control the technological revolution or will technology sweep him along toward an unplanned and unthinkable world?*
2. *Can technology deal with the crises (pollution, population, etc.) that accom-*

pany technological "progress" or have we, in this regard, misplaced our faith in science?

3. *Will man destroy himself as he continues his centuries-old "conquest of nature," or will he adopt a new respect for the laws of the natural world and come to live in nature?*

In a curriculum that centers on liberal/general education, these issues are obviously germane. They seem to be objectionable (or "irrelevant") in the study of science only insofar as science takes on the special character of professional training. In this regard, with respect to the human development criterion for content selection, Dewey notes:

> *The things which are socially most fundamental, that is, which have to do with the experiences in which the widest groups share, are the essentials. The things which represent the needs of specialized groups and technical pursuits are secondary. There is truth in the saying that education must first be human and only after that professional (Dewey 1916, p. 191).*

Finally, content selection on the basis of human development does not mean indoctrination into the values or modes of thought deemed "correct" by the school. While complete neutrality or "objectivity" is obviously impossible, there does exist a continuum along which curriculum planners are free to adopt a more "open" or less "open" stance toward inquiry and the issues of human development. Thus, the criterion under discussion is predicated on an examination of, and inquiry into, that content which impinges most significantly on the quality of human existence in contemporary society.

References

Becker, Ernest. 1967. *Beyond Alienation.* New York: George Braziller.

Bode, Boyd H. 1927. *Modern Educational Theories.* New York: The Macmillan Company.

Broudy, Harry S. 1961. *Building a Philosophy of Education.* 2d ed. Englewood Cliffs, N.J.: Prentice-Hall.

————, B. Othanel Smith, and Joe R. Burnett. 1964. *Democracy and Excellence in American Secondary Education.* Chicago: Rand McNally & Co.

Bruner, Jerome. 1960. *The Process of Education.* Cambridge, Mass.: Harvard University Press.

————. 1963. *On Knowing: Essays for the Left Hand.* Cambridge, Mass.: Harvard University Press.

Dewey, John. 1902. "The Child and the Curriculum." Chicago: The University of Chicago Press. Reprinted in Martin S. Dworkin. *Dewey on Education.* New York: Bureau of Publications, Teachers College, Columbia University, 1961.

————. 1916. *Democracy and Education.* New York: The Macmillan Company. The Free Press Paperback Edition, 1966.

Foshay, Arthur W. 1968. "A Modest Proposal." In *Strategies and Tactics in Secondary School Teaching,* edited by L. H. Clark. London: The Macmillan Company.

————. 1970. "How Fare the Disciplines?" *Phi Delta Kappan* (March).

Friedenberg, Edgar Z. 1959. *The Vanishing Adolescent*. New York: Dell Publishing Company.

Goodlad, John I. 1968. "Toward Improved Curriculum Organization." In *Contemporary Thought on Public School Curriculum*, edited by Edmund C. Short and George D. Marconnit. Dubuque, Iowa: William C. Brown Company, Publishers.

Hoover, Kenneth H. 1968. *Learning and Teaching in the Secondary School*. 2d ed. Boston: Allyn & Bacon.

Hyman, Ronald T., ed. 1973. *Approaches in Curriculum*. Englewood Cliffs, N.J.: Prentice-Hall.

Keppel, Francis. 1966. *The Necessary Revolution in American Education*. New York: Harper & Row.

King, Arthur R., Jr., and John A. Brownell. 1966. *The Curriculum and the Disciplines of Knowledge*. New York: John Wiley & Sons.

Leonard, J. P. 1950. "Some Reflections on the Meaning of Sequence." In *Toward Improved Curriculum Theory*, edited by V. E. Herrick and R. W. Tyler. Supplementary Educational Monograph No. 71. Chicago: University of Chicago Press.

Levit, Martin. 1971. "Interdisciplinary Education and Understanding the Disciplines." In *Curriculum: Readings in the Philosophy of Education*, edited by Martin Levit. Urbana: University of Illinois Press.

Packard, Vance. 1972. *A Nation of Strangers*. New York: David McKay.

Parker, J. Cecil, and Louis J. Rubin. 1968. "Process as Content." In *Contemporary Thought on Public School Curriculum*, edited by Edmond C. Short and George D. Marconnit. Dubuque, Iowa: William C. Brown Company, Publishers.

Phenix, Philip H. 1964. "The Architectonics of Knowledge." In *Education and the Structure of Knowledge*. Fifth Annual Phi Delta Kappa Symposium on Educational Research. Chicago: Rand McNally & Co.

Piaget, Jean. 1950. *The Psychology of Intelligence*. New York: Harcourt Brace Jovanovich.

Pritzkau, Philo T. 1970. *On Education for the Authentic*. New York: Thomas Y. Crowell (IEP).

Richmond, W. Kenneth. 1971. *The School Curriculum*. London: Methuen & Co.

Saylor, J. Galen, and William M. Alexander. 1966. *Curriculum Planning for Modern Schools*. New York: Holt, Rinehart & Winston.

Schwab, Joseph J. 1964a. "Problems, Topics, and Issues." In *Education and the Structure of Knowledge*. Fifth Annual Phi Delta Kappa Symposium on Educational Research. Chicago: Rand McNally & Co.

―――. 1964b. "Structure of the Disciplines: Meanings and Significances." In *The Structure of Knowledge and the Curriculum*, edited by G. W. Ford and Lawrence Pugno. Chicago: Rand McNally & Co.

Smith, B. Othanel, William O. Stanley, and J. Harlan Shores. 1957. *Fundamentals of Curriculum Development*. Rev. ed. New York: Harcourt Brace Jovanovich.

Tanner, R. Thomas. 1970. "The Science Curriculum: Unfinished Business for an Unfinished Country." *Phi Delta Kappan* (March).

Terman, Lewis M., and Margaret Lima. 1925. *Children's Reading*. New York: Appleton-Century-Crofts.

Thorndike, Robert L. 1941. *Children's Reading Interests*. New York: Bureau of Publications, Teachers College, Columbia University.

Wheeler, D. K. 1967. *Curriculum Process*. London: University of London Press.

CHAPTER 15
LEARNING ACTIVITIES

A child or an adult . . . learns not alone by doing but by perceiving the consequences of what he has done in their relationship to what he may or may not do in the future. . . . In seeing how his acts change the world about him, he learns the meaning of his own powers and the ways in which his purposes must take account of things. . . . With experience of this kind, there is that growth within experience which is all one with education.

—KATHERINE C. MAYHEW AND ANNA C. EDWARDS[1]

Meaningful learning activities represent the heart of the curriculum because they are so influential in shaping the learner's experience and thus his education. *"Learning experiences, and not the content as such, are the means for achieving all objectives besides those of knowledge and understanding"* (Taba 1962, p. 278). Good intentions, fine goals and objectives, excellent content, flawless evaluation procedures, then, are all for naught if the learning activities in which students engage do not provide them with experience whose consequences are educational.

Learning activities in many schools have traditionally been restricted to reading, listening, and responding to teachers' questions (reciting).[2] Indeed, Combs (1966) has noted that these activities are so prevalent that students have been conditioned into believing that they are not learning anything unless someone

1. See Mayhew and Edwards (1936).

2. Reading, listening, and responding to questions, of course, are all valid learning activities. However, they represent only three of a vast number of activities by which people learn. It is the almost total dependence on these activities, and not the activities themselves, that is objected to here.

is giving them information. In contrast, Combs cites as one alternative the active exploration of ideas—a discussion activity through which students are enabled to discover personal meaning. He points out that the ingestion or possession of information usually has little effect on behavior; it is rather the personal *meaning* of that information that shapes the individual's experience and determines his dispositions and conduct (see Dewey's points with respect to content and knowledge in Chapter 14).

When individuals are engaged in a quest for personal meaning, whether that meaning involves criteria for moral behavior or the dispersion of heat in an internal combustion engine, learning activities can take on an almost infinite variety of forms. Thus, the full range of possibilities for learning activities should be kept within the purview of curriculum planners. At the same time, however, planners cannot forget the constraints placed on their selection of learning activities by the necessity for maintaining congruence with foundational commitments and with other components of the curriculum. Clearly, selecting and organizing learning activities that meet all of these demanding conditions is an extremely difficult task.

Conceptions of the Nature of Learning Activities
LEARNING ACTIVITIES AND LEARNING EXPERIENCES

At the turn of the century, the terms "learning activities" and "learning experiences" did not appear in the educational literature. Rather, designations such as "recitations," "exercises," "assignments," "examples," and "problems" were used to indicate tasks that students were to perform (Tyler 1957, p. 368). Most curriculum documents of the period consisted mainly or entirely of outlines of content that was to be covered with little or even no suggestion at all of the learning activities in which students were to engage.[3] In general, it was assumed that teachers would present the content (by lecture and/or assignment) and students would demonstrate their possession of it in recitations and examination.

With the development of the field of psychology and through the work of John Dewey and other leaders in education, increased emphasis was put on the activities of learners as a crucial factor in the learning process. Thus, "by 1925, both writings of theorists and curriculum guides were commonly using the term 'learning activities' to refer to basic elements of the teaching-learning situation" (Tyler 1957, p. 368). Curricula of this period usually include listings of activities in which students are to engage in order to interact productively with course content.

Further analysis of the learning process, however, led educational writers to conclude that the term "learning activities" inadequately described the process

---

3. For example, see Special Committee of the New England History Teachers' Association (1901, 1904).

involved in the teaching-learning situation. They noted that while two students might be engaged in identical activities (e.g., reading the same book), the *experience* which each derived might be quite different. Thus, by 1935 the term "learning activities" was being supplanted by "learning experiences" in the literature because it more accurately conveyed what was occurring in the interaction between the learner and the situation. "Today almost all writers on the curriculum use the term 'learning experience,' and they seek to plan the learning situation so as to give direction to the experience the student has, that is, to his internal perception of the situation and his own interaction with it" (Tyler 1957, p. 368).

Essentially, the difference in meaning attached to the terms "activity" and "experience" is the difference between intent and result. In curriculum construction, planners can readily prescribe the learning *activities* that students will be engaged in, but they can only *hope* that these activities will result in the desired *experiences*. Of course, in order to determine how far their hopes have been realized, curriculum planners will have to assess as accurately as possible the experiences that learners have as a result of their learning activities, utilizing this data as feedback and guide for further development of ·curriculum content and activities. What this distinction suggests, then, is that at the curriculum *planning* stage, learning *activities* will be specified, but at the curriculum *evaluation* stage, resultant *experiences* will be employed to judge the effectiveness of the prescribed activities.

The above discussion suggests that, while the terms "learning activities" and "learning experiences" often are used interchangeably in the literature, a distinction needs to be made for clarity's sake. We have chosen the term "learning *activities*" in this chapter because it most accurately describes that which curriculum planners specify in constructing the third component of the curriculum document. Learning experiences, however, are no less important, but properly merit consideration at another point in the curriculum construction process. Learning experiences are treated in greater detail in Chapter 16.

RELATIONSHIP OF CONTENT AND LEARNING ACTIVITIES

In reality, content and activity never exist apart from one another.[4] Reflection on any number of common experiences will demonstrate this coexistence. For example, when we are eating, we do not ordinarily divide what we are doing into "eating" and "food." But if, for some reason, we wish to conduct an inquiry into what is happening, one of the first distinctions we make is between (1) the procedures carried on by the organism to ingest, process, and digest food; and (2) the nature of the content (food) acted upon. As Dewey points out, the distinction is not a separation in *reality*, but a separation in *thought*. Thus,

---

4. Compare the artificiality of separating content and process that was noted in the previous chapter. Process, we observed, is the (learning) activity, while content is the material acted upon.

"reflection upon experience gives rise to a distinction of *what* we experience (the experienc*ed*) and the experienc*ing*—the how" (Dewey 1916, p. 196). In terms of curriculum analysis and construction, when we give names to this mental distinction, we identify as pseudoseparate entities "content" and "learning activities."

In a functional curriculum (as distinguished from the inert curriculum document) content and learning activities always exist as a unity. When students engage in studying, learning, constructing, analyzing, feeling, thinking, etc., they must utilize some content; i.e., they study *something*, learn *something*, think *something*, and so on. Conversely, students cannot in any way deal with content unless they are engaged in some activity. (Even when assigned simply to "learn the capitals of the fifty states," for example, the implied activity is *memorizing*.) "We can distinguish a *way* of acting, and discuss it by itself; but the way *exists* only as a way-of-dealing-with-material" (Dewey 1916, p. 194).

The separation, then, of content and learning activities represents a way of dealing rationally with reality; it is not by any means intended to be a representation of reality. For purposes of curriculum planning—i.e., the selection and organization of learning activities—the distinction has the advantage of helping us to identify and clarify at least two common areas of curriculum dysfunction. The first is the one in which highly desirable and significant content is applied with deficient activities so that inadequate or counterproductive experiences and outcomes result. A daily diet of "Read Chapter X and answer the questions at the end of the chapter" is an example of a textbook activity in which good content often is undermined by a stultifying activity. The second area, a converse of the first, is one in which highly effective activities are specified in conjunction with content that is trivial or inappropriate. Having a class engage in a survey-inquiry of the student body in order to determine what the school colors should be is an example of this type of anomaly. "One can speak of effective learning only as both content and processes are fruitful and significant" (Taba 1962, p. 265).

Another important reason for making the distinction between content and learning activities at the curriculum planning stage is that criteria for selecting content often need to be kept quite separate and distinct from those employed in the selection of learning activities (Taba 1962, pp. 265, 266). For example, one important criterion for the selection of learning activities is the activity's efficacy in promoting disciplined thought. But this criterion is highly questionable as a standard for content selection. Clearly, it is possible to learn (by rote) the procedures for solving a number of types of complex algebraic word problems without understanding the logical and quantitative relationships inherent in them. On the other hand, it is also possible to understand at the most significant level the principles and logic necessary to inquire into the source of malfunction in a badly running automobile engine. This observation suggests that the "nonintellectual" subject of auto mechanics may be more productive of disciplined thought than is mathematics when the latter subject is taught using learning activities that advance only verbal learning. The power to promote disciplined thought, then, appears to reside as much or more in the quality of the learner's interaction with content as it does in the content itself. "[D]epending on the nature of the learning experiences, any subject can be reduced to *learning about* or become the means for the *how* of disciplined thinking" (Taba 1962, p. 266).

The examples cited in the paragraphs above point up the need to maintain the separateness of content and learning activities for purposes of selection and organization. In the last analysis, however, it is well to remember that content and activities in the functioning curriculum become welded into the unity of the learners' experience.

CURRICULUM LEARNING ACTIVITIES VERSUS INSTRUCTIONAL LEARNING ACTIVITIES

The curriculum plan is implemented through the medium of instruction. Regarding the distinction between curriculum and instruction in general, there is little to add to what has already been said in Chapter 1. If a teacher is more than a machine, more than an automaton following a highly specific set of directions, it is proper that he exercise both his responsibility and prerogative to determine the specific nature of the instructional strategies needed to bring the inert curriculum document to life as a functioning dynamic in the classroom setting. In other words, the teacher will (among other things) formulate the learning activities through which the curriculum plan is translated into a functional curriculum. This translation process, especially as it relates to learning activities, inevitably raises a troublesome question: Where do *curriculum* learning activities properly leave off and *instructional* learning activities begin?

It is impossible to specify at precisely what point a curriculum learning activity becomes an instructional learning activity. The best we can presently do in terms of making a judgment is governed by a criterion that falls somewhere on a general-to-specific continuum; precisely where is a matter of preference. It will be recalled from Chapter 13 that roughly the same situation ensued in distinguishing aims, goals, and objectives; fuzziness and/or overlap sometimes makes classification dubious. Furthermore, though the issue was not broached in Chapter 14, a similar problem exists with respect to separating *curriculum* content from *instructional* content.

With respect to the degree of generality or specificity employed in the designation of curriculum learning activities, a crucial factor would seem to be reliance on the translation competencies of the instructional staff. At one extreme, recent efforts to produce "teacherproof" curricula (e.g., such discipline-centered "curricula" as Physical Sciences Study Committee (PSSC) physics, Biological Sciences Curriculum Study (BSCS) biology, etc.) have resulted in documents so specific that they are viewed by many curriculum writers as *instructional,* rather than curriculum, plans. Such documents virtually constitute "programmed learning" and leave little if any instructional latitude to the teacher. On the other hand, other curriculum documents are so vague on the matter of learning activities that instructional personnel are given no guidance at all as to how the curriculum planners envision the conditions under which learners will interact with the content. Such curricula are particularly mislead-ing, since they imply by omission that process is inconsequential and that ingestion of information (content) is all that is necessary for the attainment of goals and objectives.

Until further developments in curriculum theory alleviate the difficult situa-tions noted above, a subjective sense of proportion and balance would seem to provide the best resolution of the curriculum/instruction dilemma in learning activities. The following curriculum learning activities, intended to enable learners to understand war as a human experience, are good examples of this writer's notion of "a subjective sense of proportion and balance":

> *Create maps of battles and show strategies*
> *Give reports—oral, written, or using slides and tape (audio)—on area of*
>   *their interest*
> *Role-play, creating their own situation or taking one from literature*
> *Create a newspaper, write an imaginary journal of a soldier at the front*
>   *or a civilian at home*
> *Check local newspapers and how they reported or how they are reporting*
>   *the war (letters to the editor can be noted for civilian response to war)*
> *Interview war veterans and civilians on their war experiences (this could*
>   *be done with a tape recorder)*
> *Bring in guest speakers to class for discussion*
> *Use war games and diplomatic games now available on the market*
> *Write poetry or excerpt poetry from collections from the wars (Note: Not*
>   *all poetry or literature is anti-war.)*
> *Reenact a period in all its aspects*
> *Debate a controversial issue*
> *Reconstruct conversations that might have been held—military or political*
>   *conferences or battlefront scenes*
> *Draw cartoons or Xerox cartoons from newspapers and magazines depict-*
>   *ing attitudes toward war*
> *Exhibit paintings depicting war (Herskowitz 1972, p. 54).*

These activities are clearly specific enough to provide instructional personnel with a sense of the curriculum planner's intent, while being sufficiently indefi-nite to allow for detailed development and execution in accordance with the teacher's instructional style and personality. The numerous activities designated also suggest the possibility of selection and/or addition of learning activities to meet student, as well as teacher, needs. Activities that meet these criteria will usually fulfill the requirements of *curriculum* learning activities.

Criteria for the Selection of Learning Activities
AIMS, GOALS AND OBJECTIVES

As was the case with curriculum content, the primary standard for judging the merit of proposed learning activities is how well they contribute to the attain-ment of curriculum aims, goals, and objectives. For example, if learners are intended to develop skill in problem solving, their learning activities should probably provide them with the opportunity to solve problems. Likewise, if learners are expected to develop behavior patterns that are effectively democratic, their learning activities ought reasonably to place them in genuinely democratic situations, which provide numerous opportunities for democratic decision making. Finally, the development of appreciation for literature (an *affective* disposition) probably ought to involve activities requiring responses on the *feeling* level. The point—namely, that if we want students to learn something, we ought to engage them in activities likely to lead to it—is so obvious that it seems hardly worth making. We mention it here, however, only because public school curriculum practice has so consistently violated the principle. To support the contention, we can point to certain anomalous activities that schools sometimes employ in the three learning situations cited above. For example, in many schools problem solving is "taught" by having students memorize the five steps of the "scientific method"; moreover, it is not unusual to observe "Problems of Democracy" classes conducted as though they were totalitarian states; and finally, activities in art- and literature-appreciation courses routinely take the form of cognitive inquiry—i.e., "learning *about*" the works, their authors, and their historical context. While "learning about" can certainly enhance appreciation, it is far from a sufficient basis for teaching it. Indeed, exclusively or even preponderantly used, it can result in downright rejection by students of the aesthetic values of the work under study.

THE DEWEYAN PERSPECTIVE. In utilizing curriculum aims, goals, and objectives as criteria for the selection of learning activities, great care should be taken to avoid the commonly accepted notion that ends or purposes are termini lying beyond the activity which is directed toward them. As was explained in Chapter 13, objectives are the foreseen consequences that influence our thought and that stimulate us to overt action. Thus,

> *ends arise and function within action. . . . [They] are employed to give activity added meaning and to direct its further course. They are in no sense ends of action. In being ends of deliberation they are redirecting pivots in action. . . . In a strict sense an end-in-view is a means in present action; present action is not a means to a remote end (Dewey 1922, pp. 223–225, passim).*

LEARNING ACTIVITIES AND MULTIPLE OBJECTIVES. Given this Deweyan perspective on objectives, it seems clear that the present practice of selecting a learning activity because it leads to the attainment of a particular objective (viewed as a terminal point lying beyond the activity) is inadequate, if not foolish. It amounts to initiating an activity to bring about a *single* desired consequence, while ignoring the many other consequences that inevitably follow from the activity. An example might be having students memorize the names of the six New England states in order to achieve the objective, "Students can name the six New England states"; many other consequences ensue, of course (e.g., misperception of the nature of geography, aversion to study, and boredom with school), but these outcomes are deliberately blotted from perception and ignored.

Some curriculum writers (e.g., Taba 1962, p. 278 ff.) advocate the selection of learning activities that provide for the attainment of *multiple* goals and objectives. This position, of course, represents an improvement in degree over the narrower single-objective procedure cited above; but even here, unless allowances are made for noting the unforeseen plural effects that flow from all learning activities, selection will still be rather narrowly bound by the propensity to look only for those consequences (goals) deliberately projected.

That learning activities can achieve a broad range of objectives presents both advantages and disadvantages to curriculum planners. The most obvious advantage is economy: by judicious selection, curriculum planners can consolidate into a single activity the attainment of a wide range of significant learning outcomes. For example, a single group problem-solving project can, among other outcomes, provide for: (1) problem-solving skills, such as problem formulation, hypothesizing, data gathering, data interpretation, perceiving relationships, developing generalizations, testing hypotheses, drawing conclusions; (2) group process skills, such as awareness of group process, sensitivity to others, cooperative planning procedures, division of labor, integration of effort, democratic decision making; and (3) social attitudes, such as positive dispositions toward cooperation, compromise, community, acceptance of others, and democratic processes. And all of these outcomes can be attained while learners acquire personal meaning—i.e., knowledge and understanding—from the content with which the group is engaged!

The claim sometimes is made that multiple-outcome activities are in fact less economical of time than most narrowly focused traditional activities. For example, it takes a great deal less time for a student to memorize a generalization than it does for him to develop the generalization independently through extended inquiry. This argument, however, is based on the traditional non-Deweyan view of the nature of ends. It gives consideration only to the desired (content) objective of memorizing the generalization and ignores the many other (possibly undesirable) consequences that will inevitably follow the memorizing activity. But if we recognize these consequences and compare them with the development of multiple intellectual skills that ordinarily results from inquiry activities, we cannot avoid the conclusion that the argument for narrowly focused activities is not only spurious, but is educationally unsound. Clearly, the specification of multiple-purpose activities does not necessarily promote inefficiency; rather, it simply reflects the recognition of a wider range of foreseen consequences.

Another advantage of the multiple-outcomes property of learning activities is that it encourages the selection of more varied and broadly conceived "active forms of learning" (Taba 1962, p. 280). In other words, as curriculum planners become increasingly aware of the possibilities for multiple experiences and outcomes inherent in learning activities, they will tend to specify more diverse activities that engage learners in group interaction, reflective thought, planning, generalizing, making deductions and inferences, etc., as opposed to those tasks that focus mainly on the learning of content. Furthermore, as learning activities that develop a wider range of competencies in learners become more predominant, content, because of its organic relationship with the learning activities, will tend less to be learned merely on the verbal level and will be integrated into students' experience in terms of its personal meaning.

Learning activities that center on reading, writing, and listening tend to predominate in most schools today. This focus has resulted from the almost exclusive utilization of content goals as the criteria for the selection of learning activities, as well as the failure to recognize many undesirable process outcomes that follow from such activities. If a wide variety of desirable process goals (thinking, problem solving, etc.) are to be realized at all, it is important that curriculum planners closely monitor *all* outcomes. The recognition of unintended outcomes is needed to serve as a basis for redirecting the design and specification of learning activities in the ongoing task of curriculum construction.

FOUNDATIONAL COMMITMENTS

Because they are so fundamentally a part of our lives, foundational commitments very easily fall into the background of our thoughts and become invisible. Philosophical assumptions about society, man, learning, and knowledge demand continual reexamination to prevent this from happening and to ensure that decisions about learning activities are congruent with the best thinking on these big questions. Potential learning activities should be assessed in terms of questions such as the following:

Will the activity move the student closer to an undistorted view of his society and culture?

Will the activity move the student toward a rational-critical posture toward society without alienating him from it?

Will the activity help the student to clarify the conditions of his own existence?

Will the activity have a tendency to broaden or constrict students' perceptions?

Will the activity help students to develop an openness to experience?

Will the activity enable students to tolerate ambiguity?

Will the activity help students to deal with change?

Many other questions could be added here; it seems clear, however, that an examination of learning activities in terms of these questions can help to illuminate basic assumptions and maintain congruency between foundations and the proposed learning activities. Often the difference between the selection of a significant and a trivial learning activity rests upon considerations such as these.

CONTENT

If, as was pointed out in a previous section, content and learning activities are in reality a unity, assessment of the merit of learning activities cannot avoid a consideration of content as a criterion for selection. Ideally, the proposal of a particular learning activity as a vehicle for the attainment of certain outcomes ought to be supported, at least in part, by evidence taken from a number of actual cases in which the activity was employed; and, as we have seen, these actual cases would, of necessity, have involved the utilization of particular content. But even in cases involving new and untried learning activities, hypotheses regarding the experiential consequences of the activity for learners would necessarily have to take account of alternative content possibilities with which the activity could be implemented.

Perhaps one of the most obvious examples of this point is the activity of reading. If competence in reading is a desired outcome, then learners will have to engage in certain activities—actual reading, exercises, drills, etc.—from which the most effective and productive ones, hopefully, will be chosen to occupy learners' time. But students must read some*thing*, practice with certain *materials*, perform their drills utilizing some *content*. Furthermore, and from the students' own point of view, an activity is not performed as an end in itself—e.g., reading for the sake of the *activity* of reading—but rather to fulfill some further purpose. Thus, learners engage in reading (as most of us do) mainly for the purposes intimately connected with content: getting information, experiencing vicariously, finding answers to questions, etc. In this sense, the content to be employed in the proposed reading activity becomes, in part, an important justification for the selection of that activity. These points, of course, also reinforce the notion that reading (like other learning activities) should not be viewed as a single-purpose enterprise, intended, for example, only to develop mechanical reading skills.[5] It can, and should, be designed to provide for a wide range of cognitive and affective objectives, such as identifying thematic elements, distinguishing fact from opinion, perceiving logical relationships, appreciating metaphor, and many others. To the extent that learning activities are specified in the abstract—i.e., unsupported by content—the curriculum cannot function adequately as a plan for learning.

STUDENTS' EXPERIENCE

It has become a cliché in education to say that teaching, to be effective, must begin wherever the learner is. Even Bruner, widely known for his statement that "any subject can be taught effectively . . . to any child at any stage of development," was disposed to add in a following paragraph: "The task of teaching a subject to a child at any particular age is one of representing the structure of that subject *in terms of the child's way of viewing things*" (Bruner 1963, p. 39, italics added).

---

5. As we have repeatedly pointed out, no activity ever *does* have single consequences, and to ignore its unforeseen plural effects is, to put it mildly, unintelligent.

It goes without saying, then, that curriculum planners can ignore the criterion of students' experience only at the peril of specifying dysfunctional learning activities. In instances where this disregard occurs, learners often are not even able to engage in the specified activity. Even when they *can*, however, the consequences are rarely a meaningful expansion of the learners' fund of experience. Like the verbal learning of content, meaningless activity results in little more than a mechanical adaptation to external requirements.

Several aspects of the criterion of students' experience as it applies to content selection and organization were discussed in Chapter 14. In the sections dealing with content and knowledge, logical versus psychological organization of content, and sequencing of content, the *primacy of meaning* was emphasized as the central issue in relating educational materials to students' development. The following discussions explore the ramifications of this principle as it applies in the specification of learning activities.

EXPERIENCE AS ABILITY. In most cases the specification of ineffective and dysfunctional learning activities does not result from disregard of the criterion of students' experience, but rather from overestimations of it in terms of students' ability. In other words, curriculum planners, because they tend to perceive learning tasks in terms of their own extensive experience, overlook or take for granted the many sophisticated competencies required by the activity. They assume (mistakenly) that the learners' young experience has provided them with the ability to engage successfully and meaningfully in the activities, and, unfortunately, attribute to indolence or perversity students' failure to perform successfully.

A good example of the situation described above is the assignment of "outside research papers." Even at the most advanced levels of the secondary curriculum, this activity usually is based on an inflated notion of what students' present state of attainment permits them to bring to the task. Production of a bona fide research paper requires a host of sophisticated and critical competencies ranging from problem formulation and critical analysis of data to rather high-level reading and composition skills. Because this activity is so far beyond the experience of most secondary school students (and even many college undergraduates!), the research product usually turns out to be little more than a disorganized blend of paraphrase and plagiarism. Thus, the activity of "outside research" in most cases results not only in little if any increment in the attainment of intended goals (e.g., skill in analysis, reflective thinking, organization of ideas, writing), but often in the development of adverse (unintended) dispositions and attitudes, such as diminished curiosity, apathy, cynicism, dishonesty, rebelliousness, etc.

The problems raised by the outside research activity cited above suggest that two sets of data need to be utilized by curriculum planners in designing ability-appropriate activities: (1) learners' present experience and (2) the thought-forms and skills needed to move them from their present condition toward desired, more sophisticated levels. For the research activity discussed above, one way of doing this might be a *class* research project on a question of current concern conducted under the guidance of the teacher. (Topics like "Student Rights and Responsibilities" are particularly useful because they are "real" issues, not manufactured ones for school purposes.) Problem formulation, data sources, data relevancy, related issues, and report organization, would all come under examination and discussion. "Professional" research reports, such as *The Report of the President's Commission on Campus Unrest* and the *Report of the National Advisory Commission on Civil Disorders* could be read and discussed in terms of *their* research procedures and reporting. Each student would have an opportunity to engage in many research activities and compare his findings and experiences with others in the class. Definitive procedures for conducting the inquiry would not be prescribed, but rather the productiveness of various methods would be explored and evaluated in terms of the project being conducted. Finally, the class would share in producing a research report that could be duplicated and distributed within the school or even the larger community. It should be noted that this activity is appropriate for *any* class of students at *any* stage of development, the *necessary changes having been made to adapt the activities and content to the learners' experience.*

Although not as often as it is *over*estimated, learners' ability is sometimes *under*estimated in designing activities. The repetition of certain exercises in grammar and punctuation throughout the junior and senior high school grades is an example of a *pro forma* activity that keeps students busy doing things that they are already able to do quite well. The consequences of boredom and distaste arising from *this* miscalculation, however, are generally not so destructive as the bewilderment, frustration, and failure that result from activities built on an overestimation of students' ability.

EXPERIENCE AS CULTURE. The life experience that learners bring to school with them has a culture-value dimension that is not always attuned to the culture-value system supported in the school. This cultural experience of learners has been a widely recognized "problem," but one that has little affected learning activities in most schools. Notwithstanding broad acceptance of the principle that "the curriculum should be adjusted to the child," culturally different children in most cases have found prescribed curriculum activities unyieldingly alien and have often suffered trauma in attempting to meet their demands. During the early decades of the twentieth century, for example, the children of many southern and eastern European immigrants experienced an "Americanization" process in schools that involved humiliating (and sometimes even brutal) learning activities. Today, the children of such cultural minorities as blacks, Chicanos, Indians, migrant farm workers, and the just plain poor often are forced to engage in learning activities that are not only irrelevant to their present experience, but sometimes even senseless and degrading. The following is a report of one such activity:

> *The students in a sixth-grade English class in a school on a Chippewa Indian reservation are all busily at work, writing a composition for Thanksgiving. The subject of the composition is written on the black-board for the students (and the visitor) to see. The subject: "Why We Are Happy the Pilgrims Came" (Silberman 1970, p. 173).*

Respecting the cultural differences of learners, however, does not mean abandoning the values of the curriculum. It does mean, especially at the beginning, translating the curriculum into activities which enable the learner to understand the new as it relates to his experience. "The more heterogeneous or deviate the background or the social learning of the students, the more important it is that there be a variety of bridges between what is now under-stood, the current concepts and meanings, and that which is to come" (Taba 1962, p. 283).

Thus, for ghetto children, restricted as they are within the confines of the neighborhood, the study of "geography" might begin with the project of map-ping the neighborhood and gaining some perspective as to its perimeter, nature, and relationship to the "outside." This could be followed by expeditions (prompted by the study of maps of the city) to many areas outside of the ghetto, where encounters with people, buildings, transportation, businesses, etc., could provide all manner of rich areas for comparison and contrast with the learners' ghetto experience. Ghetto (underground) publications could be read and compared with the city's mainstream daily. Discussions could follow, which would revolve around social values, poverty, racism, opportunity, educa-tion, and government. The aforementioned activities are only a few of a multi-tude that could be carried on; and they would not be carried on only for "school purposes." Activities such as these can generate vital meanings which connect with the learners' base experience, producing an expanded new experiential synthesis of concepts and values. Finally, but not the least important, it is these activities that translate the social heritage—its depravities as well as its triumphs—into experiences that are each student's own.

EXPERIENCE AS INTEREST. Learners' interests are in large measure the result of their experience, but in a certain sense interests also constitute a particular aspect of experience. We have already discussed interests rather extensively in Chapter 13 in relation to aims, goals, and objectives, and in Chapter 14 in rela-tion to content. In this section we shall elaborate on some of the basic principles treated in these two chapters with respect to their effect on the selection of learning activities.

It should be clear by now that the question is not whether interest as a component of learners' experience should or should not be a criterion for the selection of learning activities. Rather, the question is how interest functions in learning and how knowledge about learners' interests can be helpful in selecting learning activities that produce optimal educational results. "If learning is to proceed at all, the attention of the learner must be secured and his attention can be secured only through a direct or indirect appeal to his interests" (Counts 1926, p. 80).

Appeal to interest, however, does not necessarily mean, as many proponents as well as critics of the criterion have interpreted it, selecting learning activities according to learners' whims. A students' preoccupation with a new motor-scooter or a recent exciting holiday in Hawaii is no excuse for a unit of learning activities based on these immediate "interests." Interests merely reveal one aspect of the learners' present experiential status; they do not tell us the direction he should take in his educational development.

There is little danger, however, of today's curriculum activities being centered excessively on students' present interests. Rather, there seems to be considerable indication that students' interests are not given adequate consideration in the formulation of activities. Classroom activities based mainly on reading, writing, listening (to lectures), and occasionally discussion—without recourse to learners' present interests—have resulted in the mechanical performance of these tasks, boredom, and in some cases student unrest. Defense of these limited activities often is based on the argument that pandering to students' interests produces inconsequential results and that to be significant and effective, learning should be "hard," and even somewhat distasteful. Research in educational psychology, however, particularly in the areas of motivation, perception, and meaning, indicates that learning activity grounded in interest only *appears* to be easier, but in fact is more effective and significant, whether the activity involves the academically respectable reading of a classic or the less traditional survey of community attitudes toward the high school's dress code.

How, then, should interest be regarded in the selection of learning activities? Pedagogically, interests function as a bridge: "that which connects two things otherwise distant" (Dewey 1916, p. 149). At one point we have the learner at a present or initial stage of development and at the other, the learner at a future or more advanced stage in terms of curriculum goals. One of the important "means" by which the learner is moved toward the advanced stage is interest. Thus, activities, if they are to develop in the student the experiences and competencies hoped for, should *in themselves* be interesting to the learner. When they are not, intervening connections need to be made; that is, intervening activities, of interest to the learner at his present stage, are required to move him toward interest in those further activities that accomplish the hoped-for experiences.

How this theory of interests functions can be seen by taking an example from a hypothetical junior high school curriculum. Among other goals, this curriculum might propose that its preadolescent clients will develop interest and skill in reading and interpreting imaginative literature (e.g., narrative fiction), develop concern for moral values, practice critical assessment of their own values, etc. (Ultimately, these goals would translate into a sophisticated appreciation for mature literature and awareness of one's own value system.) At the same time it is known that preadolescent male students' experience has produced in them an intense interest in cars, drag racing, etc., as well as some distaste for reading, especially school reading. The judicious suggestion that these students might like reading such adolescent novels as Henry Gregor Felsen's *Crash Club* (Bantam Books, 1958), *Street Rod* (Bantam Books, 1953), or *Hot Rod* (Bantam Books, 1950) would capitalize on a genuine interest in cars, but at the same time involve them in reading well-written novels that deal seriously with many of the moral and value issues that concern adults as well as adolescents. It is important to emphasize that this technique does not suggest fixation on "car stories." Rather, the "car stories," because they contain elements that move learners in desired educational directions, *expand* interests so that the limited world of cars no longer occupies the central place in students' view of the world. Paradoxical as it may sound, it is usually through the pursuit of *interests* that interests are expanded. Thus, one student, "turned on" by Felsen's style, might request others of his works and be given *Letters to a Teen-Age Son* (Dodd, Mead & Co., 1962), a book that deals with serious adolescent problems. Another student, deeply affected by Galt's death in *Crash Club* and concerned about the issue of individual human responsibility for the death of others, might be introduced to a novel such as Walter van Tilburg Clark's *The Ox-Bow Incident* (Random House, 1940), which deals with the lynching of three innocent men. It should be noted that in both of these instances, students would be engaged in reading and in developing their reading competencies, as well as exploring important moral and value questions. At the same time, the reading activity responsible for moving them outward into expanded areas of interest, knowledge, and awareness would be "legitimate" since it was grounded in *their* genuine interest (cars). The activity, thus, is not contrived or artificial, and is easily distinguishable from certain curriculum practices which attempt to make school activities interesting by "seduction" or pandering to interests. As one example of pandering to students' interests, we might point to the utilization of car magazines. Reading automobile magazines will not promote movement toward the curriculum goals stated above, and except insofar as this activity might provide an intermediate bridge to other materials (e.g., the Felsen novels), it tends to limit possible growth opportunities for students by accentuating the centrality of cars in their view of things. To this extent the activity indulges students' present whimsy.

To sum up this section, then, interest—an important dimension of our experience—is integral to human activity. Its consideration in the design and selection of learning activities is unavoidable; yet, great care should be taken to prevent its exaggeration as the central determiner of curriculum activities. Writing more than fifty years ago, Dewey (1916, p. 149) put it this way: "The remedy is not in finding fault with the doctrine of interest, any more than it is to search for some pleasant bait that may be hitched to the alien material. It is to discover objects and modes of action, which are connected with present power."

The Organization of Learning Activities

Very little curriculum research or writing has dealt with the problem of the organization of learning activities.[6] This situation, in part, probably accounts for the fact that the organization of learning activities usually is based on tradition. For example, it is widely held that activities involving the parsing of sentences should properly precede those in which students write compositions. In the same vein, activities in which students are granted responsible freedom usually occur (if at all) only after many activities that involve precision in following directions. And, of course, activities of the English class are almost always kept separate and totally unrelated to those in history or in health. The "logic" inherent in these arrangements of activities is often at odds with what little empirical data exist, but tradition, nevertheless, usually prevails. Recommendations for reorganization, however, are often no more soundly based than the organizations they hope to supplant. Thus, many "innovations" mainly represent revolts against the tyranny of tradition rather than any carefully thought-out rationale.

How can we account for this lack of theory and research in such a critical area of curriculum construction? One reason almost certainly is the fact that the complex behaviors characteristic of educated individuals are not learned quickly or simply. Rather, they are acquired only gradually over long periods of time as a result of a large number of interrelated, conducive experiences. Thus, the large number of variables and their complex interrelationships over time make it virtually impossible to control research conditions to any significant degree. A good example of this gradual progression in significant learning (but by no means the most complex) is the ability to read critically. Starting in the early elementary grades, children learn to decode printed symbols and to pronounce printed words; as they progress through school, they move, given the appropriate learning activities, from a process that essentially consists of translation toward a much more sophisticated level of functioning that involves understanding shades of meaning, identifying central ideas, distinguishing data from conclusions, separating the descriptive from the emotive, sensing metaphor, and a host of others. Thus, "a major phase in building a curriculum is to work out an organization of the many, many learning experiences required so that the student develops these complex behavior patterns gradually, day by day, and relates them to others so as to have an increasingly unified understanding of essential knowledge and a well-integrated command of essential skills" (Tyler 1957, p. 371). In view of the complexities noted above, it is hardly surprising that the organization of learning activities has not been the subject of much research.

6. Perhaps the most notable exception to this generalization occurs in the field of reading. Here, substantial research into vocabulary, sentence structure, speech patterns, child development, etc., has resulted in the production of several commercial programs which prescribe a carefully controlled, graduated sequence of reading activities.

VERTICAL AND HORIZONTAL ORGANIZATION

Primitive as our knowledge is with respect to a theoretical rationale for the organization of learning activities, a few basic principles have emerged. One of these, as was the case with content, is that learning activities may be thought of in their vertical or horizontal organization.[7] The *vertical* organization refers to the sequencing of learning activities as students progress through the curriculum. Thus, as we discussed the example in a previous section, a guided class research activity might logically precede an outside independent research activity. The *horizontal* organization of learning activities refers to the relationship of activities carried on at a particular level of the curriculum. For example, activities involving a survey of community attitudes toward blacks for a Problems of Democracy course might be designed to coincide with the writing of short stories, essays, and poems on prejudice for an English class. The rationale for this concurrent organization of "social studies" and "English" activities might be the promotion, examination, and expression of students' affective responses to a particular social issue and its impact on their community. Coordination of the vertical and horizontal organizations is necessary if learners' educational experiences are to provide them with a unified and integrated world view.

CRITERIA FOR THE ORGANIZATION OF
LEARNING ACTIVITIES

Tyler (1950) identifies three basic criteria for the organization of learning activities: continuity, sequence, and integration. In the absence of substantive research to the contrary, these criteria have come to be widely accepted as rule-of-thumb standards for deciding on the organization of curriculum activities.

CONTINUITY. "Continuity refers to the vertical reiteration of major curriculum elements" (Tyler 1950, p. 55). Thus, if inductive reasoning skills are important as an objective, learning activities throughout the curriculum would be designed in such a way that the students have repeated and continuing opportunities to practice this activity.

SEQUENCE. Sequence is similar to continuity as a criterion, but goes beyond it. Sequence demands not only that the activity reiterate, but that it progress from the simpler to the more complex. Reading activities, for example, are organized in such a way that students must deal with increasingly more complex vocabulary and sentence structure as they proceed through the curriculum, at the same time that they continue to practice and improve on previously acquired word pronunciation skills and speed. At even more advanced levels students may be engaged in activities that require them to interpret and to critique, as well as

---

7. See the section "Problems of Scope and Sequence" in Chapter 18 for an extended discussion of vertical and horizontal organization in curriculum design.

to translate the printed page into spoken language. The criterion of sequence often appears in the literature under the nomenclature "cumulative learning" (e.g., see Taba 1962, p. 296 ff.).

It should be pointed out that appropriate sequence in learning activities often can be achieved without changing the content. A simple example of this principle is *Alice in Wonderland,* content which can be dealt with either on the nursery-tale level in elementary school or as a complex literary work on the college level. In the same manner, the concept of "interdependence" can take on increasingly sophisticated meaning for learners as they engage in increasingly mature learning activities (Taba 1962, p. 296). At an early age children acquire a simple notion of this concept through such family-centered activities as buying food at the market or watching the television repairman fix the family's set. At the high school level, through course work, extracurricular activities, part-time jobs, social interactions, etc., the concept is broadened and deepened to include political, social, economic, and even psychological interdependence from the personal through the international levels. "With each return engagement, the difficulty of the 'content' of the concept, the level of abstraction, and the complexity and precision required in using it are increased progressively" (Taba 1962, p. 296).

INTEGRATION. Tyler's third criterion addresses itself to the the horizontal relationship of curriculum activities. The intent here is for curriculum activities at any given point in the sequence to be related in such a way as to provide a unified and integrated experience for the learner. For example, activities in a biology class might relate to social studies activities involving a problem in water pollution. Or activities involving the solution of geometry problems might be integrated with map-making activities in a geography class. Ultimately, however, the success or failure of the integration of activities depends on· what happens to the learner. And this may very well mean that we will have to shift our emphasis away from relating concurrent activities, each of which is characteristic of an established subject, to totally novel learning activities that transcend subjects and are integrative in and of themselves. What this means in terms of concrete curriculum practice is hard to imagine, for while it is unfortunate, it is nevertheless true that for all of the inquiry and research that has taken place over the past fifty years, we still know relatively little about the dynamics, design, and management of effective learning activities.

References

Bruner, Jerome. 1963. *The Process of Education.* Cambridge, Mass.: Harvard University Press.

Combs, Arthur. 1966. "Today's Adolescent: His Learning." Address presented at the convention of the National Association for Core Curriculum, University of Florida, Gainesville.

Counts, George S. 1926. "Some Notes on the Foundations of Curriculum Making." In *The Foundations and Technique of Curriculum-Construction*, edited by Guy M. Whipple. Twenty-sixth Yearbook of The National Society for the Study of Education, Part II. Bloomington, Ill.: Public School Publishing Company.

Dewey, John. 1916. *Democracy and Education*. New York: The Macmillan Company.

————. 1922. *Human Nature and Conduct*. Modern Library Edition. New York: Random House. Reprinted 1950, 1957.

Herskowitz, Herbert. 1972. "Paperbacks in the Social Studies: Beyond the Textbooks with Paperbacks." In *The Paperback Goes to School*, edited by Dominic Salvatore. New York: Bureau of Independent Publishers and Distributors.

Mayhew, Katherine C., and Anna C. Edwards. 1936. *The Dewey School: The Laboratory School of the University of Chicago, 1896–1903*. New York: Appleton-Century-Crofts.

Silberman, Charles E. 1970. *Crisis in the Classroom*. New York: Random House.

Special Committee of the New England History Teachers' Association. 1901, 1904. *A History Syllabus for Secondary Schools*. Boston: D. C. Heath & Company.

Taba, Hilda. 1962. *Curriculum Development: Theory and Practice*. New York: Harcourt Brace Jovanovich.

Tyler, Ralph W. 1950. *Basic Principles of Curriculum and Instruction*. Chicago: University of Chicago Press.

————. 1957. "The Curriculum—Then and Now." *The Elementary School Journal* (April), pp. 364–374.

CHAPTER 16
EVALUATION

'Tis with our judgments as our watches, none
Go just alike, yet each believes his own.

—ALEXANDER POPE

Evaluation, the fourth component of the curriculum, is probably the most narrowly viewed aspect of the educational enterprise. In most curriculum books that deal with the topic, it is almost always treated exclusively in terms of the evaluation of student achievement, often in connection with assigning "grades" or "marks." Even in a comprehensive text, which accords curriculum evaluation far broader scope than most treatments of curriculum, the focus of evaluation is principally on "the degree to which pupils attain . . . objectives" (Taba 1962, p. 312).

Of course, there is substantial truth in the claim that "the proof of the pudding is in the product." But while the evaluation of student achievement (product evaluation) certainly constitutes an important *part* of curriculum evaluation, it by no means approaches what may generally be conceived of as comprehensive curriculum evaluation. (A comprehensive evaluation, for example, would also emphasize such considerations as the correspondence between stated objectives and curriculum content and even an evaluation of the objectives themselves.) Preponderant reliance on product evaluation is appropriate mainly in situations which involve training and the technical model of curriculum development.[1]

Product Evaluation: The Technical Model

What passes for curriculum evaluation today is almost always "product evaluation" centered on the student and based on the technical model of curriculum

---

1. See the section "Training: the Technical Model" in Chapter 13.

development. It will be recalled that in the technical model, learners, viewed as "raw material," are subjected to certain curricular and instructional treatments in order to produce a "finished product" that meets predetermined objectives. Since judgments of curriculum effectiveness are based almost entirely upon an assessment of the degree to which curriculum objectives are attained by learners, "curriculum evaluation" based on this model in fact turns out to be little more than an estimation of goal achievement. The fallacy inherent in this narrow concept of evaluation is pointed up in the following example: "An American History curriculum, K–14, which consisted in the memorization of names and dates would be absurd—it could not possibly be said to be a good curriculum, no matter how well it attained its goals" (Scriven 1967, p. 52).

Narrow and inadequate though it may be as the *sole* basis for comprehensive curriculum evaluation, however, product evaluation provides important data for comprehensive curriculum evaluation. Clearly, one criterion by which curriculum effectiveness is legitimately judged is its "payoff"—that is, the quality of the "product" that it turns out. For this reason, the process, which is in fact a highly complex one, merits careful study by curriculum planners. In the following sections we shall discuss some of the more prominent aspects of product evaluation.

MEASUREMENT AND EVALUATION DISTINGUISHED

Judgments regarding the degree to which learners have achieved curriculum objectives will be most valid if they are based on empirical evidence. This empirical evidence often takes the form of educational measurement, defined as "the process that attempts to obtain a quantified representation of the degree to which a pupil reflects a trait" (Ahmann and Glock 1967, p. 11). Measurement data are basically descriptive in nature and usually are expressed in numerical terms in order to avoid the value connotations that are connected with words. Thus, an individual's height and weight, recorded at seventy-two inches and ninety-seven pounds, simply provides measurement data without implying that the individual is short or tall, light or heavy.

Evaluation, in contrast to measurement, constitutes a value judgment. For example, we may offer the evaluation—i.e., the judgment—that an individual is "underweight for his height" and support the evaluation with the measurement data reported in the previous paragraph. Of course, in order to make the evaluation "stick," it will be necessary to demonstrate that most people who are seventy-two inches tall weigh more than ninety-seven pounds (or that most ninety-seven-pound people are shorter than seventy-two inches). Even the simple example illustrated above suggests that good evaluations, generally, are based on a great deal of information derived from many sources.

It should be clear from this discussion that while "measurement" and "evaluation" are distinct in meaning, they are decidedly related terms. Measurement comprises a substantial part of the more inclusive process of evaluation.

TESTS

The most common resource for measurement data in schools is paper-and-pencil tests. Thus, tests provide the bulk of the data on which product evaluations usually are made. A test is ordinarily defined as a group of questions or tasks to which learners are asked to respond—orally, in writing, or sometimes even in pantomime. It is presumed to consist of "a representative sample of all possible questions and tasks related to the trait measured by the test . . ." (Ahmann and Glock 1967, p. 14). But measurement need not always involve testing (e.g., teachers' responses on checklists and rating scales related to learner achievement can also constitute measurement data); and evaluations need not even be based on tests at all. Tests constitute a particular kind of measurement that can provide useful data for curriculum and learner evaluation, but when they are overemphasized, they can distort curriculum evaluation and even unintentionally influence curriculum goals and outcomes (e.g., "test anxiety" might inhibit the attainment of a "creativity" goal).

INDIRECT NATURE OF MEASUREMENT

The discussion of behavioral objectives in Chapter 13 pointed up the significance of operationalism in the process of empirically determining the degree to which curriculum objectives had been achieved. Many of the same issues of operationalism underlie the process of measurement.

When we measure the length of a piece of paper or a board to be cut, the element being measured is clear, observable, "obviously present and measurable" (Ahmann and Glock 1967, p. 21). The process is one of direct measurement. But when we utilize a test to measure some psychological trait—such an anxiety, self-concept, creativity, intelligence, or history achievement—we are *inferring* the presence of the trait from observable responses to the measuring instrument. In other words, we are inferring the presence of the trait from what we assume to be the *effects* of the trait.

The rationale used in constructing measuring instruments is quite nicely illustrated by the procedures to which we all subscribe in judging the "intelligence" of friends and acquaintances. For example, if asked to justify our opinion that a friend is "highly intelligent," we may point out that he holds a master's degree, that his income is above average, that he "catches on quickly" to difficult riddles, that he is a fascinating conversationalist, and that he reads profound philosophical treatises. In principle, we have "measured" our friend's intelligence by counting up a significant number of observable behaviors and achievements which we consider to represent the effects of intelligence. On a more formal basis, this is the very same procedure employed by psychologists wishing to construct a measuring instrument for general intelligence. Starting with an analysis of the concept "general intelligence" they would go on to identify a number of second-order constructs such as are represented in Figure 16-1.

FIGURE 16-1
Measuring the intangible construct "intelligence."

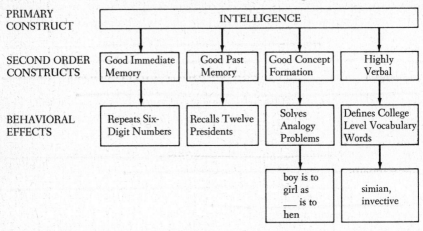

These second-order constructs would then be translated into observable behaviors. Thus, as we do, the psychologists infer the presence of intelligence from the manifestation of behaviors that are taken to represent the effects of intelligence. Of course, the example presented in Figure 16-1 is grossly oversimplified; but it places into sharp profile one of the basic questions raised by the indirect nature of measurement: Are the specified behaviors, and *only* the specified behaviors, the effects of the hypothesized construct? The answer, of course, must depend on one's definition of the construct; and the only possible conclusion is that the construct being measured is defined by the test that measures it. This notion that, in effect, "IQ is whatever the IQ test measures" is borne out by research with intelligence tests. It has been found that two of the most highly developed and reliable individual IQ tests (the Stanford-Binet and the Wechsler Intelligence Scale for Children [WISC]) correlate only .60 to .80 (Ahmann and Glock 1967, p. 380). These statistics indicate that the two tests indeed define "intelligence" in significantly different ways and so are measuring different (although apparently overlapping) constructs.

The implications of this problem of indirect measurement are significant for curriculum evaluators. In the first place, it seems clearly imperative that curriculum workers know not only what *construct* a test is measuring, but what *effects* are being taken as evidence of the construct's presence. Clearly the behaviors represented in Figure 16-1 are an inadequate index of any sophisticated conception of intelligence. Correspondingly, an inspection of the behaviors demanded by most achievement tests (both standardized and informal) raises serious questions with respect to the inferences that can legitimately be drawn about student "achievement" in the areas being tested. Additionally, the fact that all psychological traits are inferred from behavior should place anyone using this measurement data on warning that the process is so highly complex that measurement data can rarely be relied on to provide definitive answers to the questions posed by evaluation. "All too frequently, the crudeness of the information produced by measuring procedures prevents us from even ranking pupils" (Ahmann and Glock 1967, p. 26). This does not mean that psychological measurement ought to be abandoned; it does mean that extreme caution and prudence need to be exercized in drawing inferences from measurement data.

STANDARDS FOR PRODUCT EVALUATION

Given a sufficient quantity and wide variety of data on which to base student evaluations, what standards should be used to judge relative success or failure? Basically, there exist four standards for evaluation:[2] the absolute maximum standard, the absolute minimum standard, the relative standard, and the multiple standard.

THE ABSOLUTE MAXIMUM STANDARD. An absolute standard is an arbitrarily set level of achievement against which all students are evaluated. It may be set either at a *maximum* or *minimum* level. At the *maximum* level, the standard is out of reach of all but the most able students. The percentage system of evaluation prevalent in most public schools is an example of the absolute maximum standard: 90 to 100 percent "correct" responses to curriculum tasks represents an "excellent" level of achievement. All students theoretically can achieve this fixed level, but rarely do more than a very few reach it. On the other hand, all may theoretically "fail" by achieving less than the 70 percent correct responses that represents the customary fixed level for "passing." Sometimes the majority of the class actually does fall below this level. If the absolute maximum standard is taken seriously, actual student achievement does not call into question the legitimacy of the standard. If all fail, the student raw material is judged to be inferior; if many achieve high evaluations, the students are viewed as high-quality raw material. (In actuality, however, the "absolute" standard often is "adjusted" to bring about a "reasonable" distribution of achievement levels.) The maximum absolute standard is most appropriate to product evaluation within the framework of the technical model of curriculum.

THE ABSOLUTE MINIMUM STANDARD. The minimum level of the absolute standard usually is set at a point that ensures success for virtually all students in the program. Students who do not achieve mastery of curriculum objectives at the minimum level are retaught until the standard is met. A curriculum is not judged to be effective unless all students achieve *all* the objectives that have been prescribed for them. When the minimum standard is exclusively employed as the evaluation criterion, the problem of "grading" or sorting of students is eliminated. As the exclusive criterion of evaluation, the minimum absolute standard is most appropriate in the training paradigm. Indeed, the minimum absolute standard is advocated very strongly by many proponents of behavioral

2. I am indebted to Kenneth H. Hoover (1968, pp. 553–555) for the basic schema used to classify evaluation standards.

objectives under the nomenclature of "performance standards" or "learning for mastery" (e.g., see Bloom, Hastings, and Madaus 1971, pp. 5–57).

Sometimes the minimum standard is used as a mastery base which ensures a "passing" grade for students, but which many students may go beyond in order to achieve "higher grades." Depending upon the standards used to determine the "higher grades" the total product evaluation may be useful in either the technical or humanistic model.

THE RELATIVE STANDARD. The relative standard is most familiar in connection with "scaling grades" on the "normal curve." This standard of product evaluation judges each student against the relative performance of the group. Thus, the group's mean performance (in conjunction with the standard deviation) operates as a kind of sliding scale against which individual achievement is judged. Unlike the absolute standard, it is highly competitive, since high achievement in this relative situation consistently demands achievement higher than that of most others in the class. Often, competitive pressure builds to the point of getting in the way of learning or, more significantly, of producing learning outcomes that are unintended and undesirable (e.g., the attitude that *any* measures that enable one to "beat the competition" are acceptable).

Another problem associated with the relative standard of evaluation is that it assumes that all competitors are essentially equal in the ability to succeed, i.e., that every person in the class has the potential for being top scorer in the competition. The assumption, of course, is false. Some individuals have more ability in math, some in language subjects. Some students have reading difficulties, others lack prerequisite skills. Thus, the contest is "stacked" so to speak so that it is reduced to competition only among the most able few. The result for the less able usually is discouraging and demoralizing. Indeed, many just quit, so that the evaluation of these students represents a rejection of achievement rather than lack of it. (Ironically, their rejection of the contest makes the bona fide competitors look even better than they would if the less able in fact competed.) The conclusion, of course, is simply that a competitive situation is good (and valid) only for those who really believe they have a chance to win.

A relative standard for product evaluation, however, has certain advantages in terms of feedback for guidance in curriculum revision. For example, the relative standard provides us with a normative base line that can serve as a guide with respect to reasonable expectations for student achievement. To illustrate: when the mean measurements taken for a science curriculum project consistently fall below the 30 percent level for correct answers, the greater probability is that one or more components of the curriculum (or instruction) is drastically dysfunctional, rather than that the students are very weak. Perhaps the objectives are far too ambitious; perhaps the content is inappropriate; perhaps the learning activities are badly sequenced; or perhaps the measurement instruments are faulty. In any case, the relative standard has provided the kind of data that direct us to "check up" on the curriculum—to reexamine and revise the curriculum plan. But for the time being, at least, students are not penalized with the low grades they might have received under an absolute standard. Individual levels of achievement are adjusted to the relative performance of the group.

THE MULTIPLE STANDARD. The fourth standard for product evaluation, the multiple standard, consists of the growth that each student undergoes from the inception of instruction to the point of evaluation. Figure 16-2 shows graphically how this evaluation standard operates. While student A's final achievement after instruction is 2 units more advanced than student B's (9 compared with 7), A began instruction at a point that was 4 units in advance of B (6 compared with 2). Thus, the bars representing each student show that B's actual growth is 2 units greater than A's (a growth of 5 units for B compared with only 3 units for A). Strictly speaking, then, under the multiple standard of evaluation, B's achievement would be rated higher than A's.

Although the multiple standard is the most "individualized" and therefore the "fairest" standard to use, there are many problems associated with its use. The measurement of clearly defined, operationally stated objectives *after instruction* is a difficult task. To attempt to measure a variety of traits at the inception of instruction for the purpose of determining each student's general stage of development is virtually impossible. Then, too, "units of achievement" rarely proceed at equivalent intervals; i.e., the degree of growth between units 3 and 4, for example, cannot be assumed to be equivalent to the degree of growth between units 6 and 7. Finally, the extensive use of the multiple standard is highly impractical when one thinks about the large numbers of students to be evaluated. For a teacher having responsibility for five classes of thirty-five to forty students there is little opportunity to implement the procedure.

Implementation of the multiple standard of product evaluation, however, *is* feasible in a highly restricted training situation, but it is usually not well suited in principle to the purposes of the technical model. For example, the preassessment of a learner's stage of development in reading a foreign language can be done in a fairly precise manner; but for training purposes, a postinstructional evaluation based on a minimum absolute standard or a relative standard would be more appropriate. We should note, however, that a foreign language curriculum built on the humanistic model might very well employ the multiple standard.

One final note on the human dimension in product evaluation is appropriate.

FIGURE 16-2
The Multiple standard of evaluation.

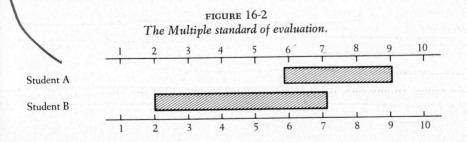

To the extent that human relationships are taken into account in the development and implementation of curriculum, they supplement, enrich, and sometimes even transcend evaluations based on precise, recordable data. Broad new insights; a revised *Weltansicht*; or feelings of warmth or excitement about a teacher, another student, or a new idea may represent a far more significant learning outcome than all those represented by the data amassed through conventional instruments.

The point is illustrated in the story of Andy and Bill, two sixth-grade boys. They had completed a current events lesson in which one of the facts learned was that seventy-six American soldiers had been killed in Viet Nam the previous week. The evaluation of the lesson was a quiz, and one of the questions was: "How many American soldiers were killed in Viet Nam last week?" Both boys answered "seventy-six" and were given full credit for the "correct answer."

The information that seventy-six American soldiers had been killed was school data for Bill. He might forget it the next day, or he might always remember it; but at least for now it was only a statistic. But eight weeks before this school lesson Andy and his family had received word that his older brother Ken had been killed in Viet Nam, and only four weeks before, Ken's body had arrived home. The news of his brother's death and the funeral constituted an emotionally significant experience for Andy. Because of it, the information that seventy-six young men "like Ken" were now dead had a terrific impact on him. Recalling Ken and the relationship he had had with him—playing catch, going for rides, building shelves for his room, talking about sports and school and even politics—Andy was overwhelmed by the enormity of seventy-six dead Kens and of the holocaustic meaning of mass killing and war. Questions began to flood into his brain: What happens to a person when he dies? What happens to all those dead people? What does it mean to be alive? Why are we here, living in this world? Why do wars start?

The evaluation of the kind of powerful incipient learning suggested by the above questions does not ordinarily occur through the vehicle of conventional evaluation instruments because the kinds of data it requires are not available from these sources. The information necessary for assessing many of the most important curriculum outcomes of liberal education resides in the human relationships developed during the course of curriculum implementation. Given a conducive relationship between teacher and learners, unexpected questions, feelings, and ideas are channeled back to the teacher as a consequence of interactions. Such data serve as an invaluable guide in the revision and evolution of the curriculum. It is in informal situations involving sensitivity to the messages inhering in human interaction that the multiple standard of evaluation is by far the most appropriate.

Which of the four standards of evaluation is best? The question is probably an inappropriate one. While the absolute maximum standard is probably not defensible in any situation, conditions usually call for some combination of the other three. Evaluations which utilize a variety of standards tend to reflect most accurately the multidimensional richness of human learning.

EVALUATION VERSUS GRADING

Before concluding this section on product evaluation, a few words regarding the distinction between evaluation and "grading" are in order. Grading, whether by letter, number, or other symbolic representation, is a kind of shorthand system for recording and reporting the evaluation of individual student achievement. Grading (the shorthand record-keeping system) is convenient to the degree that mass education involves keeping achievement records and periodically communicating educational progress for large numbers of students. But while certain inferences may be drawn from grades, grades do not constitute, and should not be confused with, evaluation. Product evaluation—the evaluation of student learning—is far too complex an enterprise to be reduced to a single symbol. An effective evaluation that would constitute a comprehensive representation of a student's educational progress would include, among other factors, measurement and other relevant data; an analysis of the student's interests, capabilities, and achievement; and conclusions based explicitly on appropriate combinations of minimum, relative, and multiple standards.

But while a system of grading does not constitute an evaluation, it nevertheless influences (sometimes significantly) curriculum outcomes. For example, the "ABCDF" system has been criticized for increasing student anxiety because of its built-in threat of failure. In addition, it has been said to be punitive and to have discouraging effects because it continues to reduce the student's grade-point average long after he has "caught on" and is doing creditable academic work. One alternative to this traditional way of grading is the ABC no-entry system, which removes the threatening and punitive aspects of failure by simply "not counting" course work that is not satisfactorily completed. The proponents of this system claim interest only in degrees of successful performance (ABC), not in degrees of inadequate performance (DF).

Another "innovation" in grading is the "pass-fail" system, which simply reduces the five-point (ABCDF) scale to a two-point (P-F) scale. It is said of the P-F system, however, that it is just as anxiety producing and punitive as the ABCDF system, but it is worse because it encourages mediocrity by not recognizing and rewarding excellent performance.

The problems of grading have been responded to in a variety of ways, including the call to "abolish grades." But recent calls by school reformers to abolish grades have not seemed to take into account the distinction between *grading* and *evaluation* made in the previous paragraphs. To abolish evaluation would be unthinkable, if not impossible. Even if we could operate without making judgments about the value of what we were doing in curriculum, it is doubtful that intelligence would permit such a course. With respect to our present systems of grading, however, abolition might be a real possibility. The reason is that the systems not only fail to communicate student evaluations reasonably clearly, but their side effects are punitive, threatening, discouraging, and in a general sense antithetical to much of what we are trying to achieve in education. (See "Goals and Roles of Evaluation" in the following section for an extended treatment of this issue.) In view of these conditions, it would seem that we ought to be able (1) to devise better record-keeping systems than we have, and (2) to interpret these shorthand systems far more intelligently than we do. Thus, curriculum planners should be urged to experiment on a broad scale with shorthand systems that would serve the recording and reporting requirements of mass education and at the same time avoid the adverse effects on curriculum outcomes that are so prevalent in present procedures.

Comprehensive Curriculum Evaluation

Comprehensive curriculum evaluation is an enormously complex undertaking that defies attempts to codify the process either in terms of sequence or components. The reason for this distressing state of affairs is that comprehensive curriculum evaluation involves not only the assessment of a written document (the "inert curriculum" or curriculum plan) but more important, of the implemented curriculum as a functional corpus of phenomena involving the interaction of students, teachers, materials, and environments. To make matters worse, most of the significant aspects of the implemented curriculum have to do with intangibles, such as thought processes, attitudes, meanings, relationships, feelings, etc., which can only be inferred from tangible behaviors that we assume (sometimes mistakenly) to be the effects of the constructs in which we are most interested. Furthermore, the implemented curriculum can only be assessed in terms to a large degree controlled by the instructional medium through which it is executed or made operative. This condition injects into the evaluation process a whole new series of variables which must be taken into account.

Other difficulties arise when we consider that the "inert curriculum," i.e., the document which constitutes the total curriculum plan, often does not even exist. Most often, an established curriculum is already operative in the school setting and the curriculum staff is challenged to change the old for some new plan. But the new curriculum plan as a finished document usually exists only hazily in the minds of the curriculum staff, and pilot implementation begins (as it should) with just a portion of each of the four curriculum components formulated and intact. Evaluation of this embryonic plan *and* its preliminary implementation, then, proceeds in tandem fashion, the feedback alternately provided by each aspect contributing data useful in further development of both the inert and functional curricula. Thus, while it is sometimes convenient to think of the curriculum plan as a full-blown document ready to be implemented afresh in a virgin school setting, reality rarely permits such an ideal situation. Even where the "old" curriculum might exist complete in document form, it usually is obsolescent and therefore largely irrelevant to much of the curriculum operative in the school.

The above paragraphs suggest just some of the many practical operational difficulties associated with comprehensive curriculum evaluation. But as a matter of principle, it should also be clear that, because curriculum evaluation is a component of the total curriculum, its design and procedures will be significantly affected (as is the total curriculum design) by such foundational factors as philosophy, cultural analysis, conceptions of the nature of man, and other values. Hence, the design for a comprehensive curriculum evaluation cannot be legislated abstractly and no single "method of evaluation" can be proposed as an appropriate instrument for the evaluation of all curricula. In short, the nature of the curriculum evaluation will be substantially determined by the intent and design of the curriculum to be evaluated.

In spite of this limitation on the preplanning of a standard procedure for curriculum evaluation, certain recurring principles and issues in evaluation can be cited that will provide guidance to planners as they design the evaluation component for a specific curriculum plan. The following sections briefly explore some of the most significant issues connected with comprehensive curriculum evaluation.

GOALS AND ROLES OF EVALUATION

Clarity about the function of evaluation in curriculum is essential if the evaluation is to contribute what it should to the implemented curriculum. Scriven (1967, pp. 40–43) draws the distinction between the *goals* of evaluation and the *roles* of evaluation. The principal goal of evaluation is the determination of how well a curriculum performs when measured against certain criteria or when compared with another curriculum. Arriving at this overall determination, of course, implies a number of more specific subgoals. But the ultimate purpose of evaluation is essentially the same, whether we are trying to evaluate "coffee machines or teaching machines, plans for a house or plans for a curriculum" (Scriven 1967, p. 40).

The *roles* of evaluation as it operates in a particular sociological or curricular context, however, can (and probably should) vary enormously. Depending upon how the evaluation is designed and executed, it can perform differentially (play a variety of roles) in the curriculum development process, in the execution and implementation of curriculum, or even in the political/economic arena, where many important curriculum decisions are ultimately made. The particular role played by evaluation, of course, will have important effects on the curricular end product. It is the wide variety of roles that curriculum evaluation can play that makes it difficult to prescribe in advance a generalized sequence of procedures for curriculum evaluation.[3]

3. Scriven (1967, p. 40) proposes a generalized evaluation methodology: "The evaluation activity consists simply in the gathering and combining of performance data with a weighted set of goal scales to yield either comparative or numerical ratings, and in the justification of (a) the data-gathering instruments, (b) the weightings, and (c) the selection of goals." The latitude allowed for by the conceptual breadth of this generalized methodological sequence provides little specific guidance in particular curriculum evaluation situations.

The variety of roles that evaluation can play is illustrated simply and concretely by observing its operation in any school situation. Evaluation plays a motivational role for some students; for others it plays a threatening and coercive role. From the teacher's point of view, evaluation often operates as a lever or a control device; and from the school's point of view, it performs as an instrument for sorting and classifying students into "homogeneous" groups. It should be noted that *none* of these roles is inherent in the *goals* of evaluation, nor is any of them necessarily a consequence of evaluation: the roles are dependent upon how evaluation is executed and used in a particular curriculum setting.

We can now see that arguments for the abolition of evaluation (or grades) are based mainly on what turns out to be inappropriate roles assigned to evaluation. Inappropriate roles, however, are not always (or even usually) a matter of conscious intent. They may emerge as a result of accident or as a matter of unconscious value orientation. As a result, planners need to be aware of the roles that their evaluation procedures assume as the development of curriculum proceeds.

Of course, curriculum evaluation can and should play a variety of appropriate and productive roles even as it moves toward its principal *goal* of assessment of curriculum quality. One such role (connected with the process of curriculum development) might be ongoing improvement of the curriculum (and instruction). But if the evaluation component, as designed and administered, for some reason operates as an anxiety-producing agent among the teachers who are implementing the curriculum, the actual role of evaluation may turn out to be exactly the reverse of what was intended. Again, sensitivity to the roles of evaluation has to be a continuing concern of curriculum workers.

One final note is necessary with respect to the relative emphasis that should be accorded evaluation goals as opposed to evaluation roles. Excessive concern about evaluation roles has often resulted in the dilution of evaluation "to the point where it can no longer serve as a basis for . . . the estimation of merit, worth, value, etc. . . ." (Scriven 1967, pp. 41, 42). For example, when the goals of content evaluation in a sex education program (i.e., the scrupulous determination of the merit of the content) are blunted because a favorable verdict on highly controversial content would play an antagonistic role in the school's community public relations program, then evaluation has failed to function properly in the curriculum development process. While it is certainly prudent to take political considerations into account in the *implementation* of curriculum, educational criteria ought to predominate as the basis for essentially *curriculum* decisions, such as those concerning the relative merit of content. Certainly, the realities of the school setting often make it necessary to be content with "half a loaf," but politics, economics, and other factors by no means require the dilution of evaluation goals to the extent that we delude ourselves into thinking that half a loaf is a whole one. Such predetermined closure in the curriculum development process is self-defeating because it often turns out to be nothing more than a self-fulfilling prophesy.

The goals of evaluation, then, need to be kept clearly in view, but in the

Deweyan "ends-in-view" sense. The *roles* of curriculum evaluation, because they constitute *other consequences* of evaluation design and execution, are important factors whose impact should be influential in the development of the evaluation component of the curriculum.

SUMMATIVE AND FORMATIVE EVALUATION

The principal distinctions between summative and formative evaluation have to do mainly with (1) purposes, (2) time, and (3) level of generalization (Bloom, Hastings, and Madaus 1971, p. 61). Since these characteristics are relative rather than absolute, the definitions of summative and formative evaluation should be taken in a relative sense.

Summative evaluation, as its name implies, is conducted in order to obtain a comprehensive assessment of the quality of a completed curriculum. Thus, summative evaluation ordinarily takes place at the completion of the curriculum development process and provides a terminal judgment on the completed product in overall, general terms.

Formative evaluation, by contrast, while providing assessments of curriculum quality, is conducted during the curriculum development process for the additional purpose of providing data that can be used to "form" a better finished product. Thus, formative evaluation takes place at a number of intermediate points during the development of a curriculum and in connection with relatively more specific aspects of it. We might say of both summative and formative evaluation that their *roles* in curriculum development are a major consideration in their use.

From the definitions of these two terms, it is obvious that they do not represent radically new concepts in evaluation. What constitutes summative evaluation has appeared under the label of "terminal," "outcome," and "product" evaluation; and the principles of formative evaluation have been discussed under such labels as "continuous" or "ongoing" evaluation. Nevertheless, the distinction is an important one, and one that is especially valuable in curriculum construction.

It seems clear that for curriculum development purposes, formative evaluation is a far more useful tool than is summative evaluation, although both types are necessary. The problem with summative evaluation is that once a curriculum has been established in a relatively completed form, everyone connected with it resists anything that suggests the necessity for major changes. On the other hand, because curriculum is an evolutionary phenomenon, formative evaluation is a uniquely well-suited instrument in the guidance of its evolution. Its particular strength is that it encourages a Deweyan ends-means position with respect to goal reassessment and the examination of unintended outcomes. In short, formative evaluation, as feedback and guide, operates to keep the curriculum development process "open."

One final note on the utilization of summative evaluation is in order. Summative evaluation should not be perceived exclusively as a one-time only procedure which always occurs "at the end." Comprehensive summative evaluations can (and probably should) occur at certain infrequent but strategic points during the curriculum development process. Such intercessions provide an opportunity to step away from the flow of curriculum development activity and assess *in toto* the emerging curriculum product. It is sometimes valuable at these times to bring in outside evaluators in order to gain a fresh perspective on the entire project.

GOAL EVALUATION

Curricula that provide for evaluation of the degree to which stated aims, goals, and objectives are attained are abundant; those, however, that also include procedures for the evaluation of the goals themselves are conspicuous by their rarity. This condition is astonishing since it seems very clear that those responsible for school curricula should certainly be held accountable for the outcomes that they say their curricula should produce. The conclusion seems unavoidable, then, that evaluation of the merit of curriculum aims, goals, and objectives themselves should constitute a significant part of the evaluation component.

A number of issues connected with the evaluation of aims, goals, and objectives were discussed in Chapter 13. For example, the section on "The Problem of Ends and Means" dealt with the philosophical framework in which purposes should be considered and the section on "Sources of Aims, Goals, and Objectives" discussed certain criteria against which the value of curriculum purposes might be assessed. These considerations will be very helpful in reevaluating curriculum purposes as the process of curriculum development evolves. Other considerations that should come into play as the curriculum plan is tested in school situations can be briefly noted here.

PHILOSOPHICAL ASSUMPTIONS. Questions such as the following should recurringly arise in the evaluation of curriculum purposes: What assumptions are being made when a particular purpose is singled out as a desirable curriculum outcome? Are the reasons given the "real" reasons, or simply "good" reasons? Curriculum purposes should be continually reassessed in the light of an ongoing inquiry into the basic philosophical commitments of the people responsible for curriculum construction.

SOCIAL/CULTURAL ANALYSIS. Inquiry in this foundational area is basic to both goal formulation and goal assessment. Because cultures are evolving continually and because perceptions of the culture's value orientations are themselves in an evolutionary state, an active dialectic between curriculum aims, goals, and objectives and cultural analysis is necessary throughout the development of the curriculum. To avoid the limiting effects of cultural encapsulation, sociological and cultural analysis should be conducted in the light of an ongoing inquiry into philosophical assumptions.

THE EDUCATED PERSON. The central purpose of the curriculum is, in the last analysis, the development of the educated person. Thus, whether we are conscious of it or not, stated aims, goals, and objectives in a very real sense constitute a composite definition of this ideal type. Certainly, it seems desirable (if not imperative) that curriculum purposes be continually reassessed in the light of maximally conscious reflection on our best and most noble conceptions of what man can become.

VALUES. Closely connected with the three considerations of goal evaluation discussed above is values. In assessing particular goals and objectives, such questions as the following should receive careful and honest thought: What values are we reaffirming when we place a priority on a particular goal or objective? Are these values consonant with our best conceptions of the educated person, of the ideal society, and of the good life? To what extent does this goal or objective represent acquiescence to tradition, some level of government, a business or labor group, a religious organization, a political party, an influential patriotic society, an "aroused" taxpayers' association, or some other special-interest force? It may be that awareness and honesty with respect to values will reveal with embarrassing transparency the degree to which our aims, goals, and objectives have been influenced by special-interest forces to the detriment of a reasoned and principled determination of curriculum purposes.

The four centers of reflection discussed above represent basic considerations in goal evaluation. Of course, a large number of other considerations, such as material well-being, the freedom-responsibility continuum, and learning theory, might be utilized. Many factors such as these would be identified as a result of feedback acquired from pilot implementation of the curriculum plan. The crucial consideration, however, is awareness that statements of aims, goals, and objectives are never finished products, but require frequent reevaluation, not only for the obvious reason of keeping curriculum direction contemporary and up to date, but for the more important reason of correcting for the prior biases to which all human beings are subject. For if curriculum construction is the dynamic life process that it should be, planners will themselves move closer to the ideal of the educated person as they engage in the process of curriculum building.

EVALUATING THE COHERENCE OF CURRICULUM

The problem to be considered in this section is the same one touched on in the section "Relationship of Aims, Goals, and Objectives" in Chapter 13. There, we noted that curriculum planners had an obligation to demonstrate that specific objectives were reasonably consistent with stated goals, and that these goals were in turn congruent with the ultimate curriculum aims that students were to attain. As an example of inconsistency between levels of purpose, take a curriculum goal like "Students will be competent writers of expository prose" and one of the curriculum objectives that is commonly subsumed under it:

"Students will write out from memory (1) the definition of a preposition and (2) the ten most commonly used prepositions." Tradition notwithstanding, the behavior required by the subsumed objective both logically and in terms of reported research seems to bear little relationship to the behavior sought in the longer-range curriculum goal.

The lack of coherence between levels of purpose discussed above represents one of the most prevalent causes of curriculum dysfunction. In the following sections we will discuss some other of the more common points of inconsistency; but planners need to be aware that inconsistency can occur within and between any of the dozens of elements and operations involved in curriculum and instruction. Because a functioning curriculum is a dynamic and organic whole, its effectiveness depends to a large degree on the coherence of its interrelated components.

CONSISTENCY OF PURPOSES AND EVALUATION. Discrepancies between evaluation procedures and stated purposes are perhaps the most visible area of dysfunction in curriculum coherence. Pace (1958, pp. 78, 79) describes one such discrepancy that serves as a classic example of the kind of inconsistency that ordinarily, though unintentionally, occurs in this area. He reports that the stated purposes of a certain freshman college course in "Responsible Citizenship" included "critical thinking" and "analysis of complex ideas and relationships." These purposes were quite clearly communicated, and the teaching procedures and student activities both in and out of class were fully congruent with them. For example, in class discussions students were "encouraged, rewarded, and given frequent opportunity for the exercise of critical thinking and the analysis of complex ideas and relationships . . . ," traits clearly associated with "responsible citizenship." But he goes on to say that a "major portion of the final examination typically consisted of true-false and multiple-choice questions requiring the recall of historical information, definition of terms, and similar factual material contained in required readings." Clearly, the evaluation was dysfunctional because it assessed behavior that was essentially quite different from that which the course was intended to develop. Furthermore, student word-of-mouth concerning the evaluation procedures in the course would very likely be responsible in future offerings for diverting energies from the kind of activity that fulfilled stated objectives to memorization and other behaviors that resulted in "payoff"— i.e., good grades. In so altering their behavior, the students would, in effect, be demonstrating that they had learned what many experienced curriculum evaluators know: If you want to find out what the purposes of a curriculum *really* are, do not read the statement of objectives; look at the final exams.

It should be pointed out that the evaluation described above was not *entirely* dysfunctional since the learners were probably expected (quite properly) to have a reasonable command of the facts and information important for critical thinking and analysis. But knowledge of facts constituted only a fraction of the total range of objectives; not only were most of the objectives not evaluated, but the most important ones, involving higher mental and attitudinal outcomes, were not considered. This condition of inconsistency between stated purposes and evaluation occurred because the evaluation program lacked *scope* or *comprehensiveness*.

Lack of scope or comprehensiveness has been described as "the most flagrant deficiency of current evaluation programs" (Taba, 1962, p. 317). This condition usually occurs because most of our evaluating devices tend to be inadequate for assessing the higher-level complex areas of human psychological functioning: e.g., such areas as reflective and intuitive thinking, creativity, social attitudes, aesthetic valuing, and moral development. The result is that evaluation becomes centered on those objectives that are most easily evaluated. It is no accident, for example, that in the language arts curriculum objectives in spelling receive intensive evaluative attention, while such critically important outcomes as development of aesthetic taste in literature (which are given heavy emphasis in statements of purpose) are virtually omitted from evaluation programs. Clearly, insistence on precision in evaluation can result, not only in a deceptive assessment of curriculum outcomes, but in the suppression of significant intended learning outcomes.

Precision in curriculum evaluation certainly is a characteristic that should be sought. But lack of a precise measuring instrument is never a good reason for narrowing the scope of an evaluation. Indeed, the learning outcomes that represent the highest levels of human development are least amenable to precise measurement, but to exclude them from the evaluation is effectively to suppress their attainment and thereby to subvert the best intents of the curriculum. A comprehensive evaluation program—one that is consistent with the full range of curriculum purposes—will be precise where it is possible to be, but whenever necessary, will accept as valid the best rough approximations of goal attainment it can get in the interests of balance and consistency.

CONSISTENCY OF ALL CURRICULUM ELEMENTS. Although not as conspicuous as inconsistencies between goals and evaluation, lack of correspondence among all of the other curriculum components is common and contributes significantly to curriculum incoherence and dysfunction. Inconsistencies can occur between goals and content, goals and learning activities, content and learning activities, learning activities and evaluation, etc. Indeed, inconsistencies can occur at so many junctures in the curriculum plan that it would be virtually impossible to provide a complete account of them here. The following few examples, however, will furnish some insight into the nature of the more common discrepancies among curriculum elements and show how these discrepancies operate to undermine curriculum effectiveness.

Inconsistencies often occur between curriculum objectives and learning activities. For example, "Students will understand the use of the scientific method of inquiry" is an objective often found in science curricula. An activity that would seem congruent with this stated objective might be a rather extended project in which each student formulates a problem and then uses the groping, but nevertheless structured, model of inquiry to reach some tentative solution. It is not unusual, however, to find that the activity connected with the above objective is merely learning by rote "the five steps of the scientific method." Such an activity, clearly, is not functional in helping students to reach the objective, but rather promotes the "ingestion of information," or as Dewey has put it, "verbal learning."

Another discrepancy that is common to many curricula occurs between learning activities and evaluation. An example of this inconsistency was noted in the previous section. College students who had engaged in critical thinking and analysis of ideas in classroom activities were evaluated on the basis of recall of information. While the activity appeared to be valuable and productive, no real evidence of its value was available because the evaluation was inconsistent with the activity. Of greater import is the possibility that the dysfunctional evaluation might, in the future, be responsible for student rejection of apparently productive activities.

The final example of curriculum incoherence that we shall present occurs between goals and content. A curriculum goal found in many statements of purpose is that "Students will develop an appreciation of (visual) art." Although this goal is essentially affective, the content of many art appreciation curricula is heavily cognitive. It usually is specified in terms of an historical survey of art and includes information relating to cultural background material, biographical data about the artists, and analyses of selected works. The assumption, of course, is that "knowledge about" automatically transfers to "appreciation of." Certainly appreciation is enhanced by knowledge, but experience clearly indicates that "knowledge about" is insufficient either to initiate or support desired affective dispositions. Other visual art content, organized differently, clearly is demanded by this objective.

The dysfunctional effects of incongruous content are nowhere more striking than in the poetry appreciation sections of most high school English courses. Here, students become proficient in identifying all of the poetic meters, from iambic pentameter to dactyl hexameter; they can define a host of poetry terms: ballad, imagery, couplet, blank verse, lyric, etc.; and they can adeptly recite the rhyme schemes of the Italian and Elizabethan sonnets. Yet they leave school despising poetry! Surely, other factors (e.g., the adverse disposition to poetry in American culture) contribute to this lack of appreciation for poetry; but the mechanical content of poetry courses, so alien to the nature and function of poetic values, undoubtedly is counterproductive in achieving stated goals.

These few examples demonstrate the need for curriculum planners to build into the evaluation component provisions for assessing the internal consistency of the curriculum plan. Unfortunately, no shortcuts exist for avoiding the tedious task of continually checking and cross-checking curriculum components to ensure congruence among all the elements of the plan.

CONSISTENCY OF CURRICULUM COMPONENTS AND FOUNDATIONAL COMMITMENTS. In evaluating the curriculum, provision should be made for frequent references to commitments in the foundational areas: the culture, the individual, learning theory, and epistemology. For example, we might ask: Do the objectives reflect movement toward the kinds of society and individuals for which we hope? Does the content and its organization reflect our beliefs about the nature of knowledge? Are the proposed learning activities consistent with our notions of how human beings learn? Perhaps most important, because it can affect the very design of the curriculum, is the consideration: Is the evaluation itself congruent with our foundational and theoretical commitments?

Enough has been said about the derivation of aims, goals, and objectives in Chapter 13 for us to recognize their especially close ties to philosophical and theoretical commitments. But a *continual* reevaluation of purposes in terms of these commitments is made necessary for two related reasons: first, because of the tentative nature of the curriculum purposes themselves (Dewey's concept of purposes as "ends-in-view"); and second, because of the evolutionary character of cultures and individuals. We are never at the same place (psychologically as well as physically) as we were a little while ago. Added experience affords us more information, new insights, and a generally broader perspective on man and culture. Given these two considerations, it is unthinkable that periodic reassessment of purposes would not take place.

Content, too, as we noted in Chapter 14, is dependent on foundational commitments. But it is all too easy, when immersed in the day-to-day particulars of selecting and organizing content to lose sight of larger theoretical concerns and to fall back (unconsciously) on the more familiar criteria of custom and tradition. The temptation of a traditional body of well-defined and organized content ready for automatic transfer into the curriculum is hard to resist; and a hard, critical assessment of the degree to which this content really matches foundational commitments all too often gives way to rationalization. The development of content based on a novel epistemology or organizational pattern is a highly demanding task because it requires broad knowledge of the traditional disciplines coupled with epistemological imagination. To avoid the ubiquitous influence of unexamined (or invisible) custom and tradition, curriculum planners need constantly to examine the congruence between the content they propose for inclusion in the curriculum and the foundational positions they claim to have assumed.

A few comments with respect to consistency between curriculum evaluation and theoretical foundations will round out this section, although we will by no means have provided a complete discussion of curriculum coherence. Evaluations that are not consistent with foundational commitments not only provide misleading assessments of curriculum effectiveness, but, because of unintended roles, can produce outcomes that are antithetical to the foundational beliefs of the producers of curriculum. For example, take a situation in which students have demonstrated in an evaluation that they have an excellent cognitive grasp of democratic concepts and values. The curriculum then is judged to be effective by the planners, whose social and individual commitment has been based on the democratic ideal. The evaluation may be misleading, however, because while the students have demonstrated *knowledge about* democratic functioning, they were not evaluated in terms of their dispositions to *behave* democratically. Indeed, where emphasis is placed exclusively on intellectual performance, and evaluations rigidly focus on individual achievement and competition, the outcomes, in attitudinal terms, may in fact be extremely antidemocratic. It is all too true that many students learn authoritarianism in "Problems of Democracy" classes.

Coherence of curriculum elements is a central concern of evaluation. Because of the complexity of the curriculum enterprise, however, its achievement is elusive, and even in optimal situations only partial. Increased attention to evaluation in this area, however, can help to produce far more functional curricula than those that have customarily resulted from emphasis on product evaluation.

COLLECTING EVALUATION DATA

Most established procedures geared to collecting information for curriculum evaluation have to do with product (i.e., student) evaluation. Taba (1962, p. 329) notes three sources for such evidence: "standardized tests, nonstandardized or teacher-made paper and pencil tests, and informal devices." Paper-and-pencil tests, both standardized and informal, are the predominant source of evaluation data in most schools. There are many reasons for this: paper-and-pencil tests are purported to be objective, economical, easy to administer, and they provide a "norm" against which individual achievement can be judged. But there are a number of limitations inherent in paper-and-pencil tests, also. Some of these were discussed in the first section of this chapter, "Product Evaluation: The Technical Model," and have to do with such matters as the indirect nature of measurement and the inferences that can legitimately be drawn from test performance. Other significant limitations, however, have to do with the limited range of objectives that paper-and-pencil tests measure and the fact that complex and novel forms of mental functioning are generally beyond their capability to measure. Within the framework of limitations that are conceded, however, paper-and-pencil tests do provide data for curriculum evaluation, and deserve serious consideration, though not the emphasis *ad absurdum* that they have customarily received.

Informal evaluation devices, a third source of product evaluation data, are useful in assessing complex objectives, novel or unique objectives, student interests, and other outcomes of curriculum. For example, Taba (1962, p. 330) suggests as sources of evidence, "records of all sorts, classroom observations, student products, diaries, essays and simple classroom exercises. . . . [W]hen students describe what they saw on a trip or react to a story they read, these reactions . . . can be analyzed for the levels of awareness or social attitudes displayed. . . ."

The above constitute sources of data for product evaluation. What are some sources of evidence that can be used in evaluating the curriculum as a whole? The topics of this section of the chapter, of course, suggest a major source: the curriculum document itself, including the statement of purposes, content, learning activities, and evaluation. Such questions as the following should be generated as the curriculum is brought under the scrutiny of evaluators: What is the theoretical rationale for the document? Is the document a coherent whole? How were curriculum purposes derived? Is the content (learning activities, evaluation) consistent with purposes? Since the curriculum document represents the plan for learning, judging its merit is a critical first step in the evaluation process.

But the less tangible functional curriculum, as it is field tested with students and teachers in an instructional setting, is also a source of data crucial for effective curriculum evaluation. Unlike the curriculum document, however, the functional curriculum cannot be directly studied; it has to be observed as it operates through people, materials, and environments. In such a setting, therefore, teachers become a valuable source of information for curriculum evaluators. Information ordinarily is secured from teachers by means of interviews, questionnaires, and a wide variety of other structured and unstructured devices, both written and oral. (Perhaps the most valid information is acquired when evaluators have developed sound interpersonal relationships with teachers and teachers' feelings and perceptions are freely and honestly expressed in informal discussions.) Teachers' perceptions of content, instructional materials, learning activities, relevance, student enthusiasm, and the like can yield valuable insights when compared (or contrasted) with the evaluators' perceptions of the functioning curriculum in these areas.

Students, too, are an important source of evaluation data. As with teachers, information is secured from both structured and unstructured instruments. Particularly if they are sure that their responses to evaluation instruments will not be used to determine individual grades, students will respond with a candor that can quite accurately reflect the flavor of the experience they are having as a result of their interaction with the curriculum. Again, comparing and contrasting students' perceptions with those of teachers and curriculum planners can provide entirely new (and even startling) appreciations of the dynamics of the functioning curriculum.

A third source of information for evaluating the functioning curriculum is the curriculum material utilized in instruction, including texts, paperbacks, films, slides, periodicals, and the like. Evaluators, of course, need to determine the appropriateness of these in terms of the intent and character of the curriculum plan; but shared observations of how they are used in the functional curriculum may very well provide the more important assessment of their value. Curriculum materials do not constitute a curriculum, and it is common knowledge that teachers using identical materials can, in effect, produce radically different operating curricula in terms of learning activities, students' experiences, and eventual outcomes. This relatedness of curriculum materials and the way they are used demonstrates once again the complexity of the curriculum enterprise and the difficulties encountered specifying procedures for comprehensive curriculum evaluation.

Space does not permit elaboration on all possible sources of curriculum evaluation data. For example, follow-up studies of graduates of the curriculum and/or their associates is very important if a summative evaluation is to have any real validity. The seven sources discussed, however, would appear to be minimal if a reasonably comprehensive evaluation is desired. In addition, it should be noted that as a matter of policy, unsolicited evidence from whatever source should be given serious attention: letters, phone calls, or visits from parents; testimony from school personnel, students, or lay people; or even "letters to the editor" in the local paper often constitute important data.

VALIDITY OF EVALUATIONS

An evaluation will be valid only to the extent that the evidence it employs accurately describes what it claims to describe. For example, if a measuring instrument purports to yield a score reflecting the degree to which students can *interpret* historical data, but requires in its questions only the *recall* of data, it is not describing what it claims to describe. As a consequence, an evaluation of curriculum effectiveness in the area of historical interpretation would not be valid in this instance since there is no basis for such an evaluation. Clearly, curriculum evaluators need to ensure the validity of the data they use in judging curriculum quality.

A second aspect of the problem of validity was touched on in a previous section, "Consistency of Purposes and Evaluation." In that section, it will be recalled, an example was given of an evaluation that was distorted because it was based only on *some* (rather than all) of the curriculum objectives to be achieved. Validity was impaired in this case because the evaluation lacked scope or comprehensiveness.

A third factor that needs to be considered in order to ensure the validity of curriculum evaluation is the incidence and nature of unintended outcomes. The issue of unintended outcomes was touched on briefly in Chapter 13. There, it was noted that a whole range of consequences, in addition to those outcomes we intend to reach, are ushered in as students interact with the functional curriculum. But because evaluators have a (quite natural) tendency to focus on the extent to which stated objectives are achieved, and because a high degree of awareness and sophistication is required for the identification of *all* outcomes, this aspect of comprehensive evaluation—the identification and evaluation of unintended outcomes—is perhaps the most difficult to achieve.

Taba reports an incident that points up this need to be aware of the "total pattern of educational outcomes":

> a school which was greatly concerned with the development of scientific objectivity and critical thinking had stressed the use of reliable and dependable materials of unquestioned objectivity. After administering a battery of tests on thinking, the staff discovered to its amazement that the students were highly gullible. They had a tendency to accept as true almost anything in print because they had no opportunity to compare poor and good sources. An exclusive diet of excellent and dependable ideas cultivated an unquestioning attitude (Taba 1962, pp. 314, 315).

Taba's example demonstrates that validity in comprehensive curriculum evaluation involves not only assessing the attainment of all stated goals and objectives, but of identifying and judging the merit of the full range of consequences issuing from the implemented curriculum. Clearly, unless the evaluation takes into account all curriculum outcomes, it will not provide an accurate picture of curriculum quality.

A fourth and final factor in evaluation validity has to do with the proportional weighting of product evaluation and other areas of curriculum assessment in the total evaluation design. We have noted previously, for example, that curriculum evaluation has traditionally consisted almost exclusively of product (or "payoff") evaluation. But we have argued in this section on comprehensive curriculum evaluation that while product evaluation is a necessary part of curriculum evaluation, it is not in itself sufficient. Thus, we have stressed the need to give attention to the direct evaluation of such curriculum elements and characteristics as the objectives themselves, content, learning activities, component consistency, and even evaluation. Scriven (1967, p. 53 ff.) has classified these procedures as "intrinsic evaluation" to distinguish them as a class from "product evaluation." The validity question to be dealt with, then, becomes: How much weight in the evaluation design is to be accorded product evaluation as opposed to intrinsic evaluation?

Although it is obviously impossible to prescribe a desirable mix of product and intrinsic evaluation that will prove optimally valid for all curricula, it seems clear that something approaching a 50:50 proportion might be a good place to start in terms of developing an evaluation rationale for a particular curriculum. Clearly, product evaluation is essential if we are at all interested in what the curriculum actually does. But product evaluation, because of its essentially summative nature, provides little help with the questions that get raised at formative stages of development. For example: Is there a good match between content and goals? Is the (product) evaluation consistent with the content? Are students responding negatively to the content because it is not contemporary or because it is poorly organized for learning efficiency? What is the reason for a particular (undesirable) unintended outcome? If goal attainment turns out to be relatively good, how adequate are goals in terms of the possibilities for optimal student development?

Such questions require that curriculum evaluators go beyond the relatively precise, empirical procedures of product evaluation and assess curriculum effectiveness in the far more value-loaded and nebulous areas of intrinsic evaluation. Of course, we should expect the reliability (i.e., the accuracy) of a comprehensive evaluation (as compared with a purely product evaluation) to suffer somewhat from the inclusion of considerations that are not ordinarily susceptible to operationally defined criteria; but it seems clearly more desirable for the evaluation to reflect a balanced, if somewhat opaque, view of the total curriculum than to insist on clarity and precision to the extent that we get an accurate picture of only segments of it. An analogue of this point would be the argument that a rough pen-and-ink sketch of a man provides a more valid impression of his physical nature than an extremely clear color photograph of a hand, a nose, and an ear. By taking the sketch and photograph together, however (as we would combine an intrinsic and a product evaluation), validity and reliability are improved.

The four aspects of curriculum evaluation validity that we have discussed above suggest that validity is a quality essential for an evaluation to possess. To the degree that an evaluation lacks validity, it is of no use whatever.

References

Ahmann, J. Stanley, and Marvin D. Glock. 1967. *Evaluating Pupil Growth*. 3d ed. Boston: Allyn & Bacon.

Bloom, Benjamin S., J. Thomas Hastings, and George F. Madaus. 1971. *Handbook on Formative and Summative Evaluation of Student Learning*. New York: McGraw-Hill Book Company.

Hoover, Kenneth H. 1968. *Learning and Teaching in the Secondary School*. 2d ed. Boston: Allyn & Bacon.

Pace, C. Robert. 1958. "Educational Objectives." In *The Integration of Educational Experiences*, edited by Nelson B. Henry. Fifty-seventh Yearbook of the National Society for the Study of Education. Chicago: University of Chicago Press, chap. IV.

Scriven, Michael. 1967. "The Methodology of Evaluation." In Ralph W. Tyler, Roger M. Gagné, and Michael Scriven, *Perspectives of Curriculum Evaluation*. AERA Monograph Series on Curriculum Evaluation, No. 1. Chicago: Rand McNally & Co.

Taba, Hilda. 1962. *Curriculum Development: Theory and Practice*. New York: Harcourt Brace Jovanovich.

IV
CURRICULUM DESIGN AND ENGINEERING

Part IV concludes our study of the curriculum field with discussions of curriculum design, development, implementation, and change. Chapter 17 introduces the topic of curriculum design with an analysis of six prototypes that have had at least some currency in practice in American school settings. The discussion is continued in Chapter 18 with a description of two challenging, but as yet untested, proposals representing radical departures in curriculum design. This chapter closes with a critical treatment of five major problems of curriculum organization.

Chapters 19 and 20 deal with processes of curriculum engineering—namely, curriculum development and implementation. The former chapter begins with an expository discussion of curriculum development and goes on to analyze eight contemporary models for implementing curriculum development activities. Chapter 20 ends the discussion with a consideration of five crucial issues affecting curriculum development.

Our study of the curriculum field is concluded in Chapter 21, the epilogue, where the nature and function of individual decision making in curriculum change is examined. This chapter emphasizes the importance of personal commitment, individual conscience, and responsible risk taking for the realization of significant curriculum change.

CHAPTER 17

CURRICULUM DESIGN: REPRESENTATIVE PROTOTYPES

The design element is central in many applied fields. "Utmost sim-plicity" is sometimes seen as a desirable characteristic of good design. Our concern in curriculum planning is more than just simplicity. We seek a larger context in order to cope with necessary diversity and complexity.   —PAUL R. KLOHR

Curriculum design, as stressed in Chapter 1, is a term that refers to a *substantive*—in particular, the structure, pattern, or organization of the curriculum. It presents the question, "What general structure of the curriculum can be developed so that autonomy of the parts does not result in anarchy in the program as a whole?" (Bellack 1965, p. 321). Its major concerns are the nature and arrangement of the four basic curriculum components: aims, goals, and objectives; content; learning activities; and evaluation. Thus, the central problems of curriculum design are scope, sequence, continuity, and integration (Taba 1962, p. 382).

Curriculum design manifests itself along two basic dimensions of organization: horizontal and vertical. Horizontal organization (sometimes referred to as scope and integration) is concerned with the side-by-side arrangement of curriculum components. For example, combining the content and learning activities of eleventh-grade history, economics, political science, and sociology into a unified eleventh-grade course in social studies is a matter of horizontal design. In contrast, vertical organization (sometimes referred to as sequence and continuity) is concerned with the longitudinal arrangement of curriculum elements. An example of vertical design is the placement of addition-skills development in the first grade and subtraction skills in the second. A more extensive discussion of these design topics appears in Chapter 18, in the section "Critical Problems of Curriculum Design."

Even a cursory survey of current school curricula will reveal that little, if any, serious attention is paid to organization and design and that generally speaking, fashion exerts a disproportionate influence on curriculum offerings. Courses such as sex education, black studies, environmental education, and economic education are added incrementally "to make the curriculum more relevant"; new sequences are effected on a piecemeal basis "to reverse permissive, anti-intellectual trends"—as when algebra and foreign languages are moved downward from the junior high to the elementary level; and mini-courses proliferate at a breath-taking rate "to meet the specific individual needs and interests of students." The result is a kind of disjointed clutter of specialized subjects which often operates to impede, rather than to foster, education.

This situation strongly suggests the need for some sort of internal consistency. The curriculum that we present our students should appear as a sensible and coherent whole at each grade level and across the grades from kindergarten through senior high school.[1] It is this overarching concern for the cohesiveness and coherence of the *total curriculum* that best characterizes the essence of curriculum design.

We have previously noted that curriculum construction—i.e., decisions that eventuate in a curriculum design—should be based on a thorough examination and assessment of the four foundational areas. Without diminishing the importance of that principle, we should also note that curriculum-construction decisions need in addition to be based on the best knowledge derived from analysis of current designs. It is only on the basis of such knowledge that the elements and problems peculiar to curriculum design can be adequately handled.

Unfortunately, attempts to analyze, and thereby to understand, current curriculum designs are hampered because of the apparent irregularity and randomness (noted above) in much of the curriculum with which we are familiar. We are faced with a veritable "verbal jungle":

> *Subject-centered, experience-centered; correlated, integrated, fused; broad fields, major social functions, centers of interest; core, unit, problem—in many combinations and under as many logics—these are among the terms used to describe modern curriculum designs (Stratemeyer et al. 1957, p. 86).*

Despite the confusion propagated by this profusion of terminology, however, we shall see that almost all curriculum designs can be classified as modifications and/or combinations of three basic categories: (1) subject-centered designs, (2) learner-centered designs, and (3) problem-centered designs.[2] Within each

1. It should be pointed out, however, that a neat and tightly structured curriculum design grounded in a unitary principle (e.g., "communication" or "interpersonal relations") will almost certainly eventuate in a grossly oversimplified program with undesirable consequences of its own. (Taba 1962, p. 414).

2. I am indebted to Stratemeyer et al. (1957, pp. 86–105) and Smith, Stanley, and Shores (1957, pp. 225–387) for their analyses of curriculum designs. The schema presented here is an adaptation of the work of these authors.

category a few prototypical designs can be identified. For example, among the subject-centered designs are the subject design, the disciplines design, and the broad fields design. Among the learner-centered designs are the activity/experience design, the open classroom design, and the humanistic design. And grouped under problem-centered designs are the areas of living design, the personal/social concerns of youth design, and the core design. Perfect replicas of these prototypes are rarely, if ever, encountered in practice. Indeed, we probably should not expect to find the theoretically pure in the world of reality. Yet it will prove useful to describe the characteristics of some of these prototypes since a knowledge of them will enable us to discuss and analyze with much less confusion the multitude of mixed designs that we find operative in the schools. Perhaps more important, however, a knowledge of the prototypes will make us more alert to the problems of curriculum design and to inconsistencies and discontinuities in our own designs.

Representative Curriculum Designs
SUBJECT-CENTERED DESIGNS

While it is a dangerous oversimplification to attribute blanket foundational positions to groups of similar curriculum designs, it frequently is conceded that subject-centered designs tend to grow out of absolutist (i.e., other-worldly and earth-centered) philosophical assumptions. Supporters of these designs customarily view society as a (properly) hierarchical structure, with individuals (often perceived as being "naturally evil" and requiring control) finding their appropriate places in it according to well-defined and generally fixed divine and/or physical laws. Learning, like all other phenomena, typically is conceived as a mechanistic process which conforms to these laws.

The three subject-centered curriculum designs described below all have in common the utilization of *content* as a basis for both the horizontal and vertical structure of the curriculum. Consequently, other curriculum components (aims, goals, learning activities, etc.) have little impact on their organization. However, each of the three designs is characterized by certain distinct qualities that differentiate it from other designs in this grouping.

THE SUBJECT DESIGN. The subject design[3] is probably the oldest and most widely employed form of curriculum organization. Its origin in Western education is the seven liberal arts of classical Greece and Rome, the *trivium* and *quadrivium*[4] of which, broadly interpreted, were the subjects of instruction purported to

---

3. Chapter 14, "Content," elaborates on many of the topics and issues inherent in the subject design.

4. It will be recalled that the *trivium* consists of grammar, rhetoric, and dialectic, and that the *quadrivium* includes arithmetic, geometry, astronomy, and music. See Chapter 6 for a description of these subjects as they were originally conceived.

encompass the full sweep of knowledge essential to the educated man. The modern subject design dates from the 1870s and the work of St. Louis school superintendent William Torrey Harris. This influential and highly respected educator, steeped in the classical tradition, established a subject orientation to curriculum design that virtually controlled curriculum making in the United States until the second decade of the present century (Cremin 1971, p. 210).

In its purest form, the subject design organizes the curriculum into a variable number of subjects, each of which purportedly represents a specialized and homogeneous body of content. The basis for the organization is usually, but not necessarily, the divisions of labor in research: physics, chemistry, history, literature, philosophy, etc. However, since its inception in the nineteenth century, many "practical" areas, such as homemaking, typing, and auto mechanics, have come to be accepted as legitimate "subjects."

The essence of the subject design is the *inherent* nature of its organization. This, it is claimed, has been *discovered* by the content specialists, whose work, over the centuries, has resulted in the totality of all the subjects—the classified and categorized cultural heritage of civilized man. The subjects, then, represent knowledge in its most logical, economical, useful, real, and easily digestible form; those who possess it to the greatest degree are the ones who are best equipped to deal with the problems of life.

It is easy to see from the above that the scope of the subject design will be determined by the range of subjects worthy of inclusion in the curriculum and by the content included in each subject. Likewise, sequence becomes a function of the logic of the subject matter, although the maturity of students to handle particular content also plays a significant role.

It is assumed in the subject design that each subject consists of a single and distinctive kind of content. Philosophical and philological research, however, have demonstrated the error of this assumption. Moreover, the classification of subjects has been shown to be so extremely complex (see Chapter 14) that about all we can say with any confidence about the nature of a subject is that it is a *relative* construct. Take, for example, the "subject" of English: English really includes the somewhat disparate "subjects" of grammar, spelling, literature, rhetoric, etc. Grammar, in turn, may be subdivided into the specialized "subjects" of phonology, morphology, syntax, prosody, etc. In a reverse direction, the "subject" biology (which, incidentally consists of botany and zoology) has recently been combined with chemistry to form the new subject of biochemistry. Thus, the entire matter of what constitutes a subject presents a problem even to those proponents of the subject design who limit their definition to "the divisions of labor in research."

Typically, the subject curriculum leans heavily on verbal activities. This is so, say subject-design proponents, because knowledge and ideas, the data of the subjects, are best communicated and stored in verbal form. Thus, the subject design tends to emphasize such procedures as lecture, discussion, exposition, explanation, recitation, questioning, written exercises, oral reports, term papers, etc. Although in practice some variations of the subject curriculum attempt to provide activities that develop such skills as critical thinking and valuing, the basic structure of the design so encourages content coverage that the traditional emphasis is on memorization and the acquisition of information.

In its present form, the subject design assumes a hierarchy of value inherent in the subjects. Although proponents of the subject design have debated among themselves over which subjects are the most important (e.g., the humanities versus the sciences), they generally agree that the academic subjects are naturally superior to the "practical" ones.[5] For example, Conant (1959, pp. 47, 48, 57), recommends a minimum academic program for *all* high school students that includes four years of English, three to four years of social studies, and a year each of science and mathematics. (He recommends a far more rigorous minimum program for the academically talented.) These subjects, presumably represent the irreducible base of knowledge for the citizen; they are the subjects whose value is not only greater than the others', but virtually indispensable.

An important issue raised by the hierarchy problem is one that we have discussed in previous chapters: the distinction between general (liberal) education and special (vocational/professional) education. The issue is reflected in one of the essential characteristics of the subject design—the variable availability to students of its subjects. Some subjects are required of *all* students, some are required only of *certain classes* of students, some may be elected *only* by certain students, and some may be elected by *anyone*.

The subjects required of *all* students are called constants (Smith, Stanley, and Shores 1957, p. 235) and constitute the common elements or general education component of the curriculum. Presumably, these are the essential subjects (as judged by varying criteria) and most commonly include English, American history and/or government, and perhaps a year of mathematics or science. The subjects required only of certain students might be foreign language, algebra, and physics for college preparatory students; or typing, business math, and shorthand for commercial students. These courses constitute the special education program inasmuch as they are designed to develop skills and knowledge for particular professional or vocational purposes. The third category of subjects— the electives restricted to certain classes of students—may be viewed as developing nonessential or specialized vocational/professional expertise. For example, calculus and fifth-year French might be elective for qualified college preparatory students, while advanced typing and medical office practice might be available to qualified commercial students. Finally, electives that are open to all students (e.g., typing, ceramics, and photography) reflect concern for generally avocational interests and thus for the personal development aspect of liberal education.

The appearance in the discussion above of such subjects as typing, shorthand,

---

5. There has been an increasing tendency to view all subjects—whether mathematics or typing, chemistry or home economics—as having equal value. See Rockefeller Brothers Fund (1958). This report decries the trend toward "democracy of subject matters" and proposes certain priority subjects.

ceramics, and photography reveals the considerable broadening of the modern subject design that has occurred in American schools over the past seventy years. But while the addition of these new subjects is claimed to represent curricular innovation, it should be pointed out that in fact no innovation in basic design has necessarily taken place. The inherent logic of classified segments of content continues as the controlling factor in determining organization and design, and very often the expository-explanatory procedures used to implement the older academic subject design continue to be followed as well.

The chief argument in favor of the subject design is that it is the most systematic and effective organization for acquainting youth with the essentials of the cultural heritage. By studying the organized bodies of subject matter, students can build their store of knowledge most efficiently and economically (Taba 1962, p. 386). This argument, of course, is based on the twin assumptions that (1) the inherent "logic" of a subject corresponds to the psychological processes that human beings employ in learning it, and (2) that such organization facilitates the storage and retrieval of subject matter for future utilization in life situations. Recent psychological research tends to refute both of these assumptions.[6]

Other arguments in favor of the subject design tend to be practical in nature.[7] In the first place, most teachers (especially secondary teachers) have a college experience that orients them toward the subject design. Since the design is the one employed by virtually all colleges and universities, teachers, on the basis of familiarity alone, feel most comfortable with it. Moreover, "It allows for the maximum direct use of their college work and provides the security that comes with a feeling of competence" (Stratemeyer et al. 1957, p. 89). Put another way (and perhaps more fairly), the subject design is uniquely suited to take advantage of the teacher's subject matter expertise, an important, but often neglected, aspect of curriculum implementation.

A second practical advantage of the subject design is that textbooks and other teaching materials generally are organized by subjects so that the material to be learned is clearly laid out. It is unfortunately a truism that the availability of

6. See the section "Logical and Psychological Content Organization" in Chapter 14.

7. We need to distinguish "in principle" arguments (such as the one above) from "practical" arguments because the latter tend to lean primarily on feasibility and/or expediency rather than on a fundamental justification. While a particular design may be easy to implement because of practical considerations, it may not, in principle, be worth implementing. On the other hand, a design which seems to be highly meritorious in principle may be well worth fighting for even against overwhelming practical disadvantages. Along the same lines we should point out that a design that has fared poorly in its implementation should not be discarded or condemned immediately as untenable. More effective implementation might have made it work. "A pure-form organization is open to criticism only if its basic theory is untenable, or if it is impossible *under any conditions* to translate into practice. Practice, of course, is open to criticism if it departs significantly from the theory" (Smith, Stanley, and Shores 1957, p. 227, italics added).

suitable curriculum materials has always been an influential factor in the determination of design.

A third practical advantage is that the subject design is buttressed by tradition: parents tend to support a curriculum that they are familiar with and therefore feel is "academically sound." Furthermore, colleges, in their entrance requirements and academic accounting, place a heavy emphasis on subject matter divisions.

Finally, the inherent nature and organization of the subject design make it easy to administer. A teacher whose subject is chemistry, for example, can be assigned his own specially equipped chemistry laboratory in which to dispense his subject efficiently. The same is true of English, mathematics, home economics, and woodshop. Moreover, class scheduling can conveniently be compartmentalized to correspond to subject requirements: forty minutes each for English and mathematics, eighty minutes for chemistry and home economics.

In effect, the four practical advantages cited above argue in favor of maintaining the status quo because it is more convenient to do so. Such reasoning is not entirely legitimate. Every curriculum design must ultimately stand the test of its own inherent values.

What are the major weaknesses attributed to this most prevalent of all curriculum designs? First it is claimed that the very nature of the design tends to fragment knowledge and therefore the understanding of students. It "consists not of a body of knowledge unified by a dynamic purpose, but rather a collection of fragments of information selected to give the learner an orderly coverage of various aspects of the different subjects" (Smith, Stanley, and Shores 1957, p. 224). True, relationships *within* history or *within* biology may be taught, but the relationship of history to biology, literature, music, and other fields of human endeavor are not provided for in the design. Concepts and facts are learned in the isolation of subject-pure compartments with little opportunity to relate them to anything that might give them perspective and meaning. As a matter of fact, their meaning and utility is in most cases confined to the preparation of assignments and the passing of tests.

Because of the lack of integration inherent in the subject design, critics argue that adverse educational consequences result:

> it is unlikely that the fullest development of the intellectual aspects of personality can be attained. . . . If the average pupil ceases to grow intellectually, and if he remains politically immature, knowing and caring little about social strategy—this stagnation and apathy are probably due in part to the specialized and restrictive character of the subject curriculum (Smith, Stanley, and Shores 1957, p. 245).

A second major criticism of the subject design is its detachment from the concerns and events of the real world. Of course, teachers aware of the need for "relevance" may attempt to relate aspects of their subject to world affairs, but this is often difficult and usually impossible when the orderly coverage of a

predetermined body of subject matter is the basis of instruction. Such important considerations of life and education as poverty, racism, war, pollution, conservation of resources, urbanization, and energy are no respecters of subject
matter boundaries. Nor does a systematic acquaintance with the cultural heritage *qua* subjects ensure the transfer of skills and ideas needed to deal effectively with these physical and social problems.

> *The products of the subject curriculum know more about the crusades
> than they know about the management of modern industry; more about
> the structure of the earthworm than about their own bodies and the status
> of public provisions for their health; more about the exploits of Napoleon
> than about the nature and workings of their own economic and political
> systems . . . (Smith, Stanley, and Shores 1957, p. 248).*

We should hasten to point out that the content of the subject areas is
admittedly an extremely valuable source of knowledge for dealing with the
affairs of life. But it is quite a different matter to assume that its organization
for purposes of storage, retrieval, and research (i.e., as subjects) is also the best
organization for the education of youth.

A third major criticism of the subject curriculum is that it gives inadequate
consideration to the needs, interests, and experience (in Lewin's words, the
life space) of students. Since mastery of the subjects is the central aim of the
subject design, only students whose experience and interest meshes with the
subjects as presented tend to profit meaningfully from the curriculum. Others
(and this probably includes a significant majority) either "play the game" for
purposes of social approval or become problem students in one way or another.
True, teachers of a subject-design persuasion who bring a knowledge of educational psychology to their work attempt to provide for students' interests by adjusting and differentiating course content and assignments. Nevertheless, the very
nature of the subject design precludes significant deviation. As a result, the
experience, needs, and interests that students bring with them to school can be
provided for only in a very limited way. Many examples of this difficulty with
the subject design can be given: How is a teacher to deal with a student whose
experiential background renders him incapable of interacting meaningfully with
the literature prescribed for his grade level? What is to be done about an intellectually underdeveloped seventh-grade youngster who does not have the skills
needed to cope with seventh-grade mathematics? And what can be said to the
student who responds with revulsion or boredom to the study of earthworms,
spiders, and frogs?

The importance of beginning instruction on the *student's* own psychological
ground is a well-established pedagogical principle. When, as is commonly the
case in the subject design, students are coerced through marks, promotions, and
other external forces to learn subject matter in a form that is alien to their
experience, they usually *also* learn to despise the school, the subject, and the
people who teach it to them. Though unintended, this is indeed a sad fate

for so noble an institution, so great a cultural heritage, and so honorable a profession.

A fourth major criticism of the subject design is that it is an inefficient arrangement of the curriculum for learning and for use. This argument was suggested above in rebutting the claim that the subject design is the most efficient and economical organization of the curriculum. Aside from pointing once again to the discussion of the logical and psychological organization of subject matter presented in Chapter 14, we can conclude our exposition of this criticism with this keen observation:

> *The plain fact is that the organization of ideas—or for that matter any-thing else—depends upon the purpose. Since the purposes of the learner are seldom the purposes implied by the subject curriculum, the organiza-tion is of necessity often alien to the centers of interest about which the experiences of the learner crystallize (Smith, Stanley, and Shores 1957, p. 248).*

The final serious criticism of the subject design involves the limited scope of its goals and its passive concept of learning (Taba 1962, p. 390). It is well known that the earliest form of this design heavily stressed the passive memoriza-tion of facts and details with virtually no attention paid to habits of thinking or valuing. While research in child development and educational purposes over the past fifty years has mitigated somewhat the extremes of this emphasis, data retention has generally continued as the central curriculum outcome of this design.

Clearly, it is not enough for any age, let alone our own highly complex tech-nological age, to fill youths' heads with a smorgasbord of information. Cur-riculum design must take into account the *process goals* of both intellect and affect. The first includes logical thinking: hypothesizing, data selection and evaluation, generalization, transfer of facts and ideas to new and different situa-tions, critical assessment of conclusions, etc. The second involves being sensitive to people, values, and feelings. A curriculum of logically ordered predigested content develops neither the powers of intellect nor feeling; at its best it pro-duces masters of information.

Our final note on the subject curriculum has to do with a practical disadvan-tage of the design: i.e., its tendency to proliferate subjects. As our culture has become more sophisticated over the years, the demand for new subjects (quite properly) has grown formidably. In the academic domain, for example, such subjects as psychology, sociology, and anthropology have been added to the high school curriculum. In the practical domain, driver training, homemaking, cos-metology, and computer technology are widely offered. It has been estimated that in 1930 the number of subjects offered in American schools was 300. By 1957, it had grown to 500. With the advent of the currently popular mini-course, it is estimated that the number of courses presently offered in American schools exceeds 700! While the curricular diversity demonstrated by this condition is certainly to be admired, one wonders whether it is at all possible to make any kind of coherent educational sense of it.

THE DISCIPLINES DESIGN. While the subject design is a product of the late nineteenth century and reached its zenith before 1925, its offspring, the disciplines design,[8] did not appear until after World War II. It rapidly grew in popularity, however, attaining its greatest influence during the mid-1960s. When, in the late 1960s and early 1970s, student revolts and other protest movements caused its basic assumptions to be called into question, enthusiasm for the design waned. Its influence is still discernable, however, in many elementary and secondary schools.

Like its parent the subject curriculum, the disciplines design is predicated on the inherent organization of content. However, there is an important difference. While the subject design is not at all clear on the principles used to establish what a subject is (e.g., such diverse areas as mathematics, home economics, and driver training are all accepted as "subjects"), the disciplines design makes a point of specifying the criteria by which a body of knowledge is determined to be a discipline. Thus, King and Brownell (1966, pp. 67–94), among the most forceful proponents of the disciplines design, define a discipline as an autonomous *community of discourse* marked by the following isomorphic features: a community of persons, an expression of human imagination, a domain, a tradition, a mode of inquiry, a conceptual structure, a specialized language or other system of symbols, a heritage of literature and a network of communications, a valuative and affective stance, and an instructive community. This definition is not nearly so rigorous as it sounds,[9] but what it adds up to is that a discipline generally is considered to be one of the traditional *academic* areas of inquiry: physics, psychology, and literature, for example, but not industrial arts, homemaking, and accounting. The disciplines design, then, is predicated on the assumption that the school is "a microcosm of the world of intellect," the cornerstone of which is "the primacy of the intellectual claim on the content of the curriculum" (King and Brownell 1966, p. 119).

Emphasis on the disciplines has resulted, not surprisingly, in content disciplinarians—i.e., physicists, biologists, historians, etc.—taking a strong hand in curriculum building. The propagation of large numbers of curriculum projects (such as the Physical Sciences Study Committee [PSSC], the Biological Sciences Curriculum Study [BSCS], and the School Mathematics Study Group [SMSG]) are examples of this phenomenon and are discussed in greater detail elsewhere in the text. The point, however, is that this condition has

8. Very often, little or no distinction is drawn between the subject and the disciplines design. Taba (1962), for example, treats the disciplines design incidentally, as a "new emphasis on content," and Saylor and Alexander (1974) discuss it in a section titled, "Designs Focused on Disciplines/Subjects." This writer, however, believes that the disciplines design constitutes a distinct and significant curriculum reform movement that warrants its own expository treatment.

9. See the section "The Architectonics of Content" in Chapter 14.

resulted in a quest for disciplinary purity: thus, English is replaced by grammar, rhetoric, and literature; science by physics, chemistry, and biology: and social studies by history, geography, and economics.

While proponents of the disciplines design view an intimate acquaintance with the disciplines of knowledge as the basis of humanistic, liberal education, they stress the *understanding* of disciplinary elements rather than, as in the subject design, merely the possession of data and information. Students are encouraged to see the basic logic or *structure* of the discipline—the relationships of its key concepts, ideas, and principles—and to understand its characteristic mode(s) of inquiry. This, it is said, enables students "to attack unfamiliar problems and to grasp the relationship of new phenomena not previously encountered to phenomena already experienced" (Goodlad 1966, pp. 33, 34). Furthermore, the expository procedures and passive memorization characteristic of the subject design are replaced in the disciplines design with the "discovery" approach to learning; and insofar as students are permitted to "discover" at their own rates, individual differences are provided for in the design. In these respects, then, the disciplines design is not as some claim, a throwback to the older subject design, but a new synthesis of the subject organization with important elements of Deweyan progressivism.

The basic argument in favor of the disciplines is essentially that of the subject design: it is the most systematic and effective organization for transmitting the cultural heritage (the essence of liberal education). Disciplinarians would also add that it is the only organization that preserves the intellectual integrity of man's knowledge. A second argument is that it offers students subject matter in a form that is reasonable: not a set of facts and principles to be memorized and recalled on demand, but concepts, relationships, and intellectual processes derived from students' own activities and thinking. This is understanding in its best sense, and pursued in sufficient breadth and depth, it produces the intellectually liberated person.

In spite of its efforts (quite often successful) to overcome the intellectual passivity and preoccupation with facts that stigmatize the subject curriculum, the disciplines design, by virtue of its inherent organization, remains subject to the same five basic criticisms as its older counterpart. First, it presents students with a fragmented curriculum, providing no vehicle for the integration of knowledge. To leave the problem of making some kind of coherent sense out of the compendium of disciplines that students are expected to learn in school is simply to beg one of the most formidable questions of curriculum design. Second, and perhaps most devastating, the disciplines design does not address itself to the relationships between schooling and life. One can be steeped in physics, history, and literature, for example, and have very little insight into the problems of crime, poverty, the subjection of women, and political corruption in our society. No curriculum that detaches itself from the realities outside the school can claim significance as an educative vehicle.

The third criticism of the disciplines design is that it gives inadequate consideration to the interests and experience of students. While individual differences sometimes are provided for *within* each discipline in terms of assignments and/or rate of progress, the design has been geared almost exclusively to the vocational/professional goals of the college bound. In this respect, the disciplines design is unequivocally an elite curriculum designed for the "academically talented," with no provisions at all for the great majority whose formal education ends after the senior year of high school.

The fourth criticism of the design is that it is an inefficient arrangement of the curriculum for learning and use. While in many respects it represents an improvement over the sometimes artificial linear logic of the subject design, its insistence on the structure of the discipline as an organizing principle fails to take into account the varied learning styles that psychological research has demonstrated to exist. Finally, the disciplines design is limited in the scope of its goals, which, though broader than those of the subject curriculum, are still narrowly academic and intellectual. Perhaps the best statement of this criticism comes from Jerome Bruner, formerly a leader and one of the foremost proponents of the disciplines movement, who now virtually repudiates the disciplines design:

> *I believe I would be quite satisfied to declare, if not a moratorium, then something of a de-emphasis on matters that have to do with the structure of history, the structure of physics, the nature of mathematical consistency, and deal with curriculum rather in the context of the problems that face us. We might better concern ourselves with how these problems can be solved, not just by practical action, but by putting knowledge, wherever we find it and in whatever form we find it, to work in these massive tasks. . . . The issue is one of man's capacity for creating a culture, society, and technology that not only feed him but keep him caring and belonging (Bruner 1971, pp. 29, 30).*

THE BROAD FIELDS DESIGN. This third variation of the subject-centered designs first appeared in the second decade of the twentieth century (Smith, Stanley, and Shores 1957, p. 255). Essentially, it represents an effort to overcome the fragmentation and compartmentalization of the subject curriculum by combining two or more related subjects into a single broad field of study. For example, at the elementary level, reading, writing, spelling, speaking, and composition are combined as language arts; and at the secondary level, physics, chemistry, biology, astronomy, and geology are combined as general science. The rationale is to provide students who live in a world of burgeoning specialized information with a comprehensive view of broad related areas for the purpose of general (and liberal) education.

The broad fields design has become a standard pattern of organization in most elementary schools[10] and a significant factor in the curricula of many secondary schools. Content organized as broad fields is employed to a somewhat lesser degree at the college level, but it does appear in the form of introductory

---

10. The popularity of the disciplines design during the 1960s was responsible for the partial reorganization of many elementary school curricula along disciplinary lines.

or survey courses, such as Introduction to Physical Science and Survey of Western Civilization.

Two main advantages are claimed for the broad fields design. First, because it is ultimately based on the separate subjects, it provides for an orderly and systematic exposure to the cultural heritage. This advantage it shares with the subject curriculum. But it also integrates separate subjects, thereby enabling learners to see relationships among various elements in the curriculum. This second advantage is the special strength that the broad fields design claims over the subject curriculum.

With respect to the integration claimed for the broad fields design, it is worth noting that in practice, combining subjects into a broad field often amounts to little more than the compression of several separate subjects into a single course with little actual unification taking place. Thus, a high school humanities course may consist mainly of a series of condensed topics from history, literature, art, and music sequentially strung out over the duration of a semester. While this result is not necessarily built into the broad fields design, it is one that has commonly occurred and poses a distinct danger. Broad fields, in their best sense, involve a thoroughgoing reorganization of related subject areas so that the focus is on a coherent and integrated whole.

The practical arguments heard in favor of the subject curriculum also often are marshaled in defense of the broad fields design. Broad fields, it is said, are sufficiently similar to college courses so that teachers feel competent and comfortable with them. Furthermore, text materials in the broad fields are readily available. The design has had sufficient currency to make it acceptable to parents and colleges, and it is a relatively easy form of curriculum organization to administer in practice.

Even assuming the optimal degree of integration in a broad fields design, the perennial curriculum issue of breadth versus depth is bound to arise. It is obvious, for example, that a year's study of general science will provide students with a more varied range of science concepts than will a year's study of biology. But granting equally effective instruction, the students who study biology will certainly have a much firmer grasp of that subject than the general science students. As a result, opponents of the broad fields curriculum claim that it lacks depth and cultivates superficiality by providing students with only a smattering of information from a variety of subjects. Proponents of broad fields, however, claim the superiority of the design on the basis that its breadth provides the general education appropriate for everyday life. Some school systems have attempted to reconcile this breadth-depth dilemma by employing the broad fields design at the elementary level, using the middle or junior high school as a kind of halfway house, and implementing a separate subjects design in the high school.

Aside from the criticism that it lacks depth, the broad fields design is subject to the same general criticisms as the other subject-centered designs: to one degree or another, it, too, is fragmented insofar as it does not provide for integration between broad fields (e.g., between general social studies, general science, general arts, language arts, etc.). It is by its nature divorced from the real world, is weak in providing for the experience and interests of students, and does not adequately account for the psychological organization by which learning takes place. Finally, though less so than the subject curriculum, the broad fields design tends to stress the goals of content coverage and acquisition of information, offering little opportunity for the achievement of either cognitive or affective process goals.

LEARNER-CENTERED DESIGNS

While learner-centered designs sometimes are founded in an other-worldly ontology (e.g., Rouseau's assumptions), they are much more frequently the result of man-centered philosophical thought. Supporters of these designs are likely to view society in *extremely* democratic terms and perceive the individual human being as a "naturally good," even sacred, entity. The favored learning theories tend to be perceptual-gestaltist in character.

Because learner-centered designs emphasize individual development, their organizational patterns grow out of the needs, interests, and purposes of students. Although a number of notable attempts have been made to implement learner-centered curricula, examples of this design are far more common in the literature than they are in practice.[11] This, perhaps, is as much due to the heavy demands the design makes on teacher competence as it is to conventional rejection of its philosophical foundations.

Two basic characteristics differentiate designs in this category from those classified as subject centered: First, learner-centered designs take their organizational cues from *individual students* rather than from content. Second (and this follows from the first) learner-centered designs are *not preplanned*, but evolve as teacher and students work together on the tasks of education (often termed "growth"). Thus, the organization of the curriculum for a particular group of students will depend upon the concerns, topics, or problems that *they* center on; and the sequence will depend on where the learners are and how far they can go with the problems and situations that arise (Stratemeyer, et al. 1957, p. 104).

Clearly, given the ground rules, an almost limitless number of variations on the basic model is possible. Among the best known of these are the activity, experience, and child-centered designs of the progressive era and more recently, the open, free, alternative, and humanistic designs proposed in reaction to the disciplines emphasis of the 1960s. Because these specific designs, being grounded in common assumptions about the proper focus of education, are quite similar, we propose in this section to describe only one prototype of the learner-centered designs. Out of respect for tradition, and because it best describes the rationale

11. Learner-centered designs tend to be more characteristic of particular private, quasi-private, and "alternative" schools than they are of the public schools. Perhaps the most widely publicized experiment in learner-centered curriculum is A. S. Neill's private English boarding school, Summerhill.

of this design, we shall call this prototype the activity/experience design, although we should make it clear that it is an equally appropriate model to use in describing some of the more recent open and humanistic designs.

THE ACTIVITY/EXPERIENCE DESIGN. Although this design traces its origin to eighteenth-century Europe and the work of Rousseau and Pestalozzi (see Chapter 3) it did not become a factor in modern public school curriculum design until the flowering of the progressive movement in the 1920s and 1930s.[12] Even then, it was the pattern of organization employed in only a few scattered elementary schools, and it never gained any kind of serious consideration at the secondary level.

The appropriateness of the name "activity/experience" for this pattern of curriculum organization is found in the rationale for the design.

> *People learn only what they experience. Only that learning which is related to active purposes and is rooted in experience translates itself into behavior changes. Children learn best those things that are attached to solving actual problems, that help them in meeting real needs or that connect with some active interest. Learning in its true sense is an active transaction* (Taba 1962, p. 401).

From this rationale, the principal features of the activity/experience design are readily deduced. First, as mentioned above, the structure of the curriculum is determined by learners' needs and interests. By this is meant learners' *own immediate felt* needs and interests, not, as is so often the case, adults' conceptions of what students need or what their interests *ought* to be. Thus, an important task of the teacher implementing the activities/experience design is (1) to discover what the interests of his students are and (2) to help *them* select the most significant of these for study. This is by no means a simple task. It is made even more difficult, however, by the necessity of distinguishing between learners' "genuine" needs and interests and their whims and fancies. The former impulses are characterized by proponents of the design as the more stable potentialities of individual development, while the latter, they admit, are only fleeting stimuli not worthy of curricular response.

These difficulties in determining needs and interests have been responsible for stimulating a great deal of research in child and adolescent growth and development, the purpose being to illuminate the dominant needs and interests of young people. This is not to say that the intent is to impose on learners the interests generalized from research; rather, the intent is to make available knowledge that will help teachers to discover their students' most compelling needs and interests. Clearly, then, a thorough acquaintance with child and

---

12. Pioneers in the development of the modern activities/experience design were Dewey's Laboratory School at the University of Chicago (1896); Meriam's University Elementary School at the University of Missouri (1904); and Collings' experimental schools in McDonald County, Missouri (1917). (See Smith, Stanley, and Shores (1957, pp. 265–269), for a brief description of the curricula of these schools.)

adolescent growth and development is a *sine qua non* for the activities/experience curriculum designer (the teacher).

The second basic feature of this design flows from the first. If students' own needs and interests determine curriculum structure, then curriculum cannot be preplanned in the manner of subject-centered designs; curriculum structure will take shape only as teacher and students plan together the goals to be pursued, the resources to be consulted, the activities to be carried out, and the assessment procedures to be followed. This cooperative planning is so central a feature of the activity/experience design that the term "teacher-pupil planning" has almost become a synonym for it in educational circles.

No definitive advance planning, however, does not mean no preparation whatever. As Smith, Stanley, and Shores (1957, pp. 274, 275) point out, the teacher is responsible for several major tasks which require extensive planning: discovering students' interests, guiding students in the selection of interests, helping groups and individuals to plan and carry out learning activities, and assisting learners to appraise their experience. In short, the teacher must prepare in advance to help learners decide what to do, how to do it, and how to evaluate the results.

A third major characteristic of the activities/experience design is its focus on problem-solving procedures for learning. In the process of pursuing their interests, students encounter certain difficulties or barriers that must be overcome. These difficulties constitute problems which, being real, become challenges that students eagerly accept. In attacking these problems and finding their solutions, students achieve the learnings that represent the major values of this curriculum: realness, significance, immediacy, vitality, and the relevance of activity and experience.

The problem-solving focus of this design contrasts starkly with the emphasis on the exposition of content found in most subject-centered curricula. Subjects and disciplines are viewed as highly useful resources, not bodies of knowledge to be consumed; they are *means* to solving problems rather than *ends* in themselves. Thus, the learning activities component of the curriculum is accorded far more attention in this design than in subject organizations, where primary consideration is given to the content component. Also, *process objectives* (e.g., the constituent skills of problem solving) get much more emphasis here than they do in subject-centered curricula, which tend to focus primarily on *content objectives*. Because of its emphasis on activity and process, the activity/experience curriculum is often condemned for being devoid of content. This is an illegitimate criticism, however, because the design employs substantial content from every field of knowledge, except that its organization is modified to suit the requirements of problem-solving situations.

The principal strengths claimed for the activity/experience design are generally the obverse of criticisms made of subject-centered designs. First, because school activities are based on students' needs and interests, motivation is intrinsic, and does not need to be externally induced. Facts, concepts, skills, and processes are learned because they are important for students, not because they are needed for college or because the teacher will be testing for them. In short, learning is real and meaningful—"relevant," as some observers would have it. A second advantage is that the activities/experience curriculum provides for the individual differences of students. A student may join a class group if its interests coincide with his own; on the other hand, he may decide to pursue an individual project if his needs and interests are unique. Third, the problem-solving activities emphasized in this design provide students with the process skills they will need to cope effectively with life outside school. Indeed, insofar as the curriculum deals with the real needs of students, it actually constitutes "life itself," rather than "preparation for life." And what better "preparation" for life than grappling with the concerns of life itself?

Critics of the activities/experience design, however, have grave reservations concerning its educative efficacy. In the first place, they maintain that a curriculum based on students' felt needs and interests cannot possibly provide an adequate preparation for life. This is so because many understandings vital for effective functioning in the modern world are certain to be omitted if students are allowed to exclude from their curriculum anything that does not immediately interest them. Moreover, while they concede that numerous important skills and concepts are learned effectively through this design, they contend that by and large it neglects the critical *social goals* of education. Are there not *some* aspects of the cultural heritage, they ask, that *all* students should be required to encounter?

A second weakness of the activity/experience design often cited is its inherent lack of a definitive horizontal structure. If the subjects or disciplines organization is abandoned in favor of interest categories, what will the organizing principle of the curriculum be? As Smith, Stanley, and Shores (1957, p. 292) so aptly point out, "Merely to say that the activity curriculum will be based on children's interests does not provide a framework of categories for a curriculum pattern." Although numerous attempts have been made to deal with this problem, none has been found to be entirely satisfactory. Indeed some supporters of subject-centered curricula note (with some justification) that the so-called fragmentation of their curriculum designs seems far less a fault than the virtual antipattern of the activities/experience design.

In all fairness, however, we should point out that the activities/experience design need not be, and usually is not, totally disorganized. For example, Dewey's laboratory school curriculum was structured around four human impulses: the social impulse, the constructive impulse, the impulse to investigate and experiment, and the expressive or artistic impulse; Meriam's elementary-school curriculum employed four other categories: observation, play, stories, and handwork; and more recently, "centers of interest," such as home life, the natural world, the local community, and food, have been used as organizing principles. Although "centers of interest" do not actually describe the way that children's interests are organized, they do reduce learning activities to a manageable number of particular categories for design purposes (Smith, Stanley, and Shores 1957, pp. 267–296, passim). Actually, experimentation with

the activities/experience curriculum has resulted in greatly expanded understanding of children's interests, and further work may eventually turn up the
knowledge we need to do a more creditable job of organization in terms of
interest categories.

A third criticism of the activities/experience design is its inherent lack of
continuity (sequence). Traditionally, sequence in curriculum design has been
based on many factors: maturation, experiential background, prerequisite learning, utility, and difficulty—in addition to interest (Smith, Stanley, and Shores
1957, p. 302). However, when the only basis relied on for curriculum design is
students' interests, which shift erratically over time in response to diverse (and
often uncontrollable) genetic and environmental factors, continuity in learning
is difficult to maintain. Even when interests do not shift, problems result. For
example, students have been known to repeat an activity year after year with
only slight modification as a result of interests fixed in a particular area.

Attempts to overcome the problem of continuity have taken two general
directions. First, efforts have been made to discover the "natural" sequential
order of child and adolescent mental development. The work of the psychologist
Jean Piaget is perhaps the most notable current example of this trend. Valuable
as the knowledge yielded by such research is, however, it does not presently
constitute an adequate basis for sequence in curriculum design. Indeed, since
mental development appears to be heavily influenced by environmental (as well
as maturational) factors, it is doubtful that such research can *ever* comprise the
exclusive basis for curriculum sequence.

The second direction taken to overcome the continuity problem has been
research in centers of interest for various age groups. If general classes of interests could be ascertained for each age group, then a sound basis for sequence
in the activities/experience design would be established. Unfortunately, while
certain common interests have been found to exist within particular age groups,
individual interests are so varied that either (1) they cannot all be fit into a
reasonable number of centers-of-interest categories, or (2) the centers-of-interest
categories must be expanded to the point that they become virtually unmanageable. In any case, interests have been demonstrated to depend so much on
environmental conditions (for example, contrast the corpus of interests characteristic of a Kansas farm boy, a Watts-ghetto black, and a Boston suburbanite)
that questions of value preempt all attempts to base sequence on centers of
interest, even if they could be definitively classified.

In addition to in-principle arguments citing its neglect of social goals and its
weaknesses in organization and sequence, the activities/experience design has
been subject to a number of practical criticisms. First, the design demands an
extraordinarily (perhaps impossibly) competent teacher. Not only must he
possess an unusually extensive liberal education (a subject matter specialist
will not do at all), but he must be exceptionally well versed in the intricasies
of child growth and development and interpersonal relations. Because the design is so unstructured and depends so heavily on teacher-pupil interaction,
anything less than the highest level of teacher performance results at best in

meager and inconsequential learning, and at worst in utter chaos. Related to this criticism, of course, is the argument that colleges are not organized to prepare teachers to function with the activities/experience design, particularly at the secondary level.

A second practical disadvantage of the design is that textbooks and other teaching materials, being organized by separate subject areas, generally are not geared to its requirements. Moreover, the effective implementation of the design requires such an abundance of all types of materials that (1) the teacher cannot possibly be knowledgeable enough about all of them to use them effectively, and (2) the cost of supplying the required wealth of resources is prohibitive.

Finally, it is argued that the design contradicts the entire academic structure. How can students reared on this curriculum adjust to the subject specialization they will find in college? Perhaps even more to the point, will they be acceptable in terms of college entrance requirements?

These caveats notwithstanding, many educators with a deep-rooted commitment to the humane and open principles underlying the activities/experience curriculum have moved with vigor and determination to make the design operational. The program of the Wilson Campus School at Mankato State College in Minnesota is an example:

> *Pupils can go duck hunting whenever they want during the duck season, take vacations anytime during the year, work, sleep, stay at home, and generally "do their thing" as long as it does not hurt others. . . . [They have a] choice of teachers, choice of courses, daily schedules, optional attendance, freedom of dress, and individualized evaluation (no report cards). . . .*
>
> *The schedule is a daily smorgasbord menu. The student selects as much as is needed or desirable, when it is needed, for as long as it is needed. . . . Each day a new schedule is developed for students to select the opportunities which they desire to pursue. They may go home for part of the day, if that best suits their needs (Glines 1970, pp. 187–189).*

While such practices inevitably raise questions about the educative effectiveness of the curriculum, they accurately reflect the spirit of the activity/experience design.

PROBLEM-CENTERED DESIGNS

Problem-centered designs, like the learner-centered ones just described, are rooted in man-centered philosophical assumptions. While a democratic view of society is basic to their structure, it is a less individualistic view, with greater emphasis being placed on group welfare. The individual may be viewed as "naturally good," but more typically the assumption is made that he is neutral. Transactional-gestaltist learning theories predominate.

By "problem-centered designs" we mean designs focused on the problems of living, both individual and social. Because this basic organizing principle is so broad and inclusive, designs in this category exhibit a large number of variations on the theme, focusing, for example, on such areas as persistent life situations, major social functions, contemporary social problems, areas of living, the personal and/or social concerns of youth, and even social action projects for the reconstruction of society. As these names suggest, one of the chief criteria used to compare problem-centered designs is the relative degree of emphasis they place on individual as opposed to social needs.

Generally speaking, designs in this category, unlike learner-centered designs, are essentially *preplanned*. We say "essentially," however, because most of them, as a result of their concern with *genuine* life problems, specify that, to a degree, adjustments should be made when necessary to accommodate the concerns and situations of learners. In this respect problem-centered designs evidence a flexibility not readily apparent in their subject- and learner-centered counterparts.

The horizontal organization of problem-centered curricula is determined by the scope and classification of problem areas to be studied;[13] therefore, content, because it is selected on the basis of relevance to the problem, almost always cuts across subject lines. Sequence, too, is determined by the classification of problems, but it also is based to a large degree on the needs, concerns, and abilities of students. These characteristics make it clear that, unlike the designs previously described, problem-centered curricula stress both *content and the development of learners*.

With the possible exception of the personal/social concerns of youth design, curricula in this category tend, in one form or another, to emphasize the major life activities and problems of mankind. Thus we propose to focus our first description in this section on a prototype curriculum called "the areas-of-living design." With only minor adjustments, many of which we shall note below, this model will adequately describe many of the variations of problem-centered designs previously cited.

The second design to be considered in this section is the core curriculum. Characteristically a problem-centered design, the core is noteworthy because it represents a special application of problem-centered principles and because of its relatively widespread implementation.

Although it may appear to be a distinct design related to learner-centered curricula, the personal/social concerns of youth design is essentially similar to the areas-of-living design. Its organization is based on an analysis of the common problems which adolescents presently face and which they are *likely to face in the future*. It is *preplanned* by adults and stresses *both content and individual development*. Because it evidences so many features in common with the areas-of-living curriculum, this design will not receive separate consideration.

THE AREAS-OF-LIVING DESIGN. Interest in areas of living as a basis for organizing the curriculum can be traced to the nineteenth century and Herbert Spencer's (1885) signal essay, "What Knowledge Is of Most Worth?" (see Chapter 13). Spencer, it will be recalled, proposed that the curriculum prepare people to

---

13. As noted above, horizontal organization may be modified to accommodate students' needs.

function effectively in the five basic areas of living common to all societies: (1) direct self-preservation, (2) indirect self-preservation (e.g., securing food, shelter, etc.), (3) parenthood, (4) citizenship, and (5) leisure activities. As we know, a firmly entrenched subject curriculum precluded any actual reorganization in this direction.

Another important statement advocating that curriculum prepare people in the areas of living was made in 1918 by the eminent Commission on the Reorganization of Secondary Education.[14] This commission proposed a classification of areas of living that gained prominence as "The Seven Cardinal Principles." These are health, command of fundamental processes, worthy home membership, vocation, citizenship, worthy use of leisure time, and ethical character. More recently, the Educational Policies Commission of the National Education Association (1944, pp. 249, 250) has recommended that the curriculum prepare students in six major categories of life: civic responsibility and competence, economic understanding, family relationships, intelligent consumer action, appreciation of beauty, and language proficiency.

Pioneer efforts to implement the areas-of-living design date to the late 1920s, when sociological studies of American life (e.g., Lynd and Lynd (1929)) were beginning to focus attention on the common activities of men and how well (or badly) these activities were performed. By emphasizing common social functions,[15] the areas-of-living design represented an attempt to overcome the inherent weaknesses of the subject design while at the same time avoiding the basic disadvantages of the activities/experience design. In other words:

> *organizing the curriculum around the activities of mankind will not only bring about a needed unification of knowledge but will also permit such a curriculum to be of maximum value to students' day-by-day life, as well as to prepare them for participation in a culture (Taba 1962, p. 396).*

But the most prominent feature of this design, the reorganization of traditional subject matter around areas of living, is at the same time one of its most fundamental problems: What are the essential areas of living that will constitute the organizing principle of the curriculum?

We have already noted the very brief lists of essential areas proposed by two famous commissions. Another well-known plan, one that received much more extensive development, is the *Tentative Course of Study for Virginia Public Schools,* published by the Virginia State Board of Education in 1934. This publication (no longer in use) identifies the major areas of social life as follows:

Protection and conservation of life, property, and natural resources
Production of goods and services and distribution of the returns of production

14. See the section "Special Influences on the Secondary Curriculum" in Chapter 3.

15. The areas-of-living design often is identified in the literature as "the social functions design."

Consumption of goods and services
Communication and transportation of goods and people
Recreation
Expression of aesthetic impulses
Expression of religious impulses
Education
Extension of freedom
Integration of the individual
Exploration

These eleven areas of living constitute the scope of the curriculum for all grade levels (except that the last three are included only in the secondary program). The sequence of the curriculum is governed by a "center of interest" for each grade level, about which the areas of living are clustered. The theory is that the child's sociological center of interest moves consecutively from his immediate home environment, to the school, to the community, and ultimately toward an expanding social and scientific world. Thus, in grade 1, the center of interest is "Home and School"; in grade 2, "Community Life"; in grade 3, "Adaptation of Life to Environmental Forces"; in grade 4, "Adaptation of Life to Advancing Physical Frontiers," etc. While the original document is substantially more detailed, this brief outline will suffice to convey the flavor of a typical areas-of-living design.

Perhaps the most extensive recent effort to develop a design based on areas of living is the "persistent life situations" curriculum proposed by Stratemeyer et al. (1957, pp. 155–165). These authors have prepared a detailed "Master List of Persistent Life Situations" which delineates the scope of a complete and balanced curriculum. While they point out that their list represents only one of many possible analyses of man's activities, they emphasize that since persistent life situations have been its focus, the list should be a useful reference against which to check other plans. A condensed version of the master list is presented below.

A. *Situations calling for growth in individual capacities*
  1. *Health*
    a. *Satisfying physiological needs*
    b. *Satisfying emotional and social needs*
    c. *Avoiding and caring for illness and injury*
  2. *Intellectual power*
    a. *Making ideas clear*
    b. *Understanding the ideas of others*
    c. *Dealing with quantitative relationships*
    d. *Using effective methods of work*
  3. *Responsibility for moral choices*
    a. *Determining the nature and extent of individual freedom*
    b. *Determining the responsibility to self and others*

4. Aesthetic expression and appreciation
   a. Finding sources of aesthetic satisfaction in oneself
   b. Achieving aesthetic satisfaction through the environment
B. Situations calling for growth in social participation
   1. Person-to-person relationships
      a. Establishing effective social relations with others
      b. Establishing effective working relations with others
   2. Group membership
      a. Deciding when to join a group
      b. Participating as a group member
      c. Taking leadership responsibilities
   3. Intergroup relationships
      a. Working with racial and religious groups
      b. Working with socioeconomic groups
      c. Dealing with groups organized for specific action
C. Situations calling for growth in ability to deal with environmental factors and forces
   1. Natural phenomena
      a. Dealing with physical phenomena
      b. Dealing with plant, animal, and insect life
      c. Using physical and chemical forces
   2. Technological phenomena
      a. Using technological resources
      b. Contributing to technological advance
   3. Economic-social-political structures and forces
      a. Earning a living
      b. Securing goods and services
      c. Providing for social welfare
      d. Molding public opinion
      e. Participating in national and local government

It is doubtful that agreement on a master classification of areas of living will ever be achieved. Yet, different as the various classification schemes are, they clearly exhibit many common topics of concern. It may very well be that in principle, this degree of broad agreement is all that is desirable in the interest of maintaining flexibility for areas-of-living designs.

Besides being a preplanned reorganization of content that cuts across traditional subject matter lines, what are some other salient features of the areas-of-living design? First, like the activities/experience design, it focuses on problem-solving procedures for learning. As a result, process objectives (e.g., analysis skills, human relations skills, etc.) and content objectives are functionally integrated, while the passive acquisition of information for its own sake is discouraged. This does not mean, as opponents of this design frequently argue, that students do not learn subject matter. On the contrary, the design draws very heavily on the content of the traditional subjects and disciplines, but it utilizes such content in a form that illuminates the problematic areas of living under study. The following is an excellent account of how content is made functional and integrated with process objectives as a consequence of problem-solving procedures:

> *Twelfth grade John may have fewer opportunities to study economics as a field of knowledge than he would were he under a curriculum design organized by subjects. However, through explanation of the economic problems he has faced over the years, he may actually bring to DECID-ING WHAT WORK TO DO and MANAGING MONEY* [these are to two subproblems in Stratemeyer's life-situations classification scheme] *more comprehensive generalizations. These might include insights into the factors that make for salary differences, the role of government in securing better working conditions, the history and present status of organized labor, the regulations under which banks operate and the reasons why, the purposes of insurance, the basis for tax and social security payroll deduction, the values and hazards in setting up his own independent enterprise.* John's understandings, skills, and insights are learned in the ways in which he is likely to use them. (Stratemeyer et al. 1957, p. 131, emphasis added).

Another feature of this design is that it utilizes the experience and immediate situations of learners as a gateway to the basic areas of living. In this respect it differs significantly from the activities/experience design. That curriculum, *as a matter of principle*, bases its content and learning activities on students' felt needs and interests. In contrast, the areas-of-living design, *as a matter of strategy*, employs students' immediate concerns as a starting point. This is simply the recognition and utilization of a fundamental law of learning. Although the same strategy has been called for in subject-centered designs that take account of contemporary learning theory, the difficulties encountered with it have been legion. The reason is obvious: there is little actual relationship between the separate subject areas and the life experience of students. But this is not the case with the areas-of-living design. Every student's experience is closely related to the basic areas of living; indeed, in a certain sense, it is a special instance of them. We might even say that a well-formulated areas-of-living design comprises a generalized summary of every student's social experience. Thus, the design is able to bring student interest and curriculum goals into the closest functional relationship.

The above account of the areas-of-living design suggests many of the advantages frequently claimed for it. Nevertheless, we shall briefly enumerate the most important of these for the sake of clarity. First, this design presents subject matter in an *integrated* form. It does this by cutting across the separate subjects and focusing on the related categories of social life. Second, because it is organized around the problems of individuals living in society, this design encourages problem-solving procedures for learning. Thus, process objectives, such as critical-thinking skills, receive their proper emphasis, and the acquisition of information for its own sake is discouraged. Third, this design presents subject matter in a *relevant* form. Content is put to use in the solution of real-life problems, rather than consumed for its own (or the teacher's) sake. This is another way of saying that under this curriculum students transform content into *knowledge*; they discover and internalize *meanings*. Fourth, this design presents content in a *functional* form. Because it is employed in the solution of students' own problems, it provides them with learnings that are directly applicable to future life situations. It is said of this curriculum design that more than any other, it brings the learner and society into close relationship. In so doing, it makes the greatest contribution to the development of individuals and the improvement of society. A fifth and final advantage claimed for the areas-of-living design is related to the second: because it is relevant, students do not need to be prodded by extrinsically applied motivational devices. They are learning about what most concerns them: the facts and processes of their own existence in the real world.

Among the difficulties attributed to the areas-of-living design is the one previously mentioned: How are we to determine what, in fact, are the scope and sequence of the essential areas of living? As we have seen, many different (and sometimes conflicting) organizational schemes have been proposed. Because of this difficulty, another problem has arisen: The somewhat arbitrary specification of one or another schema for the organization and sequence of life's activities suggests a kind of artificiality that has, in fact, resulted in *lack* of integration and continuity. Indeed, units developed around separate areas of living have sometimes been so discrete as to produce much the same kind of fragmentation that is characteristic of the subject curriculum. In part, this has been the result of faulty implementation, and is therefore subject to correction; on the other hand, it is unquestionably due, to some extent, to fundamental difficulties with the analysis of areas of living.

The design has also been criticized on the basis that it does not provide an adequate exposure to the cultural heritage—this, as might be expected, from the proponents of the subject curriculum, who advocate the traditional "logical" arrangement of content. The stand one takes on this issue, of course, depends on one's philosophical position. Advocates of the areas-of-living design, however, would maintain that their curriculum is not only as adequate an exposure (in terms of current social needs), but one that is better integrated, more relevant, and more functional as well.

A fourth criticism of the areas-of-living design is directed at the foregoing defense of it: Since the curriculum is based on the areas of current social life, it has a tendency to indoctrinate youth into existing conditions and thereby to perpetuate the social status quo.

> There is no assurance that study within such areas as "getting a living," "conserving and improving material conditions," or "living in and improving the home" would be oriented to deliberately considered and criticized social values. The study of such areas does not, in and of itself, assume anything in particular with respect to values, standards of right and wrong, or relative worth of several ways of earning a living . . . (Smith, Stanley, and Shores 1957, p. 371).

While it does tend to encourage, by omission, acceptance of the status quo, the areas-of-living design cannot be said necessarily and inherently to foster such a consequence. If, in the best tradition of education, it is formulated deliberately to cultivate the critical analysis and evaluation of current social life, it can develop citizens who are eminently competent to participate in directing the evolution of their society.

Beyond these criticisms of the design's utility as a general education instrument, however, is the question of whether a curriculum of this type is adequate to produce the wide variety of specialists needed by a technologically sophisticated society. Stratemeyer et al. (1957, pp. 137–140), noting that general and special education are never entirely discrete, argue for the combined general-*and* special-education efficacy of their persistent life-situations design. Their argument is essentially that "any persistent life situation may be faced under circumstances calling for special competence." This is true, of course, but the point does not directly address the "need-for-specialization" issue. Other proponents of areas-of-living concede the basically *general* nature of the design, but contend that education in special areas (including vocational subjects and the academic disciplines) can easily be added to the areas of living on an elective basis to provide for special-interest and professional/vocational needs. This proposal of elective special courses *in addition to* a general areas-of-living common curriculum verges on describing one variety of the core curriculum, a design to be treated in the following section.

Finally, the areas-of-living design is subject to many of the same practical objections leveled against the activity/experience design: First, teachers are not prepared to function effectively with the design; second, textbooks and other teaching materials needed to implement the design are not readily available; and third, parents and colleges are not ready to accept the departure from tradition that the design represents.

THE CORE DESIGN. The concept of core originated around the turn of the century as a reaction against the fragmentation and "piecemeal learning accumulated from separate subjects" (Smith, Stanley, and Shores 1957, pp. 311, 312). To achieve coherence of the total curriculum, a unifying core of studies was proposed to which the other subjects would be related and subordinated. Thus, the "Ziller plan" made the cultural studies—biblical and profane history and literature—the core about which the other subjects were organized, while the "Parker plan" emphasized the sciences—minerology, zoology, anthropology, and history—in the core. As we shall see, this subject-centered concept of core continues to dominate several contemporary designs presently classified as core curricula.

In the late 1920s, however, the progressive movement evolved a radically different theory of core. On the assumption that the curriculum should foster individual development and democratic social competence, the progressives proposed a core of studies that would center on common individual and social needs. Out of this educational tradition grew what has come to be called the areas-of-living (social functions) core and the social problems core. In addition, the activity/experience branch of the progressive movement developed core designs that utilized principles drawn from learner-centered (activity/experience) designs.

With this kind of historical background, it is not surprising that the term "core" has come to be used in a wide variety of ways. To make matters even worse, many other terms, such as "common learnings," "unified studies," "basic education," and "block-time classes," often are employed as synonyms for core design. In spite of the confusion surrounding the term "core," however, certain generalizations about all curricula bearing this designation can be made. Moreover, although agreement among curriculum specialists is far from universal, a few core designs generally are accepted as authentic or "true" core, while certain others are regarded merely as segments of other types of curricula that pass as "core" because they are required of all students. In this section we hope (1) to clarify the concept of core and (2) to describe the features that properly characterize this pattern of curriculum organization.

To begin with, the core, or universally required, component of any so-called core curriculum is intended to provide common learnings, or general education, for all students. That is, it constitutes the segment of the curriculum that teaches the common concepts skills, and attitudes needed by all individuals for effective functioning in society.[16] This common-learnings feature of core has led to the term sometimes being used to refer to *any* program of general education. As a result, when we are told that a school is employing a core design, about all we can be assured of is that the curriculum is structured somewhat along the lines illustrated in Figure 17-1. This figure shows the required core of general studies surrounded by several varieties of specialized optional courses. On the basis of this usage of the term "core," there is very little that can be assumed about the goals, content, and organization of a core curriculum.

Obviously, while required common learnings is an essential feature of the core design, this characteristic is far from constituting a sufficient, clear, or precise definition of it.

Another common characteristic of core curricula is what Vars (1968, p. 515) calls its "body"—that is, its administrative framework, the block-time class. Whatever diversities of curriculum design are embodied in various core curricula, virtually all[17] employ a block of time consisting of two or more normal periods for teaching the core component. While a team of subject specialists sometimes is given responsibility for the block-time class, most often it is handled by a single teacher who also functions as the class's homeroom teacher.

> *Block time [with a single teacher] has been especially well received at the junior high school level. It provides a transition between a self-contained*

---

16. Because the core design was invented expressly to provide needed, but lacking, general education, its development has occurred primarily at the secondary level, where the curriculum has traditionally been regarded as excessively specialized and fragmented. Almost no core activity has taken place at the elementary level since the curriculum there consists almost entirely of basic common learnings.

17. The principal exception is the "core" consisting of required separate subjects.

FIGURE 17-1
Skeletal structure of the core design.

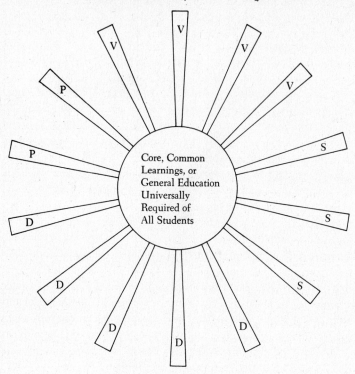

V = Vocational course, e.g.,
     auto mechanics, cosmetology

S = Special-interest course,
     e.g., ceramics, music
     appreciation

P = Preprofessional course,
     e.g., business law,
     premedical biology

D = Academic discipline course,
     e.g., physics, sociology

*elementary school program and a departmentalized high school, and it
facilitates teacher advisement and guidance at a time when youngsters are
going through the stresses and strains that accompany adolescence (Vars
1968, p. 516).*

It is important to emphasize at this point that just as required common
learnings do not in themselves constitute a sufficient criterion for identifying an

authentic core curriculum, neither does the block-time class. The block-time class is an administrative device that does not substantially affect curriculum design. Thus, as we shall see, several curricula that pass as core principally on the basis of common learnings and/or block-time classes generally are not considered authentic core designs.

Aside from these two properties—(1) required general education taught in (2) a block-time class by a teacher who assumes responsibility for the homeroom and guidance functions—curricula passing as core designs vary significantly. Depending on the fineness of distinction that a curriculum analyst wishes to make, the number of different so-called core designs can vary from four to perhaps a dozen or more. Alberty and Alberty (1962, pp. 204–225) describe five different core types; Taba (1962, p. 408), six; and Smith, Stanley, and Shores (1957, pp. 337–381), six. We find that at least six significantly different types of curriculum design are currently being identified as core curricula. These are (1) the separate subjects core, (2) the correlated core, (3) the fused core, (4) the activity/experience core, (5) the areas-of-living core, and (6) the social problems core.

1. *The separate subjects core.* Perhaps the most commonly encountered of the so-called core designs, the separate subjects core consists of a series of required individual subjects separately taught by subject matter specialists. In the junior high school two "core" subjects (usually English and social studies) are sometimes taught by a single teacher in a block-time class. In effect, the separate subjects core is merely a segment of the subject curriculum that is required of all students. It does not legitimately represent a distinct curriculum design. Since it makes no provision for the integration of content, it cannot be traced even to the earliest core initiatives described above. An example of the separate subjects core is a curriculum that requires English, American history, and general science of all tenth graders, but makes no systematic attempt to demonstrate their relationships. Because it is really only a variant of the subject curriculum, the separate subjects core manifests the same characteristics, strengths, and weaknesses as that design.

·2. *The correlated core.* Firmly planted in the subject-centered tradition, the correlated core curriculum attempts to provide common learnings in a coherent form by showing the relationships among the two or more subjects included in the core. Most often, English and American history or social studies are the subjects employed. Less frequently, mathematics and science also are correlated.

In practice, two fairly distinct forms of correlated core have emerged. First, in schools where subjects are taught separately by subject matter specialists, content of the separate core subjects that can be related is brought together and taught concurrently. For example, when the American history teacher is treating the Civil War period, the English teacher is dealing with the literature of that era; or when students are studying communism in their social studies class, they are reading biographies of Marx and Lenin in their English class.

The second pattern of correlated core to emerge employs what Alberty and Alberty (1962, pp. 207, 208) call the "overarching theme." In this variant, the basic content of the subjects is retained, but it is selected and organized with reference to broad themes, problems, or units.[18] Although it is sometimes utilized by schools staffed with subject matter specialists, this type of correlated core usually appears in block-time classes. An example of a theme used to correlate concepts from social studies and science is The Conservation of Natural Resources. In such a unit the social studies elements might include the pioneers' use of the land and forests, waste in deep-pit and strip-mining of coal, and the automobile and private transportation in America; correlative elements from science might include the technology of soil conservation, the chemistry of coal and other sources of energy, and the efficiency of the internal combustion engine. It should be emphasized that in the correlated core curriculum, the topics to be dealt with are *not* primarily determined by such factors as student interest, relevance to social issues, or even relationship to one another. Rather the scope and sequence of the curriculum is governed by the content of the subjects involved. This being the case, the correlated core generally is regarded as a variation of the broad fields design previously described, and as such, its characteristics, strengths, and weaknesses are essentially the same.

3. *The fused core.* Also rooted in the subject-centered tradition, the fused core is based on the total integration or "fusion" of two or more separate subjects. For example, history, geography, economics, sociology, and anthropology may be combined and taught as "social studies"; physics, chemistry, botany, and zoology, as "general science"; or American history and American literature as "American studies." In the latter instance, the core ordinarily is divided into a series of epochs, such as The Colonial Period, The Early National Period, The Westward Movement, and The Industrial Revolution. The literature of each period is presented in the context of the period's political, economic, and social characteristics, and composition, spelling, and other language arts are taught functionally, as tools for developing a basic understanding of the period (Alberty and Alberty 1962, p. 210).

Because it is impossible to integrate subjects that are only tenuously related, the fused core rarely represents the entirety of common learnings. Indeed, mathematics and science are seldom found in this type of "core," although they often are required as separate subjects outside the block-time class.[19]

It seems clear that, insofar as the major characteristic of the fused core is maximal unification or integration of separate subjects, it differs from the correlated core more in degree than in kind. Moreover, it may be noted that inasmuch as unification of related subjects is also the chief property of the broad fields design, the fused core actually represents not much more than a

---

18. Some curriculum specialists (e.g., Taba 1962, p. 408) classify this variant of correlated core as a distinct core design. However, the fact that it is basically grounded in established subject content that is reorganized primarily to demonstrate interrelationships qualifies it as a variant of correlated core.

19. The curriculum described in this paragraph would most properly be classified as a combination "fused/separate subjects core."

segment of broad fields that is made a universal requirement taught in a block-time class. Indeed, all three of the so-called core curricula that we have thus far described are actually variants of subject or broad fields designs. In spite of claims to the contrary, they are rarely regarded as authentic core designs by curriculum specialists.

4. *The activity/experience core.* A product of the progressives' learner-centered tradition, the activity/experience, or "unstructured," core defines general education in terms of the immediate felt needs and interests of learners. Like other learner-centered designs, this one eschews all preplanning and formal structure, basing ultimate curriculum content and organization on the classroom planning and decision making of students and teachers. Needless to say, this type of core design is much less frequently encountered than the subject-centered designs described above. Only a very few elementary schools and a trifling number of secondary schools are organized on this basis.

As we might expect, the activity/experience core is almost always taught in an extended block-time class. Due to the philosophy underlying the design, individual interests usually are accommodated in the core class, though specialized courses frequently are offered on an elective basis, usually in areas that cannot be handled by the core teacher. An example of activity/experience core is a project designed to eliminate pollution in a local river or stream. Both students and teacher decide on the project, plan the activities, and establish criteria for evaluation.

While proponents of this unstructured design hail it as the only "true" core, most curriculum specialists regard it as the activity/experience curriculum scheduled into a block-time class. Their rationale is that, even though the design frequently deals with content in terms of problem areas, it is primarily learner centered rather than problem centered. Indeed, its principal characteristics, strengths, and weaknesses virtually duplicate those of the activity/experience design.

5. *The areas-of-living core.* Also rooted in the progressive tradition, the areas-of-living or "social functions" core is a preplanned, required program of general education based on problems arising out of the common activities of man in society. Insofar as the areas-of-living design was described in a previous section, we need not repeat the description here. Suffice it to say that this type of design generally is regarded as an authentic core design because it is (1) problem centered rather than subject or learner centered, (2) essentially preplanned (3) comprised of integrated, required common learnings (general education), and (4) customarily taught in a block-time class by a teacher who also serves a guidance function. While it draws heavily on the subject areas for its content, its basic orientation is the common needs, problems, and concerns of learners as participants in their own and their society's development. This type of core sometimes makes allowances for student-teacher planning; when such planning takes place, however, it is always within the framework set by the basic curriculum structure.

An example of the areas-of-living core is a unit on community health. Such a unit would stress the health problems of students and relate them to the immediate and wider community. Drawing upon the content of the subject areas, it might utilize concepts from biology and chemistry in a study of nutrition—personal, community, national, and worldwide; ideas from sociology and political science in a study of waste-disposal regulations; or material from history and anthropology in determining the basis and evolution of community and national public-health programs.

The advantages of the areas-of-living core as a program for general education are much the same as those claimed for the areas-of-living design: it integrates and unifies content, encourages problem-solving procedures in learning, presents subject matter in a relevant and functional form, and fosters intrinsic motivation in students. Additionally, Alberty and Alberty (1962, pp. 220, 221) note that this core design makes possible a direct attack upon the needs of youth and the problems which beset them in our present-day confused culture. It also helps to break down the social-class barriers maintained in subject-centered curricula, fosters democratic practices in the classroom, and encourages the use of the community as a laboratory for learning.

Although a large number of curriculum specialists view this type of core as the most promising design for general education in contemporary society, it has been adopted by only a very small proportion of secondary schools (recent estimates range from 4 to 13 percent). The reasons, according to Alberty and Alberty, are not hard to find. Primarily, the areas-of-living core represents a significant departure from subject-centered curriculum designs and often is attacked (unjustly) for its "radicalism," neglect of "fundamentals," and so-called soft pedagogy. In addition, it calls for hard-to-find resource materials in the place of conventional textbooks, and for teachers whose training is quite different from that of most. Perhaps most significantly, however, it may be that authentic core designs are not popular because American society has simply accepted the idea that general education is useless (read "worthless—without cash value"). If the increasing vocationalism and specialization of our secondary and college curricula are any indication, it would appear that, as a people we are far more interested in "learning a living"[20] than in learning how to live. But economic security and material well-being are not necessarily humanizing. Insofar as a sound general education, and not specialized competence, provides the skills and knowledge needed to assess and regulate the quality of our individual and collective lives, our preference for lucrative special skills at the expense of personal/social wisdom can only result in disaster, if not for us, then for our children. However technologically advanced it is, no society unwilling to contemplate the basis of its existence deserves to be called civilized.

6. *The social problems core.* A product of the progressive movement, the social problems core is similar to the areas-of-living core—so similar, in fact, that Smith, Stanley, and Shores (1957, p. 372) comment, "more than a casual

---

20. "Learn a Living" is an advertising slogan adopted by Kent State University and certain other colleges to promote increased enrollments.

analysis is required to determine whether or not a particular core program takes its organizational pattern from social functions or from social problems." There is one critical difference, however, between these two designs: while areas-of-living categories are based upon such universal (and noncontroversial) human activities as "maintaining health," "earning a living," and "conserving natural resources," social problems categories are derived from the crucial (and controversial) issues that beset men at every level of contemporary social life. They are not necessarily universal in scope (Smith, Stanley, and Shores 1957, p. 372).

What makes a social problem *crucial* (and, incidentally, controversial) is the extent of its influence on the entire direction of society. For example, the question of what proportion of our national economic resources should be expended on environmental protection is a crucial social problem because the solution that we arrive at will affect the way people live for generations to come. Other clearly *crucial* social problems include poverty; world hunger; population control; energy conservation; inflation; racism; the status of women; integrity in government; and war, nuclear weapons, and world government.

Social concerns such as those listed above become problems because individuals and social groups preceive them differently and therefore advocate conflicting solutions. Since perceptions are in large measure governed by the desires and values of individuals, these factors become important in both the definition and solution of the problem. This means that the resolution of any social issue involves the modification of individual values.

We noted earlier that because the areas-of-living design is based on the universal activities of man, it has a tendency to sanction and indoctrinate current ideas (the "conventional wisdom") about society and life. In other words, it supports the status quo by omitting a critical consideration of existing conditions. In contrast, the social problems core, by centering on crucial and controversial issues, stimulates the critical examination of conflicting personal and social value systems.

This contrast between the two core designs is well illustrated in the way that each would deal with a hypothetical unit on "Occupations." The areas-of-living core would emphasize the investigation of such factual elements of the topic as available occupations, their contribution to the economy, and perhaps the skills that they require. The social problems core, however, would *in addition* consider the value dimension of the occupational structure. It would raise such questions as: Why are football stars paid twenty times more than medical researchers? What are the moral responsibilities of ad writers? Why is teaching generally considered a low-status occupation in our society? Are there some occupations available that ought to be eliminated? And are there some desirable alternatives that should be added to the existing array of occupations? Clearly, while the areas-of-living core focuses principally on *what is*, the social problems core is also vitally concerned with *what should be*.

The construction of a curriculum unit on a crucial social problem demands that attention be given to a sequence of four fairly definitive phases. The pattern is illustrated in the following four questions.

1. *What is the existing situation?*
2. *What are the probable consequences of the continuance of this state of affairs?*
3. *What is the ideal situation, given certain accepted values?*
4. *If #3 is different from #2, what individual and group action is needed to alter the present course of events?*

One of the best contemporary examples of what a social problems core looks like uses this four-phase pattern with "the disillusionment of youth with our society" as a prototypical social problem:

> *Youth's rejection of adult culture—"the whole, rotten, stinking mess of it"—has become a significant social movement. This movement has assumed international proportions—practically every modern, industrialized nation has felt its impact. Any school that has not made this social movement a subject of serious study on the part of its youthful clientele is about as irrelevant as it can get (Metcalf and Hunt 1970, pp. 358–361).*

Since young people today will be in the prime of life by the year 2000, Metcalf and Hunt urge that they begin to think now about the kind of society they want by that time. Thus, they propose a social problems curriculum structured on the following four questions:

1. *What kind of society now exists, and what are the dominant trends within it?*
2. *What kind of society is likely to emerge in the near future . . . if present trends continue?*
3. *What kind of society is preferable, given one's values?*
4. *If the likely and prognosticated society is different from the society that one prefers, what can the individual, alone or as a member of groups, do toward eliminating the discrepancy between prognostication and preference, between expectation and desire? (Metcalf and Hunt 1970, p. 360).*

Metcalf and Hunt's proposal in effect constitutes a plan for an integrated total social problems core. Its components are the specific problems of society that contribute to the larger unifying problem of the kind of society we have, as contrasted with the one that we want. This framework provides an excellent medium for developing the primary thrust of the social problems core: i.e., learning value standards and how to use them in the process of critical thought.

We have noted elsewhere in this text that historically, no system of education has ever existed free from control of the state. Since the social problems core encourages the scrutiny of current social policy and brings under critical examination the basic value orientation of the culture, we should not be surprised that it has received considerable criticism. The charge, however, that the social problems core aims at remaking society in accordance with prescriptions handed down by curriculum planners and educationists is based on a misconception of the design and is not correct. As Smith, Stanley, and Shores (1957, pp. 380,

381) point out, teachers and students are limited in their capacity to "solve" social problems, and schools can seldom be geared to the resolution of such issues. To claim (as has recently been done) that they *should* engage in large-scale social activism means turning teachers and students into politicians, and this, of course, overreaches the legitimate function of education. Rather, the primary thrust of the social problems core is to emphasize the rigorous study of social problems and to develop habits of critical thinking. Thus, students are prepared (among other things) for effective adult participation in directing the course of their society.

Aside from its emphasis on conflicting values, the social problems core is quite similar to the areas-of-living design: It is problem centered, essentially preplanned, comprised of required common learnings, and customarily taught in a block-time class. Consequently, substantially the same advantages and disadvantages are attributed to both designs. It is worthwhile to note, however, that social problems categories are by their nature far less stable than areas-of-learning categories, which do not vary noticeably over time. Thus, social problems core requires a greater degree of ongoing revision to keep it current and relevant than does the areas-of-living (or any other) design.

The scope of the social problems core is, of course, tied to the identification of crucial contemporary social problems. This raises several questions: What criteria will be used to identify crucial problems? Once identified, how will they be organized? And, is there an integrating framework that can accommodate all manner of social problems? As we have seen, Metcalf and Hunt's overarching problems—"What kind of society do we have—and want?"—suggests one answer to the question of an integrating framework. But much more research is needed in the social problems area if adequate responses to the question of scope are to be made.

The sequence of this core design will of course be governed by such psychological factors as maturity, experiential background, prior learnings, interests, and difficulty. However, the problem of sequence as it applies to "what social values and goals should guide public thought and action in dealing with social issues . . . has not been solved" (Smith, Stanley, and Shores 1957, p. 385).

Of all the so-called core designs, only the last two—areas-of-living and social problems—generally are regarded as "authentic," problem-centered core designs. Probably because of the controversial nature of its content and aims, social problems core has had far less currency, both in the literature and in practice, than its more popular counterpart. Some curriculum specialists, however, believe that the social problems core represents the ideal design for general education in a democracy.

References

Alberty, Harold B., and Elsie J. Alberty. 1962. *Reorganizing the High-School Curriculum.* 3d ed. New York: The Macmillan Company.

Bellack, Arno A. 1965. "What Knowledge Is of Most Worth?" *The High School Journal* (February).

Bruner, Jerome S. 1971. "The Process of Education Reconsidered." *Dare to Care/ Dare to Act*, edited by Robert R. Leeper. Washington, D.C.: The Association for Supervision and Curriculum Development.

Conant, James B. 1959. *The American High School Today*. New York: McGraw-Hill Book Company.

Cremin, Lawrence A. 1971. "Curriculum Making in the United States." *Teachers College Record* (December).

Dewey, John. 1916. *Democracy and Education*. New York: The Macmillan Company.

Educational Policies Commission. 1944. *Education for All American Youth*. Washington, D.C.: National Education Association.

Foshay, Arthur W. 1970. "How Fare the Disciplines?" *Phi Delta Kappan* (March).

Glines, Don. 1970. "Implementing a Humane School." *Educational Leadership* (November).

Goodlad, John I. 1966 "Directions of Curriculum Change." *NEA Journal* (December).

King, Arthur R., Jr., and John A. Brownell. 1966. *The Curriculum and the Disciplines of Knowledge*. New York: John Wiley & Sons.

Lynd, Robert S., and Helen Lynd. 1929. *Middletown.* New York: Harcourt Brace Jovanovich.

Meriam, J. L. 1920. *Child Life and the Curriculum*. New York: Harcourt Brace Jovanovich.

Metcalf, Lawrence E., and Maurice P. Hunt. 1970. "Relevance and the Curriculum." *Phi Delta Kappan* (March).

Rockefeller Brothers Fund, Inc. 1958. *The Pursuit of Excellence*. A Panel Report V of the Special Studies Project, America at Midcentury Series. New York: Doubleday & Company.

Saylor, J. Galen, and William M. Alexander. 1974. *Planning Curriculum for Schools*. New York: Holt, Rinehart and Winston.

Smith, B. Othanel, William O. Stanley, and J. Harlan Shores. 1957. *Fundamentals of Curriculum Development*. Rev. ed. New York: Harcourt Brace Jovanovich.

Spencer, Herbert. 1885. "What Knowledge Is of Most Worth?" In Herbert Spencer, *Education: Intellectual, Moral and Physical*. New York: John B. Alden, Publisher.

Stratemeyer, Florence B., Hamden L. Forkner, Margaret G. McKim, and A. Harry Passow. 1957. *Developing a Curriculum for Modern Living*. 2d ed. New York: Teachers College Press.

Taba, Hilda. 1962. *Curriculum Development: Theory and Practice.* Harcourt Brace Jovanovich.

Vars, Gordon F. 1968. "The Core Curriculum: Lively Corpse." *The Clearing House* (May).

White, Emerson E. 1896 "Isolation and Unification as Bases of Courses of Study." *Second Yearbook of the National Herbart Society for the Scientific Study of Teaching*. Bloomington, Ill.: Pantograph Printing and Stationery Co.

Whitehead, Alfred North. 1929. *The Aims of Education and Other Essays*. New York: The Macmillan Company.

CHAPTER 18
CURRICULUM DESIGN:
ALTERNATIVES AND PROBLEMS

Recent Alternatives in Curriculum Design

The six curriculum designs described in Chapter 17 have received extensive discussion in the literature and at least some testing under classroom conditions. The two designs presented in this chapter represent challenging theoretical proposals based on radical approaches to curriculum design. Needless to say, many details of these designs remain to be worked out when (and if) experimentation with them occurs.

THE "UNENCAPSULATION" DESIGN

The unencapsulation design is an adaptation of Joseph Royce's proposals for mitigating the effects of encapsulation. Encapsulation, it will be recalled, refers to a general human condition in which the individual believes that he has an accurate perception and understanding of reality when in fact, because of various limitations, he has only a partial and distorted image of what is really "out there." (See Chapter 10.) The aim of this design, therefore, is to produce the hypothetical "better man" whose behavior is governed by sound and balanced knowledge rather than distorted perceptions and unconscious prejudices. Clearly, this is a design for general education; it makes no provision for vocational and other aspects of special education.

According to Royce, sound and balanced knowledge is acquired only where all avenues of thought and perception are employed in developing concepts and ideas. Although he admits that there are actually a great many theories of knowing, he maintains that in a psychological sense the human organism can know only in terms of *four* basic processes: rationalism, intuitionism, empiricism, and authoritarianism (Royce 1964, p. 13).[1] Thus, a curriculum for unencapsulation would be organized around these four basic ways of knowing. (Such a design, incidentally, would be characterized as highly *process* oriented and would contrast markedly with most other designs, which take their organizing principles from various arrangements of *content*.)

Royce (1964, p. 13 ff.) briefly describes each of the four ways of knowing and the criteria that each employs to establish the authenticity of knowledge:

Rationalism (thinking) is a system which holds anything illogical to be false. Conversely, sharply logical thinking is said to lead to truth. Thus, the criterion for authentic knowledge in this category of knowing is a logical/illogical continuum.

Empiricism (sensing) is the route to knowledge that employs sensory experience as the criterion of truth. If something cannot be seen, smelled, touched, heard, etc., it does not exist. Furthermore, "truth" is said to be apprehended when we sense objects accurately, but when we misperceive them, we are left only with illusions and false concepts. Thus, the criterion for authentic knowledge in this category is a perception/misperception continuum.

Intuitionism (feeling), which Royce admits is considerably more difficult to define than the other three, is a process of knowing by "immediate" or "self-evident" apprehension. In this connection one often is said to have a "feeling" or "hunch" that something is true. For example, a doctor may have an intuitive "feel" that his patient's symptoms indicate a particular disease, or a motorist on an unfamiliar road may "sense" that he ought to take the right, rather than the left, fork in the road. Although psychology is still very much in the dark regarding intuition, it has been suggested that it may be a process of conveying knowledge via symbol rather than sign (symbols reflect a many-to-one relationship, while signs reflect a one-to-one relationship). For example, a red traffic light is a "sign" meaning one thing: "stop." But a painting or symphony conveys meaning via symbols which can be apprehended by those who have a "feel" for such communication, but which are meaningless to others. Another analysis of intuition (Bruner 1963, pp. 55–68) proposes that sound intuition rests on a solid background of knowledge—a familiarity that gives intuition something with which to work. It means skipping (analytical) steps, leaping out, and taking shortcuts. Whatever research ultimately reveals the precise nature of intuitionism to be, Royce (1964, p. 16) believes that it will certainly include "a complicated mixture of our total psychobiological equipment." The criterion for authentic knowledge via intuition is presented as an insight/no-insight continuum.

Authoritarianism (believing) is the path to knowledge which is founded on the proposition that something is true if the Bible, Plato, Einstein, Freud, or

---

1. Although these processes are substantially distinct, each one actually contains elements of the other three.

some other authority "said so." In fact, authoritarianism is the route to knowledge on which most of us are forced to rely. If man had to test rationally, empirically, or intuitively every item of knowledge that he believed, the task would be absurdly overburdening. (How many of us, for example, take it on authority that the earth spins on its own axis while moving in a circular path around the sun, and how many have checked out this knowledge empirically and rationally?) Clearly, the credibility of our knowledge source is a vital dimension of authoritarianism. As a consequence, the criterion for authentic knowledge in this category is an ideology/delusion continuum.

Royce states (1964, p. 75), "We can escape encapsulation only to the extent that we can educate away from it." This means, of course, bringing individuals into awareness of their psychological limitations and the limitations on perception imposed by the culture. The vehicle for such an education is the curriculum design diagramed in Figure 18-1. In this diagram we find the curriculum organized around the four ways of knowing rather than around subjects, broad

FIGURE 18-1
Curriculum design based on Royce's four processes of knowing.

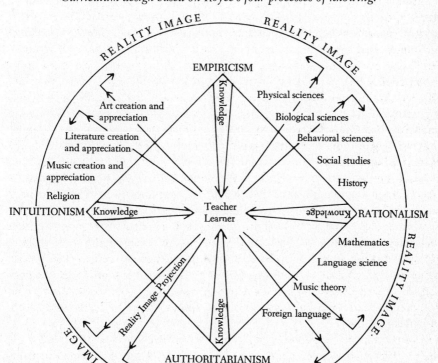

fields, students' needs, social problems, etc.[2] The teacher and learners are depicted at the center of a universe of knowledge which has the potential for presenting human beings with an undistorted image or reality, and thus the basis for wise decision making. By utilizing in the curriculum a balance of all ways of knowing (rather than emphasizing one or two ways as we now do), it is theorized that students (and teachers) will project increasingly more accurate images of reality, thus becoming increasingly unencapsulated.

The scope and sequence of the curriculum design proposed in Figure 18-1 is far from being clearly worked out. Translating this theoretical conception into the concrete objectives, content, learning activities, and evaluation procedures that might constitute *the* curriculum is a monumental task in curriculum construction which would involve many people in a long-term evolutionary process. The significance of the proposal, however, lies in the fact that a coherent theoretical design based on serious consideration of the foundational areas is the platform on which it is proposed that curriculum construction and development work proceed. This approach to curriculum planning is quite different from that which ordinarily is taken, in which alterations of existing designs are made with virtually no attention to overall design so that over a period of time the curriculum assumes the proportions of an incoherent hodgepodge. Whether the unencapsulation design will ever be taken seriously is highly problematical; nevertheless, at this point it represents a legitimate and viable alternative to designs in current use.

BECKER'S HUMANISTIC DESIGN

The humanistic design[3] is a general education design similar in thrust to the unencapsulation curriculum described above. Becker advocates educating away from *alienation* (his term for roughly the same concept as encapsulation), but in addition intends for his curriculum to educate toward an ideal human being whose characteristics approximate those of the individual discussed in Chapter 10. In that chapter, the ideal was described as authentic, self-reliant man in integrated community. Becker's emphasis on content rather than process, however, results in a subject-centered ("broad fields") design, with content organized around three broad areas: (1) the individual dimension of alienation, (2) the social and historical dimension of alienation, and (3) the theological dimension of alienation. It is because the aims and content of this curriculum

2. The traditional subjects—*qua* organizations of content—are included in the diagram to suggest the *approximate* location of familiar segments of present curricula in this unfamiliar design. It should be emphasized that such clusters of content might not be recognizable in an unencapsulation curriculum.

3. Becker presents his design as a university curriculum. With the necessary changes, however, it is quite applicable to the elementary and secondary levels of schooling. Indeed, without such initial application, it is difficult to imagine its effectiveness at the university level. It should be emphasized here that a thorough understanding of his curriculum requires a careful reading of his profound work (see Becker 1967).

center almost exclusively on man that it deserves quite properly to be called "humanistic" (although that term has been so loosely used in recent years that its precise meaning with regard to curriculum design is generally obscure).

The theme that gives unity and coherence to Becker's humanistic design is the question: What is man? Although admittedly unanswerable in the usual sense, the question provides the curriculum with a most significant challenge.

> *The more we learn [about the nature of man], the more it will contribute to our wonder; the more competent we become, the more humble and respectful . . . the more we try to discover man, the more we will discover men. . . . When we gradually discover that we are united with all things, we may learn our closeness with one another; when we find out all there is to know about how we came to be as we are, we will value above all that which we are not yet; when we begin to value this, we will have prepared for the openness that alone could bring a new world into being (Becker 1967, pp. 257, 258).*

The scope of Becker's curriculum is very well defined. As noted above, it consists of three "broad fields." The first broad field (if it may be so called) is "The Individual Dimension of Alienation." This block of content "is supposed to show the individual the history of his estrangement from himself, from reliance on his own powers" (Becker 1967, p. 258). It teaches how man is basically an animal, and how he developed from other animals; the growth of perception and language; the development of the self—those concepts, according to Becker (1967, p. 258) presently included in such courses as "Human Development," "Developmental Psychology," "Personality," "Social Psychology," and "Culture and Personality."

Although Becker (1967, p. 259) does not detail the learning activities through which students are to interact with this content, he is acutely aware of the need to make it meaningful to their individual lives. Presumably, this would entail personalization through discussions and other such vehicles in order to relate the content to students' personal experience.

The second "broad field" of this humanistic design is "The Social and Historical Dimension of Alienation." Inasmuch as individual life history is an integral part of social historical development (and vice versa), the two broad fields evidence some overlap. However, the emphasis of each is quite distinct. The second broad field teaches the student how he is trained to function in a social role and how he earns his feeling of value by filling the status available to him in society; in short, how he is reduced to the role of performer in the larger social scene (Becker 1967, p. 26).

"The Social and Historical Dimension of Alienation" is made up of two main subjects of study: (1) *the history and sociology of the state* and (2) *historical psychology*. With regard to the former, Becker (1967, pp. 263–268) notes that the student would be taught first the historical events that led to the great unequal scramble that we presently call the "civilized state" and second, how the social system functions as an interrelated dramatic fiction. Thus, according to

Becker, he would understand how man has been prevented from achieving self-reliance in the community of men.

With respect to the second subject of study, historical psychology, Becker states that the student would learn how society limits the range of social meanings open to man: for example, how it has promoted the fetishism of commodities and sex; how it has encouraged scapegoating as a clumsy and easy way to attain social unity; and how it has fostered all of the "social manias" that result in irrational, rather than rational, conduct. This broad area of the curriculum, of course, draws its content from such conventional subjects and disciplines as history, sociology, social psychology, and anthropology.

Becker (1967, p. 262) points out that the overlap of the individual and social dimensions provides a natural integration of the two broad fields. However, he is also aware of a serious problem of content selection in the social dimension because of "the crushing mountain of knowledge" represented by its contributing subjects. What criterion, then, will be used to determine which content to include and which to exclude? For Becker the answer is obvious: Since the content must be meaningful in the students' life, he advocates bringing the human person up front, putting him in the center, establishing him as a locus of control (Becker 1967, p. 262). This is equivalent to what contemporary curriculum planners refer to as "student input," and it plays a central and significant role in this humanistic design.

The third and final "broad field" in Becker's humanistic curriculum is "The Theological Dimension of Alienation." Becker is aware that secularists, scientists, and sectarian religionists oppose the introduction of theology as a required course in the curriculum. But he points out that the particular theological point of view he is advocating is not one of *belief*, but one that is "subject to the critical requirements of all universal knowledge: empirical control, examination and discussion, full and free debate aiming at potential refutation" (Becker 1967, p. 272). Thus, he maintains that criticisms of the theological dimension per se are not well founded.

This third broad field of study is intended to teach the student the direction in which he can experience the maximum exercise of his freedom; that is,

> *to contribute our own energies to the eternal meaning of the cosmos, the freedom to bathe our daily life in the highest possible intensity and scope of meanings; and these must be divine, self-transcendent meanings (Becker 1967, p. 273).*

Thus, theology is seen as a natural complement to this humanistic curriculum because it invests the individual and society with significance beyond the daily routines of life. In so doing, it gives full support to the communitarian ideal by showing how a true community differs from a mere collection of individuals (Becker 1967, p. 274). And it pulls together the individual, social, and historical perspectives of the curriculum by providing a transcendent ideal which holds out a solution to the problem of alienation.

It is doubtful that the humanistic curriculum proposed by Becker will receive more than incidental acknowledgment by the educational establishment, much less serious consideration by society at large. In the first place, it is built on a highly sophisticated interlocking set of concepts, a *Weltanschauung*, so to speak, beyond the intellectual powers of many educational professionals even to grasp. Thus, it often is ridiculed as naive, impractical, unrealistic, etc. If it *were* understood, however, it would most likely be bitterly attacked as a threat to our society and its values (which it is), and suppressed with an unrelenting vigor. We should recall that historically speaking, no educational system has ever escaped control by the state (curricula, traditionally, have reflected societies, as we have seen), and a curriculum which, successfully implemented, can transform a society would simply not be permitted.

Like the unencapsulation design, Becker's humanistic curriculum is far from being worked out in detail. Translating the grand design into the specifics of daily objectives, content, learning activities, and evaluation involves long-term commitment, deep thinking, and classroom experimentation. This does not mean, however, that beginnings cannot be made, if desired, conducive to gradual change and evolution. We should remember that, having thought through the foundations and organizational coherence of a more desirable curriculum design, we must always begin implementation in the arena of present practices.

In closing this section on "Recent Alternatives in Curriculum Design," we should note that many novel (and not so novel) designs have been proposed in recent years by writers concerned with curriculum. Interested students may wish to consult the following resources for expositions of alternative curriculum designs: (1) Hyman (1973—short expositions of eleven different designs); (2) Wilson (1971); (3) Broudy, Smith, and Burnett (1964); (4) Phenix (1964); and (5) Dewey (1916).

Critical Problems of Curriculum Design

GENERAL VERSUS SPECIAL EDUCATION DESIGNS

The initial consideration in curriculum design is the determination of whether the focus is to be on general or special education, or both. We have indicated elsewhere that general and special education are not discrete, that elements of both occur in all curricula, regardless of their intent. However, it is important for design purposes to establish clearly if the curriculum is chiefly to train for specific skills and knowledge or to educate for community participation and human development. If the former, design will tend to be determined mainly by the demands of the special area: its content and skills, and the techniques by which these are most efficiently transmitted to learners. In driver training or film developing, for example, curriculum objectives are, relatively speaking, clear and specific enough so that content, learning activities, scope, and even sequence can be developed from regularized, explicit procedures. The design, in effect, reflects a conceptualization based on logico-empirical and technical considerations. In contrast, a design intended to emphasize general education must take into account such factors as cultural norms, human ideals, ethics, and life style. These value issues are so deep-rooted and complex that a general-education design can properly be articulated only after long and difficult inquiry into substantive foundational issues. Even after such an inquiry, problems of scope, sequence, and integration are far from easily handled. In short, the fact that designs for general education represent commitments to preferred life styles needs constantly to be kept in the foreground so that the full moral import of the curriculum never is underestimated.

Because of the distinction between general and special education and the need for both, it seems appropriate to suggest that all public school curricula be formulated in terms of the basic core design diagramed in Figure 17-1. This is not to say that all curricula should have a core patterned on the general education component of a core design, but that public school curriculum design should include provisions for a general education core (whatever its design) as well as an appropriate complement of special education alternatives.

MAINTAINING RELATIONSHIPS AMONG CURRICULUM COMPONENTS

Another major problem area in curriculum design has to do with maintaining a relationship among the four components of curriculum; aims, goals, and objectives; content; learning activities; and evaluation. To begin with, it takes a good deal of keen observation and clear thinking just to maintain a good correspondence between long-range aims or goals and the more immediate contributory objectives to be stipulated in the design. For example, consider the difficulty of formulating the optimal schedule of specific objectives contributing to the attainment of the long-term goal, "ability to employ inductive reasoning in problem-solving situations." Second, it is even more difficult to maintain (at the same time) a clear-cut relationship between curriculum goals and content, learning activities, and evaluation. For example, given a curriculum goal in literature that calls for the development of empathy and the capacity to identify with human values, problems, and dilemmas, care must be taken to devise a variety of learning activities with high potential for attaining the goal, and not (as is often done) to overemphasize activities that center on the intellectual analysis of the literature read (Taba 1962, p. 424). In the same vein, the evaluation of students' achievements on this literature objective will most likely require quite unconventional devices in place of, or in addition to, the usual paper-and-pencil tests that require only recall of literary material.

One way of graphically demonstrating the necessary relationships of curriculum components is suggested in Figure 18-2. In addition to indicating that each of these curriculum components is related to all of the others, it suggests that decisions about any one will have a bearing on decisions about the others.

FIGURE 18-2
Relationship of curriculum components.

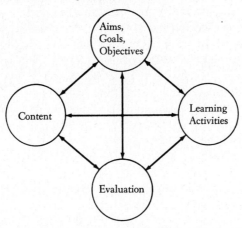

PROBLEMS OF SCOPE AND SEQUENCE

A third critical problem of curriculum design centers on the two basic dimensions introduced at the beginning of Chapter 17: horizontal and vertical organization, or, in the terminology of the curriculum field, scope and sequence. Scope, it will be recalled, refers to the extent and arrangement of curriculum elements that occur at the same time, while sequence describes their progressive, level-to-level organization over a period of time. These two factors in design may be graphically represented by the diagram in Figure 18-3. This diagram indicates that the scope of the curriculum gradually expands as learners move through it (from levels 1 through 8). Moreover, the scope of the curriculum changes from level to level as some elements are dropped or reduced, and others are added or expanded. At level 1, for example, learners interact with elements A, B, C, D, E, and F in varying degrees of emphasis (the wider the area, the greater the emphasis). By the time they proceed to level 4, however, elements A and F have been eliminated and elements G, H, J, and K have been introduced in varying degrees of emphasis. It should be made clear that Figure 18-3 tends to oversimplify the dimensions of scope and sequence insofar as it does not indicate (1) vertical *progress* from one level to another and (2) *relationships among elements* at given levels of the sequence.

The principal design problem associated with *sequence* is the difficulty of developing *cumulative and continuous* learning as students move through the curriculum. According to Taba (1962, p. 429), this problem has been particularly resistant to solution because sequence has traditionally been considered only in terms of content, with little or no attention being given to the sequence of processes—i.e., the skills and competencies that students should develop in their interaction with content. For example, in spite of many "logical" arguments in support of the vertical arrangement of its content, the conventional science se-

FIGURE 18-3
Curriculum scope and sequence.

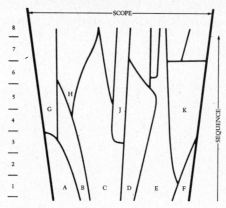

quence of first biology, then chemistry, then physics mandated by most secondary schools makes very little sense in terms of cumulative student development from a process (or even from a content) standpoint. This failure to pay serious attention to sequence in terms of the cumulative development of intellectual and affective processes has resulted in innumerable curriculum difficulties, among which we may identify poor articulation among the levels of schooling, perennial complaints at each level of poor preparation at the preceding one, misplaced expectations, and generally reduced student development (Taba 1962, p. 429).

The principal design problem associated with *scope* is the difficulty of integrating the variety of learnings that students undergo at a particular level of the curriculum. Enough has already been said about fragmentation and the compartmentalization of learnings from English, mathematics, history, and science, for example, to preclude the need for further elaboration here. Suffice it to say that the problem of integration has resisted solution in part for the same reason that the problem of cumulative development in sequence has—failure to pay sufficient attention to the interrelationship of intellectual and affective processes. While specific, nontransferable skills can certainly be claimed for each of the separate curricular areas, a broad range of reading, thinking, expression, aesthetic, and interpersonal processes are common to all of them. These common processes need to be identified and utilized as integrating elements to bolster the horizontal coherence of the curriculum.

Another problem associated with scope has to do with the breadth-or-depth dilemma that was raised in the section describing the broad fields design. The broader the scope, for example, the less possibility there exists for depth. This dilemma, it should be noted, applies whether we are dealing with scope in terms of content or process learnings. It also is related in many significant ways to our basic epistemology and learning theory. But given the chronological framework in which curriculum must be set, it is difficult to avoid consideration of the breadth-or-depth problem of design.

IDENTIFICATION OF ORGANIZING CENTERS

A fourth problem of curriculum design, the problem of determining the *organizing centers* of the curriculum, is related to scope and sequence problems insofar as it defines to some extent scope and sequence possibilities. We are already somewhat familiar with a variety of macrodesign organizing centers as a result of our discussion of representative curriculum designs. Among others, we should briefly recall the separate subject, the broad field, the learner's need, and the contemporary social problem as typical organizing centers.

Goodlad (1963, pp. 25–50) has proposed that *two* organizing concepts be used to deal with scope and sequence problems. The first of these he calls the *organizing center*. This may be a book, event, problem, epoch, experiment, or field trip selected to achieve one or more curriculum objectives with a specific group of learners. Either narrow or broad in scope, the organizing center defines the substance of the learning that is to occur at a given level of schooling.

Goodlad calls his second organizing concept the *organizing element*. This is the thread running through a series of organizing centers, "holding them together like beads on a string." An organizing element may be a concept, generalization, skill, mode of inquiry, or other developmental theme about which specific organizing *centers* are longitudinally clustered. For example, the concept of energy might be an organizing element which is developed through organizing centers on magnets in the primary years, and further expanded through a study of the solar system in high school. It is fair to say that the organizing element controls sequence by guiding the upward progression of students, while the organizing center defines scope by specifying content, materials, procedures, etc., at each level of the curriculum.

As we have seen earlier in this chapter, determining what the organizing centers of a curriculum design are to be is a process involving assumptions and beliefs in the foundational areas. Subject, learner, and problem centeredness are conclusions that evolve from basic value orientations. Inasmuch as the nature of organizing centers profoundly influences design possibilities, it is most difficult to deal with the technical problem of manipulating centers of organization without prior consideration of their specific nature.

THE PROBLEM OF BALANCE

A fifth problem of curriculum design is one that has been alluded to above: the problem of maintaining *balance* in the curriculum. Balance, of course, means ensuring that appropriate weight is given to each aspect of the design so that distortions due to overemphasis and underemphasis do not occur. Banal as such a consideration may appear, it is noteworthy that most designs are remarkably weak in this respect.

A great deal of controversy in curriculum design has traditionally centered on the question of how much emphasis, respectively, should be accorded to subject matter on the one hand, and learners on the other. This is, of course, a question of balance. As we have seen, some curriculum designs are heavily subject centered, while others are fundamentally learner centered. In the former case, emphasis on content usually results in the conclusion that arithmetic, for example, is an important subject that can be learned by first-graders; therefore, that subject is systematically taught, beginning in the first grade. The result is frequently frustration and failure, with the victims of an inflexible curriculum being charged with responsibility by reason of stupidity, indolence, recalcitrance, or worse. In the latter instance, where primary emphasis is placed on learners, first-graders are customarily taught what *they* are interested in learning and consequently may not be introduced to arithmetic until much later on. Even then, the subject will probably not be taught systematically, but rather functionally, in accordance with learners' needs and interests. The result here is frequently number illiteracy and other basic educational inadequacies.

Reasonable consideration of the balance factor in design suggests that neither of these "either-or" positions is very satisfactory, and that a renewed, non-ideological inquiry into the problem is long overdue.[4] Some previously discussed "problem-centered" designs, of course, represent efforts in this direction, but their practical results have been somewhat less than spectacular. The reason is that balance in this case is not a simple matter of more or less emphasis but rather a very complex process involving the integration of two diverse factors: subject matter and learners. A great deal of work still remains to be done in the development of designs that respect the logic and authority of knowledge and at the same time provide for the humane development of learners.

Balance is also a factor in the development of the four curriculum components. For example, subject-centered designs tend to overemphasize content to the neglect of objectives, learning activities, and evaluation. When objectives are defined in these designs, they are usually quite narrow, mainly stressing ingestion of content. Also, learning activities center on the memorization of information, and evaluation follows suit by measuring only the quantities of data that students retain. In contrast, core curricula often overemphasize learning activities, but are deficient in the specification of content (Taba 1962, p. 422). Objectives and evaluation in these designs also tend to be underemphasized, probably because their breadth of scope makes them difficult to handle. The main difference in emphasis between the subject and the core designs, however, probably derives from the former's propensity to view learning in terms of content, and the latter's tendency to view it as process. We may note, finally, that the fascination with curriculum outcomes that dominates many current "competency-based" designs has resulted in curricula that are mainly comprised of objectives and evaluation, with extremely superficial consideration given to the components of content and learning activities.

---

4. Dewey's (1916) work probably represents the best contemporary approach to curriculum design in which subject matter and learners are accorded proper balance.

The distinction between content and process learnings mentioned above represents another point which requires special attention if balance is to be maintained in curriculum design. As we have noted earlier in connection with the problem of scope and sequence, traditional designs have tended to overemphasize content learning to the neglect of many important intellectual and affective processes. Content and process are inextricably linked, of course, but inadvertent overemphasis of either results in distortions that permeate the entire design structure.

The five problems of curriculum design described above reflect one writer's conception of the major issues in curriculum organization. For comparison and contrast, we present below the seven fundamental questions of curriculum design proposed by Stratemeyer and associates.

FUNDAMENTAL QUESTIONS IN CURRICULUM

1. *How can balanced development be assured? What guarantees can there be that important areas of life in which students or teacher are insensitive to problems will not be neglected?*
2. *How can there be continuous growth from year to year without undesirable repetition or undesirable gaps in learning?*
3. *How can desirable depth of knowledge be assured? How is it possible to prevent learners from ending up with a smattering of superficial knowledge about many areas and little of the depth they need for genuine understanding?*
4. *How will the depth of command of special subject areas important to individual learners be assured? Where will the persons with specialized talents come from—the scientists, historians, linguists, artists, teachers, statesmen, philosophers of the future?*
5. *How can it be guaranteed that children and youth will become acquainted with the broad cultural resources which are part of our heritage and become skilled in drawing upon and using these resources in meeting life situations?*
6. *How can there be guarantees that choices of problems are not trivial and do not represent transitory interests rather than basic concerns?*
7. *How can there be genuine group problems? Will there not actually be many times when extrinsic motivation will be needed if group study is desired? Does the point of view not logically lead to work that is completely individualized? (Stratemeyer et al. 1957, pp. 110, 111).*

While some of the problem areas that we have identified are omitted from the above list (and vice versa), areas of correspondence are clearly substantial. Treatments of design problems by other writers show a similar correspondence. Consequently, it is fair to say that curriculum specialists appear to know what the design problems are, but they have not yet been able to formulate effective solutions for them.

References

Becker, Ernest. 1967. *Beyond Alienation.* New York: George Braziller.

Broudy, Harry S., B. Othanel Smith, and Joe R. Burnett. 1964. *Democracy and Excellence in American Secondary Education.* Chicago: Rand McNally & Co.

Bruner, Jerome S. 1963. *The Process of Education.* Cambridge, Mass.: Harvard University Press.

Dewey, John. 1916. *Democracy and Education.* New York: The Macmillan Company.

Goodlad, John I. 1963. "Toward Improved Curriculum Organization." In *Planning and Organizing for Teaching.* Project on the Instructional Program of the Public Schools. Washington, D.C.: National Education Association, chap. II.

Hyman, Ronald T., ed. 1973. *Approaches in Curriculum.* Englewood Cliffs, N.J.: Prentice-Hall.

Phenix, Philip H. 1964. *Realms of Meaning.* New York: McGraw-Hill Book Company.

Royce, Joseph T. 1964. *The Encapsulated Man.* New York: D. Van Nostrand Company.

Stratemeyer, Florence B., Hamden L. Forkner, Margaret G. McKim, and A. Harry Passow. 1957. *Developing a Curriculum for Modern Living.* 2d ed. New York: Teachers College Press.

Taba, Hilda. 1962. *Curriculum Development: Theory and Practice.* Harcourt Brace Jovanovich.

Wilson, L. Craig. 1971. *The Open Access Curriculum.* Boston: Allyn & Bacon.

CHAPTER 19

CURRICULUM DEVELOPMENT: REPRESENTATIVE MODELS

The concept of lay persons determining the ends and professionals determining the means of education is too simple a generalization for most situations. —JOHN I. GOODLAD

Introduction

It will be recalled from Chapter 1 that curriculum work in real school settings consists of three essential processes: curriculum construction, curriculum development, and curriculum implementation.[1] Curriculum construction is defined as the decision-making process that determines the nature and design of the curriculum; curriculum development as procedures for carrying on the construction process; and implementation as the process of putting into effect the curriculum produced by curriculum construction and development.

These three processes, it should be emphasized, are neither discrete nor sequential, but occur both in parallel and in alternating tandem. They make up a highly complex and organic cluster of curricular phenomena that requires skillful orchestration of participants and components in order to bring about desired results. Thus, while it is convenient to discuss these three processes separately for the sake of clarity and understanding, practice demands that they be dealt with concurrently and in combination.

Chapters 5 through 16 of this text were concerned essentially with the process of curriculum construction—the basis for decision making in the areas of (1) foundations and (2) components of the curriculum. Our final three chapters, on the other hand, will focus on the dynamics of curriculum development and the forces that affect curriculum implementation and change. One may legiti-

1. These are the three processes that curriculum specialists refer to collectively as *curriculum engineering.*

mately ask why the curriculum construction process merits as many as twelve chapters, while development, implementation, and change—the "doing" aspect of curriculum work—are treated in only three. The answer is twofold: First, the construction process, which emphasizes the valuing, foundational, "theoretical" aspect of curriculum work, has been generally neglected by curriculum writers. The reason, very likely, is that American culture has stressed the *"do* something" aspect of affairs to such a degree that the reflective, understanding component of human behavior has suffered proportionately.[2] If anything has characterized curriculum work in the United States, it is the propensity to implement a plethora of "innovations" with little thought given to their theoretical soundness or value orientation. Therefore, a deliberate effort has been made here to provide a full and comprehensive basis for understanding the curriculum itself, about which a great deal is known, but is rarely brought to bear in practice. The point is that an in-depth understanding of our selves, our values, our culture, and our relationships with physical and social environments provides us with the best possible basis for intelligent decision making in the action realms of development and implementation.

Our second point more directly addresses the relatively briefer treatment accorded curriculum development, implementation, and change. Unfortunately, very little is known about these processes and it is for this reason, rather than neglect, that we are able to treat them in only three chapters.

> *Little has been learned about development processes from curriculum development projects. We do not have even a rudimentary taxonomy of curriculum developments and we do not know such things as these: what organization of personnel is most suitable to maintain an idea throughout development; when, and under what conditions, different actors perform best; what the critical decision points are; and whether different patterns of decision give different outcomes (Connelly 1971, p. 165).*

In spite of the rudimentary state of our knowledge about the curriculum-engineering processes, a variety of patterns for curriculum planning and implementation have emerged since the advent of curriculum as a field of study. Some of these have been widely employed in curriculum work, while others have received little currency outside of the literature. The following section presents a brief description of the most prominent models for curriculum engineering with the caveat that they represent theoretical prototypes which rarely, if ever, occur in pure form when put into practice.[3]

---

2. See, for example, *Don't Just Do Something* (1972). The point of the title is that we need to *understand* situations before acting on them.

3. The serious student may wish to consult the following authors for alternative classifications of curriculum engineering models: Lippitt (1965, pp. 15–23), O'Hanlon (1973/74, pp. 64–71), and Doll (1964, pp. 258–298).

Models for Curriculum Engineering
THE ADMINISTRATIVE (LINE-STAFF) MODEL

The earliest, and probably the most familiar, pattern of curriculum development is the administrative model.[4] Because it utilizes "top down, line-staff" procedures, initiatives for curriculum development usually originate with a high-level official, often the superintendent. Having decided that a program of curriculum development and implementation is needed, he arranges meetings with key subordinates and, if necessary, seeks approval for the project from the board of education. These critical steps ordinarily culminate in the formation of a steering committee made up of top administrative officers (assistant superintendents, principals, and supervisors) and key teachers. The charge of this steering committee is to formulate general plans, develop guiding principles, and prepare a statement of philosophy and objectives for the *entire* school district. In addition, the steering committee may provide for the organization of lay advisory committees to work with school personnel in formulating plans, principles, and objectives.

Having developed a broad curriculum policy, the steering committee selects and appoints from the teaching staff the working committees responsible for the construction of the curriculum. These are the committees that formulate the specific curriculum goals and objectives, content, learning activities, etc.—all in accordance with the policy guidelines laid down by the steering committee. Customarily, this work has been done after regular school hours and without additional compensation. These conditions often are identified as being responsible for (1) disillusionment with curriculum work on the part of many teachers and (2) the generally poor quality of curriculum that results from the process.

When the committees of teachers have completed the curriculum-construction process, the curriculum documents which they have produced are reviewed either by the steering committee or another high-level committee appointed for that purpose. This committee serves several functions: It provides for coherence of scope and sequence in the K–12 program by coordinating the work of the separate teachers' committees; it ensures the orthodoxy of the whole vis-à-vis the curriculum policy set by the steering committee; and it makes such emendations of style and form as may be required prior to sending the materials for publication.

With the curriculum plan in its revised and final form, another committee of administrators (usually building principals) and teachers is appointed to implement or "install" it. This committee acquaints those professional personnel who were not engaged in the production of the curriculum with its philosophy, rationale, objectives, and methodology. As the new curriculum is tried out under

4. The administrative, grass-roots, and demonstration models of curriculum engineering are classifications identified and described by Smith, Stanley, and Shores (1957, pp. 426–436). These authors note that the administrative model was used to revise the curriculum in the city of Denver in 1923.

actual teaching conditions, its effectiveness is monitored through class visits, discussions, pupil evaluation, and other means, and modifications are made as indicated by the results (Smith, Stanley, and Shores 1957, p. 428). Following this period of implementation and modification, the "new" curriculum is declared to be an operative reality in the school system.

Because curriculum development in the administrative model is conceived, initiated, and directed from the top downward along hierarchical line-staff channels, it has been widely criticized as being undemocratic in principle. This criticism aside, however, experience with the model has shown that it is not a very effective means for bringing about and sustaining significant curriculum change. The reasons are fairly complex and have a great deal to do with the fact that curriculum change is "people change" and cannot be brought about merely by fiat or by organizational manipulation (e.g., the formation of committees). More specifically, however, it has been pointed out that a major weakness of the administrative model is its assumption of the "two-phase" concept—i.e., the concept that changes from an old to a new curriculum take place uniformly at a given time throughout the school system in two distinct phases—(1) the preparation of a new curriculum document and (2) the installation or implementation of the document. The following is one comment on the fallacy of this uniform, two-stage process:

> As experience in curriculum programs increased, the concept of change on a "uniform front" was one of the points at which radical modification occurred. . . . Thus there developed the conception of change on a "broken front." This recognized that modifications in practice have small beginnings, with a few teachers taking the lead in the difficult process of testing new ideas. As new practices are demonstrated to be feasible, more teachers take over their use. . . . (Caswell et al. 1950, pp. 51–52).

Because of the criticisms noted above, the administrative model rarely is advocated among curriculum specialists. However, many school districts continue to employ its managerial line-staff principles (under less authoritarian-sounding nomenclatures) to "get the job done."

THE GRASS-ROOTS MODEL

The grass-roots model of curriculum engineering contrasts with the administrative model on many significant points. For example, it is initiated by teachers in individual schools, employs democratic group methods of decision making, proceeds on a "broken front," and is geared to the specific curriculum problems of particular schools or even classrooms.

The intensely democratic orientation of the grass-roots model is responsible for generating what have probably become the curriculum establishment's two least-questioned axioms: First, that a curriculum can be successfully implemented only if the teachers have been intimately involved in the construction and development processes, and second, that not only professional personnel, but students, parents, and other lay members of the community must be included in the curriculum planning process. To deny the validity of either of these claims (neither of which has been satisfactorily demonstrated) is not necessarily to deny *any* role to teachers or lay participants; rather it is to suggest the need to define more precisely the *appropriate* role that administrators, teachers, curriculum specialists, and nonprofessionals should play in curriculum engineering.

The primacy of the teacher as the key to effective curriculum engineering is reflected in the four principles on which the grass-roots model is based:

1. *The curriculum will improve only as the professional competence of teachers improves.*
2. *The competence of teachers will be improved only as the teachers become involved personally in the problems of curriculum revision.*
3. *If teachers share in shaping the goals to be attained, in selecting, defining, and solving the problems to be encountered, and in judging and evaluating the results, their involvement will be most nearly assured.*
4. *As people meet in face-to-face groups, they will be able to understand one another better and to reach a consensus on basic principles, goals, and plans* (Smith, Stanley, and Shores 1957, p. 429).

These principles become operative as teachers are encouraged to work "cooperatively" in the planning of new curricula. "Encouragement" occurs when administrators provide "leadership," free time, materials, and other stimuli conducive to curriculum planning. In some districts "workshops" are organized to foster the process: at year's end, workshops tend to focus on curriculum review and needs assessment, while prior to school opening they may result in the construction of new curricula. Ideally, of course, the workshops include administrators, teachers, students, parents, and other lay members of the community, in addition to consultants and special resource personnel. Participants work on the curriculum problems peculiar to their own local situations and resolve these problems democratically, by consensus. It is worth noting here that because teachers are so intimately involved in the planning and decision-making processes, their knowledge and commitment precludes any need for the special implementation procedures demanded by the administrative model.

The primary weakness of the grass-roots model of curriculum engineering is that it applies the method of participatory democracy to a highly technical, complex, and specialized process. This is not to say that the community and public interest need not be provided for, or that teachers have no role in curriculum engineering. It *is* to say, however, that a "one man-one vote" rationale will not necessarily result in good decisions in situations where it is necessary to bring to bear the authority of specialized knowledge. In short, the appropriate roles and functions of participants in the process needs far more precise definition than is provided by what is essentially a democratic governance model. Having made that point, however, it is also necessary to note that the grass-roots model has contributed immeasurably to broadening the base of curricular decision

making, and in that regard it is at least partly responsible for increased respon-
siveness of curricula to community desires.

THE DEMONSTRATION MODEL

Proposals for extensive changes in the curriculum often are perceived as threats
to the security, status, and general welfare of the people affected by them. Thus,
because the demonstration model is designed to introduce curriculum innovation
on a small scale, it is advocated specifically for situations in which a broad,
systemwide program of curriculum revision is likely to be met by strong opposition either from the faculty or the community.

According to Smith, Stanley, and Shores (1957, p. 435), the demonstration
model occurs in two forms. In the first, a separate unit of teachers is organized
within the school and charged with the development of experimental curriculum
projects. The ultimate purpose of this unit, a kind of internal research and
development (R and D) team, is to produce new segments of curriculum with
the hope that their demonstrated merit will result in adoption by the entire
school. Insofar as this form of the model is initiated and organized by the
administrative hierarchy, it represents a variation of the administrative model
of curriculum engineering.

The second form of the demonstration model is less formally constituted than
the first. Here, a few teachers who are dissatisfied with the existing curriculum
decide to experiment in certain areas for the purpose of generating alternative
curriculum practices. The more "successful" curriculum units created by this
informal R and D team then are proposed for adoption on a schoolwide basis.
Clearly, this form of the demonstration model is representative of the grass-
roots approach to curriculum engineering.

There are several advantages associated with the demonstration model. First,
because curriculum produced by this process has undergone testing in protected
experimental situations, it can provide a school or school system with "workable"
alternatives to present practices. Second, as we have noted above, change in the
form of specific, workable segments of curriculum tends to mitigate the head-on
resistance that often develops in the face of proposals for total or systemwide
revision. Third, the small-scale nature of the demonstration model facilitates a
"broken front" approach to curriculum innovation that avoids the hiatus between
document and implementation inherent in the administrative model. Finally,
the demonstration model, especially in its grass-roots form, "capitalizes on the
initiative and resourcefulness of teachers, and gears the administrative resources
to the needs and interests of teachers in the development of new programs"
(Smith, Stanley, and Shores 1957, p. 436).

The principal weakness of the demonstration model is that it creates new
antagonisms to replace the ones that it avoids. For example, as Smith, Stanley,
and Shores (1957, p. 436) note, teachers who are not participants in the curriculum development process tend to perceive the experimental teachers with
suspicion and distrust. They may regard them at best as a well-meaning but

misguided group, or at worst as a "fair-haired," self-serving, opportunistic elite. Resentments such as these, of course, do not bode well for the adoption of even the most meritorious curriculum innovations. Consequently, an important component of the demonstration model is provision for open lines of communication between experimental teachers and the "regular" faculty, the primary goal being the *prevention* of resentments, rather than their neutralization. In any case, it is essential that the experimental unit at some point "demonstrate" the merit of their work to the satisfaction of the faculty, parents, and students if their curriculum innovations are to become more than experimental curiosities.

BEAUCHAMP'S SYSTEM

Beauchamp (1964, pp. 116–139) identifies a series of five critical decision-making areas that in effect constitutes a model for curriculum engineering. The first of these is the *arena for curriculum engineering*, a term which defines the scope of the development effort. For example, the arena may be a single classroom, a school, local school system, an entire state, or as is the case in some European countries, an entire nation. Decisions regarding the arena largely are settled by such external considerations as legal statutes and de facto circumstances. For example, while legal responsibility for education in the United States is vested in state governments, curriculum decisions have been left substantially to local authorities. Both state and federal governments, however, are becoming increasingly influential in determining curriculum policy. Furthermore, whatever arena is selected for the construction process, implementation must, by its nature, always be dealt with in the arena of the individual classroom. In spite of these limitations, though, considerable latitude in choosing arenas does exist. For example, whether the construction arena is to be a single school or an entire school system is still very much an open question. Unfortunately, Beauchamp's model provides little guidance on this kind of an open question.

The second phase in Beauchamp's system is the *selection and involvement of people*. Beauchamp (1964, p. 118) points out that historically, four different categories of people have been involved in curriculum planning in the United States. These are (1) specialized personnel, such as central-office curriculum specialists or outside subject matter specialists, (2) representative groups composed of specialized personnel and selected classroom teachers, (3) all professional personnel in the school system, and (4) all professional personnel plus representative lay citizens. As we shall attempt to show below,[5] Beauchamp's categories tend to describe the somewhat mythical conventional wisdom of the educational establishment. They represent groups of people who "go through the motions" of curriculum making, but do not in fact affect its substance in any significant way. Rather, it is a different set of actors who have the greatest impact on the curriculum: textbook writers and publishers; local, state, and national political figures; unions and corporations; and a wide variety of other

5. See the section "Political Realities of Curriculum Development" in Chapter 20.

special-interest groups, from the John Birch Society to the National Organization for Women, to name just a few. This is not to say that local professionals
have *no* control over the curriculum that is taught; after all, teachers have been
known to subvert a wide variety of imposed curriculum innovations. But it *is*
to say that, as a group with limited power and influence that generally willingly
(and unconsciously) conforms to the more conventional values of the culture,
school personnel cannot easily construct and implement curricula that *really*
represent alternatives, even if they wish to do so.

It is obvious that phase two of Beauchamp's model, the selection and involvement of people, depends to a considerable degree on the arena for curriculum
engineering. If the arena is to be the entire nation (as it is in France, for
example), it would be foolish for national planners to call for the participation
of local school personnel in the curriculum construction process (although
classroom teachers would play a significant role at the implementation stage).
On the other hand, if the arena is a single school, there seems little reason to
involve state, much less national authorities. Beyond the limitations imposed by
the arena, however, considerable latitude exists, and in a country like ours,
where curriculum planning is in effect delegated to local districts by the legally
constituted state authorities, the possibilities, including the political realities,
are intriguing. For some reason, however, controversy among educationists has
tended to center on a single aspect of this issue: Should *everyone*—administrators, teachers, students, and interested lay members of the community—be
involved in curriculum planning?

As we noted in the section on the grass-roots model, the ideological appeal
of participatory democracy has led to strong advocacy in the curriculum literature
for total (and often *full*) participation of all professional and lay members of
the community. With regard to teachers, the argument in favor of involvement
most frequently heard is that participation in planning is essential for commitment and effective implementation. This, of course, is a *logical* point, unsub-
stantiated by research, that does not account for *alternative* means of securing
commitment and effective implementation. Beauchamp wisely counsels caution
with regard to teacher involvement, but on other grounds.

> The theorist or practitioner who debates and decides on this involvement
> should know beforehand the teacher-load problems that it carries in its
> wake. The conventional impression of the job of the teacher is that his
> sole responsibility is to develop instructional strategies and carry them out
> with his class or classes . . . To think of involving teachers additionally
> in anything as complicated as a curriculum system . . . is impossible unless
> ways and means [are found] for teachers to participate . . . unencumbered
> by teaching responsibility (Beauchamp 1964, p. 120).

This position clearly allows for teacher involvement in curriculum planning,
but sets up certain practical preconditions.

With regard to the participation and role of lay citizens in curriculum planning, advocates "make much of the fundamental authority and responsibility of
school patron groups . . ." (Beauchamp 1964, p. 121), while opponents cite lay

citizens' lack of technical expertise in complex curriculum-engineering processes. Neither of these arguments is sufficiently comprehensive nor convincing, but most debate in this area falls into the category of unsupported "value judgment." Whatever group is being considered for involvement in the planning process, the question of participation will have to be handled on at least three levels: (1) *Should* the groups be involved in curriculum planning? (2) If so, what *role* should it play? (3) Is it possible to develop ways and means for that role to be effectively executed?

The third sequential area in Beauchamp's model for curriculum engineering is *organization and procedures for curriculum planning*. This area defines the procedures to be followed by those who establish curriculum goals and objectives, select the content and learning activities, and determine the overall design. The problems entailed in this area of engineering are reasonably manageable when the arena is limited (e.g., a single small school) or when the people involved are relatively homogeneous (e.g., a committee of specialized personnel); however, the problems here become overwhelmingly complex when large numbers of diversified people are involved in systemwide programs of curriculum development and implementation.

Beauchamp (1964, pp. 128–131) divides this third area into five successive phases: The first phase is the formation of a "curriculum council" to act as an overall coordinating agency. The second phase involves the appraisal of present practices. Phase three embraces the study of new and alternative curriculum content, and phase four provides for the formulation of criteria for decisions about what shall go into the curriculum. The fifth and final step of this area of curriculum engineering consists of designing and writing the new curriculum. The five-phase procedure described above "incorporates most of the activities proposed by curriculum authorities and used in projects reported by school systems" (Beauchamp 1964, p. 131).

The fourth critical area of Beauchamp's system is *curriculum implementation*. Since Beauchamp raises many of the same questions and problems related to this area of curriculum engineering that we have alluded to in previous sections, there is no need to repeat them here. He does, however, make the noteworthy point that while many curricula have been planned, far fewer have been systematically implemented. This condition underscores one of the major weaknesses of most curriculum projects: a great deal of time, effort, and even money is expended in producing a curriculum document, but because of fundamental flaws in the development process, implementation atrophies, and the documents end up gathering dust on a closet shelf or in a desk drawer. As we shall see below, some engineering models are designed specifically in terms of the "broken-front" concept to increase the probability that the curriculum plan will become an operational reality in the classrooms.

The fifth and final area that Beauchamp identifies is *curriculum evaluation*. This area has at least four dimensions: (1) evaluation of the teachers' use of the curriculum, (2) evaluation of the curriculum design, (3) evaluation of student outcomes and (4) evaluation of the curriculum (engineering) system. Data collected from this evaluation system are used to improve the engineering process and to provide for curriculum continuity and growth from year to year (Beauchamp 1964, pp. 138, 139).

Comprehensive as it is, Beauchamp's system leaves unanswered many questions concerning curriculum-engineering processes. Furthermore, the "top-down" organizational orientation of the model leads us to conclude that in many respects it closely resembles the administrative model described by Smith, Stanley, and Shores. One reason, as Beauchamp himself notes, is that his system incorporates procedures that have become well established in school practice, and school practice, as we know, overwhelmingly has favored the administrative framework. But it is time now that we turn our attention to another model of curriculum engineering, one that represents a radical departure in sequence and that is considered by many curriculum specialists to be a unique and promising alternative.

TABA'S INVERTED MODEL

In its most simplified form the traditional sequence of curriculum engineering calls for selected committees (1) to examine foundational areas and develop a statement of foundational commitment, (2) to formulate an overall curriculum design based on stated commitments, (3) to construct curriculum units consonant with the overall design framework, and (4) to implement the curriculum at the classroom level. Taba (1962, p. 439) believes that this essentially "deductive" process "tends to reduce the possibilities for creative innovation because it limits the possibilities of experimentation from which new ideas and concepts of curriculum can emerge." She points out that when change begins with a redesign of the overall framework, a pattern is fixed before thorough reexamination and testing of what goes into the pattern. Second, with a traditional sequence curriculum committees may *deduce* what seem to be appropriate curricular plans, but until implementation occurs some time in the future, there is no way of discovering if substantial portions of the design—indeed, even the design itself—are empirically unsound. For example, providing activities that achieve multiple objectives, establishing a balance between breadth and depth of content, or formulating developmental sequences necessary for achieving complex objectives can only be managed on a logical, not an empirical, level. Third, because they do not evolve from empirical testing, the curricula produced by the traditional process tend to consist of very general, and often abstract, prescriptions for instruction—"sketchy schemes" as Taba (1962, p. 442) calls them— that provide little guidance for conversion into instructional practice.

These three problems suggest what perhaps is the most significant deficiency of the traditional sequence in curriculum engeering: the gap that it creates, at both ends of the engineering process, between theory and practice:

> *theoretical designs of curricula are developed with meager foundation in experimentation with practice, and implementation is carried on with insufficient understanding of theory. This gives theory an unreal quality and fosters black and white thinking (Taba 1962, p. 441).*

Taba cites the development/implementation of the core curriculum as an example of this dysfunction in the theory-practice nexus. The core curriculum was designed to promote (1) the integration of content and (2) relationships with students' life needs. In practice, however, it has generally remained an administrative reorganization; blocks of time in which separate subjects (usually English and social studies) are taught, and in which life problems, when included, are treated in isolation and at the expense of sound and valid content. In short, the form, rather than the substance, of core was implemented because a deductive engineering sequence resulted in the separation of theory and practice (Taba 1962, p. 441).

To deal with these problems, Taba advocates an inversion of the traditional sequence. Instead of starting with a general design framework, she proposes that the first step be the planning by teachers (and others) of specific learning-teaching units.[6] These units, after undergoing testing/implementation in the classroom, are to be used as an empirical basis for determining overall design. Such a sequence helps to bridge the gap between theory and practice because the production of teaching-learning units combines theoretical competence and practical experience in teaching (Taba 1962, pp. 441, 442). A second advantage claimed for Taba's inverted sequence is that curricula evolved from concrete teaching-learning units prepared by teachers are more easily introduced to school faculties. This is because they are easier to understand than the abstract, general curricula produced by the traditional sequence. A third advantage of Taba's inverted model is that curricula consisting of both a general framework and tangible teaching-learning units are more likely to affect classroom practice than do current curriculum plans, which "stop short" of the specific guidance afforded by teaching units.

Taba has developed a five-step sequence for engineering curriculum change by the inverted model. The first step is the experimental *production of pilot units* by groups of teachers. Taba (1962, p. 458) notes that the production of pilot units establishes a link between theory and practice by requiring (1) that the planning be based on theoretical considerations worked out in the light of available research, and (2) that concurrent experimentation in classroom settings be carried on to provide empirical data against which theoretical principles may be assessed. An eight-step sequence is prescribed for pilot-unit production (Taba 1962, pp. 347–379):

1. *Diagnosing needs*
2. *Formulating specific objectives*
3. *Selecting content*
4. *Organizing content*
5. *Selecting learning experiences [activities]*
6. *Organizing learning experiences [activities]*
7. *Evaluating*
8. *Checking for balance and sequence*

6. This inversion of the conventional sequence, particularly when it is initiated by classroom teachers, makes Taba's model a variant of the grass-roots approach to curriculum engineering.

The second step of Taba's model is the *testing of experimental units.* Although the units have been tried out in classrooms by teachers involved in the engineering process, they need "to be tested in different classrooms and under varied conditions to establish their validity and teachability . . ." (Taba 1962, p. 458). The testing step provides data regarding needed modifications and suggests alternative content and activities to be used with varying student populations. For example, adequate breadth for one group may turn out to be excessive for another, or learning activities appropriate in one classroom may be quite wrong in another. Teachers who were involved in unit production are able to help those who are testing the units by demonstrating specific procedures and materials, and by providing information and insights derived from their own experience with the units during step one. This training function, carried on by peers, encourages effective implementation of the *substance* of the new curriculum, as opposed only to its *form.*

The third step of Taba's model is the *revising and consolidating* of the curriculum units. On the basis of the data gathered during the testing step, units are generalized for use in all types of classroom situations. They also are examined for theoretical consistency. This is particularly important, for the individual units should, taken together, represent a coherent whole based on a consistent rationale. If the units encompass all grade levels of a particular subject—e.g., social studies—they comprise a sequential subject-area curriculum. On the other hand, if the units encompass all areas of study for a given year, they comprise a horizontally coordinated segment of curriculum. Taba (1962, p. 459) is careful to point out that the step of revising and consolidating is a task that most appropriately falls within the province of curriculum coordinators and curriculum specialists.

Step four of Taba's model, *developing a framework,* is analogous to, but not equated with, developing the overall curriculum design. When a broad range of unit groupings has been produced, curriculum specialists or others competent in the theoretical aspects of curriculum construction examine them for overall scope, sequence, and coherence. They make adjustments in the curriculum on the basis of such questions as the following: Do the central ideas and concepts gradually extend toward increasing maturity and complexity? Is the content of successive units adequate in scope? Do learning activities provide opportunities for the cumulative development of intellectual skills and emotional insights? In effect, this step of Taba's engineering process takes a grouping of revised, consolidated unit plans, and with necessary changes having been made, structures them into an overall and coherent curriculum. Included in the final document at this stage of the engineering process is a statement of the theoretical rationale of the curriculum, including the philosophy on which it rests.[7]

7. Step four need not encompass the total curriculum of an entire school system, and indeed, Taba's text suggests that she is discussing only a significant segment of such a curriculum. Logically, however, the end of curriculum engineering is the formulation and implementation of a *total* curriculum, and we have treated Taba's model here as if this were the ultimate goal.

The final step in Taba's model is the *installation and dissemination of the new units*. Naturally, the more the new curriculum differs from the accustomed one, the greater will be the difficulties encountered in its implementation. Training teachers to use the new curriculum may be accomplished in a variety of ways: intensive workshops, in-service courses, and "other in-service training devices to develop the necessary content background, the requisite teaching skills, and an understanding of the theory underlying the new program" (Taba 1962, p. 459). Responsibility for the installation step is assigned to the administrative staff of the school. Even under the best conditions, a period of several years is needed to produce and install a curriculum using Taba's inverted sequence of engineering.

Taba concedes that in all probability, no school system could afford system-wide reform utilizing the model described above. Such curriculum engineering efforts would most likely have to be concentrated in some reasonably limited area such as the lower elementary grades, social studies, or science education. The criterion for selecting the area for redesign might be need, teacher concern, obsolescence, or some other problematic condition.

As noted above, the major strength of Taba's model inheres in its provision for the integration of theory and practice. There is little question that the customary procedure of producing volumes of documents intended for implementation all at once at some future time has encouraged massive discrepancies between what is written (theory) and what is done (practice).[8] By providing for a thinking-doing situation in which the two functions are contiguous and reciprocal, Taba's model encourages consistent translations of thought and word into overt curricular behavior. And, as we have emphasized many times, it is only when we are able to make such translations that we are operating on an aware and intelligent (as opposed to an unconscious and encapsulated) level.

Having emphasized the major strength of Taba's model, however, we are constrained to observe that while a rearrangement of organizational factors can in some cases facilitate a reassessment of theory in the light of ongoing practice, it rarely, by itself, constitutes a stimulus powerful enough to dislodge the familiar and settled thought patterns that are mainly responsible for existing discrepancies. For example, if we presently include formal English grammar in the language arts curriculum on the theoretical basis that it promotes effective speaking and writing, participation in steps one and two of Taba's engineering model is not likely to alter that conviction, particularly if it represents (as it often does) a rationalization for familiarity, security, affinity, and comfort with the content of English grammar. Only a confrontation of self with ideas can produce the effective integration of theory and practice that Taba desires, and while her inverted model may facilitate that confrontation, it is neither a necessary nor sufficient condition for it.

8. If, indeed, anything is done at all: the frequent relegation of the new curricula to the closet shelf or the desk drawer represents the ultimate gap between theory and practice.

Another aspect of Taba's model that raises problematic questions is its final step: the installation and dissemination of new units. Indeed, we might observe that this step appears to reflect a style of curriculum implementation that has been the object of Taba's own criticism. While it is true that the participation and cooperation of administrators are important to the successful implementation of new curricula, we must once again point out that the creation of congenial organizational arrangements is far from sufficient to ensure the substantive kind of implementation that is desirable.

It is puzzling that Taba does not make more of the advantages to implementation generated by the initial steps in her sequence. As we have noted earlier, teachers' participation in curriculum experimentation and testing makes them an integral (and substantive) component of the curriculum engineering process, rather than passive (and merely formal) instruments of execution. Contacts they have with experimental units at the early stages of curriculum planning and testing not only operate to reduce anxiety and resentment toward innovation, but also tend to improve current curricular effectiveness and to diminish the adjustment needed later on when the new curriculum is adopted in its revised form. In effect, we may regard Taba's first two steps as important contributions to the implementation phase. (One might even speculate that the implementation phase, far from being a separate step occurring toward the end of the engineering sequence, should be organically integrated into the development/construction process. But this goes well beyond what is called for in Taba's model.)

Lest we appear to be hypercritical of Taba, we readily concede that her model, in purely organizational terms, goes a long way toward stimulating reassessment of conventional patterns in curriculum engineering. In particular, her concern for the theory-practice nexus, the congruous translation of curriculum into instruction, and the differentiation of roles in the engineering process combine to distinguish her model as a milestone in the field of curriculum engineering.

ROGERS' INTERPERSONAL RELATIONS MODEL

When Crosby (1970, p. 388) wrote, "Curriculum change is 'people change,'" she was expressing a viewpoint that is accepted by most curriculum specialists, but, as we have seen, is seldom given heavy emphasis in models for curriculum development and change. Carl Rogers, although he is not a professional educationist,[9] has prepared a model for curriculum development that centers on "people change." Although it lacks most of the technical components that curriculum specialists would like to see addressed (e.g., the specifics of content, learning activities, and implementation), it represents an intriguing contribution to the literature of curriculum engineering.

9. Carl Rogers is a psychologist whose ideas have played a central role in the theory and practice of many curriculum specialists. He is best known for his "nondirective," "humanistic" approach to teaching and curriculum planning. His most influential books include *On Becoming a Person* (1961) and *Freedom to Learn* (1969).

Rogers' model is predicated on the need—if society is to meet the challenges of the contemporary world—to create and maintain a climate conducive to change. He holds that "we cannot rest on the *answers* provided by the past, but must put our trust in the *processes* by which new problems are met." Thus, a curriculum is needed that will "develop individuals who are open to change, who are flexible and adaptive, [and] who have learned how to learn . . ." (Rogers 1967, p. 717).

Such a curriculum, of course, can be constructed and implemented only by professional educators who themselves have become open, flexible, and process-oriented. What is needed to produce this type of professional, is an educational system characterized by "a climate conducive to personal growth, a climate in which innovation is not frightening, in which creative capacities of administrators, teachers, and students are nourished and expressed rather than stifled" (Rogers 1967, p. 718). The tool for effecting this needed change is the "intensive group experience," an experience resulting from what is variously referred to as sensitivity training, the basic encounter group, or the T- (for training) group.

The intensive group ordinarily is made up of from ten to fifteen people plus a "facilitator" or leader. It is relatively unstructured and provides an environment of freedom for personal expression, interpersonal communication, and exploration of feelings. Each participant is encouraged to put aside defenses and façades and to relate directly and openly to the other members of the group. According to Rogers, the experience produces significant intrapersonal and interpersonal benefits:

> *Individuals come to know themselves and each other more fully than is possible in the usual social or working relationships; the climate of openness, risk-taking, and honesty generates trust, which enables the person to recognize and change self-defeating attitudes, test out and adopt more innovative and constructive behaviors, and subsequently to relate more adequately and effectively to others in his everyday life situation (Rogers 1967, p. 718).*

Employing the intensive group experience as the vehicle for his plan, Rogers charts a sequential model for curriculum change that is "revolutionary" in the sense that it promotes basic changes in people. The first step is the selection of a target educational system. The only criterion for this selection is that one or more individuals in a position of power (e.g., a school board member, superintendent, or other high-level administrator) be willing to involve himself in an intensive group experience. With this commitment, an opportunity will have developed for involving a group of administrators and board members in a one-week retreat, usually at a secluded resort away from the interruptions and distractions of daily business. Preferably, participation would be voluntary, but "if the administration decided that all staff members above a certain level must attend, this would be acceptable" (Rogers 1967, p. 721). An outside, experienced facilitator (provided by an organization such as the National Training

Laboratories or the Western Behavioral Sciences Institute) would be responsible for guiding the group sessions.

It is impossible, of course, to describe the scenario of these one-week encounters, much less, as Rogers puts it "to convey intellectually the quality of the relationships which develop." But on the basis of his past experience, he makes the following observations:

> . . . I think of administrators who have worked together for twenty years, and discover they have never known each other at all as persons; of negative feelings which have "loused up" planning and work for years, which can now safely be brought into the open, understood, and dissolved; of positive feelings which have always seemed too risky to voice . . . of personal tragedies and problems which make understandable the armor plate behind which some individuals have hidden . . . the intense sense of community which develops, in place of the alienation each has felt . . . (Rogers 1967, p. 721).

What are the long-term outcomes of such a week-long intensive group experience? They are numerous, of course, and may vary considerably. But a summary of the most significant ones listed by Rogers (1967, p. 722) will convey a sense of the new directions taken by the administrator in the execution of his professional duties:

1. *He is less protective of his own beliefs and can listen more accurately.*
2. *He finds it easier and less threatening to accept innovative ideas.*
3. *He has less need to protect bureaucratic rules.*
4. *He communicates more clearly and realistically to superiors, peers, and subordinates because he is more open and less self-protective.*
5. *He is more person oriented and democratic.*
6. *He openly confronts personal emotional frictions between himself and colleagues.*
7. *He is more able to accept both positive and negative feedback and use it constructively.*

The second phase of Rogers' model involves intensive group experiences for teachers. These, of course, follow much the same pattern as the ones in which administrators were participants. While Rogers emphasizes the desirability of a week-long experience at a secluded site, he acknowledges that staff size, financial resources, and a variety of other circumstances may make it necessary to entertain alternative arrangements—e.g., a long (holiday) weekend at a site near enough to allow participants to spend the night at home. Again, it is desirable that participation in the experience be voluntary, and as Rogers notes, there should be no expectation that every teacher will participate, especially at the first invitation to do so. However, compelling changes in the behavior and personal relations of previous participants may well provide a stimulus for those who are uninformed or skeptical about intensive group processes.

The effects of the experience for the teacher, of course, will parallel those listed above for the administrator. In addition, Rogers (1967, p. 724) lists the following specifically teacher-related outcomes:

1. *He is more able to listen to students.*
2. *He accepts innovative, "troublesome" ideas from students, rather than insisting on conformity.*
3. *He pays as much attention to his relationships with students as he does to course content.*
4. *He works out problems with students rather than responding in a disciplinary and punitive manner.*
5. *He develops an equalitarian and democratic classroom climate.*

The third phase of Rogers' model is the development of an intensive group experience for a class or course unit. Because the number of students involved makes the retreat format impractical, Rogers suggests an arrangement by which five full days are devoted to the experience. An outside facilitator might help to provide a climate of freedom, but the prior experience of teachers and administrators would presumably contribute significantly to the success of the venture. The effects on the student of such an experience may be summarized as follows (Rogers 1967, pp. 724, 725):

1. *He feels freer to express both positive and negative feelings in class.*
2. *He works through these feelings toward a realistic solution.*
3. *He has more energy for learning because he has less fear of constant evaluation and punishment.*
4. *He discovers that he is responsible for his own learning.*
5. *His awe and fear of authority diminish as he finds teachers and administrators to be fallible human beings.*
6. *He finds that the learning process enables him to deal with his life.*

The fourth step in this interpersonal model calls for the involvement of parents in intensive group experiences. Rogers suggests that this phase be carried on concurrently with the previous one so that parents can be effectively informed of the direction being taken by the school system. Groups might be convened for members of the PTA or for parents of students involved in class groups. Because of the practical problems involved with scheduling parent groups, Rogers suggests weekend group experiences, three-hour evening sessions on a weekly basis, or even a twenty-four hour marathon as alternatives to the week-long retreat. The purpose of these groups is to enrich parents' relationships with one another, their children, and the school, and to clarify the intensive group program being carried on. Although Rogers admits that only a tiny proportion of parents can be reached through intensive group sessions, he is hopeful that those who *have* been will serve as favorable interpreters of the program to the rest of the community.[10]

The culmination of Rogers' interpersonal model is the convening of what he calls "vertical groups." Until now, groups have consisted essentially of peer participants; but successful curriculum change can occur only when effective relationships prevail both horizontally *and* across status-role lines. Thus, Rogers (1967, p. 725) prescribes vertical encounter groups consisting of two board members, two administrative officers, two parents, two teachers, two excellent students, and two failing students or dropouts. Because the traditionally adversary role relationships among vertical-group participants can jeopardize the successful functioning of the group, Rogers would include only individuals who have been involved in a previous intensive experience. In addition, he suggests that a theme, such as, "The _____ Schools: What I like and do not like about them, and what I want them to be" be used to focus the group's interaction.

Rogers testifies (1967, p. 725) that vertical group encounters have been conducted "with extremely rewarding results." Members of such groups incorporate broader understandings of self and others, to some degree become more flexible, and find that they are involved in genuine self-change. It is this kind of change that not only transforms the curriculum, but "contains the yeast of a revolution in the [total] educational climate" (Rogers 1967, p. 726).

In closing the description of his human relations model, Rogers emphasizes the importance of scheduling the sequence of group experiences over a reasonably short period of time. This is necessary to prevent the dissipation of their impact. He suggests at least ten "workshops" during the first academic year of the program, each "workshop" consisting of from one to ten encounter groups. This minimum, clearly, would involve hundreds of individuals—a substantial proportion of the total number of administrators, teachers, and student body.

There is no denying the importance of human relations in curriculum engineering. Indeed, a major criticism of most engineering models is their infatuation with administrative organization to the detriment of intangible, yet substantive, human factors. At the same time, however, one must raise serious questions regarding the adequacy of Rogers' model. Paraphrasing Bettelheim's oft-quoted statement that "Love is not enough," we might observe of Rogers' plan that "Good will is not enough." In curriculum engineering, substantial provision must be made for the rational and systematic examination of values, concepts, principles, procedures, and data. One idea (or principle or procedure) is *not* necessarily as good as another, and in a great many specific instances, its inferiority (or superiority) can be demonstrated. In a situation like this, to avoid conflict—to "compromise" or "smooth things over" for the sake of harmonious human relations—would not only violate intellectual integrity, but most likely would lead to adverse consequences. While Rogers' model may facilitate

10. Probably because of the inherent diversity of parent groups, Rogers does not provide a list of specific outcomes expected for these participants. We may presume, however, that the effects are generally quite similar to those noted for the other groups.

adaptive change, it does not supply us with a reasoned basis for *directing* change.

Rogers, of course, is not arguing for harmony at all costs. He simply is maintaining that our relations with people improve if we are able to get some perspective on how *they* feel and how *they* see things. This improvement in relations, of course, not only results in more effective social functioning, but in superior decision making. The decisions are better because they are based on reasonably accurate perceptions of reality rather than on anxiety, expectations, status roles, and defense mechanisms. The desirability of this "unencapsulated" perspective has been dealt with elsewhere in this text, and there is no need to elaborate on it or to reaffirm its importance here. But beyond exhorting us to listen, empathize, and be ourselves, Rogers offers little guidance in answering some of the most difficult curriculum-engineering questions with which we are faced: How and at what point are the hard decisions about content and learning activities to be made? What role in such decisions is to be taken by administrators, teachers, parents, and students? Will the encounter-group organization be employed exclusively as the decision-making vehicle? And, not the least important, what criteria can be used to evaluate the merit of the various proposals made in the curriculum construction/implementation processes?

A final note of caution is in order with regard to Rogers' system of basic encounter groups. Ironically, the very instrument which is designed to overcome the impersonality and bureaucratic role playing characteristic of most administrative organizations may itself become a formalized vehicle for role playing. As is the case with many innovations that in principle represent a departure from routinized practice, the basic encounter group has "caught on," been popularized, and become a part of the system that it was intended to overcome. Now, participants play (albeit unconsciously) at authenticity, aping the solicitude of professional facilitators and acting out the role of concerned listener and empathizer. Old wine, new bottles—and a preeminent example of how institutionalization can reduce even the antisystematic to a routine formula. It leads one to wonder how necessary (or even conducive) the basic encounter group is in developing the human relations dimension of curriculum engineering.

For all of the problems inherent in Rogers' human relations model, it represents an important contribution to curriculum literature because it puts the human dimension up front where it belongs. Curriculum change, ultimately, *is* "people change." And the quality of interaction among participants in the engineering process is certain to show up in the curricular experience of students.

THE SYSTEMATIC ACTION-RESEARCH MODEL

The systematic action-research model of curriculum engineering has been developed in great detail by Smith, Stanley, and Shores (1957, pp. 436–497). It is based on the assumption that *curriculum change is social change,* that it is "a process involving the personalities of parents, students, and teachers, the structure of the school system, and the patterns of personal and group relations among members of the school and community" (Smith, Stanley, and Shores 1957, p. 438). As a consequence of this assumption, the model is built on considerations involving three critical factors: human relations, school and community organization, and the authority of professional knowledge. In this respect it is superior to Rogers' model, which focuses only on human relations in encounter groups, and to most of the other models that we have discussed, which tend to overemphasize organizational arrangements.

With regard to the human relations aspect of their model, Smith, Stanley, and Shores (1957, p. 439) note that the curriculum exists in the context of an "extensive web of expectations" among members of the community. Just as individuals expect a doctor, minister, mother, or businessman to behave in certain ways, they look for particular patterns of response from the government, church, business establishment, television industry, or school. In the case of the latter, parents, students, laymen, and teachers all have certain ideas about what and how the school teaches, the way children ought to be educated, and just what role the curriculum should play in all of this.[11] Thus, an effective curriculum engineering program will attempt to determine and to take into account the various sentiments, expectations, and ideas that people have with regard to the curriculum and will attempt to deal with them in the context of human relations. This does not mean that the model advocates the psychological manipulation of people in order to achieve predetermined ends of the engineering process; it simply means that the engineering process should include some mechanism for ensuring that the highly influential variables of individual and group perceptions are not omitted from consideration. One way of achieving this result (without overemphasizing it) is through a procedure called *action-research*.

Action-research is a cyclical "kernel" procedure that is recurringly applied in working through the systematic action-research model of curriculum engineering. An adaptation of the "scientific method" described in an earlier chapter, action-research ordinarily is stimulated when a specific (curriculum) situation is perceived to be problematical or disturbing in some way. As this situation is surveyed, its relationship to a multitude of other aspects of the school and community ordinarily emerges, and it soon becomes clear that a more widespread and systematic inquiry is needed if the initial problem is to be fully understood and resolved. At this point, step one of the action-research procedure is invoked.

This first step involves a careful examination of the curriculum problem: first, wide-ranging fact-finding activities in order to clarify the problem; and second, broad inquiry seeking the identification of factors, forces, and conditions that must be dealt with if the problem is to be resolved. Lewin (1948, p. 205) notes that the inquiry launched in step one usually modifies perceptions concerning the nature of the initial (stimulus) problem. Furthermore, successful completion of this first step yields two important elements for subsequent action:

---

11. The concept of *encapsulation* is analogous to the unexamined "expectations" that Smith, Stanley, and Shores are dealing with here.

(1) an "overall plan" of how to deal with the problem as redefined, and (2) a decision regarding the *first* action to be taken.

The second step in the action-research procedure consists of implementing the decision regarding the first action to be taken. This action is followed immediately by data-gathering and fact-finding activities. These fact-finding activities serve four important functions: First, they provide data for evaluation of the initial action with regard to its effectiveness in achieving expected goals. Second, they give curriculum planners new insights into the nature of the problems they face and the strengths and weaknesses of the procedures they are using. In short, they enable planners to learn and to become more effective problem solvers. Third, the data gathering is useful in reassessing and modifying the overall plan. Finally, it serves as a valuable resource for determining the second action to be taken. This very important fact-finding step clearly establishes the centrality of knowledge as a critical factor in the systematic action-research model.

As an example of how this process works, suppose that in consequence of step one, an overall curriculum-engineering plan were conceived that called for parents' involvement in the ongoing planning effort. Suppose, too, that the first action decided on was the convening of exploratory meetings with selected parents to inform them of the overall plan and to determine appropriate roles for them to play. The data gathering and fact finding immediately following this round of meetings might lead to the following conclusions (among others) in each of the four areas cited in the previous paragraph: (1) While flattered with the invitations to take part in ongoing curriculum planning, parents were reluctant to make the substantial time commitment needed for effective participation because they were involved in so many other personal and community activities. (2) The exploratory meetings might have been unsuccessful because the overall plan was presented to parents in the technical jargon of education and as a result had a chilling and intimidating effect on them. In further contact with the lay community, it is decided, technical jargon will have to be avoided. (3) The overall plan is modified so that the role of parents becomes one of reacting to major policy decisions rather than intimate participation in the ongoing planning and execution of the engineering process. (4) The second action is decided on: a public relations campaign (press, mailings, radio interviews, and public meetings) to inform the community of the major contours of the incipient curriculum effort.

From this account of the action-research step two, it is not difficult to guess the next step in the procedure: implementation of the second action followed by fact-finding reconnaissance. Again, planners will evaluate this second action, learn more about the process in which they are engaged, further develop and/or modify the overall plan, and determine the next action to be taken. This, then, is the recurrent cycle of steps that represents the heart of Smith, Stanley, and Shores' systematic action-research model.

Before proceeding to a description of the contextual framework in which the action-research kernel is placed, it is worthwhile to pause and compare the characteristics of action-research with those of the more familiar theoretical/ laboratory type of research. Of course, both types of research hold in common the principle of unbiased investigation as a basis for understanding phenomena; they both employ well-established canons of logic and inquiry so that methodologically the two types of research are equally "scientific." But whereas the findings of theoretical research are not intended (necessarily) to affect people directly or immediately, the chief aim of action-research is "the immediate modification of social practice" (Smith, Stanley, and Shores 1957, p. 446).[12] Action-research, then, is not so much different from theoretical research in principle, but rather in terms of the time frame it allows to produce anticipated practical results. We might also note on this score that since theoretical research is not particularly concerned with immediate applications, it is ordinarily accompanied by extensive experimental controls and meticulous precision in procedures. Action-research, on the other hand, willingly sacrifices experimental control and precision in the interest of effecting immediate social (or other) change.[13]

How does action-research fit into an overall model of curriculum engineering? Smith, Stanley, and Shores propose that it be the methodology for implementing each of the four phases of their formal systematic model:

1. *A diagnostic study of the school-community situation to ascertain the constellation of forces that maintains the present curriculum.*
2. *The induction of change in the existing equilibrium so as to loosen up the established constellation of forces.*
3. *The control of various forces in order to move the level of curriculum practice in the desired direction and to the desired amount.*
4. *The establishment of the new constellation of forces to sustain the new curriculum (Smith, Stanley, and Shores 1957, p. 444).*

The authors caution that the analysis of curriculum change into these four discrete steps is, of course, an oversimplification. Only in the crudest terms is it possible to describe each phase as a discrete, sequential process. For example, a diagnostic study of the school community (phase one) is itself a change-inducing activity (phase two). Moreover, many intermediate and correlative steps are suggested by each of the four noted above. Nevertheless, in approaching an overwhelmingly complex activity such as curriculum engineering, it is necessary to impose some kind of simplified (theoretical) pattern on the interacting forces of reality if some perspective on meaning is to be developed. This is the function well served by the four phases identified by Smith, Stanley, and Shores.

The limitation of space has precluded the presentation of more than a super-

12. It is in this regard that the human relations factor assumes major proportions in the systematic model of curriculum engineering.

13. It should be noted that control and precision are both relative and may legitimately be increased or decreased according to the demands and purposes of the research being conducted.

ficial account of the systematic action-research model. Nevertheless, it should be clear that Smith, Stanley, and Shores' proposal is a process-oriented one that leans heavily on trust in the capability of professionals and laymen to build and implement quality curricula through the processes of action-research. In this respect the model is highly democratic. Although it eschews the tightly structured top-down orientation of most administrative models, it is a far cry from the laissez-faire looseness characteristic of grass-roots proposals. Discipline is maintained because recommended procedures do not neglect the factors of school and community organization, human relations, and the authority of knowledge.

The paragraph above suggests that the systematic action-research model avoids the flaws of other models and successfully deals with the central problems of curriculum engineering. This is essentially true. Can we assume, then, that it is possible to implement an effective curriculum-engineering project by meticulously following the procedures advocated by Smith, Stanley, and Shores? Unfortunately, it would be a mistake to make any such supposition.

In the first place, the engineering of a dynamic and vital curriculum adequate to the challenges of our times cannot occur as a result of following instructions. Instructions, or rules, are rarely sufficient in curriculum engineering. Although they are clear, easy to understand, and therefore easy to follow, they are worthy only of robots—or computers.

In the second place, Smith, Stanley, and Shores do not supply instructions to be followed. A careful reading of their proposal shows that they offer, rather, principles on which to base decisions. But the fact that the systematic model provides us with principles rather than rules presents its own kind of problem. Principles are meaningless unless and until they are confronted in actual social situations; their real meaning can be understood only by those who have worked with them and consciously experienced their operation in life. To cavalierly treat principles as rules or instructions is to invite disaster in any curriculum enterprise. Yet, it is only the confrontation of principles in real-life situations that enables us to function on the highest levels of human awareness. Herein lies the paradox of Smith, Stanley, and Shores' proposal: Because it takes into account people, social organization, and knowledge, and deals with these factors on the level of principled decision making, it has the best potential for producing a dynamic and functional curriculum. But because it rests ultimately on processes involving the intellectual and social growth of people, it is the most difficult to implement.

EMERGING TECHNICAL MODELS

We have noted earlier the predominance of scientific-technical and business-efficiency values in American culture. It should come as no surprise, then, that current trends in curriculum engineering favor procedures based on these orientations. Kirst and Walker (1971, p. 486) identify three emerging models that reflect such orientations.

THE BEHAVIORAL ANALYSIS MODEL. An outgrowth of the time-and-motion studies conducted in the early decades of this century, the behavioral analysis model begins with the activities that students are being trained (*sic*) to engage in and analyzes them into a hierarchy of molecular capabilities, the sum of which constitutes the desired complex behavior. Next, instructional sequences are designed that lead students step by step through the hierarchy toward the complex behavior. This model, clearly, emphasizes Skinnerian procedures controlled from inception to execution by specialists. Its adoption requires the authority of strong administrative organization.

THE SYSTEMS ANALYSIS MODEL. Also known by such names as program planning, cost-effectiveness analysis, and PPBS (program planning and budgeting systems), systems analysis is a descendant of the business-efficiency movement in education. The first step in this model is to specify the complete set (or a complete subset) of achievements (outputs) desired of students. Second, instruments for measuring these outputs are constructed. Inputs necessary for teaching students to attain specified output levels then are identified and their cost estimated. Finally, the relative costs and benefits of different educational programs are quantitatively compared. The most obvious weakness of this model lies in the lack of inherent correspondence that exists between the educational enterprise and the business enterprise.

THE COMPUTER-BASED MODEL. An outgrowth of America's infatuation with scientific empiricism and computer technology, the computer-based model consists of identifying a large number of curriculum units each containing a multitude of desired outcomes. Students and teachers are asked to complete questionnaires relating to these units, and the results, along with aptitude and achievement data on each student, are stored in the computer. The computer utilizes these data to make initial content prescriptions for each student. Again, student and teacher reactions are fed into the computer with aptitude and achievement information, and the machine—in theory, at least—"automatically changes its decision-rules to optimize achievement subject to constraints of interest and involvement" (Kirst and Walker 1971, p. 486). Although no such system is presently in full use, simple prototypes are, and it is predicted that fully operational computer-based curriculum engineering will soon be available. There is, of course, no question regarding the effectiveness of the computer in handling large quantities of data. What is highly problematical with regard to the legitimacy of this model is the kind and quality of the data on which decisions are made.

References

Beauchamp, George A. 1964. *Curriculum Theory.* 2d ed. Wilmette, Ill.: The Kagg Press.

Caswell, Hollis L., and Associates. 1950. *Curriculum Improvement in Public School*

Systems. New York: Bureau of Publications, Teachers College, Columbia University.

Connelly, F. Michael. 1971. "Some Considerations on the Status, Relationship to Research, Character, and Study of Curriculum Development: An Overview." In *Elements of Curriculum Development*, edited by F. Michael Connelly. Monograph Supplement to *Curriculum Theory Network*, No. 7. Toronto: The Ontario Institute for Studies in Education.

Crosby, Muriel. 1970. "Who Changes the Curriculum and How?" *Phi Delta Kappan* (March).

Doll, Ronald. 1964. *Curriculum Improvement: Decision-Making and Process*. Boston: Allyn & Bacon.

Don't Just Do Something: A Collection of Major Articles Selected from the Center Magazine. 1972. Santa Barbara, Calif.: The Center for the Study of Democratic Institutions.

Kirst, Michael W., and Decker F. Walker. 1971. "An Analysis of Curriculum Policy-Making." *Review of Educational Research* (December).

Lewin, Kurt. 1948. *Resolving Social Conflict*. New York: Harper & Row.

Lippitt, Ronald. 1965. "Roles and Processes in Curriculum Development and Change." In *Strategy for Curriculum Change*, edited by Robert R. Leeper. Washington, D.C.: The Association for Supervision and Curriculum Development.

O'Hanlon, James. 1973/74. "Three Models for the Curriculum Development Process." *Curriculum Theory Network*, Vol. 4, No. 1. Toronto: The Ontario Institute for Studies in Education.

Rogers, Carl R. 1967. "A Plan for Self-Directed Change in an Educational System." *Educational Leadership* (May).

Smith, B. Othanel, William O. Stanley, and J. Harlan Shores. 1957. *Fundamentals of Curriculum Development*. Rev. ed. New York: Harcourt Brace Jovanovich.

Taba, Hilda. 1962. *Curriculum Development: Theory and Practice*. New York: Harcourt Brace Jovanovich.

CHAPTER 20
CRUCIAL ISSUES IN CURRICULUM DEVELOPMENT

Issues should not be seen as threats. They should be seen as opportunities for gaining new insights. —GLENN HASS, KIMBALL WILES, AND JOSEPH BONDI

Political Realities of Curriculum Development

Existing literature in curriculum development deals almost exclusively with questions of how curriculum is planned and implemented at the local level. The assumption seems to be that professionals (teachers, administrators, and perhaps consultants) make the curriculum, that the role of parents (and often students) is crucial, and that local leadership and initiative are significant factors in curriculum quality (see, for example, the models described in the previous chapter). The result is that almost all curriculum specialists approach problems of curriculum engineering from a "rational scientific" or "human relations" point of view, seeking the resolution of conflicts on the basis of analysis, reason, and principle. Indeed, the language used by specialists to describe the process is replete with such terms as "decision making," "planning," "research and development," and "management" (Kirst and Walker 1971, p. 481). Rarely is curriculum development viewed as a policy-making activity, and almost never is it placed in the context of *political* policy making,[1] although the "influence" of politics sometimes is acknowledged.

Substantial evidence exists, however, to suggest that this conventional view

1. "Political" as it is used in this section is not confined to phenomena involving government; it refers more broadly to all the processes by which conflicts among competing public policies (and their underlying values) are resolved. These processes include, but are not limited to, lobbying, bargaining, exerting economic pressure, promoting legislation, organizing demonstrations, and compromising.

of curriculum development may be little more than a monumental myth. On the basis of an extensive analysis of the sources and processes of innovation in curriculum, Pellegrin (1966, p. 15) concludes:

> *the greatest stimuli to changes in education originate in sources external to this field. What I have shown is that the sources of innovation lie largely outside the local community, and in most instances outside the education profession.*

This statement suggests that curriculum development is not merely "influenced" by political phenomena, but that it may itself be a political process in many ways (Kirst and Walker 1971, p. 480). Indeed, history presents us with many macrocosmic examples: when, in the early decades of the century, immigration was a national political issue, the curriculum emphasized Americanization; when totalitarianism threatened democratic institutions in the 1930s, education for democracy had its heyday; and when, following World War II, the cold war and Sputnik challenged America's technological supremacy, curricula for scientific excellence quickly were assembled to meet the challenge. Although federal influence over curriculum policy has theoretically been virtually nonexistent until recent years, these examples demonstrate that national political issues have in fact significantly affected curriculum for a long time. The key political (and curriculum development) question is: through which specific channels?

In order to answer this question we shall rely heavily on Kirst and Walker (1971, pp. 488–498), whose extensive survey of the field has produced a clear, concise analysis. These authors have identified a number of important sources that are presently determining curriculum policy and have classified them into three broad categories: (1) groups that establish minimum curriculum standards, (2) alternative generators, and (3) groups demanding curriculum change.[2]

GROUPS THAT ESTABLISH MINIMUM
CURRICULUM STANDARDS

At least four different groups, only one of them governmental, exercise political pressure to maintain minimum curriculum standards.[3] The first of these, *private accrediting agencies* such as the North Central Association, employ on-site visits and written reports of findings to enforce the maintenance of minimum curriculum standards. Their evaluation guidelines are highly specific and in effect constitute a particular value judgment of what the curriculum

2. See also Larsen and Toy (1955). These authors classify the forces affecting curriculum development as state agencies, the federal government, the profession, accrediting agencies, special-interest groups, business and labor, patriotic groups, social and religious groups, and the community.

3. It should go without saying that the imposition of minimum curriculum standards effectively limits the local district's prerogatives in determining curriculum content.

should be. Because loss of accreditation can have disastrous consequences for the prestige and standing of a school, these associations' curriculum recommendations are difficult to resist. Many observers view accrediting agencies as forces supporting traditional curriculum and inhibiting significant change.

Private testing agencies are another group that exerts a "standardizing" influence on the curriculum. Educational Testing Service, for example, is a $20-million-a-year enterprise whose College Board tests are taken by over a million students. While these tests do not entirely control curriculum content, they certainly place important limitations on it at the local level. Furthermore, standardized tests of reading, math, and spelling administered at the elementary level have a substantial influence on presecondary curriculum since most schools want their students to compare favorably with national norms.

A third, and widely recognized influence on curriculum standards are the *state departments of education*. While the control exercised by these legal agencies varies tremendously from state to state, as a group they constitute a substantial political force. Surveys have shown, for example, that a majority of states mandate courses in alcohol and drug abuse, about half require that the curriculum include United States history and physical education, and many legislate courses in other specific subjects.

Finally, *associations of teachers of special subjects* are an effective lobby for determining local curriculum policy. This is especially true of more recently developed, nonacademic subjects such as vocational education, home economics, and driver education. The power of these associations (often NEA state affiliates) is effectively characterized below:

> *Suppose a local board, aware of the obsolescence and flaccidity of much that passes for vocational training . . . decides to reduce its program in these areas. In theory this is one of its sovereign rights. In practice several things occur to change its mind. First the vocational education lobby goes to work on other members of local government and on the state legislature or state department of education to protect the extensive interests of vocational education teachers. Second the regional accrediting association comes to the aid of the status quo and makes threatening noises, suggesting and then perhaps demanding, on pain of disaccreditation . . . that the board rescind its decision. Third, the NEA state affiliate "investigates" and through its considerable power "persuades" the board to a different view (Koerner 1968, pp. 126, 127).*

Koerner's account, which leaves little to the imagination, is an accurate representation of how political pressures are brought to bear in the curriculum arena.

ALTERNATIVE GENERATORS

Notwithstanding the constraints imposed by the standard setters described above, many alternatives to present curriculum practices are possible. However, even within a framework bounded only by minimum standards, local educators are not free to employ any alternative they would like, whatever its educational merit may be. Curriculum alternatives, it turns out, are themselves largely determined by external sources. For example, if a school district wished to offer a course in black history twenty years ago, not only would a very unusually trained teacher need to be identified, but he would have to develop virtually single-handedly all of the curriculum materials for the course. While a few schools might attempt to meet such a formidable challenge, most would not. The point is that circumstances had not yet made the production of black history materials a profitable venture, and lacking such materials, the alternative of black history was simply not feasible. As the foregoing example suggests, money plays an important role in the generation of curriculum alternatives, and as we shall see below, it underlies the political influence of many influential sources of curriculum alternatives.

One of the most important sources of curriculum alternatives is *suppliers of curriculum materials*—principally *textbook publishers*, of course, but increasingly producers of all sorts of printed, electronic, visual, and mechanical devices for classroom use. The depth of publishers' influence on curriculum is demonstrated by a recent study of textbook use in Texas. This research reveals that 75 percent of a student's classroom time and 90 percent of his homework time is spent using textbooks. In such circumstances, it is hardly an exaggeration to say that the textbook *is* the curriculum.

Publishers, however, do not themselves always exercise control over textbook content. It is no secret that biology textbooks for the southern and western markets often are bound minus the chapter on evolution, just as history books are shipped to some school districts with the "Negro history" section deleted. In this regard, publishers clearly do not wield the power over curriculum content that often is attributed to them.

Some observers point out that while textbooks continue to exert significant influence on local school curricula, they are increasingly being supplanted by a wide range of nontext materials being produced and marketed by a rapidly expanding *corporate education industry*. "IBM has bought SRA, Xerox has bought American Educational Publications, GE and Time have formed General Learning, RCA has bought Random House, and CBS has bought Holt, Rinehart and Winston" (Kirst and Walker 1971, p. 496). Considering the unprecedented technology that these conglomerates have at their disposal, there is no reason to believe that a vast array of new curriculum materials— programs, packages, films, tapes, software, and hardware—will not flow from their offices and plants. The potentially powerful effects of these materials on local school curricula are difficult at this point even to imagine. One thing is certain, however: the well-organized and well-financed marketing techniques employed by the corporate giants will make their products very difficult for local schools to resist.

A second powerful influence on curriculum development is the *federal government*. Although its direct interest in public education is of relatively recent vintage, some estimates place present federal spending on curriculum construction substantially in excess of the amount allocated for that purpose

by states, local districts, and private enterprise. The influence of federal involvement, largely through 'the efforts of the National Science Foundation, can be
roughly gauged when we consider that over 50 percent of our schools are
offering the new physics and chemistry curricula and about 65 percent the
new biology. It is interesting to note, however, that virtually all federal money
has been used to update and improve existing curricula, not to develop radical
alternatives. Thus, "we have new math, new physics, new biology, new social
studies, and new English, but not psychology, sociology, economics, philosophy,
problems of modern living, interpersonal relationships, sex education, or film-
making and -viewing" (Kirst and Walker 1971, p. 493).

A third political force determining the direction of curriculum alternatives
is represented by *private foundations*. Like the federal government, private
foundations are relatively new to curriculum development. However, unlike
the federal government, such agencies as the Ford, Rockefeller, Carnegie, and
Kettering foundations have funded curriculum development projects in many
unconventional areas, such as photography, individual programming, and
psychology. The Kettering Foundation's Institute for Development of Educational Activities, Inc. (I/D/E/A) is a good example of such an innovative
curriculum project.

University professors are another influence on local curriculum policy. Coming from a variety of subject areas, they have contributed principally as subject
matter experts (e.g., in constructing the "alphabet soup" curricula of the
1960s). But in recent years psychologists have been more active in providing
the learning-process dimension for curriculum projects. That education faculty
have not been significantly involved in these projects is a datum well worth
pondering.

Although university professors as a group are quite diverse and therefore do
not represent an organized position on curriculum,[4] the *professional organizations to which they belong* do take consistent positions and are often extremely
influential. For example, the American Association for the Advancement of
Science and the American Institute for Biological Sciences are largely responsible for getting evolution into biology textbooks in spite of the concerted
objections of fundamentalists. And it was the American Mathematical Society
that initiated and financed the original School Mathematics Study Group
(SMSG) curriculum.

In surveying the political influences on curriculum innovation, we should
not overlook the effect that *professional educators and their journals* have on
curriculum development. Although many of the contributions published in
these journals fall into the category of specific instructional techniques rather
than broadly based curriculum practice, they often make an impact on local
policy. Publications of the Association for Supervision and Curriculum Devel-

---

4. One possible exception is their tendency to emphasize the *intellectual* in curriculum
to the detriment of the physical, moral, and aesthetic.

opment advocating curricula for cultural pluralism and world peace are good examples of curricular alternatives offered by the profession.

GROUPS DEMANDING CURRICULUM CHANGE

The agents described in the previous section induce curriculum change by developing innovations and offering them as alternatives to present practices. That is, they operate in such a way as to make change possible. In contrast, the groups discussed in this section *demand* change, and demand that it occur in a particular direction. Generally, these groups are not significant producers of curriculum materials.

One of the most consistently active groups in this category is the Council for Basic Education (CBE). As its name implies, CBE advocates increased emphasis on fundamental intellectual skills and knowledge and criticizes the schools for diverting valuable time to insignificant activities such as film making and folk dancing, for overemphasizing social adjustment at the expense of intellectual discipline, and for appropriating responsibilities that properly belong to the home, the church, and other societal agencies. The council makes extensive use of popular writing, conferences, journalism, and other media to influence board members, PTA's, and voters. Although no research is available on the effectiveness of the council's activities, there can be little doubt that they have had an impact on the curriculum policies of some school districts.

Other organizations frequently identified as lobbies for curriculum change are the Chamber of Commerce (Junior Achievement programs), the National Association of Manufacturers, the AFL-CIO, the John Birch Society, and the Daughters of the American Revolution. Generally sporadic in their activities, these organizations can wield effective power over curriculum policy, particularly in a crisis environment. The John Birch Society, for example, has precipitated many an anticommunist *cause célèbre* after scrutinizing school texts and finding "incredible quantities of pro-communist propaganda." Many years ago, when this writer was a high school English teacher, he was *required* to assign his classes a 500-word essay on "What It Means to Be an American" because the local DAR had decided to hold an essay contest in the schools. It is in situations such as these that one suddenly is confronted with the political power of external curriculum agents and realizes the vulnerability of school, teacher, and student.

In the light of these considerations, the conclusion seems unavoidable that the conventional treatment of curriculum development as a purely professional enterprise is inadequate, if not entirely spurious. This is so first, because it ignores the reality of extraprofessional political forces, and second, because it sidesteps "the [hard] political questions of who should have a say in determining curriculum at what stages in which ways with what impact" (Kirst and Walker 1971, p. 481). Furthermore, there seems to be little doubt that the identification of these varied and far-flung sources of curriculum policy serves seriously to undermine the myth of local control in curriculum development. What it seems to suggest is that if we wish to initiate curriculum change in a significant way, we had best consider the political strategies as well as the formation of schoolwide or systemwide "curriculum committees." This should not be viewed as cause for despair, however, for it is no disgrace to use political processes when the game turns out to be political.

> The fact of the matter is that any group with sufficient talent and re-
> sources can prepare curriculum materials and possibly start a trend that
> will sweep these other sources either aside or along (Kirst and Walker
> 1971, p. 498).

The Role of the Teacher in Curriculum Development

More nonsense has probably been promulgated about the role of the teacher in curriculum development than in any other area of the curriculum field. For example:

> We see the teacher as a very active participant in the planning of the
> total program of the school center. . . .
>
> [E]ach teacher *takes part in planning the total program of the school,
> possibly at district and state levels as a member of committees, councils,
> and other groups, and* always *as a member of the faculty of a particular
> school* (Saylor and Alexander 1974, pp. 43, 61, emphasis added).

With this kind of curriculum involvement it is hard to imagine the teacher having time for much of anything else, especially teaching. Ironically, however, the real situation is very much a reversal of Saylor and Alexander's prescription. If we know anything at all about teachers' responsibilities, we know that excessive class loads and unreasonably heavy nonprofessional duties prevent them from having time for much, if any, curriculum work at all.

But lack of time is only part of the problem. We have studies of curriculum innovation indicating that teachers simply are not oriented toward developing new curricula, or indeed even toward developing new patterns of classroom operation for themselves:

> It is a unique school indeed in which teachers discuss their classroom
> problems, techniques, and progress with one another and with their
> principal. In most schools teachers practice their own methods—rarely
> hearing, or even caring, if one of their colleagues is experimenting with
> some new teaching device or technique (Chesler et al. 1963, p. 76).

This would seem to suggest that teachers themselves do not view curriculum development as one of their professional responsibilities.

Finally, as we have noted elsewhere, some writers have raised questions regarding teachers' competency to make many of the decisions necessary in the curriculum-engineering process. While no one would argue that teachers are not competent to take *any* part in curriculum construction and development, the implication of Saylor and Alexander's statement that they can (and should) function adequately in *all* aspects of it is certainly to be regarded with some suspicion.

Yet, in another sense, the teacher's role in determining what the curriculum shall be is in fact enormous. It is a pitifully naive professional who assumes that what appears in the textbook, or curriculum guide, or course of study, is what is taught. In fact, research indicates that the reverse is true. For example, studies of the implementation of some recently developed science curricula show that teachers present the subject in ways that are significantly different from the conceptions intended by the curriculum writers (Kirst and Walker 1971, p. 493). Amusingly, the realization that teachers exercise considerable control over the operational curriculum has led some sardonic curriculum workers to attempt to produce "teacherproof" curricula. Needless to say, the attempt has always failed.

The unavoidable fact of ultimate teacher control over the operational curriculum is, perhaps, what has led Pritzkau (1959, p. 3) to write "curriculum improvement [is] equated with teaching." If this be the case, then we cannot help but conclude that the same must certainly be true for the engineering process. Thus, in spite of the constraints of teachers' limited knowledge of curriculum work, their apparent indifference to curriculum responsibilities, and their lack of time, their ultimate control over curriculum at point of implementation is a fact that curriculum engineers cannot avoid reckoning with in the engineering process.

But the argument for the involvement of teachers in curriculum development can be made on the basis of moral principle as well as practical necessity. For example, Oliver (1965, p. 49) writes: "Since there are many people who are affected by curriculum decisions, the democratic concept of education is that those who will live by a decision should have a share in the making of it." While Oliver's implied analogy between curriculum engineering and participatory democracy is a somewhat tenuous one, few professionals would argue that teachers should have *no* part in curriculum engineering or that it should be the exclusive preserve of curriculum specialists and/or administrators. Thus, the question seems not to be whether teachers should participate at all, but rather: What role should and can they properly be expected to play? It is this question that has not been systematically dealt with either in philosophical or empirical terms. And it is for this reason that the role of the teacher in curriculum development has received such vague and exaggerated treatment in the literature.

Beginnings are being made, however, to clarify the role of the teacher in curriculum development. Reports of curriculum development projects have begun to appear from which it is possible to generate testable hypotheses and research designs. For example, Whiteley (1971, pp. 43–46), writing in a recent publication devoted entirely to the process of curriculum development, reports a Canadian project that makes the teachers' role in curriculum development its central concern. Observing that teachers for the most part fail to understand new curricula while curriculum developers tend to lose touch with teachers' most recent thinking, Whiteley argues that the "functional separation" of classroom teachers and curriculum specialists is inadequate for curriculum development. His remedy for this professional hiatus is a procedure that he calls "the preimplementation study of curriculum programs." This preimplementation study, which was tested in the development of an English Curriculum Program for the Canadian province of Saskatchewan, is comprised of five major elements:

1. Timing and personnel: *The preimplementation study occurs prior to field trials of the new curriculum and involves "a large proportion" of teacher implementers.*
2. Purpose: *The purpose of the study is to promote the integration of the new curriculum in the minds of teachers, primarily in terms of applicability and feasibility.*
3. Structure: *Teachers and curriculum makers meet to discuss the new program. The discussion is conducted in terms of five interconnected areas of concern—philosophical, sociological, technological, psychological, and evaluative.*
4. Curricular areas: *Each of the five areas cited above represents a set of concerns in the development and implementation of curriculum programs. The* philosophical *area involves views of man, learning, and knowledge that appear to underlie curriculum aims, goals, and objectives; the* sociological *area denotes the concepts and principles to be assimilated by the learner; the* technological *area relates to the materials used to transmit curriculum content; the* psychological *denotes teacher and student activities for implementing the curriculum. And the* evaluative *involves procedures for determining success and for correcting deficiencies, based on use.*
5. Growth potential: *The preimplementation study is intended not only to foster development and integration of the new curriculum (see "Purpose," above), but also to foster the professional development of involved teachers.*

Whiteley (1971, p. 45) summarizes the benefits of preimplementation study as "(1) the development of adequate, feasible, and cohesive final programs, (2) teacher understanding and acceptance of final programs, and (3) the professional growth of practicing teachers."

Unfortunately, Whiteley does not comment on the actual results of preimplementation study as it was applied in Saskatchewan. Nevertheless, his proposal deserves serious consideration because it clearly defines the teacher's role in curriculum engineering, because it is a reasonable approach to the question, and because it presents several researchable hypotheses. Two observations, however, seem worthwhile to make. First, since Whiteley's proposal does not provide for broad teacher participation until just prior to the first field testing of the new curriculum, it seems clear that he does not intend teachers to be involved in the main work of curriculum construction.[5] In essence, this means that teacher influence is brought to bear primarily at the point where teacher competence is strongest: applicability and feasibility of the new curriculum for teaching. This does not, of course, obviate the possibility, indeed, the likelihood, of curriculum modification in terms of the five curricular areas noted in element #4, above. It does, however, emphasize that "the teacher's primary role in the curriculum development process is teaching in the classroom" (Anderson 1965, p. 57). The second observation to be made (and this is essentially a practical consideration) is that released time for teachers to participate in this kind of curriculum work will have to become far more common than it presently is if they are to be effective participants in preimplementation studies of new curricula.

A somewhat different point of view on teacher participation in curriculum engineering is expressed by Herron (1971, pp. 47–52), who reports research suggesting that "teachers, as a group, have little knowledge of the foundational aspects, or rationale, of . . . new programs. What they do with them, therefore, bears little resemblance to the uses for which they were designed." Thus, Herron emphasizes that effective implementation of new curricula can occur only when implementers (i.e., teachers) fully understand (and agree with) the theoretical basis of the new curriculum.

The traditional response to this problem in effective implementation has been the in-service workshop or the summer institute. Such devices, it will be noted, are similar in timing, purpose, and function to Whiteley's "preimplementation study." But Herron points out that in-service workshops and summer institutes usually do not work because they are not able to produce in teachers effective understanding of the new curriculum's foundational rationale. What is required is that "those individuals who are going to teach the program [be] involved in many phases of its creation, evaluation, and revision" (Herron 1971, pp. 50, 51). This means presenting teachers with a variety of philosophical, psychological, sociological, and methodological "choice points" in curriculum construction and making them aware of the consequences of various alternatives at each choice point. In effect, it makes teachers the curriculum decision makers at every stage of the construction process.

Herron's position, insofar as it advocates "total involvement" of all teachers in all phases of curriculum engineering, is very close to that of Saylor and Alexander. From Herron's point of view, only total participation in the construction of a curriculum provides an adequate understanding of its theoretical rationale—a *sine qua non* for effective implementation. Even if this happens to be the case (which, it being merely a hypothesis, is by no means obvious),

5. While all, or most, teachers are not included in the curriculum-construction process, selected teacher-representatives do work with specialists, consultants, and others in the construction of the new curriculum. This arrangement provides for appropriate teacher "input" at all stages of the engineering process.

practical considerations (e.g., teachers' lack of time, competence, inclination, etc.) militate against total participation by teachers. Nevertheless, Herron's observation concerning the importance of theoretical understanding in effective implementation is a point worth further consideration. Emphasis on such understanding may well provide a key breakthrough in defining the appropriate role of the teacher in curriculum development.

A final word on the human side of teacher involvement in curriculum development: It is natural for people to reject what they do not know or what is forced upon them, whatever its merit may be. This is as true of new curricula as it is of anything else. The notion of "teacherproof" curricula, for example, is an affront to both the teaching profession and to teachers as individuals. Whatever the "appropriate" role of the teacher turns out to be, it will be unacceptable unless it affords teachers the dignity due them as professionals and human beings.

Curriculum Engineering as Research and Development (R & D)

The establishment of research and development (R & D) centers[6] funded by both private and public sources is a recent phenomenon in curriculum engineering. The movement received its greatest impetus in the 1960s when the United States government provided substantial grants for the organization of several R & D centers. Recent reductions in federal funding, however, have caused a decline in R & D activity. Although the comparative success of R & D centers in accomplishing needed educational reform is still a much-debated question, a few specialists believe that they have greater potential for effecting curriculum change than any of the more traditional methods of curriculum engineering.

The establishment of R & D centers is based on at least five major premises (Chase 1971, pp. 143, 144): First, R & D centers perform functions (i.e., curriculum research and development) that are either neglected or poorly performed by other educational agencies such as schools, universities, and departments of education. Second, R & D centers are obligated to engage in activities that result in products and processes useful in the achievement of specified curriculum goals or the solution of important curriculum problems. Third, the centers' *research* is conducted to discover knowledge to be used for specific purposes, not to pursue knowledge for its own sake; furthermore, *development* is regarded successful only to the extent that specified criteria are

6. Although the R & D center is regarded by some curriculum specialists as a particular "model" for curriculum engineering, the variety of purposes, characteristics, and organizations exhibited by R & D centers, as well as their relative recency (and very often transience), precludes their classification as a definitive model at this time. The description of R & D centers presented in this section is based on research conducted and reported by Chase (1971, pp. 142–163).

met. Fourth, effective research and development depends on teams of qualified specialists working over extended periods of time. Insistence on instant results (a characteristically American tendency) is detrimental to significant research and development; real progress can be made only after long-term analysis and problem solving, goal clarification, and painstaking adaptation of means to ends. Finally, the expenditure of public (and other) funds for research and development is justified by an evaluation process that holds R & D centers accountable, but which does not impede their research activities.

According to proponents, the promise of R & D operations as effective vehicles for curriculum change lies primarily in the characteristics that distinguish them from other methods of curriculum engineering. For example, R & D operations generally represent

> *a systematic attempt to work out cycles of need assessment, specifications of objectives, analysis of alternative strategies and treatments leading to choices among alternatives, construction of partial or tentative systems among prototypes on the basis of testing in clinical and experimental situations, installation and testing under field conditions in a variety of situations, and continuing evaluation and refinement (Chase 1971, pp. 144, 145).*

No other method of curriculum engineering is designed to promote quite so consistently this systematic recycling of research and development processes until the desired effects are achieved. And, according to its proponents, it is this emphasis on systematic, "scientific" recycling of R & D activities that provides the greatest potential for curriculum change and improvement.

A second, and related, characteristic of R & D operations is their "attention to all the major elements in learning environments" (Chase 1971, p. 145). In other words, R & D operations tend to treat curriculum in all-inclusive terms, specifying not only instructional materials and media, but physical settings and the development of "relevant behaviors" for teachers and other school personnel, family groups, and community volunteers. If this sounds like an attempt at total management of the entire learning environment, both human and nonhuman, we should not be surprised. "Systematic" and "scientific" (more accurately, *technical*) approaches commonly attempt to control all possible variables in order to reduce the probability of unintended effects. Considering the philosophical foundations of the curriculum, however, it is questionable whether the purely technical paradigm is appropriate in curriculum engineering. Indeed, many curriculum specialists would hold that avoidance of value questions can have deleterious moral consequences, to say nothing of the lack of intelligence such avoidance manifests. Moreover, in terms of curriculum theory, the total control suggested above goes well beyond *curriculum* engineering, being more appropriately termed the detailed prescription of programmed (teacherproof) *instruction*. It is this second characteristic of existing R & D operations that mark them as highly technical approaches to curriculum engineering.

A third characteristic of R & D operations is their attempt to link many different organizations and institutions in the implementation effort. Thus, attention increasingly is being given to the potential contributions of such sources as state departments of education, parents, civic groups, industries, ethnic leaders, and community social agencies. This experimental stance toward the involvement of indirect, but substantial, influences on the curriculum is a desirable quality which, unfortunately, is lacking in many of the more traditional curriculum implementation procedures we have reviewed.

Subscribers to the R & D concept quite correctly reject the widely accepted notion that such piecemeal practices as the introduction of new media; the revision of curriculum guides; the regrouping of students; and the adoption of programmed instruction, team teaching, modular scheduling, and computer-assisted instruction can result in significant curriculum reform. Such "band-wagons," they point out, have produced little real change. In contrast, they propose the R & D center as a long-term commitment to the production of new curriculum materials and the careful adaptation of these to particular schools and communities. Thus, curriculum engineering becomes a coherent, reconstructive, and incremental process in which R & D centers and adopting schools function reciprocally not only to produce needed curriculum change, but to carry on a sustained effort for rational curriculum evolution.

With regard to the role of the school in R & D efforts, Chase (1971, pp. 146, 147) points out that R & D centers will be successful only to the degree that there exists in "adopting agencies" a particular orientation or set of conditions. He describes this set of conditions in terms of three basic requirements:

1. An ongoing assessment of the educational needs of the school's clientele. *This needs assessment should be conducted in such a way that it proceeds from the identification of the symptomatic effects (e.g., low achievement, poor attendance, and high dropout rate) to the underlying causes of curriculum deficiency.*
2. The identification of specific goals. *These goals grow out of the needs assessment cited above and should be perceived as important by the school's clientele, as well as by the professional staff.*
3. A willingness to search for means to attain the goals. *The search, of course, will draw heavily on the resources of the R & D center, which will also have been involved in the needs assessment and the goal setting.*

By requiring the foregoing set of conditions for effective reciprocal operations between school and R & D center, Chase simply makes the rather obvious point that unless the school adopts the same orientation to curriculum engineering as that employed by the R & D center, the desired curriculum changes cannot be brought about effectively. The conditions cited, of course, represent a purely "systematic" or "technical" approach to curriculum engineering—i.e., (1) assess the situation, (2) set goals, and (3) select the most effective means to achieve stated goals. As we have noted above, however, this purely technical paradigm is an inadequate procedure for dealing with the complexities of curriculum engineering.[7]

Beyond the fact that R & D centers have tended to develop a purely technical approach to curriculum engineering, the R & D principle as a vehicle for curriculum development has important potential. In the first place, R & D centers need not necessarily represent only the technical paradigm of curriculum engineering. They might experiment with a number of different approaches and thereby become centers for all sorts of curriculum-development research—philosophical and aesthetic, as well as empirical. Second, the R & D center can bring together in a single institution a group of professionals who represent a broad spectrum of expertise in curriculum development. It is not entirely inappropriate to use the metaphor of "critical mass" to describe the generation of significant new theory and practice that occurs when the best minds are brought together and provided opportunities to interact. Finally, the R & D center is in a unique position to provide client schools with a disinterested (unencapsulated) perspective on their curriculum situations. As we have suggested so often in this text, unconscious bias, or encapsulation, is probably the most significant obstacle to real curriculum reform. Of course, the perceptions of a school's professional staff (as well as other "insiders") are always an important ingredient in curriculum development; but "insiders," who are very likely to be biased (encapsulated), would undoubtedly benefit considerably from exposure to the viewpoints of astute "outsiders."

The real potential of R & D centers, unfortunately, will probably not be actualized in the very near future. As mentioned earlier, funding for R & D agencies both from government and private sources is becoming increasingly scarce. With regard to support at the federal level, "Uncertainties regarding national policy, frequent changes in personnel in HEW and the Office of Education, short-range funding, and burdensome reporting and review processes often have proved frustrating . . ." (Chase 1971, p. 159). Another impediment to the development of R & D centers is the reluctance of highly trained specialists to commit themselves to ventures which, as we have seen, have only tenuous prospects for long-term survival, much less significant development. It seems appropriate to observe, however, that colleges and schools of education, which already possess substantial specialized talent and resources, might take the initiative in the establishment of university-based R & D centers. Many obstacles to this course of action exist, of course, but the university would appear to be a "natural" locus for R & D activities in conjunction with surrounding local school districts. Indeed, some curriculum specialists have noted

---

7. For discussions which detail the inadequacy of the purely "scientific" or "technical" approach in the solution of human problems see the following sections: "Some Definitions of Theory" and "Scientific Theory and Curriculum Theory" in Chapter 4; "The Nature of Knowledge: Earth-Centered Philosophies" in Chapter 6; "Man: Free or Determined?" in Chapter 9; "The Problem of Ends and Means" and "Training versus Education" in Chapter 13. While the technical approach is *useful* and often *necessary*, it is not *sufficient* for dealing with curriculum problems.

that failure of teacher-training institutions to respond to the obviously critical need for curriculum reform in public schools may very well result in a decline in their status and influence vis-à-vis state departments of education and teachers' organizations. Finally, R & D centers will probably not expand rapidly as a major force in curriculum development and change because of impediments arising from the relatively low state of the science, technology, and arts on which educational research and development depend (Chase 1971, p. 160). One consequence of this low state of development in curriculum arts and sciences is that strategies and techniques of curriculum construction, evaluation, and dissemination emanating from R & D centers have not been strikingly more successful than those resulting from other, more conventional, procedures. While this condition is, of course, not attributable to any inherent defect in the R & D concept, it unquestionably operates to dampen enthusiasm for R & D operations, which, by their nature, have tended to be relatively expensive enterprises.

Leadership in Curriculum Development

Research studies involving "leadership" indicate that its nature and function are quite different from popular conceptions. For example, when the teachers in a large public school were asked who was "in charge" of their school (i.e., who was their "leader"), an overwhelming majority identified the principal. An examination of the *functions* performed by principal, guidance counselors, teachers, and other school personnel, however, showed that *no* individual or group performed a leadership role. Rather, the school operated, as it were, "under its own power," a bureaucratic organization functioning according to a network of written and unwritten "rules." In this particular case, the teachers had confused *status* and *visibility* with the exercise of authority. Furthermore, their error may very well have grown out of the mistaken assumption that a functioning organization presupposes a leader who is "in charge." Studies of many bureaucratic organizations show that this assumption cannot be made.

THE NATURE OF LEADERSHIP

Most people view the quality of leadership in much the same way that they conceive intelligence: as an *inherent* and *unitary* capability, sometimes learned, but often genetic in origin. Thus, they talk of a "born leader"—an individual whose talent enables him to command respect, to persuade others to accept his decisions and policies, and to direct the tasks that followers will perform. But research suggests that defining leadership as a set of qualities or traits inherent in the individual is much less realistic (and productive) than viewing it as a *functional* role played by an individual at a particular time in connection with a particular group of people.[8] In this context leadership is defined as functions

8. This section is based mainly on the distinction between *functional* and *status* leadership drawn by Smith, Stanley, and Shores (1957, pp. 459–463).

that promote the purposes of the group and foster its growth. Thus, "leadership is being exercised when a group member is helping the group to define and to meet its needs. And that person is the leader who at a given moment is most effectively helping the group in these respects" (Smith, Stanley, and Shores 1957, p. 459). This concept of "circular" or "revolving" leadership maximizes group potential because it utilizes the talents and resources of all members of the group. No one person, after all, can know more than every other member of the group about every curricular problem the group faces. At the same time it is abundantly clear that some members of the group will be more skillful at clarifying issues and facilitating movement toward solutions than others. It is these individuals who tend most frequently to emerge as functional leaders of the group.

Functional leaders, however, are not the only individuals who assume leadership roles. As Smith, Stanley, and Shores (1957, p. 460) point out, organizations, including school systems, usually are based on a hierarchical pattern of status and authority positions that defines official channels of communication and power. The teacher carries out the *principal's* directives, and the principal obeys the *superintendent's*. In such instances, individuals assume leadership positions *ex officio*, as it were, and by virtue of *status* acquire the power and influence not only to initiate and encourage certain courses of action, but to change, inhibit, or check certain others.[9] Even from these brief descriptions, it is obvious that a clear distinction exists between *functional* and *status* leadership.

Functional leadership is not conferred; it is earned by virtue of certain individual actions that directly move a group in the direction of its goals. But a status leader may either facilitate, inhibit, or, as was the case in the research reported in the opening paragraph of this section, play no role at all in the group's movement. Only in the first instance do the roles of functional and status leadership coincide. This represents an ideal *leadership* situation: the convergence of formal authority and integral function to produce the best possible conditions for effective curriculum development.

But what is the nature of a status leader who lacks the skills and knowledge required for functional leadership? Because of perceived, and real, demands that he "take charge" of the situation, the status leader is apt to use his official position to achieve curriculum development chiefly by fiat. Often this exercise of arbitrary power feeds upon itself so that by a series of incremental steps—sometimes in spite of himself and, ironically, out of fear—he becomes an outright authoritarian, feared and often despised by his subordinates. The results are usually extremely rigid (and repressive) curriculum practices, such as meticulously prescribed learning activities, lock-step progression through highly specific content, and evaluation chiefly in terms of tangible particulars. In other cases, the status leader who has a command of sophisticated manage-

9. For an excellent analysis of the locus, sources, and parameters of campus power, see Lindquist and Blackburn (1974).

ment skills may *seduce* his subordinates into accepting his decisions and directives, thereby creating what is known as a paternalistic relationship between himself and his subordinates. Perceptive professionals, however, sense the authoritarianism that underlies the status leader's exhortations to "cooperate with the group" and resent the arbitrary imposition of his curriculum directives. Finally, there is the status leader who, because of a desire to be liked, anxiety, incompetence, or sheer laxness, eschews any influential role at all in curriculum decision making. This type of leader creates a laissez-faire climate which in the absence of bureaucratic systematization or other functional leadership can result in chaotic curriculum conditions. In such a "do-your-own-thing" environment there is little incentive for group work, and curriculum coherence—difficult to maintain even under the best conditions—gives way to individual idiosyncrasies and even aberration.

What, then, is the character of the status leader who also performs a functional leadership role in curriculum engineering? Although it is impossible at this stage of our knowledge precisely to define his qualities, we at least can stipulate that he should possess extensive understanding of the main curriculum topics explored in the chapters of this text: curriculum theory and history, foundations, anatomy, design, and engineering. Just as important, however, it would seem reasonable to expect that he would also possess a number of other competencies vital to translating theory into effective curriculum practice. For example, he should be skillful in working with individuals and groups in face-to-face situations. This includes, among other abilities, identifying and meeting individual and group anxieties and needs, facilitating growth in others' sensitivity to interpersonal and group processes, and dealing effectively with individual and group conflicts. In short, it means recognizing the relativity of his own, as well as others', perceptions in dealing with curriculum problems. Second, the functional leader should be adept at initiating and sustaining rigorous intellectual inquiry. By a variety of research procedures— objective survey instruments, document analysis, case studies, personal interviews, and just plain reflection—he will attempt to search out the basis of curriculum problems, the attitudes of lay and professional groups, the loci of power and influence in school system and community, and other data necessary for sound curriculum development. He would bring to his inquiry, of course, the self-examining open orientation that we have previously characterized as "unencapsulation" and "authenticity." Finally, the status leader who performs a functional leadership role should possess a number of the "practical" skills that one usually associates with the politics of the real world. For example, he will be sensitive and astutely responsive to political parties; taxpayers' associations; racial, ethnic, and religious groups; labor unions; business organizations; and other vested interests affecting curriculum at local, state, and national levels. Being aware of the substantial impact of the mass media, the functional status leader will have a "feel" for the correct timing of news releases; he will be able to assess the possible consequences of public statements; and he will find ways to project a reasonably favorable image (when appropriate) of the school and its curriculum. This is not to say that cynicism, expedience, or manipulation are part of the functional leader's character. It simply means that the environment in which we, and the curriculum, exist contains many factors which, though they may be perceived as uncongenial, cannot be ignored. The exercise of intelligence demands that these factors be taken into account in the decision-making process. On what basis they are dealt with can be determined only by the application of the standards of conduct demanded by one's moral code. The code endorsed in this text, of course, draws its principles from man-centered philosophies (see Chapter 6) and a "synoptic view of man" (see Chapter 10). Whatever code he employs, however, the functional leader will carefully weigh the value dimension of the decisions he makes as he deals with the forces affecting the course of his curriculum development program.

LEADERSHIP OF THE PROFESSION IN CURRICULUM DEVELOPMENT

Elsewhere in this text the question of participation in curriculum engineering has been raised. It was suggested that since schools are institutions created by society to fulfill a social need, the question is not whether extraprofessional groups should participate in the process, but what role they should play. Whatever those roles may be, and agreement on them is far from having been reached, it seems clear that they are properly subordinate to the role of the education profession *when, and only when, the profession functions adequately in its leadership role.* There are several reasons justifying a leadership role for the profession in curriculum engineering, some of them obvious, others less so. Among the most obvious is the fact that members of the profession are students of, and purportedly authorities in, the technical aspects of education. For example, they have been schooled in such areas as the psychology of learning processes, the nature of the reading act, techniques of effective information transmission, and so on. While no claim is made that the profession's level of expertise in these matters is entirely adequate, it is certainly demonstrably higher than that of any other segment of the lay community.

Another obvious ground supporting the profession's leadership role in curriculum engineering is its collective expertise in the content of the cultural heritage—that is, the disciplines of knowledge. While other segments of the society may possess superior expertise in certain areas (e.g., medical practitioners and electrical engineers), the profession's collective mastery of the areas of knowledge that constitute the content of education is greater than that ordinarily found in the lay community.

But there are other reasons justifying professional leadership in curriculum engineering that are less obvious—often, unfortunately, even to members of the profession. One of these is the fact that since teaching is an inescapably moral enterprise, teachers should be avid students of social and educational values, and more specifically, of the foundational areas of the curriculum. As most of us are painfully aware, a propensity for searching inquiry into the value basis of curricular practice is not a characteristic of many professionals in education. Yet, at bottom, it is these values, often unconscious and the result of long-term enculturation, that are the most important determinants of the curriculum.

> *Values are involved in almost every controversy, and certainly they are involved in every act of teaching and every curriculum change. The selection of educational objectives, the materials and methods of instruction, and the administration and operation of the school necessarily require choices among values (Smith, Stanley, and Shores, 1957, p. 455).*

There is little doubt that our school curricula generally reflect the unexamined values imbedded in our national and local communities. But in the last analysis, the profession's responsibility must be to the world community and mankind. This argument rests not only on an "altruistic" basis, admirable as that value may be; it is made in the name of enlightened self-interest and survival, for in the interdependent world that we have created there can be no other basis for education. Professional curriculum makers cannot avoid consideration of the larger questions of man and the basis of his existence, his social relations, and his cosmic destiny.

In those cases where the local, or even national, community demands that ideas not conforming to its particular social, political, economic, or religious philosophy be proscribed from the curriculum, the profession has an obligation to exercise its leadership—indeed, its power as an organized group—to subject the values in question to open discussion and debate. No curriculum, of course, can be value free; nor should it be. But only when the profession insists on a self- and social-critical stance toward curriculum making will schools become more than instruments of propaganda and indoctrination. Acquiescence in practices that impede the free exploration of ideas can only lead to the effective strangulation of education.

Unfortunately, as we have already noted, school systems have not distinguished themselves in the defense of freedom of inquiry or expression.[10] Very likely, this has been at least partly due to the profession's neglect of foundational values as a vital area of study. The result has often been the embarrassing anomaly of the courts—in a large number of cases—having to impose freedom on what theoretically ought to be the most liberal institution in the society. But until the profession acknowledges and accepts its obligation to become proficient in the analysis of social and educational values, curricu-

---

10. One of the saddest commentaries on the state of freedom of expression in public schools is the Supreme Court case of *Tinker v. Des Moines Independent Community School District.* In this case three students were suspended for wearing black armbands to protest United States involvement in the Viet Nam war. In finding for the plaintiffs, Mr. Justice Fortas stated, "the wearing of armbands . . . was closely akin to 'pure speech.' . . . It can hardly be argued that either students or teachers shed their constitutional rights . . . at the schoolhouse gate."

lum will remain an instrument of the state, controlled for the most part by people (and forces and events) whose purposes have little to do with the ideal ends of education.

Even supposing, however, that the education profession became aware of the necessity to be self- and social-critical and to take a leadership role in freeing the curriculum from the constraints of narrow and parochial values: How should they *exercise* this leadership? In the words of Smith, Stanley, and Shores (1957, p. 456), "It is one thing to know *what* to do, it is quite another thing to know *how* to do it." This issue brings us to the fourth and final justification for professional leadership in curriculum engineering: the profession's unique opportunity, as yet unfulfilled, to generate school and community action on the implementation of curriculum reform. What we are talking about here are the skills of effective curriculum engineering: sensing anxiety in others, alleviating hostility, diagnosing the sources of individual conflicts, fostering cooperation among special-interest groups, facilitating intragroup processes; in short, the whole range of human relations skills that make the difference between successful curriculum development and the apathy, resentment, hostility, bickering, disillusion, and final collapse that all too often, despite glowing public accounts to the contrary, mark curriculum reform projects. Since the profession of education, virtually by definition, centers on effective human interaction, it seems reasonable to propose that professional educators be especially adept in this critical area of curriculum work.

To summarize this section on professional leadership, then, our argument is that the profession has the prerogative, as well as the obligation, to assume a leadership role in curriculum engineering by virtue of its expertise (or potential expertise) in (1) technical skills and knowledge, (2) the content of education, (3) social and educational values, and (4) knowledge and skills in curriculum engineering processes.

Consultants in Curriculum Development and Implementation

The services of consultants in curriculum development projects have been used by school systems almost since the time that such projects first were introduced in the 1920s. The proper or most effective use of consultants, however, has received little attention in the literature so that their role, while sometimes influential in practice, has never been clearly defined. The prevailing confusion over the appropriate role of consultants can be demonstrated from this writer's experience with a curriculum development project when he was a secondary English teacher in a New England school system. Early in the school year the superintendent announced that the high school curriculum was to be "revised" and that a group of consultants from a nearby prestigious university would visit the school once a week (2:30 to 5:00 P.M.) during the school year to work with the faculty. With no other orientation than this, it is understandable that the faculty looked forward to its first meeting with a mixture of curiosity, anxiety, perplexity, amusement, and for some, resentment. Although most had little idea of what their own role in the curriculum revision project would be, they assumed, in the light of the handsome fee paid to retain the university specialists, that the "experts" would certainly know what needed to be done and how to do it.

After the first meeting (the teachers in each subject area met with a consultant in that area) there was considerable suspicion that not only was the consultant uninformed with regard to the school's curriculum, but that he had no specific plan for revision in mind and had no intention of providing his group with any suggestions or directions for curriculum action. By the third weekly session, most teachers were convinced that though the curriculum meetings were interesting enough as "rap sessions," little in the way of hard or tangible curriculum revision would come out of them. Their prediction was confirmed when, as April approached, the consultants pointed out that the school year was coming to an end and it was essential that something concrete "be gotten down on paper." Tasks (such as assembling required reading lists for each grade and ability group, revising recommended titles for "extra-credit" book reports, and inscribing minimum standards for proficiency in composition by grade level) were assigned and summarily executed. By June each committee had contributed its "curriculum documents" to the school's aggregate curriculum plan, and with great fanfare the superintendent and the university, in a joint announcement, proclaimed the eminent success of their cooperative venture. The teachers, of course, breathed a sigh of relief and returned to the normality of the familiar curriculum.

The point of the foregoing anecdote is not to disparage consultants, superintendents, or teachers. It is merely to establish the lack of understanding that prevails with regard to the appropriate role of consultants. For the most part, the teachers had expected the "experts" to know everything about correct curriculum-engineering procedures and to tell them exactly what to do. The consultants, on the other hand, did not perceive their roles at all in leadership terms; they were nondirective resource persons being paid, as one consultant egotistically put it, "to allow my brain to be picked." Whether the whole exercise was in fact intended to be nothing more than a public-relations ploy by its initiators is really beside the point; it was allowed to become that mainly because of a lack of clarity about appropriate roles.

As indicated above, part of the problem of effective use of consultant services is that client school systems expect the consultants to solve their problems.[11] This no consultant can do because none can have at his disposal formula solutions to idiosyncratic local problems involving idiosyncratic local people. If we

---

11. In some cases it is possible for the consultant to achieve a reorganization that apparently does solve the problem. The so-called solution, however, actually amounts to the imposition of a new and perhaps more smoothly functioning system; but such a system merely represents a different type of closed curriculum.

stand by our contentions that curriculum change is people change, that psycho-cultural encapsulation is a fundamental problem in curriculum work, and that searching inquiry into unexamined values and assumptions is a requisite for effective curriculum development, we must conclude that the curriculum will change only to the extent that local professionals carefully examine their own behavior and its relationship to the local curriculum situation. Thus, the role of the consultant can only be defined in terms of the requirements of the local situation, and the consultant will be primarily concerned with initiating and fostering the processes of self-examination, interaction, and inquiry in its broadest sense.

What does this mean in terms of the conditions under which the school staff and the consultant cooperate (i.e., literally operate together)? In the first place it means that once-a-week meetings after school over a period of the academic year constitute an unreasonable constraint on curriculum-development effectiveness. As we have noted in the section on R & D centers, coherent curriculum change is a reconstructive, incremental, and evolutionary process that requires extended periods of time. Furthermore, the people involved in the process cannot be expected to function effectively if curriculum development work is handled as an overtime, uncompensated responsibility. Regular and sufficient released time and/or additional compensation for participation in weekend or vacation-time curriculum workshops must be provided. It is an affront to individual dignity to require regular staff to work overtime without compensation while paying the consultants they are expected to work with generous per diem fees. Other conditions, such as adequate meeting facilities, library resources, and curriculum materials, are of course necessary, but these two—the dignity of adequate time and compensation—are basic.

Given a physical-psychological framework within which the staff can work effectively on curriculum change, what role should the consultant play? Initially, for the consultant who is naively called in by a school system "to help with general curriculum revision,"[12] there is no alternative to an extended period of assessment. This involves deriving some understanding of where the school staff and the community "are" with regard to values, beliefs, perceptions, etc. The consultant, in other words, must "get inside" staff members' perspectives so that he can "see" the situation as they see it (Smith, Stanley, and Shores 1957, p. 473). It goes without saying that the situation as it is perceived by members of the staff and local community may be quite removed from actuality. Nevertheless, this process by which the consultant puts himself in the others' shoes is essential to breaking out of his own encapsulation and thereby getting a more accurate picture of what the situation really is.

As he comes to what he believes is an understanding of the local situation, the consultant will be tempted to impose that understanding on members of

---

12. While this is probably the least desirable and effective use of consultant services, it is probably the most common. However, in school systems that are floundering and totally unable to initiate any form of curriculum development activity on their own, it may be an appropriate—indeed unavoidable—way to utilize consultants.

the community and staff, particularly if it is very different from their own. Any attempt at such imposition is bound to fail, since people, being what they are, will either ignore it, reject it with hostility, or passively accept it only for the sake of appearances.

The consultant who understands people and how to communicate with them will usually begin by exploring the staff's perceptual fields with them: Why do you think the principal will "come down hard" if you assign that book? What leads you to believe that discrimination is not a problem in dealing with minorities in this school? What are the nonprofessional duties that prevent you from doing the kind of teaching job you would like to do? By questions, sympathetic responses (one can be honest and disagree while being sympathetic), mutual exploration, and other forms of personal interaction, the consultant stimulates staff members to ask their own questions, to examine their own assumptions, and gradually to adjust their perceptions so that the perceptions yield a less distorted and egocentric view of the curriculum situation. Of course, the consultant will undoubtedly be altering his own perceptions throughout the process. Moreover, he will surely find many individuals whose defenses and armor do not permit them to perceive the situation from a broader perspective. Nevertheless, this process of encouraging the growth of people's perspectives (as, incidentally, one's own perspective grows) is the only route by which curriculum change *qua* people change can occur.

Common as it is, the practice of calling in consultants without prior local preparation is not, as we have noted, a very efficient or economical way of using consultant services. It is far more desirable to know what one wants from the experts that are employed. Presuming that local professionals have developed some expertise in curriculum construction, development, and implementation, it is reasonable to assume that they have the capability, at least in some preliminary way, of assessing their own curriculum situation with respect to needs, desired goals, problems, and so on. Only after they have developed an orientation of this kind are they in a position to determine at what points in the development program they will be in need of what kinds of expert help. Thus, when a consultant is called in, he can focus his expertise on the specific questions and problems that beset a particular school. This is not to say that the consultant may not assist the school's staff members to reconceptualize their perceptions of the local curriculum situation or some aspect of it; nor does it mean that the consultant's methods will be any the less human-relations oriented than we have advocated above. It simply proposes that prior focusing of the consultant's role enhances his usefulness and efficiency, and avoids much of the (often expensive) confusion and groping that characterizes many consultant-client relationships in curriculum development. Clearly, though unfortunately, utilizing consultant resources in the manner described above precludes the possibility of prescribing in advance, or in the abstract, when or what kind of expert help should be employed in particular curriculum development projects.. Considering the nature of curriculum work, however, we should not be surprised. Indeed, this condition of open-endedness will probably be a far more disturbing one for professionals who view themselves as "directions followers" than for those who more properly consider themselves *decision makers.*

References

Anderson, Vernon E. 1965. *Principles and Procedures of Curriculum Improvement.* 2d ed. New York: The Ronald Press Company.

Chase, Francis S. 1971. "Educational Research and Development in the Sixties." In *Elements of Curriculum Development,* edited by F. Michael Connelly. Monograph Supplement to *Curriculum Theory Network,* No. 7. Toronto: The Ontario Institute for Studies in Education.

Chesler, Mark, Richard Schmuck, and Ronald Lippitt. 1963. "The Principal's Role in Facilitating Innovation." *Theory into Practice.* Vol. II, No. 5.

Herron, Marshall. 1971. "On Teacher Perception and Curricular Innovation." In *Elements of Curriculum Development,* edited by F. Michael Connelly. Monograph Supplement to *Curriculum Theory Network,* No. 7. Toronto: The Ontario Institute for Studies in Education.

Kirst, Michael W., and Decker F. Walker. 1971. "An Analysis of Curriculum Policy-Making." *Review of Educational Research* (December).

Koerner, James D. 1968. *Who Controls American Education?* Boston: Beacon Press.

Larsen, Roy E., and Henry Toy, Jr. 1955. "Forces Affecting the Curriculum." *NEA Journal* (December).

Lindquist, John D., and Robert T. Blackburn. 1974. "Middlegrove: The Locus of Campus Power at a State University." *AAUP Bulletin,* Winter issue (December).

Oliver, Albert I. 1965. *Curriculum Improvement.* New York: Dodd, Mead & Co.

Pellegrin, R. J. 1966. *An Analysis of Sources and Processes of Innovation in Education.* Eugene, Ore.: Center for the Advanced Study of Educational Administration.

Pritzkau, P. T. 1959. *Dynamics of Curriculum Improvement.* Englewood Cliffs, N.J.: Prentice-Hall.

Saylor, J. Galen, and William M. Alexander. 1974. *Planning Curriculum for Schools.* New York: Holt, Rinehart & Winston.

Smith, B. Othanel, William O. Stanley, and J. Harlan Shores. 1957. *Fundamentals of Curriculum Development.* Rev. ed. New York: Harcourt Brace Jovanovich.

Whiteley, Thomas. 1971. "A Model for Pre-Implementation Study of Curriculum Programs." In *Elements of Curriculum Development,* edited by F. Michael Connelly. Monograph Supplement to *Curriculum Theory Network,* No. 7. Toronto: The Ontario Institute for Studies in Education.

CHAPTER 21

EPILOGUE: INDIVIDUAL COMMITMENT AND DECISION MAKING IN CURRICULUM CHANGE

Education innovations are often due to the initiative of one person or a very few individuals. As long as that individual or group keeps working on it, the innovation survives. When they stop, it dies.
—ROBERT HALFMAN, M. L. A. MACVICAR,
W. T. MARTIN, EDWIN TAYLOR, AND
JERROLD ZACHARIAS

For the most part the past two chapters have dealt with curriculum development, implementation, and change on a social or organizational level. We have discussed models for organized curriculum engineering, political factors, research and development centers, and so on. In many situations, however, no organizational vehicle exists for directing the evolution of the school's curriculum, although individual teachers may be genuinely concerned about the curriculum that they teach, its relationship to the total school program, and its development (or lack of development) over time. Even where an organizational vehicle does exist, it may be ideologically at odds with an individual's curricular convictions and thereby be perceived as a counterdevelopmental force; or it may actually be only a pseudo-organization—i.e., merely a façade maintained for public relations purposes. What can, or should, the individual do in situations like these?

It should come as no surprise that we hold out no set of directions for individuals to follow in difficult (and "impossible") curriculum development situations. The only valid response to the question of what individuals can do to bring about desirable curriculum change is, "Think, then act." This response emphatically is not an evasion of the issue or an equivocation; it is derived from the theory (and conviction) that the individual's behavior (both in professional affairs and in the conduct of his personal life) is unavoidably the result of freely taken decisions, responsibility for which cannot be abrogated. On a broader theoretical plane this response should be recognized as an approach to individual action based on our *synoptic view of man*. Inasmuch as this perspective on the nature of the individual has already been formally presented in great detail (see Chapter 10), there is no need to repeat it here. Suffice it to say that it integrates the concepts of encapsulation, responsible freedom, self-reliance, and community. Our purpose in this section is to deal with the problem of individual commitment and decision making in curriculum change by drawing on the principles inherent in this foundational position on man.

Under the adverse conditions for curriculum development and change that prevail in most schools, teachers often are heard to comment: "The curriculum needs changing, but the system will never allow it." "Certainly the curriculum is outdated, but with five classes of thirty students each, who has time for curriculum development?" "Everybody talks about change, but nobody does anything." "What can *I, alone*, do to change the curriculum?"[1]

These questions cry out for analysis by the people making them in order that their real meanings may be revealed. Can they be taken literally, at face value, or do they simply represent (unconscious) means for dealing with (or avoiding) truth and reality? For example, when, as a teacher, I say, "The curriculum needs changing, but the system will never allow it," what assumptions am I making? How do I *know* the system will never allow change? What hard evidence do I have to support such a conclusion? Or is the conclusion really a mechanism that I use to enable me to avoid confrontation with a responsibility that I *feel* but wish to avoid?

Furthermore, what do I mean by the "system"? Is there really a faceless structure of forces that will not permit me to do as I would like? Or is the "system" a convenient, commonly accepted scapegoat that I conjure up to rationalize attitudes and behaviors born of other, less congenial and justifiable motivations and impulses? Perhaps the "system" *is* real, but *really* an agglomeration of individuals like myself who, by assuming that certain actions will not be permitted, in fact prevent those actions from taking place. (Shades of the self-fulfilling prophesy!) If so, I must ask myself why I, and others, really wish to prevent these actions from occurring. What is our real reason for opposing curriculum change?

Finally, what do I mean by change? Change can be identified as alterations in practice covering a wide range of directions. Perhaps the "system," assuming that it is a real force, will permit certain alterations but not the ones that I advocate. Is it possible that my position with regard to the direction of change is not as desirable as I believe it to be? Further, change, in whatever direction,

---

1. It has been suggested that questions such as these indicate that the individuals asking them are themselves part of the problem.

can occur in many degrees of magnitude. To insist on immediate and revolutionary change may be to invite rejection (perhaps intentionally). It may be important at this point to ask whether I have considered the maxim, "Half [or quarter or eighth] a loaf is better than none."

These questions suggest an attempt at separation of the self from its envelopment in, and dependency on, the narcotic of familiarity—in a word, from encapsulation. They are questions which represent, as Pritzkau (1970, p. 4) phrases it, putting oneself into question, relating to *what is*, and trying to ascertain the ingredients and meanings of reality. It is questions such as these that the individual must ask himself as he strikes out to assume a responsible individual role in curriculum change.

The answers that I provide to these questions will vary, of course, depending on "where I am" both psychologically and situationally. On the psychological level, my probing may make me terribly uncomfortable, but willing tentatively to admit that I have resisted doing anything about curriculum change because I was afraid to fail, or was too comfortable with familiar routines, or even because I feared the ridicule of colleagues who might label me an ambitious exhibitionist "bucking" for department chairman. On the other hand, my psychological condition may be so "closed" that I reject out of hand any suggestion that factors other than a rigid and overbearing "system" prevent me from initiating curriculum change.

On the situational level my answers to self-reflective questions will be influenced by factors inherent in the situation: e.g., state law, a highly influential community pressure group, or an excessive teaching load. Relevant situational factors usually operate as constraints, although self-reliant individuals are quick to identify those that can be used to facilitate curriculum change. It is crucial (though admittedly extremely difficult) that a reasonably clear and accurate distinction be maintained between actual constraints in the situation and those that are invented to serve convenient psychological purposes. Situational constraints, unlike psychological ones, are rarely insurmountable. The former can almost always be dealt with in one way or another with varying degrees of success by the self-reliant individual. The latter, however, almost invariably paralyze.

In response to these contentions, it often is argued that even when an individual reflects upon his encapsulated condition and recognizes his entrapment, he is not "free" to reform the curriculum as he wishes. "If I taught English as I really believe it ought to be taught," says our critic (who perceives himself as "unencapsulated"), "I'd be fired on the spot." Leaving, for the moment, the question of whether this statement itself reflects a state of encapsulation, we shall deal with it at face value, addressing the issues that it raises.

In the first place, we should point out the obvious fact that no one can be absolutely free in the sense that he may do anything he wishes. For example, we humans may not lift an automobile off the ground or fly into space unaided by mechanical devices. Yet we are a great deal freer than most of us assume. For example, we are all of us quite free, if we wish, to refrain from eating, to drive our cars on the sidewalk, to teach in the nude, to propagate children out of wedlock, or to shun the society of all other human beings. The reason most of us do not ordinarily do these things is that we are unwilling to accept their rather certain and unpleasant consequences. We *say* we are not free to do them, but what we really mean is that their consequences are undesirable and unacceptable. Thus, the English teacher who claims that he is not free to teach as he wishes is not being quite accurate; he is perfectly free to do so if he is willing to undergo the consequences of that behavior.

This argument is not merely an exercise in semantics. It is important because it reveals the value basis of our behavior. Any given situation presents us with a virtual infinity of alternative courses of action from which we are quite literally free to choose whichever one(s) we wish. The one that actually gets chosen is ordinarily the one that yields the most beneficial consequences for us, *judged according to the values that we hold*. What makes things difficult for us is that in most cases, choosing among alternative courses of action involves choosing among conflicting values, each of which may be quite important to us. For example, take the case of a young woman who, to her great dismay, observes her best friend shoplift a pair of gloves in a boutique owned by a struggling young shopkeeper. What action should she take, if any? Strict adherence to honestly tells her to report her friend so that justice may be done; wrongdoers should suffer the lawful consequences of wrongdoing. Besides, it is unfair that the victim, who can ill afford such losses in merchandise, should suffer from her friend's dishonesty. By turning her friend in, she adheres to the principles of honesty and justice and at the same time thwarts the victimization of the innocent shopkeeper.

But what of her obligation to her friend? The values of friendship and loyalty should not be lightly dismissed. Would not turning in her friend be tantamount to betrayal, an ugly principle of action? And to be guilty of betrayal in this case would certainly result in the loss of a valued relationship, a most undesirable consequence.

But to turn in her friend or do nothing are not the only possible courses of action in this situation. The young woman might approach her friend and urge her to turn herself in, to return the gloves secretly, to pay for the gloves, or to take any one of a number of different actions. Each of these alternatives, of course, will have variant consequences and will be based on different values. Nor does approaching her friend with the advice that she take a particular course of action on her own exhaust the possibilities. Our young woman may decide to seek an intermediary—a relative, minister, or other counselor—to talk with her friend; or she may decide only to warn the shopkeeper so that he may prevent further losses. Other possibilities are deciding to pay the shopkeeper for the gloves herself or even surreptitiously to "recapture" them from her friend and return them, either openly or secretively. The alternatives, obviously, are legion, but whatever decision finally is made will reveal to us a great deal about the value commitments that the young woman has made.

As it is in this hypothetical exercise in moral behavior, so it is with the individual's responsibility in curriculum development and change. He is perfectly free in most instances to take whatever course of action he wishes; what course he actually pursues will be a function of its consequences, his conscious and unconscious value commitments, and real and perceived factors in the situation. Ultimately, however, he cannot fail to accept responsibility for his decisions and his behavior.

To see what this all means for a professional dealing with curriculum, suppose that I am a teacher of civics, married with two children, who holds the conviction that my responsibility to students demands a curriculum geared to the realities of contemporary politics at all levels of government. I know that an unwritten school policy prohibits the discussion of controversial issues in the classroom (the official text presents an idealistic, and innocuous, indoctrination into American government), but over the past five years I have managed to "bootleg" many significant current political issues into the curriculum with highly salutary results from the point of view of students' learning. I know that, strictly speaking, I am violating school policy, but changing the curriculum by "subversion," as it were, seems preferable both to obeying the rules and to precipitating a confrontation on the basis of principle. To have gone the "confrontation route" by attempting to get the policy changed would surely have released a whirlwind of controversy in which passion and vituperation would undoubtedly have played a more important role than reason. Besides, the outcomes of such controversies are almost impossible to predict, and even more rigid curriculum restrictions might have eventuated.

Following the "subversion route," on the other hand, I have been able to increase the proportion of relevant current political topics each year, and from my point of view, have substantially improved the civics curriculum. The principal and most teachers know what I am doing, do not *dis*approve, and assume a posture of "looking the other way." As a matter of fact, many teachers mildly approve of the changes I have made, and some have even begun to include current controversial issues in *their* courses (a "bonus" consequence of my decision that is very gratifying to me).

What has occurred in the above situation is that I have assessed my own convictions and values, surveyed the current situation, projected alternative courses of action and their likely consequences, and on that basis chosen to act as I did. Of course, I might have elected to follow school policy, but that would have represented a different value orientation (e.g., "following the rules always takes precedence"). Alternatively, I might have chosen to follow school policy not because I valued rule following per se, but because I was not prepared to take the risks involved in violating the rules. I might have reasoned that "rocking the boat" was likely to elicit displeasure from the administration which, even if it did not result in nonrenewal of my contract, might have provoked other kinds of retaliation (e.g., assignments of extra duty, such as cafeteria supervision, detention hall, or boys' room patrol). In entertaining hypotheses such as these it is crucial that one's deliberations be as free as possible from encapsulating influences. Excessive acquiescence to authority, mild paranoia, and inordinate needs for security can significantly distort perceptions of reality to the extent that decisions clearly contrary to the best interests of all involved are executed and justified on quite rational grounds.

Obviously, in the above example I might have followed many courses of action different from the two alternatives that I entertained. Presumably, as a self- and social-critical self-reliant individual I would have examined many points and alternatives that it was not feasible to include. Nevertheless, it is hoped that the principle of operation that we have been dealing with here has been made reasonably clear: free and responsible action is based on a decision-making process that involves self- and social-critical reflection.

Simple as the above principle is to articulate, its meaning cannot be understood, nor its implementation accomplished, on a purely abstract intellectual basis. It must be examined reflectively in a variety of hypothetical situations, and exercised in a great many practical ones, before the richness and complexity of its meanings begin to emerge in terms of personal experiential knowledge. Such understanding, however, can be facilitated if we explore beforehand some of the problems that occur when individuals grapple with the process in making personal and professional decisions.

Internalization of Theory

The important distinction between conceived and operative values was made in Chapter 7. There, it will be recalled, *conceived values* were defined as those that we believe we hold, while *operative values* were identified as those that could be inferred from our behavior. With regard to the need for free and responsible curriculum decision making, it is important that the individual be able to distinguish, insofar as he is able to do so, discrepancies between what he "believes that he believes" and the beliefs that are implicit in his behavior. Put in other terms, this means aligning theory and practice. For example, "providing for individual differences" is a conceived value that has become so entrenched as a curriculum principle that virtually all professionals swear allegiance to it. Not only the legitimacy of the principle, but its meaning, generally are considered beyond question. Yet the most cursory observation of curriculum practice reveals an overwhelmingly consistent denial of the principle: uniform texts and assignments, absolute standards in evaluation, widespread use of standardized tests, and a plethora of other mass-treatment devices. As Pritzkau (1970, p. 35) notes, "the term 'teaching for individual differences' is mouthed so much as to be automatized to the point of meaninglessness."

In this particular situation it seems clear that the "theory of individualization" is merely a nonfunctioning verbalization. It will not—indeed, cannot—be translated into practice until its verbalizers recognize their schizophrenic posture and internalize the theory. Of course, examination and clarification of the theory may lead to its rejection and the subsequent formulation of a theoretical statement that is more consistent with existing practice. In any case, each individual must examine his own values and behavior honestly and attempt to determine (1) where, theoretically speaking, he prefers to stand, and (2) *what this theory means translated into practice.* This is, perhaps, one of the most crucial aspects of decision-making behavior, for self-conscious internalization of theory is the only means by which a genuine correspondence between theory and practice can be achieved in curriculum development.

The Unwarranted Separation of Thought and Action

Throughout this section we have been advocating an extensive and probing inquiry by the individual into his unconsciously held values, his perceptions of the situation, and the probable consequences of alternative courses of action before he commits himself to one of the many options open to him. It has been our contention that problems in general, and problems of curriculum development in particular, are mainly the result of decisions based on unexamined assumptions, encapsulated perceptions, and cursory and superficial thinking and planning. Yet, our position on this issue, firmly held as it may be, does not resolve a perennial problem that occurs in every situation demanding a decision: At what point is it most appropriate for the individual to terminate his inquiry and deliberation and commit himself to a particular course of action?

Unfortunately, much as we would like our decisions to be based on *all* the relevant data, they can never be entirely known. Even under the best conditions, we are forced to proceed on the basis of only partial knowledge. For example, in presenting the hypothetical case of the civics teacher above, we indicated that a decision was taken after a thorough consideration of certain values and alternatives. We also suggested, though, that other options were available. Was the civics teacher remiss in opting for "subversive" curriculum change without considering his assumptions more probingly or entertaining other alternatives? Might he, for example, upon further deliberation, have evolved a course of action for changing school policy without precipitating the confrontation he feared and wished to avoid?

The problem of the separation of thought and action can, of course, have no single answer. Failure to commit oneself to action at some given point in one's deliberations is tantamount to paralysis. We need not belabor here the oft-heard complaint brought against those who "discuss, discuss, discuss, but never *do* anything." On the other hand, it seems that premature action based on inadequate and superficial inquiry is far more common than is excessive inquiry, especially among curriculum professionals. We have already noted our distaste for that characteristically American inclination to "do *something*" even when "you do not know what to do." Such a posture, in our estimation, can be far more harmful and dangerous than the paralysis born of excessive inquiry, particularly if it becomes, as it has in our culture, the dominant procedure in decision making. One consequence of this tendency toward unreflective action is the previously noted "bandwagonism" that characterizes so much superficial "change" in curriculum today.

Whatever our inclination to explore thoroughly all aspects of a curriculum situation, it is clear that some cases, by virtue of their critical nature, allow much less time for inquiry than do others. For an example of such a situation let us return to our hypothetical civics teacher whose theoretical principles call for a curriculum that features controversial issues. Suppose that a heated and volatile scandal erupts in the local community involving "loans" and "gifts" to several city councilmen from competing road contractors. The issue is seized upon by the civics teacher as a unique opportunity to teach the realities of municipal government. Because of the high visibility of the scandal, however, word of its airing in the high school curriculum reaches influential city fathers, who exert downward pressure through the school board and superintendent to eliminate it. As a result, the principal directs the civics teacher not only to drop the issue as a curriculum topic, but for the time being, at least, to suspend discussion of all controversial issues in the classroom. Since the principal's directive with a single stroke virtually nullifies the curriculum currently in effect, the civics teacher is faced with the necessity of taking immediate action of some kind. While he recognizes the necessity of examining all aspects of the problem and projecting the probable consequences of the options open to him, he is also painfully aware that whatever decision he makes must be made quickly. Thus, the urgency of a situation (and this, like all other aspects of it, is a matter of individual perception and judgment) is a factor in determining when reflection is terminated and action is commenced.

The example above also serves to illustrate a final (and perhaps more convincing) argument against the separation of thought and action. The fact that our civics teacher commits himself to a course of action in no way necessarily signals the suspension of his thought. As he initiates the implementation of his plan for curriculum action, he will attempt to maintain an unencapsulated sensitivity to the feedback of data that the environment produces in response to his behavior. Such data provide the basis for reassessment of his decision, further examination of self and situation, and perhaps an alteration in the nature of his commitment to act. This suggests that, in reality, thought and action are not separable—that we make the determination only for the convenience of analysis. This is the view taken by such thinkers as John Dewey, who speak of the "transaction" between choice maker and his environment. If, in reality, thought and action *are* inseparable (and this certainly appears to be case), then it seems clear that awareness of the possibility of unwarranted separation in the minds of individuals can help them to avoid inadvertently slipping either into a state of paralysis (failure of action) or unreflective hyperactivity (the "do something" syndrome).

Risk Taking and Decisions of Conscience

In the previous sections we have emphasized the importance of inquiry and values in decision making and action. Even under conditions involving optimal levels of unencapsulated reflection, however, individuals always are faced with the prospect of risk. Sometimes risk means "taking a chance"—i.e., opting for a course of action whose consequences are difficult or impossible to project. Our interest, however, lies in another kind of risk taking, the kind that is often associated with courage. This kind of risk taking is not due to unknowns, but is calculated fully. It involves decisions that place individuals in personal jeopardy, but which are nonetheless taken for reasons of firmly held internalized values and principles.

To explore the dimensions of the latter kind of risk taking, the kind that is demanded in so many decision-making situations, let us return once again to our example of the civics teacher. In the previous section we left him facing a difficult decision: How should he respond to his principal's directive to cease teaching controversial issues? Knowing that he has consciously made a whole-hearted commitment to the inclusion of controversial issues in the curriculum, we can understand his reluctance to abandon a principle (internalized curriculum theory) that he "knows to be right." But continuing to teach in a manner dictated by his conscience entails considerable risk. What are the probable consequences of such a decision? In the heat of the present controversy, there is some likelihood that he will be suspended from his teaching duties, or even summarily dismissed for "insubordination." Even if drastic repercussions do not ensue, he may very possibly find that his contract is not renewed for the following year. At the very least, he can expect the eruption of substantial conflict and controversy such that he will have to pay a considerable personal price in time, tension, energy, and peace of mind.

To complicate matters, our civics teacher must consider his wife and two children (for whose support he is responsible), to say nothing of his accountability to his students. While as a matter of personal conviction he might be willing to endure the adverse material and psychological consequences of a hard-line "stand-on-principle" position, he must consider his commitments to others who are *de facto*, if not voluntary, participants in the situation. The problem raised here centers on the conflict between mutually esteemed values, a problem touched on earlier. The point is that, unfortunately, we can almost *never* talk about *a commitment* (singular), but rather are inevitably placed in the position of choosing among *commitments* (plural).

Our discussion to this point suggests that the civics teacher is too firmly committed to the controversial-issues curriculum to scuttle it for the sake (value) of personal safety. Thus, he does not view the alternative of obeying the principal's directive as a feasible course of action. Further, he is too astute an individual to do nothing but continue to teach controversial issues as he has in the recent past. While such an option certainly enables him to maintain his principles, it almost certainly invites disaster by surrendering the initiative to his antagonists and abandoning himself to the tender mercies of random events.

Nevertheless, our civics teacher, repelled by the abundant expediency he observes in American behavior, is convinced that he has to take a stand on what he regards to be a worthwhile principle. Having made such a decision, he must next consider strategies for winning his case. One course might be to enlist the resources of the local and/or state education association. Another might be legal action alleging violation of academic freedom. Another yet might be a personally conducted publicity campaign similar to that waged by candidates for public office. He would undoubtedly consider many other alternatives too numerous to list here; whatever the strategy, however, one thing about his decision is eminently clear: taking a forthright stand on his perceived right to include controversial issues in the curriculum involves total commitment to an ideal and the willingness to stretch himself to the limit for the purpose of sustaining that ideal. It not only involves considerable personal risk, but many substantial sacrifices of time, energy, comfort, and money.

To opt for an all-out stand on the basis of principle has, until recently, been urged as the only decision that is entirely honorable and "moral." Such a position probably represents an oversimplification of decision making that reflects an excess of idealism.[2] More recently, pragmatic Americans have tended to prefer decisions that are more "practical." Unfortunately, this tendency to be "practical" has developed to a point where the former excesses of idealism have been "overcorrected," as it were, and supplanted by expedience and the crassest kind of self-interest. Such admonitions as "Don't rock the boat," "Don't get involved," and "Take care of number one" testify to this trend. The *real* problem, however, is not simply a matter of choosing between principle and expedience, but of determining priorities among a number of value commitments. With regard to the case of the civics teacher, it entails asking which values he is willing to compromise (or sacrifice) in order to preserve his right to teach controversial issues. In other decision-making situations involving a principle, it means asking the general question, "Where do I draw the line and say, 'Beyond this point I will not go!'?"

This question is asked by every self-reliant individual as he makes those crucial decisions which many thinkers believe define the kind of person an individual is. Seriously considered, it explains the noble acts of courage and self-sacrifice that identify the heroes and heroines of our cultural heritage. It is also the question that, seriously considered, creates the thousands of little known and uncelebrated heroes and heroines whose tiny acts of risk and courage have humanized the conditions of our existence.

While we would certainly admire a decision by our civics teacher to stand

---

2. One of the best treatments of the problem of excessive idealism occurs in *Brand*, a play by the Norwegian playwright, Henrik Ibsen.

on principle and fight for the maintenance of his controversial curriculum,[3] we would understand a less forthright decision given the consideration of other values and commitments. Suppose, for example, that our civics teacher were not willing to subject his family to the dislocations and even hardships that might ensue from a forthright stance on his right to include controversial issues in the curriculum. Such a course, after all, would mean notoriety, financial adversity, crank phone calls, and long hours of work, consultations, and meetings that would undoubtedly keep him away from his family for abnormally long periods of time. What other options are open to him short of total capitulation? There are literally hundreds, of course, but we need only explore one to make our point. He might arrange a meeting with the principal (who he knows is quasi-sympathetic), explain the substantial decrease in curriculum quality that will occur if controversial issues are deleted, and attempt to convince him that the curriculum can be saved by eliminating only the "scandal" issue, but not the other controversial content. "If we can defuse their chief issue," the civics teacher might argue, "agitation by the anticontroversial curriculum forces will probably subside. No doubt we—or I guess you—will have to deal with *some* antagonism as a result of the retention of controversial content, but I do not think that is too high a price to pay. Surely we ought to be able to take *some* flak to maintain this curriculum." If the principal agrees (and his decision in many respects is a decision of conscience), the proposed course of action will be embarked on and hopefully will result in the predicted consequences.[4] However, the principal may *not* agree, either because he believes that the strategy suggested by the teacher will not appease the antagonists, because he is not willing to take the risk, because he does not think the curriculum is worth the fight, or any of a number of other reasons. In this event, our civics teacher must consider another course of action.

Assuming that the teacher's decision to work out a solution through the principal was "successful," though, should we judge it any less honorable than the forthright one that did not compromise at all? To answer the question we must look at the values and consequences involved. While the compromise decision involves a partial sacrifice of principle (some controversial content was eliminated from the curriculum), this solution to the problem probably averts not only a distressful situation for the teacher's family, but also the acrimony, polarization of community, and other divisive "fallout" that would occur in an outright battle on principle—this, even if the teacher wins his case! By choosing the compromise decision, the teacher is saying that he is willing to compromise (but not sacrifice) a principle in the interest of other values and considerations (namely, the welfare of his family and community harmony). He is, in

---

3. With the proviso, of course, that his strategies represent principled and prudent courses of action. Threats against the superintendent's life or firebombing the board of education, for example, are hardly justifiable strategies in this situation.

4. It may not result in the predicted consequences, however, and alternative strategies will have to be worked out in the light of what *does* occur.

effect, saying, "I will go beyond this point [his right to include *any* controversial issue], but I will *not* go beyond *this* point [his right to include *some* controversial issues]." As situations change, however, our civics teacher's position on the principle might be quite different. Faced with certain dismissal if he did not cease immediately the teaching of all controversial issues, what would his decision (of conscience) be? An unencapsulated inquiry might require him, even though in total despair, to capitulate. Inflation, recession, a family to support, a child with chronic asthma, and a less-than-hundred-dollar reserve in the bank, may leave him (in terms of his perceptions, values, and conscience) little choice. Yet, another civics teacher in exactly the same situation might stand on principle and fight, quit his job, or take any of a number of alternative courses before abandoning his principle. Indeed, in extreme cases involving basic human principles, it is not unusual for individuals to choose self-sacrifice and even suicide as preferable to living under what they perceive to be unbearably degrading circumstances.

In the course of our daily lives we are faced with a multitude of decisions of conscience ranging from the most mundane to the most significant. In almost all of these it is a presumption to tell someone what he *ought* to do in a given situation. Since our values differ not only in kind but in relative importance to us, our decisions, all else being equal, will likewise differ. Who has the right, for example, to tell the civics teacher that he is "taking the easy way out" if he follows the principal's directive and abandons his controversial-issues curriculum? This does not mean that it is improper in certain circumstances to raise questions with another person by way of clarifying values or illuminating unconsidered factors involved in his decision. Indeed, we would urge decision makers to seek such dialogue since it is supportive of expanded meanings and consciousness, and therefore operates to produce the wisest decisions. But this is quite different from making a decision for another, which no one can really do.

Nor can an individual escape responsibility for his choices by asking another to decide for him. In spite of an overwhelming tendency among curriculum workers to seek "directions to follow" in curriculum development, no such directions exist, except in the most pedestrian situations. We cannot escape our freedom, and if we decide simply to follow another's prescription, we must understand that what we have really done is to decide on a course of action without benefit of reflective thought. Such a course may be the least justifiable. In any event, it in no way releases us from full responsibility for our decision, our action, or its consequences.

But while we can neither choose for others nor delegate our choice to others, we can judge, and be judged, on the basis of the values implicit in our decisions. The individual who consistently subordinates all other values to self-interested expedience in the decision-making process is a person with whom it is patently unwise to entrust one's welfare. Such principles as loyalty, truthfulness, friendship, and compassion are not likely to play a role in his personal and group relationships or in the decisions that he makes. Conversely, the individual who ruthlessly applies a rigid set of principles in all decision-making situations is bound to perpetrate grotesque anomalies: extreme cruelty in the name of justice, or brutal candor in the name of truthfulness. Between these two extremes lies a multitude of unique personalities, the character of each dependent upon the idiosyncratic cluster of values that determine one's behavior —and our judgment of it.

In the light of this discussion on individual commitment and decision making, it seems fair to conclude that in the last analysis the direction of curriculum development and the incidence of curriculum change are ultimately dependent on each of the individuals involved in the curriculum enterprise. Of course, familiarity with curriculum theory, foundations, organization, and engineering is an important knowledge component for productive functioning in the curriculum field; but possession of such knowledge is no guarantee that it will be put to effective use. The crucial factor is acceptance by professionals of responsibility for their own roles in curriculum work.

We have suggested on numerous occasions that the organizational mode of producing curriculum change is inadequate. Such procedures inevitably result only in a superficial reshuffling of goals, content, learning activities, and so on, with little or no fundamental reexamination of values, purposes, or methods. Independent action by committed individuals, however, is also inadequate, inasmuch as it alone cannot bring about the widespread change in public school curriculum that obviously is needed. What seems to be called for is greater dialogue among committed, self-reliant professionals whose decisions invite the participation of an expanding circle of educators and foster concerted efforts for curriculum change. In other words, what is called for is individual initiative within the framework of group action. That individual commitment can be translated into organizational effectiveness is demonstrated by the existence of such groups as Common Cause, The Sierra Club, The American Civil Liberties Union, Nader's "Raiders," and in its own encapsulated fashion, the Ku Klux Klan. The creation of groups of self-reliant individuals committed to curriculum reform will not, of course, sweep away the overwhelming obstacles (such as inadequate time, lack of materials, obsolescent values, repressive administrations, and apathetic faculties) that intimidate even the most optimistic curriculum reformers. But it will create vehicles by which difficult (and "impossible") situations can be dealt with in a way that produces curriculum practices *somewhat* better, at least, than the ones we now know. In curriculum work (as in most areas of life) no miracles occur, and none should be expected.

Given these observations, it would appear that there is only one place for the initiation of curriculum work, whatever form it may take, and that is the individual. He must begin at the beginning, of course, with himself as the question. Where such a beginning will take him is impossible to say; but it is an exciting prospect to contemplate.

Reference

Pritzkau, P. T. 1970. *On Education for the Authentic.* New York: Thomas Y. Crowell Company (IEP).

INDEX

507

82 83 84 85 10 9